The New Professional Chef™

Fifth Edition

The Culinary Institute of America

The New Professional Chef™

Fifth Edition

With Forewords by

Paul Bocuse

and

Ferdinand Metz, C.M.C.

President, The Culinary Institute of America

Linda Glick Conway, Editor

VNR VAN NOSTRAND REINHOLD

New York

President and Chief Executive Officer: Judith R. Joseph
Sponsoring Editor: Pamela Scott Chirls
Designer: Monika Keano
Editorial Supervisor: Joy Aquilino
Production Director: Louise Kurtz

Color illustrations for Chapter 8 by Alex Bloch

Library of Congress Catalog Card Number 91-8711
ISBN 0-442-21982-2 (trade)
ISBN 0-442-00807-4 (academic)

Printed in the United States of America

Van Nostrand Reinhold
115 Fifth Avenue
New York, New York 10003

Chapman and Hall
2–6 Boundary Row
London, SE1 8HN, England

Thomas Nelson Australia
102 Dodds Street
South Melbourne 3205
Victoria, Australia

Nelson Canada
1120 Birchmount Road
Scarborough, Ontario MIK 5G4, Canada

16 15 14 13 12 11 10 9 8 7 6 5 4 3 2

Library of Congress Cataloging in Publication Data

Culinary Institute of America.
    The new professional chef/The Culinary Institute of
    America; Linda Glick Conway, editor.—5th ed.
       p. cm.
    Rev. ed. of: The professional chef. 4th ed. 1974.
    Includes index.
    ISBN 0-442-21982-2 (Trade).—ISBN 0-442-00807-4
    (Academic)
    1. Quantity cookery.   I. Conway, Linda Glick.
II. Culinary Institute of America. Professional
chef. III. Title.
  TX820.C85 1991
    641.5′7—dc20   91-8711
                                CIP

Contents

Part One   The Foodservice Professional   1

Chapter *1*
**Introduction to the
Foodservice Industry**
9

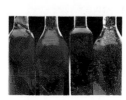

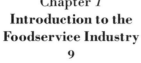

Chapter *2*
The Professional Chef
12

**Part Two   Sanitation, Nutrition, and
Equipment   18**

Chapter *3*
Sanitation and Safety
20

Chapter *4*
**Nutrition and Nutritional
Cooking**
34

Chapter *5*
Equipment Identification
48

Part Three   Product Identification   68

Chapter *6*
**Meats, Poultry, and Game
Identification**
70

Chapter *7*
**Fish and Shellfish
Identification**
84

Chapter *8*
**Fruit, Vegetable, and Fresh
Herb Identification**
98

Chapter *9*
**Dairy, Cheese, and Egg
Identification**
132

Chapter *10*
**Nonperishable Goods
Identification**
142

vii

Recipes

Dry-heat Cooking without Fats or Oils   342

PAUL BOCUSE

Lors de ma visite au Culinary Institute of America de Hyde Park, New-York, en 1989, j'ai eu l'occasion de voir et d'apprécier les méthodes d'enseignement appliquées dans cette école qui en font l'une des meilleures du monde.

Une éducation structurée donne d'excellents résultats, conduisant les élèves au titre honorable de "Chef Professionnel".

Restant convaincu que le respect des traditions pour les générations actuelles et à venir, sera beaucoup plus profitable en matière d'enseignement culinaire, permettant aux jeunes de maîtriser parfaitement les différentes techniques de base. Cette formation donnant enfin sur le marché des chefs qui savent rôtir, griller, faire une mise en place, prêts à répondre aux besoins spécifiques de leur métier.

Encore toutes mes félicitations à cet Institut.

Foreword

During my visit to The Culinary Institute of America in Hyde Park, New York in 1989, I had the opportunity to see and appreciate the training methods applied at the school, which make it one of the best in the world.

A structured education yields excellent results, leading the students to the honorable title of "Professional Chef."

I remain convinced that respect for tradition in the teaching of culinary arts will be made most effective by enabling students to perfectly master the fundamental techniques. This approach to teaching, as featured in *The New Professional Chef*, finally provides the marketplace with chefs who know how to roast, grill, prepare proper mise en place, and are ready to address all of the specific needs of their profession.

Once more, all my congratulations to the Institute.

Paul Bocuse

Foreword

There is a widespread misconception about how one becomes a chef. It is not simply the rote memorization of hundreds or thousands of recipes. Neither is it the case that a chef has access to tools and ingredients not available to those outside the profession. There is no special magic in the knives and spices found in a professional kitchen. The serious student of cooking must learn lessons of greater value and wider application than a single recipe could provide. These lessons must serve as the foundation of a career: the ability to properly grill, roast, poach; to prepare charcuterie, breads, and pastries.

The process of mastering these basic skills is not all that is involved in becoming a chef. The drive to achieve technical excellence, paired with the motivation to learn the importance of flavor, and about its subtleties, harmonies, and contrasts, moves us along on the journey from apprentice to chef. As students of cooking, we must all continue to grow through our experiences so that we can answer the questions of how much, how appropriate, when, and why. It is in searching for the answers to these questions that the student begins to develop the profound sensibility that allows him or her to distinguish the substantial from the trivial. The chef must learn to appreciate the important elements of food—their honest flavors, pleasing textures, comforting colors, and their nutritional values—so that they can speak for themselves.

The guiding principle in preparing this book has been to explain the techniques and preparations that any student of cooking must fully comprehend and assimilate in order to be truly proficient at his or her craft. These skills must then be carefully practiced and refined over the course of a lifetime.

This book should function as far more than a textbook. If we have accomplished our purpose, the serious student will be inspired to use these lessons as a springboard to continually learn more, for there is always more to learn. The youngest apprentice and the most experienced master chef alike are at their best only if they aspire toward greater perfection of technique and the most ideal combinations of flavors. As we continue to learn, we are brought at last to the realization that it is simplicity, in cooking as in all arts, that demands the greatest artistry and offers the greatest rewards.

Ferdinand E. Metz, Certified Master Chef
President
The Culinary Institute of America

Preface

The New Professional Chef represents a total reworking of our classic text, *The Professional Chef*, and as such, it is more than simply an updating of material. The motivation for this new book was our desire to incorporate into one volume as many contemporary cooking concepts as possible, while remaining true to the principles that govern all good cooking. Increased interest in nutritional cooking, working profitably with a dwindling supply of high-quality fish and shellfish, the excitement of learning about cuisines from our own and other countries—all of these elements have combined to change the way we view a culinary education.

Rather than following one specific curriculum, this book focuses on a particular subject area or technique in each chapter. By nature of its encyclopedic subject coverage, this text is suited to other courses of study, whether as part of an existing program or through independent study. An instructor may choose to use all or part of its contents; the student may use the book to advance his or her learning by employing it as a broad, basic text or as a reference tool to answer specific questions about a particular technique. The techniques as explained in this book have all been tested in the Institute's kitchens. Each represents one way of many possible variations. The fact that all variations are not included in this text does not imply that these other methods are incorrect. Experience will teach the student many "tricks of the trade."

Nor should the title of this work put it into the rarified category of books to be used only by those working in restaurant or hotel kitchens. The basic lessons of cooking are the same whether one prepares food for paying guests or for one's family and friends. Therefore, we hope that those who look to cooking for a creative outlet will come to regard this book as a valuable tool.

This book is suited to a variety of teaching situations because the material is arranged in a logical, progressive sequence, starting with a brief history of cooking and moving on through chapters devoted to the lessons that must be learned in the process of becoming a professional chef. The primary emphasis is to give a clear picture of the technique. Cooking is not always a perfectly precise art, but a good grasp of the basics gives the chef or student the ability not only to apply the technique, but also to learn the standards of quality so that one begins to develop a sense of how cooking works.

Counted among the basics in the kitchen is the ability to seek out and purchase the best possible ingredients. This material is covered thoroughly in the third section of the book, with separate chapters devoted to meats and poultry; fish; fruits, vegetables, and fresh herbs; dairy products and eggs; and nonperishable goods such as oils, flours, grains, and dried pastas. The information is presented in such a way that it can act as a quick reference to quality, seasonality, and appropriate cooking styles or techniques.

Other important culinary rudiments include the care and use of a knife and basic preparations such as roux, mirepoix, and bouquet garni. This material can be found in the chapter devoted to mise en place. The remainder of the book acts as a guide to the different cooking techniques: making stocks, soups, and sauces; grilling, broiling, roasting, sautéing, panfrying, poaching, and boiling; making salads, cooking eggs, and preparing basic forcemeats; and making breads, cakes, and pastries.

The recipes included in this book are an example of the wide range of possibilities open to the student once the basics are mastered. It should be noted that these recipes have both metric and American measurements. In the conversion from one system to another, quantities have usually been rounded to the nearest even measurement.

The recipe yields reflect real-life cooking situations; some items, such as stocks and soups, are prepared in large quantities, while others, such as sautés and grills, are prepared "à la minute," for a few portions at a time. Larger roasts, braises, stews, and side dishes generally have yields of 10 or 20 servings; any marinades, sauces, or condiments included in the recipe that are prepared in advance are normally given in quantities to produce a yield of 10 servings. These yields may not always suit the student who is using the book outside of a professional kitchen. In most cases, they can be reduced or increased in order to prepare the correct number of servings. Baking formula yields are based on specific weight ratios, however, and must be followed exactly.

Becoming a chef is a career-long process. Cooking is a dynamic profession, one that provides some of the greatest challenges as well as some of the greatest rewards. There is always another level of perfection to achieve and another skill to master. It is our hope that this book will function both as a springboard into future growth and as a reference point to give ballast to the lessons still to be learned.

Acknowledgments

The Culinary Institute of America is blessed with wonderful resources. Hailing from 20 countries, our 95 chefs and instructors have a cumulative total of 2,000 years of experience. Among our faculty are more Certified Master Chefs and Culinary Olympic Team members under one roof than anywhere else. The school is doubly blessed to have an enthusiastic, dedicated, and professional staff to keep us progressing on a daily basis.

In assembling *The New Professional Chef* we have tapped into both of these bountiful resources. This process has not always been easy, but the results show that it was well worth the effort.

We wish to acknowledge and thank the following people for their contributions to this project:

CONTENT

Wayne Almquist

Arnaldo Bagna

Adam Balogh

Vincent Bankoski

Viktor Baumann

Earl Bebo

Gunter Behrendt

Henry Biscardi

Helen Blankenship

Edward Bradley

Elizabeth Briggs

Robert Briggs

Lyde Buchtenkirch-Biscardi

Michael Bully

John Canner

Kenneth Carlson

Shirley Cheng

Howard "Corky" Clark

Anthony Colella

Monica Coulter

Richard Czack

Michael D'Amore

Philip Delaplane

Ronald DeSantis

John DeShetler

Joseph DiPerri

Dieter Doppelfeld

Bruno Ellmer

George Engel

Mark Erickson

Gregory Fatigati

Vincent Fatigati

Dieter Faulkner

Marcus Färbinger

Louis Fessy

Mary Frankini

Martin Frei

Richard Gabriel

David Geller

Hedy Gold

Stephen Gold

Craig Goldstein

Patrick Healy

Uwe Hestnar

James Heywood

Mary Elizabeth Heywood

Gilles Hezard

Julia Hill

Heinz Holtmann

Henry Iles

John Jensen

Jaime Johnson

Morey Kanner

Manfred Ketterer

Thomas Kief

Charles Koegler

John Kowalski

Rudolf Lang

Danny Lee

Jean-Pierre LeMasson

Alain Levy

Helmut Loibl

Francis Lopez

James Maraldo

Noble Masi
Joseph McKenna
David Megenis
Peter Michael
Vega Militariu
Henri Mortier
Joseph Mure
Alfred Natale
John O'Haire
Robert Pankin
Philip Papineau
Claudio Papini
Henri Patey
Italo Norman Peduzzi
Seymour Perlowitz
Catharine Powers
Paul Prosperi
Heinrich Rapp
Charles Rascoll
William Reynolds
Daniel Riedi
Timothy Rodgers
Karl Roth

David St. John-Grubb
Ivan Salgovic
Paul Sartory
Eric Saucy
Tom Schmitter
Walter Schreyer
Johann Sebald
Konstantin Sembos
Elliott Sharron
Brian Smith
David Smythe
Fritz Sonnenschmidt
Carmine Stanzione
John Stein
Gustav Stickley
Marianne Turow
Richard Vergili
Fred Von Husen
Michael Weiss
Joseph Weissenberg
Jonathan Zearfoss
Greg Zifchak

REVIEW

Wayne Almquist
Arnaldo Bagna
Vincent Bankoski
Edward Bradley
Elizabeth Briggs
Robert Briggs
Lyde Buchtenkirch-Biscardi
Howard "Corky" Clark
Anthony Colella
Monica Coulter
Richard Czack
Mark Erickson
Vincent Fatigati
Dieter Faulkner
Craig Goldstein
Julia Hill
Heinz Holtmann
John Jensen

Jaime Johnson
Rudolf Lang
Noble Masi
Peter Michael
Claudio Papini
Seymour Perlowitz
Catharine Powers
Paul Prosperi
Heinrich Rapp
Timothy Rodgers
David St. John-Grubb
Eric Saucy
Fritz Sonnenschmidt
Marianne Turow
Richard Vergili
Fred Von Husen
Joseph Weissenberg

PHOTOGRAPHY

Technique photography was produced by the faculty and Learning Resources Center of The Culinary Institute of America. Props were provided courtesy of All-Clad Metalcrafters, Inc. and The Hall China Company. Props for the cover photograph were provided by All-Clad Metalcrafters, Inc.

Learning Resources Center

Henry Woods, Director
John Grubell, Photographer
Lorna Smith, Assistant Photographer

Faculty

Viktor Baumann	Peter Michael
Edward Bradley	Henri Mortier
Elizabeth Briggs	John O'Haire
Lyde Buchtenkirch-Biscardi	Paul Prosperi
Howard "Corky" Clark	Heinrich Rapp
Vincent Fatigati	Timothy Rodgers
John Jensen	Walter Schreyer
Charles Koegler	Johann Sebald
Helmut Loibl	Fritz Sonnenschmidt
Joseph McKenna	Fred Von Husen
David Megenis	

Chapter introduction photography was produced by the team of David Kellaway, Certified Master Chef; Queenie Burns, Senior Art Director of *Restaurants & Institutions* Magazine; and Vuksanovich, Inc.

ADMINISTRATION/STAFF

Robin Plass Bruno
Carol Goldsmith
Steven Kolpan
Stephen McKee
Maryann Monachelli
Lesley Rokjer
Lisa Tippett (copyeditor)

SPECIAL ACKNOWLEDGMENTS

Preparing this book was a major effort, with everyone working together as a team. Tim Ryan, Certified Master Chef and Vice-President of Education, was the dynamic and visionary coach who kept everyone advancing toward the goal.

We would certainly be remiss to not thank Linda Glick Conway for her professionalism and guidance; and all the folks at Van Nostrand Reinhold, particularly Judy Joseph and Pam Scott Chirls, who have encouraged and supported us from the very beginning.

Finally, the Institute would like to extend a special thanks to Mary Donovan. Mary has been responsible for pulling all the pieces of this project together. She has shown consummate professionalism and determination throughout the process. Her dedication was so strong, in fact, that shortly after delivering her first child she was back reviewing galleys (in her hospital bed), causing her infant son to be nicknamed "The New Professional Baby." Without Mary's talent and tenacity this book might not have been completed.

Part One

The Foodservice
Professional

A series of historical, cultural, and technological factors has brought the foodservice industry to the position it occupies today. The first chapter provides a brief overview of these factors, which serves as background for the rest of the book. A combination of classic methods with contemporary ingredients, equipment, and expertise has brought cooking to the position of excellence and respect it now enjoys.

The professional chef is the "keeper of the flame" for the industry's reputation. Therefore, it is only appropriate that a chapter is devoted to the education, personal characteristics, and general duties of a successful chef and to the chef's responsibilities as a businessperson. The overriding qualification is professionalism, for there can be no substitute for good judgment, a dedication to service, and a sense of responsibility.

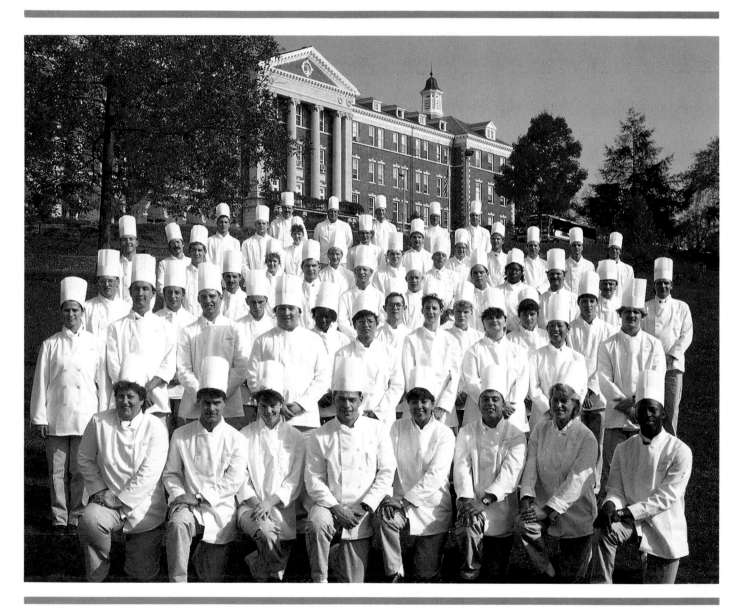

Introduction to the Foodservice Industry

The history of cooking is undoubtedly almost as old as that of mankind itself. The contemporary status of the food-service industry as a whole is a direct reflection of man's development. Almost all areas of human endeavor have had an influence.

This chapter will identify those factors that have had the most direct and visible effects: exploration and travel; the history of the political system in Europe, most notably monarchies and the subsequent development of a large and thriving middle class; and science and technology. It will also cover the evolution of the restaurant, the influence of particular individuals, social trends that affect when and why people eat out, and the range of opportunities available in the industry today.

MAJOR HISTORICAL INFLUENCES

Conquest, Travel, and Exploration

Although humans tend to seek out the familiar, reassuring foods of their native countries, travel has a broadening influence, not only on the kinds of foods that are eaten, but also on the ways in which familiar and unfamiliar foods are prepared. Although some peoples have tended to stay in one area for generations upon generations, others have roamed from one end of a continent to the other, venturing out onto the high seas and discovering new lands. The quest to conquer other lands has been one of the most potent influences in the growth and development of cooking.

The Greeks and Romans were perhaps the most effective at bringing about changes that altered completely the eating habits of most Western hemisphere inhabitants. As each nation they encountered was conquered, the delicacies and choicest goods of that country became their "property." Leavened breads, sweet wines, forcemeats, sauces, and "composed dishes" all became part of the Greek repertoire after they fought to gain control of Egypt, Persia, Babylonia, and India. When the Romans marched through what would one day become Europe, they spread their recipes for dishes that called for a variety of seasonings, pickles, cheeses, and special cakes and breads. Several of these influences can still be seen today; examples are the sweet-sour sauces of modern Italy and the sauerkraut or sauerbraten of modern Germany.

Another example of culinary influence through conquest is that of the Moors over the Spaniards. The use in Spain and Portugal of typical Moorish ingredients, such as sweet syrups, pastries, and almonds, is still evidence today of their centuries-long dominion.

As the world moved into the Dark Ages, travel began to diminish. Crusaders in the eleventh to the thirteenth centuries were still making journeys to the Holy Land, and the devout still made pilgrimages to various shrines and holy places. Most of the rich cooking styles, and the books that discussed food and cookery, were safeguarded in monasteries while the people outside their walls continued to prepare the rough, simple dishes that had sustained them for generations.

Exploration of new worlds was rather slow, and it took many decades before any real influence on the established European cuisines was felt. Eventually Europeans traveled to the Americas and the West Indies, returning with such native foods as chocolate, chilies, beans, corn, tomatoes, and potatoes, many of which were at first regarded as poisonous. A famous French agronomist, Antoine-August Parmentier (1737–1813), finally broke through the deep-seated fear of potatoes with a campaign begun in 1774. By the time the French Revolution began in 1789, they were as familiar on the French table as bread. Other new foods that seemed more familiar, or at least bore a surface resemblance to foods already available in Europe, such as the turkey, were taken up immediately and enthusiastically.

With the end of the Dark Ages came a resurgence of travel by the wealthy. At first, this was a time-consuming and hazardous undertaking. However, new modes of travel, such as improved ships able to make long sea journeys, made it possible for the noble classes to move with greater freedom, carrying their own approach to foods and cookery with them, but also being influenced by the foods that they found. The number of French chefs in Russia in the eighteenth and nineteenth centuries is a testimony to the way in which cuisines tended to travel from one part of the world to another. And Thomas Jefferson's repeated trips to Europe introduced macaroni, ice cream, and a host of new fruits and vegetables to the United States.

Immigrants traveling from one country to another, whether to escape religious persecution or to try to find a better life, also carried with them their traditional dishes and ways of cooking. People coming to the United States brought with them special drinks, breads, cakes, and other foods that eventually were intermingled with the foods brought by previous arrivals and with indigenous foods.

In the United States, the soldiers who fought in the World Wars returned to this country with a newly acquired taste for the traditional foods of France, Italy, and Germany. As the twentieth century wore on, the middle class finally was able to afford foreign travel for pleasure. Today, travel influences the types of cuisines featured in contemporary restaurants. Foods from the Caribbean, the Middle East, and previously lesser-known French and Italian regions have become more familiar as the world continues to "shrink." Chefs and patrons alike are discovering the pleasures of foods from countries as diverse as Portugal, Thailand, and New Zealand. And just as travel has made it easier for the guest to get to the food, it is also a far simpler, faster, and cheaper matter to get food from all over the world to the chef's kitchen.

Royalty and the Rise of the Middle Class

European royal families often intermarried for reasons of state and to form political alliances. With the union of these families came a blending of the customs of different countries. This mingling resulted not only in the spread of cooking styles and special dishes, but in an exchange of social etiquette as well. For example, Caterina de Medici (1519–89), a sixteenth-century Italian princess who came to France as the result of a royal alliance, brought with her chefs from Florence. The number of "Florentine" dishes in the classic French repertoire attests to their influence.

Once the monarchies and the feudal system began to decline, a change occurred in the social structure. The chefs who had once worked in royal households took positions in the wealthy homes of a newly rich and "nonnoble" class. The result was an expansion of the cuisine of the nobility, first to the upper class, and eventually to the large and growing middle class.

The gradual dissolution of strict class lines, and the ability of people to move from the lower class to the middle or upper classes, allowed the cookery of the upper class or nobility, known as *haute cuisine*, to blend with the cooking of hearth and home, *cuisine bourgeoise*. This exchange between domestic cooks and classically trained chefs in all countries produced a number of innovations and refinements. The effect was to spur growth and change, and to keep classic cooking from becoming dull and stale.

Science and Technology

From the time that man first learned to control fire, advances in science and technology have had a direct relationship to food production and preparation.

Advances in farm technology have increased yields and improved quality and availability. Animal husbandry, through the ability to breed desirable characteristics in and undesirable ones out, now allows us to raise animals that have better yield and flavor and less fat.

Equipment and tools have undergone a similar evolution, from the rudimentary cutting tools and cooking vessels that first allowed men to cook foods in liquids to the gas and electric stoves, microwave ovens, and computerized equipment of today. Refrigeration allows foods to be held longer and shipped farther, without significant loss of quality.

Scientific developments have allowed us to improve on techniques for food storage, increasing both the shelf life and wholesomeness of foods and reducing the incidence of food spoilage, contamination, and poisoning. Examples of these technical advances include pasteurization, freeze drying, vacuum packing, and irradiation.

Improved methods of transportation make possible the availability of food from other geographic areas and the ability to use foods once considered "out of season." High-quality produce is now available year-round, and special items once usable only in the area where they are produced are now available worldwide.

Nutrition, a relatively young science, has also had an impact. As we continue to learn more about how the foods we eat are converted to energy and affect the body, old cooking techniques have been updated and new techniques found. The industry is thus able to keep in step with a society concerned both with health and fitness and with dining well.

RESTAURANT HISTORY AND EVOLUTION

The first restaurant (as we know restaurants today) opened in Paris in 1765. M. Boulanger, a tavern-keeper, served a dish of sheep's feet, or trotters, in a white sauce as a restorative or *restorante*. Although he was brought to court for infringing on a separate guild's monopoly, he won the case and was allowed to continue. Once the ice was broken, other restaurants followed in fairly rapid succession.

The French Revolution (1789–99) had a particularly significant effect on restaurant proliferation, because many chefs who previously had worked for the monarchy or nobility fled the country to escape the guillotine's specter. Although some sought employment with the noble classes, others began to open their own establishments.

Restaurants became increasingly refined operations, and although they were at first frequented only by men, this would change as customs in society and in the foodservice industry as a whole changed.

The *grand cuisine*, a careful code established by Antonin Carême (1784–1833) detailing numerous dishes and their sauces in *La Cuisine Classique* (1856) and other volumes, came to restaurants much more slowly than it did to nobility's kitchens. The menus of most hotels and restaurants offered a simple *table d'hôte*, which provided little if any choice. The grande cuisine offered a *carte* (or list) of suggestions available from the kitchen. The *à la carte* restaurant had begun to make inroads on the traditional "men's club" atmosphere of most restaurants and cafes.

By the time that the Savoy Hotel opened in London in 1898 (under the direction of Cesar Ritz and Auguste Escoffier (1847–1935), grande cuisine was still the exception. These two gentlemen waged a successful campaign to assure that their *à la carte* offerings were of the finest, that their service was the best, and that it was all delivered to the guest on the finest china and crystal. As a result, people of good standing could finally be found in the dining rooms of restaurants in England, France, and elsewhere.

Today, the variety of existing dining establishments reflects the interests, lifestyles, and needs of a modern society: brasseries, bistros, "white tablecloth" places, ethnic restaurants, fast food spots, takeout companies, hotel dining rooms, banquet halls, and the list goes on.

MAJOR FIGURES

The following list of major influential figures is by no means complete. Further reading about influential people throughout the history of cooking is recommended. Refer to the Recommended Readings at the end of this book for other sources.

Anne of Austria (1601–66), wife of Louis XIII, was a member of the Spanish Hapsburg family. Her retinue included Spanish chefs who introduced sauce Espagnol and the use of roux as a thickener for sauces.

Caterina de Medici (1519–89), an Italian princess from the famous Florentine family, married the Duc d'Orleans, later Henri II of France. She introduced a more refined style of dining, including the use of the fork and the napkin. Her Florentine chefs influenced French chefs as well, most particularly in the use of spinach.

Pierre François de la Varenne (1615–78) was the author of the first cookbook to summarize the cooking practices of the French nobility. His *Le Vrai Cuisinier François* was published in 1651.

Marie-Antoine Carême (1784–1833) became known as the founder of the *grande cuisine* and was responsible for systematizing culinary techniques. He had a profound influence on the later writing of Escoffier, and was known as the "chef of kings, king of chefs."

Jean-Anthelme Brillat-Savarin (1755–1826) was a French politician and gourmet and a renowned writer. His work, *Le Physiologie de Gout (The Physiology of Taste)*, is highly regarded.

Georges Auguste Escoffier (1847–1935) was a renowned chef and teacher and the author of *Le Guide Culinaire*, a major work codifying classic cuisines that is still widely used. His other significant contributions include simplifying the classic menu in accordance with the principles advocated by Carême, and initiating the brigade system. (See the section titled "The Kitchen Brigade System," later in this chapter.) Escoffier's influence on the foodservice industry cannot be overemphasized.

Charles Ranhofer (1836–99) was the first internationally renowned chef of an American restaurant, Delmonico's, and the author of *The Epicurean*.

Fernand Point (1897–1955) was the chef/owner of La Pyramide restaurant in Vienne, France. He went even further than Escoffier in bringing about a change in cooking styles and laid the foundations for *nouvelle cuisine*.

Paul Bocuse and *Jean Troisgros*, who were the disciples of Point, and Roger Vergé and Michel Guerard, known as the "Bande à Bocuse," were innovators and popularizers of *nouvelle cuisine*. Their considerable interaction and sharing of ideas have led to contemporary cuisine's growth and development.

Contemporary Chefs and Figures

Although there have always been famous and influential chefs, teachers, and writers, the number of people holding a position of prominence in the field today is greater than ever. Every country has its trend-setting chef: Paul Bocuse in France, Fredy Girardet in Switzerland, the Roux brothers in England, and André Soltner in the United States, for example.

There are also prominent members of the food media. Some, like James Beard, Craig Claiborne, and Julia Child, have been influential teachers and have written landmark cookbooks in addition to contributing to newspapers and magazines and appearing on television.

TODAY'S CURRENTS AND TRENDS

The foodservice industry as a whole is subject to the same changes that affect our entire culture. As life-styles, economic conditions, entertainment, and saving and spending patterns change, so does the industry.

Family Structure Changes

The two-income family and increasing numbers of single professional people have brought about significant growth in the foodservice industry. These people have more disposable income but less time to cook at home, so they have tended to eat out more often. This circumstance has also spurred the growth of "carry-out cuisine" or "takeout," which is offered by gourmet shops as well as by restaurants filling orders for home consumption.

The extended family—grandparents, parents, children, and assorted aunts, uncles, and cousins all living together—is now a rarity. The traditional "nuclear" family—working father, mother at home, two children in school—is also getting harder to find. It is far more likely that both the father and mother are working, or that the family has only a single parent.

"Baby boomers" who waited until much later in life to start their families are often unwilling to give up their careers. For any family in which the major care-givers are also the major wage earners, finding ways to minimize demands on time is essential. More and more often, meals are either eaten in a restaurant or they are takeout foods.

Single professionals and the growing numbers of retired persons have shifted the demographics of this country dramatically. And though the requirements of these two groups may not be identical, they are both looking to the foodservice industry to meet their special needs as well, whether it be gourmet shops or "early-bird" specials.

Media

The print media, radio, movies, and television, as a major part of daily life, keep the average person abreast of new developments. As a society adapts to accommodate changes, the institutions and industries that serve the consumer must also change. Fads grow (and die) quickly; in fact, it is not an easy thing to distinguish between a genuine trend and a fad.

Neither a wholly positive or a negative factor, media influence has changed the expectations of guests. As a result, the industry must keep abreast of such changes in order to meet the demands of an increasingly better-informed clientele.

The Chef as "Star"

Although cooking was once considered a less desirable job, today's chefs are a new breed—respected, even admired, for their skill, craftsmanship, and artistry. Some chefs have received so much press that their names are household words. The elevation of the status of the chef helps to attract bright and talented people to the industry, adding a constant supply of new professionals. This is important, for there is a great and continually growing need for trained foodservice workers.

Increasingly Sophisticated Clientele

Today's clientele is a more widely traveled group. They have had increased exposure to other countries' foods and restaurants, which has, in turn, spurred an interest in having these cuisines available at home. The result is a growth in restaurants that specialize in previously "unknown" foods.

These consumers' "food savvy" has also had a direct impact on the types of food that are grown here or imported, such as specialty foodstuffs. Many supermarkets offer packaged and prepared "gourmet" items. Small farms and/or bakeries producing specialty produce, cheeses, and flours are becoming more widely known and appreciated. The continuing demand for such foods will provide a great avenue for industry growth.

The public's growing interest in grains, legumes, fish, vegetables, and fruits, along with a desire to decrease overconsumption of animal fat, protein, and sodium, have helped popularize "nutritional cooking." Furthermore, they have spurred fundamental changes in the preparation and presentation of traditional foods. Classic dishes from both the classical and peasant traditions are being reevaluated to reduce or eliminate fats, sodium, and cholesterol.

"New" Foodstuffs

The ongoing quest for the gastronomic new and different has resulted in a growth of new food sources. Traditional farming methods have changed to take maximum advantage of new technology and machinery, improving yields and in some instances "creating" new foods through hybridization. At the same time a renewed interest in raising specialty items has occurred. Examples of such items include the farming of traditionally wild foods, such as game and wild mushrooms.

Aquaculture (farm-raised fish and seafood) is being increasingly looked to as a source of high-quality and safe foods as the oceans, lakes, and streams throughout the world are becoming polluted and/or "fished out."

Specialty suppliers are also reviving some traditional methods of producing hand-made cheeses, smoked meats, grains, and breads. In all cases, the increasing emphasis is on ingredient freshness—a cornerstone of contemporary cooking.

Improved Farming Methods

New methods of raising farm animals have changed the character of meats so that they are leaner, more tender, and more widely available—especially poultry, veal, and lamb—than in the past. These methods are coming under scrutiny by the public and are showing some signs of change as the demand for fewer chemicals in foods increases.

Biological engineering is one answer to these demands. By creating strains of vegetables, fruits, and grains that are genetically coded to resist certain types of diseases or pests, the need for chemical fertilizers, pesticides, and herbicides could be dramatically reduced. Organic farming, composting, and other soil management practices also allow foods to be grown without the introduction of many chemicals. These methods are also important steps in helping to control the vast amounts of solid waste produced by our society.

Hydroponic gardening of a number of crops is being practiced more widely. Herbs, lettuces, and other vegetables can be successfully grown year-round. The roots are exposed to a nutrient-rich waterbath and are grown under carefully controlled conditions to maximize yield and speed growth. These crops can be brought to maturity regardless of weather conditions or season.

Dinner as Entertainment

Going out for dinner has become a form of entertainment and the restaurant has become a "destination," not just a place to have a quick meal before moving on to another activity. Rather than spending an evening at the theater followed by supper, or going dancing preceded by a light dinner, lingering over dinner at a restaurant has become "the evening."

CAREER OPPORTUNITIES

The traditional careers such as chef, sous chef, saucier, and other "back-of-the-house" positions are the first to come to mind; and as the foodservice industry continues to grow, a continual need will exist for well-trained personnel to fill these positions. Of great importance are other opportunities besides those in the back of the house, and, as will become evident, many opportunities are available to a well-trained and motivated "cuisinier."

The Kitchen Brigade System

The "brigade system" was instituted by Escoffier to streamline and simplify work in hotel kitchens. It served to eliminate the chaos and duplication of effort that could result when workers did not have clear-cut responsibilities. Under this system, each position has a station and defined responsibilities, outlined below. In smaller operations, the classic system is generally abbreviated and responsibilities are organized so as to make the best use of work space and talents. A shortage of skilled personnel has also made modifications in the brigade system necessary. The introduction of new equipment has helped alleviate some of the problems of smaller kitchen staffs. Figure 1-1 illustrates a contemporary kitchen's organization.

The chef is responsible for all kitchen operations, including ordering, supervision of all stations, and development of menu items. He or she may be known also as "chef de cuisine" or executive chef.

The *sous* ("under") chef is second in command, answers to the chef, may be responsible for scheduling, fills in for the chef, and assists the station chefs (or line cooks) as necessary. Small operations may not have a sous chef.

Station chefs *(chefs de partie)* are considered "line cooks" and include the following:

The sauté station *(saucier)* is responsible for all sautéed items and their sauces. This position is often considered the most demanding, responsible, and glamorous on the line.

The fish station *(poissonier)* is responsible for fish items, often including fish butchering, and their sauces; this position is sometimes combined with the saucier position.

The roast station *(rôtisseur)* is responsible for all roasted foods and related jus or other sauces.

The grill station *(grillardin)* is responsible for all grilled foods; this position may be combined with rôtisseur.

The fry station *(friturier)* is responsible for all fried

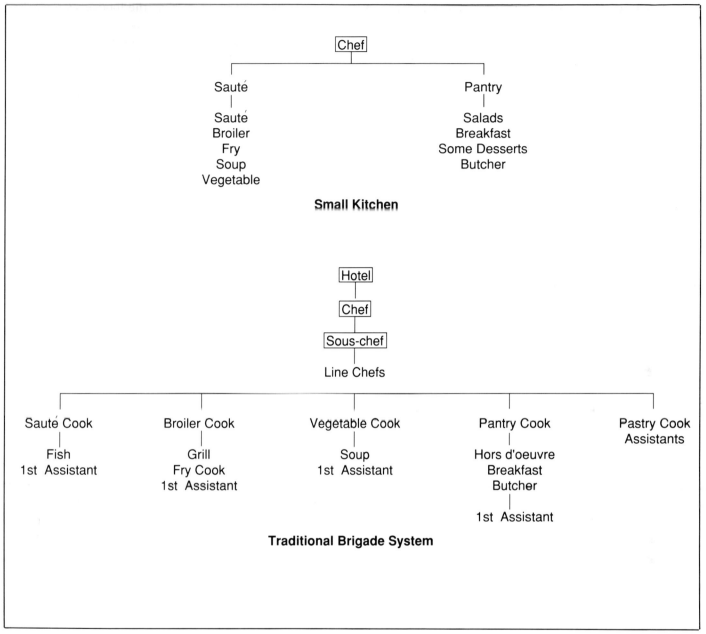

Small Kitchen

Traditional Brigade System

1-1

The organizational structures for two contemporary kitchens: the small kitchen *(top)* and the traditional brigade system *(bottom)*.

foods; this position may also be combined with rôtisseur.

The vegetable station *(entremetier)* is responsible for hot appetizers, and frequently has responsibility for soups and vegetables, starches and pastas. (In a full, traditional brigade system, soups are prepared by the soup station or *potager*, vegetables by the *legumier*.) This station may also be responsible for egg dishes.

The roundsman *(tournant)* is also known as the swing cook. This individual works as needed throughout the kitchen.

The pantry chef *(garde-manger)* is responsible for cold food preparations, including salads, cold appetizers, pâtés, etc. This is considered a separate category of kitchen work.

The butcher *(boucher)* is responsible for butchering meats, poultry, and (occasionally) fish. The boucher may also be responsible for breading meat and fish items, and is often considered part of garde-manger.

The pastry chef *(pâtissier)* is responsible for baked items, pastries, and desserts. The pastry chef frequently supervises a separate kitchen area or a separate shop in larger operations. This position may be further broken down into the following areas of specialization: *confiseur* (prepares candies, petits fours), *boulanger* (prepares nonsweetened doughs as for breads and rolls), *glacier* (prepares frozen and cold desserts), and *decorateur* (prepares show pieces and special cakes).

There are other brigade positions. The expediter or announcer *(aboyeur)* accepts orders from the dining room and relays them to the various station chefs. This individual is the last person to see the plate before it leaves the kitchen. In some operations, this may be either the sous chef or kitchen steward. The *communard* cooks for the staff; the *commis*, or apprentice, works under a chef de partie to learn the station and its responsibilities.

The Dining Room Brigade System

The other "traditional" type of foodservice industry positions are classified under the term "front of the house." The traditional line of authority in a dining room is as follows:

The *maître d'hôtel*, known in American service as the dining room manager or the food and beverage manager, is the person who holds the most responsibility for the front-of-the-house operation. The *maître d'hôtel* trains all service personnel, oversees wine selection, works with the chef to determine the menu, and organizes seating throughout service.

The wine steward *(chef de vin*, or *sommelier)* is responsible for all aspects of restaurant wine service, including purchasing wines, preparing a wine list, assisting guests in wine selection, and serving wine properly. If there is no wine steward, these responsibilities are generally assumed by the *maître d'hôtel*.

The head waiter *(chef de salle)* is generally in charge of the service for an entire dining room. Very often this position is subsumed into the positions of either the captain or the *maître d'hôtel*.

The captain *(chef d'étage)* deals most directly with the guests once they are seated. The captain explains the menu, answers any questions, and takes the order. Any tableside food preparation is generally done by the captain. If there is no captain, these responsibilities fall to the front waiter.

The front waiter *(chef de rang)* assures that the table is properly set for each course, that the food is properly delivered to the table, and that the needs of the guests are promptly and courteously met.

The back waiter or busboy *(demi-chef de rang* or *commis de rang)* is generally the first position assigned to new dining room workers. This person clears plates between courses, fills water glasses and bread baskets, replaces ashtrays, and assists the front waiter and/or captain as needed.

Nontraditional Positions

In addition to the kitchen and dining room positions, a growing number of less traditional opportunities exist, many of which do not involve the actual production or service of foods.

Consultants and design specialists will work with restaurant owners, often before the restaurant is even open, to assist in developing a menu, designing the overall layout and ambience of the dining room, and establishing work patterns for the kitchen.

Well-informed salespeople help chefs determine how to best meet their needs for food and produce, introduce them to new products, and demonstrate how to properly use new equipment that is essential to the well-run, modern kitchen.

Teachers are essential to the great number of cooking schools nationwide. Most of these teachers are chefs who are sharing the benefit of their experience with students.

Food writers and critics discuss food trends, restaurants, and chefs. It will always mean more, of course, if the writer is well-versed in the culinary arts.

Food stylists and photographers are sought after to work with a variety of publications, including magazines, books, catalogs, and promotional and advertising pieces.

Research and development kitchens employ a great many chefs. These may be run by food manufacturers who are developing new products or food lines or by advisory boards hoping to promote their product. Test kitchens are also run by a variety of both trade and consumer publications.

ESTABLISHMENTS

Chefs are needed not just in hotel dining rooms and traditional restaurants but in a variety of settings—public and private, consumer-oriented, and institutional. An increased emphasis on nutrition, sophistication, and financial and quality control means that all settings, from the "white tablecloth" restaurant to the fast-food outlet, offer interesting challenges.

Hotels often have a number of different dining facilities, including fine dining restaurants, room service, coffee shops, and banquet rooms. The kitchens are large, and there will often be separate butchering, catering, and pastry kitchens on the premises.

Full-service restaurants such as bistros, "white tablecloth," or family-style restaurants feature a full menu, and the patrons are served by trained waitstaff.

Private clubs generally provide some sort of foodservice. It may be as simple as a small grill featuring sandwiches, or it may be a complete dining room. The difference is that the guests are paying members, and the food costs are generally figured differently than they would be for a public restaurant.

Executive dining rooms are operated by many corporations. The degree of simplicity or elegance demanded in a particular corporation will determine what types of food are prepared, how they are prepared, and what style of service is appropriate.

Institutional catering (schools, hospitals, colleges, airlines, correctional institutions) often demands a single menu and a cafeteria where the guests serve themselves, choosing from the offered foods. The range of menu selections depends a great deal on the institution's needs, available monies, and the desires of those operating the cafeteria.

Caterers provide a particular service, often tailored to directly meet the wishes of a special client for a particular event, whether it be a wedding, a cocktail reception, or a gallery opening. Caterers may provide either on-site services (the client comes to the caterer), off-site services (caterer comes to the client), or both.

"Carry-out" foodservices are growing in importance as more couples, single professionals, and families try to enjoy meals at home without having to spend time preparing them. These shops prepare entrées, salads, side dishes, and desserts.

SUMMARY

It has been estimated that by the year 1995 there will be 1 million more foodservice industry jobs available than there will be trained people to fill them. This industry's evolution has been one of steady growth, increased diversification, and expanding opportunities. The interaction of new trends in foods and dining, combined with the traditions and customs of other eras and other social groups, creates new styles of cooking, new dishes, new types of eating establishments. The increasing communication between chefs and other influential individuals has stimulated growth and opened up new potentials.

It is important to have an understanding of how the industry has grown in order to have an insight into the ways in which it may continue to grow. This chapter has touched upon only some of the elements of the industry's history. The chef should not only keep abreast of new ideas, but also look to history for the lessons that can, and should, be learned.

Chapter 2

The Professional Chef

Those chefs who have made the greatest impression knew that their success depended on several character traits, some of which are inherent, some of which are diligently cultivated throughout a career. A true chef is, among other things, a lifelong student, a teacher, an artisan, and a professional. An open and inquiring mind, an appreciation of and dedication to quality wherever it is found, and a sense of responsibility are among the professional chef's cardinal virtues.

The term "chef," although it is frequently used to describe anyone who cooks, is a mark of respect. The position of chef is one that is earned through practice of the craft.

BECOMING A PROFESSIONAL CHEF

Any profession has a great many sides; the food-service industry also follows this axiom. Receiving a thorough grounding in the basics is a prerequisite for the practitioner of any craft or art, but many other important points should be considered as well.

Formal Education and Training

A sound and thorough culinary education is a logical first step in the development of one's foodservice career. In order to gain a solid grounding in basic and advanced culinary techniques and become "fluent" in the language of the trade, any aspiring chef will find formal training at an accredited school an excellent beginning. An apprenticeship and on-the-job training can be useful in place of formal training for some individuals, and as a follow-up to it for all chefs-in-training.

Learning should be an ongoing process, and is achieved in a variety of guises, all important at various stages throughout one's career.

There is no substitute for experience, and only with a great deal of practice will class-learned theory become fully developed. Continued practice, coupled with constant and critical attention, will eventually result in a mastery of technique.

Continuing Education

Continuing education, once initial training has been completed, is equally important, because the foodservice industry is constantly evolving. Attending classes, workshops, and seminars helps keep practicing cooks and chefs in step with new methods and new styles of cooking, or serves to hone skills in specialized areas.

Working with Other Chefs

Working with other professionals to share information and knowledge is another important avenue of growth. By keeping an open mind when faced with new concepts, chefs are able to incorporate fresh ideas into their own work.

In the same vein, joining professional organizations, competing in shows and competitions, reading trade magazines and journals, traveling, dining in other restaurants, and keeping current by reading mainstream magazines and newspapers are all important.

A Chef's Professional Attributes

Every member of a profession is responsible for the profession's image, whether he or she is a teacher, lawyer, doctor, or chef. The following lists a few of the many areas in which chefs are called upon to act in a manner consistent with their chosen profession.

The "Service" Concept

The foodservice industry is predicated on service; therefore, a chef should never lose sight of what that word implies. Good service includes (but is not limited to) providing good food, properly cooked, appropriately seasoned, and attractively presented in a pleasant environment—in short, making the customer happy. The degree to which an operation can offer satisfaction in these areas is the degree to which it will succeed in providing good (and ideally excellent) service. The customer must always come first.

Responsibility

Responsibility to one's self, to coworkers, to the restaurant, and to the guest should include respecting all involved resources.

When guests and employees feel that their needs are given due consideration, several valuable things will occur. Employees' self-esteem will increase and their attitudes toward the establishment will improve, both of which will increase their productivity and reduce absenteeism. Guests will enjoy their dining experience, certain that they are getting good value for their money.

Foods, equipment, staff, and the facility must be treated with care and respect. It will then be obvious to all staff members that this behavior is the norm. Waste, misuse, and abuse of any commodity is unacceptable. Personal behavior is also accountable. Abusive language, ethnic slurs, and profanity do not have a place in the professional kitchen.

Judgment

Although it is not easy to learn, a sense of what is right, whether it be combining certain ingredients in a dish, selecting menu items, or evaluating the quality of a product or finished dish, is a prerequisite for becoming a professional. This sense of what is appropriate is acquired throughout a lifetime of experience. Good judgment is never completely mastered; rather, it is a goal toward which one should continually strive.

The Uniform

A chef's uniform is an outward symbol of the profession. Looking like a professional helps to generate a feeling of professionalism. The uniform's history is an interesting one, reflecting both a practical, utilitarian outlook as well as its more romantic aspects.

The chef's checked trousers serve to disguise the inevitable spots that develop while working. The white jacket is double-breasted so that if it becomes soiled during service it can be rebuttoned to hide the dirt. Also, the double layer of fabric provides additional protection from scalds and burns. Finally, the jacket reflects the fact that the term "chef," in this country at least, does not denote gender; it is equally appropriate for men or women.

The neckerchief, tied cravat-style, originally served to absorb facial perspiration; today, it provides a "finished" look, much as a tie completes a suit. Aprons protect the uniform from spills and insulate the body from burns and scalds.

The most recognizable part of the uniform is the *toque blanche*, or hat. There are many explanations for the shape of the hat. For instance, some believe that the tall white hat may have originated at the time the Byzantine empire was under siege by the barbarians. Fleeing persecution, many men (some philosophers, some artists, some chefs to royalty) fled to Greek Orthodox monasteries for protection. In the monasteries, the headgear they wore was the same as the tall black hats of the priest's uniform so that they would not be recognized. After the threat of persecution lessened, they wore white hats, to differentiate themselves from the ordained priests. The pleats on a chef's hat also have a story—the hundred pleats are said to represent the 100 ways a chef can prepare eggs.

THE CHEF AS A BUSINESSPERSON

The primary purpose of being in business is, obviously, to make money. In the following sections, the basics of the business aspects of being a chef or foodservice operator are discussed. Because not everyone is capable of handling the increasingly complex problems of budgeting, taxes, wages, and many other business considerations, it is certainly a good idea to hire professionals trained specifically to handle these areas. In order to be sure that these professionals are able to do what a specific operation requires, the chef must be aware of how a business operates and must be realistic about what can be expected.

Cost/Accounting

Purchasing

Purchasing has a direct impact on cost control. An adequate store of supplies is needed so that the restaurant can operate efficiently. This includes not only food but nonfood items, such as cleaning supplies, small tools, and equipment. On the other hand, it is wasteful to have more supplies than can be used in a reasonable amount of time, or to own unnecessary equipment and tools. Following the nine steps outlined here will assure that foods, supplies, and equipment are purchased wisely and efficiently.

1. Develop needs. All food and equipment purchased for the kitchen should have a direct relation to the menu. First, develop a menu; if a menu already exists, analyze it carefully.

2. Develop quality and purchasing specifications. This is a precise description of the product, including trade or common names, type of container, brand names or federal grades, container size, and the unit (pound, case, bunch, can, and so on) on which the item's price is quoted. Any other pertinent specifications, such as whether meats should be aged, should also be included. These specifications should take the form of a written communication between the purchaser and the purveyor.

3. Select purveyors. It is best to have a minimum of two purveyors for any item purchased. Well-chosen purveyors can provide an operation with products of consistent quality, and will also work with an operation to help set up delivery schedules. To find a good purveyor, check with the Better Business Bureau and with other restaurant owners. The price quoted by the salesperson should be the same as the price paid upon receipt of the goods. Delivery trucks should be clean and, if necessary, properly refrigerated.

4. Organize a delivery schedule. A consistent delivery schedule means that the chef can save time and avoid wasting money. Inconsistent deliveries may force the chef to overpurchase in order to be prepared for the chance of a late delivery. Deliveries that are too frequent or too early may mean that foods cannot be used before they lose quality, leading to higher food costs and dollars lost through wasted products.

5. Develop a parstock. Parstock is the amount of stock necessary to cover operating needs between deliveries. Being overstocked can be as bad as having too little stock. If there is too much stock, valuable space and money are tied up. If there is not enough, it may be impossible to produce a given menu item.

6. Take purchase inventory. This is a physical count of what is available. This amount is then "brought to par" by ordering enough of an item to reach the level established by the parstock.

7. Forecast contingency needs. Keeping full and complete business records can help predict what times of the year, month, or week may be busier than others. Additional stock may then be ordered to cover especially high-volume times. The owner or chef in a new operation can learn some of this information by talking with other area owners or chefs. Other factors to consider are parties, banquets, and special events such as festivals in the area.

8. Take market quotes. This translates simply as continually being aware of current prices.

9. Maintain a purchase log. Keeping good records of all orders, invoices, and price lists helps to make ordering, receiving, and storing procedures efficient.

Storage

If all storage areas, no matter how small, are well-maintained and -monitored, then the amount of money lost through waste and spoilage will automatically be lowered.

Food Cost

The food and drink that are ultimately served to the guest are the raw materials of the industry. It is impossible to overemphasize how important it is for the chef to be aware of what food and drink actually cost, and to take steps to maximize the use of the raw materials. *Total utilization* is the goal. Controlling spoilage and waste is a priority because many of these materials are perishable. Keeping food costs in line is the chef's responsibility and he or she must maintain an awareness of food and beverage prices, even if the purchasing is actually done by someone else.

The chef must also be familiar with the food's expected yield. That is, he or she should know that a case of broccoli will yield a particular number of servings, once the broccoli is trimmed, peeled, cut, and cooked. The AP, or "as purchased" price, represents the amount paid for the item as delivered to the kitchen. Once all of the inedible and/or nonuseful portions of the item are removed, the EP, or "edible portion" cost, can be determined by dividing the EP weight into the AP price.

Menu Pricing

Once the chef has determined exactly what the food cost is, a variety of methods may be used to calculate the correct selling price. These methods have many variations, and different approaches to menu pricing work well for different sorts of establishments. Two of the more commonly used methods for pricing are explained below.

1. Food cost percentage. The food cost percentage reflects the idea that the cost of the food sold should fall within a range that is a specified percentage of the sales in dollars. For instance, if the food cost percentage should be approximately 25 percent, an item costing $1 per portion should sell for $4. The EP cost has been divided by the appropriate food cost percentage.

In a similar way, 25 percent (representing the food cost) may be divided into 100 percent (representing the selling price) to get 4. This number is a "factor" by which the food cost can be multiplied to arrive at the selling price as well. The 80/20 rule, a variation of this percentage method, states that 80 percent of the food cost should come from 20 percent of food sales. In both methods, the remaining 75 or 80 percent of the income from food sales must cover the other costs of doing business, such as labor, utilities, rent or mortgage, and taxes, as well as provide a profit.

2. "Follow-the-leader" pricing. Simply put, this method means that the selling price is the same as that of other restaurants of similar caliber in the area.

Menu pricing is a rather complex process and there are a number of books that can assist in determining which method is appropriate to an operation and how to use the chosen method. Such books include *The Restaurant Operator's Manual*, by Allen Z. Reich (1990, Van Nostrand Reinhold), and *The Business Chef* by Tom Miner (1989, Van Nostrand Reinhold). Also refer to the resources listed in the Recommended Readings.

Computers in the Kitchen

Unlike other labor-saving devices, such as food processors, one of the most useful tools to show up in the kitchen in recent years has no direct interaction with the food itself. The computer, however, is almost essential today to allow a kitchen and the chef to operate successfully.

One of the most basic computer functions is to assist in recordkeeping, inventory, and costing. Other applications include standardizing and, in some cases, costing out recipes, analyzing nutrients easily and quickly, and writing and printing menu copy to allow more frequent changes. This allows the chef to take advantage of an item that has a short season, or one that is exceptionally well-priced. Given a computer's many advantages to a foodservice operation, computer literacy is an important part of every chef's education.

Marketing and Customer Relations

The way in which a foodservice establishment presents itself to its customers has a definite influence on whether or not the business will succeed. The following areas of concern, although they may not appear to come directly under the chef's domain, are still areas that should be given consideration.

Menu design and layout. Menus are potent advertising pieces and should be treated as such. Some establishments may prefer a formal menu design, professionally printed on good-quality paper. Others may choose a "disposable" menu in order to allow frequent changes: computer-generated menus that the customer may take away, permanent display boards, or even chalkboards are just a few options. Each of these different styles gives a message to the customer and sets up certain expectations. Whatever the design style chosen, it should be a true reflection of the establishment's type of food and service.

Copy. Customers should be able to read and understand the menu easily, so it is important to consider the size and type of print to be used, the words used to describe a dish, and perhaps the inclusion of foreign terms. Although a good waitperson should be available to answer any questions, it is not a good idea to write a menu in such a way that the customer is uncertain about the majority of the items or is in any way intimidated.

Restaurant design and ambience. First and foremost, a foodservice establishment should be appealing to the eye and the nose. This means keeping all visible areas clean, well-lit, and well-maintained. There are additional considerations, however. Lighting should be appropriate and adequate to allow the menu to be read easily. It should be flattering to the food and to the guest, in order to promote a pleasant feeling. Chairs should be comfortable and tables should be appropriately appointed with flatware and china that are suitable to both the food and to the atmosphere of the restaurant. Music may be good for some styles of operations. It should be at a level that makes it easy to hear but not so loud that it intrudes on the meal or conversation.

Above all, it should be remembered that the service provided must be appropriate to the needs and wants of the customers, as well as to the standards and ideals of the particular establishment. Bistros and grill rooms should "feel" like bistros; "white tablecloth" restaurants need a more formal atmosphere.

SUMMARY

A chef must deal daily with a great many people: salespeople, waitstaff, kitchen staff, customers. In order to be successful in these dealings, the chef constantly must keep one key element in mind: professionalism.

This concept is not always easy to define and is actually much more simply described in terms of what it is not. Anyone can recognize behavior that is below the industry's acceptable standards.

Education, work experience, more education, more experience, and still more education are the cornerstones. Learning through daily contact with other professionals what professionalism means, and how it shows itself to coworkers and guests, will do much to elevate the chef's image. Carrying professionalism into all areas is the chef's responsibility.

Some of the subjects touched on in this chapter may not come into play on a daily basis—the method chosen for cost accounting, the type of menu to be used, the lighting that is most effective. None of these, however, are considerations a chef can afford to ignore.

Part Two

Sanitation,
Nutrition,
and Equipment

Before discussing ingredients and cooking procedures, basic information on sanitation and safety, nutrition, and equipment must be covered. The importance of maintaining sanitary conditions for food preparation and a safe kitchen environment cannot be overemphasized. An unsanitary workspace and careless work habits can cause food-borne illnesses that not only are uncomfortable and possibly dangerous for the guests, but also can be a source of negative publicity.

Nutrition is playing an increasingly important role in contemporary life. Many Americans are becoming receptive to changes in diet as part of an overall program to maintain health and general fitness and are looking for healthful items on the menu.

Selecting equipment appropriate to the establishment's needs is also an important preliminary step. The goal is to have the proper tool for the task at hand.

Chapter 3

Sanitation and Safety

The importance of sanitation cannot be over-emphasized. In a business based on service and hospitality, reputations and, indeed, livelihoods are dependent upon the customer's good will. Few things are as detrimental to that good will as an official outbreak of a food-borne illness caused by poor sanitary practices.

In addition to providing a sanitary atmosphere and adhering to procedures for safe food handling, it is also important to assure a safe working environment. This chapter covers the causes of food-borne illnesses and prevention procedures and also includes checklists to help the staff achieve sanitary and safe kitchen conditions.

SANITATION

Simply put, sanitation is the preparation and distribution of food in a clean environment by healthy food workers. The purpose of teaching sanitation is to attempt to assure that the customer will be protected from food-borne illness. In addition to damaging a business's good name, an outbreak of illness can be expensive. Possible legal costs combined with loss of revenue may well force an establishment to close.

Regulations, Inspection, and Certification

Federal, state, and local government regulations work to ensure the wholesomeness of the food that reaches the public. Any new foodservice business should contact the local health department well in advance of opening to ascertain the necessary legal requirements. A professional chef moving to a new area to work should contact local authorities for ordinances specific to that area.

Some states and local jurisdictions offer sanitation certification programs. Regulations and testing vary from area to area; in some cases, each kitchen is required to have at least one worker who has been certified. Certification is often available through certain academic institutions.

Food-borne Illness

Food can serve as the potential carrier for many different illnesses. The severity of the illness depends on the amount of contaminated food ingested and, to a great extent, on the individual's susceptibility. Children, the elderly, and anyone whose immune system is already under siege generally will have much more difficulty than a healthy adult in combating a food-borne illness.

The most common symptoms of food-borne illnesses include cramps, nausea, vomiting, and diarrhea, possibly accompanied by fever. These symptoms may appear within a matter of hours, although in some cases, one to two days may elapse before onset. In order for a food-borne illness to be officially declared an outbreak, it must involve two or more people who have eaten the same food and must be confirmed by health officials. Table 3-1 gives a detailed list of food-borne illnesses and symptoms.

Contamination Sources

The source of the contamination affecting the food supply can be chemical, physical, or biological. Insecticides and cleaning compounds are examples of chemical contaminants that may accidentally find their way into foods.

Physical contaminants include such things as bits of glass, rodent hairs, and paint chips. Careless food-handling can mean that even an earring or a plastic bandage could fall into the food and result in illness or injury.

Biological sources account for the majority of food-borne illnesses. These include naturally occurring poisons, known as toxins, found in certain wild mushrooms, rhubarb leaves, green potatoes, and other plants. The predominant biological agents, however, are disease-causing microorganisms known as pathogens, which are responsible for up to 95 percent of all food-borne illnesses. Microorganisms of many kinds are present virtually everywhere, and most are helpful if not essential; it is only a small percentage of microorganisms that are actually responsible for causing illness.

Potentially Hazardous Foods

Microorganisms require three basic conditions for growth: a protein source, readily available moisture, and a moderate pH. Many foods provide these three growing conditions, and are therefore considered to be potentially hazardous. Two other factors—available oxygen and storage temperature—will also affect a microorganism's ability to grow and reproduce but, as will be discussed below, the requirements for these two factors will vary according to the type of microorganism.

Foods do not necessarily have to be animal-based to contain protein; vegetables and grains also contain protein. The higher the amount of protein in a food, the greater its potential as a carrier of a food-borne illness. Meats, poultry, seafood, tofu, and dairy products (with the exception of some hard cheeses) are all categorized as potentially hazardous foods. Sauces such as custards, hollandaise, and mayonnaise are particularly high in egg yolks and should be handled with meticulous attention to sanitary work methods at all times.

A food's relative acidity or alkalinity is measured on a scale known as pH. Figure 3-1 shows the effect of pH on bacterial growth. A moderate pH—a value between 4.6 and 10 on a scale that ranges from 1 to 14—is best for bacterial growth, and most foods fall within that range. Salting, brining, or pickling will change a food's pH to a more alkaline measurement of 10 or more; this will mean that the food is no longer as susceptible to food-borne illness.

Preserving—the methods by which foods are smoked, salted, or air-cured—is another way to reduce the potential for bacterial growth. It is for this reason that meats were salted, smoked, or air-cured to preserve them through the winter before refrigeration became widely available.

Classification

Food-borne illnesses fall into two distinct subdivisions: intoxication and infection.

Intoxication. Food intoxication occurs when a person consumes food containing toxins produced during the pathogen's life cycle. Once in the body, these toxins act as poison. A staphylococcus intoxication and botulism are food intoxications.

Infection. In the case of an infection, the food eaten by an individual contains large numbers of living pathogens. These pathogens multiply in the body and generally attack the gastrointestinal lining. Salmonellosis is an example of a food-borne infection.

TABLE 3-1. FOOD-BORNE ILLNESSES

Disease and Incubation Period*	Symptoms	Cause	Food Involved	Preventative Measures
		Intoxicants		
Botulism 12–36 hours	sore throat, vomiting, blurred vision, cramps, diarrhea, difficulty breathing, central nervous system damaged (possible paralysis). Fatality rate up to 70%.	*Clostridium botulinum:* anaerobic bacteria that form spores with a high resistance to heat. Found in animal intestines, water, and soil.	Refrigerated, low-acid foods or improperly canned foods such as spinach, tuna, green beans, beets, fermented foods, and smoked products. Rare in commercially canned food.	Toxin is sensitive to heat, so maintain a high temperature while canning food and boil 20 minutes before serving. Do not use food in swollen cans or use home-canned food for commercial use.
Staphylococcus 2–4 hours	vomiting, nausea, diarrhea, cramps	*Staphylococcus aureus:* facultative bacteria found in the nose, throat, and in skin infections of humans.	Foods that are high in protein, moist, handled much, and left in the danger zone. Milk, egg custards, turkey stuffing, chicken/tuna/potato salads, gravies, reheated food.	Since toxin cannot be destroyed by heating, store foods below 40° and reheat thoroughly to 165°F. People with infected cuts, burns, or respiratory illnesses should not handle food, and *all* food handling should be limited. Keep food out of danger zone.
Ergotism varies	hallucinations, convulsions, gangrene of extremities	Ergot: a mold that grows on wheat and rye	Wheat and rye	Do not use moldy wheat and rye
Chemical Poisoning Minutes to hours	varied	Pesticides on fruits and vegetables, cyanide in silver polish, zinc inside tin cans, copper pans		Wash fruit and vegetables before using; stop using polish with cyanide and wash utensils after polishing; store pesticides away from food; avoid cooking and storing foods in cans since zinc is leached out of tin by acidic foods and is poisonous; don't allow food to touch copper.

* Incubation period is the time between infection and onset of symptoms.
Source: *Basic Food Sanitation*, The Culinary Institute of America, 1986, pp. 1-21–1-23.

(continued)

TABLE 3-1. FOOD-BORNE ILLNESSES *(continued)*

Disease and Incubation Period*	Symptoms	Cause	Food Involved	Preventative Measures
		Intoxicants		
Plant and Animal Poisoning varies—often rapid	varies	Aklaloids; organic acids		Make sure you can identify mushrooms. Don't ingest rhubarb leaves, too much nutmeg, green-skinned potatoes, fava leaves, raw soybeans, blowfish, moray eel, or shark liver.
Salmonellosis 6–48 hours	headache, diarrhea, cramps, fever. Can be fatal or lead to arthritis, meningitis, and typhoid	*Salmonella:* aerobic bacillus that lives and grows in the intestines of humans, animals, birds, and insects.	Egg, poultry, shellfish, meat, soup, sauces, gravies, milk products, warmed-over food	Don't hold food in danger zone for more than 2 hours. Reheat leftovers to an internal temperature of 165°F. Since *salmonella* can be killed by high temperatures, cook to proper temperatures. Eliminate rodents and flies, wash hands after using bathroom, avoid cross-contamination, especially with cooked foods.
Shigellosis 12–48 hours	diarrhea, cramps, fever, dehydration	*Shigella sonnei* and other species found in feces of infected humans, food, and water.	Beans, contaminated milk, tuna/turkey/ macaroni salads, apple cider, and mixed, moist foods	Safe water sources, strict control of insects and rodents, good personal hygiene.
Bacillus cereus 8–16 hours	cramps, diarrhea, nausea, vomiting	*Bacillus cereus:* anaerobic bacteria that produce spores and are found in soil and any food	Cereal products, cornstarch, rice, custards, sauces, meat loaf	Spores are able to survive heating, so reheat to 165°F and keep foods out of danger zone.
Streptococcus 1–4 days	nausea, vomiting, diarrhea	Various species of *streptococcus* bacteria which are facultative anaerobes. Some are transmitted by animals and workers contaminated with feces, others from the nose and throat of infected humans.	Milk, pudding, ice cream, eggs, meat pie, egg/potato salads, poultry.	Cook food thoroughly and chill rapidly. Strict personal hygiene. Use pasteurized dairy products.
Trichinosis 4–28 days	fever, diarrhea, sweating, muscle pain, vomiting, skin lesions	*Trichinella spiralis:* a spiral worm that lives in the intestines where it matures and lays eggs and later invades muscle tissue. Transmitted by infected swine and rats.	Improperly cooked pork allows larvae to live.	Cook pork to 150°F. Avoid recontamination of raw meats. If frying, cook to 170°F.

* Incubation period is the time between infection and onset of symptoms.
SOURCE: *Basic Food Sanitation*, The Culinary Institute of America, 1986, pp. 1-21–1-23.

TABLE 3-1. FOOD-BORNE ILLNESSES

Disease and Incubation Period*	Symptoms	Cause	Food Involved	Preventative Measures
		Intoxicants		
Infectious Hepatitis 10–50 days	jaundice, fever, cramps, nausea, lethargy	Hepatitis virus A: grows in feces of infected humans and human carriers. Transmitted by water and from person to person and infects the liver.	Shellfish from polluted water, milk, whipped cream, cold cuts, potato salad.	Since the virus does not grow in foods, the only control method to prevent contamination is to cook clams, etc., thoroughly to a temperature exceeding 150°F. Heat-treat and disinfect suspected water and milk. Strict personal hygiene (especially after using the bathroom).
Perfringens 9–15 hours	diarrhea, nausea, cramps, possible fever, vomiting (rare)	*Clostridium perfringens:* spore-forming anaerobic bacteria that can withstand most cooking temperatures and are found in soil, dust, and the intestinal tract of animals.	Reheated meats, raw meat, raw vegetables, soups, gravies, stews	Cool meat that is to be eaten later quickly and reheat to 165°F. Avoid cross-contamination of raw meat and cooked meat. The only way to kill spores is to pressure cook at 15 lb. steam pressure to reach 250°F.

* Incubation period is the time between infection and onset of symptoms.
SOURCE: *Basic Food Sanitation*, The Culinary Institute of America, 1986, pp. 1-21–1-23.

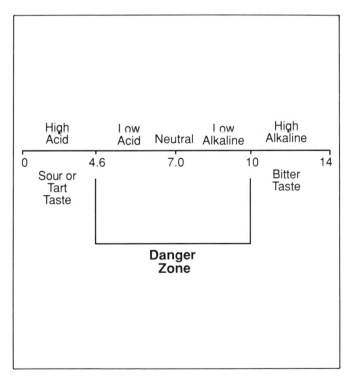

3-1

pH values for various foods. A value of less than 7 denotes an acidic food; a value above 7 indicates an alkaline food. SOURCE: *Basic Food Sanitation*, The Culinary Institute of America, 1986, p. 1-10.

Pathogens

The specific types of pathogens responsible for food-borne illnesses are fungi, viruses, parasites, and, most important, bacteria.

Fungi, which include molds and yeast, are more adaptable than other microorganisms and have a higher tolerance for acidic conditions. They are more often responsible for food spoilage than for food-borne illness. Fungi are important to the food industry in the production of cheeses, breads, and wines and beers.

Viruses do not actually multiply in food, but if food is contaminated by a virus through poor sanitation practice, consumption of that food may result in illness. Infectious hepatitis caused by eating shellfish harvested from polluted waters (an illegal practice) is an example. A chef should therefore be sure of the source of the shellfish being purchased. Shellfish harvested from safe waters will be tagged as such.

Viruses reproduce asexually. This process, known as bacteriophaging, occurs when a virus invades a cell (called the host cell) and "reprograms" it to produce not more host cells, but more viruses. The new viruses leave the dead host cells behind and invade still more cells.

Parasites are pathogens that feed and take shelter from another organism, called a host. The host receives no benefit from the parasite and, in fact, may suffer harm or even death as a result. Amoebas and various worms, such as the *Trichinella spiralis* associated with pork, are among the parasites that contaminate foods. Different parasites reproduce in different ways. An example is the parasitic worm that exists in the larva stage in muscle meats. Once consumed, the life cycle and reproductive cycle continue. When the larvae reach adult stage, the fertilized female releases more larvae, which travel to the muscle tissue of the host, and the cycle continues.

Bacteria are responsible for the majority of biologically caused food-borne illnesses. It is important to understand the classifications and patterns of bacterial growth in order to better protect food during storage, preparation, and service.

Classifying Bacteria

Bacteria are classified by their requirement for oxygen, the temperatures at which they grow best, and their spore-forming abilities.

Oxygen requirement. Aerobic bacteria require the presence of oxygen to grow. Anaerobic bacteria do not require oxygen and may die even when exposed to it. Facultative bacteria are able to function with or without oxygen.

Temperature. The effect of temperature, as well as time, on the growth of bacteria is shown in Figure 3-2. In terms of sensitivity to temperature, bacteria fall into the following categories:

1. Mesophilic bacteria grow best between 60 and 100°F (16 and 38°C). Because the temperatures of human bodies, as well as commercial kitchens, fall within that range, mesophilic (middle temperature range) bacteria tend to be the most abundant and the most dangerous.
2. Thermophilic bacteria grow most rapidly between 110 and 171°F.
3. Psychrophilic bacteria prefer cooler temperatures, between 32 and 60°F (0–15°C).

Spore-forming abilities. Certain bacteria are able to form endospores, which serve as a means of protection against adverse circumstances such as high temperature or dehydration. These endospores are not a means of reproduction, but instead allow an individ-

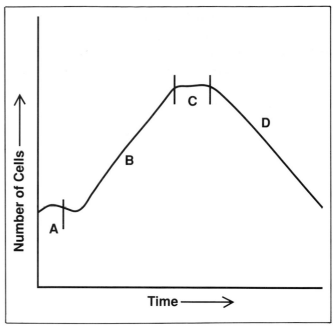

3-2

Stages of bacterial growth. The four distinct stages of growth for bacteria are (a): the *lag phase*, during which newly introduced bacteria become adjusted to their environment; (b) the *accelerated growth phase*, during which the organisms reproduce at a rapid rate due to ideal environmental conditions; (c) the *stationary phase*, during which the rate of growth equals the rate of death and there is no increase in numbers; and (d) the *decline phase*, when the essentials needed for the bacteria to live are exhausted, and the death rate exceeds the growth rate. SOURCE: *Basic Food Sanitation*, The Culinary Institute of America, 1986, p. 1-14.

ual bacterium to resume its life cycle if favorable conditions should recur.

Reproduction. Bacteria reproduce asexually by means of binary fission—one bacteria grows and then splits into two bacteria of equal size. These bacteria divide to form four, the four form 16, and so on. Under ideal circumstances, bacteria will reproduce every 20 minutes. In 12 hours, one bacterium can evolve into 72 billion bacteria, more than enough to cause illness.

Preventing Food-borne Illness

Food that contains pathogens in great enough numbers to cause illness may still look and smell normal. Disease-causing microorganisms are too small to be seen with the naked eye, so it is usually impossible to ascertain visually that food is adulterated (unfit for human consumption). Because the microorganisms, particularly the bacteria, that cause food to spoil are different from the ones that cause food-borne illness, food may be adulterated and still have no "off" odor. Although cooking food will destroy many of the micro-organisms present, careless food handling after cooking can reintroduce pathogens that grow even more quickly without competition for food and space from spoilage microorganisms.

Although shortcuts and carelessness do not always result in food-borne illness, inattention to detail increases the risk of creating an outbreak that may cause serious illness or even death. The various kinds of expenses that a restaurant can incur as the result of an outbreak of food-borne illness can be staggering. In addition, negative publicity and loss of prestige are blows from which many restaurants can simply never recover.

Cross-contamination

Many food-borne illnesses are a result of unsanitary handling procedures in the kitchen. Cross-contamination occurs when disease-causing elements are transferred from one contaminated surface to another, and can be avoided by adhering to the following practices.

Personal cleanliness. Excellent personal hygiene is one of the best defenses against cross-contamination. The employee who works with a contagious illness or even an infected cut on the hand puts every customer at risk. Food handlers should follow the guidelines contained in Figure 3-3. Any time the hands come in contact with a possible source of contamination, especially the face, hair, eyes, and mouth, they must be thoroughly washed before continuing any work. Food workers must also observe careful hygienic procedures, as shown in Figures 3-4 and 3-5.

Careful preparation and storage. Food is usually at greatest risk of cross-contamination during the preparation stage. Ideally, separate work areas and cutting boards should be used for raw and cooked foods. Equipment and cutting boards should always be cleaned and thoroughly sanitized between uses. For example, before cutting a piece of pork on a surface that was used to cut chicken, it is important to clean and sanitize not only the cutting surface, but also the knife and the steel. Wiping cloths for this purpose should be held in a double-strength sanitizing solution and placed near each workstation to encourage use. All food must be stored carefully to prevent contact of raw and cooked. Place drip pans beneath raw foods to prevent any splashing or drippage.

CHECKLIST FOR FOOD HANDLERS AND SERVERS

____ Observe fundamentals of good personal hygiene.

____ Maintain good general health; have regular physical and dental checkups. Do not handle food when ill.

____ Attend to cuts or burns immediately. Keep any burn or break in the skin covered with a clean, waterproof bandage and change it as necessary.

____ Begin each shift in a clean, neat uniform. Do not wear the uniform to or from work or school. Store the uniform and all clothing in a clean locker.

____ Keep hair clean, neat, and restrained, if necessary.

____ Keep fingernails short and well maintained, with no polish.

____ Do not wear jewelry other than a watch and/or a plain band, to reduce risk of personal injury and/or cross-contamination.

____ Do not smoke or chew gum when working with food.

____ Wash hands thoroughly (long enough to lather) when beginning a shift, after handling raw food items (for example, raw chicken), after handling any nonfood item, and upon returning to the kitchen.

____ Keep hands away from hair or face when working with food.

____ Cover face with tissue when coughing or sneezing and wash hands afterward.

____ Clean side stands, trays, and tray stands before the start of each shift and as necessary during service.

____ Handle napkins as little as possible; always fold them on a clean surface. Table linens should only be used once.

____ Carry plates, glasses, and flatware in such a way that food contact surfaces are not touched.

____ Serve all foods using the proper utensils; handle ice and rolls with tongs, never with fingers.

3-3
Sample checklist for food handlers and servers.

Proper Cooling Methods

An equally important weapon against pathogens is the observance of strict time/temperature controls. As the shaded areas in Figure 3-6 indicate, the temperature range in which foods are most susceptible to contam-

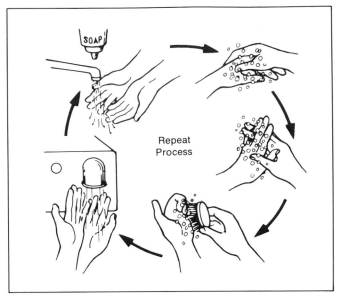

3-4

Proper handwashing procedure. Proper handwashing procedure should be observed before handling food; after
sneezing, smoking, or using the bathroom; and after touching money, garbage, or unclean surfaces. Wash hands thoroughly with soap and water, scrub nails with a brush, rinse,
and dry well. SOURCE: *Basic Food Sanitation*, The Culinary
Institute of America, 1986, p. 2-5.

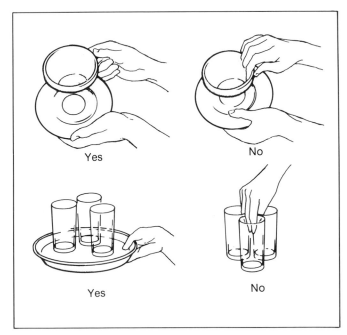

3-5

Proper ware handling. To prevent the transmission of food-
borne illnesses, limit hand contact with tableware that
comes in contact with food or the customer's mouth. Handle glasses or cups by their bases or handles—don't touch
rims. Carry utensils by their handles. Avoid touching the
rims of bowls and plates. SOURCE: *Basic Food Sanitation*,
The Culinary Institute of America, 1986, p. 2-4.

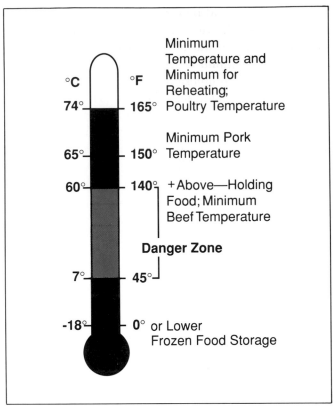

3-6

Safe reheating temperatures for foods. This illustration
shows the proper reheating ranges for various foods. Note
the "danger zone" between 45 and 140°F (7 and 60°C).
SOURCE: *Basic Food Sanitation*, The Culinary Institute of
America, 1986, p. 1-11.

ination is 45 to 140°F (7 to 60°C). This range is known
as the "danger zone," and chefs should have a clear
understanding of this concept. Foods left in the danger zone for a period longer than two hours are considered adulterated. Additionally, one should be fully
aware that the two-hour period does not have to be
continuous, but is *cumulative*, which means that "the
meter is running" every time the food enters the danger zone. Cooling and heating foods to a temperature
outside the range will not reduce the total accumulation.

Food should be prepared as close to service time as
possible. In the case of stocks, other preparations
used as ingredients for other dishes, and food prepared in advance banquets and catering, there are
specific safe handling procedures. Cooked foods that
are to be stored need to be cooled down to below 45°F
(7°C) as quickly as possible. Placing a large container
of hot stock under refrigeration will not cool it quickly
enough and may result in raising the temperature of
the refrigerator.

Hot liquids should be placed in a cold water or ice water bath, as shown in Figure 3-7, and stirred frequently so that the warmer liquid at the center mixes with the cooler liquid at the outside edge of the pot, bringing overall temperature down rapidly. Stirring also discourages potentially dangerous anaerobic bacteria from multiplying at the center of the mixture.

Semi-solid foods should be refrigerated in shallow containers to allow greater surface exposure to the cold air for quicker chilling. For the same reason, large cuts of meat should be cut into smaller portions, cooled to room temperature, and wrapped before storing.

Reheating Foods

When foods are prepared ahead and then reheated, they should move through the danger zone as rapidly as possible and be reheated to a safe internal temperature. Refer to Figure 3-6. Improperly reheated foods are frequently the culprit in food-borne illness.

Food handlers must use the proper methods and equipment for reheating potentially hazardous foods, which should be brought to the proper temperature over direct heat (burner, flat top, grill, or conventional oven) or in a microwave oven. A steam table will ade-

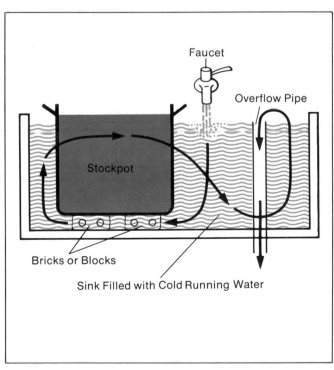

3-7

Proper cooling procedure for liquids. Heat conductors, such as metal, make better containers for cooling foods than insulators such as plastic. SOURCE: "Skill Development I and II," The Culinary Institute of America, classroom handout.

quately hold reheated foods above 140°F (60°C), but will not bring foods out of the danger zone quickly enough. Instant-reading thermometers should always be used to check temperatures. The thermometer should be carefully cleaned and sanitized after each use.

Thawing Frozen Foods

Frozen foods may be safely thawed in several ways. Once thawed, they should be used as soon as possible, and for optimum quality and flavor should not be refrozen. The best—though slowest—method is to allow the food to thaw under refrigeration. The food should still be wrapped and should be placed in a shallow container to prevent any drips from cross-contaminating other items stored near or below. If there is not time to do this, covered or wrapped food may be placed in a container under running water of 70°F (21°C).

Individual portions that are to be cooked immediately may be thawed in a microwave oven. Liquids, small items, or individual portions may also be cooked without thawing, but larger pieces of solid or semi-solid foods would become overcooked on the outside before they were thoroughly cooked throughout. Do not thaw food at room temperature; it is an invitation to pathogens.

Storing Foods

1. Refrigeration. Refrigeration and freezing units should be regularly maintained and equipped with thermometers to make sure that the temperature remains within a safe range. Although in most cases chilling will not actually kill pathogens, it does drastically slow down reproduction. Refer to Figure 3-2 and notice the lag phase that is part of the bacterial growth curve. In general, refrigerators should be kept between 36 and 40°F (2 to 4°C), but quality is better served if certain foods can be stored at specific temperatures:

Meat and poultry—32 to 36°F (0 to 2°C)
Fish and shellfish—30 to 34°F (−1 to 1°C)
Eggs—38 to 40°F (3 to 4°C)
Dairy products—36 to 40°F (2 to 4°C)
Produce—40 to 45°F (4 to 7°C)

Separate refrigerators for each of the above categories is ideal, but if necessary, a single unit can be divided into sections. The front of the box will be the warmest area, the back the coldest.

Reach-in or walk-in refrigerators should be put in order at the end of every shift. Before being put in the refrigerator, food should be properly cooled, stored in clean containers, wrapped, and labeled clearly with the contents and date. Store raw products below and away from cooked foods to prevent cross-contamination by dripping. Because air circulation is essential for effective cooling, avoid overcrowding the box and make sure the fan is not blocked.

Do not stack trays directly on top of food; this will reduce the amount of air that can circulate and may also result in cross-contamination. Use the principle of First In, First Out (FIFO) when arranging food, so that older products are in the front.

2. Dry storage. Dry storage is used for foods such as canned goods, spices, condiments, cereals, staples such as flour and sugar, as well as for some fruits and vegetables that do not require refrigeration and have low perishability. As with all storage, the area must be clean, with proper ventilation and air circulation. Foods should not be stored on the floor or near the walls, and there must be adequate shelving to prevent crowding. The FIFO system mentioned previously should be practiced and all containers should be labeled with a date. Cleaning supplies should be stored in a separate place.

Sanitizing

It is important to note the distinction between cleaning a surface or object and sanitizing it. Cleaning refers to the removal of soil or food particles, whereas sanitizing involves using moist heat or chemical agents to kill pathogenic microorganisms. During preparation, or for equipment that cannot be immersed in a sink (see Chapter 5, "Equipment Identification"), use a wiping cloth wrung out in a double-strength sanitizing solution. Small equipment, tools, pots, and tableware should be run through a warewashing machine or washed manually in a three-compartment sink. The many kinds of warewashing machines all use some sanitation method, such as very hot water (usually 180 to 195°F [82 to 91°C]) or chemical agents. Figure 3-8 shows a properly set-up three-compartment sink for hand washing of dishes and pots. The first basin is used for washing, the second for rinsing, and the third for sanitizing by means of a 30-second immersion in water of 170°F (77°C) or an immersion in a chemical sanitizer. Iodine, chlorine, and quaternary ammonium compounds are inds are all common sanitizing agents. Check the manufacturer's instructions for procedures for use.

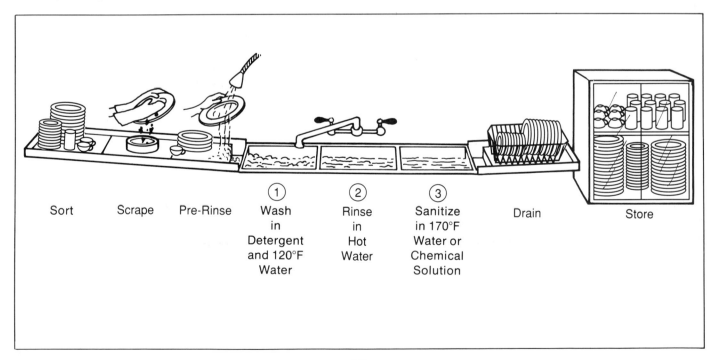

| Sort | Scrape | Pre-Rinse | ① Wash in Detergent and 120°F Water | ② Rinse in Hot Water | ③ Sanitize in 170°F Water or Chemical Solution | Drain | Store |

3-8

Proper setup for a three-compartment sink. Manual dishwashing should be done in three sinks (wash, rinse, and sanitize) away from food preparation areas. The dishes are first sorted, then scraped and pre-rinsed to remove large food particles. Dishes are washed in the *first sink*, which contains a detergent solution of at least 120°F (49°C). They are rinsed in the *second sink* in water at approximately 130°F (54°C), then sanitized in the *third sink*, which contains water at 170°F (77°C) or a chemical sanitizing solution. Dishes are then air dried and stored.

Hard water, which contains excessive amounts of iron, calcium, or magnesium, may interfere with the effectiveness of detergents and sanitizing agents and may also cause deposits that can clog machinery. Water-softening additives can prevent these problems. After sanitizing, equipment and tableware should be allowed to air dry completely because using paper or cloth toweling could result in cross-contamination.

Figure 3-9 lists daily and weekly cleaning duties for the entire kitchen. These should be carefully observed. An accumulation of dirt and grease in kitchens is not only unsanitary and unsightly, it is a source of other potential hazards. Slippery floors can cause falls that may result in injury. Improperly cleaned equipment may not function properly. Each kitchen, therefore, should develop its own cleaning schedule.

Pests

Careful sanitation procedures, proper handling of foodstuffs, and a well-maintained facility all work together to prevent a pest invasion. Besides being destructive and unpleasant, rats, mice, roaches, and flies may also harbor various pathogens. Figure 3-10 is a checklist for pest infestation prevention.

SAFETY

In addition to the precautions necessary to guard against food-borne illness, care also must be taken to avoid accidents to staff and guests. The following safety measures should be practiced:

1. Clean up grease and other spills as they occur. Use salt or cornmeal to absorb the grease, then clean the area.

2. Beware of grill fires. Do not attempt to put them out with water. Removing excessive fat and letting any marinades drain completely away from foods will help prevent flare-ups.

3. Observe caution when changing the oil in deep-fat fryers.

4. Keep fire extinguishers in proper working order and place them in kitchen areas where they are most likely to be needed.

5. Remove lids from pots so that the steam vents away from the face, to avoid steam burns.

6. Have first-aid kits and know the procedures for treating cuts and burns. Figure 3-11 is a list of first-aid supplies.

KITCHEN CHECKLIST

____ Use separate cutting boards for cooked and raw foods and sanitize after using.

____ Wash hands thoroughly after working with raw foods.

____ Use tasting spoons. Do not taste foods with fingers or with kitchen utensils.

____ Store any toxic chemicals (cleaning compounds and pesticides, for example) away from food to avoid cross-contamination.

____ Store solid or semi-solid potentially hazardous foods so that their depth is not more than 4 inches, to ensure prompt chilling.

____ Make a hand sink easily accessible, supplied with soap and paper towels.

____ Date and rotate inventory and observe a first in, first out (FIFO) policy.

____ Wrap or cover well, label, and date foods that are to be stored in refrigerators and freezers.

____ Use utensils whenever possible to cut down on unnecessary food handling.

____ Use wiping cloths and a sanitizing solution to wipe down work tables, cutting boards, and other surfaces between uses. Store the wiping cloth in a sanitizing solution, which should be changed as necessary.

____ Use side towels only for handling hot items.

____ Hold potentially hazardous foods in the danger zone (45 to 140°F [7 to 60°C]) for no more than two hours' cumulative time.

____ Prepare foods as close to service time as possible. If prepared in advance, foods should be chilled to below 45°F (7°C) as quickly as possible.

____ To reheat foods, bring them to a minimum temperature of 165°F (74°C) as quickly as possible. Steam tables, warmers, and similar pieces of equipment are not adequate for reheating.

____ Use instant-reading thermometers (and sanitize them after using) to ensure that adequate temperatures are reached.

____ Thaw frozen food in the refrigerator, under running water of 70°F (21°C), or in a microwave (provided that the food is to be thoroughly cooked immediately after thawing).

3-9

Sample kitchen maintenance checklist.

PEST INFESTATION PREVENTION

____Clean all areas and surfaces thoroughly. Wipe up spills immediately and sweep up crumbs.

____Cover garbage and remove every 4 hours.

____Elevate garbage containers on concrete blocks.

____Keep food covered or refrigerated.

____Check all incoming boxes for pests and remove boxes as soon as items are unpacked.

____Store food away from walls and floors, and maintain cool temperatures and good ventilation.

____Prevent access to facility by installing screened windows and screened, self-closing doors.

____Fill in all crevices and cracks, repair weak masonry, and screen off any openings to buildings, including vents, basement windows, and drains.

____If necessary, use insecticides, traps, poison, ultrasonic devices, and other pest control measures. Read and follow instructions carefully, or consult a professional exterminator.

3-10

Sample pest-infestation prevention checklist.

FIRST-AID SUPPLIES

____ Adhesive strips in assorted sizes

____ Bandage compresses

____ Sterile gauze dressings, individually wrapped

____ Rolled gauze bandage

____ First-aid adhesive tape

____ Cotton swabs (for applying antiseptic or removing particles from eye)

____ Tourniquet

____ Tongue depressors (for small splints)

____ Scissors

____ Tweezers

____ Needle (for removing splinters)

____ Rubbing alcohol (for sterilizing instruments)

____ Mild antiseptic (for wounds)

____ Antibiotic cream

____ Syrup of ipecac (to induce vomiting)

____ Petroleum jelly

____ Aspirin or acetaminophen

3-11

Sample checklist of first-aid supplies.

7. Make sure that all dining room and kitchen staff members know how to perform the Heimlich Maneuver. Post instructions in readily visible areas of the kitchen and the dining room.

8. Handle equipment carefully—especially mandolines, slicers, grinders, band saws, and other pieces of equipment with sharp edges.

9. Do not work while under the influence of alcohol or drugs.

10. Post emergency phone numbers for ambulance, hospital, and the fire department near every phone.

SUMMARY

Avoiding injury and illness to staff and guests is the responsibility of every employee. Failing to observe sanitation and safety procedures can:

- Damage the customer's or employee's health
- Ruin the establishment's reputation
- Lead to legal suits
- Increase insurance premiums
- Cause absenteeism
- Discourage workers

Professionals dare not take foolish chances with the public health, their reputations, or the tremendous investment of resources. In his or her attention to the details of maintaining a clean and safe establishment, the chef provides the most tangible evidence that a restaurant and its patrons are in the hands of a dedicated and responsible professional.

Chapter 4

Nutrition and Nutritional Cooking

A relatively young science, nutrition has profoundly influenced the way foods are selected, prepared, and presented. A combination of factors—including Americans' increasing consciousness of what they eat and technological advances that have encouraged people to lead more sedentary lives —has brought about a strong interest in nutrition. As a result, eating healthful foods has become a way of life for everyone, not just "fitness freaks" and those on special diets. No longer a specialty of institutional kitchens, nutritional cooking requires all cooks to be innovative. Chefs continually must adjust the ways they prepare foods and must include foods on their menus that have not been traditional restaurant fare. Making foods that are "good for you" good to eat can be one of the most enjoyable challenges in the contemporary kitchen.

THE BASICS OF NUTRITION

Nutrition is basically the study of how the body uses food—a series of interrelated steps by which food is assimilated for maintenance, for growth, and for replacement of tissue.

Building Blocks

Nutrition's building blocks are six basic nutrients: proteins, fats, carbohydrates, vitamins, minerals, and water. Nutrients are those compounds found in food that the body needs to maintain life. The body converts carbohydrates, proteins, and fats into energy, in the form of heat, which it uses to carry out innumerable functions. That energy is measured in units known as calories. A calorie is the amount of heat necessary to raise the temperature of a gram of water 1°C. Proteins and carbohydrates have 4 calories per gram; fat has 9 calories per gram.

Vitamins and minerals supply no energy but play specific roles in the body's metabolism. Water, sometimes a forgotten nutrient, is essential for the body's metabolic reactions to take place.

Carbohydrates

Carbohydrates are composed of units of individual sugar molecules and are classified as simple or complex. Simple carbohydrates are known as either monosaccharides or disaccharides. Examples include the naturally occurring sugars in milk and fruit as well as refined table sugar, maple syrup, and honey. Complex carbohydrates are polysaccharides and contain long chains of sugar units, such as those contained in starches and fibers.

Starch, as found in potatoes and cereals, is a valuable energy source that is also rich in vitamins and minerals. In fact, it is the plant's way of storing carbohydrates. Animals and humans have limited stores of complex carbohydrate, called glycogen, in the liver and muscles.

Fiber is the structural framework of plants and provides dietary fiber, of which there are two types, soluble and insoluble. Both are important. An example of soluble fiber is pectin, which may help prevent cancer, lower cholesterol levels, and control the blood sugar level in diabetics. Cellulose, an example of insoluble fiber, aids digestion by ensuring proper elimination. Table 4-1 shows the amount of fiber in a broad sampling of foods.

TABLE 4-1. FIBER CONTENT OF VARIOUS FOODS

Food	Approximate Fiber Content (grams)
Apple (small)	3
Bread, whole wheat (1 slice)	2.5
Bread, rye (1 slice)	2
Broccoli, cooked (½ cup)	2
Cantaloupe (½ medium)	2
Chickpeas, cooked (½ cup)	8
Kidney beans, cooked (½ cup)	3.5
Lentils, cooked (½ cup)	4
Lettuce (1 cup)	1
Nuts (¼ cup)	1
Oatmeal, cooked (1 cup)	2
Orange (1 small)	2
Pear (1 medium)	3
Peas, cooked (½ cup)	4
Potato, cooked (½ cup)	2.5
Prunes (2)	2
Rice, brown, cooked (½ cup)	0.5
Rice, white, cooked (½ cup)	0.2
Shredded wheat cereal (1 biscuit)	4
Strawberries (½ cup)	2.5
Tomato (½ large)	1

Source: Adapted from *Journal of Human Nutrition* 30 (1976), pp. 303–313 and *Journal of the American Dietetic Association* 86 (1986), pp. 732–743.

Proteins

Proteins are composed of nitrogen-containing chemical compounds called amino acids. The human body needs approximately 22 different amino acids for proper functioning. Fourteen are actually produced in the body; the remaining eight, known as the essential amino acids, must be supplied through diet.

Animal sources (meats, eggs, cheeses, or milk, for example) provide all eight essential amino acids, and are therefore considered complete sources of protein. Plant sources lack one or more of these essential amino acids or provide them in amounts too small to support the body, making them incomplete protein sources. To ensure a sufficient supply of protein from plant sources alone, it is necessary to eat a variety of foods (grains, legumes, and seeds and nuts, for example). Because the body does not store extra protein but converts any surplus into carbohydrates and fats, a daily supply of all eight essential amino acids is required.

Besides supplying energy, protein has a variety of other functions, such as building new tissue and replacing worn-out or injured tissue. It is also a major component of enzymes and hormones, as well as an essential part of the immune system. In addition, protein plays a role in the regulation of bodily fluids.

Fats and Oils

Fats are usually solid at room temperature and generally come from an animal source; oils are usually liquid at room temperature and come from a plant source. Their major dietary functions are to provide flavor, a feeling of fullness, and energy storage. An illustration of fat's ability to supply a feeling of fullness is the common experience people have of feeling hungry shortly after an ample meal at an Oriental restaurant, where the foods are typically low in fat.

Small amounts of fats or oils should be consumed to provide the body with what are known as fatty acids. At least one, and possibly more, of the required or essential fatty acids cannot be produced in the body. Linoleic acid is an example of an essential fatty acid.

Fats also provide the body with sterols, the most familiar of which is cholesterol. Unlike linoleic acid, the body is perfectly capable of producing all the cholesterol it needs, without receiving any through the diet.

Fats and oils are classified according to the amount of hydrogen in their chemical structure, or degree of saturation, as shown in Table 4-2. The three classifications are saturated, monounsaturated, and polyunsaturated. Saturated fat has no double bonds between carbon atoms; instead, all available bonding sites are filled with hydrogen atoms. Monounsaturated fat's structure has one double carbon bond and polyunsaturated fat has multiple double carbon bonds. Most dietary fats contain various saturations, and they are grouped according to overall degree of saturation. The type of oil consumed has a great bearing on body cholesterol levels.

1. Saturated fats are mainly fats of animal origin, although coconut oil and palm oil are two exceptions. Hydrogenated shortenings may also be saturated. (For an explanation of hydrogenation, see Chapter 10, "Nonperishable Goods Identification.") Examples of saturated fats are butter, cheese, chocolate, coconut and coconut oil, egg yolk, lard, meat, milk, palm oil, poultry, and vegetable shortening.

2. Monounsaturated fats are fats that come from plant and fish sources. Examples are avocado, olives and olive oil, nuts and nut oils, and nut butters.

3. Polyunsaturated fats come predominantly from plant sources, although a few come from fish sources. Examples are corn oil, cottonseed oil, mayonnaise, safflower oil, salad dressing, soybean oil, sunflower oil.

TABLE 4-2. CHEMICAL STRUCTURE OF FATS

Kind of Fatty Acid	Examples
Saturated (section of chain)	Butter
	Cheese
	Chocolate
	Coconut and coconut oil
	Egg yolk
	Lard
	Meat
	Milk
	Palm oil
	Poultry
	Vegetable shortening
Monounsaturated (section of chain)	Avocado
	Cashews
	Olives and olive oil
	Peanuts and peanut oil
	Peanut butter
Polyunsaturated	Almonds
	Corn oil
	Cottonseed oil
	Filberts
	Fish
	Margarine (most)
	Mayonnaise
	Pecans
	Safflower oil
	Salad dressing
	Soybean oil
	Sunflower oil
	Walnuts

C, a carbon atom.
H, a hydrogen atom.
−, a single bond.
=, a double bond.
SOURCE: "Nutrition," The Culinary Institute of America, classroom handout, 1989.

4. Cholesterol is found only in products of animal origin, such as meat, eggs, butter, lard, and cheese. Saturated fats from plant sources, such as palm kernel oil and coconut oil, do not contain cholesterol. Saturated fats of any sort, animal or plant, tend to increase the levels of cholesterol in the blood, whereas polyunsaturated and monounsaturated fats either tend to lower it, or have no effect. The factors affecting blood cholesterol levels include age, sex, exercise/activity level, stress, and consumption of foods high in cholesterol, saturated fats, and fiber.

Vitamins

Although needed only in small amounts, vitamins are an essential, but noncaloric, part of the diet. They assist in the regulation of many biological processes and play a necessary role in the release of energy from caloric nutrients. Vitamins are classified according to solubility. The fat-soluble vitamins, A, D, E, and K, may be stored in the fat stores within the body. The water-soluble vitamins, C and the B vitamins, cannot be stored in the body in appreciable amounts, so proper amounts of these vitamins should be included in the diet daily. However, one should not greatly exceed recommended daily amounts of fat-soluble vitamins (especially by taking megadoses of vitamin supplements) because these vitamins are stored by the body and it is possible to build up toxic levels.

Minerals

Minerals, also a noncaloric dietary essential, are probably the least understood nutrient. Daily requirements for other nutrients are measured in grams, but many minerals are needed in only thousandths or even millionths of a gram. Minerals have roles in building and maintaining the skeleton and muscle tissue, regulating heartbeat and fluid balance, transporting oxygen, and transmitting nerve impulses. There are two mineral classifications—macro-, or major, minerals and trace minerals. These designations reflect the amount of the mineral the body needs, not its importance. As can be seen in Table 4-3, calcium is a macromineral and iron is a trace mineral.

Recommended Dietary Allowance (RDA)

The National Research Council of the Food and Nutrition Board of the National Academy of Sciences has prepared estimates of the nutrient amounts needed to maintain good health. The RDA (Recommended Dietary Allowance) establishes recommendations for proteins, vitamins, and minerals based on the needs of different groups of people, divided according to age and sex, as can be seen in Table 4-4. There are no established recommendations for carbohydrates and fats, because the need for these nutrients varies by individual and depends on a number of factors, such as age, weight, sex, and activity level.

The USRDA (United States Recommended Daily Allowance) is a simplified version of the RDA that is used on processed food labels. (The USRDA label on food packages gives the highest recommendations in each category, excluding the requirements for pregnant women.)

TABLE 4-3. VITAMINS AND MINERALS

Vitamin RDA for Adults	Sources	Function	Deficiency/ Excessiveness	Stability
Thiamine (B₁) RDA: Men 1.4 mg Women 1.0 mg	pork, liver, legumes, fresh green vegetables	carbohydrate metabolism, maintaining healthy nerves, normal appetite	def.: beri-beri	destroyed by heat and water
Riboflavin (B₂) RDA: Men 1.7 mg Women 1.5 mg	milk, liver, lean meats, eggs, leafy vegetables	breakdown of fatty acids for energy, release of energy from food	def.: rare, except in alcohol abusers	destroyed by U.V. rays and fluorescent lights, stable in heat and acid
Niacin Men 18 mg Women 14 mg	liver, lean meats, wheat germ, leafy green vegetables	carbohydrate metabolism	def.: pellagra excess: liver damage, skin rashes, peptic ulcer	
Vitamin B₆ Pyridoxine RDA: 2 to 2.2 mg	meat, liver, whole grain cereals, vegetables	aids in synthesis of nonessential amino acids, fat and carbohydrate metabolism	def.: convulsions, anemia, depression, nausea	stable to heat, light, oxidation

Other minerals: Magnesium, chloride, sulfur, zinc, copper, manganese, chromium, fluorine, molybdenum, selenium, cobalt.

TABLE 4-3. VITAMINS AND MINERALS

Vitamin RDA for Adults	Sources	Function	Deficiency/ Excessiveness	Stability
Vitamin B$_{12}$ RDA: 3 µg	liver, meats, milk, eggs (only animal foods)	growth, blood formation, amino acid synthesis	def.: pernicious anemia	stable during normal cooking
Folacin (most common vitamin deficiency) RDA: 400 ug	green leafy vegetables, liver, milk, eggs	blood formation, amino acid metabolism	def.: megaloblastic anemia, diarrhea	unstable to heat and oxidation
Ascorbic Acid (vitamin C) RDA: 60 mg	citrus fruits, strawberries, cantaloupe, broccoli, cabbage	production and maintenance of collagen (base for all connective tissue), healing, resistance	def.: scurvy (smoking cigarettes seems to interfere with use of vitamin C)	unstable; destroyed by oxygen, water
Vitamin A (retinol) RDA: 1000 R.E.	liver, carrots, sweet potatoes, green leafy vegetables, egg yolk, milk fat	building of body cells, bone growth, healthy tooth structure, normal vision in dim light	def.: night blindness excess: joint pain, nausea, rashes	fairly stable in light and heat, easily destroyed by air and ultraviolet light
Vitamin D RDA: unknown	animal fat, fortified milk, sunlight	bone development (promotes the absorption of calcium and phosphorus)	def.: rickets excess: hypercalcemia	stable to heat, aging, and storage
Vitamin E (tocopherols) RDA: 10 I.U.	leafy vegetables, egg yolk, legumes, vegetable oils, peanuts	protects cell structure, antioxidant	def.: blood disorder (rare) excess: least toxic	destroyed by rancidity
Vitamin K RDA: unknown	cabbage, leafy vegetables, liver, vegetable oils	essential for clotting of blood	def.: lack of prothrombin (important in blood clotting) excess: jaundice	destroyed by strong acids, alkalis, and oxidizing agents
Calcium RDA: 800 mg	milk, dairy products, canned salmon w/ bones	bone and tooth formation, coagulation of blood, regulates muscle contraction	def.: osteoporosis	N/A
Phosphorus RDA: 800 mg	milk, poultry, fish, meats, cheese, nuts, cereals, legumes	energy exchange, buffer system	def.: unknown	N/A
Sodium	common salt, some canned foods, salt-cured meats, pickles	regulates electrolyte and water balance (extracellular fluid)	excess: linked to hypertension	N/A
Potassium	meats, cereals, vegetables, legumes, fruits	regulates electrolyte and water balance (intracellular fluid), muscle contractions		N/A
Iron RDA: Men 10 mg Women 18 mg	liver, meat, whole or enriched grains, green vegetables	essential for hemoglobin production, constituent of tissue cells, transporting oxygen	def.: anemia	N/A
Iodine RDA: 150 µg	iodized salt, seafoods	necessary for the formation of thyroxine (a hormone of the thyroid gland)	def.: goiter	N/A

Other minerals: Magnesium, chloride, sulfur, zinc, copper, manganese, chromium, fluorine, molybdenum, selenium, cobalt.

TABLE 4-4. RECOMMENDED DIETARY ALLOWANCES

Age (years)	Weight (kg)	(lb)	Height (cm)	(inches)	Protein (g)	Vitamin A (RE)	Vitamin D (I.U.)	Vitamin E (mg)	Vitamin C (mg)	Thiamine (mg)	Riboflavin (mg)	Niacin (mg equiv.)	Vitamin B_6 (mg)	Folacin (mg)	Vitamin B_{12} (µg)	Calcium (mg)	Phosphorus (mg)	Magnesium (mg)	Iron (mg)	Zinc (mg)	Iodine (µg)
Infants																					
0.0–0.5	6	13	60	24	kg×2.2	420	10	3	35	0.3	0.4	6	0.3	30	0.5	360	240	50	10	3	40
0.5–1.0	9	20	71	28	kg×2.0	400	10	4	35	0.5	0.6	8	0.6	45	1.5	540	360	70	15	5	50
Children																					
1–3	13	29	90	35	23	400	10	5	45	0.7	0.8	9	0.9	100	2.0	800	800	150	15	10	70
4–6	20	44	112	44	30	500	10	6	45	0.9	1.0	11	1.3	200	2.5	800	800	200	10	10	90
7–10	28	62	132	52	34	700	10	7	45	1.2	1.4	16	1.6	300	3.0	800	800	250	10	10	120
Males																					
11–14	45	99	157	62	45	1000	10	8	50	1.4	1.6	18	1.8	400	3.0	1200	1200	350	18	15	150
15–18	66	145	176	69	56	1000	10	10	60	1.4	1.7	18	2.0	400	3.0	1200	1200	400	18	15	150
19–22	70	154	177	70	56	1000	7.5	10	60	1.5	1.7	19	2.2	400	3.0	800	800	350	10	15	150
23–50	70	154	178	70	56	1000	5	10	60	1.4	1.6	18	2.2	400	3.0	800	800	350	10	15	150
51 +	70	154	178	70	56	1000	5	10	60	1.2	1.4	16	2.2	400	3.0	800	800	350	10	15	150
Females																					
11–14	46	101	157	62	46	800	10	8	50	1.1	1.3	15	1.8	400	3.0	1200	1200	300	18	15	150
15–18	55	120	163	64	46	800	10	8	60	1.1	1.3	14	2.0	400	3.0	1200	1200	300	18	15	150
19–22	55	120	163	64	44	800	7.5	8	60	1.1	1.3	14	2.0	400	3.0	800	800	300	18	15	150
23–50	55	120	163	64	44	800	5	8	60	1.0	1.2	13	2.0	400	3.0	800	800	300	18	15	150
51 +	55	120	163	64	44	800	5	8	60	1.0	1.2	13	2.0	400	3.0	800	800	300	10	15	150
Pregnant					+30	+200	+5	+2	+20	+0.4	+0.3	+2	+0.6	+400	+1.0	+400	+400	+150	a	+5	+25
Lactating					+20	+400	+5	+3	+40	+0.5	+0.5	+5	+0.5	+100	+1.0	+400	+400	+150	a	+10	+50

a Supplemental iron is recommended (30 to 60 mg).

Note: The allowances are intended to provide for individual variations among most normal, healthy people in the United States under usual environmental stresses. They were designed for the maintenance of good nutrition. Diets should be based on a variety of common foods in order to provide other nutrients for which human requirements have been less well defined.

SOURCE: Reproduced from *Recommended Dietary Allowances*, 9th ed. (1980), with the permission of the National Academy of Sciences, Washington, D.C.

Dietary Goals

In 1977, the Senate Select Committee on Nutrition and Human Needs reviewed American consumption patterns for protein, fat, carbohydrates, and a number of other nutrients and prepared a list of dietary goals. Figure 4-1 compares the percentage of nutrients in the current average diet with recommendations for changes. Recommendations include changes in carbohydrate consumption, with an increase in complex and naturally occurring simple carbohydrates and a decrease in refined simple sugars.

The goal for protein consumption remains the same as the current diet, but a decrease in animal protein and an increase of plant sources of protein is advisable. Other goals include a decrease in overall fat consumption—especially saturated fats, a decrease in cholesterol and in sugar, and an increase in fiber.

Dietary Guidelines

Nutritional theory is only useful when it results in practical applications. In order to help the public

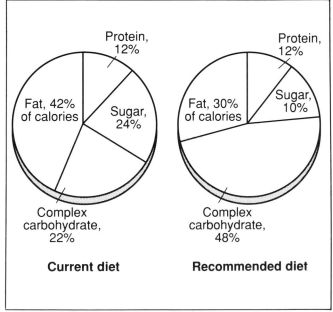

4-1

The current American diet versus the recommended diet.
SOURCE: "Dietary Goals for the United States," Washington, D.C.: Gov't Printing Office, Stock No. 052-070-03913-2.

meet the dietary goals and to provide the straightforward information needed to make nutritionally enlightened decisions, the U.S. Department of Health and Human Services and the Department of Agriculture have developed specific dietary guidelines in the form of concrete suggestions discussed in some detail here.

1. Eat a variety of foods. Nearly 50 different known nutrients are needed to maintain health. Rarely encountered in their pure form, nutrients are found in the innumerable combinations that form food. The greater a diet's variety, the better the chances are for adequate nutrition. Referring to a chart on the basic food groups, such as the one in Table 4-5, can help in making wise food choices and achieving a balance in calorie and nutrient consumption.

2. Maintain a healthy weight. Many factors are involved in determining a reasonable weight: body frame, metabolism, gender, and age.

There are various ways to determine the number of daily calories an individual needs to maintain a desirable weight, based on the interrelationship of activity level and metabolism. One example is the formula given in Figure 4-2. Weight is maintained by balancing energy intake, in the form of calories, with energy expenditure, in the form of exercise. Taking in fewer calories than are used will result in weight loss; taking in more will result in weight gain.

The need for regular exercise and maintaining a "fit" weight cannot be overemphasized. Gradual weight loss resulting from improved eating habits and regular exercise yields better long-term success than crash dieting.

3. Choose a diet low in fat, saturated fat, and cholesterol. Although most Americans are guilty of consuming too many of their daily calories in the form of fat, it is important to remember that the body does require some fat. The answer, then, is to keep dietary fat amounts at reasonable levels (no more than the

TABLE 4-5. THE FOUR BASIC FOOD GROUPS

Food Group	Recommended Number of Servings				
	Child	Teenager	Adult	Pregnant Woman	Lactating Woman
Milk	3	4	2	4	4
1 cup milk, yogurt OR Calcium Equivalent: 1.5 slices (1.5 oz.) cheddar cheese* 1 cup pudding 1¾ cups ice cream 2 cups cottage cheese*					
Meat	2	2	2	3	2
2 oz. cooked, lean meat, fish, poultry, OR Protein Equivalent: 2 eggs 2 slices (2 oz.) cheddar cheese* ½ cup cottage cheese* 1 cup cooked dried beans, peas 4 tbsp. peanut butter					
Fruit-Vegetable	4	4	4	4	4
½ cup cooked or juice 1 cup raw Portion commonly served: medium-size apple or banana					
Grain	4	4	4	4	4
whole grain, fortified, enriched 1 slice bread 1 cup ready-to-eat cereal ½ cup cooked cereal, pasta					

* Count cheese as serving of milk OR meat, not both simultaneously.
"Others" complement but do not replace foods from the four food groups.
Amounts should be determined by individual caloric needs.
SOURCE: "Nutrition," The Culinary Institute of America classroom handout, 1989.

DETERMINING CALORIC REQUIREMENTS

1. DETERMINING DESIRABLE BODY WEIGHT (DBW)

Build	Women	Men
Medium	Allow 100 lb. for first 5 feet, plus 5 lb. for each additional inch.	Allow 106 lb. for first 5 feet, plus 6 lb. for each additional inch.
Small	Subtract 10%	Subtract 10%
Large	Add 10%	Add 10%

2. DETERMINING DAILY CALORIC NEEDS

Basal Calories

DBW × 10 (Men) = _____
DBW × 9 (Women) = _____

Activity Calories

DBW × 3 (Sedentary) = _____
DBW × 5 (Moderate) = _____
DBW × 10 (Strenuous) = _____

Basal Calories + Activity Calories = Total Daily Calories _____

3. ADJUST CALORIES TO GAIN, LOSE, OR MAINTAIN WEIGHT

* *Add* zero (0) calories to maintain weight
* *Subtract* calories to *lose weight*   −
  (suggested to lose 1 to 2 lb. per week)
* *Add* calories to *gain weight*   +
  (suggested to gain ½ lb. per week)

One pound of body fat is equal to approximately 3500 calories.
   To lose 1 lb. per week, subtract 500 calories per day.
   To gain ½ lb. per week, add 250 calories per day.

TOTAL CALORIES NEEDED TO GAIN, LOSE, OR MAINTAIN WEIGHT =

4-2

Standards for determining desirable body weight, daily caloric intake, and calorie adjustment for weight maintenance. SOURCE: "Nutrition," The Culinary Institute of America, classroom handout, 1989, p. 33.

recommended 25 to 30 percent), a practice that will automatically help control the number of daily calories consumed.

Saturated fats, primarily animal fats and some of the hydrogenated fats found in processed and packaged foods, should not exceed a maximum of 10 percent of daily calories. The majority of the fats and oils (15 to 20 percent of the daily calorie allotment) consumed daily should be unsaturated. The body is then sure to receive linoleic acid, the essential fatty acid not produced by the body.

Dairy products, important as a calcium source, are also high in fats and cholesterol. They should therefore be selected with an eye to reducing cholesterol. Remember that it is not necessary to totally eliminate foods such as cream and butter. What is important is to drastically cut back on their consumption.

4. Choose a diet with plenty of vegetables, fruits, and grain products. Starchy foods provide not only energy but many vitamins and minerals as well. Because starches provide fewer calories per gram than fats, eating more starchy foods is a good way to reach a feeling of fullness and increase dietary fiber.

Increasing the amount of fruit and vegetable consumption helps raise the percentage of complex carbohydrates in the diet. In addition, many fruits and vegetables provide significant amounts of soluble and insoluble fiber. Many meals and grains are also good sources of complex carbohydrates and fiber, as well as protein.

5. Use sugars only in moderation. Foods containing refined sugars often have "empty" calories—calories with comparatively few vitamins and minerals. More than an occasional indulgence in such foods may result in undesired weight gain as well as an increase in dental problems, especially cavities.

6. Use salt and sodium only in moderation. There may be a relationship between a heavy sodium intake and an increased incidence of hypertension (high blood pressure), which is often thought to be the cause of heart attacks, strokes, and kidney disease. Family history and obesity are other important risk factors. Processed foods are notoriously high in sodium and should be avoided as much as possible. Table 4-6 shows the sodium content of a number of foods.

The recommended daily sodium consumption is 3,300 milligrams or less (1 teaspoon of table salt contains 2,000 milligrams). Saltiness is an acquired taste, and the tolerance for it increases as consumption rises. As a side effect, increased salt use reduces sensitivity to other flavors. If sodium intake is reduced gradually, the "flavor" loss is less noticeable.

7. If you drink alcoholic beverages, do so in moderation. Alcoholic beverages are high in calories but low in nutrients. Alcohol contributes 7 calories per gram—more than protein or carbohydrate and almost as many as fat—with few if any vitamins and minerals. One or two drinks a day, a total of 200 to 250 calories, is considered to be moderate. Table 4-7 lists various alcoholic beverages and their caloric content.

NUTRITIONAL COOKING

Nutritional cooking is a way both of preparing foods and of combining various dishes to provide a nutri-

tionally sound meal or overall diet. The goal is to produce foods that are attractive, tasty, and in conformance with the dietary guidelines previously outlined.

Conserving nutrients is a benefit for the customer and a challenge for the chef. There is no reliance on cream and butter to add richness and savor, salt to provide flavor, or sugar to produce a dessert finale. There are no rich and elaborate sauces, stuffings, or fillings to hide behind. The flavor of the food must be its own appeal—enhanced by new techniques for cooking meats, fish, and vegetables, imaginative uses of unfamiliar grains and legumes, and substitution of spices and herbs for much or all of the salt.

The "Positive Nutrient Profile"

This is a somewhat imposing way of saying that foods should provide as many of the best-quality nutrients as possible—a far cry from the stereotypical "hospital" food associated previously with nutrition. Nor does it have anything to do with so-called "health foods" such as bean sprouts, tofu, and brown rice.

In order to meet the most important mission of nutritional cooking—having someone actually eat the food—chefs must recognize that increasing fiber and complex carbohydrates while reducing fats, sugars,

TABLE 4-6. SODIUM CONTENT OF VARIOUS FOODS

Food	Approximate Sodium Content (milligrams)
Apple (small)	1
Beans, kidney, cooked (½ cup)	3
Beef, corned (3 oz./85 g)	800
Beef, rib roast (3 oz./85 g)	40
Bread, whole wheat (1 slice)	140
Cheese, hard (1 oz./30 g)	200
Cheese, process (1 oz./30 g)	325
Chicken breast (3 oz./85 g)	55
Egg (large)	60
Milk, skim (1 cup)	125
Mustard, prepared (1 tbs.)	190
Pasta, cooked (½ cup)	1
Potato (½ cup)	2.5
Salt (1 tsp.)	2300
Scallops (3 oz./85 g)	225
Soy sauce (1 tbs.)	1320
Tomato (½ medium)	4
Tomato juice (1 cup)	485
Tomato ketchup (1 tbs.)	160
Tuna, canned (3 oz./85 g)	680

SOURCE: Adapted from *Handbook of the Nutritional Value of Foods in Common Units*, Catherine F. Adams for the USDA, 1986. New York: Dover.

TABLE 4-7. CALORIC CONTENT OF ALCOHOLIC BEVERAGES

Beverage	Approximate Number of Calories Per Serving	Per Ounce (30 ml)
Beer (12 oz./serving)	155	13
Beer, light (12 oz./serving)	100	8
Brandy (1 oz./serving)	70	70
Liquor (gin, rum, vodka, whiskey, 1½ oz./serving),		
86-proof	105	65
100-proof	125	83
Manhattan (3¼ oz./serving)	233	72
Martini (2¼ oz./serving)	152	61
Piña colada (3 oz./serving)	450	150
Wine (3½ oz./serving),		
Champagne	71	20
Red table	76	22
Sherry	147	42
White table	80	23
Liqueur (1 oz./serving),		
Average	97	97
Irish cream	85	85

SOURCE: Adapted from "Nutritive Value of American Foods in Common Units," USDA, 1979.

and salts calls for using a wide variety of fresh, healthful foods. Logically, a chef should begin by planning a menu that incorporates these items and purchasing the necessary foods.

Once purchased, foods must be handled properly to assure the smallest possible nutrient loss. This may mean learning to prepare smaller batches of food closer to service time, or it may mean purchasing special equipment such as microwave ovens or nonstick pans. The chef will need to learn to recognize what is healthful in a cooking technique and where a less healthful technique might be successfully modified to achieve the desired result.

Other components of proper handling and preparation are selecting recipes that best showcase the foods being prepared, using a combination of new and traditional dishes to strike the right menu balance, and, where necessary, learning to modify recipes by substituting ingredients or techniques.

The final step is to present the food in the most appealing way possible. Because part of the chef's ability to regulate calorie, fat, and cholesterol amounts is to control portion sizes, it becomes important to feed the eye. Americans are conditioned to expect large steaks, enormous servings of prime rib, and "healthy" portions of fish and poultry. If a serving of pork loin, for instance, is kept at the recommended 3 to 4 ounces, it could look skimpy unless the chef plates it so that the eye sees not a tiny piece of meat but an attractive, satisfying meal.

Purchasing

There are many healthful alternatives to foods rich in fat and cholesterol. There are also ways to emphasize the more healthful aspects of a dish and de-emphasize components that are high in fats, sodium, or sugar. For example, an increased interest in ethnic foods has made it possible to feature a variety of special dishes based primarily on grains, as in the case of a main-course couscous, pilaf, or risotto. Making the right choice when purchasing food can greatly affect the nutritional content of the finished dish. Not only the natural properties of an item should be considered, but also the way in which it has been raised, grown, or processed.

1. Produce. The fresher the produce, the better. When possible, buy from local producers, especially those who may be willing to grow specialty items if they know there will be a reliable market. Organically grown fruits and vegetables are available in many areas. They may not have superior nutritional value, but they have been grown without harmful chemical pesticides, herbicides, and fertilizers. No nationwide standards exist at this time for what can be labeled "organic."

2. Dairy products. Dairy products are excellent sources of protein, as well as calcium. Unfortunately, many dairy items are also high in saturated fat and cholesterol. Select low-fat, skim, or nonfat products where feasible. Part-skim ricotta may be used to take the place of heavy cream or cream cheese in dishes ranging from sauces and stuffings to desserts. Nonfat yogurt can be drained overnight in cheesecloth to give it a better texture and used in place of fromage blanc, sour cream, or crème fraîche.

3. Meats and poultry. Meat grading standards have undergone some revision in recent years, and consequently less fatty, more healthful cuts of meat can be found to use in place of higher-fat cuts. One should be aware of the relative amount of fat in various meat cuts. For instance, the pork loin and tenderloin are extremely lean, especially after trimming away the visible fat. The shoulder or ham, however, will have much higher fat levels.

Steroids are used in raising some animals and poultry, to increase their size and thus shorten the growing period. In poultry, especially, antibiotics are often introduced as part of the feed. The result has been a growing concern over what effect this has on the food chain, specifically the final consumer. For example, because steroids will be held in the body forever, consumers and producers have become increasingly interested in free-range, or organically raised, poultry and meat. As with produce, no strict standards exist.

Sausages and preserved or cured meats often contain high sodium levels; most of them also contain nitrates and nitrites. As an alternative, look for products that are nitrite-free or use smoke-roasting (a technique discussed in the section on roasting in Chapter 18) as a means of imparting a smoky flavor without actually smoking or curing.

4. Oils. Use oils that are poly- or monounsaturated, selecting them for their cooking properties, and make sure they are of high quality. Extra-virgin olive oil or nut oils (walnut, peanut, sesame, hazelnut) contribute a unique flavor and, if used in proper amounts, can do so without having a negative effect on the meal's overall nutritional profile.

5. Meals, grains, and legumes. These ingredients have undergone a rebirth of popularity in recent years and are available in great variety. Foods such as quinoa, amaranth, millet, and a number of specialty rices (arborio, pecan, wild, popcorn, and basmati, for example) are no longer considered exotic. The less processed the grain, the higher the nutritional content (see Chapter 24, "Cooking Grains and Legumes").

6. Fish and shellfish. Expanding the number of fish entrées is a relatively simple way to increase a menu's nutritionally sound offerings. Like produce, fish must be exceptionally fresh. It is important to find out the source of the fish; farm-raised fish, for instance, are assumed to be safe. Learn as much as possible about the species available in a particular area, especially "underutilized" fish and shellfish (see Chapter 7, "Fish and Shellfish Identification").

7. Herbs and spices. The increased availability of fresh herbs and a greater range of spices have been a boon for chefs attempting to cut back on salt.

8. Additives. In broad terms, anything added to a food to enhance its flavor or keeping properties is an additive; sugar and salt, for example, can be called food additives. For the most part, however, the word is used in a negative sense—for flavor enhancers such as monosodium glutamate (MSG), BST, sulfites in wines, and nitrites. It is particularly important to read frozen and canned goods labels, to be sure those foods have not been treated with undesirable chemical additives (MSG, BHT, BHTA, to name just a few) during processing. If there are questions about what a certain ingredient might be, consult an up-to-date reference book; also refer to the list of Recommended Readings at the end of this book.

9. Specialty items. There are a number of special ingredients that can give foods a satisfying flavor. Specialty vinegars, such as balsamic or herb-flavored, have a number of applications, from deglazing a pan for a simple sauce to using it as a salt replacement. Dried fruits, such as apricots, cherries, and tomatoes, can also add a distinctive flavor and appeal. Ethnic cuisines' flavorings, such as those used for Middle Eastern, Italian, Japanese, or Chinese meals, can often be applied to different recipes.

Preparation

If the first step is purchasing nutritious foods, the second is making sure that these foods' nutritional benefits are retained through proper storage, handling, and preparation.

Exposure to air, heat, and water should be kept at a minimum until immediately prior to cooking. For this reason, keep foods properly wrapped, and trim, peel, cut, or portion them only as needed. Foods stored under proper conditions should retain most of their nutrients; however, it is still advisable to use them as soon after they are received as possible.

In preparing foods, the following points should be kept in mind:

1. Establish correct portion sizes. Most Americans are accustomed to large portions of foods high in protein, such as meat, fish, or poultry. The emphasis must shift from large meat portions to more modest servings, while increasing vegetable, grain, and legume portions.

2. Cook vegetables for the shortest possible amount of time, in the least amount of liquid. The microwave oven can often be used to prepare vegetables for the greatest possible nutrient retention, especially when small batches or individual portions are being prepared. Pan steamers are also effective.

Roasting or grilling vegetables can give them a highly desirable flavor, which can be used to advantage in a number of dishes. For example, corn roasted in the husk has a rich, nutty flavor that makes an excellent accompaniment to roasted or grilled meats, or in sauces for meats or game. Roasted garlic contributes the same flavor as sautéed garlic.

3. Learn which cooking techniques are naturally less reliant on fats and oils. Poaching, steaming, roasting, and grilling are all good choices, because they do not require any fat. Braising and stewing are also wise choices, because the foods' nutrients are retained in the sauce, which is served as part of the dish.

Smoke-roasting can give foods the taste of smoking without requiring salt-laden brines, nitrates, nitrites, or fats. The use of hardwood chips imparts a unique flavor and a mahogany color.

Some techniques that traditionally called for significant amounts of cooking fat can be modified, or a different technique can be used to achieve similar results. Instead of sautéing a chicken breast in oil, for example, dry-sauté it in a properly seasoned cast-iron pan, or one with a nonstick surface. Rather than tossing vegetables in butter to finish them before service, "sauté" them in a small amount of a flavorful, well-seasoned stock.

4. Select sauces for their ability to add to the overall value of the dish. Cream- and butter-based sauces can be replaced with vegetable-based sauces. Roux can be replaced with a small amount of a modified starch, such as arrowroot. A sauce may be replaced with a relish, such as a compote of onion or corn relish, salsa, or stewed lentils. Although a poached or steamed fish traditionally might have been served with a butter sauce, such as Hollandaise or beurre blanc, additional flavor and moisture can be added instead by serving it with a sauce made from a reduction of the cooking liquid combined with a vegetable coulis.

Analyzing Recipes

There are three ways to identify nutritionally sound recipes:

1. Learn to recognize nutritional recipes. Not every recipe in the classic repertoire is loaded with fat, salt, and sugar. It would be hard to improve on the ingredients and techniques used for producing consommés, clear vegetable soups, purees of legumes, and jus de veau, for example. Examine the ingredient list and the techniques carefully.

2. Modify existing recipes. Often, fat can be reduced or completely eliminated. Alternatively, it may be possible to use a different technique—grilling a piece of fish, for example, instead of panfrying it. Long cooking times may be unnecessary; cooking foods just to the point of doneness often can save a great many nutrients. Substitute ingredients judiciously. The following suggestions are only a beginning:

- Substitute evaporated skim milk for heavy cream in soup and sauce recipes.
- Use dried fruits instead of refined sugar to introduce sweetness.
- Use high-calorie, high-fat, or high-sodium ingredients in a way that makes the most of small amounts. For instance, a sprinkling of parmesan cheese can be used in place of salt. A small amount of whipped cream added as a soup's garnish gives the impression of more cream than if the cream were added directly to the soup.
- Use grains, vegetables, and/or legumes to stuff items, rather than traditional forcemeats that might include a high percentage of fat. Or use these same items to replace heavy sauces. A bed of stewed lentils can be served with grilled fish instead of a compound butter.
- Use egg whites, rather than whole eggs, where possible. Because egg yolks do perform specific functions, such as forming an emulsion, it may not always be possible to completely eliminate them; however, the number of yolks can often be reduced, as for a custard or omelet. Whites can serve as a binder and may replace yolks in such preparations as fresh noodle dough.

3. Develop new recipes. As chefs become willing to try new or modified techniques, foods' specific tastes, textures, and appearances will suggest new combinations. An unfamiliar vegetable, such as jicama, could spark a new idea, or an effort to modify a classic dish might result in the birth of a new one.

Becoming familiar with foods' properties and how a particular technique might affect their flavors and textures are an ongoing part of a chef's education. Experimenting with new ingredients or dishes from other cuisines is another way to inspire creation. According to Brillat-Savarin, "The discovery of a new dish does more to advance the happiness of mankind than the discovery of a new star." Nowhere is this more true than in the development of a nutritional cooking style.

Presentation

Presentation is of special importance for the proper public perception of nutritious foods because there has been a reluctance to try anything that sounds "healthy." Frequently, the diner has an almost automatic expectation that the food will be bland and unsatisfying, and will be in portions too small for a filling meal.

If a plate looks nearly empty, or is too "brown," the guest already feels cheated. A plate that has good color and texture contrasts and a look of completeness and some abundance conveys a message that the food will taste good. More detailed guidelines for presentation are covered in Appendix 1, "Menu Development and Plating Techniques."

Making Nutritional Cooking Work

A number of tools can make the implementation of a nutritional cooking program easier. Scales help keep portion sizes in line and are essential for determining whether finished dishes will meet the dietary goals. Steamers, grills, and nonstick pans allow for preparation without fats. Ice cream freezers can be used to prepare a variety of low-fat desserts, such as sorbets or ricotta-based "ice cream."

The computer is becoming prominent in many kitchens. In addition to its applications for business matters and recording orders, properly selected software can allow the chef to use a computer to fine-tune a recipe under development or evaluate an existing recipe before going to the stove. The savings of time, effort, money, and product are a distinct advantage.

Business Considerations

Nutritional cooking has tangible benefits not only on the human level but also from a business standpoint. Consumers' demands for foods that meet their dietary needs are growing. Some customers may have specific dietary requirements because of illness—heart disease or diabetes, for example. Others may prefer a vegetarian diet. Menu offerings that are appropriate for special needs may be labeled with words or a symbol as a help to the guest and an effective way of attracting business.

SUMMARY

Nutritional cooking combines a basic knowledge of nutrition principles with the successful chef's creative skills. More and more, it is becoming the mainstream of cooking. Patrons are increasingly well-educated about foods and a healthful diet, and there is a growing acceptance of foods that once might have been considered "weird" or "counterculture."

The principles and guidelines discussed in this chapter will strike many as simply common sense. Little difference exists between the aims of nutritional cooking and good cooking in general. Selecting the freshest products and preparing them in a way that further enhances the food should be the goal for any dish, no matter how it is labeled.

Chapter 5

Equipment Identification

It is indeed a poor workman who blames his tools. Knowing how to select, use, and care for tools and equipment is a crucial part of mastering basic cooking techniques. Our survey of basic examples ranges from the simplest hand tools—knives, whips, spatulas, and the like—to complex machines such as grinders, slicers, steam kettles, ovens, and refrigeration equipment. The chapter begins with a detailed discussion of the selection and maintenance of one of the chef's most important professional tools—the knife.

HAND TOOLS

Hand tools are generally composed of few, if any, moving parts, and most are designed to perform a range of functions. Knives are perhaps the most important hand tools in the professional kitchen; their proper use and care are discussed below in detail. Other kitchen tools, such as sharpening and honing tools, peelers, scoops, whips, and spatulas, are also illustrated and explained.

Knives

The importance of knives to a professional chef or cook cannot be overstated. The only piece of "equipment" more basic to cooking is the human hand. All knives should be treated with great respect and care. The following rules concerning knife care, use, and storage are automatic behavior for all true professionals.

• Keep knives sharp. Learn the proper techniques for both sharpening and honing knives. A sharp knife not only performs better but is safer to use, because less pressure is required to cut through the food. When too much pressure is exerted, there is a good possibility of the knife slipping and causing injury to the user.

• Keep knives clean. Clean knives thoroughly after using, and sanitize as necessary, so that the tool will not become a site for food cross-contamination. Keeping knives clean also helps to extend their lives. Never drop a knife into a full pot sink. It could be dented or nicked by heavy pots, and someone who reaches into the sink could be seriously injured by grabbing the blade. Do not clean knives in a dishwasher, because the handles are likely to warp and split.

• Keep knives properly stored. There are a number of safe, practical ways to store knives, including in knife kits or rolls for one's personal collection, and in slots, racks, and magnetized holders. Proper storage will prevent damage to the blade or harm to an unwary individual. Knives should be carefully dried after cleaning, then stored in sheaths to help retain their edge.

• Use an appropriate cutting surface. Wooden or composition cutting boards should always be used. Cutting directly on metal, glass, or marble surfaces will dull and eventually damage the blade of a knife.

• Use for intended purposes only and follow procedures. Always hold a knife by its handle. When passing a knife to someone else, lay it down on a work surface and allow the other person to pick it up. Do not allow the blade of a knife to extend over the edge of a table or cutting board. Refrain from using knives to open bottles, loosen drawers, and so on.

A wide array of knives is available to suit specific functions. As a chef continues to work in professional kitchens, the *batterie de cuillier* expands from the "basics" —chef's or french knife, boning knife, paring knife, and slicer—to include a number of special knives, such as a tourné knife, serrated knife, utility knife, flexible-bladed knives, and so on.

Selecting a knife of good quality that fits the hand and is suitable for the intended tasks depends on a basic knowledge of the various parts of the knife (see Fig. 5-1).

Blades

Currently, the most frequently used material for blades is high-carbon stainless steel. Other mate-

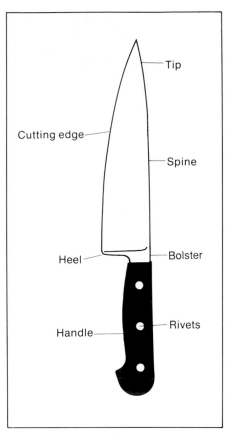

5-1

Chef's knife.

rials, such as stainless steel and carbon steel, are also available. For many years, carbon steel was used to make most knife blades. Although carbon steel blades take a better edge than either regular or high-carbon stainless steel, they tend to lose their sharpness quickly. Also, carbon steel blades will discolor in contact with high-acid foods such as tomatoes or onions. Carbon steel blades must be treated carefully to avoid discoloration, rusting, and pitting; they should be washed and thoroughly dried between uses and before storage. The metal is brittle and can break easily under stress.

Stainless steel is much stronger than carbon steel and will not discolor or rust. It is very difficult to get a good edge on a stainless steel blade, although once an edge is established, it tends to last longer than that on a carbon steel blade.

High-carbon stainless steel is a relatively recent development that combines the advantages of carbon and stainless steel. The higher percentage of carbon allows the blade to take and keep a keener edge; the fact that it is stainless steel means that it will not discolor or rust readily.

The most desirable type of blade is "taper ground." This means that the blade has been forged out of a single metal sheet and has been ground so that it tapers smoothly from the spine to the cutting edge, with no apparent beveling. Frequently used knives should be made with taper-ground blades.

Hollow-ground blades are made by combining two sheets of metal; the edges are then beveled or fluted. Although hollow-ground blades often have very sharp edges, the blade itself lacks the balance and longevity of a taper-ground blade. This type is often found on knives, such as slicers, that are used less frequently in the kitchen.

Tangs

The tang is a continuation of the blade and extends into the knife's handle. Knives used for heavy work, such as chef's knives or cleavers, should have a full tang; that is, the tang is as long as the entire handle. A partial tang does not run the length of the handle. Although blades with partial tangs are not as durable as those with full tangs, they are acceptable for less-used knives. Rat-tail tangs are much thinner than the spine of the blade and are encased in the handle (not visible at the top or bottom edges); these tangs tend not to hold up under extended use. For examples of these tangs, see Figure 5-2.

Handles

A preferred material for knife handles is rosewood, because it is extremely hard and has no grain, which helps to prevent splitting and cracking. Impregnating wood with plastic protects the handle from damage caused by continued exposure to water and detergents. Some state codes require that plastic handles be used in butcher shops, because they are considered more sanitary than wood. Care must be taken to thoroughly remove grease, however, because it adheres more closely to plastic than it does to wood.

The handle should fit the hand comfortably; a range of handle sizes is available. People with very small or very large hands should be sure that they are not straining their grip to hold the handle. Some knives are constructed to meet the needs of left-handed chefs.

Rivets

Metal fasteners called rivets are used to secure the tang to the handle. The rivets should be completely smooth and lie flush with the surface of the handle to prevent irritation to the hand and to avoid causing pockets where microorganisms could gather.

Bolsters

In some knives there is a collar or shank, known as a bolster, at the point where the blade meets the handle. This is a sign of a well-made knife, one that will hold up for a long time. Some knives may have a collar that looks like a bolster but is actually a separate piece attached to the handle. These knives tend to come apart easily and should be avoided.

Types of Knives

The number of knives that a chef will accumulate over the course of his or her career will almost undoubtedly include a number of special knives that are not discussed below. There are, for example, several special knives and cutting tools found exclusively in the bakeshop; still others are required for butchering meats and fabricating fish. This list is intended as a guide to the knives that may be found in nearly any well-outfitted knife kit. See Figure 5-3 for examples of some of these knives.

• Chef's knife, or French knife. This all-purpose knife is used for a variety of chopping, slicing, and mincing chores. The blade is normally 8 to 14 inches long.

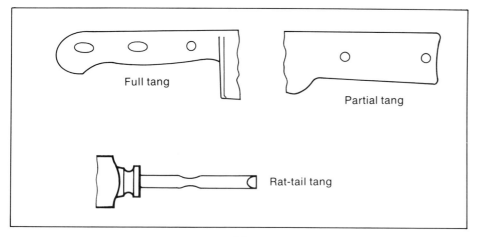

5-2

Tangs: full tang, partial tang, and rat-tail tang.

Other knives: utility, paring, boning/filleting, slicing, cleaver, and tourné.

• Utility knife. This smaller, lighter chef's knife is used for light cutting chores. The blade is generally 5 to 7 inches long.

• Paring knife. This short knife, used for paring and trimming vegetables and fruits, has a 2- to 4-inch blade.

• Boning knife. A boning knife is used to separate raw meat from the bone. The blade, which is thinner and shorter than the blade of a chef's knife, is about 6 inches long, and is usually rigid.

• Filleting knife. Used for filleting fish, this knife is similar in shape and size to a boning knife, but has a flexible blade.

• Slicer. This knife is used for slicing cooked meat. It has a long blade with a round or pointed tip. The blade may be flexible or rigid and may be taper-ground or have a fluted edge that consists of hollow ground ovals.

• Cleaver. Used for chopping, the cleaver is often heavy enough to cut through bones. It has a rectangular blade and varies in size according to its use.

• Tourné knife. This small knife, similar to a paring knife, has a curved blade to make cutting the curved surfaces of tournéed vegetables easier.

Sharpening and Honing Tools

The key to the proper and efficient use of any knife is making sure that it is sharp. A knife with a sharp blade always works better and more safely because it cuts easily, without requiring the chef to exert pressure, which may cause the knife to slip and an injury to result. Knife blades are given an edge on a sharpening stone and maintained between sharpenings by honing with a steel. Examples of two kinds of stones and a steel are shown in Figure 5-4.

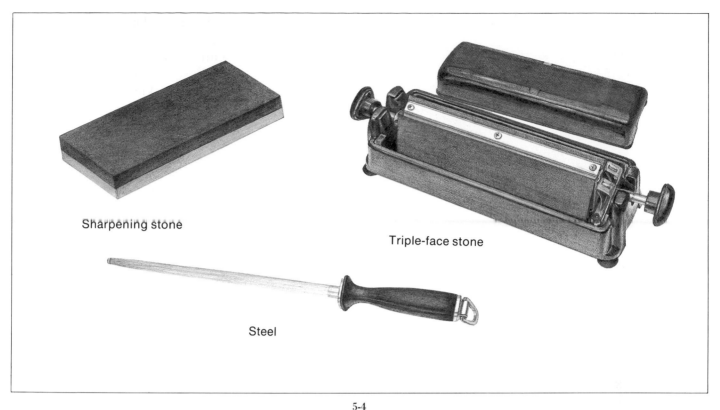

5-4

Sharpening stone, triple-face stone, and steel.

Sharpening Stones

Sharpening stones are essential to the proper maintenance of knives, and are used to sharpen the blade by passing its edge over the stone at the correct angle. The grit—the degree of coarseness or fineness of the stone's surface abrades the blade's edge, creating a sharp cutting edge. When sharpening a knife, always begin by using the coarsest surface of the stone and then move on to the finer surfaces. A stone with a fine grade should be used for boning knives and other tools in which an especially sharp edge is required. Most stones may be used either dry or moistened with water or mineral oil. Once oil has been used on a stone's surface, that practice should be continued. Three basic types of stones are commonly available:

• Carborundum stones have a fine side and a medium side.

• Arkansas stones are available in several grades of fineness and some consist of three stones of varying degrees of fineness mounted on a wheel.

• Diamond-impregnated stones are also available. Although they are expensive, some chefs prefer them because they feel these stones give a sharper edge. The standard size for sharpening stones is 8 by 2 by $^{13}/_{16}$ inches.

Before using a stone, the chef should be sure that it is properly stabilized. Place carborundum or diamond stones on a dampened cloth and allow enough room to work. A triple-faced stone is mounted on a rotating framework that can be locked into position so that it will not move. The blade should be held at a 20-degree angle to the stone's surface and the entire length of the blade should be drawn across the stone. See Figure 5-5 for a complete demonstration of how to use a sharpening stone.

Grinding wheels, electric sharpeners, leather strops (such as those used to sharpen barbers' blades), and other grinding tools may be necessary to replace or restore the edge of a badly dulled knife.

Steels

A steel should be used both immediately after sharpening the blade with a stone and also between sharpenings to keep the edges in alignment. The length of the steel's working surface can range from 3 inches for a pocket version to over 14 inches. Hard steel is the traditional material for steels. Other materials, such as glass, ceramic, and diamond-impregnated surfaces, are also available.

Steels come with coarse, medium, and fine grains and some are magnetic, which helps the blade retain proper alignment and also col-

5-5 SHARPENING A KNIFE ON A STONE

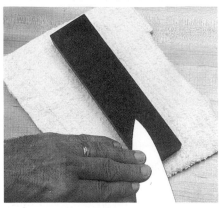

(1) Place the stone on a work surface and use the guiding hand to stabilize the knife, holding it at a 20-degree angle. Begin to draw the knife over the stone's surface.

(2) Continue to draw the knife over the entire stone in a smooth motion.

(3) Draw the knife off smoothly, making sure to pass the last few inches of blade over the stone.

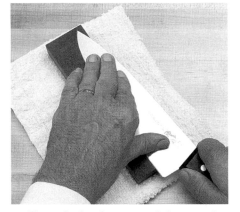

(4) Turn the knife over and sharpen the second side. Notice how the position of the guiding hand changes.

lects metal shavings. A guard or hilt between the steel and the handle protects the user, and a ring on the bottom of the handle can be used to hang the steel.

When using a steel, the knife is held almost vertically, with the blade at a 20-degree angle, resting on the inner side of the steel. The blade should be drawn along the entire length of the steel. See Figure 5-6 for a complete description of how to use a steel.

Small Tools

A number of small tools other than knives belong in a knife kit. It

should be noted that, in addition to the hand tools listed here, many others such as cherry pitters, strawberry hullers, and tomato knives (also known as witches) are used in the professional kitchen for various specific functions. Examples of each of the following are shown in Figure 5-7.

• Rotary peeler. This is used to peel the skin from various vegetables and fruits. The swivel action accommodates the contours of various products.

• Parisienne scoop (melon baller). This is specifically designed for scooping out balls or

ovals (depending upon the shape of the scoop) of vegetables and fruits.

• Kitchen fork. The fork is used to test the doneness of braised meats and vegetables, for lifting finished items to the carving board or plate, and to steady the item being carved. A kitchen fork should not be used to turn foods being sautéed, grilled, or broiled, because the tines will pierce the food and let the juices emerge.

• Palette knife (metal spatula). This is a flexible, round-tipped tool used in the kitchen and bakeshop for turning pancakes or grilled foods, spreading fillings and glazes, and a variety of other functions. A palette knife with a serrated edge is useful for preparing and slicing sandwiches.

• Whips. Whips are used to beat, blend, and whip foods. Balloon whips are sphere-shaped and have thin wires to incorporate air for making foams. Sauce whips are narrower and frequently have thicker wires. The chef should have a number of whips in various sizes.

• Offset spatula. This spatula is used to turn or lift foods on grills, broilers, and griddles. It has a wide, chisel-edged blade set in a short handle.

• Pastry bag. This plastic, canvas, or nylon bag is used to pipe out pureed foods, whipped cream, and various toppings. Pastry bags have uses in both the kitchen and the bakeshop.

Other Hand Tools

Other kitchen hand tools include (but are not limited to) those shown in Figure 5-8. These are rubber scrapers; ladles of various sizes; skimmers for skimming the surface of stocks, soups, etc.; "spiders" for lifting foods out of liquids or fats; spoons of various sorts, wooden

5-6 STEELING A KNIFE

(1) Hold the steel away from the body in one hand and hold the knife in the other. Start with the knife nearly vertical, with the blade resting on the inner side of the steel at a 20-degree angle.

(2) Pass the blade along the entire length of the steel, rotating the wrist as the blade moves. Keep the pressure even and light.

(3) Keep the blade in contact with the steel for the last few inches, so as to be properly honed.

(4) Return the blade to a nearly vertical position, this time on the outer side of the steel, to hone the second side of the knife.

(5) Use the thumb to maintain even, light pressure.

(6) Finish the second pass, making sure the entire length of the blade, including the tip, is properly honed.

and metal serving spoons, tasting spoons, and slotted or solid spoons; scoops of various sizes; hardwood rolling pins; and plastic or wooden cutting boards.

SMALL EQUIPMENT

The tools outlined in this section are available in any well-equipped kitchen. For the sake of clarity, they have been categorized here according to their general function: measuring, straining, and sifting.

Measuring Equipment

Measurements are determined in many different ways in a professional kitchen, depending upon the ingredient to be measured and the system employed by a specific recipe. This makes it important to have equipment for liquid and dry volume measures for both U.S. and metric, as well as a variety of scales for accurate measurement by weight. Thermometers should display both Fahrenheit and Centigrade temperatures. Examples of these, discussed below, are included in Figure 5-9.

• Graduated measuring pitchers. These are used for measuring liquids and are generally available in pint, quart, and gallon sizes.
• Scales. These are used to weigh ingredients for preparation and portion control. Ounce/gram and pound/kilo scales both should be available. Scales may be spring-type, balance beam, or electronic.
• Thermometers. An instant-reading thermometer is used to measure foods' internal temperatures. The stem, inserted in the food, gives an instant reading. Candy and deep-fat thermometers are also helpful.

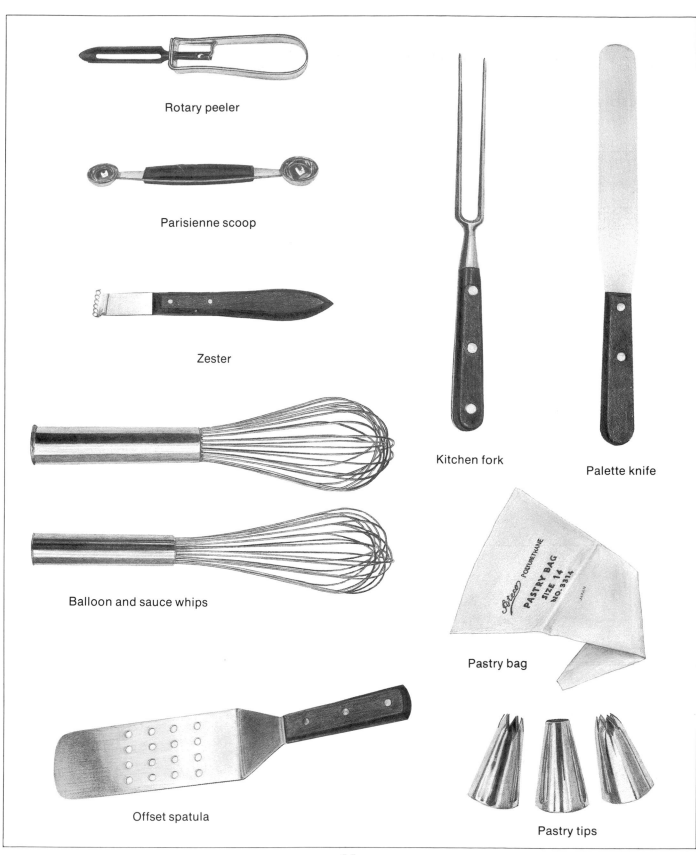

Rotary peeler

Parisienne scoop

Zester

Kitchen fork

Palette knife

Balloon and sauce whips

Pastry bag

Offset spatula

Pastry tips

5-7

Small/hand tools: rotary peeler, parisienne scoop, zester, kitchen fork, palette knife, balloon and sauce whips, offset spatula, pastry bag, and pastry tips.

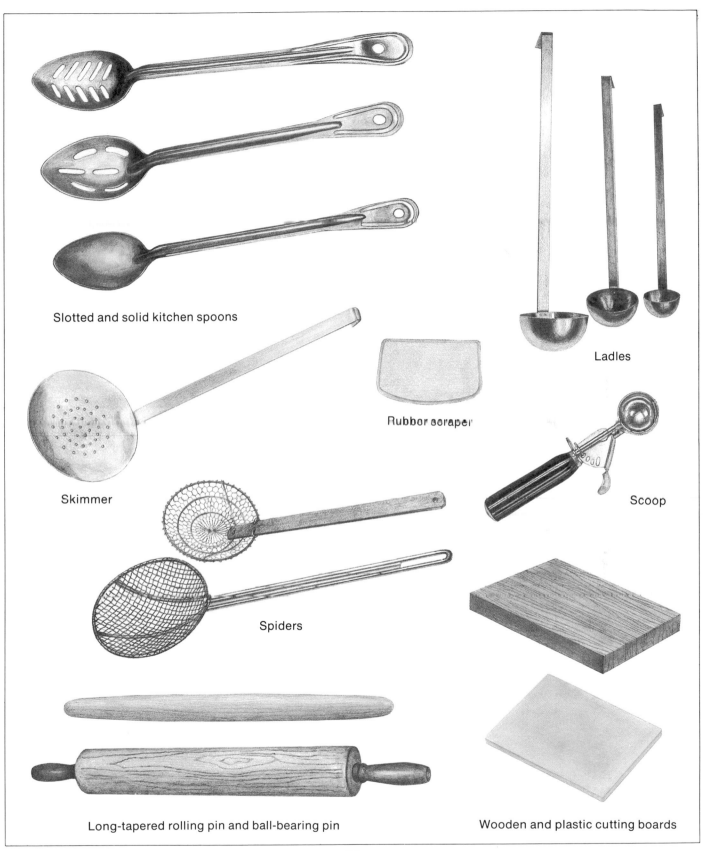

Slotted and solid kitchen spoons

Ladles

Rubber scraper

Skimmer

Scoop

Spiders

Long-tapered rolling pin and ball-bearing pin

Wooden and plastic cutting boards

5-8

Small kitchen tools: slotted and solid kitchen spoons, rubber scraper, skimmer, spiders, scoop, ladles, long-tapered rolling pin and ball-bearing pin, and wooden and plastic cutting boards.

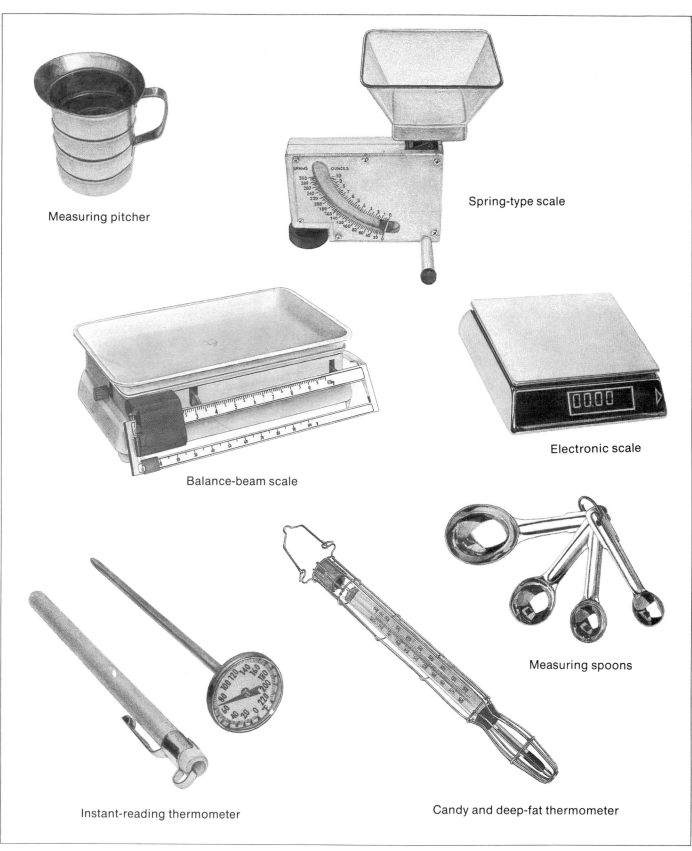

Measuring pitcher

Spring-type scale

Balance-beam scale

Electronic scale

Instant-reading thermometer

Candy and deep-fat thermometer

Measuring spoons

5-9

Measuring equipment: Measuring pitcher, spring-type scale, balance-beam scale, electronic scale, instant-reading thermometer, candy thermometer, and measuring spoons.

• Measuring spoons. Measuring spoons come in the following sizes: tablespoon, teaspoon, ½ teaspoon, and ¼ teaspoon.

Sieves, Strainers, and Chinois

Sieves and strainers are mainly used to sift, aerate, and help to remove any large impurities from dry ingredients. They are also used to drain or puree cooked or raw foods. Figure 5-10 includes examples of some of these, described below.

• Food mill. This is a type of strainer used to puree soft foods. A flat, curving blade is rotated over a disk by a hand-operated crank. Most professional models have interchangeable disks with holes of varying fineness. An exception is the Foley food mill, which has a mesh disk that is fixed in place.

Note: Many mixing machines may be used like a food mill through the addition of attachments that allow them to strain and puree foods.

• Drum sieve (tamis). This sieve consists of a tinned-steel, nylon, or stainless-steel screen stretched in an aluminum or wood frame. A drum sieve is used for sifting or pureeing. A *champignon* (mushroom-shaped pusher) or a rigid plastic scraper is used to push the food through the screen.

• Chinois. This conical sieve is used for straining and/or pureeing food. The openings in the cone can be of varying sizes, from very large to a fine mesh. A fine chinois (also known as a bouillon strainer) is a valuable piece of equipment and should be treated with great respect. It should be cleaned immediately after each use and stored properly; never drop it into a pot sink where it could be crushed or torn.

• Colander. This stainless-steel sieve, with or without a base, is

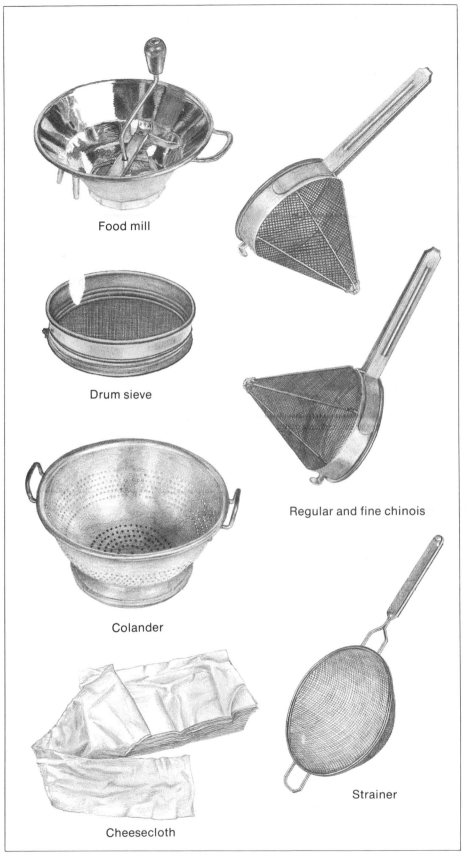

Food mill

Drum sieve

Colander

Regular and fine chinois

Cheesecloth

Strainer

5-10

Food mill, drum sieve, regular and fine chinois, colander, cheesecloth, and strainer.

used for straining foods. Colanders are available in a variety of sizes.

• Ricer. This is a device in which cooked food, often potatoes, is placed in a hopper, which is pierced with holes. A plate on the end of a lever pushes the food through the hopper walls. Garlic presses and french-fry cutters operate on the same principle.

• Cheesecloth. This light, fine mesh gauze is frequently used in place of a fine chinois and is essential for straining some sauces. It is also used for making sachets. Before use, cheesecloth should be rinsed thoroughly in hot water and then cold water to remove any loose fibers. Cheesecloth also clings better to the sides of bowls, chinois, and so forth when it is wet.

POTS, PANS, AND MOLDS

Various materials and combinations of materials are used in the construction of pots, pans, and molds. Because form and function are closely related, it is important to choose the proper equipment for the task at hand.

Pots made of copper transfer heat rapidly and evenly; because direct contact with copper will affect the color and consistency of many foods, copper pots must be lined. Great care must be taken not to scratch the lining, which is usually a soft metal, such as tin. Copper also tends to discolor quickly, and so it requires significant time and labor for proper upkeep.

Cast iron has the capacity to hold heat well and transmit it very evenly. The metal is somewhat brittle, however, and must be treated carefully to prevent pitting, scarring, and rusting. Cast iron is sometimes coated with enamel to simplify care.

Stainless steel is a relatively poor conductor of heat, but is often used because it has other advantages, including easy maintenance. Other metals, such as aluminum or copper, are often sandwiched within stainless steel to improve heat conduction. Stainless steel will not react with foods; this means, for example, that white sauces will retain a pure white or ivory color.

Blue-steel, black-steel, pressed-steel, or rolled-steel pans are all prone to discoloration but transmit heat very rapidly. These pans are generally thin, and are often preferred for sautéing foods because of their quick response to changes in temperature.

Aluminum is also an excellent conductor of heat; however, it is a soft metal that wears down quickly. When a metal spoon or whip is used to stir a white or light-colored sauce, soup, or stock in an aluminum pot, it could take on a gray color. Anodized or treated aluminum tends not to react with foods, and it is one of the most popular metals for pots used in contemporary kitchens. The surfaces of treated aluminum pans tend to be easier to clean and care for than most other metals, with the exception of stainless steel.

Nonstick coatings on pans have some use in professional kitchens, especially for those that try to offer foods that are cooked with less fats and oils. These surfaces are not as sturdy as metal or enamel linings, so care must be taken to avoid scratching during cooking and cleaning.

The following guidelines should be observed for the choice of a pan or mold.

• Choose a size appropriate to the food being cooked. The chef should be familiar with the capacity of various pots, pans, and molds. If too many pieces of meat are crowded into a sauteuse, for instance, the food will not brown properly. If the sauteuse is too large, however, the *fond* (caramelized drippings from the meat) could scorch. If a small fish is poached in a large pot, the *cuisson* (cooking liquid) will not have the proper flavor intensity. It is also easier to overcook the fish in a too-large pot. If the pot is too small, there may not be enough cuisson available for the sauce.

• Choose material appropriate to the cooking technique. Experience has shown, and science has verified, that certain cooking techniques are more successful when used with certain materials. For instance, sautéed foods require pans that transmit heat quickly and are sensitive to temperature changes. Braises, on the other hand, require long, fairly gentle cooking, and it is more important that the particular pot transmit heat evenly and hold heat well than that it respond rapidly to changes in heat.

• Use proper handling, cleaning, and storing techniques. Avoid subjecting pots to heat extremes (for example, placing a smoking-hot pot into a sinkful of water) because some materials are prone to warping. Other materials may chip or even crack if allowed to sit over heat when they are empty or if they are handled roughly. Casseroles or molds made of enameled cast iron or steel are especially vulnerable. In order to protect the "seasoning" of rolled steel pans, do not clean the surface with detergents or abrasives such as steel wool or cleansing powders.

Be sure to dry pans before storing —air drying is best—to prevent the pitting and rusting of some surfaces, as well as to keep them clean and sanitary. Proper and organized storage prevents dents, chips, and breakage, and expedites the work load, because staff can more readily find what they need.

Pots and Pans for Stovetop Cooking

Pots and pans are not only available in a variety of materials but are also produced in a number of different sizes. All must be able to withstand direct heat from a flame. A poorly produced pot will have weak spots that will eventually warp. Figure 5-11 shows standard pots, pans, and other items used for a number of different cooking procedures. Different manufacturers, however, may use different styles of handles, loops, or lids.

• Stockpot (marmite). This large pot, of medium-gauge metal, is taller than it is wide, and has straight sides. Some stockpots have a spigot at the base so that the liquid can be drained off without lifting the heavy pot. Anodized aluminum and stainless steel are the preferred materials.

• Saucepot. This pot is similar in shape to a stockpot, although not as large, with straight sides and two loop handles for lifting.

• Saucepan. This pan has straight or slightly flared sides (a pan with flared sides may be known as a *fait-tout*) and has a single long handle.

• Rondeau. This is a wide, fairly shallow pot with two loop handles. When made from cast iron, these pots are frequently known as "griswolds," and they may have a single short handle rather than the two loop handles. A brazier is similar to a rondeau and may be square instead of round.

• Sauteuse. This shallow skillet with sloping sides and a single long

Marmite with spigot

Saucepot with two loop handles

Saucepan with one long handle

Rondeau

Sauteuse

Sautoir

Omelet pan

Crêpe pan

5-11

Marmite with spigot, saucepot with two loop handles, saucepan with one long handle, rondeau, sauteuse, sautoir, omelet pan, and crêpe pan.

Double boiler (bain-marie)

Bain-marie inserts

Griswold

Fish poacher

Tiered aluminum steamer

Couscoussière

Wok

5-11 *(continued)*

Double boiler (bain-marie), bain-marie inserts, griswold, fish poacher, tiered aluminum steamer, couscoussière, and wok.

handle is often referred to as a sauté pan.

• Sautoir. This shallow skillet has straight sides and a single long handle. It is often referred to as a sauté pan.

• Omelette pan/crêpe pan. This shallow skillet has very short, slightly sloping sides, and is most often made of rolled or "blue" steel.

• Bain marie (double boiler). These are nesting pots with single long handles. The bottom pot is filled with water that is heated to gently cook or warm the food in the upper pot. The term also refers to the stainless-steel containers used to hold food in a steam table.

• Griddle. This is a heavy round or rectangular surface for griddling. A griddle is flat with no sides or handles and may be built directly into the stove. There may be a groove or indentation around the edge to allow grease to drain away.

• Fish poacher. This is a long, narrow pot with straight sides and may include a perforated rack for holding the fish.

• Steamer. This consists of a set of stacked pots. The upper pot has a perforated bottom and is placed over a larger pot, which is filled with boiling or simmering water. The perforations allow the steam to rise from the pot below to cook the food above. Tiered steamers are also available.

• Specialty pots and pans. Woks, couscoussières, paella pans, and grill pans (the latter is essentially a skillet with ridges that can simulate grilling) are among the stovetop pots and pans used to prepare special, usually ethnic, dishes.

Pots and Pans for Oven Cooking

Pans used in ovens are produced from the same basic materials as are used to make stovetop pots and pans; in addition, glazed and unglazed earthenware, glass, and ceramics are also used. The heat of the oven, less intense than that of a burner, prevents these more delicate materials from cracking and shattering due to extremes of temperature. It is important to remember not to submerge these materials into water immediately after removing them from the oven. Figure 5-12 includes some examples of pots and pans used in oven cooking.

• Roasting pan. This rectangular pan with medium-high sides is used for roasting or baking and comes in various sizes.

• Sheet pan. This shallow, rectangular pan is used for baking and may be full or half size.

• Pâté mold. A deep rectangular metal mold, the pâté mold usually has hinged sides to facilitate removal of the pâté. Special shapes (oval, triangular, and others) may be available.

• Terrine mold. The terrine mold may be rectangular or oval, with a lid. Traditionally an earthenware mold, it may also be made of enameled cast iron.

• Gratin dish. A shallow oval baking dish, this may be ceramic, enameled cast iron, or enameled steel.

• Soufflé dish. This is a round, straight-edged ceramic dish of various sizes.

• Timbale mold. This small metal or ceramic mold is used for individual portions of various molded, cooked vegetables, usually made with a custard base.

• Specialty molds. These include dariole, savarin, ring, and other molds that are used to achieve varying shapes.

5-12

Roasting pan, sheet pan, hinged pâté mold, terrine mold, soufflé mold, and timbale molds.

LARGE EQUIPMENT

Safety precautions must be observed and proper maintenance and cleaning consistently applied in order to keep this equipment functioning properly and to prevent injury or accident. Observe the following guidelines when working with large equipment:

1. Obtain proper instruction in the machine's safe operation. Do not be afraid to ask for extra help.

2. First turn off and then unplug electrical equipment before assembling or breaking down the equipment.

3. Use all safety features: Be sure that lids are secure, hand guards are used, and the machine is stable.

4. Clean and sanitize the equipment thoroughly after each use.

5. Be sure that all pieces of equipment are properly reassembled and left unplugged after each use.

6. Report any problems or malfunctions promptly and alert coworkers to the problem.

Grinding, Slicing, and Pureeing Equipment

Grinders, slicers, and cutting equipment all have the potential to be extremely dangerous. The importance of observing all the necessary safety precautions cannot be overemphasized. As these tools are essential for a number of different operations, all chefs should be able to use them with confidence. Figure 5-13 includes examples of this kind of equipment.

• Meat grinder. This is a freestanding machine or an attachment for a standing mixer. A meat grinder should have dies of varying sizes and in general will have a feed

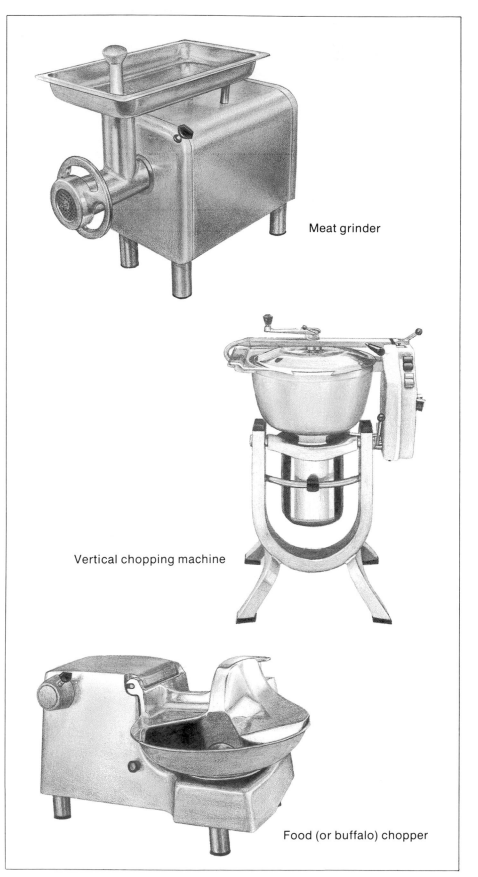

Meat grinder

Vertical chopping machine

Food (or buffalo) chopper

5-13

Meat grinder, vertical chopping machine, and food (or buffalo) chopper.

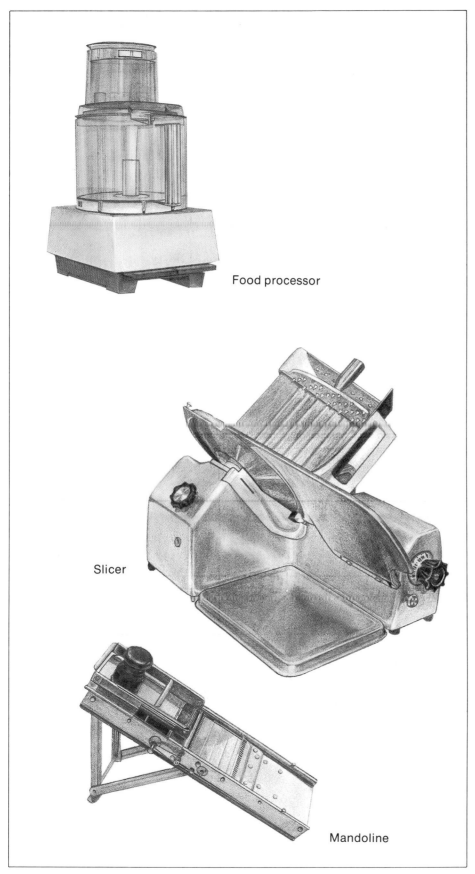

Food processor

Slicer

Mandoline

5-13 *(continued)*
Food processor, slicer, and mandoline.

tray and a pusher. All food contact areas should be kept scrupulously clean. To make sure all the food has been pushed through the worm, feed a twisted coil of plastic wrap through the feed tube.

• Vertical chopping machine (VCM). This machine operates on the same principle as a blender. A motor at the base is permanently attached to a bowl with integral blades. As a safety precaution, the hinged lid must be locked in place before the unit will operate. The VCM is used to grind, whip, emulsify, blend, or crush foods.

• Food chopper (buffalo chopper). The food is placed in a rotating bowl that passes under a hood, where blades chop the food. Some units have hoppers or feed tubes and interchangeable disks for slicing and grating. Food choppers are available in floor and tabletop models and are generally made of aluminum with a stainless-steel bowl.

• Food processor. This is a processing machine that houses the motor separately from the bowl, blades, and lid. Food processors can grind, puree, blend, emulsify, crush, knead, and, with special disks, slice, julienne, and shred foods.

• Food/meat slicer. This machine is used to slice foods in even thicknesses. A carrier moves the food back and forth against a circular blade, which is generally carbon steel. There may be separate motors to operate the carrier and the blade. To avoid injury, all the safety features incorporated in a food slicer, especially the hand guard, should be used.

• Mandoline. This slicing device is made of nickel-plated stainless steel with blades of high-carbon steel. Levers adjust the blades to achieve the cut and thickness desired. As with food slicers, be sure to use the guard—the carriage device that holds the food—to prevent injury. The mandoline can be used to make such cuts as slices, juliennes, gaufrettes, and batonnet.

Kettles and Steamers

Kettles and steamers enable a chef to prepare large amounts of food efficiently, since the heat is applied over a much larger area than is possible when a single burner is used. Cooking times for dishes prepared in steamers and large kettles are often shorter than for those prepared on a range top.

• Steam-jacketed kettle. This free-standing or tabletop kettle circulates steam through the walls, providing even heat. Units vary; they may tilt, may be insulated, and may have spigots or lids. Available in a range of sizes, these kettles are excellent for producing stocks, soups, and sauces. They are generally made of stainless steel and sometimes have a specially treated nonstick surface. Gas or electric models are available.

• Tilting kettle. This large, relatively shallow free-standing unit is used for braising and stewing. Most tilting kettles have lids, allowing for steaming as well. They are usually made of stainless steel and are available in gas or electric models.

• Pressure steamer. Water is heated under pressure in a sealed compartment, allowing it to reach higher than boiling temperature (212°F/100°C). The cooking time is controlled by automatic timers, which open the exhaust valves at the end. The doors cannot be opened until the pressure has been released.

• Convection steamer. The steam is generated in a boiler and then piped to the cooking chamber, where it is vented over the food. Pressure does not build up in the unit; it is continuously exhausted, which means the door may be opened at any time without danger of scalding or burning.

Stoves, Ranges, and Ovens

It is difficult to imagine a kitchen without a stove. The stovetop is known as the range; the oven is usually below the range. There are a number of different variations on this standard arrangement, however, just as there a number of different range tops and ovens available today.

Gas or electric ranges are available in many sizes with various combinations of open burners, flat-tops (not to be confused with griddle units), and ring-tops. Open burners and ring-tops supply direct heat, which is easy to change and control. Flat-tops provide indirect heat, which is more even and less intense than direct heat. Foods that require long, slow cooking, such as stocks, are more effectively cooked on a flat-top. Small units known as candy stoves or stockpot ranges have rings of gas jets or removable rings in a flat-top that allow for excellent heat control.

Ovens cook foods by surrounding them with hot air, a gentler and more even source of heat than the direct heat of a burner. Although many types of food are prepared in ovens, they are most commonly used for roasting and baking. Different ovens are available to suit a variety of needs, and both the establishment's menu and its available space should be evaluated before determining what type and size oven to install.

• Open-burner range. This is an individual grate-style burner that allows for easy adjustment of heat.

• Flat-top range. This consists of a thick plate of cast-iron or steel set over the heat source. Flat-tops give relatively even and consistent heat but do not allow for quick adjustments of temperature.

• Ring-top range. This is a flat-top with removable plates that can be removed to widen the opening, supplying more or less heat.

• Convection oven. Hot air is forced through fans to circulate around the food, cooking it evenly and quickly. Some convection ovens have the capacity to introduce moisture. They are available in gas or electric models, in a range of sizes, with stainless-steel interiors and exteriors and glass doors. Special features may include infrared and a convection-microwave combination.

• Conventional/deck ovens. The heat source is located on the bottom, underneath the deck, or floor, of the oven. Heat is conducted through the deck to the cavity. Conventional ovens can be located below a range top or as individual shelves arranged one above another. The latter are known as deck ovens, and the food is placed directly on the deck, instead of on a wire rack. Deck ovens normally consist of two to four decks, though single-deck models are available. Some deck ovens have a ceramic or firebrick base. Deck ovens usually are gas or electric, although charcoal and wood-burning units are also available. The basic deck oven is most often used only for roasting, but several variations are available for other purposes.

Additional styles of ovens include pizza ovens, rotary ovens for spit roasting, conveyor ovens, and rotating deck ovens. Two other oven/range features, the griddle and the grill, are part of the traditional commercial foodservice setup.

• Griddle. Similar to a flat-top range top, a griddle has a heat source located beneath a thick plate of metal, generally cast-iron or steel. The food is cooked directly on this surface. A griddle may be gas or electric.

• Grill/broiler/salamander. In a grill, the heat source is located below the rack; in a broiler or salamander, the heat source is above. Some units have adjustable racks, which allow the food to be raised or lowered to control cooking speed. Most units are gas, although electric units with ceramic "rocks" create a bed of coals, producing the effect of a charcoal grill. Salamanders are small broilers, used primarily to finish or glaze foods.

Refrigeration Equipment

Maintaining adequate refrigeration storage is crucial to any foodservice operation; therefore, the menu and the available refrigeration storage must be evaluated and coordinated. All units should be maintained properly, which means regular and thorough cleaning, including the insulating strips. Such

precautions will help reduce spoilage and thus reduce food costs. Placing the units so that unnecessary steps are eliminated will save time and labor. Both of these factors will save money for the operation.

• Walk-in. This is the largest style of refrigeration unit and usually has shelves that are arranged around the walls. It is possible to zone a walk-in to maintain appropriate temperature and humidity levels for storing various foods. Some walk-ins are large enough to accommodate rolling carts for additional storage. The carts can then be rolled to the appropriate area of the kitchen when needed. Some units have pass-through or reach-in doors to facilitate access to frequently required items.

Walk-ins may be situated in the kitchen or outside the facility. If space allows, walk-ins located outside the kitchen can prove advantageous, because deliveries may be made at any time without disrupting service.

• Reach-in. A reach-in may be a single unit or part of a bank of units, available in many sizes. Units with pass-through doors are especially helpful for the pantry area, where salads, desserts, and

other cold items can be retrieved by the waitstaff as needed.

• On-site refrigeration. These are refrigerated drawers or undercounter reach-ins, which allow foods on the line to be held at the proper temperature during service. This eliminates unnecessary walking, which can create a hazard during peak periods.

• Portable refrigeration. This is basically a refrigerated cart that can be placed as needed in the kitchen.

• Display refrigeration. These are display cases that are generally used in the dining room for desserts, salads, or salad bars.

SUMMARY

The chef employs a broad selection of hand tools and equipment, all of which must be treated with knowledge and respect. The knife is decidedly the most important hand tool the chef will use, especially the chef's, or French, knife.

Choosing the proper equipment for a particular task is fundamental. In the case of complex machinery, it is especially important that the chef or foodservice employee know the proper procedures and safety precautions before beginning to use the equipment.

Part Three

Product
Identification

Before beginning to cook, a chef must first learn to select high-quality ingredients and then handle them so as to maintain that quality. This section provides a brief encyclopedia of the most commonly stocked foods. For meats, poultry, and game, the chef should know the different cuts and the inspection and grading standards. For fish and shellfish, one must learn the properties of the many species available, and the most suitable cooking techniques.

Fruits and vegetables must be purchased on the basis of freshness and seasonality. Dairy products and eggs, highly perishable ingredients, must always be selected on the basis of quality and freshness. Cheeses, the least perishable dairy products, are covered here under the categories of fresh, semi-soft, soft, hard, and grating.

Nonperishable goods comprise a broad range of items, including grains, meals, flours, legumes, nuts and seeds, flavorings, condiments, and beverages. Convenience foods of various sorts are also discussed.

Chapter 6

Meat, Poultry, and Game Identification

or most restaurants, the purchase, preparation, and service of meats is one of the most expensive—but also one of the most potentially profitable—areas of the business. Determining which meat cuts are best for a particular style of cookery or cooking technique and selecting meats suitable for a particular menu will be covered in this chapter.

Also discussed are poultry and game, which enjoy increased popularity because of their comparatively low levels of saturated fats and cholesterol. Variety meats, traditionally not as popular in the United States as in other countries, are also currently enjoying some increased consumer acceptance.

Often the difference between turning a profit and losing money will depend upon wise purchasing of meats. This chapter will cover the following basic information: inspection, grading, and quality standards, primal cuts, and market or purchase standards.

MEAT BASICS

The meat, poultry, and game cuts that a restaurant should buy will depend upon the nature of the particular operation. A restaurant featuring predominantly à la minute preparations—especially those with a preponderance of grilled or sautéed items—will need to purchase extremely tender (and more expensive) cuts. A restaurant that uses a variety of techniques may be able to use some less tender cuts, for example, the veal shank in a braise such as osso bucco.

The degree to which a kitchen is capable of storing meats, the available equipment, the kitchen staff's capability to butcher, or "fabricate," larger cuts, and the volume of meat required will determine whether it is more economical to purchase large pieces, such as whole legs of veal, or prefabricated meats, such as veal already cut into a top round, or perhaps even precut scallopini, which have been trimmed and cut into portions (known as "pc").

Storage

Meats, poultry, and game should be loosely wrapped and stored under refrigeration. When possible, they should be held in a separate unit, or at least in a separate part of the cooler. They should always be placed on trays to prevent them from dripping on other foods or onto the floor.

The chef should separate different kinds of meats; for example, poultry should not come in contact with beef, or pork products in contact with any other meats. This will prevent cross-contamination.

Meats packed in Cryovac® (a special type of plastic wrapping) can be stored directly in the Cryovac, as long as it has not been punctured or ripped. Once unwrapped, meats should be rewrapped in air-permeable paper, such as butcher's paper, because air-tight containers promote bacteria growth that could result in spoilage or contamination. Variety meats, poultry, and uncured pork products, which have short shelf lives, should be cooked as soon as possible after they are received. Meat stored at the proper temperature and under optimal conditions can be held for several days without a noticeable quality loss.

Inspection and Grading

Government inspection of all meats is mandatory. Inspections are required at various times—on the farm or ranch, at the slaughterhouse, and, again, after butchering—to assure that the animal is free from disease, and that the meat is wholesome and fit for human consumption.

Grading, however, is not mandatory. The U.S. Department of Agriculture (USDA) has developed specific standards used to assign grades to meats, and also trains graders. The packer may, however, choose not to hire a USDA grader and may assign his own grade instead.

Depending upon the particular animal, the grader will consider the overall carcass shape, the ratio of fat to lean, ratio of meat to bones, color, and marbling of lean flesh.

The eight USDA beef grades are Prime, Choice, Select, Standard, Commercial, Utility, Cutter, and Canner. The five grades for veal are Prime, Choice, Good, Standard, and Utility. Lamb is rated Prime, Choice, Good, or Utility. Pork may receive a federal grade as well (USDA 1, 2, or 3), but this grading system is less widely used. The grade placed on a particular carcass is then applied to *all* the cuts from that animal.

Poultry is also given a mandatory inspection for wholesomeness and may be graded as USDA A, B, or C. The following factors determine that grade: shape of the carcass; ratio of meat to bone; freedom from pinfeathers, hair, and down; and number (if any) of tears, cuts, or broken bones.

General Carcass Divisions

The obvious step after slaughtering the animal is to cut the carcass into manageable pieces. Certain exact standards govern where the carcass is to be divided. The first large cuts, known as primal cuts, are then further broken down into other cuts—steaks, roasts, shanks, etc.

As the illustrations of the cuts of beef, pork, veal, and lamb indicate (see Fig. 6-1), the divisions follow a similar pattern, whichever animal is being butchered, with only minor variations by type.

- The leg. This is known as the "round" for beef and the "ham" for pork.
- The loin. In general, the most tender and most expensive cuts come from this area. Because it is the smallest part of the animal, there is far less yield, which means the prices are higher. Pigs are bred specifically to have a long loin; thus, the cut for the pig's primal loin is far larger than for other animals.
- The rib. Another prized part, in addition to the loin, is the rib. This section, along with the loin, is generally the least exercised portion of the animal and is thus more tender.
- The shoulder. The shoulder, like the leg, does have some tender cuts. For the most part, however, the shoulder meat is not well suited

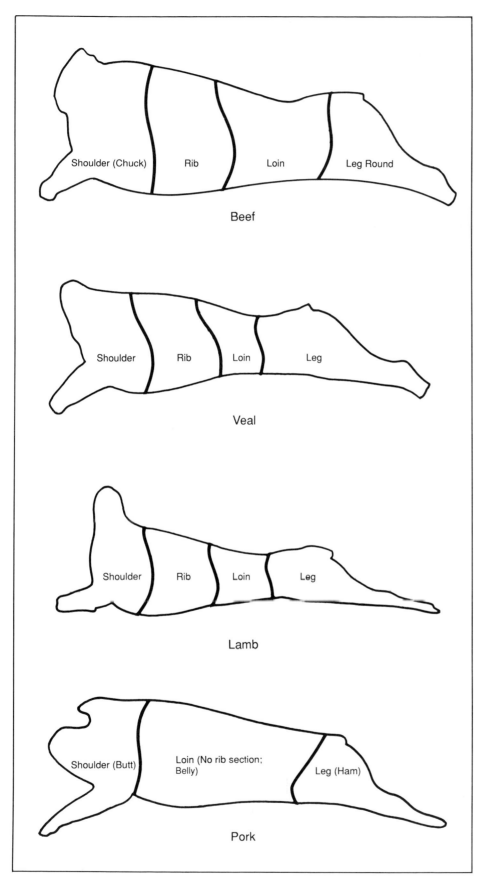

Shoulder (Chuck) | Rib | Loin | Leg Round

Beef

Shoulder | Rib | Loin | Leg

Veal

Shoulder | Rib | Loin | Leg

Lamb

Shoulder (Butt) | Loin (No rib section; Belly) | Leg (Ham)

Pork

6-1

Relations of major carcass divisions for beef, veal, lamb, and pork.

to dry-heat techniques such as grilling and sautéing. Shoulder cuts are more frequently prepared with moist or combination methods such as braising or stewing.

MARKET FORMS

Market forms of meat are those cuts of meat that are ready for sale. They may be an entire primal cut itself (a leg of veal, for example, or a loin of pork) or they may have been fabricated from the primals (a top round of beef, for example). In some cases, the amount of actual fabrication necessary to prepare market forms for sale may be quite minimal; perhaps only some scrap or trim will be removed. In other cases, it may be more dramatic: Some cuts are fully boned and trimmed before they are ready for sale. The amount of work done to prepare a cut for sale will, in part, determine its price. With the exceptions of venison, rabbit, and other game, all market forms of meat are assigned quality grades; only beef and lamb have yield grades.

Beef

After slaughter and post-mortem inspection, beef is first assigned both a USDA quality grade and a yield grade, which reflects the yield of usable meat versus fat trim. Yield Grade 1 is the highest yield; 10 is the lowest. The carcass is then split down the backbone to divide it into two sides. The sides are further divided into the forequarter and the hindquarter.

The forequarter contains four primal cuts: the rib, the chuck (shoulder), the brisket, and the foreshank. The hindquarter contains two primal cuts: the loin and the round (leg). These primal cuts may be sold as is, or, as is more often the case, they will be broken down into their market forms. Various cuts of beef are shown in Figure 6-2.

In addition to the illustrated cuts, ground beef and the parts such as the oxtail, liver, heart, tongue, and other organ meats may also be sold. Some cuts may be cured (corned beef, for example, usually from the brisket) or dried.

Beef may be "aged," a process that gives the meat a darker color, a more tender texture, and a full flavor. Boneless cuts such as steaks may be aged in plastic (Cryovac), or the entire side, forequarter, or hindquarter may be hung in a climate-controlled area to age. Aged beef is more expensive, however, because a significant moisture and weight loss reduces ultimate yield.

Veal

Veal is an offshoot of the dairy industry. Cattle butchered from the age of one day up to 14 to 15 weeks are sold as veal. The cuts are similar to those for beef; however, veal has a paler flesh and a more delicate taste.

Veal may be split in two halves, or it may be cut into a foresaddle and a hindsaddle, which is accomplished by splitting the carcass at a point between the eleventh and twelfth ribs.

The primal cuts for veal are the shoulder (chuck), shank, rack (rib), loin, and leg. Organ meats (offal) from veal are highly prized, especially the sweetbreads, liver, calf's head, and brains. Various cuts of veal are shown in Figure 6-3.

Oven-ready rib roast, or "prime rib"   Boneless rib roast

Tenderloin   Flank steak

Bottom round   Top round

Strip loin

Top butt, sirloin

Top butt

Boneless brisket

Chuck (shoulder)

Eye of round

Knuckle

Shank, bone in

6-2

Market forms of beef *(from top left, opposite page):* oven-ready rib roast, or "prime rib"; boneless rib roast; strip loin; top butt, sirloin; top butt; tenderloin; flank steak; boneless brisket; chuck (shoulder); eye of round; bottom round; top round; knuckle; and shank, bone in.

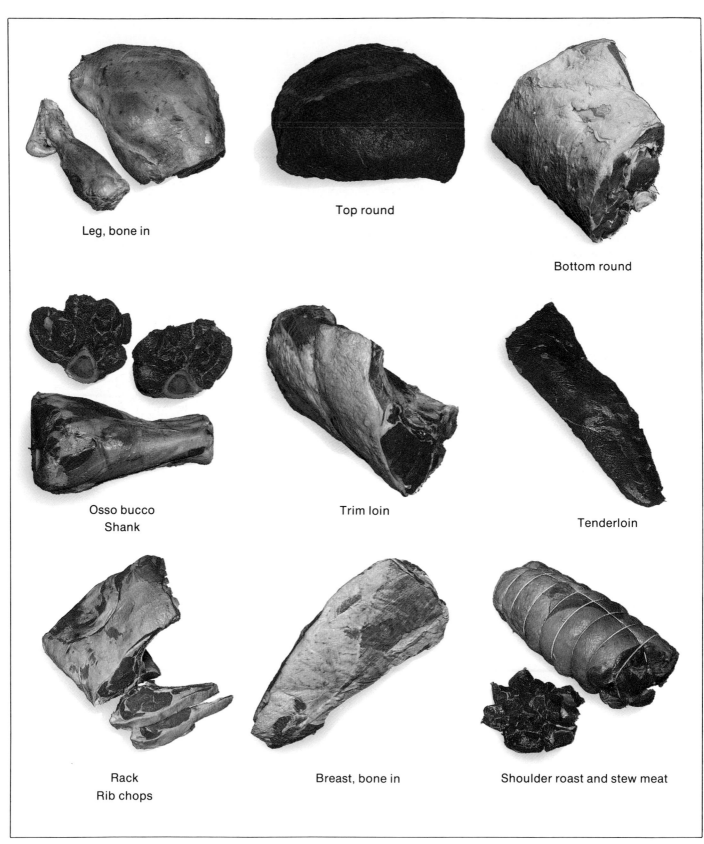

Leg, bone in

Top round

Bottom round

Osso bucco
Shank

Trim loin

Tenderloin

Rack
Rib chops

Breast, bone in

Shoulder roast and stew meat

6-3

Market forms of veal: leg, bone in *(shank shown on lower left)*; top round; bottom round; osso bucco *(top)*, shank *(bottom)*; trim loin; tenderloin; rack *(top)*, rib chops *(bottom)*; breast, bone in; and shoulder roast and stew meat.

Pork

Pigs raised today are bred to produce leaner meat cuts. They are slaughtered and butchered in facilities that handle no other type of meat, to prevent the spread of disease and infection, such as trichinosis.

The pork carcass, once split into two halves along the backbone, is divided in a slightly different manner from most other meats. Instead of a primal rib, the loin is cut long.

Pork's primal cuts are: the ham (leg portion), the shoulder butt, and the loin. Important subprimal pork cuts include the spareribs, bacon or side pork, jowl, and clear-plate fatback. Various pork cuts are shown in Figure 6-4.

Lamb and Mutton

Lamb has grown in popularity over the last several years, and the impression that it will have a "sheepy" flavor is fading fast because of improved methods for breeding, raising, and feeding sheep. Improved breeding techniques mean that lamb is no longer available only in the spring (the traditional time for "lambing" or "dropping young").

Because the lamb is slaughtered when still quite young, it is tender, and most cuts can be cooked by any method. Spring lamb and hothouse lamb are not fed grass or grain because once the lamb begins to eat grass, the flesh loses some of its delicacy. As the animal ages, the flesh will darken in color, take on a slightly coarser texture, and have a much more pronounced flavor. Sheep slaughtered under the age of a year may still be labeled lamb; if slaughtered after that, however, they must be labeled mutton.

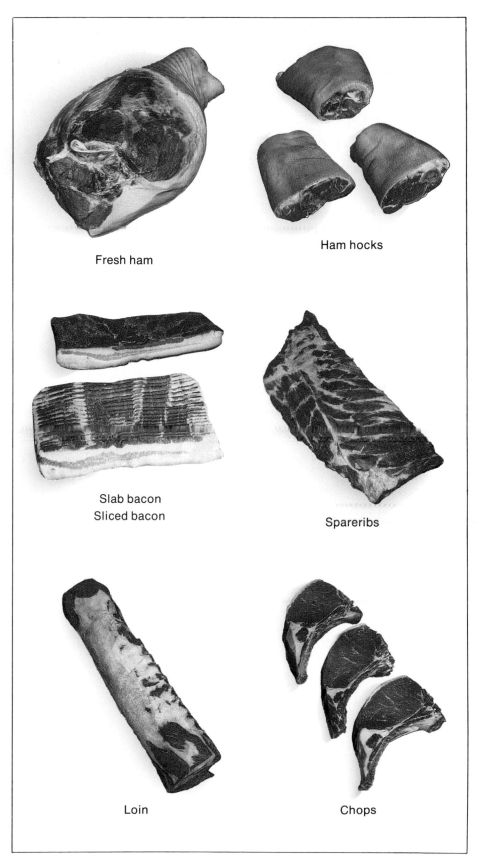

Fresh ham

Ham hocks

Slab bacon
Sliced bacon

Spareribs

Loin

Chops

6-4

Market forms of pork: fresh ham; ham hocks; slab bacon *(top)*, sliced bacon *(bottom)*; spareribs; loin; chops.

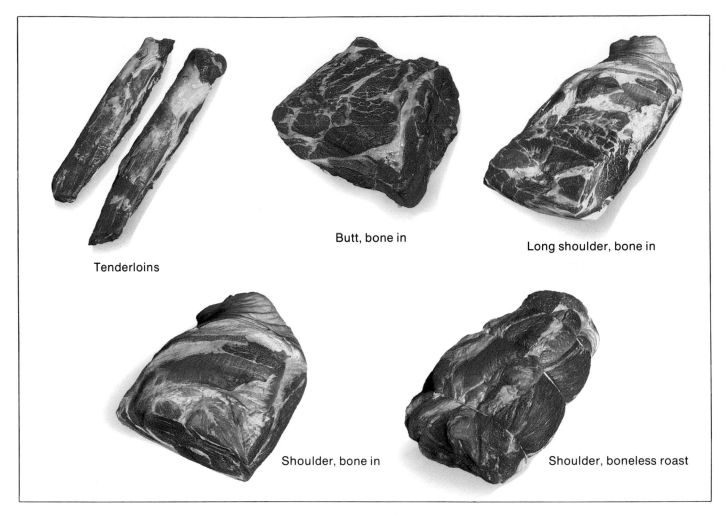

Tenderloins

Butt, bone in

Long shoulder, bone in

Shoulder, bone in

Shoulder, boneless roast

6-4 *(continued)*

Market forms of pork: tenderloins; butt, bone in; long shoulder, bone in; shoulder, bone in; and shoulder, boneless roast.

Like veal, lamb is also cut into a foresaddle and hindsaddle and may also be cut into sides. The major lamb cuts are: rib (known also as rack), square-cut shoulder, breast, shank, loin, and leg. Various lamb cuts are shown in Figure 6-5.

Venison and Large, Furred Game

Fallow deer (a farm-raised deer) produces a lean, tasty meat with less fat and cholesterol than beef. The loin and the rib are quite tender and can be suitable for most cooking techniques, especially roasting, grilling, and sautéing. The haunch and legs are more exercised, and are best when prepared by moist-heat or combination techniques.

Depending upon the area of the country, other types of game—including wild boar, elk, and bear—may also be available. The same general rules that determine how to cook a red meat cut will work for these meats:

1. Cuts from less exercised portions of the animal may be prepared by any technique and are frequently paired with dry-heat methods such as grilling or roasting.

2. Well-exercised areas of the animal, such as the leg (or haunch), shank, and shoulder are best when cooked by moist-heat or combination methods. These cuts are also used for preparing pâtés and other charcuterie items (see Chapter 29, "Charcuterie and Garde-manger"). Various venison cuts are shown in Figure 6-6.

Rabbit

Rabbit, raised domestically, is available throughout the year. The loin meat is delicate in flavor and color, and has a tendency to dry out if not handled carefully. Traditional preparation methods include roasting, braising, and "jugging," which preserves the meat by cooking and storing it in fat. The loin and legs are often prepared by two separate techniques—the loin is roasted or

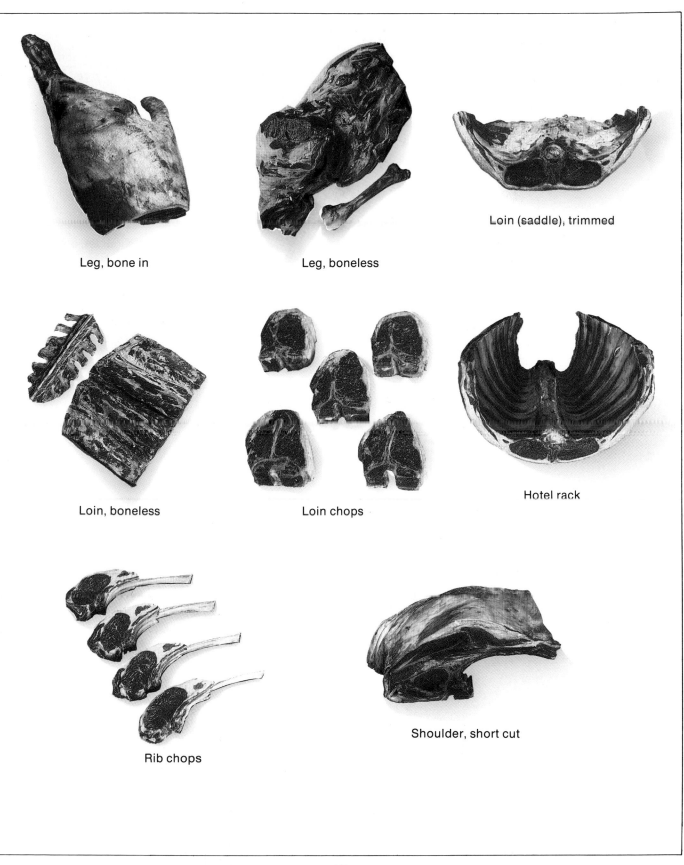

Leg, bone in

Leg, boneless

Loin (saddle), trimmed

Loin, boneless

Loin chops

Hotel rack

Rib chops

Shoulder, short cut

6-5

Market forms of lamb: leg, bone in; leg, boneless; loin (saddle), trimmed; loin, boneless; loin chops; hotel rack; rib chops; and shoulder, short cut.

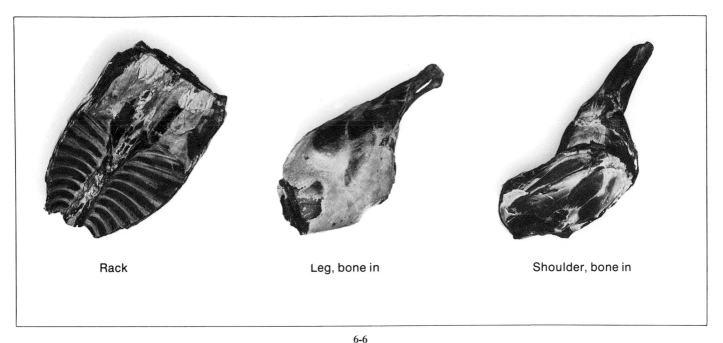

6-6

Market forms of venison: rack; leg, bone in, and shoulder, bone in.

sautéed and the legs, which are more exercised, are cooked by stewing or braising. Figure 6-7 shows a rabbit carcass.

Domestic Poultry

As better rearing methods have been perfected, chicken and other poultry, once reserved for special occasions, have become commonplace in restaurants and homes. Poultry production is now a big business, with breeding, care, and feeding all scientifically controlled.

After slaughter and post-mortem inspection, the birds are plucked, cleaned, chilled, and packaged. They can be purchased whole or in parts. The younger the bird, the more tender its flesh will be. As birds age, their flesh toughens, and the cartilage in the breast hardens. The windpipe and bill of ducks and geese will also harden.

It is possible to purchase "free-range" poultry and game. Raised in large yards, these birds are more

well-exercised than their "factory"-raised counterparts. The meat of free-range birds is generally darker in color, and some prefer its flavor and texture.

Poultry is classified by size and age (maturity), as shown in Table 6-1. See also Figure 6-8 for examples of both domestic poultry and waterfowl.

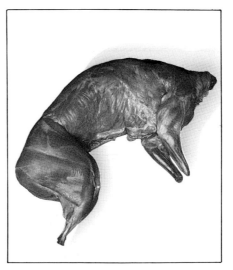

6-7

Rabbit.

Various Game Birds

Traditionally, chefs could only obtain most game birds during the hunting season, usually late fall and early winter. Today many game birds are raised on farms year-round. However, many game birds, especially those allowed "free range," will still be at their best from October through December or January. Poultry are domesticated; that is, their habitat and breeding are carefully controlled by humans. Game birds are "wild" species. They may also be farm-raised, but their characteristics are usually not reproductively controlled. Examples of game birds are shown in Figure 6-9.

Young fowl should have soft, smooth, pliable skin. The breast-bone cartilage should be flexible, as it is for domestic fowl. The flesh should be tender, with a slight "gamy" taste. The types of game birds most often used today in cooking are the following:

TABLE 6-1. POULTRY CLASSIFICATION

Name	Description	Age	Weight
Rock Cornish Game Hen	Very tender, suitable for all cooking techniques	5–6 weeks	¾ to 2 lb. (.34 to .9 kg)
Broiler	"	9–12 weeks	1½ to 2 lb. (.34 to .9 kg)
Fryer	"	9–12 weeks	2½ to 3½ lb. (.7 to 1.6 kg)
Roaster	"	3–5 months	3½ to 5 lb. (1.6 to 2.3 kg)
Stewing Hen	Mature female bird, requires slow, moist cooking	Over 10 months	3½ to 6 lb. (1.6 to 2.7 kg)
Capon (Castrated Male)	Very tender, usually roasted or poêled	Under 8 months	5 to 8 lb. (2.3 to 3.6 kg)
Young Hen or Tom Turkey	Tender, suitable for most cooking techniques	5–7 months	8 to 22 lb. (3.6 to 10 kg)
Yearling Turkey	Fully mature but still tender, usually roasted	Under 15 months	10 to 30 lb. (4.5 to 14 kg)
Broiler or Fryer Duckling	Very tender, usually roasted, but suitable for most techniques	Under 8 weeks	2 to 4 lb. (.9 to 1.8 kg)
Roaster Duckling	Tender, usually roasted	Under 16 weeks	4 to 6 lb. (1.8 to 2.7 kg)
Young Goose or Gosling	Tender, usually roasted	Under 6 months	6 to 10 lb. (2.7 to 4.5 kg)
Guinea Hen or Fowl	Related to pheasant; tender, suitable for most techniques	About 6 months	¾ to 1½ lb. (.34 to .7 kg)
Squab*	Light, tender meat, suitable for sauté, roast, grill; as bird ages, the meat darkens and toughens	3–4 weeks	Under 1 lb. (under .45 kg)

* Domestic pigeon that has not begun to fly.

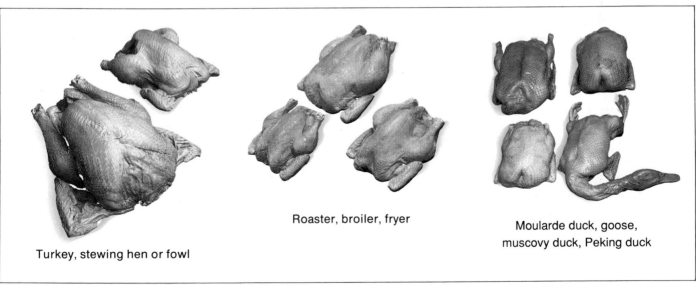

Turkey, stewing hen or fowl

Roaster, broiler, fryer

Moularde duck, goose, muscovy duck, Peking duck

6-8

Domestic poultry and water fowl: turkey, stewing hen or fowl; roaster, broiler, fryer; moularde duck *(top left)*, goose *(top right)*, muscovy duck *(bottom left)*, and Peking duck *(bottom right)*.

• Quail. The smallest of the game birds, these are traditionally spit-roasted, poêléed, or poached.

• Snipe/woodcock. The snipe is available in three sizes, large, common, and small, and has traditionally been considered by gourmets to be one of the finest of all game birds.

• Wild duck. Teal, a small duck, is considered a delicacy. As wild duck ages, the flesh may take on a fishy or oily taste.

• Pheasant. One of the meatiest of all game birds, the pheasant may be roasted or braised. Domestically raised pheasant will not have a pronounced gamy flavor.

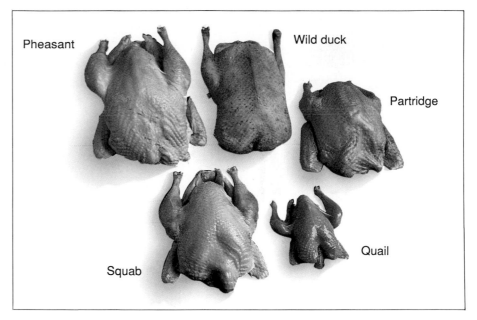

6-9

Game birds: *(top row, left to right)* pheasant, wild duck, partridge; *(bottom row, left to right)* squab, quail.

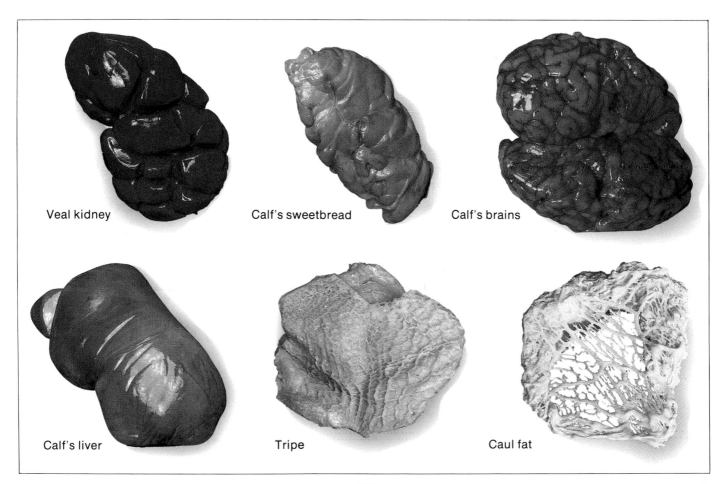

6-10

Offal meats: veal kidney; calf's sweetbread; calf's brains; calf's liver; tripe; and caul fat.

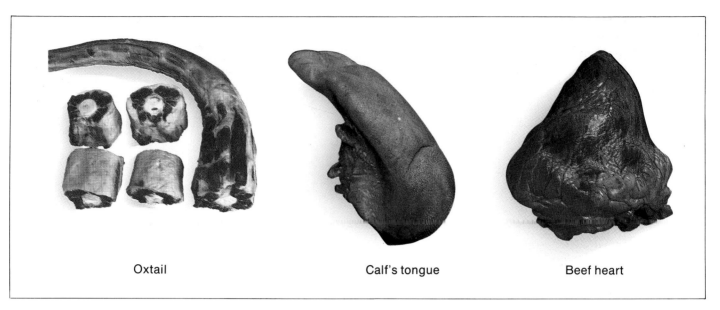

Oxtail   Calf's tongue   Beef heart

6-10 *(continued)*

Offal meats: oxtail; calf's tongue; and beef heart.

Offal Meats

Offal meats are the "innards" of virtually any animal. At one time, butchers gave these meats away as pet food. As palates have become more discriminating and clientele have become less squeamish, demand for these meats has increased and their prices have risen greatly in a relatively short time. Offal meats are divided into two categories, organ meats and muscle meats.

The liver, sweetbreads, brain, and kidneys are commonly available organ meats. Foie gras is the fattened liver of a special breed of duck or goose; it has always been prized for its succulence and rich flavor. Sweetbreads, which have a particularly misleading name, are actually a veal or lamb thymus gland and bear no resemblance to a cinnamon bun.

Muscle meats include the heart, tongue, tripe, and oxtail. These meats are best when cooked slowly in a liquid. Examples of some kinds of offal meats appear in Figure 6-10.

Kosher Meats

Kosher meats are specially slaughtered, bled, and fabricated in order to comply with religious dietary laws. In this country, only beef and veal forequarters, poultry, and some game are customarily used for kosher preparations. In order to be considered kosher, the animal must be slaughtered by a single stroke and completely bled, and all veins and arteries must be removed. Removing them from the loin and leg of beef or veal would essentially mutilate the flesh, which is why the hindquarter of these animals is not generally used.

SUMMARY

Meat traditionally has been a large component of the typical American diet. In spite of the negative publicity meat has received, continued nutritional studies have come to the commonsense conclusion that meat is not harmful, as long as it is eaten in prudent amounts. Many restaurants have learned to serve reasonable portions, instead of thick chops and plate-sized steaks.

As consumers eat smaller portions, they will look for better quality, improved flavor, and tenderness. Methods of raising, grading, and butchering meats are constantly improving in response to industry demands. Meats are becoming less fatty, with a better proportion of lean meat to both fat and bone.

The knowledgeable foodservice operator recognizes the importance of purchasing appropriate cuts for menu items, maximizing the cuts' portion yield, and eliminating waste. Observing these guidelines assures that the guest will perceive the meal as healthful and a good value. The chef should refer to further chapters in this book on the best ways to fabricate and prepare various meats.

Chapter 7

Fish and Shellfish
Identification

ish were once plentiful and inexpensive, but due to various factors, including nutritional concerns, pollution of fishing beds, and the search for variety, demand has begun to outstrip supply. Fish's dietary importance is gaining credibility, even among Americans who traditionally have favored red meats, and fish have become popular entrées. The chef should be familiar with many fish, including under-utilized varieties that until quite recently were grouped together as "trash fish" or "junk fish." Although not well-known, these fish can be excellent alternatives to species that are no longer available either because of over-fishing or because their habitats have become polluted. The chef can also purchase fish grown by "aquaculture." Farm-raised fish such as catfish, salmon, and trout, and shellfish, such as oysters, raised in special beds, are good examples.

FISH BASICS

The chef should select absolutely fresh fish of the best quality. The first step in this process is assessing the purveyor or market. The fishmonger should properly handle, ice, and display the fish and should be able to answer any questions regarding the fish's origin and its qualities: lean or oily, firm-textured or delicate, appropriate for moist-heat methods or able to withstand a grill's heat.

Purchasing

Fish can be transported rapidly from the source to the consumer, but to ensure that fish are of the best quality, the chef should apply as many as possible of the following tests, which are listed in approximately their order of importance. If a fish smells fresh and looks fresh, but has a slight browning of the gills, it may still be acceptable. If a fish smells bad, no matter how clear the eyes or firm the flesh, reject it. Figure 7-1 illustrates some of the steps in checking fish quality.

1. Smell the fish. It should have a fresh, clean "sea" aroma, appropriate to the fish. Very strong

7-1 CHECKING FISH QUALITY

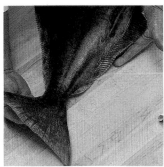

(1) The fins and tail should be moist, full, and flexible.

(2) Press the fish with a fingertip.

(3) The gills should have a good red color.

(4) Check the belly cavity of gutted fish.

odors are a clear indication that the fish is aging or was improperly handled or stored.

2. Feel the skin. The skin should feel slick and moist. The scales, if any, should be firmly attached.

3. Look at the fins and tail. They should be moist, fresh, flexible, and full, and should not appear ragged or dry.

4. Press the flesh. It should feel firm and elastic; if there is a visible finger imprint, the fish is not fresh.

5. Check the eyes. Eyes should be clear and full. As the fish ages, the eyes will begin to lose moisture and sink back into the head. (Note: The wall-eyed pike's eyes should appear milky.) This test should be used in conjunction with as many others as possible.

6. Check the gills. They should have a good red to maroon color, with no traces of gray or brown, and should be moist and fresh-looking. The exact shade of red will depend on the fish type.

7. Check the belly. There should be no sign of "belly burn," which occurs when the guts are not removed promptly; the stomach enzymes begin to eat the flesh, causing it to come away from the bones. There should also be no breaks or tears in the flesh.

8. Check live shellfish for signs of movement. Lobster and crab should move about. Clams, mussels, and oysters should be tightly closed. As they age, they will start to open. Any shells that do not snap shut when tapped should be discarded; the shellfish are dead. If a bag contains many open shells the delivery should be rejected.

Storage

Ideally, the chef should purchase only the amount of fish needed for a day or two at most, and should store it properly as described below. When the purveyor is only able to make deliveries once or twice a week, then proper storage becomes a critical concern.

Under proper storage conditions, fish and shellfish can be held for several days without losing any appreciable quality. When the fish arrives, the following things should be done.

1. Check the fish carefully for freshness and quality. The fish may be rinsed at this point; scaling and fabricating should be delayed until close to service time.

2. Place the fish on a bed of shaved or flaked ice in a perforated container; stainless steel or plastic is preferred. The fish should be belly down, and the belly cavity may be filled with shaved ice as well.

3. Cover with additional ice; the fish may be layered, if necessary, with shaved or flaked ice.

4. Set the perforated container inside a second container. In this way, as the ice melts, the water will drain away.

Fish should not be left sitting in a pool of water. Shaved or flaked ice is preferred, because the water can drain away more quickly, keeping the fish dry and avoiding bruising of the flesh. The fish should be thoroughly drained and re-iced daily. Figure 7-2 demonstrates some of the steps in proper fish storage.

• Clams, mussels, and oysters should be stored in the bag in which they were delivered, but should not be iced. They last better at a temperature range close to 40°F (4°C). The bag should be closed tightly and lightly weighted to keep the shellfish from opening up.

• Scallops out of the shell and fish purchased as fillets should be stored in plastic containers set on or in the ice. They should not be in direct contact with the ice, however, because as it melts much of the flavor and texture of the scallop or fish would be lost.

• Crabs, lobsters, and other live shellfish should be packed in seaweed or damp paper upon delivery. They can be stored directly in their shipping containers until they are to be prepared, if a lobster tank is not available. Do not allow fresh water to come in direct contact with lobster or crab, as it will kill them.

• Frozen fish, including glazed, whole fish (fish repeatedly coated with water and frozen so that the ice builds up in layers, coating the entire fish) and frozen shrimp, should be stored at 0°F (−18°C) until they are ready to be thawed and cooked. (Storage at −10°F (−2°C) is ideal and will greatly extend shelf life.) Do not accept any frozen fish with white frost on its

edges. This indicates freezer burn, the result of improper packaging or thawing and refreezing of the product.

Market Forms

Butchering fresh fish is relatively simple, and many restaurant chefs will probably prefer to do this, retaining the bones and head for stocks or fumet. As with meats, the available working space and the staff's level of skill in butchering should be evaluated. Most fish are too expensive to be cut up carelessly, and the extra money spent on buying fish fillets may balance out the money lost through waste. Fish may also be purchased frozen, smoked, pickled, or salted. In Chapter 13, instructions will be given for cutting fish into their market forms, as well as into other cuts. Four of the following market forms, widely available, are shown in Figure 7-3.

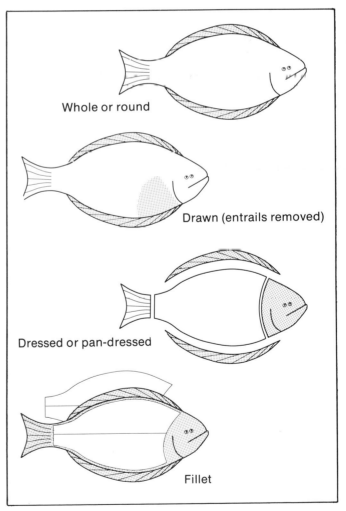

7-3

Market forms of fish: whole or round, drawn, dressed or pan-dressed, and fillet.

7-2 PROPER FISH STORAGE

(1) A perforated stainless-steel container that can be set in a hotel pan is ideal for storing fish.

(2) Hold the fish belly-down in a bed of shaved ice.

• Whole or round fish (round here does not refer to the fish category called round, which is based on skeletal type; see "Categories"). This is the fish as it was caught, completely intact.

• Drawn fish. The viscera (guts) are removed, but head, tail, and fins are still intact.

• Dressed fish. Viscera, scales, and fins are removed. The head and tail may also be removed, depending upon the fish. Also known as pan-dressed, these fish are usually small, about ½ to ¾ pound.

• Steaks. These are cross-section cuts, with a portion of the backbone in each cut. The skin is generally not removed. Steaks are usually available only from large round fish (for example, salmon, tuna, or swordfish), although one flat fish, the halibut, may also be cut into steaks.

• Fillets. This is a boneless piece of fish, removed from either side of the backbone. The skin may or may not be removed before cooking, but when purchased, the fish's skin should be attached to be sure that the fish received is the one that was ordered.

• Shucked. Shucking is the removal of a mollusc or fish from the shell; this term also refers to its market form sold as meat only, along with natural juices known as liquor. Molluscs such as oysters, clams, and mussels may be available shucked; scallops are nearly always sold shucked.

CATEGORIES

There are numerous different fish species and even greater numbers of names for these fish, not all of which may be of culinary importance. The name a fish will go by depends upon the region in which it is sold. However, basic groupings can be used to sort fish and shellfish. Once these groupings are explained, appropriate selection becomes a much easier matter.

The skeletal structure of finfish can also be used as the initial way to separate fish types into more readily understandable subjects. There are three basic skeletal types, two of which are shown in Figure 7-4.

1. *Round fish*, such as trout, bass, perch, salmon; these have a backbone along the upper edge with two fillets on either side. A round fish has one eye on each side of its head.

2. *Flat fish*, such as the various flounders and Dover sole; these have a backbone that runs through the center of the fish with four fillets, two upper and two lower. Both eyes are on the same side of the head.

3. *Nonbony fish*, such as ray, skate, sharks, and monkfish, which have cartilage rather than bones.

Shellfish can also be broken into distinct categories, also based on their skeletal structure:

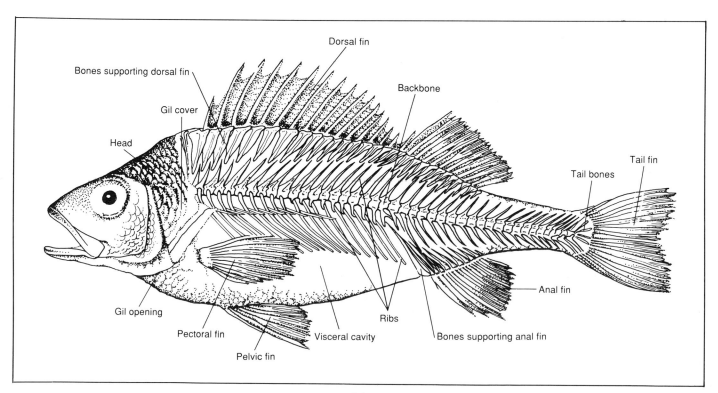

7-4a

The basic skeletal structure of a round fish.

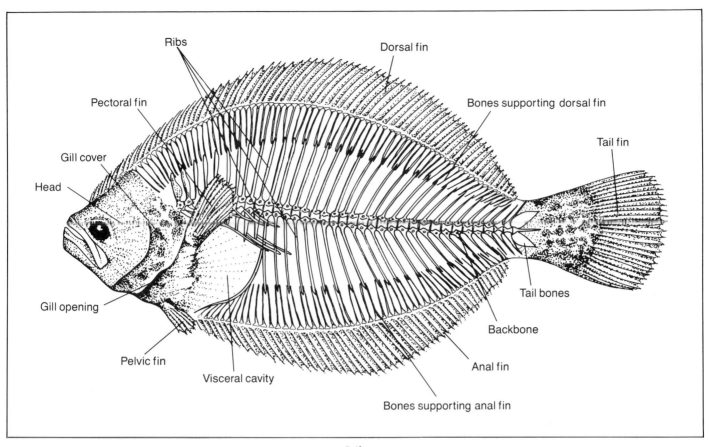

7-4b

The basic skeletal structure of a flat fish.

1. *Univalves* (single-shelled), such as abalone and sea urchins;

2. *Bivalve* (two shells joined by a hinge), such as clams, mussels, oysters, and scallops;

3. *Crustaceans* (jointed exterior skeletons or shells), such as lobster, shrimp, and crayfish;

4. *Cephalopods*, such as squid and octopus. The name translates as "head-footed," and is a reflection of the fact that the tentacles and arms are attached directly to the head.

COMMONLY AVAILABLE FISH

Within these fairly broad categories are a wide range of flavors and textures. Some fish are naturally lean; others are more "oily"; some have extremely delicate and subtle flavors; others are robust and "meaty."

The best way to pair a fish with a cooking technique is to consider the flesh. For example, oily fish—bluefish and mackerel, for example—are often prepared by dry-heat techniques such as grilling or broiling. Fish with moderate amounts of fat (tuna, salmon,

trout) work well with any technique. Very lean fish, such as sole or flounder, are most successfully prepared by poaching or sautéing.

Knowing how to work with fish and shellfish is a skill that takes time and experience to truly master. There are some classic preparations, however, that combine certain fish with specific techniques. This information will be included in the list that follows. Obviously, it is only a starting point.

Round Fish

Anchovy

The most common form for the anchovy is the canned fillet packed in oil, with or without a caper. In addition, they are sold as anchovy paste or smoked fillets and may also be available fresh. The salted and oil-packed fillet is a classic component in Caesar salad.

Black Sea Bass

This fish feeds primarily on shrimp, crabs, and molluscs. It has firm, well-flavored flesh that can be prepared by all cooking techniques. Considered to hold a close resemblance to a Mediterranean fish called the sea bream, black sea bass generally weigh from 1½ to 3 pounds but may be larger in the fall. Other bass—striped bass, seabass, pike, and red snapper, for example, are not necessarily related by family—but share culinary similarities.

Figure 7-5 shows a black sea bass, as well as striped bass, pike, and red snapper.

Bluefish

A fish with a relatively strong flavor and oily flesh; it should be drawn as soon as possible after it is caught and should be very fresh. Young bluefish, known as "snappers," generally have an excellent flavor, as they feed on molluscs and shrimp. The flesh has a loose, flaky texture and is excellent broiled or grilled. The strip of dark-colored flesh in the fillet has a more pronounced flavor and tends to hold any pollutants or contaminants.

Brown Trout

This fish, which has a firm flesh with a white to deep-pink color, is very similar to salmon in terms of culinary applications.

Catfish

Catfish are farmed and marketed under carefully controlled conditions. Catfish should be skinned before cooking and are commonly sold as skinless fillets. The flesh is delicately flavored, lean, and very firm, almost rubbery in texture. This fish can be prepared by any cooking technique; a traditional preparation is dipped in cornmeal and panfried.

Cod

Cod has a lean, white flesh. The cod family has a number of distinct species, each with different identifying marks. Cod may be poached, used in chowder, or steamed, and is also available salted (known as *baccala*). Finnan haddie is split, smoked haddock, a species of cod. Atlantic cod, turbot, haddock, cusk, whiting, hake, and pollock are all members of the cod family. Figure 7-6 shows two species of cod.

Dolphin Fish (Mahi Mahi)

This fish, harvested from the Pacific Ocean, has firm flesh with a sweet, delicate flavor. It can be prepared by all cooking techniques and is excellent in ceviche. The skin should be removed before cooking.

7-5

Black sea bass, striped bass, pike, and red snapper *(top to bottom)*.

7-6

Haddock *(top)* **and cod** *(bottom)*.

Eel

Eel has a rich, oily flesh. Eels spawn in the Sargasso Sea, which is part of the North Atlantic, and then begin the journey back to either Europe or America. They are available live, whole, skinned, in fillets, smoked, and jellied. One of the most famous eel dishes is a French stew known as *matelote*. Figure 7-7 shows an eel.

Groupers

There are several kinds of grouper, all members of the sea bass family. One of the most commonly available is red grouper. Grouper has lean, firm, white flesh that is best when sautéed, panfried, steamed, or shallow-poached. The skin should be removed before cooking.

Haddock (see Cod)

Mackerel

This is an oily, soft-textured fish, once regularly sold salted. Spanish and king mackerel both are considered fish of eating quality, but the Spanish mackerel is conceded to be the best. The flesh flakes easily when cooked. Mackerel may be prepared by all cooking techniques but are commonly broiled. Figure 7-8 shows Spanish and Boston mackerel.

Perch

Perch has a lean and delicate flesh. The best perch are harvested from the fresh waters of lakes and reservoirs. Small perch may be deep-fried and served whole; large fish are cut into fillets and then either panfried, steamed, or shallow-poached.

Pompano

Considered by some as one of the finest-eating saltwater fish, pompano is becoming increasingly expensive. Pompano has firm, well-flavored flesh and is often broiled or prepared *en papillote*. Most pompano comes from the Gulf of Mexico.

Salmon

This firm, moderately oily fish has a distinctively colored flesh, ranging from light pink to a deep orange-pink. A number of different species, including cohoe,

king, and Atlantic, are available. The Atlantic species is commonly farm-raised. Salmon may be prepared using any technique and among the more popular presentations are poached, baked in pastry *(coulibiac)*, and grilled. Salmon is available fresh, smoked, or cured as "gravad lox." Salmon shares flavors, textures, and culinary treatments with trout. Figure 7-9 shows both Atlantic and cohoe salmon, as well as a rainbow trout.

7-7
Eel.

7-8
Spanish *(top)* and Boston mackerel *(bottom).*

7-9

Rainbow trout *(top)*, Atlantic salmon *(center)*, and cohoe or silver salmon *(bottom)*.

Shad

Shad usually enter the rivers of the Atlantic coast from the Gulf of St. Lawrence to northern Florida from December to May. The flesh of both sexes, which is sweet and white but extremely bony, and the roe of the female are highly regarded. A traditional preparation method for shad and shad roe is to sauté or pan-fry them with bacon. The American Indians used to smoke-roast the fish, a technique referred to as "planking."

Snappers

There are a number of different snappers. One of the most popular is red snapper, which has become greatly reduced in overall supply. True red snapper comes from the Gulf of Mexico and adjacent Atlantic waters. Among other desirable snapper species are silk, mutton, mangrove, gray, beeliner, pink, and yellowtail. The flesh is firm, moist, and finely textured. Almost any preparation technique can be used; snapper is often prepared *en papillote* or baked.

Striped Bass

The flesh of striped bass is sweet and relatively firm. Some freshwater species are landlocked in the United States, but those fished from clean saltwater tend to have the best texture and flavor. Unfortunately, because striped bass can tolerate polluted waters, its sale has been severely restricted. A hybrid striped bass is farm-raised and has a darker and oilier flesh than saltwater striped bass.

Swordfish

Swordfish has an extremely firm texture with a unique flavor. Commonly cut into steaks and grilled, swordfish has a lot of characteristics similar to shark, a nonbony fish that is usually less expensive. Swordfish's darker strip of flesh has an umbrella-shaped pattern, which is one way to distinguish it from shark, which has a round pattern. The distinction between swordfish and mako shark steaks is clearly illustrated in Figure 7-10, which also includes tuna. Tuna has the same kind of meaty flavor and firm texture as swordfish and shark.

Tilefish/Golden Bass

This fish has a texture and flavor that has been compared to lobster, an apt reflection of the fish's crustacean diet. Tilefish can be cooked by any technique and is occasionally smoked.

7-10

Mako shark steak *(top left)* has a round pattern of dark flesh; swordfish *(top right)* has an umbrella-shaped pattern. A piece of tuna is also shown *(bottom)*.

Trout

Along with catfish, salmon, oysters, mussels, and clams, trout are farm-raised in large quantities. In fact, with the exception of some special trout species, such as the steelhead, all trout sold in restaurants come from commercial hatcheries. Rainbow trout and brown trout are among the most commonly available species. They are excellent when pan-fried in a manner similar to catfish, roasted, or poached. *Truite au bleu* is a famous trout preparation: freshly killed trout is poached in a vinegar court bouillon until the blue color is barely set. Smoked trout is also readily available. (See Fig. 7-9, above, for an example of a rainbow trout.)

Tuna

Tuna's flesh is similar to that of swordfish in texture, but it separates more readily. Its flavor is unique, and the flesh's color ranges from a deep pinkish-beige to a dark maroon. A member of the mackerel family, tuna has the distinctive strip of darker colored flesh along its back. Tuna is often roasted or cut into steaks and grilled. Also popular is canned tuna—albacore or light meat, packed in either oil or water. Canned tuna is essential for *tonnato* sauce and salade Niçoise. (Fig. 7-10, above, shows a piece of tuna fillet.)

Wall-eyed Pike

Most famous for its use in *quenelles de brochet*, pike has sweet, white, firmly textured flesh that is relatively lean but stands up well to dry-heat techniques. It is also commonly poached or used to prepare mousses or terrines. It should not be confused with pickerel, a fish of virtually no culinary importance.

Flat Fish

Flounder

Flounder is often sold in the United States under the market name of "sole": lemon sole, gray sole, white sole are all forms of flounder, a flat, disk-shaped fish with both eyes on the same side of its head. Plaice, another flounder species, is often sold as dab (sand dab, roughback). Flounder is generally quite delicate, with a tendency to flake readily. It is particularly suited to shallow poaching and steaming and is also commonly cut into "fingers" and deep-fried. Readily available whole, flounder is also sold cut into quarter fillets and skinned. Figure 7-1 shows a variety of flat fish—a flounder, a halibut, and a Dover sole—which all have a lean, delicate flesh.

Halibut

Halibut has firm, white meat with a delicate flavor. The halibut can grow to be quite large and may be cut into steaks or fillets. A halibut of 10 to 40 pounds is considered small; they can grow to be over 200 pounds. (See Fig. 7-11, above.)

Sole

One of the only true soles is the Dover sole, a flat fish with a compact, oval shape and firmly textured, delicately flavored flesh. Dover sole is so highly esteemed that hundreds of different dishes have been devised to feature it. Dover sole is available fresh or frozen. Note that although many species of flounder have been dubbed "sole," they should not be confused with Dover sole. (See Fig. 7-11, above.)

Turbot

A diamond-shaped fish esteemed for its snowy white, moist, finely textured flesh, turbot also may grow large enough to cut into steaks or fillets. It is generally steamed or poached to highlight its delicacy and whiteness.

7-11

Flounder *(top)*, halibut *(center)*, and Dover sole *(bottom)*.

Nonbony Fish

Monkfish

This fish has been known by a number of names, including angler fish, goosefish, lawyer fish, and belly fish. The French name is *lotte*. It is available as the fillet from the tail. Monkfish has a firm, dense texture and sweet taste. Suitable for any cooking technique, it is commonly used in fish stews such as cioppino and bouillabaisse. A piece of monkfish tail (the most commonly available form) is shown in Figure 7-12.

Shark

Mako and blue shark are commonly available, and other types of shark, including yellowtip and black-fin, are becoming important in the marketplace. Shark may sometimes be sold to the unwary as sword-fish. Be sure to check the pattern of the strip of dark-colored flesh and only pay for what was ordered; shark is generally less expensive than swordfish. The flesh of shark is sweet and relatively firm and moist, but the skin is extremely tough. Shark is commonly made into steaks and grilled, broiled, or sautéed. (For an example of how a shark steak should look, refer to Fig. 7-10.)

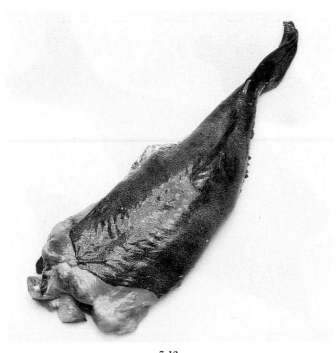

7-12
Monkfish.

Skate/Ray

The flesh of the skate or ray is sweet and firm and has been compared to scallops. It is sold as wings, which should be skinned prior to sautéing, although they may be poached with the skin on. Skate wings are easier to skin after poaching. One famous presentation method is to sauté the skate and serve it with *buerre noir*.

Univalves

Abalone

The abalone has one shell and a suction cup that attaches firmly to rocks; it must be pried loose. Available from California, state law prohibits the exportation of live abalone, so most of the country must rely on frozen or canned abalone. The meat, which is cut into steaks and pounded before sautéing or grilling, becomes extremely tough if overcooked.

Conch

True conch comes from the Caribbean and is more accurately classified as a gastropod—a large class of mollusc. Conch is sold out of the shell and may be sold ground. It is used in salads, ceviche, chowders, and fritters. Further north, the whelk, which is much smaller and grayish in color, is sold as conch.

Bivalves

Clams

Clams are available in the shell, shucked (and possibly frozen), and canned. Clams sold as "live" should definitely be checked for tightly closed shells, to make sure they are alive. They should have a sweet smell. Clams, like oysters, may be marketed by the name of the bed from which they were taken and local preferences for species will vary. The following terms are commonly applied to clams:

• Bean clam or "coquina." This clam is used for broths or soups.
• Hardshell clam or quahog. There are two kinds of hardshell clams. Little Neck (not to be confused with littleneck) are small hardshell clams often eaten raw on the half shell. Cherrystones are the next largest size and are also commonly eaten raw. If hardshell clams are more than 3 inches in diameter, they are generally referred to as quahogs and are used for chowder or fritters.

• Littleneck. These clams, also known as manilla clams, are found on the Pacific coast and are generally steamed.

• Soft-shell clams. Generally steamed and used in fritters, these clams are also the traditional clam for use in New England clam chowder.

Some commonly available clams are illustrated in Figure 7-13.

Mussels

Most commercially available mussels are farm-raised and are sold live in the shell. Mussels are commonly prepared *à la marinière* (steamed with wine, garlic, and lemon) or as the major component of Billi-bi soup (a velouté soup garnished with mussels), although there are a great many other presentations. See Figure 7-14.

Oysters

Oysters are sold live in the shell or shucked. As with clams, they are generally marketed by the name of the beds from which they were harvested, and local preference will vary greatly. Some of the most famous

presentations include raw on the half shell, oyster stew, oyster omelets, and oysters Rockefeller, a dish that includes spinach and Pernod. A grouping of oysters is shown in Figure 7-15.

7-14
Mussels.

7-13
Clams: Topneck *(upper left)*, littleneck *(upper right)*, chowder clam *(lower left)*, and cherrystone *(lower right)*.

7-15
Oysters: two Atlantic varieties *(upper left corner)*; two Pacific oysters (Olympia) *(upper right corner)*; two Belon oysters (French) *(foreground)*.

Scallops

Three species of scallop are of commercial importance: bay scallops, sea scallops, and calico scallops. Sea scallops can become quite large (2 to 3 inches in diameter); bay and calico scallops are smaller. Bay scallops are generally considered superior in quality to calicos. Most scallops are sold shucked. See Figure 7-16 for an illustration of scallops. Occasionally, shucked scallops with the roe attached may be found; less frequently, they are sold still in the shells. Coquilles St. Jacques is customarily thought of as a cream-based scallop gratin; it is also the name for scallop in French, and refers to the fact that St. James wore the shell of the scallop as his personal emblem.

Crustaceans

A grouping of crustaceans appears in Figure 7-17.

Crab

Common kinds of crab include blue, Dungeness, king, and spider. Blue crab, which is found on the Atlantic Coast, especially around the Chesapeake Bay, is sold live, or as pasteurized or canned meat. In the spring through late summer, when the crab molts, blue crab are sold as "soft-shelled crabs," which are

7-17

Crustaceans, including sea- and fresh-water varieties: cooked Dungeness crab, a Pacific variety *(upper left corner)*; American lobster *(upper right corner)*; blue crab (Atlantic variety) *(second row from top, left side)*; shrimp *(third from top, left side)*; prawn *(bottom left corner)*; and crayfish *(lower right corner)*.

commonly panfried or sautéed. Hard-shelled crab may be boiled or steamed. The meat may be removed and used in a variety of preparations, including one of the most famous, crab cakes. She-crab soup is made from the roe and meat of female crabs, identifiable by their broad "aprons" and the red tips on their claws.

Dungeness crab is common on the Pacific Coast. King crab and spider crab are valued mainly for their legs, although the whole crab can be used. Only one claw per stone crab can be harvested, however, in order to help save the species. Fishermen simply twist off the claws (which grow back) and return the crab to the sea. Legs and claws are cooked and frozen on the ship in most cases and the claw may be cracked (especially in the case of stone crab).

Crayfish

Freshwater crayfish is widely available year-round because it can be farmed. Crayfish may be purchased live or precooked and frozen (whole, or tail meat only). Crayfish are used extensively in Creole and Cajun

7-16

Scallops in the shell *(top row)*; bay scallops with roe *(middle row)*; shucked sea scallops *(bottom row)*.

cooking and are also a classic garnish. Etouffé and jambalaya are two of the most popular crayfish dishes.

Lobster

American lobster is generally the most prized; it is available live or cooked and canned. The meat is firm and succulent and virtually the entire lobster is edible. The female contains the roe, considered a delicacy; both sexes possess the tomalley, another prized part. To determine the sex of the lobster, feel the appendages where the tail meets the body. In the female they will be soft and feathery, whereas in the male they are rigid. The female's tail or abdomen is generally broader.

Other types of lobster include the rock lobster (often sold as frozen tails, rock lobster is the market name for spiny lobster), Dublin prawn, and lobsterette.

Shrimp

Shrimp is probably one of the most popular crustaceans. Shrimp are most commonly available frozen, as fishermen generally remove the heads and flash-freeze the shrimp on the boat in order to preserve flavor and quality. Fresh shrimp are highly perishable, but they may be available in some regions of the United States, notably the Gulf of Mexico and Chesapeake Bay regions, and there are both saltwater and freshwater species. The flesh has a sweet flavor and a firm, almost crisp texture.

Shrimp are sold according to the number in a pound, known as the "count." The count ranges include three per pound; 10 to 15; 21 to 25; 26 to 30; 31 to 35; and on up to over 100 per pound.

Some common presentations include cold "cocktails," deep-fried (tempura), baked, sautéed, and grilled.

Cephalopods

Octopus

Octopus is firmly textured with a sweet "marine" flavor. It is generally sold fresh, and cleaned of its ink and beak, but may also come frozen. Octopus may be prepared in a number of dishes, including ceviche, chowders, and salads.

Squid

Squid is one of the most widely available forms of seafood. It has always been an established part of Mediterranean and Oriental cuisines and is continuing to gain popularity in the United States. Squid are available in a range of sizes; small squid are frequently stuffed and cooked whole in a sauce, whereas large squid are cut into rings, fried, and served with a spicy sauce. There are many different presentations, however, because squid are suited to most cooking techniques.

Miscellaneous Items

Caviar

Real caviar is the salted roe from the sturgeon. It is available fresh (must be carefully refrigerated) or pasteurized and canned. For additional information, see Chapter 27, "Hors d'Oeuvre, Appetizers, and Salads."

Frogs' Legs

These are the hind legs of frogs that are usually farm-raised. Frogs' legs are sold in pairs. One classic dish is frogs' legs sautéed *à la provençale*.

SUMMARY

In response to an ever-increasing consumer demand, more fish are available commercially (many of them farm-raised) than ever before. The chef should purchase the freshest, most flavorful fish available and prepare them in a manner which highlights the particular taste of the fish.

This chapter has provided information to help the chef select and store fish properly. Chapter 13, "Fish and Shellfish Fabrication," will demonstrate the many ways in which fish can be cut. Once fish is properly fabricated, it must then be paired with an appropriate cooking technique, sauce, and accompaniment to create a dish that appeals on all levels—appearance, texture, and taste.

Although some species of fish are becoming more and more scarce, the sea still is able to provide a large supply, as long as the chef is willing to give a previously unfamiliar variety a try.

Chapter 8

Fruit, Vegetable, and Fresh Herb Identification

Fruits, vegetables, and herbs have always been an important part of the human diet, although at one time the European artistocracy spurned vegetables as peasant food, preferring to demonstrate their "superiority" with an ostentatious consumption of rarer and more costly meats.

The Roman Catholic tradition of fasting caused even wealthy people to seek alternatives to meat. Today, vegetables, fruits, and fresh herbs play an important role in meeting the requirements of consumers interested in maintaining overall health and fitness.

In order to help chefs and restaurateurs take advantage of the abundance of fresh produce now available, this chapter offers information about the most commonly used fruits, vegetables, and herbs. Included is information on identification, availability, determination of quality, proper storage, and, where possible, grading of fruits, vegetables, and herbs.

GENERAL GUIDELINES

Selection

As with selection of almost any food, certain guidelines apply to fresh fruits, vegetables, and herbs. They should, obviously, look fresh. What constitutes a fresh appearance varies, however, from one item to another. In general, fruits and vegetables should be free of bruises, mold, brown or soft spots, and pest damage; they should have colors and textures appropriate to their type; and any attached leaves should be unwilted. Fruits should be plump, not shriveled.

Specific information on choosing high-quality produce is given in the individual tables that cover commonly used fruits, vegetables, and herbs. These tables appear in the appropriate sections of this chapter.

Grading

Since it is usually not possible to examine produce until it has been delivered to the restaurant, one way to help ensure quality is to buy according to grade. The grading information in the tables is based on U.S. Department of Agriculture standards. Grades are listed in descending order of quality. (A is the highest grade, in other words.) Lower-grade items, particularly fruits, may be used successfully in preparations such as baked pies and puddings, where appearance is not a factor.

Some items are graded according to state standards, so the chef should try to obtain local grading information from state agricultural departments. When the quality of fresh produce cannot be guaranteed, one possible solution is to buy frozen fruits and vegetables. Most vegetables and some fruits are available frozen, and these are preferable to poor-quality fresh produce. Peas, corn, spinach, and most berries, for example, freeze well.

Seasonality/Availability

Traditionally, chefs have selected fruits and vegetables when they are "in season," because they are at their best then. However, the chef is no longer limited to the "seasons" and availability of only locally grown produce, because improved shipping methods have extended fruits' and vegetables' seasons. Some items ship particularly well, especially those that do not have to ripen completely on the vine. Examples are asparagus, head lettuces, broccoli, some melons, apples, and citrus fruits.

Most produce will still have noticeably better quality and flavor the closer the purchaser is to the source. Items such as sweet corn, apricots, peaches, and strawberries that have been shipped are definitely inferior to locally grown counterparts, despite continued efforts to develop strains that combine good shipping qualities with superior flavor.

Another advantage to using local growers is that so-called "boutique" farmers may have specialty produce (wild lettuces, golden beets, yellow tomatoes, for example) that are not available through large commercial purveyors.

More and more vegetables can be grown hydroponically, that is, in nutrient-enriched water rather than soil. Hydroponic growing takes place indoors under regulated temperature and light, so any growing season may be duplicated. Hydroponically grown lettuces, spinach, herbs, and tomatoes are all readily available. Although they have the advantage of being easy to clean, these products may have a less pronounced flavor than conventionally grown fruits and vegetables.

A good number of restaurants try to grow as many fresh herbs as possible on the premises, and some large operations may devote space to more extensive gardening to ensure absolute freshness.

Storage

Once the produce has been obtained, following certain storage guidelines can assure and even extend its life. If proper purchasing practices are observed, most foodservice establishments will not store produce more than three or four days. The length of storage time depends on the business's volume, the kind of available storage facilities, and delivery frequency. The ideal is to let the purveyor handle the produce as long as possible.

With a few exceptions (bananas, potatoes, dry onions), ripe fruits and vegetables should be refrigerated. Unless otherwise specified, produce should be kept at a temperature of 40 to 45°F (4 to 7°C), with a relative humidity of 80 to 90 percent. The ideal situation is to have a separate walk-in or reach-in refrigerator for fruits and vegetables.

Most fruits and vegetables should be kept dry, because excess moisture can promote spoilage. Produce should therefore not be peeled, washed, or trimmed until just before it is used. The outer leaves of lettuce, for example, should be left intact; carrots should remain unpeeled. Leafy tops on green vegetables like beets, turnips, carrots, and radishes should be removed and either discarded or used immediately; even after harvesting, the leaves absorb nutrients from the root and increase moisture loss.

Fruits and vegetables that need further ripening, notably peaches and avocados, should be stored at room temperature, 65 to 70°F (18 to 21°C). Once produce is ripe, it should be refrigerated so it does not become overripe.

Certain fruits (including apples, bananas, and melons) and avocados emit ethylene gas as they sit in storage. Ethylene gas can accelerate ripening in some unripe fruits, but can also promote spoilage in fruits and vegetables that are already ripe. For this reason, unless being used deliberately as a ripening agent, ethylene-producing fruits should be stored separately. A general practice that prevents this kind of spoilage is to store fruits in one refrigerator and vegetables in another whenever possible. When separate storage space is unavailable, store ethylene-producing fruits in sealed containers.

Some fruits and vegetables, including onions, garlic, lemons, and melons, give off odors that can permeate other foods. Dairy products are particularly susceptible to odor absorption and should always be stored away from fruits and vegetables. Certain fruits, such as apples and cherries, also absorb odors. They too should be well-wrapped or stored separately.

Many vegetables begin to lose quality after three or four days. Although citrus fruits, most root vegetables, and hard squashes have a longer storage life, most restaurants do not hold even these items for more than two to three weeks.

FRUITS

In general fruits are designated under that name because they are sweet and because they are customarily used in sweet dishes, such as puddings, pies, and jellies. They also may be used to flavor essentially savory dishes, in both classic and contemporary preparations. Sole Veronique (sole with green grapes), for example, is a classic French fish preparation.

Historically, fruits were used with meat and fish to mask undesirable flavors; today, fruits are often used to cut the richness of some meats—especially pork and duck—or to brighten the delicate flavors of veal or fish.

Fruits have often been served as a natural companion to cheese and as a dessert, either fresh or poached. They are available fresh, frozen, and, in some cases, dried.

The discussion of fruits is organized according to common characteristics—purchasing factors, texture, and structure—rather than by strict botanical guidelines. Peaches, plums, and cherries, for instance, belong to the same botanical group and have some similarities, but their handling and use in the kitchen justifies placing them in separate categories. An alphabetical listing appears in Table 8-1.

TABLE 8-1. FRUITS

Item (Types)	French and Italian Names	Grade and Peak Season	Purchasing Factors	Pack and Weight*
Apples (See Table 8-2 for types)	*Pomme; mela*	U.S. Extra Fancy, No. 1, No. 2 Year-round	Firm, good color; no soft spots, bruises, or brown spots; no mealy, brown-fleshed fruits; well-shaped.	Carton 38–42# (variable count loose or tray-packed fruit) Carton 34–43# (variable count cell-packed fruit)
Apricots	*Abricot; albicocca*	U.S. No. 1, No. 2 June–July	Plump, firm but not hard, uniform size and golden-yellow color, juicy, ripe.	Lug (4 per row) 24–28# Flat (5–9 per row) 12#
Bananas	*Banane; banana*	U.S. No. 1, No. 2 Mar.–June	Plump, yellow, green tips; little or no brown on skin; ripen in house.	Box 40# (115 avg. count for No. 1 grade)
Berries Blackberry Blueberry Cranberry Raspberry Strawberry	 *Mure; mora* *Myrtille; mirtillo* *Canneberge/airelle rouge; mirtillo rosso* *Framboise; lampone* *Fraise; fragola*	U.S. No. 1 (Strawberries only No. 1, Combination, No. 2) May–Aug. (exact season varies by type)	Bright, clean, fresh appearance; solid and plump; full, ripe color; clean; no caps or stems (except strawberry, gooseberry, and currant); no mold or wetness.	Basket ½ pint, pint, or quart (usually trays of 12 pints) about 10#

* Count, where applicable.

(continued)

TABLE 8-1. FRUITS (*continued*)

Item (Types)	French and Italian Names	Grade and Peak Season	Purchasing Factors	Pack and Weight*
Cherries	*Cerise; ciliegia*	U.S. No. 1, Commercial May–Aug.	Bright, fresh, plump, good color for type, firm but not hard, juicy, dry, no mold.	Lugs 20# Calif. Lugs 18# Flat 12#
Dates	*Datte; dattero*	No Federal Grades Year-round	Fresh: Plump, shiny, not sticky. Dried: Plump, wrinkled, sticky.	Bulk (pitted, hydrated) 15# Chopped 30# Macerated 40#
Figs	*Figue; fico*	U.S. No. 1 June–Oct.	Fully ripe, fairly soft; no bruises, fermentation odor; skins not hard or wet.	Flat 5#
Grapefruit	*Pamplemousse; pompelmo*	U.S. Fancy, No. 1, Combination, No. 2, No. 3 Nov.–May	Firm but slightly springy; plump, well-shaped; heavy for size; skin smooth and thin, minor skin blemishes will not affect quality.	Texas: 7/10 bushel 38–42# 1⅗ bushel 76–84# Florida: ⅕ bushel 40–50# Calif. & Ariz.: Carton 38–42#
Grapes	*Raisin; uva/acino*	U.S. Fancy, Extra No. 1, No. 1 Year-round	Plump; mature; fresh-looking; good color for type; berries attached to stems; no dry, brittle stems; sweet.	Lug/carton 12, 17, or 23#
Kiwi	N/A	U.S. Fancy, No. 1, No. 2 Year-round	Fuzzy, brown skin; firm but not hard.	Carton/flat 7 or 20# average
Lemons	*Citron; limone*	U.S. #1, Combination, No. 2 Year-round	Fine-textured skin; firm fruit; heavy for size; good, uniform color.	Carton 37–40# (variable counts 63–235, 115 used most often)
Limes	*Limon; limetta*	U.S. #1, Combination Year-round	Heavy for size, plump, smooth skin, uniform deep-green or yellow-green color.	Carton 10, 20, or 38# (variable counts 72–28, 48, 54, and 63 used most often)
Mangos	*Mango; mango*	No Federal Grades May–Aug.	Red, green, yellow, orange, or combination of colors; firm to fairly soft; bumpy, slightly rough skin.	Flat 10 or 12# (variable count 8–30)
Melons	*Melon; melone*	U.S. No. 1, Commercial, No. 2 Apr.–Dec./Jan.	Heavy for size; fragrant (winter melons and watermelons are less aromatic); firm but not hard, plump; smooth and slightly sunken stem end; no sloshing when shaken.	May be purchased by crate or count
Cantaloupe	*Cantaloup; cantaloupe*		Full slip, well-developed netting, light gold to light gray-green background color.	½ crate 38–41# (23 count) crate 75–85# (46 count)
Casaba	N/A		Soft creamy white, sweet and juicy flesh; yellowish rind with soft blossom end.	6–8 count 25–30#
Crenshaw or Spanish	N/A		Yellowing rind with softening at blossom end.	6–8 count 25–30#

* Count, where applicable.

TABLE 8-1. FRUITS

Item (Types)	French and Italian Names	Grade and Peak Season	Purchasing Factors	Pack and Weight*
Honeydew	N/A		Light-yellow rind that yields slightly to pressure; green flesh	6–8 count 25–30#
Santa Claus	N/A		Slight yellowing of rind with softening at blossom end; yellow-green flesh	4–5 count 25–30#
Persian	N/A		Distinct netting; bleached gray rind; slightly soft, full slip.	4–5 count 25–30#
Watermelon	*Melon d'eau; cocomero*		Large, heavy, firm, symmetrical, green or green-and-yellow-flecked skin; yellow or white area on bottom acceptable.	Each 28–32# Carton 78–80# (3–5 count)
Nectarines	*Brugnon; pescanoce*	U.S. Extra No. 1, No. 1 June–Aug.	Plump, firm but not hard; creamy yellow to yellow-orange skin with red blush; fragrant.	Lug 19–23# Lug/carton 25 or 35# (variable count 50–84)
Oranges	*Orange; arancia*	U.S. Fancy, Choice, No. 1, Combination, No. 2, No. 3 Year-round	Firm, heavy for size; fine-textured skin well-colored (surface green or minor blemishes do not affect quality); thick skins for navel oranges, thin skins for juice oranges.	Calif. & Ariz.: Carton 37–45# (variable count 48–163) Florida: ⅘ bushel carton 37–45# (variable count 32–56) Texas: ⁷⁄₁₀ bushel carton 38–44# (variable count 56–144) 1⅖ bushel carton 82–87#
Papayas	*Papaya; N/A*	U.S. No. 1, No. 2 Year-round	Yellow to deep orange flesh; smooth, thin skin from green to yellow or orange when ripe; somewhat soft.	Carton/flat 10# (8–14 count)
Peaches	*Peche; pesca*	U.S. Extra No. 1, No. 1 Apr.–Oct.	Plump; firm but not hard; creamy yellow to yellow-orange skin with red blush; fragrant.	Lug/carton 19–23# (variable count 50–80) Box 17–18# (variable count 40–65)
Pears	*Poire; pera*	U.S. Extra Fancy No. 1, Fancy No. 2 Year-round	Firm but not hard; clean; no blemishes (russeting acceptable on most varieties).	Box/carton 44–46# (variable count 70–165) Tight-fill carton 36# (variable count 70–165)
Persimmons	*Kaki; cachi*	No Federal Grading Oct.–Dec.	Well-shaped; plump; smooth; soft; good color; stem and cap attaches; yellow to dark-red color; slight wrinkling of skin indicates ripeness.	Flat 11–13#
Pineapples	*Ananas; ananas*	U.S. Fancy, No. 1, No. 2 Year-round	Crowns with flat, dry bottom; some yellow skin; fragrant; heavy for size.	Hawaiian: ½ carton 20# (variable count 4–7) Carton 40# (variable count 8–18) Puerto Rican: Carton 40# (variable count 14–16)

* Count, where applicable.

(continued)

103

TABLE 8-1. FRUITS *(continued)*

Item (Types)	French and Italian Names	Grade and Peak Season	Purchasing Factors	Pack and Weight*
Plums	*Pruneau; susina/prugna*	U.S. No. 1 May–Sept.	Plump; firm to slightly soft; good color for type; no cuts, bruises, sunburn, or stickiness.	Lug/carton 28#
Pomegranates	*Grenade; melagrana*	No Grade Sept.–Nov.	Firm; heavy for size; plump; tough but thin skin (showing outline of seeds); pink to bright red.	Lug 26–28#
Rhubarb	*Rhubarbe; rabarbaro*	U.S. No. 1	Fresh, firm, crisp, tender, pink to red, thick stalks; hothouse type should be almost stringless and have trimmed top and mild flavor.	Bulk (by #) Box 5# (Also frozen in various-size bags and boxes)
Tangerine/ mandarin	*Mandarine; mandarino*	U.S. Fancy, No. 1, No. 2, No. 3 Oct.–May	Heavy for size; loose skin causing slightly puffy appearance; no wet spots or mold.	Florida: Bushel carton 45# (variable count 80–210) California: ½ bushel carton 27–32# (variable count 72–165)

Apples and Pears

Apples and pears grow in similar ways, have similar structures, and are the most commonly used and available fruits. Apples and pears have seeds arranged in a pod, located in the center of the thickest portion of the fruit. Both grow on trees, rather than bushes or vines. They are harvested when still slightly immature and allowed to mature off the tree. Apples and pears are divided into two groups: summer fruits, which last only a short season, and winter fruits, which store well for longer periods of time. Although in most cases their flesh is different—the crispness of apples contrasted with the juicy smoothness of pears

TABLE 8-2. SELECTED APPLE VARIETIES

Variety	Color	Flavor and Texture	Peak Season	Uses
Delicious, Golden	Golden-yellow with blush	Sweet, semi-firm	September to May	All-purpose
Delicious, Red	Deep red	Sweet, fairly firm	September to June	Fresh, pie, sauce, freeze
Granny Smith	Green	Crisp, tart	April to July	All-purpose
Greening, Rhode Island, and North West	Green	Firm, mild, tart-sweet	October to March	Pie, sauce, bake, freeze
Jonathan	Bright red, with some yellow-green	Tender, tart, flavorful	September to January	Fresh, pie, sauce, freeze
McIntosh	Red with some yellow-green	Tender, semi-tart	September to June	Fresh, pie, sauce, bake, freeze
Rome Beauty	Bright red	Firm, mild, tart-sweet	October to June	All-purpose
Winesap	Bright red with some yellow-green	Firm, tart-sweet, flavorful	October to June	Fresh, freeze, pie, sauce, bake

—both can be considered "quintessential" fruits. There are hundreds of varieties of apples, with the most commercially available being Red and Golden Delicious, Rome, McIntosh, and Granny Smith. Table 8-2 indicates which varieties are best for eating out of hand, cooking, and baking.

Pears are to the French what apples are to the Americans. They also come in many varieties, although in fewer than apples. The most commonly available are Bartlett, Bosc, d'Anjou, and Seckel. The flesh of pears is extremely fragile. Because they are usually picked for shipping before they have ripened, it is difficult to find perfectly ripe pears in the market. They will become softer after picking but will not actually ripen. For this reason, pears are often poached whole or used in a sorbet to compensate for their underdeveloped flavor. A few apple and pear varieties are shown below.

Red Delicious apple　　　*Golden Delicious apple*

Williams pear　　　*Conference pear*

Berries

Most berries, especially strawberries, raspberries, and blueberries, are very fragile and must be inspected carefully when purchased. Juice soaking through the carton bottom means that the berries on the bottom have been squashed and may be moldy. Berries range in texture and flavor from the dryness and sourness of cranberries to the softness and sweetness of raspberries. Such special kinds as currants, gooseberries, elderberries, boysenberries, and cloudberries may be available occasionally. For additional information on particular varieties, refer to Table 8-3. Three kinds of berries are illustrated below.

Strawberries　　　*Blueberries*　　　*Raspberries*

TABLE 8-3. BERRIES

Name	Description	Name	Description
Blueberry	Round; dark bluish-purple with a dusty, silver-blue "bloom"; rough area at blossom end; whitish flesh; minute, edible seeds.	Gooseberry	Smooth, semi-translucent; usually green but may be golden, red, purple, or white. Red and purple varieties tend to be sweeter. Some varieties are fuzzy-skinned.
Boysenberry	Hybridized from various types of raspberry. Looks and tastes like raspberry, but twice the size.	Mulberry	Resembles but is unrelated to the raspberry and has smaller seeds; juicy and sweet with a slightly musty flavor.
Cloudberry	Orange-red, cold-weather raspberry; grown in Scandinavia and other cool climates.	Raspberry	Conical clusters of tiny fruits (drupes), each enclosing its own hard but edible seed. Three varieties: black, red, and white; tart-sweet and juicy. One variety, the dewberry, is matte. Red: bright, semi-translucent red; shiny or matte; often slightly fuzzy.
Cranberry	Oval; shiny, red skin; white to rosy flesh; fairly dry and sour.		
Currant	Small, shiny berry; red, black, or white. Red: bright, semi-translucent crimson; generally the sweetest. Black: very dark purple. All varieties high in pectin.		
Elderberry	Small purple-black berry that resembles the black currant.	Strawberry	Succulent, red berry; seeds on surface of skin. Various sizes and types available.

Cherries

Cherries are grown in numerous varieties and come in many shades of red, from the light crimson of Queen Anne to the almost black Bing. They vary in texture from hard and crisp to soft and juicy, and flavors run the gamut from sweet to sour. Two kinds of cherries are shown below.

Royal Anne cherries

Early Rivers cherries

Citrus Fruits

Citrus fruits are characterized by their thick skins, which contain aromatic oils, and their segmented flesh, which is extremely juicy. Grapefruits, lemons, limes, oranges, and tangerines are the most common citrus fruits. They range in flavor from the sweetness of oranges to the tartness of lemons. Three common citrus fruits are shown below.

Oranges come in three basic varieties: thin-skinned, thick-skinned, and bitter. Thin-skinned oranges have smooth skin that is somewhat difficult to peel. They are usually plump and sweet, which makes them ideal for juicing. Varieties include the small Va-

lencia and the blood orange (with orange skin and red pulp). Thick-skinned oranges include the navel, which is large, seedless, and easy to peel, and consequently makes the best eating orange. Bitter oranges like Seville and Bigarade are used almost exclusively for making marmalade. In fact, a hollandaise sauce variation flavored with the juice and rind of a bitter orange is called bigarade sauce.

Grapefruits have yellow skin with an occasional rosy blush where the sun hits them. They are juicy and tart-sweet and are available with either white (actually yellow) or pink flesh. Pink grapefruits are generally slightly sweeter than white varieties.

Orange

Grapefruit

Lime

Grapes

Grapes are juicy fruits, most with seeds, some without, that grow in clusters on vines. Technically, they are berries, but because they include so many varieties and have so many different uses, they are grouped separately. Of the many kinds available for both eating and wine-making, two of the most popular are Californian Seedless, which are appropriate for both cooking and eating out of hand, and Napoleon Red, a good table variety (see below).

Californian Seedless grapes

Napoleon Red grapes

Melons

Melons are fragrant, succulent fruits, most of which are related to squashes and cucumbers. They also come in many varieties and range from the size of an orange to that of a watermelon. The four major types are cantaloupes, watermelons, winter melons (honeydew, casaba, crenshaw), and muskmelons. Examples of the three former types appear below.

Honeydew

Cantaloupe

Watermelon

Peaches, Apricots, and Nectarines

Peaches are sweet and juicy, have a distinctively fuzzy skin, and come in many varieties. All peaches fall into one of two categories—clingstone or freestone. Clingstone peaches have flesh that clings to the pit, whereas the flesh of freestone peaches separates easily. Peach flesh comes in a range of color, from white to creamy yellow to yellow-orange to red, with a whole host of combinations possible.

Apricots resemble peaches in some ways. They have slightly fuzzy skin but are smaller, with somewhat drier flesh. They range in color from yellow to golden-orange and some have rosy patches.

Nectarines are similar in shape, color, and flavor to peaches, but they have smooth skin and their flesh may closely resemble the flesh of plums in texture. All three fruits are shown below.

Peach   *Apricot*   *Nectarine*

Plums

Plums can be anywhere in size from as small as an apricot to as large as a peach. The possible colors include green, red, purple, and various shades in between. When ripe, they are sweet and juicy, and some have sour skins that contrast nicely with their succulent flesh. Plums fall into two categories—dessert and cooking. Cooking plums are generally drier and more

acidic than dessert plums, but both types can be eaten raw. Greengage, a sweet plum with green skin and flesh, is a popular dessert variety. Damson, which has purple skin with a silver-blue bloom (faint blush on the skin), is probably the most well-known cooking plum. Three kinds of plums are shown below.

Santa Rosa plum   *Greengage plum*   *Damson plum*

Rhubarb

Although technically a vegetable, rhubarb has been classified here as a fruit because of the way it is used. Known as "pie plant," it grows in long stalks with broad, somewhat curly leaves. Only the reddish-green stalks are eaten. (The leaves should not be used because they contain large quantities of oxalic acid, a toxic compound.) Rhubarb is crisp and very sour, so it is usually cooked and sweetened. In addition to being served as a dessert, it is classically combined with rich, oily fish such as mackerel or bluefish. A stalk of rhubarb is illustrated below.

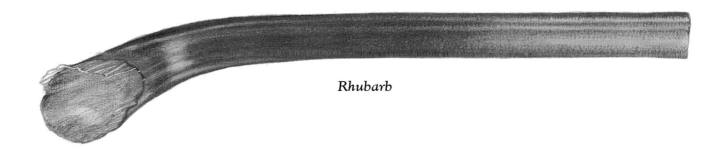

Rhubarb

Tropical Fruits

A wide variety of fruits fall into this category, which is named for the general climatic conditions under which the fruits are grown. Bananas are the most common. Unlike most fruits, they are almost always picked green and allowed to ripen en route from the plantation to the ultimate buyer. In this category are found dates, figs, kiwis, mangos, papayas, plantains, pomegranates, and passion fruit. Four of these are shown below.

Passion fruit

Mango

Papaya

Fig

TABLE 8-4. VEGETABLES *(continued)*

Item (Types)	French and Italian Names	Grade and Peak Season	Purchasing Factors	Pack and Weight*
Peas, Inedible Pod (Green, Garden, Petite Peas)	*Pois/petits pois; piselli*	U.S. No. 1, Fancy Apr.–July	Bright pods, green, somewhat velvety, young- and fresh-looking, crisp; grown locally.	Bushel 28–30# Carton/tub 30# Lug 10#
Pepper, Bell (Green, Red, Yellow, White, Purple)	*Poivron; peperone*	U.S. Fancy, No. 1, No. 2 June–Sept.	Mature; firm; thick flesh; good, uniform color, size, and shape; fresh, shiny appearance.	Bushel 26–30# Box 10#
Peppers, Chili (Anaheim, Ancho/ Poblano, Jalapeño, Serrano, Others)	*Piment rouge; N/A*	Year-round	Fresh: see peppers, bell. Dried: should be dark and may be wrinkled; they should show no moisture or other signs of rot.	½ crate 10# Bushel crate
Potatoes, Chef (White and Red)	*Pomme de terre; patata*	U.S. No. 1 Extra, No. 1 Size B, No. 2 Year-round	Firm; smooth; clean; shallow eyes; uniform size, shape, and color; green patches; no wet spots.	Carton 50# (counts in multiples of 10 from 60–120) Sack 50 or 100#
Potatoes, New (White and Red)	*Pommes nouvelle; patine novelle*	U.S. Fancy, U.S. No. 1 Year-round	See chef potatoes. Thin skin, may be ragged; small (under 1½ inches in diameter).	Carton 50# (120 or more count)
Potatoes, Russet	N/A	U.S. No. 1 Extra, No. 1 Size B, No. 2 Year-round	As for chef potatoes. Large; long; cylindrical or flattened; rough, netted skin; mealy flesh.	Carton 50# (90–100 count)
Potatoes, Sweet	*Pommes douce; patane*	U.S. Extra No. 1, No. 1, Commercial, No. 2 Year-round	Smooth, well-shaped; bright orange color; no blemishes or soft spots.	Carton 50# (variable count)
Radicchio (Red-leaf Chicory)	*Barbe de capucin; radicchio, barba di capuccino/trevisano*		Small, round heads; magenta leaves with white ribs and veins; crisp-tender; no cuts, bruises, or rot.	Carton 20# (20–24 count)
Radish	*Radis; ravanello*	U.S. No. 1, Commercial	Well-shaped, smooth, firm, crisp-tender; fairly mild flavor; uniform size; even color (bright red, white); crisp tops.	Cello pack 8 ounces Basket (w/tops) (2 dozen count) Basket (w/o tops) (2–2½ dozen count)
Salsify (White or Black) Oyster Plant	*Salsifis; scorzonera*	No Federal Grades Fall–Winter	Medium size (6 inches long or smaller); straight, firm, crisp, fresh tops.	
Shallot	*Echalote; scalogno*	U.S. No. 1 Year-round	Dry, papery skin; bronze color; firm; bulbous; purple inner skin; no mold, browning, or rot.	Bag 5 or 10#
Sorrel, French	*Oseille; acetosella*		See spinach.	
Spinach, Leaf	*Epinard; spinaci*	U.S. No. 1, Commercial Mar.–May	Clean, fresh, crisp-tender, good color, flat or curly leaf, no bruising or discoloration, should be packed with ice.	Carton/crate 20–22# (8-count [10-ounce] cello bag)
Squash, Summer or Marrow (Zucchini, Yellow, Pattypan, Others)	*Courgette; zucca (zucchini)*	U.S. No. 1, No. 2 July–Nov.	Heavy for size; no blemishes or soft spots; tender rind (easily punctured); small (6 inches or under are best).	Carton 20 or 80# Bushel carton 50#

* Count, where applicable.

TABLE 8-4. VEGETABLES

Item (Types)	French and Italian Names	Grade and Peak Season	Purchasing Factors	Pack and Weight*
Squash, Winter (Acorn, Butternut, Hubbard, Pumpkin, Spaghetti, Others)	*Gourde; zucca*	U.S. No. 1, No. 2 July–Nov.	Heavy for size; no blemishes, cracks, or soft spots; hard rind.	Individually (especially large squash like Hubbard) Carton 20 or 80# Bushel carton 50#
Tomato (Red: Cherry, Plum, Beefsteak; Green; Yellow)	*Tomate; pomodoro*	U.S. No. 1, Combination, No. 2, No. 3	Mature or vine-ripened; deep, even color; well-shaped; plump; smooth; no blemishes.	Flat 18–20# (40 or 60 count) Lug 28–30# (108, 126, or 147 count) Carton 25# Cherry: Tray 14–20# (12-count [1-pint] trays)
Turnip	*Navet; rapa* (White Turnip, to distinguish from Rutabaga)	U.S. No. 1, No. 2 Oct.–Mar.	Medium size (1¾ to 2½ inches); smooth, firm, good color (white at tip, purple near top); no blemishes; few leaf scars around crown, few fibrous roots at base.	½ bushel 25# Bag 25 or 50# Carton 43–47# (24-bushel count)
Rutabaga (Yellow Turnip)	*Choux-navet; navone*	U.S. No. 1, No. 2 Oct.–Mar.	Fairly smooth; no blemishes; light-yellow to buff color; almost always waxed.	Carton/bag 50#
Watercress	*Cresson (de fontaine); crescione*	U.S. No. 1 Year-round	Crisp, bright green; clean; packed with ice.	Case (12-bunch count)

* Count, where applicable.

Avocados

These egg- to pear-shaped vegetables have green to black leathery skin, which can be smooth or bumpy. Avocado flesh is buttery smooth, delicately flavored, green near the skin, and yellow toward the center. Cut surfaces must be treated with lemon or lime juice to prevent browning. An avocado is shown below.

Haas avocado

Cabbage Family

The cabbage family *(brassicas)* include broccoli, Brussels sprouts, cauliflower, kale, kohlrabi, collard greens, and many kinds of cabbage. (Four of these are illustrated below.) All have a similar flavor. Turnips and rutabagas are also members of the *brassica* family, but they are more commonly thought of as root vegetables.

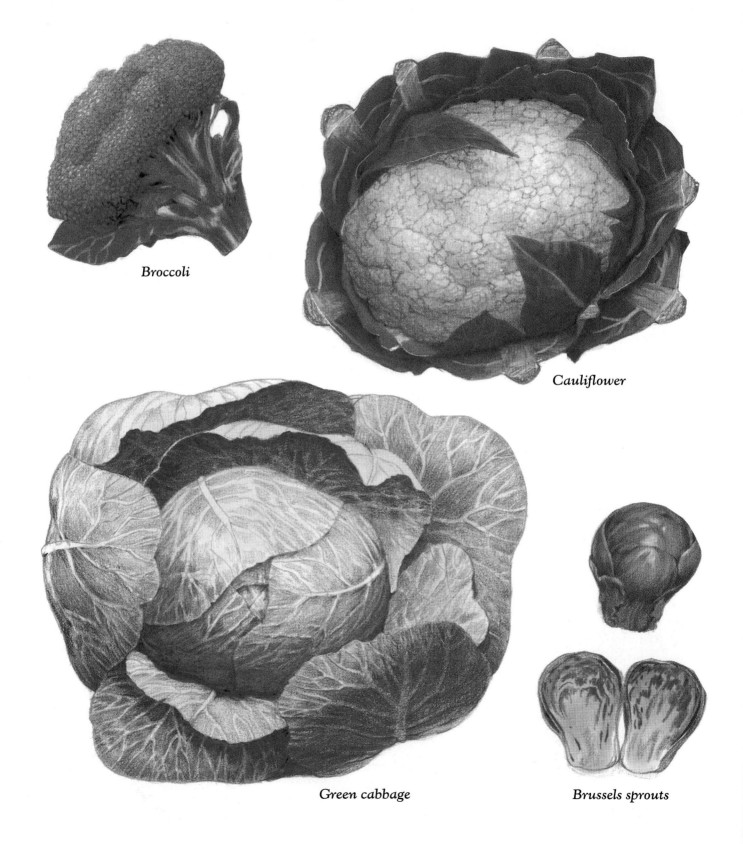

Broccoli

Cauliflower

Green cabbage

Brussels sprouts

Cucumbers, Squashes, and Eggplant

Cucumbers, eggplant, and the many squash varieties are all members of the gourd family. They have fairly tough rinds, thick flesh, and flat, oval seeds. Summer squashes (zucchini, yellow, crookneck, pattypan) are picked when they are immature to insure a delicate flesh, tender seeds, and thin skins. Winter squashes (acorn, butternut, hubbard, pumpkin, spaghetti) are characterized by their hard rind and seeds. Several of these gourd-family vegetables are illustrated below.

Cucumber

Acorn squash

Eggplant

Spaghetti squash

Leafy Vegetables

The most common examples of this category are lettuces of all sorts. Other members include endive, spinach, swiss chard, radicchio, and watercress. Beet greens, dandelion greens, and sorrel are among the less common leafy vegetables. For additional information, refer to Table 8-5.

Spinach

Chicory

Butterhead lettuce

TABLE 8-5. SALAD GREENS

Name	Description	Flavor	Name	Description	Flavor
Arugula	Medium size; tender; rounded to slightly elongated; medium-green leaves	Pungent	Lettuce, Leaf	Crisp-tender, usually curly leaves; loose cluster with no heart; red or green	Mild
Dandelion	Jagged, toothy, medium-green leaves; young leaves lighter green, more tender and milder	Somewhat bitter	Lettuce, Romaine	Elongated head, crisp leaves, fairly tender heart	Fairly mild
			Radicchio	Fairly tender, magenta leaves; white ribs and veins; small, cabbage-like head	Slightly bitter
Endive, Belgian	Tight, elongated head, blanched white to pale yellow-green	Slightly bitter	Sorrel, French	Small to medium-sized, semi-curly, spade-shaped leaves; white to green stems; contains oxalic acid, which can be toxic in large amounts, so it should be eaten in moderation	Tart, lemony
Endive, Curly	Thick, narrow leaves with very jagged, curly edges; crisp, semi-shiny; medium- to deep-green outer, pale-green inner leaves; loose, bushy head	Bitter			
Escarole	Flat, curly-edged, light- to medium-green leaves; loose head	Bitter	Spinach	Tender, deep-green leaves may be small and rounded to large and spade-shaped, flat or curly; ribbed stems removed before use	Fairly mild
Lettuce, Butterhead	Tender, slightly curly leaves; loose, round head of leaves	Mild	Sprouts, Mustard/ Radish	Small, round leaves on slender stalks; delicate texture	Peppery, pungent
Lettuce, Iceberg	Crisp, pale-green leaves; very compact head; firm core or heart	Very mild	Watercress	Small, round leaves on slender stalks; delicate texture	Peppery, pungent

Mushrooms

Mushrooms are a type of fungus, many of which are edible. They consist, in most cases, of a stem and a round or parasol-shaped cap. Both cultivated and wild varieties are available. Be sure to obtain wild mushrooms from a reputable source, to avoid getting poisonous ones. Many wild mushrooms are available dried as well as fresh and some of the more common ones are chanterelles, morels, shiitake, and wood ear. For additional information, refer to Table 8-6.

Most mushrooms are completely edible, but if the stem is tough or has a sticky skin it should be trimmed away. A common "domestic" mushroom and two wild species are illustrated below.

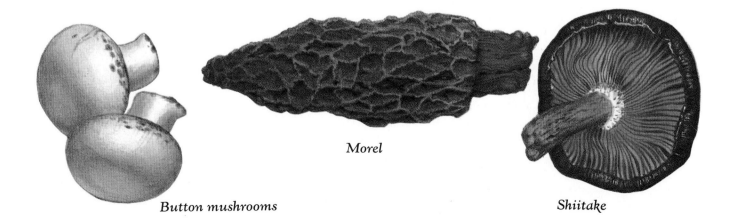

Button mushrooms   *Morel*   *Shiitake*

TABLE 8-6. MUSHROOMS

Name	French and Italian Names	Description*	Flavor
Boletus	*Bolete/cepe; porcini*	Rounded, golden-brown caps, usually fused to bulbous, white stems; tender, smooth, cream-colored flesh stays pale when cooked. Highly perishable; sticky caps may be peeled. Types: cepe or cep, porcini, and bolete.	Earthy to meaty
Chanterelle	*Chanterelle; gallinaccio/cantarello/ finferlo*	Trumpet-shaped with yellowish stem and frilly, brown cap. Convoluted shape holds dirt; should be washed and dried well. Requires longer cooking than most mushrooms. Available fresh and dried.	Delicate, fruity aroma
Enokidake (Japanese)	N/A	White to pale straw–colored with long, slender stems and tiny caps. Available fresh and canned.	Slightly fruity
Morel	*Morille; spugnole*	Delicate, spongy flesh; blunt, deeply pitted, cone-shaped caps. Various sizes. Pale tan to dark brown or gray. Tends to hold dirt; may be washed using a small brush. Available fresh and dried.	Earthy to nutty or spicy
Oyster (Oak Mushroom)	N/A	Smooth, cream to gray caps; short, creamy-white stem and gills. Grows horizontally on tree trunks; fan-shaped like an oyster shell. Ranges in size from as small as a dime to several inches across. May require longer cooking than most other types. Available fresh and dried.	Peppery raw; mild cooked
Shiitake (Chinese Black Mushroom)	N/A	Umbrella-shaped, cream-colored stem and gills, dark-brown cap with possible cream-colored cracks. Available fresh and dried.	Earthy, slightly meaty; woodsy aroma
Truffle	*Truffe; tartuffo*	Roughly round, various sizes; colors: white, black, gray, and brown. Black truffles of Perigord considered best; Piedmontese white truffle rated a close second. Available fresh and canned (whole and in pieces).	Pungent to piquant; white: garlicky; aromatic
Wood ear (Tree Ears, Cloud Ears, Chinese Black Fungi)		Flat, slightly translucent, ruffled, black. Firm, gelatinous texture. Usually dried, sometimes fresh.	Mild

* Appearance, types, purchase form

Onion Family

Onions and their relations belong to the *allium* family. All varieties share a pungent flavor and aroma and are used as seasonings. Some types are also used as vegetables. Onions fall into two main categories, reflecting the state in which they are used: cured (dried) and fresh (green). Five members of the onion family are illustrated on the opposite page.

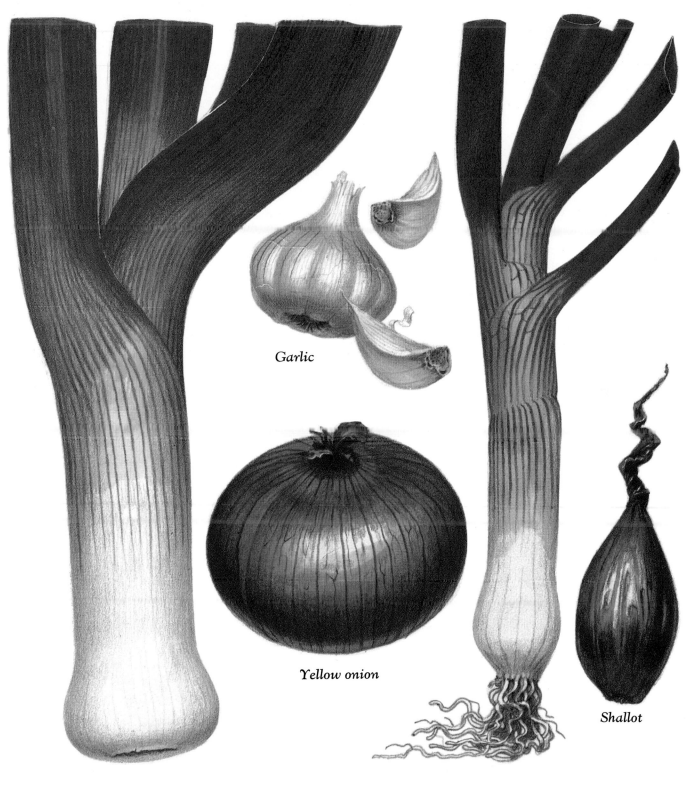

Garlic

Yellow onion

Shallot

Leek

Scallion

123

Peppers, Bell

Bell, or sweet, peppers are named for their shape and come in many colors—green, red, yellow, even creamy white and purple (three of the colors are shown below). All start out green and ripen to one of the other colors (peppers do not ripen after picking).

All are similar in appearance and flavor, although the red and yellow varieties tend to be sweeter than the others. Bell peppers are hollow, except for whitish ribs and a core with a cluster of small seeds. Both ribs and core are removed before use.

Red bell pepper   *Green bell pepper*   *Yellow bell pepper*

Peppers, Chili

Chili peppers (*chiles* in Spanish) are related to bell peppers, but they are usually smaller and contain spicy, volatile oils. Most of their fire is in the seeds, so seeded chilies will be less hot than whole ones.

Chilies are available fresh, canned, and dried (whole, flaked, and ground). Popular varieties include anaheim, ancho/poblano, habanero, and serrano, all of which are illustrated below.

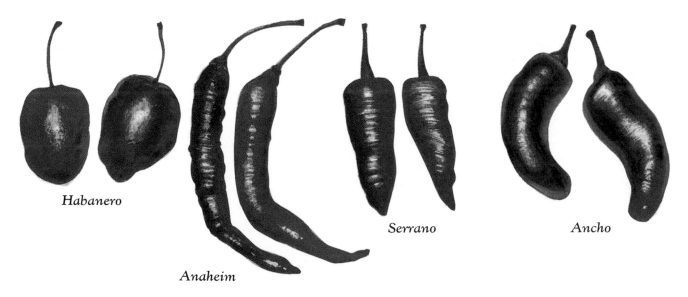

Habanero   *Serrano*   *Ancho*

Anaheim

Pod and Seed Vegetables

These vegetables include fresh legumes, such as peas, beans, and bean sprouts, as well as corn and okra. All are best eaten young and fresh, when they are at their sweetest and most tender. Once picked, they begin to convert their natural sugars into starch. They can lose their sweetness as soon as a day after being harvested; after a few days, they become mealy.

If possible, purchase pod and seed vegetables from local growers to minimize lag time between picking and serving. This is especially important with peas and corn, which are highly perishable. Peas, beans, and corn are also available in dried form, as discussed in Chapter 10, "Nonperishable Goods Identification." Some fresh peas and beans are eaten whole, when the pods are still fleshy and tender—for example, sugar snap peas, snow peas, green beans, and wax beans. In other cases, the peas or beans (such as limas, scarlet runners, and black-eyed peas) are removed from their inedible pods. Four members of the pod and seed vegetable group are illustrated below.

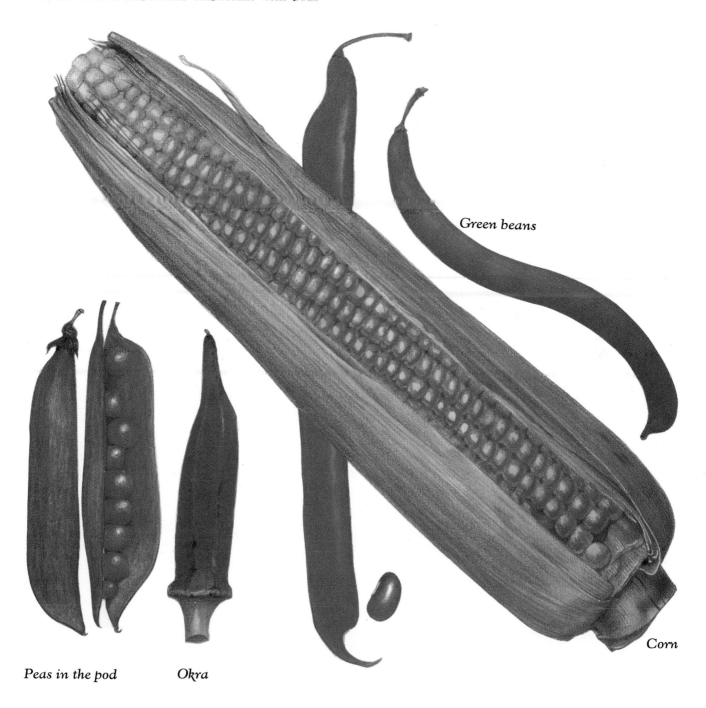

Green beans

Corn

Peas in the pod   *Okra*

Roots and Tubers

Roots and tubers serve as nutrient reservoirs for their plants. Consequently, they are rich in sugars, starches, vitamins, and minerals. Popular root vegetables include beets, carrots, celeriac, parsnips, radishes, rutabagas, and turnips. Tubers, which are enlarged, bulbous roots capable of generating a new plant, include potatoes, sweet potatoes, yams, and Jerusalem artichokes. Three roots and two tubers are illustrated below.

Roots and tubers should be stored dry and unpeeled. If they come with greens attached, these should be fresh at the time of purchase and cut off as soon thereafter as possible. If stored properly, most roots and tubers will keep for several weeks.

Beet

Chef's potato

Sweet potato

Turnip

Radish

Shoots and Stalks

This family consists of plants that produce shoots and stalks used as vegetables and includes artichokes, asparagus, celery, and fennel. The stalks should be firm, fleshy, and full, and should have no evidence of browning or wilting. Some of these vegetables are illustrated below.

Artichoke

Fennel

Asparagus

Tomatoes

These succulent "vegetables" are actually berries. They are grown in hundreds of varieties, in colors from green to yellow to bright red. Basic types include small, round cherry tomatoes, oblong plum tomatoes, and large beefsteak tomatoes, all of which are illustrated below. All have smooth, shiny skin, juicy flesh, and small, edible seeds. Most tomatoes grown commercially are picked unripe and allowed to ripen in transit, but vine-ripened tomatoes are far superior and may be obtained locally, in season.

Beefsteak tomato

Plum tomato

Cherry tomato

HERBS

Herbs are the leaves of aromatic plants and are used primarily to add flavor to foods. The chart in Table 8-7 contains basic information on each of the most common culinary herbs, including flavor, purchase forms, and possible uses. Some of the most widely used herbs are shown below and on the opposite page.

Selection

Most herbs are available both fresh and dried, although some (thyme, bay leaf, rosemary) dry more successfully than others. Aroma is a good indicator of quality in both fresh and dried herbs. An herb's scent can be tested best by using the fingers to crumble a few leaves and then smelling those leaves. A weak or stale aroma indicates old and less potent herbs. Fresh herbs also may be judged by appearance. They should have good color (usually green), fresh-looking leaves and stems, and no wilt, brown spots, sunburn, or pest damage.

Proper Use

Herbs can be used to flavor numerous preparations. They should enhance and balance, not overpower, a dish's flavors. Only occasionally, and with a purpose, should the herb's flavor be dominant. When used with discretion, herbs can transform the taste of plain foods into something special. Overuse or inappropriate use can cause, at best, a dish that tastes of nothing but herbs and, at worst, a culinary disaster.

Certain herbs have a special affinity for certain foods. Guidelines stating which herbs are most effectively paired with which foods are not cast in stone, but following them can familiarize the chef with the way herb-food combinations work and can serve as a springboard for future experimentation (see Table 8-7).

Fresh herbs should be minced or cut in chiffonade as close to serving time as possible. They are usually added to a dish toward the end of the cooking time, to prevent the flavor from cooking out. Dried herbs are usually added early in the process. For uncooked preparations, fresh herbs should be added well in advance of serving, to give them a chance to blend with the other elements.

Storage

In general, herbs should be stored by wrapping loosely in damp paper or cloth. If desired, the wrapped herbs may then be placed in plastic bags to help retain freshness and reduce wilting of leaves, and should be stored at 35 to 45°F (2 to 7°C). Some herbs, especially watercress and parsley, may be held by trimming the stems and placing the bunch in a jar of water. Wrap damp toweling around the leaves to prevent wilting.

Foodservice operations that grow herbs may have an excess at certain times of the season. These may be used for making compound butters, pestos, or flavored vinegars or oils.

Parsley   *Tarragon*

Rosemary

Oregano

Thyme

Sage

Chives

TABLE 8-7. HERBS

Name	French and Italian Names	Flavor	Purchase Forms*	Affinities
Basil	*Basilique; basilico*	Spicy with hints of clove and mint	Fresh, dried, bottled, pesto	Chicken, rabbit, lamb, shellfish, tomatoes, green beans, summer squash, potatoes, eggplant, parmesan and mozzarella cheese, pasta, rice, soups, stews, sauces (especially pesto)
Bay	*Laurier; lauro*	Pungent and piney	Dried, extract	Stocks, soups, stews, braises, boiling/poaching liquid for fish and shellfish, tomato and other sauces, marinades Extract: baked goods, sausage
Chervil	*Cerfeuil; cerfoglio*	Parsley-like with a hint of anise	Fresh, [dried]	Veal, eggs, cheese, sauces (especially for fish), soups, stews, peas, carrots, spinach, garnish, substitute for parsley
Chives	*Ciboulette, civette, cives; porrini*	Mild oniony	Fresh, [dried]	Garnish (snipped, whole, to tie items in bundles), poultry, shellfish, veal, eggs, cheese, other dairy products, potatoes, onions, asparagus, peas, artichokes, cauliflower, tomatoes
Coriander	*Coriandre; coriandolo*	Pungent with sage and citrus notes and soapy aftertaste	Fresh, [dried], seeds	Curries, stir-fries, pilafs, marinades, stews, sauces and relishes, shellfish, most meats and poultry, tomatoes, onions, beets, potatoes, chilis, garlic, mint
Dill	*Aneth; N/A*	Tangy	Fresh, [dried], seeds	Salads, garnish, soups, sauces (especially for fish and chicken), eggs, cheese, other dairy products, potatoes, cucumbers, cabbage, carrots, green beans
Fennel	*Fenouil; finocchio*	Anise/licorice	Fresh, seeds	Fish and shellfish, lamb, sausage, grains, eggs, cheese, salads, salad dressings, cabbage, beans, burnt on wood or charcoal to flavor grilled items
Marjoram	*Marjolaine; maggiorana*	Pungent with a hint of balsam	Fresh, dried	Most meat and poultry, forcemeats, stuffings, fish, soups, salads, sauces and dressings, tomatoes, mushrooms, eggplant, most green vegetables
Mint	*Menthe; menta*	Spicy-sweet, menthol	Fresh, [dried], extract	Peppermint: tea (leaves), confectionery (usually oil or extract) Spearmint: beverages (tea, fruit drinks, juleps), jelly and sauces (for lamb, veal, and other sweet and savory dishes), fruit salads and desserts, peas, cucumbers, eggplant, potatoes, carrots
Oregano	*Origan; origano*	Strong, rich, pungent	Fresh, dried	Tomato sauces, beef, veal, pork, poultry, game, fish, shellfish, tomatoes, mushrooms, bell peppers, onions, summer squash, potatoes, salads, garlic

* Brackets indicate that a certain form is available but that it is considered inferior to other forms given.

TABLE 8-7. HERBS

Name	French and Italian Names	Flavor	Purchase Forms*	Affinities
Parsley	*Persil; prezzemolo*	Mild, somewhat carrot-like	Fresh, dried	Salads, garnish, numerous cooked and uncooked preparations, pairs well with garlic and most other herbs
Rosemary	*Romarin; rosmarino*	Pungent, piney, with hints of ginger and mint	Fresh, dried	Poultry, lamb, beef, veal, pork, game, some fish, cheese, eggs, tomatoes, mushrooms, squash, peas, spinach
Sage	*Sauge; salvia*	Camphor with bitter and citrus notes	Fresh, dried	Meats (especially pork), poultry, game, some fish, stuffings, eggs, beans, lentils, batter-fried (young leaves), artichokes, tomatoes, eggplant, onions, green beans, squash, cabbage
Savory	*Sariette; Santoreggia*	Summer: pungent, thyme-like; Winter: pungent, hint of pine	Fresh, dried	Summer: lamb, sausages, stuffings, soups, herb butter and vinegar, beans, lentils, rice, green beans, peas, cabbage, eggplant, most root vegetables Winter: forcemeats, game, soups, beans, grains
Tarragon	*Estragon; dragoncello, targoncello, estragone*	Strong, grassy, anise/licorice	Fresh, dried, vinegar	Fish, chicken, most meats, forcemeats, potatoes, tomatoes, onions, leeks, mushrooms, peas, salads, salad dressings, herb butter and vinegar, sauces (especially béarnaise), eggs, most dairy products
Thyme	*Thym; timo*	Delicate with a hint of clove	Fresh, dried	Fish, chicken, most meats, forcemeats, stuffings, soups, stocks, stews, tomatoes, eggplant, mushrooms, onions, leeks, asparagus, green beans, broccoli, herb butter and mayonnaise

* Brackets indicate that a certain form is available but that it is considered inferior to other forms given.

SUMMARY

This chapter has stressed the importance of selecting fresh, blemish-free produce of the best quality and then storing it properly until the time of use. If purchasing of fruits, vegetables, and herbs is done effectively, the foodservice establishment will have enough to meet its needs but not so much that its inventory spoils.

The range of available fresh produce has been widened by improved shipping capabilities, although locally grown items are always preferable. In addition to providing superior quality, local growers can extend the available produce range, through farming of more exotic items not handled by large commercial purveyors. Herb and vegetable gardening on the foodservice operation's premises offers attractive possibilities, if the establishment has the space and manpower.

Chapter 9

Dairy, Cheese, and Egg Identification

A concentrated source of many nutrients—especially protein and calcium—dairy products and eggs hold a prominent place on menus, on their own and as key ingredients in many preparations. Milk and milk products are not only used as beverages but as ingredients in many dishes. Béchamel sauce, for example, is based on milk. Cream, crème fraîche, sour cream, and yogurt are used to finish sauces and in many baked goods. Cheeses may be served as is, perhaps as a separate course with fruit, or as part of another dish. Eggs are considered a very versatile food and appear on menus throughout the day—from morning breakfast dishes to dessert soufflés served at midnight. Eggs' unique composition makes them useful in the preparation of numerous sauces, especially emulsified ones such as hollandaise and mayonnaise.

PURCHASING AND STORAGE

Although dairy products and eggs are two separate kinds of products, freshness and wholesomeness are important for both. Both are also highly perishable. For these reasons, careful purchasing and storage procedures are extremely important.

Table 9-1 provides holding temperatures and average shelf life of eggs and various dairy products. Milk and cream containers customarily are dated to indicate how long the contents will remain fresh enough to use. Because the freshness period will vary, the chef should not combine, or "marry," milk and cream from separate containers, to avoid contamination.

When used in hot dishes, milk or cream should be brought to a boil before being added to other ingredients. If milk curdles, it should not be used. Unfortunately, detecting spoilage by simply smelling or tasting unheated milk is often impossible.

When considering storage arrangements for dairy products, flavor transfer is a particular concern. Storing all milk, cream, and butter away from foods with strong odors is preferable, when feasible. Cheeses should be carefully wrapped, both to maintain moistness and to prevent the odor from permeating other foods and vice versa.

Eggs should be refrigerated and the stock rotated to assure that only fresh, wholesome eggs are served. The chef should inspect eggs carefully upon delivery, making sure that shells are clean and free of cracks. Eggs with broken shells should be discarded because of the high contamination risk.

DAIRY PRODUCTS

Milk

Milk is invaluable in the kitchen, whether it is served as a beverage or used as a component in dishes. U.S. federal regulations govern how milk is produced and sold, to assure that it is clean and safe to use.

Most milk sold in the United States has been pasteurized. In pasteurization, the milk is heated to 145°F (63°C) for 30 minutes, or to 161°F (72°C) for 15 seconds in order to kill bacteria or other organisms that could cause infection or contamination. Milk products with a higher percentage of milkfat are heated to either 150°F (65°C) for 30 minutes or to 166°F (74°C) for 30 seconds for ultrapasteurization.

The date stamp on milk and cream cartons is 10 days from the point of pasteurization. For example, if milk was pasteurized on October 10, the date on the carton would read October 20. If the product has been properly stored and handled, it should still be fresh and wholesome on the stamped date.

Milk is also generally homogenized, which means that it has been forced through an ultra-fine mesh at high pressure in order to break up the fat globules it

TABLE 9-1. PROPER STORAGE TIMES AND TEMPERATURES OF DAIRY PRODUCTS AND EGGS

Product	Storage Time	Temperature (°F)
Milk, fluid, pasteurized (whole, low-fat, skim, other unfermented)	1 week	35–40
Milk, evaporated		
Unopened	6 months	60–70
Opened	3–5 days	35–40
Milk, sweetened, condensed		
Unopened	2–3 months	60–70
Opened	3–5 days	35–40
Milk, nonfat dry		
Unopened	3 months	60–70
Reconstituted	1 week	35–40
Buttermilk	2–3 weeks	35–40
Yogurt	3–6 weeks	35–40
Cream		
Table or Whipping	1 week	35–40
Ultrapasteurized	6 weeks	35–40
Whipped, Pressurized	3 weeks	35–40
Ice cream	4 weeks	−10–0
Butter	3–5 days	35
Margarine	5–7 days	35
Cheese, unripened, soft	5–7 days	35–40
Cheese, ripened, soft, semi-soft	5–7 days	35–40
Cheese, ripened, hard	2–3 months	35–40
Cheese, very hard, grated	2–3 months	35–40
Cheese foods	2–3 weeks	35–40
Cheese, process, sealed		
Unopened	3–4 months	60–70
Opened	1–2 weeks	35–40
Eggs, whole, in shell	5–7 days	33–38
Eggs, whole, fluid	2–3 days	29–32
Eggs, frozen	1–2 months	−10–0
Eggs, dried	1–2 months	40

Adapted from Eva Medved, *Food Preparation and Theory*, which was adapted from various USDA publications.

contains. This fat is then dispersed evenly throughout the milk, preventing it from rising to the surface. Milk may also be fortified with vitamins A and D (low-fat or skim milk is almost always fortified, because removing the fat also removes fat-soluble vitamins).

State and local government standards for milk are fairly consistent. Milk products are carefully inspected before and after production. Farms and animals (cows and goats) are also inspected, to assure that sanitary conditions are upheld. Milk that has been properly produced and processed is labeled "grade A."

Milk comes in various forms and is classified according to its percentage of fat and milk solids. Table 9-2 describes these kinds of available milks and creams.

Cream

Milk, as it comes from the cow, goat, or sheep, contains a certain percentage of fat, known alternately as milkfat or butterfat. Originally, milk was allowed to settle long enough for the cream, which is lighter than the milk, to rise to the surface. Today, a centrifuge is used to spin the milk. The cream is driven to the center where it can be easily drawn off, leaving the milk behind. Cream, like milk, is homogenized and pasteurized, and may also be stabilized to help extend shelf life. Some chefs prefer cream that has not been stabilized or ultrapasteurized because they believe it will whip to a greater volume.

Two forms of cream are used in most kitchens: heavy (whipping) cream and light cream. Half and half, a combination of whole milk and cream, does not contain enough milkfat to be considered a true cream; its milkfat content is approximately 10.5 percent. Descriptions of these three are included in Table 9-2.

Ice Cream

In order to meet government standards, any product labeled as ice cream must contain a certain amount of milkfat. For vanilla, it is no less than 10 percent milkfat. For any other flavor, the requirement is 8 percent. Stabilizers can make up no more than 2 percent of ice cream. Good-quality ice cream may contain several times more fat than is required by these standards. Ice creams that contain less fat should be labeled "ice milk."

The best ice cream has a custard base (a mixture of cream and/or milk and eggs), which gives it a dense, smooth texture. It should readily melt in the mouth, and when the ice cream melts at room temperature,

there should be no separation. The appearance of "weeping" in melting ice cream indicates an excessive amount of stabilizers.

Other frozen desserts similar to ice cream are: sherbet, sorbet, granite, frozen yogurt, and frozen tofu. Sherbet does not contain cream, and so it is far lower in butterfat than ice creams; however, it does contain a relatively high percentage of sugar in order to achieve the correct texture and consistency during freezing. Some sherbets will contain a percentage of either eggs or milk, or both. Although the word "sherbet" is the closest English translation of the French

TABLE 9-2. FORMS OF MILK AND CREAM

Form	Description	Type of Container
Milk		
Whole	Contains no less than 3% milkfat	Bulk, gallon, half-gallon, quart, pint, ½ pint
Low-fat	Usually contains 1% or 2% milkfat and is generally labeled accordingly	Same as whole milk
Skim	Contains less than 0.1% milkfat	Same as whole milk
Powdered or Dry	Milk from which water is completely removed. Made from either whole or skim milk and labeled accordingly.	50# bulk, 24 oz. bulk
Evaporated	Milk that has been heated in a vacuum to remove 60% of its water. May be made from whole or skim milk and is labeled accordingly.	14.5 oz., 10 oz., or 6 oz. cans
Condensed	Evaporated milk that has been sweetened	Same as above
Cream		
Heavy or Whipping	Must contain at least 35% milkfat. Light whipping cream is occasionally available, containing 30% to 35% fat.	Quarts, pints, ½ pints
Light	Contains between 16% and 32% fat	Same as heavy cream
Half and half	Contains between 10.5% and 12% fat. Used as a lightener for coffee.	Same as heavy cream and in portion sizes

word "sorbet," sorbets are commonly understood to contain no milk. Granites, the simplest forms of "ices," are basically flavored syrups that are allowed to freeze; once solid, they are scraped to produce large crystals or flakes. Frozen yogurts often contain stabilizers and a high percentage of fat. Test a variety of these products to determine which brand offers the best quality for the best price.

Butter

Anyone who has accidentally overwhipped cream has been well on the way to producing butter. Although traditionally butter was churned by hand, today it is made mechanically by mixing cream that contains between 30 and 45 percent milkfat at a high speed. Eventually, the milkfat clumps together, separating out into a solid mass, that leaves a fluid referred to as buttermilk. The solid mass is butter.

The best-quality butter, labeled "grade AA," is made from sweet cream and has the best flavor, color, aroma, and texture. Grade A butter also is of excellent quality. Grade B may have a slightly acidic taste, as it is made from sour cream. Both grades AA and A contain a minimum of 80 percent fat. The best-quality butter has a sweet flavor, similar to very fresh heavy cream. If salt has been added, it should be barely detectable. The color of butter will vary depending upon the breed of cow and time of year, but is usually a pale yellow. The cow's diet will vary from season to season, affecting the color and flavor of the butter.

The designation "sweet butter" indicates only that the butter is made from sweet cream. If unsalted butter is desired, be sure that the package is so marked. Salted butter may contain no more than a maximum of 2 percent salt. The salt can aid in extending butter's shelf life but can also mask a slightly "old" flavor or aroma. Old butter will take on a very faintly cheesy flavor and aroma. As it continues to deteriorate, the flavor and aroma can become quite pronounced, and extremely unpleasant, much like sour or curdled milk.

Fermented and Cultured Milk Products

Yogurt, sour cream, crème fraîche, and buttermilk are all produced by inoculating milk or cream with a bacterial strain that causes fermentation to begin. The fermentation process thickens the milk and gives it a pleasantly sour flavor.

Yogurt is made by introducing the proper culture into milk (whole, low-fat, or skim may be used). Available in a variety of container sizes, yogurt can be purchased plain or flavored with different fruits, honey, coffee, etc.

Sour cream is a cultured sweet cream that contains about 16 to 22 percent fat. It comes in containers of various sizes, beginning with a half-pint.

Crème fraîche is similar to sour cream but has a slightly more rounded flavor, with less bite, and tends to curdle less readily than sour cream when used in hot dishes. This product is made from heavy cream with a butterfat content of approximately 30 percent, which contributes to its higher cost. Although crème fraîche is available commercially, many operations make their own by heating heavy cream, adding a small amount of buttermilk, and allowing the mixture to ferment at room temperature until thickened and lightly soured.

Buttermilk, strictly speaking, is the by-product of churned butter; but despite its name, it contains only a very small amount of butterfat. Most buttermilk sold today is skim milk to which a bacterial strain has been added. Usually sold in pints or quarts, buttermilk is also available as a dried powder for baking uses.

Cheese

The variety of cheeses produced throughout the world is extensive, ranging from mild, fresh cheeses (pot cheese or cottage cheese) to strongly flavored, blue-veined cheeses (Roquefort or Gorgonzola) to hard grating cheeses (Parmesan or Romano).

Cheeses are used in many dishes, and selecting the right cheese for the intended effect is important, because cheese can be quite expensive.

Most cheeses are made through the following procedure: Milk is combined with the appropriate starter (generally rennet, an enzyme), which causes the milk solids to coagulate into curds. The remaining liquid is known as the whey. The curds are then processed in various ways, depending on the type of cheese desired. They may be drained and used immediately, as fresh cheese, or they may be pressed, shaped, inoculated with a special mold, and aged.

Categories

Cheese is made from a variety of different milks—cow's milk, goat's milk, sheep's milk, even buffalo's milk. The type of milk used will help to determine the cheese's ultimate flavor and texture. The most commonly recognized categories of natural cheese are listed in Table 9-3, which provides details on the type of milk used, shape and color, flavor, and texture. Natural cheeses are produced by inoculating milk with a bacterium or mold and allowing it to ferment and ripen. The term "natural" indicates that cheeses made by this traditional method are considered "living" in much the same way that wine is considered living, that is, the cheese will continue to grow, developing or aging to maturity (ripening), and finally spoiling (overripening). Processed or pasteurized cheeses and cheese foods, on the other hand, do not ripen and age. There are a number of categories into which kinds of cheeses may be grouped. They are:

- Fresh cheese (Fig. 9-1), such as cottage cheese or fresh goat's cheese, is moist and very soft, and usually has a mild flavor.
- Soft cheese (see Fig. 9-1), such as Brie or Camembert, usually has a surface mold. The cheese ripens from the outside to the center and the rind is edible. When fully ripe, it should be nearly runny, with a full flavor.

TABLE 9-3. SELECTED NATURAL CHEESES

Type/Milk Used	Shape and Color	Flavor	Texture
Asiago (whole or part-skim cow's)	Cylinder or flat block, lt. yellow	Mild to sharp	Semi-soft to hard (depending on age)
Bel Paese (whole cow's)	Wheel, lt. yellow	Mild, buttery	Semi-soft, creamy, waxy
Bleu/Blue (whole cow's or goat's)	Cylinder, white with blue-green veins	Piquant, tangy	Semi-soft, possibly crumbly
Bleu de Bresse (whole cow's or goat's)	Wheel, lt. yellow with blue veins	Piquant but mild for blue	Soft, creamy, slightly crumbly
Brick (whole cow's)	Block, lt. yellow	Mild to pungent (depending on age)	Semi-soft, elastic, with many tiny holes
Brie (pasteurized, whole or skim cow's)	Disk, lt. yellow	Buttery to pungent	Soft, smooth, with edible rind
Bucheron (raw goat's)	Log, white	Slightly tangy	Soft, creamy
Camembert (raw or pasteurized whole cow's)	Disk, lt. yellow	Slightly tangy	Soft, creamy, with edible rind
Cheddar (whole cow's)	Wheel, lt. or med. yellow	Mild to sharp (depending on age)	Hard
Cheshire (whole cow's)	Cylinder, lt. or med. yellow (may have blue marbling)	Mellow to piquant	Hard
Cottage (whole or skim cow's)*	Curds, white	Mild	Soft, moist
Cream (whole cow's, plus cream)	Block, white	Mild, slightly tangy	Soft, creamy
Edam (whole or part-skim cow's)	Loaf or sphere (may be coated with wax)	Mild to tangy (depending on age)	Hard, may be slightly crumbly with tiny holes
Emmenthaler (Swiss); (raw or pasteurized, part-skim cow's)	Wheel, lt. yellow	Mild, nutty	Hard, smooth, shiny with large holes
Feta (sheep's, goat's, or cow's)	Block, white	Tangy, salty	Soft, crumbly
Fontina (whole cow's or sheep's)	Wheel, med. yellow	Nutty flavor, strong aroma	Hard
Gjetost (whole cow's and goat's)	Small block, lt. brown	Buttery, caramel, slightly tangy	Hard, creamy

* Cream may be added to finished curds.

(continued)

TABLE 9-3. SELECTED NATURAL CHEESES *(continued)*

Type/Milk Used	Shape and Color	Flavor	Texture
Gorgonzola (whole cow's and/or goat's	Wheel, med. yellow with blue marbling	Tangy, piquant	Semi-soft, dry for blue
Gouda (whole cow's)	Wheel (may be coated with wax)	Mild, creamy, slightly nutty	Hard, smooth, may have tiny holes
Gruyère (whole cow's)	Wheel, lt. yellow	Sharp, nutty	Hard with medium holes
Havarti (cream-enriched cow's)	Loaf or wheel, med. yellow	Buttery (may be flavored with dill or caraway)	Semi-soft, creamy, with small holes
Jarlsberg (whole cow's)	Wheel, lt. yellow	Sharp, nutty	Hard with large holes
Limburger (whole or low-fat cow's)	Block, lt. yellow, brown exterior	Very strong flavor and aroma	Soft, smooth, waxy
Monterey Jack (whole cow's)	Wheel or block, lt. yellow	Mild to pungent	Semi-soft to very hard (depending on age)
Montrachet (raw goat's)	Log, white	Slightly tangy	Soft, creamy
Mozzarella (whole or skim cow's)	Irregular sphere, white	Mild	Tender to slightly elastic (depending on age)
Muenster (whole cow's)	Wheel or block, lt. yellow (rind may be orange)	Mild to pungent (depending on age)	Semi-soft, smooth, waxy with small holes
Neufchâtel (whole or skim cow's)**	Block, white	Mild, slightly tangy	Soft, creamy
Parmigiano Reggiano/ Parmesan (part-skim cow's)	Cylinder, lt. yellow	Sharp, nutty	Very hard, dry, crumbly
Pont-l'Évêque (whole cow's)	Square, lt. yellow with edible golden-yellow crust	Piquant, strong aroma	Soft, supple, with small holes
Port-Salut (whole or low-fat cow's)	Wheel or cylinder, white with russet exterior	Buttery, mellow to sharp	Semi-soft, smooth
Provolone (whole cow's)	Pear, sausage, round, other, lt. yellow to golden-brown	Mild to sharp (depending on age), may be smoked	Hard, elastic
Ricotta (whole, skim, or low-fat cow's)***	Soft curds, white	Mild	Soft, moist to slightly dry, grainy
Ricotta Salata (whole sheep's)	Cylinder, off-white	Pungent	Hard
Romano, Pecorino (whole sheep's, goat's, or cow's)	Cylinder	Very sharp	Very hard, dry, crumbly
Roquefort (raw sheep's)	Cylinder, white with blue-green marbling	Sharp, pungent	Semi-soft, crumbly
Sap Sago (buttermilk, whey, and skim cow's)	Flattened cone, lt. green	Piquant, flavored with clover leaves	Very hard, granular
Stilton (whole cow's)	Cylinder, med. yellow with blue-green marbling	Piquant, but mild for blue	Hard, crumbly
Taleggio (raw cow's)	Square, lt. yellow	Creamy	Semi-soft with small holes

** May have added cream.
*** May have added whey.

• Hard cheeses (Fig. 9-2), such as Gruyère, Cheshire, and Cheddar, have a drier texture than semi-soft cheeses and a firm consistency. They will grate easily.

• Semi-soft cheeses (Fig. 9-3), such as Gouda or Edam, are more solid than soft cheeses but do not grate easily. They are often coated with wax to preserve moisture and extend shelf life.

• Grating cheeses (Fig. 9-4), such as Sap Sago, Parmesan, or Romano, are typically grated or shaved rather than cut into slices because of their crumbly texture.

• Blue-veined cheeses (Fig. 9-5), such as Roquefort and Gorgonzola, have consistencies that range from smooth and creamy to dry and crumbly. Their blue veining is the result of injecting a special mold into the cheese before ripening.

EGGS

Eggs are one of the kitchen's most important items. From mayonnaise to meringues, soups to sauces, appetizers to desserts, they are prominent on any menu.

The egg's basic structure includes the outer shell, the white, and the yolk. Various other membranes

9-1

Soft and fresh cheeses: *(top row)* Brie and Neufchâtel; *(center row)* aged goat's cheese and Camembert; *(bottom row)* peppered fresh cheese, fresh goat's cheese, and herbed goat's cheese.

9-2

Hard cheeses: *(clockwise from upper left)* Appenzeller, Asiago, Emmenthaler, Provolone, and Gruyere.

9-3

Semi-soft cheeses: *(clockwise from upper left)* Jarlsberg, Gouda, Bel Paese, Morbier, Colby, and Raclette.

9-4

Grating cheeses: *(clockwise from upper left)* Parmesan, Romano, and Sap Sago.

9-5

Blue-veined cheeses: *(clockwise from upper left)* Gorgonzola, Bresse Bleu, domestic blue cheese, and Roquefort.

help keep the yolk suspended at the center of the white and help prevent contamination or weight loss through evaporation. The white consists almost exclusively of protein and water; the yolk contains protein and, in addition, significant amounts of fat and a natural emulsifier called lecithin.

Grading, Sizes, and Forms

Eggs are graded by the U.S. Department of Agriculture on the basis of external appearance and freshness. The top grade, AA, indicates that the egg is fresh, with a white that will not spread unduly once the egg is broken, and a yolk that rides high on the white's surface. The yolk is anchored in place by membranes known as the *chalazae*.

Eggs come in a number of sizes: jumbo, extra large, large, medium, small, and pee wee. Table 9-4 gives the weight of each standard size by the dozen and by the 30-dozen case. This table can be used as a guide

for substitutions; for example: to determine how many eggs of one size can be used in a recipe that calls for eggs of another size.

Younger hens produce smaller eggs, which are generally of a better quality than larger eggs. Medium eggs are best for breakfast cookery, where the cooked egg's appearance is important.

Eggs are also sold in several processed forms: bulk, or fluid, whole eggs (which sometimes includes a percentage of extra yolks to obtain a specific blend), egg whites, and egg yolks. These products generally are available in liquid or frozen form. Dried, powdered eggs are also sold and may be useful for some baked goods.

Egg substitutes may be entirely egg-free or may be produced from egg whites, with dairy or vegetable products substituted for the yolks. These substitutes are important for people who require a reduced-cholesterol diet.

TABLE 9-4. WEIGHTS FOR STANDARD EGG SIZES

	Jumbo	Extra Large	Large	Medium	Small	Pee wee
Minimum weight per dozen	30 oz.	27 oz.	24 oz.	21 oz.	18 oz.	15 oz.
Minimum weight per 30-dozen case	56 lb.	50½ lb.	45 lb.	29½ lb.	34 lb.	28 lb.

SUMMARY

Most cuisines rely heavily on dairy products and eggs. Although we do not know exactly when man discovered the various ways milk could be used, it is clear that, through long use, milk products have become so familiar that they are often given little thought.

Eggs are one of nature's most miraculous foods. They are useful for a great number of culinary functions: thickening, coloring, adding moisture, forming emulsions, foaming, and adding nutritive value to (enriching) other foods.

Although it is tempting to take dairy products and eggs for granted and select them automatically, the chef should understand the characteristics of and different uses for them. Quality and freshness are major factors, and these ingredients should always be selected wisely and handled with care.

Chapter 10

Nonperishable Goods
Identification

The term "nonperishable goods" is somewhat misleading. Although the discussed staple items do have long shelf lives, most of them are of the best quality when they are relatively fresh. A broad spectrum of nonperishable goods, also known as "dry goods," forms part of any foodservice operation's basic operating needs. Descriptions of basic nonperishable items, information about their available forms, and purchasing and storage standards are all covered. In addition, the following products are discussed: grains, meals, and flours; dried legumes; dried pasta and noodles; nuts and seeds; sugars, syrups, and other sweeteners; oils and shortenings; vinegars and condiments; coffee, tea, and other beverages; dry goods for baking; dried herbs and spices; and cooking wines, liqueurs, and cordials. The characteristics of various canned, frozen, and other convenience foods will also be given.

PURCHASING AND STORAGE

Well-organized kitchens maintain a parstock of dry goods, that is, enough of an item is stored to assure that all menu offerings, as well as any items for special events, can be prepared from what is on hand. There should also be a slight overstock, in case of an unusually busy weekend or for other contingencies. Excessive overstock, however, can monopolize valuable storage space.

Nonperishable goods may be purchased in bulk, sold by the case, or come in single units. The best way the chef can be sure that his or her foodservice operation is properly outfitted but not overstocked is to talk to various purveyors. It can then be determined which one is best able to supply what is needed, at the best cost and in a timely fashion.

Inspect all dry goods as they arrive, just as carefully as produce, meats, and fish are inspected, to ensure that the delivery matches the order. Check bags, boxes, cans, or other containers to make sure they are intact and clean and that they are not dented, broken, or in any way below standard.

Store dry goods in an area that is properly dry, ventilated, and accessible. All goods should be placed above floor level, on shelving or pallets. Some nonperishable items, such as whole grains, nuts and seeds, and coffee (if it is not vacuum-packed) are best stored in the refrigerator, or even the freezer.

GRAINS, MEALS, AND FLOURS

This broad category extends from whole grains such as rice and barley to ground cornmeal and pastry flour. Grains are of great importance to many cuisines, as is discussed in Chapter 24, "Cooking Grains and Legumes." Wheat and corn are of primary importance in Western countries, such as the United States and Canada. Rice is fundamental to many Eastern cuisines. In fact, in many Eastern countries, the word for rice is the same as that for food.

Whole grains are grains that have not been milled. Milled grains have had the germ, bran, and/or hull removed, or have been polished. Whole grains tend to have a shorter life span than milled grains and, therefore, should be purchased in amounts that can be used in a relatively short period of time—two to three weeks. Although processed, or milled, grains tend to last longer, some of their nutritive value is lost during processing.

When the whole grain is milled, it is essentially crushed into successively smaller particles. Various methods are used for milling: crushing between metal rollers, grinding between stones, or cutting with steel blades in an action similar to that of a food processor. Grains ground between stones are called "stone-ground"; they may be preferred in some cases, because they retain more of their nutritive value due to a lower temperature during this milling process than in others.

Milled grains that are broken into coarse particles may be referred to as "cracked." If the milling process continues, meals and cereals (cornmeal, farina, cream of rice) are formed. Finally, the grain may be ground into a fine powder, known as "flour."

Table 10-1 lists some of the major grains, their available forms, and some major uses or preparations. Figure 10-1 shows a selection of flours; Figure 10-2 displays various grains.

DRIED LEGUMES

These foodstuffs, seeds from pod-producing plants, have many uses in the contemporary kitchen. Although in theory they have a lengthy shelf life, as do most nonperishable items, they are best when used

10-1

Flours and meals: *(top row, from left to right)* semolina, light rye flour, durum wheat flour; *(middle row, from left to right)* bleached flour, yellow cornmeal, buckwheat; *(bottom row, from left to right)* whole wheat, unbleached flour, white cornmeal.

TABLE 10-1. GRAINS, MEALS, FLOURS, AND OTHER STARCHES

Name	French and Italian Names	Purchase Form	Major Uses or Dishes
Wheat	*Froment; frumento*		
Whole		Unrefined or minimally processed whole kernels	Side dish
Cracked		Coarsely crushed, minimally processed kernels	Side dish, hot cereal
Bulgur		Hulled, cracked hard or soft wheat; parboiled and dried	Side dish, salad (tabbouleh)
Semolina	*Semoule; semolino/ semola*	Polished wheat kernel (bran and germ removed), whole or ground	Pasta, flour, couscous (below)
Couscous	*Couscous; cuscusu*	Semolina pellets, often parcooked	Side dish (often served with stew of same name)
Farina	*Farine*	Polished, medium-grind wheat kernels	Breakfast cereal
Bran	*Son; crusca*	Separated outer covering of wheat kernel; flakes	Added to baked goods, prepared cereals, and other foods to increase dietary fiber
Germ		Separated embryo of wheat kernel; flakes	Added to baked goods and cereals to boost flavor and nutrition
Wheat Flour, Whole	*Farine; farina*	Finely ground, whole kernels	Baked goods
All-purpose		Finely ground, polished kernels; usually enriched; may be bleached	Baked goods, thickener, other kitchen uses
Bread		Finely ground, polished hard wheat kernels; usually enriched; may be bleached	Bread dough
Cake		Very finely ground, polished soft wheat kernels; usually enriched and bleached	Cakes and other delicate baked goods
Pastry		Very finely ground, polished soft wheat kernels; usually enriched and bleached	Pastry and other delicate baked goods
Self-rising		Very finely ground, polished soft wheat kernels to which baking powder and salt have been added; usually enriched and bleached	Cakes and other baked goods not leavened with yeast
Rice	*Riz; riso*		
Brown		Hulled grains, bran intact; short, medium, or long grain; may be enriched	Side dish, other
White		Polished grains, usually enriched; long or short grain	Long grain: side dish. Short grain: pudding, risotto.
Converted		Parcooked, polished grains, may be enriched	Side dish, other
Basmati		Delicate, extra-long grain, polished	Side dish, including pilaf
Italian Short-grain		Short grain, polished; types include Piedmontese and Arborio	Risotto
Wild	*Zizanie*	Long, dark-brown grain not related to regular rice	Side dish, stuffings, other

(continued)

TABLE 10-1. GRAINS, MEALS, FLOURS, AND OTHER STARCHES *(continued)*

Name	French and Italian Names	Purchase Form	Major Uses or Dishes
Glutinous		Round, short grain, very starchy; black (unhulled) or white (polished)	Sushi, other Oriental dishes
Rice Flour		Very finely ground polished rice	Thickener
Corn	*Maïs; granoturco*		
Hominy		Whole, hulled kernels; dry or canned	Side dish including succotash, in soup or stew
Grits		Cracked hominy	Side dish, hot cereal, baked goods
Meal	*Farine de maïs; farina gialla*	Medium-fine ground, hulled kernels; white or yellow	Baked goods, coating, polenta
Masa Harina		Corn processed with lime to remove hull, medium ground; dry, dough, raw, or cooked tortillas	Tortillas and other Mexican dishes
Cornstarch	*Farine de maïs; farina finissima di granoturco* (corn flour)	Very finely ground, hulled kernels	Thickener, coating
Barley			
Pot or Scotch	*Orge mondes; orzo*	Coarse, whole kernels; ground (barley meal)	Side dish, hot cereal, soups; meal: baked goods
Pearl	*Orge perle; orzo*	Polished, whole kernels; ground (barley flour)	Side dish, hot cereal, soups; flour: baked goods
Buckwheat	*Blé noir/blé sarrasin; grano saraceno*	Whole, coarsely cracked (kasha), flour	Whole: side dish; flour: pancakes, baked goods
Millet	*Millet*	Whole, flour	Side dish, flat breads
Oats	*Avoine*	Rolled, cut (oatmeal, below)	Hot cereal, baked goods
Oatmeal		Ground coarse or fine	Filler in sausages, baked goods
Oat Bran		Separated outer covering of grain, flakes	Added to cereals and baked goods for dietary fiber
Rye	*Seigle*	Cracked, flour	Cracked: side dish; flour: baked goods
Sorghum	*Sorgho; sorgo*	Whole, flour, syrup	Porridge, flat breads, beer; syrup and molasses
Other Starches			
Arrowroot		Fine, starchy powder made from a tropical root	Thickener
Filé or gumbo		Fine, starchy powder made from sassafras leaves	Thickener (especially in Creole dishes such as gumbo)

within six months of purchase. In some cases, they may be dried versions of beans and peas that are also available fresh, canned, or frozen.

Store dried legumes in a cool, dry, well-ventilated area. Before using, discard any beans or peas that appear moldy, damp, or wrinkled. It should be noted that as beans age they will take longer to cook.

Table 10-2 includes a description, common purchase forms, and major uses for the most common dried legumes. Figure 10-3 shows various kinds.

10-2

Grains: *(top row, from left to right)* long-grain brown rice, wild rice, kasha; *(middle row, from left to right)* short-grain rice, barley, quinoa; *(bottom row, from left to right)* cracked wheat (bulgur), brown rice, couscous.

10-3

Dried legumes: *(top row from left to right)* yellow split peas, Great Northern beans, kidney beans; *(middle row, from left to right)* pinto beans, brown lentils, black-eyed peas; *(bottom row from left to right)* green split peas, navy beans, and black beans.

TABLE 10-2. DRIED LEGUMES

Name	French and Italian Names	Description	Purchase Form	Uses
Beans	*Feves/haricots; fagioli*			
Adzuki (azuki)		Small, reddish-brown with white ridge on one side; slightly sweet flavor	Dried	Oriental dishes
Black (turtle)		Shiny, brownish-black; medium-sized; rounded kidney shape	Dried, canned	Mexican dishes
Black-eyed Pea (pigeon pea)		Cream-colored with black patch around hilum; medium-sized; kidney-shaped	Fresh, dried, or canned	Caribbean, soul food, and Southern dishes (including Hoppin' John)
Cannelini (white kidney beans)	*Haricots blancs; cannelini*	Medium-sized; white; smooth, long, kidney-shaped; a type of haricot	Dried, canned	Soups, Italian dishes
Chickpea	*Pois chiche; ceci;* Spanish: *garbanzo*	Medium-sized, acorn-shaped, light tan to brown	Dried, canned	Middle Eastern and Mediterranean dishes, salads
Fava (broad bean)	*Faba;* N/A	Large; flat; brown	Raw, dried	Mediterranean dishes (including falafel)

(continued)

TABLE 10-2. DRIED LEGUMES *(continued)*

Name	French and Italian Names	Description	Purchase Form	Uses
Flageolet	*Flageolet*	Medium-sized; smooth, flat oval; green or white; a type of haricot	Dried	
Kidney	*Haricot rouge; fagiole rosso*	Long, curved (kidney-shaped); pink to brown	Dried, canned	Mexican dishes, chili, salads
Lima	Butter bean	Medium-sized; flat; white, light-green	Canned, frozen	Side dishes, including succotash
Mung		Small, round; green or yellow	Fresh or dried; whole, skinless, split, sprouted	Oriental dishes
Navy		Small; smooth, rounded; white; a type of haricot	Dried, canned	Soups, baked beans
Pigeon Pea		Small; nearly round; off-white with orange-brown mottling	Dried, canned	African, Indian, and Caribbean dishes
Pinto	*Borlotti*	Medium-sized; kidney-shaped; mottled pink	Dried, canned	Latin American dishes, including refried beans, Italian *pasta e fagioli*
Soissons	*Soissons*	Medium-sized; oval; white; a type of haricot	Dried	Cassoulet
Soy	*Soya/soja; seme di soia*	Medium-sized; rounded; black or yellow	Fresh or dried; salted, fermented, soy sauce, other (see below)	Oriental dishes
Bean Products Bean Paste, Soy		Thick sauce of fermented soybeans, flour, and salt	Bottled or canned, whole and ground beans	Oriental dishes
Bean Paste, Hot		Soybean paste with crushed chili peppers	Bottled or canned	Oriental dishes
Bean paste, sweet/red		Pureed red beans and sugar	Bottled or canned	Sweet Oriental dishes (such as dumplings)
Miso		Japanese soybean paste	Foil pouches, jar	Japanese soups and sauces
Tofu (Soybean Curd)		Off-white; soft, curdled bean protein	Cakes, packed in water or pressed	Oriental dishes
Lentils	*Lentilles; lenticchia*	Small, green, brown, yellow, orange, dark green (Puy)	Dried, canned soups	Soups, stews, side dishes, purees
Peas, Garden	*Pois; pisello*	Fresh: (see vegetables); dried: green or yellow, smooth or wrinkled	Fresh, frozen, dried, canned	Fresh/frozen: side dish, purees, soups, other; dried: soups, purees

DRIED PASTA AND NOODLES

Dried pasta is a valuable "convenience food." It stores well, cooks quickly, and comes in an extensive array of shapes, sizes, and flavors. This range of shapes and flavors provides a base for a number of preparations, from a simple spaghetti dish to Oriental and Middle Eastern specialties.

Pasta and noodles are made from a number of different flours and grains. Good-quality dried pastas from wheat flour are customarily made from durum semolina. Many pastas are flavored or colored with vegetables, such as spinach, peppers, or tomatoes. Table 10-3 includes the names, shapes, and common uses for various kinds of dried pasta and noodles.

TABLE 10-3. DRIED PASTA AND NOODLES

Name (Italian/English)	Description (Shape, Base Flour*)	Major dish(es)
Acini di pepe/Peppercorns	Tiny, pellet-shaped; wheat flour	Soups
Anelli/ Rings	Medium-small, ridged, tubular pasta cut in thin rings; wheat flour	Soups
Arrowroot Vermicelli	Very thin, Chinese noodles; arrowroot starch dough enriched with egg yolks	Oriental dishes
Cannelloni/Large Pipes	Large cylinders	Stuffed with cheese or meat, sauced, and baked
Capellini/Hair	Very fine, solid, cylindrical; the finest is *capelli d'angelo* (angel's hair); wheat flour	With oil, butter, tomato, seafood, or other thin sauce; soup
Cavatappi/Corkscrews	Medium-thin, hollow, ridged pasta twisted into a spiral and cut into short lengths; wheat flour	With medium and hearty sauces
Cellophane Noodles	Very thin, transparent noodles; in bunches or compressed bundles; mung bean starch	Oriental dishes: fried crisp for garnish, boiled for lo mein
Conchiglie/Shells	Large or medium, ridged shell shape; *conchigliette* are small shells; wheat flour	Filled with meat or cheese and baked; *conchigliette*: soups
Cresti di Gallo/Cocks' Combs	Ridged, hollow, elbow-shaped noodles with a ruffled crest along one edge; wheat flour	With hearty sauces
Ditali/Thimbles	Narrow tubes cut in short lengths; *ditalini* are tiny thimbles; wheat flour	With medium-texture sauces; *ditalini*: soups
Egg Flakes	Tiny, flat squares; wheat flour	Soups
Egg Noodles	Usually ribbons in varying widths; may be cut long or short, packaged loose or in compressed bundles; may have spinach or other flavorings; wheat flour dough enriched with egg yolks	Buttered, casseroles, some sauces, rings, and puddings
Elbow Macaroni	Narrow, curved tubes cut in short lengths (about 1 inch); wheat flour	Macaroni and cheese, casseroles
Farfalle/Butterflies	Flat, rectangular noodles pinched in center to resemble butterfly or bow; may have crimped edges; *farfallini* are tiny butterflies	With medium or hearty sauces; baked; *farfallini*: soups
Fettuccine	Long, flat, ribbon-shaped, about ¼ inch wide; wheat flour	With medium heavy, rich sauces (e.g., alfredo)
Fiochetti/Bows	Rectangles of flat pasta curled up and pinched slightly in the center to form bow shapes	With medium and hearty sauces
Fusilli/Twists	Long, spring- or corkscrew-shaped strands; thicker than spaghetti	With tomato and other medium-thick sauces

* Where base flour is listed as wheat, usually durum semolina is used. Wheat pastas may be made from other flours, including whole wheat and buckwheat, and they may be flavored with vegetable and/or herb purees.

(continued)

TABLE 10-3. DRIED PASTA AND NOODLES *(continued)*

Name (Italian/English)	Description (Shape, Base Flour*)	Major dish(es)
Lasagne	Large, flat noodles about 3 inches wide; usually with curly edges; wheat flour	Baked with sauce, cheese, and meat or vegetables
Linguine	Thin, slightly flattened, solid strands, about ⅛ inch wide; wheat flour	With oil, butter, marinara, or other thin sauces
Maccheroni/Macaroni	Thin, tubular pasta in various widths; may be long like spaghetti or cut into shorter lengths	With medium and hearty sauces
Mafalde	Flat, curly-edged, about ¾ inch wide; sometimes called *lasagnette* or *malfadine*; wheat flour	Sauced and baked
Manicotti/Small Muffs	Thick, ridged tubes; may be cut straight or on an angle; wheat flour	Filled with meat or cheese and baked
Mostaccioli/Small Mustaches	Medium-sized tubes with angle-cut ends; may be ridged *(rigati)*; wheat flour	With hearty sauces
Orecchiette/Ears	Smooth, curved rounds of flat pasta; about ½ inch in diameter; wheat flour	With oil and vegetable sauces or any medium sauce; soups
Orzo/Barley	Tiny, grain-shaped; wheat flour	Soups
Pastina/Tiny Pasta	Miniature pasta in any of various shapes, including stars, rings, alphabets, seeds/teardrops	Soups, buttered (as side dish or cereal for children)
Penne/Quills or Pens	Same as mostaccioli	With hearty sauces
Rice Noodles	Noodles in various widths (up to about ⅛ inch); rice sticks are long, straight ribbons; rice vermicelli is very thin; rice flour	Oriental dishes
Rigatoni	Thick, ridged tubes cut in lengths of about 1½ inches	With hearty sauces; baked
Rotelle/Wheels	Spiral-shaped; wheat flour	With medium or hearty sauces
Ruote/Cartwheels	Small, round, 6-spoked wheels; *ruotini* are small wheels; wheat flour	With hearty sauces; *ruotini:* soups
Soba (Japanese)	Noodles the approximate shape and thickness of *fedeli* or *taglarini*; buckwheat flour	Oriental dishes, including soups, hot and cold noodle dishes
Somen (Japanese)	Long, thin, noodles; resemble *tagliarini*; wheat flour	Oriental dishes, including soup
Spaghetti/Little Strings	Solid, round strands ranging from very thin to thin; very thin spaghetti may be labeled *spaghettini*; wheat flour	With oil, butter, marinara, seafood, or other thin sauces
Tagliatelli	Same as fettuccine; may be mixed plain and spinach noodles, called *paglia e fieno* (straw and hay)	With rich, hearty sauces
Tubetti lunghi/Long Tubes	Medium-small (usually about as thick as elbow macaroni), tubular, may be long or cut in lengths of about an inch; *tubettini* are tiny tubes	With medium and hearty sauces; *tubettini:* soups
Udon (Japanese)	Thick noodles, similar to somen; wheat flour	Oriental dishes
Vermicelli	Very fine cylindrical pasta, similar to capellini; wheat flour	With oil, butter, or light sauce
Ziti/Bridegrooms	Medium-sized tubes; may be ridged *(rigati)*; may be long or cut in approximately 2-inch lengths *(ziti tagliate)*; wheat flour	With hearty sauces; baked

* Where base flour is listed as wheat, usually durum semolina is used. Wheat pastas may be made from other flours, including whole wheat and buckwheat, and they may be flavored with vegetable and/or herb purees.

SUGARS, SYRUPS, AND OTHER SWEETENERS

Once a symbol of wealth and prosperity, sugar is now so commonplace and inexpensive that it takes a good deal of effort to avoid using it. Sugar is extracted from plant sources (sugar beet or sugar cane) and then refined into the desired form. Most syrups (maple syrup, corn syrup, molasses, and honey) are also derived from plants.

Table sugar has a number of important roles in the kitchen and bakeshop, in addition to being required on the table to sweeten beverages.

Syrups and other sweeteners, such as honey and sugar substitutes, may also be necessary, depending on a particular kitchen's menu and the guests' needs. Table 10-4 lists many sweeteners, a description of each, and their possible purchase forms.

COFFEE, TEA, AND OTHER BEVERAGES

A good cup of coffee or tea is often the key to a restaurant's reputation. The chef should identify brands and blends that best serve the establishment's specific needs. Whereas some operations prefer to select whole coffee beans, others may be better served by buying preground, portioned, vacuum-packed coffee. Many restaurants serve brewed, decaffeinated coffee, and some offer espresso and cappuccino, regular and decaffeinated.

Teas come in many varieties, including decaffeinated and herbal teas. Most are blends and are available in single-serving bags or in loose form.

Although coffee and tea generally keep well, they will lose a lot of flavor if stored too long or under improper conditions. Whole beans or opened containers of ground coffee should be kept cool (ideally, refrigerated); teas should be stored in cool, dry areas, away from light and moisture.

Prepared mixes (powdered fruit drinks or cocoa mixes, for example) also should be kept moisture-free. Frozen juices and other beverages should remain solidly frozen until needed. Canned juices should be kept in dry storage. Remember to rotate stock, and check all cans, boxes, and other containers for leaks, bulges, or mold.

TABLE 10-4. SUGARS, SYRUPS, AND OTHER SWEETENERS

Name	French and Italian Names	Description	Purchase Form
Sugar	*Sucre; zucchero*		
Brown	*Cassonade*	Granular, refined sugar with some impurities left in or some molasses added; light to medium brown; moister than white sugar; slight molasses flavor	Bulk
Muscovado		Granular, brown sugar, which has undergone little processing; soft and moist; dark brown with pronounced molasses flavor	Bulk
Demerara	*Cassonade à gros cristaux*	Partially refined sugar in large crystals, golden brown, dissolves slowly	Bulk
Turbinado		Coarse granular sugar that is slightly more refined than demerara sugar; golden	Bulk
White, Coarse/ Preserving		Pure, refined sugar in large crystals; dissolves slowly	Bulk
White, Granulated, 4X	*Sucre cristallisé; zucchero cristallizzato*	Pure, refined sugar in small, evenly sized crystals	Bulk, packets
White, Superfine/ Bar, 6X	*Sucre en poudre; zucchero semolato*	Pure, refined sugar in very small crystals; dissolves quickly	Bulk

(continued)

TABLE 10-4. SUGARS, SYRUPS, AND OTHER SWEETENERS *(continued)*

Name	French and Italian Names	Description	Purchase Form
White, Confectioners, 10X		Very finely powdered, pure refined sugar; usually mixed with a small amount of cornstarch to prevent clumping	Bulk
White, Lump/Cube	*Sucre cassée*	Pure, refined, granulated sugar pressed into small cubes or tablets	Cubes
Molasses	*Mélasse; molassa*	Thick, dark-brown liquid by-product of sugar refining; rich flavor but less sweet than sugar (types: sulfured, unsulfured, blackstrap)	Bulk
Honey	*Miel; miele*	Thick, pale-straw to deep-brown liquid (creamed honeys are moist and granular); may be packaged with honeycomb, whole or in pieces; sweeter than sugar	Bulk, packets
Syrup Corn	*Sirop; sciroppo*	Liquified sugar extracted from corn; less sweet than sugar [types: light (pale yellow) and dark (deep amber)]	Bulk
Maple	*Sirop d'erable; sciroppo d'acero*	Liquified sugar made from the concentrated sap of the sugar maple, golden brown	Bulk
Treacle	*Mélasse; melassa*	A liquid by-product of refining, not widely used in the United States; light or dark, flavor resembles molasses	Bulk
Flavored		Sugar or other syrup with added flavoring [common types: cassis (black currant), grenadine (pomegranate), maple]	Bulk, packets

DRY GOODS FOR BAKING

Chocolate

Chocolate is produced from beans, known as cocoa beans, which grow in a pod on the cacao tree. For the ancient Aztecs, cocoa beans served not only to produce drinks and as a component of various sauces, but also as currency. Today the word "chocolate" usually applies to sweets—cakes, candies, and other desserts—although it is also used in a variety of savory entrées, such as *mole poblano*, a chocolate chicken dish of Spanish origin.

The chocolate extraction process is lengthy, and has undergone a great deal of refinement since the days of the Aztecs. The first stage involves crushing the kernel into a paste, completely unsweetened, called chocolate liquor. The liquor is then further ground to give it a smoother, finer texture, and sweeteners and other ingredients may be added. The liquor may be pressed, causing cocoa butter to be forced out. The cocoa solids that are left are ground into cocoa powder. Cocoa butter may be combined with chocolate liquor to make eating chocolates or it may

be flavored and sweetened to make "white chocolate." Table 10-5 lists the various kinds and forms of chocolate.

Chocolate should be stored, well-wrapped, in a cool, dry, ventilated area. Under most conditions it should not be refrigerated, since this could cause moisture to condense on the surface of the chocolate; if the weather is hot and humid, however, it may be preferable to refrigerate or freeze the chocolate to prevent loss of flavor. Sometimes stored chocolate develops a white coating, or bloom; the bloom merely indicates that some of the cocoa butter has melted and then recrystallized on the surface. If properly stored, chocolate will last for several months. Cocoa powder should be stored in tightly sealed containers in a dry place. It will keep almost indefinitely.

Leaveners

Leaveners are used to give foods a light, airy texture. Chemical leaveners, such as baking soda (sodium bicarbonate) and baking powder (a combination of baking soda, cream of tartar, and talc), work rapidly.

TABLE 10-5. CHOCOLATE AND RELATED PRODUCTS

Type	Description	Purchase Form
Chocolate liquor	The chocolate-flavored portion of chocolate; obtained by grinding and liquefying chocolate nibs	(See Chocolate, unsweetened)
Cocoa butter	The vegetable fat portion of chocolate; removed for cocoa; added for chocolate	Plastic at room temperature
Cocoa	Chocolate from which all but 10%–25% of the cocoa butter has been removed	Bulk and cans
Cocoa, Dutch process	Chocolate from which all but 22%–24% of the cocoa butter has been removed; treated with alkali to reduce its acidity	Bulk and cans
Cocoa, breakfast	Cocoa (above) with at least 22% cocoa butter	Bulk and cans
Cocoa, low-fat	Cocoa (above) with less than 10% cocoa butter	Bulk and cans
Cocoa, instant	Cocoa (above) that has been pre-cooked, sweetened (usually about 80% sugar), and emulsified to make it dissolve more easily in liquid; may have powdered milk added	Bulk and cans
Chocolate, unsweetened (bitter/baking)	Solid chocolate made with about 95% chocolate liquor, 5% cocoa butter, and 5% sugar and other flavorings	Blocks or bars
Chocolate, bittersweet	Solid chocolate made with 35%–50% chocolate liquor, 15% cocoa butter, and 35%–50% sugar; interchangeable with semi-sweet chocolate; may have added ingredients, such as nuts, fillings, stabilizers, emulsifiers, and/or preservatives	Blocks, bars, chunks, and chips
Chocolate, semi-sweet	Solid chocolate made with about 45% chocolate liquor, 15% cocoa butter, and 40% sugar; interchangeable with bittersweet chocolate; may have added ingredients (see above)	Blocks, bars, chunks, and chips
Chocolate, sweet	Solid chocolate made with 15% chocolate liquor, 15% cocoa butter, and 70% sugar; may have added ingredients (see above)	Blocks, bars, chunks, and chips
Chocolate, milk	Solid chocolate made with 10% chocolate liquor, 20% cocoa butter, 50% sugar, and 15% milk solids; may have added ingredients (see above)	Blocks, bars, chunks, and chips
Chocolate, coating (couverture)	Solid chocolate with 15% chocolate liquor, 35% cocoa butter, and 50% sugar; high-fat content makes it ideal for coating candy, pastries, and cakes	Blocks, bars, chunks, and chips
Confectionery, coating	Solid, artificial chocolate made with vegetable fat other than cocoa butter; usually contains real chocolate flavoring in chocolate-flavored types; other flavors available	Blocks, bars, chunks, and chips
Chocolate, white	Solid chocolate made with cocoa butter or other vegetable fats, sugar, milk solids, and vanilla flavoring; contains no chocolate liquor; may contain artificial yellow color and/or other added ingredients (see above)	Blocks, bars, chunks, and chips
Chocolate syrup	Chocolate or cocoa, sugar and/or other sweeteners, water, salt, other flavorings	Bulk, bottles, and cans
Chocolate sauce	Same as chocolate syrup but thicker; may have added milk, cream, butter, and/or other thickeners	Bulk, bottles, and cans
Carob	A dark-brown, somewhat chocolate-like flavoring produced from the carob bean; unsweetened carob is somewhat sweet, so it requires less added sugar than chocolate (about ¾ usual amount)	Blocks, bars, chunks, and powder

Baking powder is usually double acting, which means that one reaction happens in the presence of moisture, when liquids are added to dry ingredients, and a second occurs in the presence of heat, as the item bakes in the oven.

Yeast also leavens foods, by the process of fermentation, which produces alcohol and carbon dioxide. The gas creates a number of small pockets, and the alcohol burns off during baking.

Chemical leaveners should be kept perfectly dry. Dried yeast can be held for extended periods, but fresh yeast has a short shelf life of only a few weeks under refrigeration.

Thickeners

Thickeners are used to give a liquid a certain amount of viscosity. The process of forming an emulsion is one way to thicken a liquid, as is the process of reduction. In addition, various thickening ingredients can be used. These include the following:

• Arrowroot is a starchy root that is ground and highly refined. A lesser amount of arrowroot than of cornstarch may be used to achieve the same degree of thickening.
• Cornstarch is a refined, finely ground corn flour.
• Filé gumbo powder, which is powdered sassafras root, is used in Cajun and Creole cookery.
• Gelatin is a protein that, when properly combined with a liquid, will cause the liquid to gel as it cools. It is available in powdered form and in sheets.

Thickeners should be stored in tightly sealed containers in dry storage. They will keep almost indefinitely.

Extracts and Other Flavorings

The chef uses a variety of flavorings for cooking and baking. They may be either extracts, which are alcohol-based, or emulsions, which are oil-based. Herbs, spices, nuts, and fruits are used to prepare both extracts and emulsions. Common flavors include vanilla, lemon, mint, and almond.

Alcohol-based extracts can lose their potency if they are allowed to come in contact with air, heat, or light. To preserve flavor, store in tightly capped dark jars or bottles away from heat or direct light. Oil-based emulsions are more stable, but should also be stored in cool, well-ventilated areas in tightly capped jars or bottles to preserve freshness and flavor.

NUTS AND SEEDS

With the exception of the peanut, which grows underground in the root system of a leguminous plant, nuts are the fruits of various trees. They are available in various forms—in the shell, roasted, shelled, blanched, sliced, slivered, chopped, and as butters.

Nuts have a number of culinary uses, adding a special flavor and texture to dishes. They are relatively expensive and should be stored carefully to keep them from becoming rancid. Nuts that have not been roasted or shelled will keep longer. Shelled nuts may be stored in the freezer or cooler, if space allows. In any case, they should be stored in a cool, dry, well-ventilated area and checked periodically to be sure they are still fresh. Table 10-6 lists commonly available nuts and seeds.

Some of the seeds used in the kitchen are considered spices (celery or fennel seed, for example), and others, including sesame seeds and poppy seeds, are covered in Table 10-6. Seeds are usually available whole or as a paste and should be stored in the same manner as nuts.

OILS AND SHORTENINGS

Oils are produced by pressing a high-oil-content food such as olives, nuts, corn, avocados, or soybeans. The oil then may be filtered, clarified, or hydrogenated in order to produce an oil or shortening that has the appropriate characteristics for its intended use.

The hydrogenation process causes the oil to remain solid at room temperature, when it is known as shortening. A shortening labeled "vegetable shortening" is made from vegetable oil, whereas one labeled just "shortening" may contain animal products.

Several different oils and shortenings are required in every kitchen. Oils for salads and other cold dishes should be of the best possible quality, with a perfectly fresh flavor. First pressings of olive oil or nut oils are often chosen for these purposes, because of their delicate flavors.

Cooking oils may have a neutral flavor; those used for frying should have a high smoking point as well. Shortenings used for baking should also be neutral in flavor.

Oils and shortenings should be stored in dry storage away from extremes of heat and light. Table 10-7 lists commonly available oils and shortenings and their accepted uses. Table 10-8 displays selected fats and oils and their melting and smoking points.

TABLE 10-6. NUTS AND SEEDS

Name	French and Italian Names	Description	Purchase Form
Almond	*Amande; mandorla*	Teardrop-shaped seed of a fruit that resembles the apricot. Pale-tan, woody shell. Bitter and sweet types available. Bitter require cooking; sweet may be used raw or cooked.	Whole in shell; shelled: whole, blanched, slivered, ground, almond paste, other products
Brazil	*Noix du Bresil; noce del Brasile*	Large, oval nut; grows in clusters of segments. Each segment is a hard, wrinkled, three-sided, brown seed containing the rich nut.	Whole in shell; shelled
Cashew	*Noix d'acajou; anacardio*	Kidney-shaped nut that grows as the appendage of an apple-like fruit, which is not usually eaten. It is always sold hulled, as its skin contains irritating oils similar to those in poison ivy.	Shelled; raw or toasted
Chestnut	*Marron; marrone*	Fairly large, round to teardrop-shaped nut; hard, glossy, dark-brown shell.	Raw (whole in shell); canned: whole in water or syrup, pureed
Coconut	*Noix de coco; cocco*	Melon-sized fruit that grows on a type of palm. The woody, brown seed is covered with hairy fibers and surrounds a layer of rich, white nutmeat. The inside of the nut is hollow and contains thin, white juice (coconut water).	Whole in shell, flaked (may be sweetened), coconut cream, other products
Hazelnut or filbert	*Noisette; avellane/nocciola*	Small, nearly round nut; shiny, hard shell with matte spot where cap was attached. Nutmeat rich and delicately flavored.	Whole in shell; shelled: whole, chopped
Macadamia		Nearly round, rich, sweet nut native to Australia.	Shelled and roasted in coconut oil
Peanut or goober	*Cacahouette; arachide*	Seed grows inside a fibrous pod among the roots of a leguminous plant.	Whole in shell; shelled: whole, skinned; raw or roasted; peanut butter
Pecan		Medium-brown, smooth, glossy, oval-shaped shell. Two-lobed nutmeat has a rich flavor.	Whole in shell; shelled: halved, chopped
Pine nut	*Pomme de pin; pinoli/pignoli*	Tiny, cream-colored, elongated kernel is the seed of a Mediterranean pine. Fairly perishable.	Shelled: raw or toasted
Pistachio	*Pistache; pistacchio*	Cream-colored shell; green nutmeat with distinctive, sweet flavor.	Whole in shell: roasted, usually salted, natural or dyed red; occasionally shelled, chopped
Poppy seeds		Tiny, round, blue-black seeds with a rich, slightly musty flavor.	Whole
Pumpkin seeds		Flat, oval, cream-colored seeds with semi-hard hull and soft, oily interior	Whole in shell; shelled; raw or toasted
Sesame seeds	*Sésame*	Tiny, flat, oval seeds; may be black (unhulled) or tan (hulled); oily with rich, nutty flavor.	Whole: hulled or unhulled; paste *(tahini)*

(continued)

TABLE 10-6. NUTS AND SEEDS *(continued)*

Name	French and Italian Names	Description	Purchase Form
Sunflower seeds		Small, somewhat flat, teardrop-shaped seeds;. oily, light-tan seed with woody, black-and-white shell; grown primarily for oil	Whole in shell; shelled
Walnut	*Noix; noce*	Mild, tender, oily nutmeat; grows in convoluted segments inside hard, light-brown shell. White walnuts, or butternuts, and black walnuts are North American varieties. Butternuts are richer and black walnuts stronger in flavor.	Whole in shell; shelled: halved, chopped; pickled (whole)

TABLE 10-7. OILS AND SHORTENINGS

Name	Description/Uses	Name	Description/Uses
Butter-flavored oils	Vegetable oils (usually blended) flavored with real or artificial butter flavor for use on griddles.	Oil sprays	Vegetable oils (usually blended) packaged in pump or aerosol sprays for lightly coating pans, griddles.
Canola oil	A light, golden-colored oil, similar to safflower oil. Low in saturated fat. Multi-purpose.	Peanut oil	A pale-yellow refined oil, with a very subtle scent and flavor. Some less refined types are darker with a more pronounced peanut flavor. These are used primarily in Oriental cooking.
Coconut oil	A heavy, nearly colorless oil extracted from fresh coconuts. Used primarily in blended oils and shortenings. Health concerns have caused a reduction in the use of coconut oil, which is high in saturated fats.	Rapeseed oil	Extracted from the seeds of a variety of turnip (the same plant as the vegetable broccoli rab). Used in salads and cooking, mostly in the Mediterranean region and India; also used in margarine and blended vegetable oils.
Corn oil	A mild-flavored refined oil. It is medium-yellow colored, inexpensive, and versatile.		
Cottonseed oil	This pale-yellow oil is extracted from the seed of the cotton plant.	Safflower oil	A golden-colored oil with a light texture. Made from a plant that resembles the thistle. Usually refined.
Frying fats	Blended oils or shortenings (usually based on processed corn or peanut oils) designed for high smoke point and long fry life. May be liquid or plastic at room temperature.	Salad oil	Mild-flavored vegetable oils blended for use in salad dressings, mayonnaise, etc.
Grapeseed oil	This light, medium-yellow, aromatic oil is a by-produce of wine making. It is used in salads and some cooking and in the manufacture of margarine.	Sesame oil	Two types: a light, very mild, Middle Eastern type and a darker, Oriental type pressed from toasted sesame seeds. Oriental sesame oil may be light or dark brown. The darker oil has a more pronounced sesame flavor and aroma. Oriental sesame oil has a low smoke point so it is used primarily as a flavoring rather than in cooking.
Lard	Solid animal fat. May be treated (deodorized) to neutralize flavor.		
Olive oil	Oil varies in weight and may be pale-yellow to deep-green, depending on fruit used and processing. Cold-pressed olive oil is superior to refined. Oil from the first pressing, called "virgin" olive oil, is the most flavorful. Also classified according to acidity: extra-virgin, superfine, fine, virgin, and pure, in ascending degree of acidity. "Pure" olive oil, and that labeled just "olive oil" may be a combination of cold-pressed and refined oil.	Shortening/Baking fat	Blended oil solidified using various processes, including whipping in air and hydrogenation. Designed for plasticity and mild flavor. May have real or artificial butter flavor added. Usually emulsified to enable absorption of more sugar in baked goods. May contain animal fats unless labeled "vegetable shortening."

(continued)

TABLE 10-7. OILS AND SHORTENINGS *(continued)*

Name	Description/Uses	Name	Description/Uses
Soybean oil	A fairly heavy oil with a pronounced flavor and aroma. More soybean oil is produced than any other type. Used in most blended vegetable oils and margarines.	Vegetable oil	Made by blending several different refined oils. Designed to have a mild flavor and a high smoke point.
Sunflower oil	A light, odorless, and nearly flavorless oil pressed from sunflower seeds. Pale yellow and versatile.	Walnut oil	A medium-yellow oil with a nutty flavor and aroma. Cold-pressed from dried walnuts. More perishable than most other oils; should be used soon after purchase. Used primarily in salads.

VINEGARS AND CONDIMENTS

Vinegars and most condiments are used to introduce sharp, piquant, sweet, or hot flavors into foods. They may be used as an ingredient or served on the side, to be added according to a guest's taste. A well-stocked kitchen should include a full range of vinegars, mustards, relishes, pickles, olives, jams, and other condiments. In general, vinegars and condiments should be stored in the same manner as oils and shortenings.

DRIED HERBS AND SPICES

Many of the herbs discussed in Chapter 8, "Fruit, Vegetable, and Fresh Herb Identification," are also available in dried form. Some herbs, such as rosemary, sage, and bay leaves, dry successfully, whereas others will retain very little flavor.

Dried herbs are often stored incorrectly, which compounds the problem of flavor loss. They are often stored too close to the top of the range, are kept for

TABLE 10-8. SELECTED FATS AND OILS

Name	Uses	Melting Point	Smoking Point* (in degrees F)	Name	Uses	Melting Point	Smoking Point* (in degrees F)
Butter, whole	Baking, cooking	95	300	Peanut	Frying, margarine, salad dressings, shortening	28	440
Butter, clarified	Cooking	95	300				
Coconut	Coatings, confectionery, shortening	75	350	Safflower	Margarine, mayonnaise, salad dressings	2	510
Corn	Frying, salad dressings, shortening	12	450	Shortening: Emulsified, vegetable	Baking, frying, shortening	115	325
Cottonseed	Mayonnaise, salad dressing, shortening	55	420	Soybean	Margarine, salad dressings, shortening	−5	495
Frying fat	Frying	105	465				
Lard	Baking, cooking, specialty items	92	375	Sunflower	Cooking, margarine, salad dressings, shortening	2	440
Olive	Cooking, salad dressings	32	375				

* Note: The smoking point of any oil will be reduced after it is used for cooking.

too long, and are purchased in overly large quantities. A chef should buy only the amount of dried herbs that can be used within two or three months, and should store them away from heat. Herbs that have a musty or "flat" aroma should be discarded. If at all possible, the chef should try to find fresh herbs.

Spices are aromatics produced primarily from the bark and seeds of plants. Most spices' flavors are quite intense and powerful. Spices are nearly always sold in dried form and may be available whole or ground. In addition, the chef may use spice blends, such as curry powder, quatre épices, chili powder, and pickling spice.

Whole spices will keep longer than ground spices, although most spices will retain their potency for about six months if they are properly stored. They should be kept in sealed containers in a cool, dry spot, away from extreme heat and direct light. Check spices from time to time to be sure they are still potent, discarding any that have lost their flavor or have become stale or musty smelling. For optimum flavor,

purchase whole spices and grind them as close as possible to the time they are to be used.

Table 10-9 lists commonly available spices and appropriate uses for each.

SALT AND PEPPER

Salt was once one of the most prized of all seasonings. The expression "below the salt" shows its importance as an indicator of class differences. The nobles, who sat at the head of the table ("above the salt") were allowed to use salt; the lesser folk, sitting "below the salt," relied on herbs to flavor their food. Salt is today readily available in numerous forms, as shown in Table 10-10.

Pepper was at one time the single most expensive seasoning in the world. Today, most kitchens require a number of different peppers for different uses. Not all of the peppers listed in Table 10-10 are related botanically; however, they all share a pungent, fiery

TABLE 10-9. SPICES

Product	Uses/Affinities	Product	Uses/Affinities
Allspice	Braises, forcemeats, fish, pickles, desserts	Fenugreek	Curries, meat, poultry, chutney
Anise	Desserts and other baked goods, liqueur	Ginger	Fresh: Oriental dishes, curries, braises Ground dry: Some desserts and baked goods
Caraway	Rye bread, pork, cabbage, soups, stews, some cheeses, liqueur (*Kümmel*)	Horseradish	Sauces (for beef, chicken, fish), egg salad, potatoes, beets
Cardamom	Curries, some baked goods, pickling	Juniper	Marinades, braises (especially game), sauerkraut, gin, and liqueurs
Cayenne	Sauces, soups, most meats, some fish and poultry	Mace	Some forcemeats, pork, fish, spinach, other vegetables, pickles, desserts, and baked goods
Celery seed	Salads (including cole slaw), salad dressings, soups, stews, tomatoes, some baked goods	Mustard	Pickling, meats, sauces, cheese and eggs, prepared mustard
Chili powder	Chili and other Mexican dishes, curries	Nutmeg	Sauces and soups (especially cream), veal, chicken, aspics, spinach, mushrooms, potatoes, other vegetables, desserts (especially custards), baked goods
Cinnamon	Desserts, some baked goods, sweet potatoes, hot beverages, curries, pickles, and preserves	Paprika	Braises and stews (including goulash), sauces, garnish
Cloves	Stocks, sauces, braises, marinades, curries, pickling, desserts, some baked goods	Pepper	Stocks, sauces, meats, vegetables, universal seasoning
Coriander seeds	Curries, some forcemeats, pickling, some baked goods	Saffron	Poultry, seafood, rice pilafs, sauces, soups, some baked goods
Cumin	Curries, chili, and other Mexican dishes	Star anise	Oriental dishes, especially pork and duck
Dill seeds	Pickling, sauerkraut	Turmeric	Curries, sauces, pickling, rice
Fennel seeds	Sausage, fish and shellfish, tomatoes, some baked goods, marinades		

TABLE 10-10. SALT AND PEPPER

Name	Description	Name	Description
Salt		Pepper	
Rock salt	An unrefined, coarse salt not added directly to foods but used in some ice-cream machines.	Black peppercorns	Available as whole berries, cracked, or ground. The Telicherry peppercorn is one of the most prized. Mignonette or shot pepper is a combination of coarsely ground or crushed black and white peppercorns.
Table salt	All-purpose salt made by grinding refined rock salt into fine crystals. May be fortified with iodine and treated with magnesium carbonate to prevent clumping.	White peppercorns	Black peppercorns are allowed to ripen and then husks are removed. May be preferred for pale or lightly colored sauces. Available in same form as black peppercorns.
Sea salt	Made by allowing sea water to evaporate, leaving behind salt crystals. Available refined or unrefined, in whole crystals or ground. In its unrefined state, it may be known as *sel gris*, French for "gray salt."	Green peppercorns	Unripe peppercorns that are packed in vinegar or brine; also available freeze-dried (they must be reconstituted in water before use).
Kosher salt	Pure refined rock salt, also known as "coarse salt" or "pickling salt." Because it does not contain magnesium carbonate, it will not cloud items to which it is added. Kosher salt is required for "koshering" foods that must meet Jewish dietary guidelines.	Cayenne	A special type of chili, originally grown in Cayenne in French Guiana. The chili is dried and ground into a fine powder. The same chili is used to make hot pepper sauces.
Curing salt	A blend of 94% salt and 6% sodium nitrite. Used in a variety of charcuterie items, especially those to be cold-smoked. Usually dyed pink to differentiate it from other salts. Saltpeter, which is potassium nitrate, is occasionally used in place of curing salt.	Chili flakes	Dried, whole red chili peppers that are crushed or coarsely ground.
MSG (monosodium glutamate)	A flavor enhancer, without a distinct flavor of its own. Associated with the "Chinese Restaurant Syndrome," MSG causes severe allergic reactions in some people.	Paprika	A powder made from dried sweet peppers (pimientos). Available as mild, sweet, or hot. Hungarian paprikas are considered superior in flavor.

flavor and aroma. Freshly ground pepper is preferable, because it is more pungent and has a fresher flavor.

Salt and pepper should be stored in dry storage, away from moisture. In very humid weather, salt may cake together; mixing a few grains of rice in with the salt will help to prevent this. Whole peppercorns will retain their flavor indefinitely, releasing it only when crushed or ground. Check ground or cracked pepper for pungency if its age is in question.

WINES, CORDIALS, AND LIQUEURS

A general rule of thumb for selecting wines, cordials, and liqueurs for use in cooking and baking is this: If

it is not suitable for drinking, it is not suitable for cooking.

Among the common ones used in the kitchen are brandies and cognacs, champagne, dry red and white wines, port, sauternes, sherry, stouts, ales, beers, and sweet and dry vermouth. For baking purposes, the chef should keep on hand bourbon, cassis, fruit brandies, gin, Kahlua, rum, and scotch. Items listed for the kitchen can, of course, be used in the bakeshop, and vice versa.

Purchase wines and cordials that are affordably priced and of good quality. Table wines (burgundies, chablis, and chardonnays, for example) lose their flavor and become acidic once opened, especially when subjected to heat, light, and air. To preserve flavor, keep them in closed bottles or bottles fitted with pouring spouts, and refrigerate when not needed. Fortified wines (madeiras, sherries, and ports, for example) are more stable than table wines and can be held in dry storage if there is not enough room to refrigerate them. The same also applies to cordials, cognacs, and liqueurs.

PREPARED, CANNED, AND FROZEN FOODS

Each chef should determine how and when he or she may use convenience foods, depending upon the requirements and capabilities of the kitchen and the quality of the convenience foods available. It may make sense, for example, to purchase prepared and frozen doughs (puff pastry, brioche, phyllo dough), instead of producing them on the premises. Other commonly used convenience foods include frozen vegetables such as corn, peas, and spinach.

Canned products also have valid uses in the contemporary kitchen. Depending upon the season, some items may be of better quality than below-standard fresh produce and may provide the highest quality. An obvious example is canned tomatoes, which are often superior to out-of-season fresh tomatoes. Quality, determined by good taste, yield, price, and color, will vary from product to product. There are standard sizes for canned products, as shown in Figure 10-4. Figure 10-5 explains the names, sizes, volumes, and weights of these cans.

Other convenience foods that may have a place in the kitchen include mayonnaise and prepared bases. In all cases, remember to choose products that are of good quality.

For storage purposes, frozen goods should be kept solidly frozen until they are needed. Canned goods should be rotated on the shelves to assure that the "first in" is the "first out" (FIFO rule).

10-4

Standard can sizes.

CAN SIZES AND VOLUMES

Can #	Fluid Ounce Volume	Cups (approx. ½ pint)
6	4.75	½
303, also #1	15.6	2
303, cylinder	19.0	2⅓
2	19.9	2½
2, cylinder	23.0	3
2½	28.5	3½
5	56.0	7
10	103.7	12¾
1 gallon	128.0	16

To fill a #10 can, you would need approximately:
  2 x #5 cans
  3½ x #2½ cans
  6 x #303 cans, cylinder
  5½ x #2 cans
  6½ x #1 (or 303 regular)

10-5

Can sizes, volumes, and weights.

SUMMARY

The menu should be evaluated carefully to determine what sorts of dry goods will be required and what the appropriate parstock is. Overstocking is just as costly an error as not having a product on hand. No food is at its best when it has been stored for too long. Proper purchasing and storing procedures should be consistently applied to ensure that all items will be at their peak of flavor, appearance, and freshness.

Chapter 11

Meat Fabrication

Very few kitchens have enough refrigeration space to accommodate sides of beef, whole lambs, or entire veal legs. Nor are they usually equipped with band-saws and the other tools required for some types of butchering. The simple meat fabrication techniques presented in this chapter, however, are probably feasible for most chefs. The steps outlined here will enable the chef to refine the cuts obtained from the butcher. Fabrication is, therefore, essentially a fine-tuning of the raw product.

There are definite advantages to fabricating items on the premises. Purveyors may not always be able to cut meat exactly to specification or may be unsure of the exact definition of a particular menu term. For example, they may be familiar with the term "cutlet" but not have a clear idea of what a paillard is. For this reason, the ability to cut medallions, noisettes, paillards, and other "menu cuts" is a skill worth mastering. It also allows the chef to control portion size and to be sure that each portion's quality is the same each time—which is important to the establishment's reputation.

IMPORTANT POINTS

This chapter covers methods for fabricating all kinds of meats: beef, veal, lamb, pork, and large game. The general divisions of the animal —the loin, leg, rib, shoulder—are the same whether it's a leg of veal or lamb; the fabrication procedure for one applies to the others. For purposes of illustration only one method will be presented, except for tying a roast, where two will be illustrated.

Most of the included techniques do not require any special knowledge of the bones in a cut of meat or of the animal's overall anatomy, although reference to sections of Chapter 6, "Meats, Poultry, and Game Identification," will be helpful. Certain skills will undoubtedly take more time than others to learn. The chef should also keep in mind that although most trim can be used to prepare other kitchen items (soups, sauces, stocks, salads, and forcemeats, to name a few) more meat is available to sell if trim is kept to a minimum. Minimal equipment, essentially a sharp knife and a clean cutting board, is required for these techniques.

TYING A ROAST

This is one of the simplest and most frequently required types of meat fabrication. The chef uses this technique to ensure that the roast will be evenly cooked and that it will retain its shape after roasting. Although simple, the technique is often one of the most frustrating to learn. For one thing, knot tying is not always an easy thing to do. There are no awards given for neatness, however. As long as the string is taut enough to give the roast a compact shape without tying the meat too tightly, the result will be fine. There is one trick to keep in mind that will make initial attempts easier. Leave the string very long so that it will wrap easily around the entire diameter of the meat. In the second technique, the string is left attached to the spool, and is only cut when the entire roast is tied.

Both techniques illustrated here are appropriate for boneless or bone-in roast. The choice of technique is largely a matter of personal preference; some chefs find one method easier than the other. See Figures 11-1 and 11-2 for two ways to tie a roast. In both cases, a pork loin is used.

11-1 TYING A ROAST

(1) A length of string long enough to wrap completely around the meat is secured by passing it between the fingers and crossing one end over the other end of the string.

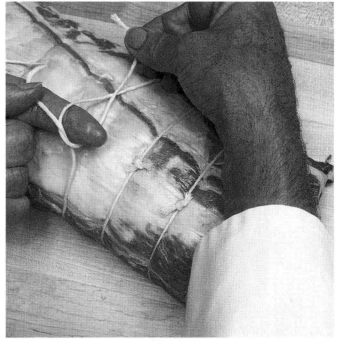

(2) Make a loop by passing the end not held between the fingers underneath the fingertip.

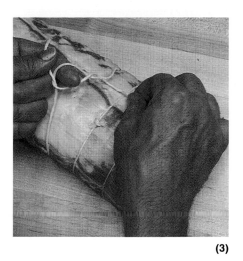

(3)

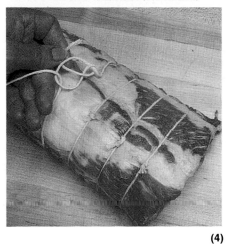

(4)

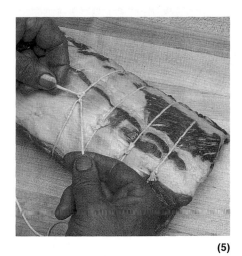

(5)

(3) Continuing the same motion, now loop the string back underneath itself.

(4) Still working with the same end of the string, pass the tail of the string back through the opening where the fingertip was.

(5) Pull both ends of the string to tighten well. The string should be pressing firmly against the meat.

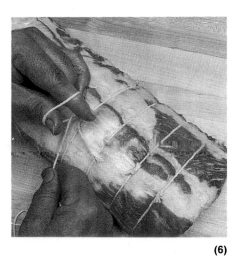

(6)

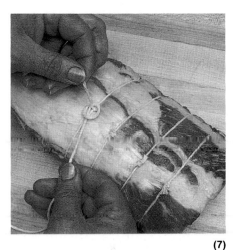

(7)

(6) Loop one end of the string completely around the thumb and forefinger, and pull the other end of the string through the loop. Hold the loop's tail firmly between the thumb and forefinger of the other hand.

(7) Pull both ends of the string to tighten securely. Trim any long string tails so that the knots are neat.

(8) Continue to knot lengths of string at even intervals until the entire piece of meat is securely tied.

(8)

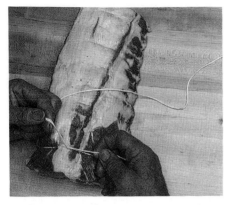

(1) Begin by tying the string around one end of the meat. Leave one end uncut. Any other knot that holds securely may be used.

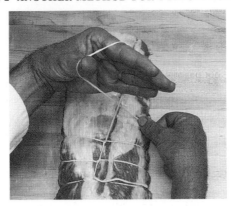

(2) Hold one hand over the meat. Pass the string around the outspread fingers and thumb so that the string comes from behind the fingers, then around the thumb, and back behind itself.

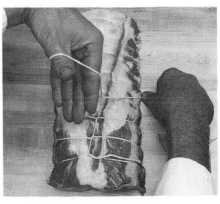

(3) Twist the loop around so that the base of the loop twists back on itself.

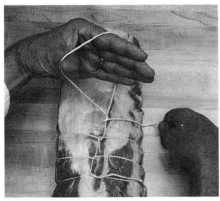

(4) The hand is now spread open so that the loop will enlarge.

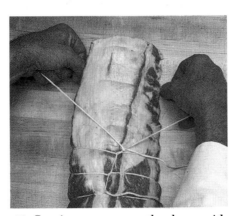

(5) Continue to open the loop wide enough so that it can pass easily around the meat, completely encircling it.

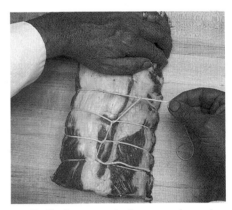

(6) Pull the string's loose end so that the loop is securely tightened around the meat. Continue until the entire piece of meat has been secured with loops.

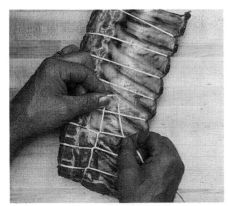

(7) Turn the piece of meat over. Pass the loose end of the string through the loop, then pass it back through underneath the loop. Pull the string tight and continue down the length of the meat.

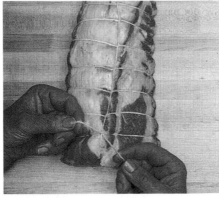

(8) Once the string has been wrapped around each loop from one end to the other, turn the meat back over. Cut the loose end and tie the string securely to the first loop.

(9) This shows the finished loin. Note that all of the loops are evenly spaced and that the meat is evenly shaped. This photo shows the side of the meat that would be placed down during roasting or braising.

TRIMMING AND BONING A PORK LOIN

A whole pork loin will often cost less per pound than a trimmed boneless loin. Removing the fat and bones is relatively easy, and the bones and any lean trim can then be roasted and used to prepare a rich brown jus or stock. It may take some time at first to learn how to properly trim and bone a roast. The novice should cut slowly, and be sure to stop and examine the roast between cuts. It is not necessary to remove the entire covering of fat with a single stroke. Pass the knife close to the bones, scraping them clean so that as little meat as possible is left on the bones. Use the tip of the knife to cut around joints and between bones, and the flat part of the blade for longer, sweeping strokes.

Once the loin, or any other suitable cut of meat, such as the top round or tenderloin, has been boned and trimmed, it can then be used to prepare a wide variety of menu cuts, including medallions, scallops, and *émincé*.

Medallions are small, round, medal-shaped pieces of meat cut most often from the tenderloin. Noisettes, so named because they are essentially little "nuts" of meat, are also cut from the tenderloin; in fact, the terms noisette and medallion are often used interchangeably to refer to a small, boneless, tender cut of meat. The term *grenadin* indicates a large cut from the loin.

When used in reference to meat, the term "scallop" means simply a thin boneless cut of meat which may come from the loin, the tenderloin, or any other sufficiently tender cut of meat, such as the top round. These cutlets are often pounded to insure an even thickness over their entire surface so that they can be rapidly sautéed or panfried. A *paillard* (derived from the French term for a straw bed) is a pounded cutlet that is grilled rather than sautéed or panfried. Figure 11-3 shows this procedure.

11-3 TRIMMING AND BONING A PORK LOIN

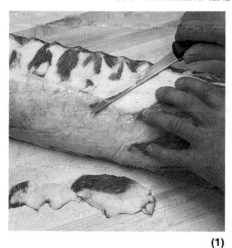

(1)

(2)

(1) Remove the excess fat covering the edge of the loin to expose the tips of the rib bones.

(2) Make smooth strokes along the bones to free the meat. Pull the meat away to make it easy to see.

(3)

(4)

(3) When all the meat is freed from one side of the bones, turn the loin over and free the meat from the other side. Here the tenderloin is being gently cut from the bones.

(4) The fully boned loin: tenderloin *(left)*, boned loin *(center)*, and bones *(right)*.

TRIMMING A TENDERLOIN

The loin is one of the most expensive cuts of meat, so care should be taken to leave the meat as intact as possible. The chef should use a very sharp knife and pay close attention to be sure that only silverskin, fat, and gristle are removed, not edible meat. It is important to completely remove the silverskin. This tough membrane, which gets its name from its translucent appearance and somewhat silvery color, tends to shrink when exposed to heat and could cause uneven cooking. A tenderloin of pork is shown in Figure 11-4 and a tenderloin of beef in Figure 11-5. The same techniques can be applied to veal and lamb tenderloins.

BUTTERFLYING MEATS

This technique creates a cut of meat that is thin enough to cook very rapidly, making it ideal for grilling or sautéing. A whole pork tenderloin that has been properly trimmed is shown in Figure 11-4. This same technique can be applied to thick cuts from the loin, tenderloin, and, in some cases, the leg. Be sure to remove all bones, silverskin, sinew, and gristle before butterflying the meat. Butterflied cuts of meat, including tenderloins, boneless poultry breasts, and legs of lamb, will very often taper from a thick "head" to a thin "tail." When this cut is opened and flattened (its shape similar to that of a butterfly), it is usually lightly pounded to achieve an even thickness for quick and even cooking. The meat, when cut, should be of an even thickness throughout.

11-4 TRIMMING AND BUTTERFLYING A PORK TENDERLOIN

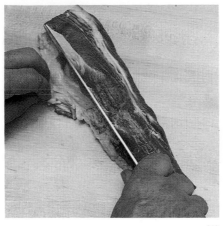
(1)

(2)

(1) Trim away all visible fat from the meat (here, pork). Be careful to trim only fat and not meat. Pulling the fat away from the meat will make it easy to see the line of separation.

(2) Use a sharp chef's knife to make an even cut through the meat's center, holding the blade parallel to the work surface. Use fingertips to gauge where the blade is.

(3) Open the piece of butterflied meat. It should be of an even thickness throughout.

(3)

11-5 TRIMMING AND CUTTING BEEF TENDERLOIN

(1) Work the tip of a boning knife under the silverskin; hold the end of the silverskin tight against the meat, and glide the knife blade just underneath. Angle the blade upward slightly so that only the silverskin is cut away.

(2) The trimmed tenderloin *(top row)*, along with a breakdown into some commonly used cuts—*(center row, from left to right)* châteaubriand, three pieces of filet mignon; *(bottom row, from left to right)* two medallions, tip of tenderloin.

SHAPING A MEDALLION

Cuts from the boneless loin or tenderloin of beef, veal, lamb, or pork may be known interchangeably as medallions, noisettes, or grenadins. Special terms that are generally used only in conjunction with beef tenderloin cuts include *tournédo* and *châteaubriand*.

Medallions are then wrapped in cheesecloth and molded to give them a compact, uniform shape. Not only does this give the meat a more pleasing appearance, but it also allows even and uniform cooking of the medallion. Figure 11-6 demonstrates shaping a medallion.

11-6 SHAPING A MEDALLION

(1) To make medallions, cut pieces of the desired size, generally between 3 and 7 ounces. Wrap the meat in a single layer of clean cheesecloth.

(2) Gather the cheesecloth and twist it slightly to begin to shape the meat.

(3) Use the flat side of a chef's knife to press the meat, while pulling the cheesecloth up and against the blade's dull edge.

(4) This photo clearly illustrates the benefits of shaping the tenderloin. The shaped piece *(right)*, is more attractive, but most important, the meat will cook more evenly.

CUTTING AND POUNDING SCALLOPS

There are a great many names for this cut. The term used is determined more by the type of dish being prepared than on the actual cut of meat. "Cutlet," *scallopine* (Italian), and *escalope* (French) are words for the same cut, in different languages, and are used as appropriate to the particular menu's style. In Figure 11-7, the side of a cleaver is used to pound the scallops; however, a small, heavy skillet or pot or a smooth, lightweight mallet could also be used. Be careful not to tear or overstretch the meat while pounding it. The technique is demonstrated here on a loin of veal.

CUTTING ÉMINCÉ

This French word translates as "minced," a good description of the cut (although different from the finely chopped vegetable cut). The strips are usually no more than ⅛ inch thick, ½ inch wide, and 1 to 2 inches long. The meat is generally sautéed, so the cut of meat used should be one of the most tender. A loin of veal is shown in Figure 11-8, but this same technique can be used for beef, lamb, or even pork. Be sure to trim the meat completely before cutting it into émincé.

FRENCHING A RACK OF LAMB

This technique is one of the more complicated covered in this chapter, although once it is understood it is not especially difficult to master. Trimmed and frenched racks or chops can be ordered from a meat purveyor if desired, but the chef can exercise greater control over the trim loss if this is done in

(1) Trim the meat completely, removing all visible fat, sinew, gristle, and silverskin. Cut pieces of approximately the same thickness and weight (ranging from 1 to 4 ounces, generally).

(2) Place the meat between two layers of plastic wrap. A pounding and pushing motion is used to make sure that the finished scallopini is evenly thinned. Increased surface area and decreased thickness promote rapid cooking.

the kitchen. This same technique can be used to french individual rib chops (lamb, veal, or pork). Any lean trim can be used to prepare au jus or saved for use in a stock. Figure 11-9 demonstrates this technique.

BONING A LEG OF VEAL

Although this procedure may look difficult, it is possible to do it successfully by following the natural "seams" in the meat as much as possible. These seams are formed between separate muscles. Cutting along the seams will produce the cuts shown in Figure 11-10. The chef should follow the seams all the way to the bones and should cut through the ligaments at the joint of the knuckle and leg bones.

DISJOINTING A RABBIT

Rabbit is a relatively lean, mildly flavored meat that can be used for a number of preparations. The loin

and rib sections tend to be dryer than the legs, in much the same way that the chicken breast can be drier than the legs. By first removing the legs and shoulder, as demonstrated in Figure 11-11, two different cooking methods can be applied to one rabbit—moist heat for the legs, dry heat for the loin— to achieve the most satisfactory results.

Cut the meat into evenly shaped pieces that are approximately 2 inches square. Use a sharp knife to cut away thin pieces, known as émincé.

11-9 FRENCHING A RACK OF LAMB

(1) Make an even cut about 3 inches from the meat's eye through the fat covering, all the way down to the bone.

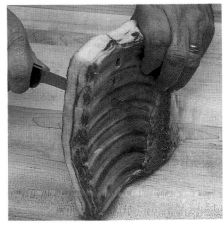

(2) Set the rack on one end and make a stabbing cut between each bone, using the initial cut as a guide.

(3) Use a boning knife tip to score the membrane covering the bones, which will allow them to break through the membrane easily.

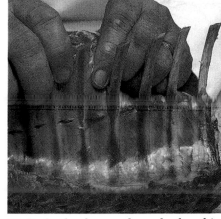

(4) Push the bones through the thin membrane. The thumbs are placed against the fleshy side of the bone and forefingers are positioned between them.

(5) Lay the rack so that the bones are facing down. Make an even cut to remove the meat surrounding the bone ends. This should pull away easily.

(6) The completely frenched rack. The exposed bones are perfectly clean. If any meat or membrane remains, scrape the bones with a knife.

WORKING WITH VARIETY MEATS

In recent years, as Americans have become less squeamish about organ meats, a steady increase in demand has arisen for properly prepared liver, kidneys, sweetbreads, and other kinds of variety meats. These cuts may be difficult for the ordinary consumer to find in a grocery store, or even a butcher's shop. Furthermore, many people are uncomfortable with, or unsure of, proper preparation techniques.

Sweetbreads, for example, need to be thoroughly rinsed in cold water to remove all traces of blood. They are then blanched in a court bouillon, peeled, and then pressed to give them a firmer, more appealing texture. The sweetbreads can then be prepared *à la meunière* (floured and sautéed) or combined with wild mushrooms and a cream sauce.

Liver also needs some advance preparation; it is important to remove any silverskin, tough membranes, or gristle before grilling or sautéing. When subjected to intense heat, the silverskin will shrink more rapidly than the meat, causing the liver to pucker and cook unevenly.

Kidneys will not necessarily taste like urine, as long as they are perfectly fresh and properly handled to allow their unique flavor to come through. After they are rinsed, they are cut in half and all fat and veins are removed to eliminate the possibility of any undesirable flavors. In some cases, recipes may indicate that the kidneys should be blanched first to remove these flavors.

Tongue is a muscle meat that can be quite tough unless it is gently simmered in a flavorful broth or bouillon until it is very tender. Allowing the tongue to cool in the liq-

11-10 BONING A LEG OF VEAL

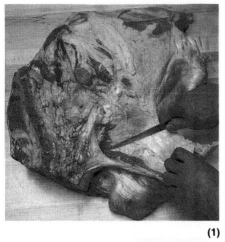

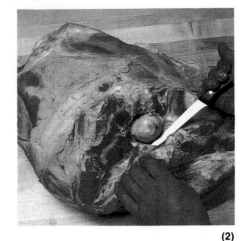

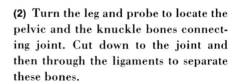

(1)

(2)

(1) Pull the flank away from the leg, and use a boning knife to cut through the tissue and fat connecting the leg.

(2) Turn the leg and probe to locate the pelvic and the knuckle bones connecting joint. Cut down to the joint and then through the ligaments to separate these bones.

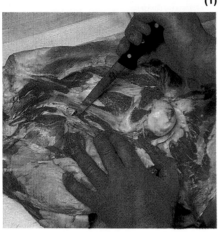

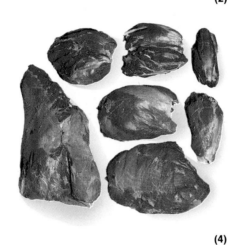

(3)

(4)

(3) Follow the meat's natural seams and cut through the meat to the bones. Cut and scrape the meat away from all the bones as cleanly as possible.

(4) The separate cuts shown here are the top round *(bottom right)*, the bottom round *(bottom left)*, the shank *(top row)*, the knuckle *(center)*, and the eye round *(middle right)*.

11-11 DISJOINTING A RABBIT

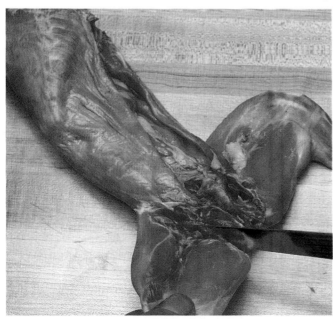

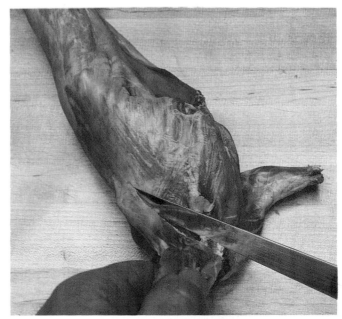

(1) Pull the leg away from the body and then cut through the meat and the joint to separate the leg from the loin.

(2) Pull the shoulder away from the body. Cut through the breast and the joint to completely separate the foreleg from the body.

174

uid will bolster its flavor. Once cooled, the tongue should be carefully peeled to remove the skin. Then, it can be used in a variety of ways: as a garnish, or as part of a choucroute or a stew.

Marrow—the soft, inner substance of bone—is often used as a garnish for a variety of sauces, soups, and other dishes. The bones should first be sawed into reasonable lengths to make it easier to remove the marrow. The bones are first rinsed under cool running water until all traces of blood have been eliminated and the water runs clear. Then the marrow can be removed from the bone.

Fabrication techniques for preparing sweetbreads, calf's liver, veal kidneys, tongue, and marrow are shown in Figures 11-12 through 11-16.

11-12 CLEANING AND PRESSING SWEETBREADS

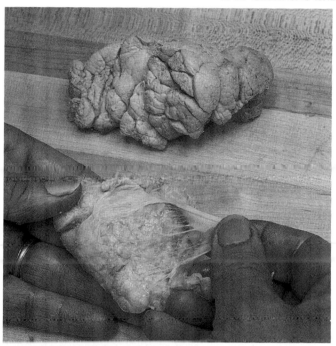

(1) Once the sweetbreads have been properly blanched and cooled, use the fingers to pull away the heavy membrane.

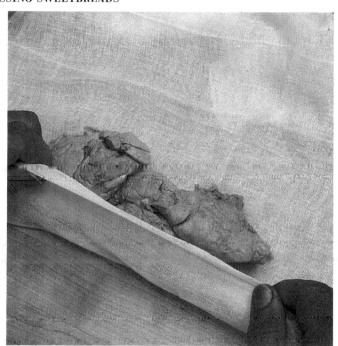

(2) Wrap the sweetbreads in clean cheesecloth and roll them up. Tie the ends with string.

(3)

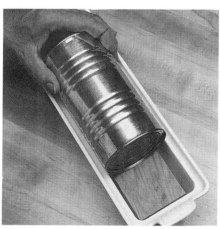

(4)

(3) Place the wrapped sweetbreads in a terrine or other container and top with a flat item, such as a clean length of board as used here.

(4) Top the board with a weight. Refrigerate. As the weight pushes out the excess moisture, the sweetbreads will take on a firm, compact texture and shape.

11-13 CLEANING LIVER

(1)

(2)

(1) The skin, a light membrane covering the liver, is easy to peel away. Use the other hand to steady the liver.

(2) Work the tip of the blade under the sinew, being sure to leave as much of the meat as possible. Holding the loose end of the cut will help prevent cutting away too much flesh.

11-14 CLEANING KIDNEYS

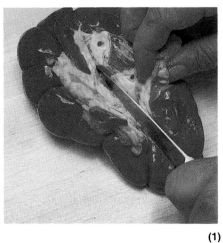

(1)

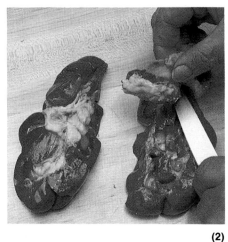

(2)

(1) Make a cut through the center of the kidneys, dividing them into two equal pieces.

(2) Lift away the kidney fat and use the tip of a sharp knife to cut it away from the kidneys.

11-15 PEELING TONGUE

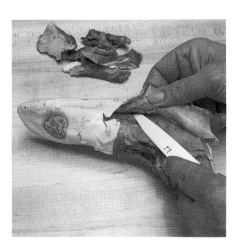

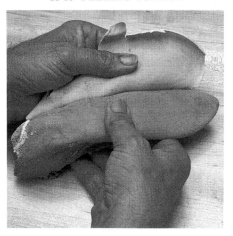

(1) Use the tip of a knife to trim the skin from the underside. Lift it away from the tongue as the cuts are made to prevent removing too much meat.

(2) The skin will peel away easily from the tongue's top.

(3) The completely peeled tongue is shown.

176

11-16 REMOVING MARROW FROM BONES

(1) Place the marrow bones in a container and cover with cold water. Add salt to help draw away any excess blood and other impurities.

(2) After the marrow bones have soaked for a few hours, push the marrow out using the thumb.

(3) The marrow is completely freed.

SUMMARY

There are a great many more fabrication techniques than could be covered in this chapter. This chapter has focused on smaller, day-to-day tasks such as trimming, pounding, and shaping. A chef might be well-advised to hone his or her butchering skills by obtaining additional training. Butchering techniques that are used in the breakdown of the entire carcass would allow the chef an even greater control over the types of meats and any special cuts that might be offered. The greater the chef's skill, the less that will be spent for these cuts. This area of expertise should not be overlooked, as it is an effective way to help a restaurant keep high food costs down and increase its profit percentage.

Restaurants are often perceived as places having a special cut of meat, or a type of meat that is not easily found in typical supermarkets. Whether it be a larger cut of meat that has been made over into smaller, customized "menu cuts" such as paillards or tournédos, or an unusual item such as sweetbreads, the menu is enhanced by including these offerings.

THE BASICS

Even if a restaurant chef does relatively little fabricating of other meats, he or she will often do a lot of poultry fabrication. Fabrication of poultry is often much easier than for other meats primarily because the bones are relatively small and the joints are easy to cut through. Young birds are the easiest to fabricate since they are usually much smaller and their bones are not completely hardened. The size and breed of the bird will also have some bearing on how easy or difficult it will be to fabricate; chickens are generally far more simple to cut up, for example, than are pheasant. The tendons and ligaments in chickens are less well-developed, except in the case of free-range birds, which move freely about an enclosed yard.

Although the procedure for boning a duck, for instance, is very similar to that used in boning a Cornish game hen, carcass shapes do differ from breed to breed. A duck has shorter legs and a long, barrel-shaped chest. The game hen, since it is small, will require smaller, more delicate cuts than a turkey. A quail, one of the smallest birds, requires all of a chef's skill and care to avoid mangling the tiny morsels of meat that cling to delicate bones.

The bones and trim remaining after fabrication can be used in a variety of ways; the wings made into hors d'oeuvre, any lean trim for forcemeat preparation, and the bones for making stock.

When working with any type of poultry, the chef should keep all tools and work surfaces scrupulously clean because of the potential for cross-contamination.

• Keep poultry under refrigeration when it is not being fabricated.
• Be sure that the cutting board has been thoroughly cleaned and sanitized before and after using it to cut up poultry.
• Clean and sanitize knives, poultry shears, and the steel before and after cutting poultry.
• Store poultry in clean, leak-proof containers, and do not place poultry above any cooked meats. If the poultry drips on the food below it, it will become contaminated. For added safety, it may be a good idea to place a drip pan underneath the container holding the poultry.

The essential tools for cutting up poultry are a clean work surface, a boning knife, and a chef's knife. Some chefs are comfortable using poultry shears to cut through joints and smaller bones. In the illustrations for this chapter, the boning knife is used to cut through bones and joints and to scrape meat free from the bone (known as "frenching"). The heel of the chef's knife is used to cut through tougher bones, or to remove the joint at the end of drumsticks so that they can also be frenched.

DISJOINTING AND BONING POULTRY

Most poultry can be purchased already broken down, but there are distinct advantages when the chef does the cutting. There is less overall waste, since any scrap of trim can be put to use in other areas of the kitchen, including pantry preparations, soups, and stocks.

When using the technique for disjointing and boning, the chef starts with the whole bird. First the legs are cut away from the body, and then the thigh and drumstick bones are removed from the leg meat. Finally, the breast is cut away from the rib cage. These steps in the disjointing and boning process are shown in Figures 12-1 and 12-2.

12-1 DISJOINTING AND BONING THE LEGS

(1) Lay the chicken on its back on a flat work surface. Using a sharp knife, make a cut between the leg and the breast.

(2) Bend the leg away from the body and press fingertips into the back of the joint to pop the joint loose. Continue to cut the leg away from the breast.

(3) Make a cut completely around the end of the drumstick to sever the flesh, tendons, and skin from the bone.

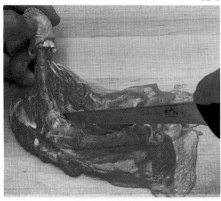

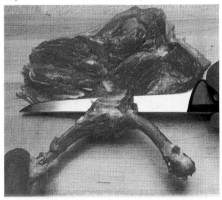

(4) Cut along the natural seams in the meat to expose the drumstick and thigh bones. Use the knife tip to cut the meat away from the bone.

(5) When the bones are completely exposed from the top, run the point of the knife blade underneath them to free them from the meat.

(6) Pull the leg bones away from the meat. Cut the joint that joins the thigh bone and the drumstick bone away from the meat. The leg is now completely boneless.

12-2 REMOVING THE BREAST

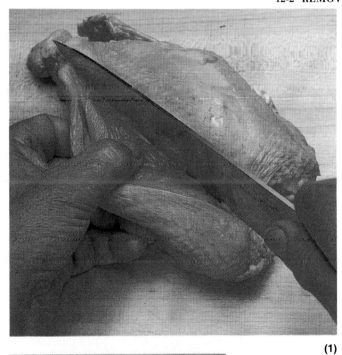

(1)

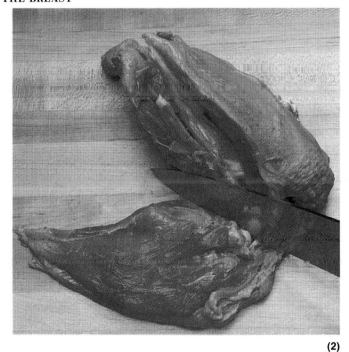

(2)

(3)

(1) Make a cut along one side of the breast bone to free the breast from the rib cage. Pull the meat away from the bones as the cut is made so that as little meat as possible is left on the bones.

(2) Make a cut through the joint that attaches the wing to the rib cage. At this point, the chicken breast may be made into suprêmes, or the wings and skin may be completely removed.

(3) Boneless, skinless chicken breasts. To make paillards, slice in half horizontally and pound the slices as shown in Chapter 11, Fig. 11-7.

PREPARING A SUPRÊME

A suprême is a boneless, skinless poultry breast, usually from a chicken, pheasant, partridge, or duck. One wing joint, often frenched, is left attached to the breast meat. The preferred cooking techniques include sautéing, shallow poaching, and grilling. Figure 12-3 demonstrates the technique for fabricating a suprême; in Figure 12-4 the completely boned bird is shown.

CUTTING POULTRY INTO HALVES, QUARTERS, AND EIGHTHS

Cutting into halves is an especially important technique for use on smaller birds, such as Cornish game hens and broiler chickens, that are to be prepared by grilling. These birds are small enough to cook through completely before the skin becomes scorched or charred. One half of the bird is usually a sufficient serving for a single portion. If the bones are left intact during grilling, they provide some protection against scorching and help to prevent shrinkage.

This technique is also used to cut ducks in half after they have been roasted. In many restaurants, the ducks needed for an evening's service will be roasted in advance, then halved and partially deboned; at service, then, it is necessary only to reheat the duck and crisp the skin in a hot oven. The wing tips and backbone should be saved for use in the preparation of stock.

By cutting a 1½- to 3-pound bird into quarters, pieces of a size suitable for sautéing, grilling, and panfrying are produced. This relatively simple procedure involves cutting the legs away from the body and halving the breast and removing it from the rib cage.

When a bird is cut into eighths, the chef then has two drumsticks, two thighs, two wing portions, and two breast portions. Broiler or fryer chickens to be panfried or deep-fried are usually cut into eighths so that they will cook evenly and thoroughly before their exterior becomes charred. This is also a popular way to fabricate poultry for stewing, braising, or barbecuing. Figures 12-5, 12-6, and 12-7 show these techniques.

TRUSSING POULTRY

There are several different methods for trussing, or tying, poultry, some involving trussing needles, some requiring only string. The object of trussing any bird is to give it a smooth, compact shape so that it will cook evenly and retain moisture. Figure 12-8 demonstrates how to truss a chicken.

12-3 MAKING A SUPRÊME

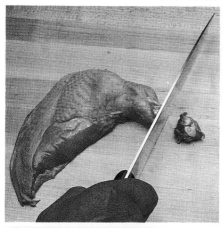

(1)

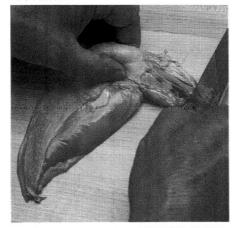

(2)

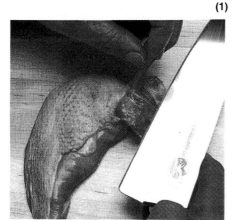

(3)

(1) Cut away the first two wing joints. Then use the heel of a chef's knife to cut the end of the remaining wing joint.

(2) Scrape the meat away from the wing bone, leaving as little meat as possible on the bone.

(3) Cut the meat away from the wing bone.

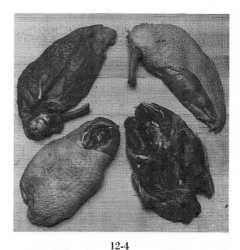

12-4

The completed boned chicken.

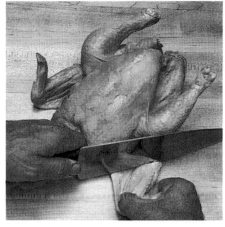

(1) Cut away the first two wing joints by cutting across them with a heavy knife. These wing tips may be reserved for use in stock.

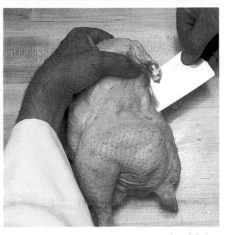

(2) Lay the chicken on one side. Make a cut along one side of the backbone, working from the neck to the tail.

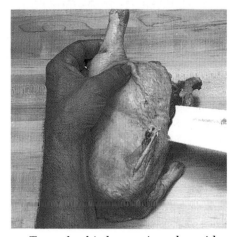

(3) Turn the bird onto its other side. Make another cut along the backbone, this time cutting from the tail toward the neck.

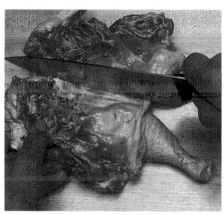

(4) Open the bird out flat, with the skin side facing down. Make a cut through the breast on one side of the keel bone to separate the bird into halves.

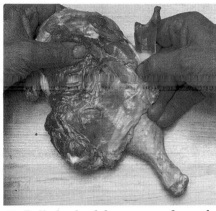

(5) Pull the keel bone away from the chicken completely. The bone may separate into two portions; be sure that it is all removed.

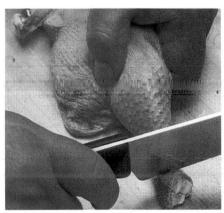

(6) Use the heel of the chef's knife to cut away the end of the drumstick.

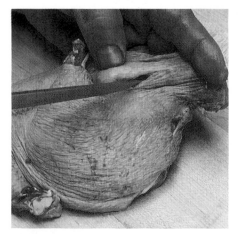

(7) Slit the skin covering the thigh with a boning knife tip to make a pocket.

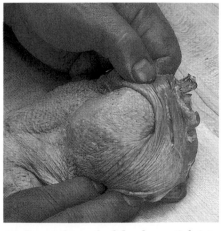

(8) Insert the end of the drumstick into the slit to hold the leg secure during cooking.

(9) The properly halved chicken.

12-6 CUTTING A BIRD INTO QUARTERS

(1)

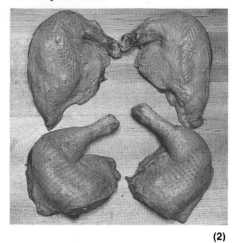

(2)

(1) Follow steps 1 through 5 of Figure 12-5 to separate the bird into halves. Then make a diagonal cut to separate the breast from the leg.

(2) The quartered chicken.

12-7 CUTTING A BIRD INTO EIGHTHS

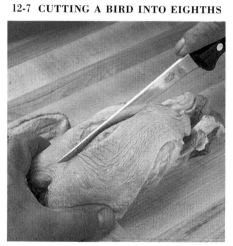

(1) Cut the entire leg away from the body, as shown in Figure 12-1, steps 1 and 2. Then make a cut through the joint connecting the drumstick and the thigh. A thin line of fat over the joint will act as a cutting guide.

(2) Make a cut through the breast on one side of the keel bone.

(3) Pull the breast away from the bones, cutting the meat free.

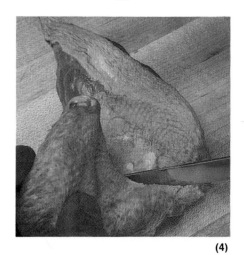

(4)

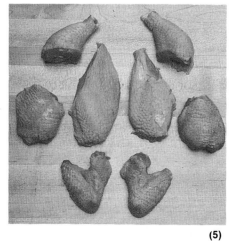

(5)

(4) Cut the wings away from the breast.

(5) The bird cut into eight pieces.

184

12-8 TRUSSING A BIRD

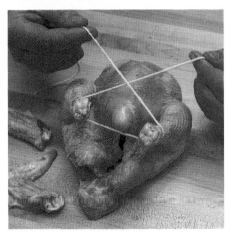

(1) Cut away the first two wing joints. Pass the middle of a long piece of string underneath the joints at the end of the drumstick, and cross the ends of the string to make an X as shown.

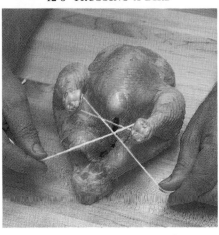

(2) Pull the ends of the string down toward the tail and begin to pull the string back along the body.

(3) Pull both ends of the string tightly across the joint that connects the drumstick and the thigh and continue to pull the string along the body toward the bird's back, catching the wing underneath the string.

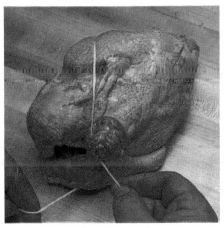

(4) Pull one end of the string securely underneath the backbone at the neck opening.

(5) Tie the two ends of the string with a secure knot.

(6) A properly trussed bird.

SUMMARY

Mastery of the techniques covered in this chapter will allow the chef to work confidently on a variety of poultry and game birds. The increasing availability of a high-quality bird—whether domestically raised poultry, free-range chickens, or farm-raised quail—makes these techniques particularly valuable to any restaurant. To be able to offer perfect roast chickens, Cornish game hen suprêmes, or a grilled paillarde of duck, the chef must be able to properly truss, trim, and cut birds. When done on the premises, poultry fabrication ensures that the operation is getting the best quality for the best possible price.

Chapter 13

Fish and Shellfish Fabrication

Fish and shellfish have become very popular on most menus and demand continues to grow. The chef may wish to do as much fabricating as possible on the premises. This will certainly help control costs, because every time a fish wholesaler puts a knife to a fish, its cost to the kitchen, and ultimately to the guest, goes up.

Fish and shellfish fabrication includes such techniques as scaling, gutting, and cutting round and flat fish into steaks and fillets. Although the more fabrication the chef can do, the more money can be saved, the flip side of this consideration is that if a poor job is done, there will be more waste. If the chef does not have the ability or time, buying prepared fillets and steaks or already shucked oysters and clams is more cost-effective.

The days of inexpensive fish in great abundance are probably gone. It is, therefore, especially important to make use of this valuable resource in the most profitable way. If fish can be cleaned, filleted, and fully fabricated with little trim loss, and if the trim can be put to good use in a mousseline, a filling, canapés, or soups, then fish can still be considered an excellent value.

THE TECHNIQUES

A number of techniques can be used to fabricate a particular fish, and the methods shown in this chapter are not always the only way to proceed. Different methods can achieve virtually the same results. Time, practice, and experience will help determine which technique works best in a particular situation. Most fish fall into one of two categories: round and flat. The basic procedure for scaling—the first step in preparing the fish before any further fabrication is done—applies to all types of fish. Methods differ slightly, however, for gutting round fish and flat fish. Similarly, the technique for filleting a round fish is different from that used for a flat fish. In determining how to fabricate, knowledge of the particular fish's specific properties is important (see Chapter 7, "Fish and Shellfish Identification").

The techniques shown here are not exceptionally difficult, nor do they require much special equipment. A sharp flexible filleting knife, needlenose pliers, and a clam and oyster knife are the customary tools.

FISH

Scaling and Trimming Fish

Not all fish have scales; however, for those that do, the scales should be removed before proceeding with fabrication. Scales are difficult to see if they are adhering to flesh rather than to skin.

The best way to remove scales is with a fish scaler, but other tools can be used if a scaler is not available. The chef should work from the head toward the tail and should have water flowing over the fish to help keep the scales from flying around. The fish should not be

13-1 TWO WAYS TO SCALE A FISH

(1) Hold the fish (a salmon is shown here) under running water. Working from the head toward the tail, scrape the scales away with a fish scaler.

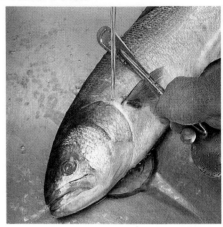

(2) If a fish scaler is not available, use the handle of a kitchen spoon.

pinched too tightly, as this could bruise the flesh. Figure 13-1 demonstrates two ways to scale a fish: in one a fish scaler is employed, in the other, a spoon handle.

The fins and tail can be cut away with either a sharp knife or a pair of scissors. This step is usually done to "pan-dress" the fish. A pan-dressed fish may often have the head cut away as well, but if the fish is to be filleted or cut into steaks, this step may not be necessary. In Figure 13-2, the procedure to cut off the fins is demonstrated.

13-2 CUTTING FINS FROM FISH

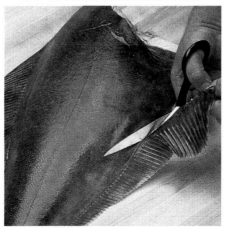

Use kitchen shears or a sharp knife to cut the fins and tail away from the fish (in this example, a halibut).

Gutting a Fish

Frequently, the fish's viscera (guts) will be removed soon after it is taken from the water, right on the fishing boat. The viscera's enzymes can begin to break down the flesh rapidly, leading to spoilage. If the fish has not been gutted, this step should be performed right after the fish has been scaled. The methods for gutting both round and flat fish are shown in Figures 13-3 and 13-4. A salmon is used to demonstrate the technique for round fish and a flounder is used for the flat fish example.

Pan-Ready Fish

Pan-ready fish are most frequently prepared by panfrying the whole fish as one portion. This means that the fish is generally no larger than 12 ounces after it has been scaled, trimmed, and gutted. The head is usually left on the fish during cooking, though it may be removed before it is served to the guest, either in the kitchen or at tableside by the waiter. Pan-ready round and flat fish are shown in Figure 13-5.

13-3 GUTTING A ROUND FISH

(1) Make a slit in the fish's belly.

(2) Pull the guts away.

(3) Rinse the belly cavity thoroughly under running, cold water to remove all traces of viscera and blood.

13-4 GUTTING A FLAT FISH

(1) Cut around the head, making a V-shaped notch.

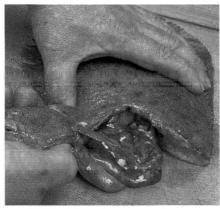

(2) Pull the head away from the body, twisting it. The guts will come away with the head.

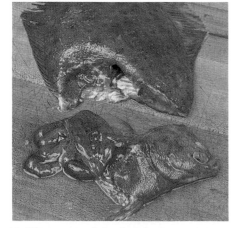

(3) The guts and the head are now completely separated from the fish.

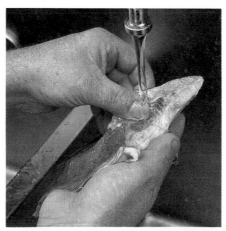

(4) Rinse the belly cavity thoroughly under running, cold water to remove all traces of viscera and blood.

Filleting a Fish

Fillets are one of the most common fabrications for fish. These boneless and (usually) skinless fish pieces can be sautéed, grilled, baked, formed into paupiettes, or cut into tranches or goujonettes. The techniques for both round and flat fish are shown in Figures 13-6 and 13-7. A round fish will yield two fillets; flat fish yield four. Several pieces of equipment are needed for this technique, including a filleting knife, a chef's knife, and needle-nose pliers.

Tranche

A tranche is simply a slice of the fillet. It is cut by holding the knife at an angle while cutting to expose more surface area and give the piece of fish a larger appearance (see Fig. 13-8). A tranche can be cut from any relatively large fillet of fish; for example, salmon, halibut, or tuna are often cut into tranches. Though this cut is normally associated with sautéed or panfried preparations, it is perfectly acceptable to grill or broil a tranche.

13-5 PAN-READY FISH

(Left) A pan-ready round fish (in this example, a trout). *(Right)* A pan-ready flat fish (in this example, a flounder).

13-6 FILLETING A ROUND FISH

(1) A salmon is used throughout this sequence. Using a flexible filleting knife, make a cut from behind the gill, angling the knife toward the head.

(2) Change to a chef's knife, and cut from the head toward the tail. Keep the blade edge slightly angled so that the blade makes a clicking sound as it nicks against the bones. Turn the fish and repeat this step. It may be a little more difficult to remove the second fillet.

(1)

(2)

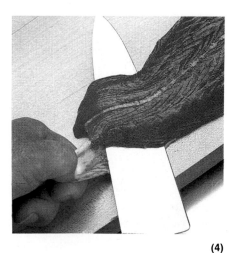

(3) Use the filleting knife to remove the belly bones. With a smooth stroke, work from the center toward the edge. Angle the blade up against the bones.

(4) Place the fillet skin-side down near the edge of the work surface. Use a chef's knife. Starting at the tail end, hold the skin very taut with one hand. Use a gentle "sawing" motion and angle the blade slightly toward the skin so that none of the flesh will be left attached to the skin.

(3)

(4)

190

(5) Continue cutting the skin away. It is important to hold the skin tautly.

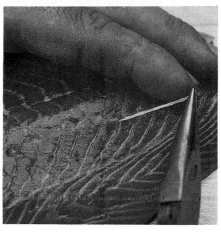

(6) The intramuscular bones can be easily located by running a finger down the fillet's center. Use needlenose pliers to pull them out.

(7) The completed salmon fillet. Note that no flesh is left attached to the skin and all surfaces are very smooth.

13-7 FILLETING A FLAT FISH

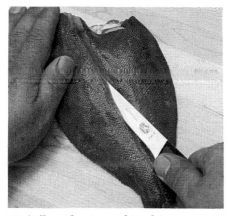

(1) A flounder is used in this sequence. Use a filleting knife to make the initial cut down the backbone. Position the fish so that the head is pointed away from the edge of the work surface. Angle the blade so that it is pointed toward the fish's outer edge.

(2) Work from the head toward the tail. Make smooth strokes along the bones to remove the first fillet. Keep the blade angled slightly so that the cut is very close to the bones.

(3) When the first fillet has been removed, turn the fish around so that the head is closest to the edge of the work surface. Cut the second fillet away from the bones, working again from the tail toward the head.

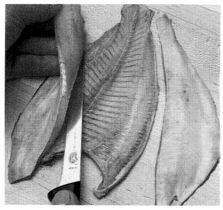

(4) *(Far left)* Turn the fish over and remove the bottom fillets using the same procedures explained in steps 2 and 3.

(5) All four fillets have been removed. Note that the skeleton (or rack, as it is sometimes known) has very little flesh.

(4)

(5)

13-8 CUTTING A TRANCHE

Fillet the fish first, removing all intramuscular bones. Hold the knife at approximately a 45-degree angle and, with a very sharp slicer, slice across the fillet. The greater the angle of the knife, the more surface area will be exposed.

13-9 CUTTING GOUJONETTES

Make even, finger-sized cuts from the prepared fillet.

Goujonette

The name for this cut is derived from the French name for a small fish, the *goujon*. Goujonettes are small strips cut from a fillet, often breaded or dipped in batter and then deep-fried. This cut has approximately the same dimensions as an adult's index finger (see Fig. 13-9). Goujonettes are normally cut from lean white fish, such as sole or flounder, and are served with a piquant sauce, such as rémoulade sauce or tartar sauce.

Paupiette

A paupiette is a thin, rolled fillet, often filled with a forcemeat or other stuffing. It should resemble a large cork (see Fig. 13-10). Paupiettes are generally made from lean fish, such as flounder or sole, although they may also be made from some moderately fatty fish, such as trout or salmon. The most common preparation technique for paupiettes is shallow-poaching.

Cutting Steaks

Steaks are simply cross-cuts of the fish and are relatively easy to cut. The fish is scaled, gutted, and trimmed of its fins. The size of the steak is determined by the cut's thickness. *Darnes*, from the French, are thick steaks. There are few flat fish large enough to cut into steaks; the halibut is one flat fish that can be fabricated in this fashion. Figure 13-11 demonstrates the techniques for cutting a round fish (salmon, in this case) and a flat fish (halibut) into steaks.

(1) Prepare a fillet and trim as necessary. Then roll the fillet, working from the head to the tail. Place the rolled fish on one of its edges.

(2) If desired, the fillet can be spread with a mousseline forcemeat before rolling.

13-11 CUTTING ROUND FISH AND FLAT FISH INTO STEAKS

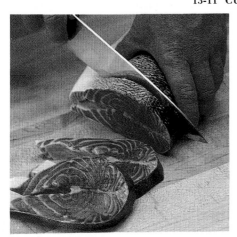

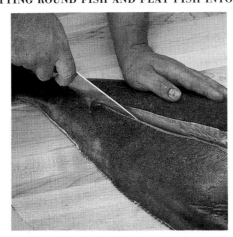

(1) Scale and gut the round fish (see Figs. 13-1, 13-2, and 13-3). Then, using a sharp chef's knife, make crosswise cuts through the fish to make steaks of the desired size.

(2) Do the initial preparation for flat fish (scaling, gutting, trimming—see Figs. 13-1, 13-2, and 13-4) and then cut the fish in half along the backbone with a chef's knife.

(3) Make crosswise cuts through the halved fish to the size desired.

SHELLFISH

Cleaning Shrimp

Shrimp are cleaned by removing the shell and then the vein that runs along the back of the shrimp, either before or after cooking. Shrimp that has been boiled or steamed in its shell will be moister and plumper than shrimp that has been peeled and deveined before cooking. Shrimp that will be served cold—in appetizers or salads, for example—can be cooked in the shell. Shrimp dishes that are sautéed or grilled usually call for the shrimp to be peeled and deveined before cooking. The shrimp would cool too rapidly if they had to be peeled in the kitchen before being served to the guests. If the shrimp were still in the shell when served in a sauce, they would be messy for the diner to handle. The greatest advantage to peeling and deveining raw shrimp before sautéing is that the shrimp will not be as easy to overcook as they might be if they were left in the shell. The technique shown in Figure 13-12 uses raw shrimp, but can also be used for cooked shrimp.

Working with Cooked Lobster

It is easier to remove the meat from a lobster that has been partially or fully cooked. When the lobster is raw, the flesh clings tightly to the shell and is very soft. It is therefore too easy to tear the flesh when trying to remove it. This does not mean, however, that the lobster must be completely cooked. Blanching the lobster lightly in a steam bath, in boiling water, or in a hot oven is all that is required to firm the flesh enough to pull it cleanly from the shell. Shown in Figures 13-13, 13-14, and 13-15 are techniques for halving a lobster and removing the tail and claw meat.

13-12 PEELING AND DEVEINING SHRIMP

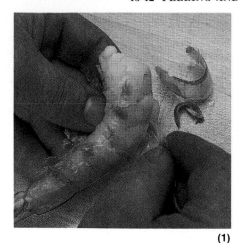

(1)

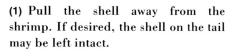

(2)

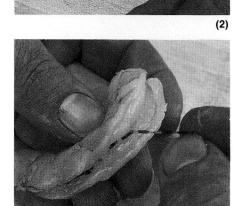

(3)

(1) Pull the shell away from the shrimp. If desired, the shell on the tail may be left intact.

(2) Make a shallow cut along the outer curve of the shrimp to expose the intestines, known as the vein. To butterfly shrimp, make a deeper cut, but leave the inner edge and the tail intact.

(3) Pull away the intestine and discard. The shrimp is now peeled and deveined.

Cleaning and Picking Crayfish

Crayfish share many similarities with lobster, but they are much smaller. Crayfish are especially popular in Cajun and Creole dishes. Like shrimp, they may be simply boiled or steamed and peeled after cooking when the meat is easy to remove from the shell. It is relatively simple to remove the vein from the crayfish before cooking, though this may be done afterward, if preferred. Techniques for removing the vein and peeling the tail meat are shown in Figure 13-16.

Cleaning a Soft-shelled Crab

A seasonal favorite, soft-shelled crabs are considered a great deli-

cacy. They are not especially difficult to clean once their various parts are identified. Soft-shelled crabs are commonly prepared by sautéing or panfrying, and the shell may be eaten along with the meat. The technique for cleaning a soft-shelled crab is shown in Figure 13-17.

Cleaning and Opening Clams, Oysters, and Mussels

Clams and oysters are often served "on the half shell," so it is important to be able to open them with ease. In addition, freshly shucked oysters and clams are often used for cooked dishes, such as oysters Rockefeller or clams casino. Mussels are rarely served raw, but the method for cleaning them before

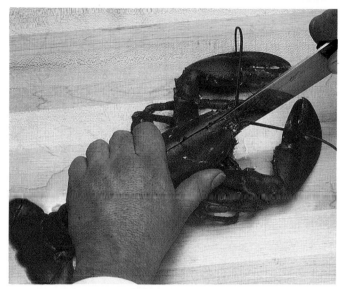

(1) When the lobster is cool enough to handle, cut cleanly through the back with a heavy chef's knife.

(2) The halved lobster. In some presentations, the shell is emptied and the edible lobster portions are diced, combined with a sauce or stuffing, and returned to the shell.

13-14 REMOVING THE LOBSTER TAIL

(1) *(Right)* Pull the tail section away from the body. If desired, reserve all edible body portions for other use.

(2) *(Below, left)* Use kitchen shears to cut away the tail's shell on the underside.

(3) *(Below, right)* Pull the meat in one piece from the shell. It can be cut into slices or medallions, or presented whole.

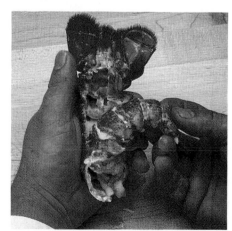

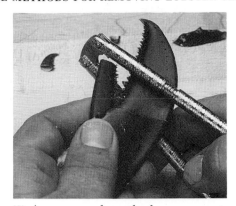

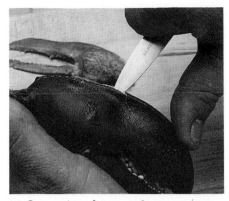

(1) With a mallet, pound the shell, using only enough force to crack it. Do not crush the shell or mangle the meat. Pull the shell away from the meat.

(2) As a second method, use a nutcracker to crack the shell. Pull some of the shell away, and then gently work out the claw meat in one piece.

(3) In version three, a sharp paring or utility knife is used to make a cut along the shell's outer curve. Open the shell away from the meat, and gently remove the claw meat in one piece.

13-16 CLEANING CRAYFISH

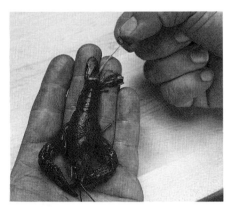

(1) To remove the intestine from uncooked crayfish, gently twist the middle fan of the tail to the left and right, then pull it away from the tail. The intestine will come away, as shown.

(2) Poach or steam the crayfish, and allow to cool until they can be handled. Pull the tail section away from the body.

(3) Crack open the shell and pull the tail meat away.

13-17 CLEANING A SOFT-SHELLED CRAB

(1) Peel back the pointed shell and scrape away the gill filament on each side.

(2) Cut the head off approximately ¼ inch behind the eyes and squeeze gently to force out the green bubble; the fluid there has an unpleasant flavor.

(3) Bend back the tail flap (or apron) and pull with a slight twisting motion. The intestinal vein should draw out of the body at the same time.

(4) The cleaned crab with the gill filaments, head, and tail flap removed.

steaming and poaching is similar to that used for clams. Unlike clams and oysters, mussels have a dark, shaggy beard that is normally removed before cooking.

The chef should scrub all molluscs well with a brush under running, cold water before opening them. Any shellfish that remain open when tapped should be dis-

carded because they are dead. If the shell feels unusually heavy or light, it should be checked. Occasionally, empty shells or shells that have filled with clay or sand will be found. Opening clams and oysters and cleaning mussels are demonstrated in Figures 13-18, 13-19, and 13-20.

Cleaning Squid and Octopus

The increased acceptance of these cephalopods on menus demonstrates their growing popularity in recent years. When properly fabricated and cooked, they are tender, sweet, and flavorful: The mantle can be cut into rings to sauté, panfry, or deep-fry; or it may be left

13-18 OPENING A CLAM

(1)

(1) Hold the clam with the hinged edge resting directly in the palm of one hand. Insert the edge of a clam knife between the shell's two halves. Use the fingers holding the clam to firmly press the knife into the shell. Twist the knife slightly to open the shell.

(2) Use the knife point to scrape the meat into one shell. Break away the shell's top half.

(3) Gently release the clam from the lower shell by scraping with the knife point.

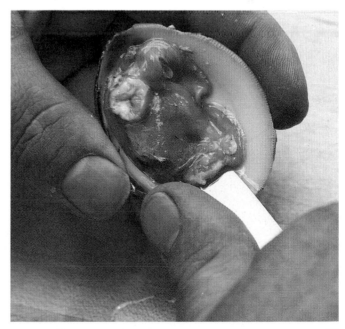

(2) (3)

(1) Oysters to be served on the half shell should be thoroughly scrubbed under cold running water. Use a brush to remove all dirt and sand.

(2) Hold the oyster on a side towel to prevent slippage. Insert the point of an oyster knife into the shell's "hinge."

(3) Use one end of the side towel to hold the oyster steady as the knife is pushed further into the shell. Twist the knife to pop the shell open.

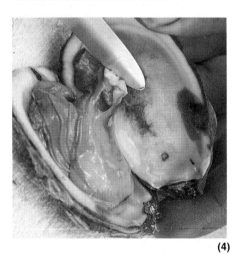

(4) Scrape the oyster meat from the top shell.

(5) Use the knife tip to loosen the meat. Note the generous amount of liquor in the shell of this fresh oyster. Place the oyster on a bed of chipped or shaved ice or seaweed to keep the shell level and prevent the loss of any liquor.

(4)

(5)

(1) Using a brush with stiff bristles, thoroughly scrub the mussel to remove all sand, grit, and mud from the outer shell.

(2) Pull the beard away from the shell.

(3) The scrubbed mussel with the beard removed.

whole to grill or braise, with or without a stuffing. If desired, the ink sac can be saved and used to prepare various dishes, such as pasta *(calamares en su tinta)* and risotto (Catalan-style black rice). Cleaning procedures for these two shellfish are demonstrated in Figures 13-21 and 13-22.

Cleaning a Sea Urchin

Sea urchins are a spiny marine fish that may not be available in all areas of the country. They are considered a delicacy in many cuisines, especially French and Japanese. When working with these creatures, the chef should always wear thick rubber gloves to protect his or her hands. Figure 13-23 shows how to clean a sea urchin.

13-21 CLEANING A SQUID

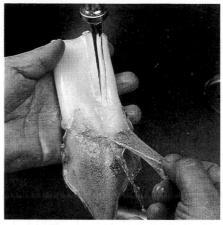

(1)

(2)

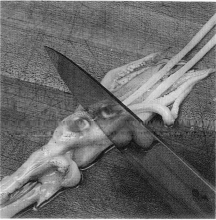

(3)

(4)

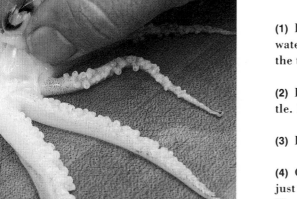

(5)

(1) Pull the mantle and the tentacles apart under running water. The eye, ink sac, and intestines will come away with the tentacles.

(2) Pull as much of the skin as possible away from the mantle. Discard the skin.

(3) Pull the transparent quill from the mantle and discard.

(4) Cut the tentacles away from the head by making a cut just above the eye. If desired, the ink sac may be reserved. The rest of the head should be discarded.

(5) Open the tentacles to expose the beak. Pull it away and discard. The tentacles may be left whole, if they are small, or cut into pieces appropriately sized for various preparations.

(2) Peel the skin away from the body by pulling firmly.

(3) Pull the suction cups away from the tentacles. The octopus is now cleaned and ready to use.

(1) Use the tip of a filleting knife to cut around the eye and lift it from the octopus.

13-23 CLEANING A SEA URCHIN

(1) Wear a heavy rubber glove to protect the hand from the shell's spines. Use scissors to cut away the shell top.

(2) Use a spoon to loosen the viscera and spoon them away.

(3) The orange-colored roe remains. It is ready to be eaten as is or may be used in other preparations.

13-24 SKINNING AN EEL

(1) Use a sharp filleting knife to make an incision completely around the fish just behind the fins nearest the head.

(2) Hold the head with one hand and grasp the skin with a clean towel in the other. Pull the skin away in one piece. If the skin should tear, repeat as necessary, loosening the skin with a knife as needed.

Skinning an Eel

This is not one of the easiest of tasks, because the eel's skin is quite firmly attached. It may take several attempts to accomplish the job. The skin must be removed because it is tough and slippery. The best-known preparation for eel is matelote, an eel stew. Figure 13-24 demonstrates the technique for skinning.

SUMMARY

With continued practice, the chef should find it increasingly easy to trim fish and then fabricate them into the appropriate form: fillets, steaks, fingers, pan-ready, or drawn. This is the absolutely best way to be certain that the fish served is perfectly fresh, properly trimmed, and cut to suit the menu.

The techniques demonstrated in this chapter on round fish, flat fish, and a variety of shellfish can be adapted to suit virtually any aquatic creature. A flounder is handled in much the same manner as a halibut; a crayfish is very similar to a lobster. When the kitchen staff is able to fabricate fish, it is also possible to take advantage of some of the less commonly known species, especially those that have only recently been accepted. These are the fish that are being offered as replacements for the popular fish that are being "fished out." The skills required to clean, shuck, and prepare a variety of shellfish is also crucial to allow the chef the freedom to choose widely from the full array that may be available. Basic skills in fish fabrication are learned through practice and repetition, but once learned, are invaluable.

Part Five

Basic
Preparations

This section begins the process of teaching cooking techniques. The procedures in Chapters 14 and 15 concern basic preparations that form the foundation or building blocks of cooking. They are as simple as chopping vegetables for mirepoix or as time-consuming as making stock.

Chapter 14, "Mise en Place," focuses on one of the most important points of the book—having the necessary ingredients at hand and in an appropriate state before the preparation of a dish begins. Less tangible—but no less important—mise en place implies a feeling of overall preparedness.

In the remaining chapters in this section, the basic techniques necessary to prepare a full repertoire of stocks, soups, and both classic and contemporary sauces are explained.

The format used in this section will be continued throughout the book, with slight variations. The explanation of each technique begins with a mise en place section. Next comes the method, which, once mastered, can be considered a basic theme that has countless variations. Following the method are guidelines for evaluating quality.

Mise en Place

*ise en place* is a French phrase that translates as "to put in place." For the truly professional chef, it means far more than simply assembling all the ingredients, pots and pans, plates, and serving pieces needed for a particular period. Mise en place is also a state of mind. Someone who has truly grasped the concept is able to keep many tasks in mind simultaneously, weighing and assigning each its proper value and priority. This assures that the chef has anticipated and prepared for every situation that could logically occur during a service period.

The techniques, terms, preparations, and skills covered in this chapter represent only the most basic elements of mise en place, gathered together for easy reference. They include knife skills, common seasoning and flavoring combinations, and techniques for mixing, shaping, and cooking. Each additional chapter imparts its own lessons on the meaning of mise en place.

KNIFE SKILLS

Knife skills include basic cuts that are used every day and more complicated special techniques. Even before anything is cut, however, knife skills include the ability to choose the proper knife for a given task, handle the knife with care, and properly maintain it. Different types of knives and their maintenance are discussed and illustrated in Chapter 5, "Equipment Identification."

Holding the Knife

Depending on the particular task and the specific knife, there are grips for holding the knife. The three basic holds are:

1. Gripping the handle with all four fingers and holding the thumb gently but firmly against the side of the blade.
2. Gripping the handle with three fingers, resting the index finger flat against the blade on one side, and holding the thumb on the opposite side to give additional stability and control.
3. Gripping the handle with four fingers and holding the thumb firmly against the blade's back. (See Fig. 14-1 for examples of these holds.)

In all cases, the hand not holding the knife, the *guiding hand*, guides the object being cut, prevents slippage, and helps to control the cut's size (see Fig. 14-2). The fingertips hold the object, with the thumb held back from the fingertips and the fingertips tucked under slightly. The knife blade then rests against the knuckles, preventing the fingers from being cut.

14-1 THE THREE KNIFE GRIPS

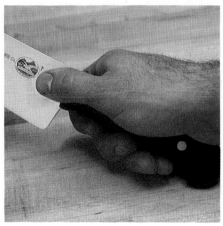

(1) The first knife grip.

(2) The second knife grip.

Basic Cuts

The basic cuts include coarse chopping and mincing, julienne or batonnet, dicing, rondelle, and oblique or roll cut. The aim should always be to cut the food into pieces of uniform shape and size because unevenly cut items take different amounts of cooking time and spoil the dish's look. The basic cuts are illustrated in the chart in Figure 14-3. They are also discussed in the following pages, with step-by-step methods. It should be noted that the dimensions indicated in Figure 14-3 are recommended guidelines. It is important that the chef be completely familiar with these cuts and able to execute them properly.

Coarse Chopping

Coarse chopping is usually used for such items as mirepoix, which will not be part of the finished presentation since they are normally strained out of the dish and discarded (see Fig. 14-4). The method is as follows:

1. Trim the root and stem ends and peel the vegetables if necessary.

(3) The third knife grip.

14-2 POSITION OF THE GUIDING HAND

The fingers of the guiding hand, left, are bent inward toward the palm, and the thumb is held well back.

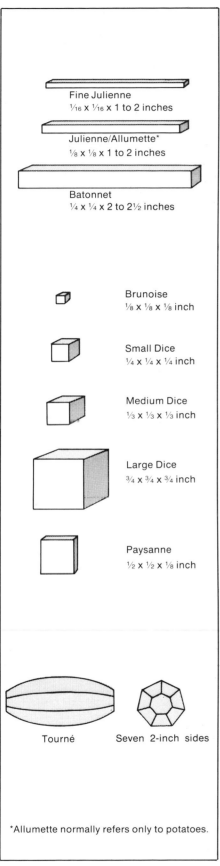

Fine Julienne
1/16 x 1/16 x 1 to 2 inches

Julienne/Allumette*
1/8 x 1/8 x 1 to 2 inches

Batonnet
1/4 x 1/4 x 2 to 2½ inches

Brunoise
1/8 x 1/8 x 1/8 inch

Small Dice
1/4 x 1/4 x 1/4 inch

Medium Dice
1/3 x 1/3 x 1/3 inch

Large Dice
3/4 x 3/4 x 3/4 inch

Paysanne
1/2 x 1/2 x 1/8 inch

Tourné   Seven 2-inch sides

*Allumette normally refers only to potatoes.

14-3
Basic knife cuts.

14-4 COARSE CHOPPING

The pieces of this cut are relatively even in size.

2. Slice or chop the vegetables at nearly regular intervals until the cuts are relatively uniform. This need not be a perfectly neat cut, but all the pieces should be roughly the same size.

Mincing

This is a relatively even, very fine cut that is especially appropriate for herbs and other flavoring ingredients such as garlic and shallots. (See Figs. 14-5 and 14-6 for different examples of mincing.) The method is as follows:

1. Gather herbs or roughly chopped garlic or shallots in a pile on a cutting board and position the knife above the pile.

2. Keeping the tip of the blade against the cutting board, lower the knife firmly and rapidly, repeatedly chopping through the herbs or vegetables.

3. Continue chopping until desired fineness is attained.

Julienne and Batonnet

Julienne and *batonnet* are long, rectangular cuts. Related cuts are the standard *pommes frites* and *pommes pont neuf* cuts (both are names for french fries) and the *allumette* (or matchstick) cut. The differences between these cuts is the size of the final product. (See Fig. 14-7 for examples of julienne, batonnet, dice, and paysanne.) The method is as follows:

1. Trim the vegetable so that the sides are straight, which will make it easier to produce even cuts. (The trimmings can be used, as appropriate, for stocks, soups, purees, or any preparation where the shape is not important.)

14-5 MINCING

(1) Coarsely chopped garlic *(left)* and finely minced garlic *(right)*.

(2) Mincing shallots. A series of parallel cuts are made through the peeled and halved shallot.

(1) Remove the leaves from the stems before mincing.

(2) Mince the leaves, using a rocking motion of the blade. The tip of the blade is held in place with the free hand.

(3) Finely minced parsley.

14-7 JULIENNE, BATONNET, DICE, AND PAYSANNE

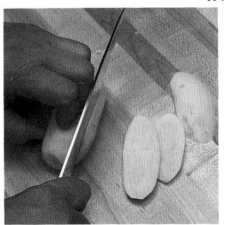

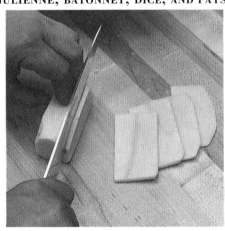

(1) Square off the sides of the vegetable.

(2) Slice the vegetable lengthwise to yield slices of even thickness.

(3) Stack the slices and make even, parallel cuts to yield julienne or batonnet.

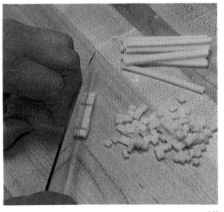

(4) Parallel, crosswise cuts of the proper thickness produce a fine dice.

(5) Use the first three steps to produce a thick batonnet and make a final thin cut to produce the typical paysanne.

(4)

(5)

208

2. Slice the vegetable lengthwise, using parallel cuts of the proper thickness.

3. Stack the slices, aligning the edges, and make parallel cuts of the same thickness through the stack. To make batonnet, the cuts should be thick. To make a fine julienne, the cuts should be very thin.

Dice

Dicing is a cutting technique that produces cube-shaped products. Different preparations require different sizes of dice, from *brunoise* (a fine dice) to a large dice. (Dicing is illustrated in Fig. 14-7.) The method is as follows:

1. Trim and cut the vegetable as for julienne or batonnet.

2. Gather the julienne or batonnets and cut through them crosswise at evenly spaced intervals.

Paysanne/Fermière

This cut resembles the thin, square wooden tile used in the game of Scrabble® (see Fig. 14-7), and it is often used for vegetables that are to garnish soups, stews, and braises. Although the size may vary, depending on the vegetable being cut and its intended use, a cut of 1-inch square and ¼-inch thick is customary. The method is as follows:

1. Trim and cut the vegetable as for batonnet.

2. Make even, thin, crosswise cuts in the batonnets, at roughly 1-inch intervals.

Rondelle

Rondelles, or rounds, are simple to cut. The shape is the result of cutting a cylindrical vegetable, such as a carrot or cucumber, crosswise. The basic rondelle shape, a round disk, can be varied by cutting the vegetable on the bias to produce an elongated or oval disk, or by slicing it in half for half-moons. If the vegetable is scored with a channel knife, flower shapes are produced. The method is as follows:

1. Trim and peel the vegetable if necessary.

2. Make parallel slicing cuts through the vegetable at even intervals. (See Fig. 14-8 for the basic rondelle cut and two variations.)

Diagonal

This cut (refer to Fig. 14-8) is often used to make vegetables ready for stir-fries and other Asian-style dishes. Because it exposes a greater surface area of the vegetable, employing this cut shortens cooking time. The method is as follows:

1. Place the peeled or trimmed vegetable on the work surface.

2. Make a series of even parallel cuts on the bias.

14-8 RONDELLE AND DIAGONAL CUTS

The carrot is being sliced straight across to yield a rondelle cut. In the background, carrots have been sliced on a diagonal.

Oblique or Roll Cut

This cut (Fig. 14-9) is used primarily with long, cylindrical vegetables such as parsnips, carrots, and celery. The method is as follows:

1. Place the peeled vegetable on a cutting board. Make a diagonal cut to remove the stem end.

2. Hold the knife in the same position and roll the vegetable 180 degrees (a half-turn). Slice through it on the same diagonal, forming a piece with two angled edges.

3. Repeat until the entire vegetable has been cut.

Special Cuts

The cuts explained in this section are more advanced than the standard cuts and require more practice. In some cases, using a special knife—for example, a tourné knife with a curved blade—may be helpful.

Tourné

Turning vegetables (*tourner* in French) requires a series of cuts that simultaneously trim and shape the vegetable. The shape may be

14-9 OBLIQUE OR ROLL CUT

To make this cut, the knife should be held at the angle shown here.

similar to a barrel or a football. Turned vegetables are traditionally given different names, depending on their size. *Printanière* (the size of a large marble) and *jardinière* (the size of a quail's egg) are two of the more common names for turned cuts. For a step-by-step illustration of how to *tourné*, see Figure 14-10. The method is as follows:

1. Peel the vegetable, if desired.
2. Cut into pieces of manageable size. Cut large round or oval vegetables, such as beets and potatoes, into quarters, sixths, or eighths (depending on their size), to form pieces slightly larger than 2 inches. Cut cylindrical vegetables, such as carrots, into 2-inch pieces.
3. Using a paring or tourné knife, carve the pieces into barrel or football shapes. The faces should be smooth, evenly spaced, and tapered so that both ends are narrower than the center.

Chiffonade

The *chiffonade* cut is used for leafy vegetables and herbs. The result is a finely shredded product, often used as a garnish. For an illustration of the chiffonade cut, see Figure 14-11. The method is as follows:

1. When cutting tight heads of greens, such as Belgian endive or head cabbage, core the head and cut it in half, if it is large, to make cutting easier. For greens with large, loose leaves, roll individual leaves into tight cylinders before cutting. For smaller leaves, stack several leaves on top of one another.
2. Use a chef's knife to make very fine, parallel cuts to produce fine shreds.

Decorative Cuts

These cuts are primarily used for garnishes, to improve the appearance of a finished dish.

Fluting

This technique, illustrated in Figure 14-12, takes some practice to master, but the result makes an attractive garnish. It is customarily used on mushrooms. The method is as follows:

1. Hold the mushroom between the guiding hand's thumb and forefinger. Place the blade of a paring knife at an angle against the mushroom cap center. Rest the thumb of the cutting hand on the mushroom and use it to brace the knife.
2. Rotate the knife toward the cap edge, to cut a shallow groove. At the same time the knife blade is cutting, the guiding hand turns the mushroom in the opposite direction.
3. Turn the mushroom slightly and repeat the cutting steps. Con-

14-10 TOURNÉ

(1) First, section the vegetable into pieces of a desirable length, then use the tip of a paring knife to whittle away pieces of the vegetable.

(2) The finished tourné *(above, right)*. The trimmings show the curved cuts that are made to produce an oval or football shape.

14-11 CHIFFONADE

Make very fine, parallel cuts to produce fine shreds.

tinue until the entire cap is fluted. The trimmings should be pulled away.

4. Trim away the stem.

Fanning

The fan cut, illustrated in Figure 14-13, uses one basic, easy-to-master cut to produce complicated-looking garnishes. It is used on both raw and cooked foods, such as pickles, strawberries, peach halves, zucchini, avocados, and other somewhat pliable vegetables and fruits. The method is as follows:

14-12 FLUTING

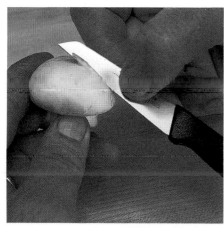

(1) Begin fluting by holding the mushroom in one hand and the blade of a paring knife in the other, as shown.

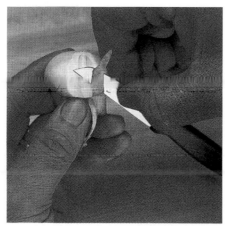

(2) Continue with a rotating motion, making closely spaced parallel strokes.

(3) The fully fluted mushroom cap.

(4) Trimming away the stem. Fluted mushroom caps are shown in the background.

1. Leaving the stem end intact, make a series of parallel vertical slices through the item.

2. Spread the cut item into a fan shape.

Special Peeling and Cutting Techniques

Techniques that are more involved than the preceding cuts are needed in the preparation of certain vegetables. These include peeling and dicing an onion, peeling and mashing garlic and shallots, mincing parsley, preparing tomato concassé, and peeling peppers.

Peeling and Dicing an Onion

Because onions grow in layers, they require a special technique (see Fig. 14-14), instead of the dicing method used on solid foods. The method is as follows:

1. Use a paring knife to remove the stem end. Peel off the skin and the underlying layer, if it contains brown spots. Trim the root end but leave it intact.

2. Halve the onion lengthwise through the root. Lay it cut-side

14-13 FANNING

Make parallel cuts, but leave one end intact. Spread the "leaves" of the fan apart gently.

14-14 PEELING AND DICING AN ONION

(1) Trim the stem end and pull back the papery skin.

(2) Trim a narrow slice from the root end and cut the onion in half from stem to root end.

(3) Make even, parallel cuts through the onion with a chef's knife, leaving the root end intact.

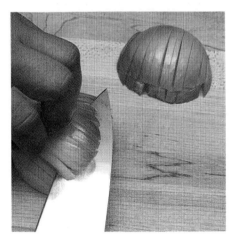

(4) Make a horizontal cut through the halved onion.

(5) Make parallel slices to produce an even-sized dice.

down and make a series of evenly spaced, parallel, lengthwise cuts with the tip of a chef's knife, again leaving the root end intact. The closer the cuts, the finer the dice will be.

3. Make two or three horizontal cuts parallel to the work surface, from the onion's stem end toward the root end, but do not cut all the way through.

4. Make even, crosswise cuts with a chef's knife, all the way through, from stem to root end.

Peeling and Mashing Garlic and Shallots

Mashed or minced shallots and

garlic are required in many preparations; for example, as a component in the aromatic bed for shallow-poached items, or in the reduction used to flavor emulsion sauces. It is important to have enough prepared to last through a service period. To prevent bacterial growth, store uncooked, minced shallots or garlic covered in oil under refrigeration. A step-by-step illustration of peeling and mashing garlic appears in Figure 14-15. The method is as follows:

1. To loosen the skin, crush the garlic clove or shallot bulb between the knife blade's flat side and the cutting board, using the heel of the

hand. Peel off the skin and remove the root end and any brown spots.

2. Mince the clove or bulb fairly fine, or coarsely chop, as for herbs. (If desired, sprinkle the garlic or shallot with salt before mincing. This makes mashing easier by providing abrasion and absorbing excess juice and oil.)

3. Hold the knife at an angle and use the cutting edge to mash the garlic or shallot against the cutting board. Repeat this step until the item is mashed to a paste.

4. To hold, place in a jar, cover with a layer of oil, and refrigerate.

Note: Large quantities may be minced in a food processor.

Zesting Citrus Fruit

The zest, the outer portion of a citrus fruit's peel or rind, is used to add color, texture, and flavor to various preparations. The zest includes *only* the skin's brightly colored part, which contains much of the fruit's flavorful and aromatic volatile oils. It does not include the underlying white pith, which has a bitter taste (see Fig. 14-16). The method is as follows:

1. Use a paring knife, swivel-

14-15 PEELING AND MASHING GARLIC

(1) Crush the garlic clove between the work surface and the flat edge of the blade.

(2) Pull away the papery skin.

(3) Mince the garlic, then hold the knife at an angle against the board and drag the blade inward, scraping the garlic repeatedly against the board.

14-16 ZESTING CITRUS FRUIT

(1) Use a zester to remove small strips of zest, without removing any of the bitter pith.

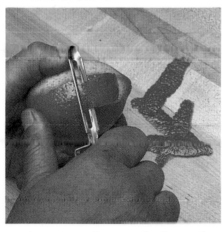

(2) A rotary peeler can also be used to remove the zest.

(3) The larger pieces can then be cut into a fine julienne with a chef's knife.

bladed peeler, or zester to remove only the peel's colored portion.

2. If julienne or grated zest is called for, use a chef's knife to cut or mince the zest.

Preparing Tomato Concassé

Tomato concassé is required in the preparation or finishing of a number of different sauces and dishes. If required it should be made in advance, but only enough to last through a single service period.

Once peeled and chopped, tomatoes will begin to lose some of their flavor and texture. A step-by-step illustration of this technique appears in Figure 14-17. The method is as follows:

1. Cut away the stem ends and pull the skin away using a paring knife. (This blanching and peeling technique is also used for peaches and apricots.)

2. Bring a pot of water to a roll-

ing boil. Drop the tomatoes into the water. After 10 to 30 seconds (depending upon the tomatoes' age and ripeness), remove them with a slotted spoon, skimmer, or spider. Immediately plunge them into ice water. Pull away the skin.

3. Halve each tomato crosswise at its widest point and gently squeeze out the seeds. (Plum tomatoes are more easily seeded by cutting lengthwise.)

4. Cut the flesh into dice or julienne, as desired.

14-17 TOMATO CONCASSÉ

(1) Drop the tomato into rapidly boiling water.

(2) Immediately remove with a slotted spoon and plunge into ice water.

Peeling Sweet or Hot Peppers

Numerous dishes call for peeled peppers because the outer skin is overly tough for these preparations. There are four basic methods for peeling peppers.

1. Peeling with a swivel peeler. This method is used when peeled, raw peppers are needed.

- Section the pepper with a knife, cutting along the folds to expose the unpeeled skin.
- Remove the core, seeds, and ribs and peel with a swivel peeler.

(3) Pull away the skin.

(4) Cut the tomato in half across the belly (the widest portion) and squeeze out the seeds.

(5) Coarsely chop the flesh into the desired size.

14-18 PEELING PEPPERS BY CHARRING

(1) Hold the pepper in a gas flame with a kitchen fork.

(2) Wrap immediately in plastic wrap to "steam."

(3) Use a paring knife to help peel away charred skin.

2. Peeling charred peppers. This technique is used to roast and peel small quantities (see Fig. 14-18).

- Hold the pepper over the flame of a gas burner with tongs or a kitchen fork or place the pepper on a grill. Turn the pepper and roast it until the surface is evenly charred.
- Place in a plastic or paper bag or under an inverted bowl to steam the skin loose.
- When the pepper is cool enough to handle, remove the charred skin, using a paring knife if necessary.

3. Peeling oven- or broiler-roasted peppers. This method is used for larger quantities (see Fig. 14-19).

- Halve the peppers and remove stems and seeds. Place cut-side down on an oiled sheet pan.
- Place in a very hot oven or under a broiler. Roast or broil until evenly charred.
- Remove from the oven or broiler and cover immediately, using an inverted sheet pan. This will steam the peppers, making the skin easier to remove.

- Peel, using a paring knife if necessary.

4. Peeling deep-fried peppers. This is a quick method for charring small quantities (see Fig. 14-20).

- Using tongs or the double basket method, submerge the peppers in oil that has been heated to 325°F (165°C).
- Deep-fry the peppers for about a minute, until they are blistered all over. The peppers may char.
- Remove from the deep fat, drain, and let cool.
- Peel away the skin, using a paring knife if necessary.

14-19 PEELING PEPPERS BY OVEN-ROASTING OR BROILING

(1) Place halved peppers on a lightly oiled sheet pan and put under a broiler.

(2) Cover with a second sheet pan.

14-20 PEELING PEPPERS BY DEEP-FRYING

(1) Place peppers in frying basket.

(3) Deep-fry until peppers are blistered all over.

(2) To keep peppers fully submerged, use doubled baskets.

(4) Remove and drain well before wrapping.

Standard Sachet d'Épices

Yield: Sufficient to season approximately 1 gallon (3.75 liters) of stock

Parsley stems, chopped	3 or 4	3 or 4
Thyme leaves, dried	½ teaspoon	½ gram
Bay leaf	1	1
Peppercorns, cracked	½ teaspoon	1 gram
Garlic clove, crushed (optional)	1	1

Place all ingredients on a piece of cheesecloth approximately 4 inches square. Gather up the edges and tie with butcher's twine, leaving a long tail of string to tie to the stockpot handle.

NOTE: Cloves, dill, tarragon stems, and other herbs and spices may be included, according to the recipe or desired result.

Liquid Marinades

Liquid marinades add flavor and some moisture. The ingredients vary, depending on how it will be used, but the basic ratio is three parts oil to one part acid, plus the desired seasonings and aromatics. Almost any oil can be used, depending on the desired effect. Commonly used acidic ingredients include vinegar, fruit juice, wine, and beer.

Aromatics or other flavoring combinations such as a mirepoix may be included. Some marinades are cooked before use, others are not. Often the marinade is used to

14-21
Bouquet garni.

14-22
Standard sachet d'épices.

14-23
Oignon piqué *(left)* and oignon brûlé *(right).*

flavor an accompanying sauce. To use a liquid marinade, the chef should:

1. Prepare the ingredient(s) to be marinated and place it (them) in a hotel pan large enough to hold the ingredient(s) comfortably.

2. Add the marinade and turn the ingredient(s) to coat evenly.

3. Marinate for the length of time indicated by the recipe, type of main product, or desired result.

Dry Marinades

A dry marinade is a mixture of salt, crushed or chopped herbs, spices, and occasionally other aromatics, such as citrus zest. In some cases, the marinade is mixed with oil to make a paste. The marinade is rubbed over the food—usually meats and fish—and the coated item is then allowed to stand, under refrigeration, to absorb the marinade's flavors. Dry marinades are often left on the food during cooking to create a savory crust.

THICKENERS

The consistency of liquid preparations, such as soups, sauces, and braising liquids, often needs to be adjusted to achieve a desired texture. The following techniques and preparations provide ways to thicken liquids.

Reduction

Reduction, a process that removes some or all of the water in a liquid, not only thickens but also concentrates the liquid's flavor. Liquids can be reduced to varying degrees, typically defined by how much liquid is cooked off. For example, reducing by half means half of the liquid is cooked off. To reduce by

Liquid Marinade for Salmon

Yield: Approximately 1½ cups (360 milliliters)

Extra-virgin olive oil	1 cup	240 milliliters
Lime juice	of 2 limes	of 2 limes
Lemon juice	of 1 lemon	of 1 lemon
Wine vinegar	1 ounce	30 milliliters
Shallots, minced	3 tablespoons	45 grams
Pink peppercorns, cracked	2 tablespoons	6 grams
Salt	to taste	to taste
Pepper	to taste	to taste

Combine all ingredients. Use to marinate thinly sliced salmon.

Dry Marinade for Salmon

Yield: 3 pounds, 4 ounces (1.5 kilograms)

Kosher salt	2 pounds	910 grams
Brown sugar	1 pound	455 grams
Curing salt	2 tablespoons	30 grams
Garlic powder	2 tablespoons	5 grams
Onion powder	2 tablespoons	5 grams
Bay leaf, ground	2 tablespoons	5 grams
Allspice, ground	2 tablespoons	5 grams
Mace, ground	2 tablespoons	5 grams
Cloves, ground	1 tablespoon	3 grams

Combine all ingredients. Use to coat salmon fillets. To remove, rinse the fish and pat dry.

three-fourths means to cook off three-fourths of the liquid, leaving one-fourth of the original volume. To reduce *au sec* (to dry) means to reduce until nearly all of the liquid has evaporated.

Heavy pots are recommended, especially for reductions au sec, because as more water evaporates, the reduction is more likely to scorch. When reducing large amounts, it is advisable to transfer it to a succession of smaller pots as it reduces, thereby minimizing the risk of scorching by keeping the liquid from spreading over a large surface area. It is often advisable to strain the liquid as it is transferred. The method is as follows:

1. Place the liquid in a heavy pot.

2. Bring it to a simmer and cook until the desired amount has evaporated.

3. When reducing au sec, keep the heat very low near the end of cooking and watch the reduction carefully to prevent scorching.

Slurries

A slurry is simply a starch (flour, arrowroot, cornstarch, or rice flour) dissolved in cold liquid. The mixture should have the consistency of heavy cream. The method is as follows:

1. Blend the starch thoroughly with one to two times its volume of cold liquid. If the slurry has stood for a while, be sure to stir it well before mixing it into the hot liquid, as the starch tends to settle.

2. Bring the hot liquid to a simmer or a low boil.

3. Gradually add the slurry, stirring or whisking constantly to prevent lumping and scorching.

4. Bring the mixture to a boil and cook just until the sauce

Standard Reduction

Yield: 3 to 4 ounces (90 to 120 milliliters)

Mushroom stems, chopped	4 ounces	115 grams
Parsley stems	10 to 12	10 to 12
Bay leaf	3	3
Peppercorns	10 to 12	10 to 12
Thyme sprigs, fresh	2	2
Shallots, minced	2	2
Garlic cloves, minced	3	3
Wine (dry, white or red)	6 ounces	180 milliliters
Water	1 ounce	30 milliliters

1. Combine all the ingredients with enough wine to cover by ½ inch.

2. Reduce over moderate heat by half. Add the water.

3. Strain; cool and reserve.

reaches the desired thickness and clarity.

Roux

Roux is prepared by cooking together a fat and a flour. This mixture is often prepared in advance in large quantities for use as needed. Butter is the most common fat, but chicken fat, vegetable oils, or fats rendered from roasts may also be used. Different fats will have a subtle influence on the finished dish's flavor.

The standard proportion of fat to flour is one to one by weight, but depending on the types of fat and flour used, this proportion may need to be adjusted slightly. Cooked roux should be moist but not greasy. A common description is "like sand at low tide." There are three basic types of roux, differing according to the length of time they are cooked: white roux, pale or blond roux, and brown roux.

The procedure for preparing roux is demonstrated in Figure 14-24. The method is as follows:

1. Melt the butter or other fat in a pan over moderate to low heat.

2. Add the flour and stir until smooth.

3. If necessary, add a small amount of flour to achieve the proper consistency.

4. Cook, stirring constantly, to the desired color. Roux should be glossy in appearance.

- White roux should be barely colored, or chalky.
- Pale or blond roux should be a golden straw color, with a slightly nutty aroma.
- Brown roux should be deep brown, with a strong nutty aroma.

5. If the roux will not be used right away, cool and store it, tightly wrapped, in the refrigerator.

14-24 ROUX

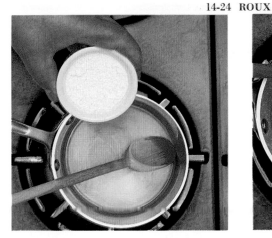

(1) Add flour to hot clarified butter.

(2) Cook the roux, stirring constantly.

(3) Roux should be glossy in appearance.

(4) Three stages: pale roux *(top)*, blond roux *(bottom right)*, and brown roux *(bottom left).*

White Roux

Yield: 2 pounds (910 grams)

Clarified butter, oil, or other fat	1 pound	455 grams
All-purpose flour	1 pound	455 grams

1. Heat the clarified butter or oil in a rondeau over moderate heat.

2. Add the flour all at once. Stirring constantly, cook over low heat until the roux is a very pale ivory, approximately 8 minutes.

VARIATIONS

Blonde Roux: Cook the roux for an additional 2 or 3 minutes, until roux becomes golden in color.

Brown Roux: Continue to cook the roux until it is browned and has a pronounced nutty aroma.

Note: Larger quantities of roux may be made in the oven in a rondeau or brazier. The fat is melted and the flour added as in the previous method. The pan is then placed in a moderate (350 to 375°F/175 to 190°C) oven and cooked to the desired color. It should be stirred occasionally during the cooking time.

Combining Roux with Liquid

1. Be sure that the roux and liquid temperatures are different—hot liquid and cold roux or cold liquid and hot roux—to help prevent lumping. Add one to the other gradually and whip constantly to work out lumps. Figure 14-25 demonstrates both ways of adding roux and also shows a properly cooked roux.

2. Gradually return the soup or sauce to a boil, whisking occasionally.

3. Reduce the heat and simmer, stirring occasionally, at least 20 minutes, to cook out the taste of the flour.

Note: To test for the presence of starch, press a small amount of the sauce to the roof of the mouth with the tongue. It should not feel gritty or gluey. If it does, continue cooking until the starch is completely cooked out.

Beurre Manié

Beurre manié, a French term for kneaded butter, is a mixture of equal amounts (by weight) of softened whole butter and flour. Sometimes called "uncooked roux," it is used to quickly thicken sauces and stews. Beurre manié produces a thin to medium consistency and a glossy texture. It is traditionally used in vegetable dishes (peas *bonne femme,* for example) and fish

Beurre Manié

Yield: 6 ounces (175 grams)

Butter	3½ ounces	100 grams
Flour	2½ ounces	75 grams

1. Allow the butter to soften until pliable.

2. Add the flour and, using a wooden spoon, work to a smooth paste. (An electric mixer may be used for larger quantities.)

3. Use immediately or wrap tightly and refrigerate.

14-25a COMBINING ROUX WITH A LIQUID

(1) Hot stock is added to the cold roux away from direct heat.

(2) A whip is used to work out all lumps.

14-25 b ANOTHER METHOD FOR COMBINING ROUX WITH A LIQUID

(1) Cold stock is added to hot roux in a pot directly over heat.

(2) Proper consistency and sheen after the roux is cooked out.

stews (known as *matelotes*). The method is as follows:

1. Allow the butter to soften until it is pliable but not melted—it should still be cool and "plastic."

2. Add an equal weight of flour and work to a smooth paste. Use a wooden spoon when working with small amounts; the friction of the wood against the bowl helps to work the butter and flour together quickly. When making large quantities, use an electric mixer.

3. If the beurre manié will not be used right away, store it, tightly wrapped, in the refrigerator.

Liaison

A liaison is a mixture of egg yolks and cream that is used to both thicken and enrich sauces and soups. A liaison also adds flavor to a sauce or soup and gives it a smooth texture and golden color.

Liaisons are never added directly to hot liquids; the heat could cause the yolks to scramble. To avoid this, some of the hot liquid is added to the liaison to raise its temperature gradually. This process, illustrated in Figure 14-26, is known as "tempering" the liaison. The tempered liaison is then added to the hot liquid.

The basic ratio in a liaison is three parts cream to one part egg yolk, by weight. A combination of 8 ounces (240 milliliters) heavy cream and three egg yolks is sufficient to thicken and enrich 24 ounces (720 milliliters) of liquid. Sour cream or crème fraîche may be substituted for the heavy cream. The method is as follows:

1. Gradually add about one-third of the hot liquid to the liaison.

2. Return the tempered liaison to the hot liquid, stirring constantly.

14-26 TEMPERING A LIAISON

(1) Gradually incorporate about one-third of the hot liquid into the liaison.

(2) Return the tempered liaison to the remainder of the hot liquid.

Liaison

Yield: Approximately 8 ounces (240 milliliters), sufficient to thicken 24 ounces (720 milliliters) of liquid

Heavy cream	8 ounces	240 milliliters
Egg yolks	3	3

Combine ingredients. Be sure to temper liaison before adding to hot liquid by adding a little hot liquid to the liaison to gradually raise the temperature.

NOTE: Sour cream or crème fraîche may be substituted for heavy cream.

3. Slowly bring the mixture to just below simmering (180°F/82°C).

Note: Liaison-thickened soups and sauces are difficult to hold because the egg yolks could easily scramble if they become too hot. Ideally, the liaison should be added just before service. If the sauce or soup must be held for service, it should be kept between 140 and 180°F (60 to 82°C).

Gelatin

Gelatin is used to stabilize foams and to thicken liquid-based mixtures that will be served cold. Approximately 2½ ounces (75 grams) of any type of gelatin will thicken about 1 gallon (3.75 liters) of liquid. More gelatin will be required if the liquid contains sugar or acidic ingredients, which inhibit gelling. (Gelatin is described in Chapter 10, "Nonperishable Goods Identification.") The method is as follows:

1. Soak the gelatin in cool liquid before using. This process, called "blooming," allows the gelatin to soften and to begin absorption of the liquid.

2. Melt the dissolved gelatin crystals. This may be done by placing the gelatin-liquid mixture over a warm water bath or by heating it in a microwave oven on a low-power setting. If the gelatin is to be combined with a hot liquid, it may be tempered with some or all of that liquid to melt the crystals.

3. Combine the dissolved gelatin with the liquid. Stir well to disperse throughout the mixture. Chill until the mixture is set.

BASIC INGREDIENTS AND APPAREILS

Some ingredients (butter, for example) need to be refined before they are ready for use at the time of service; others need to be combined with additional ingredients. An appareil is a mixture of ingredients used as one component in preparing a given dish.

Clarified Butter and Rendered Fat

Clarified butter is pure butterfat. It can be heated to a higher temperature than whole butter without burning or breaking down because the milk solids, which scorch easily, have been removed.

Because it has some butter flavor, clarified butter is often used for sautéing, sometimes in combination with a vegetable oil to further raise the smoking point, and also to make roux. Clarified butter may also be used as a sauce, usually with seafood; in this application it is known as "drawn butter."

When whole butter is clarified, some of its volume and flavor is lost because water and milk solids make up about 20 percent of the volume. One pound (455 grams) of whole butter yields approximately 12 ounces (340 grams) of clarified butter.

Clarifying Butter

As the butter heats, the milk solids and water will sink, some impurities may rise to the surface, and the butterfat will become very clear. The process of clarifying butter is illustrated in Figure 14-27. The method is as follows:

1. Melt the butter in a heavy saucepan over moderate heat.
2. Remove the pan from the heat.
3. Skim the surface foam.
4. Pour or ladle off the butterfat into another container, being careful to leave all of the liquid in the pan bottom. Discard the liquid.

Note: For *beurre noisette*, or brown clarified butter, continue to cook until the milk solids appear golden. Brown clarified butter will have a delicate, nutty aroma.

Alternate Method

1. Heat the butter in a saucepan or bain-marie until the butter and milk solids separate.
2. Refrigerate in the bain-marie until the butterfat has hardened.
3. Bore a hole through the hardened butter with a serving spoon handle. Pour away the water and milk solids.
4. Remelt the butter as needed for service.

Rendering and Clarifying Fat

Occasionally the fat from ducks, geese, or pork may be required for such dishes as confits or cassoulet. Salt pork, another example, should be gently rendered, or melted down, so that the fat can be used to smother the aromatic vegetables used in the preparation of soups, stews, and braises. Properly clarifying a roast's fat and drippings is

14-27 A METHOD OF CLARIFYING BUTTER

(1) Melt the butter and skim the foam.

(2) Ladle the clear butterfat into a separate container.

(3) Do not mix the milk solids into the clear butterfat.

(4) The three stages of butter as it is clarified: *(left)* melted butter, *(center)* butter separating, *(right)* fully clarified butter.

essential for the preparation of a good pan gravy. The method is as follows:

1. Cube the fat, if necessary.
2. Place the fat in a sauteuse. Add about ½-inch of water to the uncooked fats if there are no drippings present.
3. Cook over low heat until the water evaporates and the fat is released. (This is the actual clarifying process.)
4. Remove the cracklings, if any, with a slotted spoon (they may be reserved for garnish).

5. Use or store the rendered fat under refrigeration. A caramelized fond from the drippings should remain when preparing pan gravies.

Duxelles

A *duxelles* is a mixture of finely chopped and sautéed mushrooms that also includes shallots, leeks, and white wine. It may be used as a flavoring, stuffing, or coating. It should be moist enough to hold together but not runny.

Pesto

Pesto is a mixture of an herb and an oil, pureed into a smooth, thick paste. Italy, specifically Genoa, claims to have first developed this sauce.

Pesto customarily contains basil and oil and may also contain grated cheese, nuts, or seeds, depending upon the individual recipe. Contemporary renditions may replace some or all of the basil with cilantro, oregano, or other herbs. Pesto may be used as a sauce for pasta and other foods, as a soup garnish, or as a dressing or sauce ingredient.

Persillade

Persillade is a mixture of breadcrumbs, minced parsley, and garlic used as a coating for roasted and grilled items. It protects the meat, seals in the juices, and provides textural contrast. Usually, a small amount of melted butter or oil may be rubbed into the persillade to help the ingredients adhere better. *Persillé* is the French term used to describe items coated with this appareil.

Pâte à Choux

Pâte à choux, or cream puff dough, is the base for such desserts as profiteroles, éclairs, and Paris-Brest. It is also combined with pureed potatoes in savory dishes such as *pommes dauphines* and as a base for savory soufflés. A step-by-step illustration of the procedure for making pâte à choux appears in Figure 14-28. The method is as follows:

1. Bring water and butter to a rolling boil.
2. Add flour to boiling water and butter.

Duxelles

Yield: Approximately 12 ounces (340 grams)

Clarified butter	½ ounce	15 grams
Shallots, chopped	½ tablespoon	7 grams
Mushrooms, finely chopped	12 ounces	340 grams
Parsley, chopped	1 teaspoon	1 gram

1. Heat the butter in a small sauté pan.
2. Add the shallots and sweat.
3. Using cheesecloth or paper toweling, squeeze all juices from the mushrooms.
4. Add the mushrooms to the pan and cook until they are browned and dry.
5. Add parsley; add salt and pepper to taste.

Pesto

Yield: Approximately 1 cup (200 grams)

Basil leaves, fresh	1 cup + 2 tablespoons	60 grams
Garlic cloves	3	3
Pine nuts, toasted	1 tablespoon	7 grams
Olive oil	1 tablespoon	15 milliliters

Puree all ingredients in a blender or food processor; add water to adjust consistency, if necessary.

Persillade

Yield: 5 ounces (140 grams)

Garlic cloves, minced	4	4
Parsley, chopped	⅓ cup	12 grams
Bread crumbs, fresh	2 ounces	55 grams
Vegetable oil or melted butter	as needed	as needed

Combine all ingredients. Use immediately or store.

14-28 PÂTE À CHOUX

(1) Add flour to boiling water and butter.

(2) Cook over moderate to low heat.

(3) Add the eggs, one at a time.

Pâte à Choux

Yield: Approximately 12 ounces (340 grams)

Water	4 ounces	115 grams
Butter	2 ounces	55 grams
Salt	¼ tablespoon	4 grams
Flour, sifted	3 ounces	85 grams
Eggs	2 to 3	2 to 3

(4) The proper finished consistency.

1. Combine the water, butter, and salt in a heavy saucepan and bring to a boil.

2. Reduce heat to low. Add the flour. Stir the mixture with a wooden spoon until it pulls away from the pan sides.

3. Remove from heat and continue to stir. (When making large amounts, place in the bowl of a mixer and beat with a paddle attachment.)

4. Add eggs one at a time; beat until smooth after each addition.

5. Use immediately or cool and refrigerate for later use.

3. Cook over moderate to low heat until mixture pulls cleanly away from the pot sides. Remove from heat.

4. Add the eggs, a few at a time, and work into a smooth batter.

BASIC COOKING TECHNIQUES

Instead of explaining the most basic cooking techniques each time they appear in a method or recipe, they are outlined in this section, for easy reference. These techniques may be executed at various kitchen stations.

Separating Eggs

Before beginning this procedure, the chef should have available one container for the yolks, one for the clean whites, and a small bowl. A step-by-step illustration of the technique appears in Figure 14-29. The method is as follows:

1. Crack open the egg over a small bowl.

2. Transfer the egg back and forth between the halves of the shell, letting the white drop into the small bowl.

3. Place the yolk in its container.

4. Inspect the egg white. If there are traces of yolk, reserve it separately for use in omelets, quiches, and other preparations. If the white is clean, transfer it to the whites' container.

Whipping Egg Whites

In order to obtain the maximum volume from whipped egg whites, all traces of fat must be eliminated because fat (including that contained in the yolks and any grease on the bowl or whip) inhibits foaming. Rinse bowls and whips with white vinegar to remove grease and then rinse well with hot water. Due to the chemical reaction of the copper and the egg whites, copper bowls tend to increase volume and stability and should be used if available. An example of the different kinds of peaks obtained from whipping appears in Figure 14-30. The method is as follows:

1. Begin whipping the egg whites by hand or machine at moderate speed. Tilt the bowl to make whipping by hand easier, resting the bowl on a folded towel to prevent slipping.

2. When the whites are quite foamy, increase the speed.

3. Whip to the appropriate stage.

- Soft peak. When the whisk or beater is pulled up through the egg whites, a droopy, rounded peak will form. At this stage, the surface of the whites looks moist and glossy.
- Medium peak. Whites beaten to the medium peak stage have a moist surface and form a rounded but fairly stable peak. At this stage, sugar and other flavorings may be added.
- Stiff peak. When the whisk or beater is lifted out of the egg whites, they will stand up in stiff, stable peaks. It is crucial to stop beating while the surface is still moist and glossy.

Note: Never overbeat egg whites. Overbeaten egg whites may still re-

14-29 SEPARATING EGGS

(1) Crack open the egg over a small container.

(2) Transfer the egg back and forth between the halves of the shell.

14-30 WHIPPING EGG WHITES

(1) Soft peaks will mound slightly.

(2) Medium peaks will hold but the ends will droop over.

(3) Stiff peaks will stand up firmly.

(4) Overbeaten whites lose their glossy appearance and will not hold a defined peak.

semble those at the stiff peak stage, but their surface looks dry and they have lost their elasticity. If the whites are beaten further, the egg protein will gather into globs and the moisture will weep out.

Whipping Cream

To whip cream, follow the same general technique as for whipping egg whites. The cream should be cold when it is whipped. Chilling the bowl and beaters in advance also aids in achieving the greatest volume. For best results, sugar and other flavorings should be added after the cream is whipped to at least a soft peak.

Like egg whites, cream can be overbeaten. Overbeaten cream first develops a grainy texture. Eventually lumps will form and, if whip- ping continues, the cream will turn to butter (see Fig. 14-31).

Folding Whipped Items (Foams) into a Base Appareil

The foam should be gently folded into the base, using a rubber spatula or a whip, to assure a smooth, light, and foamy batter. A step-by-step illustration of this procedure appears in Figure 14-32. The method is as follows:

1. Have the base appareil in a large bowl to accommodate the folding motion.

2. Add about one-third of the beaten egg whites or cream and fold in, using a circular motion, going from the side to the bottom of the bowl and back up to the surface.

3. Add the remaining whipped item, folding just until blended.

14-31 WHIPPING CREAM

(1) Soft peaks will mound when dropped from the whip.

(2) Medium peaks retain marks of the whip and will hold a soft peak that droops over.

(3) Stiff peaks will form distinct mounds that hold their shape.

(4) Overbeaten heavy cream has a curdled appearance.

MISCELLANEOUS TECHNIQUES

There are a number of techniques that have a variety of applications in the kitchen and the bakeshop.

For example, a bain-marie setup would be used in the kitchen to prepare terrines or savory custards; in the bakeshop, this same technique is used to prepare steamed puddings and flans.

Bain-marie/Water Bath

Items such as custards and terrines are cooked in a water bath to assure gentle, even cooking. To set up a bain-marie, place a deep pan large enough to hold the baking dish comfortably on an oven rack. Add the baking dish. Pour in enough boiling water to come halfway to two-thirds of the way up the side of the dish. (The boiling water is poured in after the baking dish has been placed in the oven to avoid scalding spills.) Adjust the oven temperature as necessary to keep the water temperature between 180 and 190°F (82 and 88°C). See Figure 14-33 for an example.

Cutting Parchment Liners

Parchment paper is often used to cover items that will be shallow-poached or braised. The parchment traps some of the steam and allows foods to cook gently and evenly, but does not hold in so much steam that temperature and pressure will build to the point at which delicate foods might overcook and break apart. The method outlined below and illustrated in Figure 14-34 is for cutting a round of parchment and lining a ring mold.

14-32 FOLDING WHIPPED INGREDIENTS INTO A BASE

(1) Add about one-third of the beaten whites or cream to the base appareil.

(2) Use a whip to gently fold the mixtures together.

(3) The light and very smooth mixture after thorough folding.

14-33

The proper setup for a bain-marie.

1. Cut a square of parchment paper a little larger than the pan's diameter.

2. Fold the square in half to form a triangle.

3. Continue folding in half until a long triangle about an inch wide at its widest point is formed.

4. Position the triangle's narrow end above the pan's center and cut away the part that extends beyond the pan edge.

Cutting Parchment for a Ring Mold

1. Follow steps 1 to 4 in the method for cutting parchment to line a round pan (above).

2. Position the triangle's point above the center of the ring mold and cut off the point at the mold's inner edge.

14-34 MAKING A PARCHMENT LINER

(1) Fold the parchment in half to form a triangle.

(2) Continue folding into successively smaller triangles.

(3) Hold the point at the pan's center and trim away the parchment that extends beyond the rim.

(4) Unfold the paper.

(5) Hold the triangle point in the center of the ring mold opening and make a cut at the inner and outer rims.

14-34 MAKING A PARCHMENT LINER
(continued)

SUMMARY

Mastering the basic skills covered in this chapter forms the foundation of a chef's training. This cannot be stressed too much. These skills will be used throughout a cooking career, from the apprentice's assignment of trimming vegetables to the saucier's perfection of his or her art. The importance of what may seem to be only minor details will continue to grow as a chef becomes more experienced.

(6) Open the paper.

Chapter *15*

Stocks

Among the most basic of preparations found in any professional kitchen are stocks. In fact, they are referred to as *fonds de cuisine*, or the "foundation of cooking." An essential component in many major cooking techniques, stocks form the base for various soups and sauces and are used in numerous other applications.

The preparation of quality stocks illustrates a primary culinary principle: A basic technique, properly understood and carefully executed, can be used to produce a variety of products. In other words, learning a basic method is more important than knowing a great number of recipes. The specific ingredients will vary from recipe to recipe; the technique will not.

This chapter clearly illustrates the proper preparation technique for stocks. All stocks have certain essential components: a major flavoring ingredient, liquid, aromatics, and mirepoix.

A STOCK'S CHARACTERISTICS

A stock is a flavorful liquid made by gently simmering bones or vegetables in a liquid to extract their flavor, aroma, color, body, and nutritive value. When bones (or vegetables), flavorings, and aromatic ingredients are combined in the proper ratio and simmered for an adequate amount of time, the stock develops the aforementioned characteristics that are peculiar to a stock type.

Brown stocks achieve their deep, rich color and aroma when bones and meat are browned during a preliminary roasting process. White stocks, made from unbrowned bones, remain relatively clear and should not have a strong color. The color of vegetable stocks varies according to the amount and type of vegetables used.

A stock's taste should be definite enough to allow for ready identification but not strong enough to compete with the other ingredients used in a finished dish (a cream soup or braised items, for instance). Fish stock, chicken stock, and brown stock tend to have the most assertive flavors. White veal stock is considered "neutral" in flavor and can be used as a "universal" stock.

Types

White stock is a clear, relatively colorless liquid made by simmering poultry, beef, or fish bones and the appropriate aromatics in water to extract the water-soluble proteins such as gelatin that provide flavor and body.

Brown stock is an amber liquid made by first browning poultry, beef, veal, or game bones and aromatic vegetables and then proceeding as for white stock.

Fumet, a highly flavored stock, is generally made with fish bones. This stock is prepared by using a technique known as the sweating method, in which bones and mirepoix are allowed to gently cook before the liquid is added.

Court bouillon ("short broth") is an aromatic vegetable broth that frequently includes wine and/or vinegar. Court bouillon is most commonly used for poaching fish, although it may also be used for cooking vegetables, especially those to be served chilled or *à la grecque.*

Essence is essentially the same as a fumet but uses highly aromatic products, such as celery and morels.

Glace (glaze) is a reduced stock. As a result of continued reduction, the stock acquires a jellylike or syrupy consistency and its flavor becomes highly concentrated. Glaces serve as a sauce base or are used to bolster other foods' flavors. They may be made from various stocks; the most common is glace de viande, made from brown veal stock.

Remouillage (a re-wetting) is a stock made from bones that have already been used (those used for a jus lié, for example, or for making stock). This second stock is less strong and is usually reduced to make a glace. Remouillage may also replace water in the making of a stock.

Broth or *bouillon* is the liquid that results from simmering meats. Bouillon is simply the French term for broth. The base liquid is often a stock. Bouillon may be used as a soup or as the basis for other soups (especially consommé), stews, and braises.

Examples of these stocks appear in Figures 15-1 through 15-4.

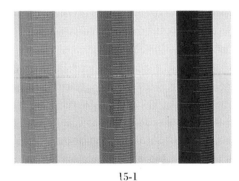

15-1

White beef stock *(left),* chicken stock *(center),* and brown veal stock *(right).*

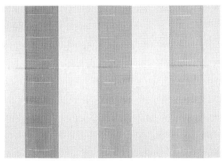

15-2

Court bouillon *(left),* fish stock *(center),* and fish fumet *(right).*

15-3

Essence *(left)* and glace de viande *(right).*

15-4

Proper color for remouillage *(left)* and broth *(right).*

USES

The three major uses of stocks are:

- as a base for sauces and soups
- as a base for stews and braises
- as a cooking medium for vegetables and grains

MISE EN PLACE

Components

Major flavoring ingredients. The major flavoring ingredients are usually bones and trimmings for meat or fish stocks. Vegetables are used for vegetable essences and court bouillon. The bones used may be fresh or frozen, although fresh is naturally preferable.

Bones should be cut into 3-inch lengths for quicker and more thorough extraction of flavor, gelatin, and nutritive value. Most bones may be purchased pre-cut into the proper length. If a kitchen staff does at least some meat or fish fabrication, the bones should be reserved. Heavy bones should be cut with a band saw; a cleaver will cause them to splinter. Chicken and fish bones can be cut with a heavy knife or cleaver.

The vegetables for a vegetable stock or court bouillon should be prepared according to type. For example, mushrooms should be trimmed and wiped to remove dirt, celery should be trimmed and rinsed, and tomatoes should be peeled.

Liquid. Water is the most frequently used liquid for making stock; it is certainly the most readily available. Remouillage is the best choice for the most richly flavored stock. Occasionally wine is added to a stock, especially to a fish fumet. For best results, the liquid should be cold when it is combined with bones or vegetables.

The ratio of liquid to flavoring ingredient is important, and the following figures are standard.

- For chicken, beef, veal, and game stock: 8 pounds of bones to 6 quarts of water yield 1 gallon of stock. One pound of mirepoix is required.
- For fish/shellfish stock or fumet: 11 pounds of bones or shells to 5 quarts of water and 1 pound of mirepoix yield 1 gallon. Many chefs prefer to use white mirepoix; mushroom trimmings may also be added. White wine may replace up to 2 quarts of the water.
- For vegetable essences: Since vegetables do not all have the same intensity of flavor there are no exact ratios, but approximately 1 pound of vegetables is required to properly flavor 1 quart of water.

Mirepoix. This should be properly trimmed and cut into a size that will allow for good flavor extraction. Fish fumet and court bouillons should have a mirepoix that has been cut small. Stocks that will simmer for over 2 hours may use a large-cut mirepoix. Figure 15-5 shows relationship of size of mirepoix to cooking time.

Aromatics. Stocks should include either a standard sachet d'épices or bouquet garni. Other herbs, spices, and aromatic vegetables may be included to impart special flavors.

15-5 RELATIONSHIP OF MIREPOIX SIZE TO COOKING TIME

The mirepoix on the right is cut small for quick-cooking fumets and essences. The mirepoix on the left is cut larger for longer-cooking stocks, and although the volume appears greater when the cuts are smaller, the weights are identical.

Chefs' opinions vary as to the use of salt in preparing stocks. Some feel that it may be used sparingly, especially if the stock will not be further reduced; others believe salt should never be added. If salt is used, only enough should be added to bring out the basic stock flavor without imparting a salty taste.

Additional optional aromatics may introduce various flavors, depending upon the desired result. For example, fish fumet is often prepared with mushroom trimmings and stems. Refer to specific recipes for guidance. The proper mise en place for a variety of stocks appears in Figure 15-6. Proper color in chicken stock and white beef stock has been achieved by replacing some of the carrots with parsnips. For the brown veal stock, the bones and mirepoix have been roasted to a deep brown. The mirepoix for the fish fumet has been cut very fine to release the flavor quickly.

Preparing Bones

Not only do bones need to be the correct size, they may also need to be blanched, browned, or sweated, according to the type of stock they are intended for.

Blanching Bones

Frozen bones used for white stocks are generally blanched to remove any impurities that might cloud the finished stock. The method is as follows:

1. Place the bones in a stockpot.
2. Cover them with cold water.
3. Bring the water to a slow boil. Skim the surface as necessary.
4. Once a full boil has been reached, drain the bones through a sieve or allow the water to drain away through a spigot. Discard this water.

15-6 MISE EN PLACE FOR VARIOUS STOCKS

(1) Chicken stock.

(2) White beef stock.

(3) Brown veal stock.

(4) Fish fumet.

5. Rinse the bones thoroughly to remove any debris or scum.
6. Proceed with the recipe.

Browning Bones and Mirepoix

Bones may be browned in a rondeau on the stovetop when working with small amounts. A large quantity of bones may be more efficiently browned in the oven, which promotes more even browning with less chance of scorching. The method is as follows:

1. Prepare the mirepoix and reserve.
2. Preheat oven to 400°F (205°C).

3. Rinse the bones and dry them well.
4. Place a thin layer of oil in a pan, and place over direct heat or in the oven to preheat.
5. Add the bones in a single layer. Cook until evenly browned, stirring or turning occasionally. Properly browned bones are shown in Figure 15-7.
6. Transfer the bones to the stockpot and continue with the recipe.
7. Place the mirepoix in the pan used for the bones. Cook until evenly browned. Stir occasionally. Add a tomato product after the mirepoix has browned, if desired, and cook out briefly, until the to-

15-7

Properly roasted bones for brown stock.

mato lightly caramelizes (a process known as *pincé*). Reserve the browned mirepoix and add to the stock during the last hour of cooking time.

8. Deglaze the pan with water and add it to the stock.

Sweating Bones or Shells

Bones or shells are used in fumets. The proteins present in fish bones and shellfish shells can take on an unacceptable flavor if allowed to cook too long. Sweating is a procedure that starts flavor release quickly. The stock, therefore, can be cooked in less than 45 minutes, with a full extraction of body and flavor. The method is as follows:

1. Heat a small amount of oil or clarified butter in a rondeau.

2. Add the bones or shells and mirepoix.

3. Cook over moderate heat, stirring occasionally, until the flesh on the fish bones turns opaque, or the shells have bright color, and moisture is released from the mirepoix.

BASIC PREPARATION METHOD

The recipes at the chapter end will indicate proper ingredients and required amounts for specific stocks. As stated before, although the ingredients may vary, the technique does not. Once the major flavoring ingredient has undergone any required preliminary steps (such as blanching, sweating, or browning),

all stocks, essences, fumets, and court bouillons are prepared the same way. Figure 15-8 demonstrates the step-by-step procedure for making a chicken stock.

1. Combine the major flavoring ingredient(s) with cold liquid(s) and bring to a simmer. The stock will throw scum to the surface as it develops. This should be skimmed away as necessary throughout the simmering time to develop a clear stock with a good flavor.

2. Add the mirepoix and aromatics at the appropriate point.

- Add them at the start of cooking time for stocks, fumets, essences, and court bouillons simmered for less than 1 hour.
- Add them for the last hour of cooking time for stocks simmered for more than 2 hours.

3. Simmer for the appropriate time. Developing a good flavor, aroma, color, and body is important.

4. Drain the stock through a sieve or colander into an appropriate container for cooling. A stock's clarity is better preserved if the major flavoring ingredients and mirepoix are disturbed as little as possible. If the pot does not have a spigot, ladle the stock from the pot rather than pouring it through a sieve. This is a safer procedure, because it is less likely to spill or splash. Discard the bones, mirepoix, and aromatics.

5. Cool the stock in a cold water bath. Stirring from time to time helps the stock cool more rapidly. For an explanation of how to properly cool stocks, refer to Chapter 3, "Sanitation and Safety."

6. Store the stock in appropriate containers. Be sure to properly label and date stocks. It is not necessary to remove any fat from the

(1) Adding cold water to the bones.

(2) The proper ratio of bones to water. The proper amount of headroom allows for expansion of the stock and for easy skimming.

(3) Skimming the surface of the stock.

(4) Adding mirepoix to the stock. Sachet d'épices is attached to the handle to make it easy to remove later.

(5) The proper surface action of the simmering stock.

(6) Cooking completed: The rings on the pot's side show the proper reduction.

15-9 STORING STOCK

(7) Straining the stock. Cheesecloth should be well-rinsed and then wrung out.

Once cooled, place the stock in suitable storage containers, cover tightly, and label and date it.

Chicken Stock

Yield: 1 gallon (3.75 liters)

Chicken bones, cut into 3-inch lengths	8 pounds	3.75 kilograms
Cold water or remouillage	6 quarts	5.75 liters
Mirepoix	1 pound	450 grams
Standard sachet d'épices	1	1
Salt (optional)	to taste	to taste

1. Rinse the bones; blanch them if they are frozen.
2. Combine the bones and water.
3. Bring them slowly to a boil.
4. Skim the surface, as necessary.
5. Simmer the stock for 5 hours.
6. Add mirepoix and sachet d'épices (and salt, if used); simmer an additional 1 to 2 hours.
7. Strain, cool, and store according to text directions for basic stock method.

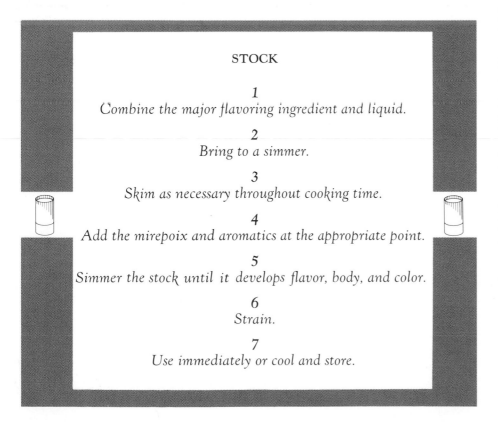

STOCK

1
Combine the major flavoring ingredient and liquid.

2
Bring to a simmer.

3
Skim as necessary throughout cooking time.

4
Add the mirepoix and aromatics at the appropriate point.

5
Simmer the stock until it develops flavor, body, and color.

6
Strain.

7
Use immediately or cool and store.

stock surface until after it is thoroughly chilled. The fat will harden and form a protective seal. When the stock is to be used, the fat can easily be lifted away and discarded. Proper storage is shown in Figure 15-9.

EVALUATING QUALITY

Stocks may be evaluated on the basis of four criteria: flavor, color, aroma, and clarity.

Flavor. If the correct procedure and ratio of bones, mirepoix, and aromatics to liquid has been followed, the flavor should be well-balanced, rich, and full-bodied. The major flavoring ingredient should dominate; for example, chicken stock should taste like chicken. The flavors of the mirepoix and aromatics should be unobtrusive. A stock's flavor should be fresh; all stocks should be checked before they are used in another preparation. To do this, reboil a small amount and taste it.

Color. White stocks and fish fumet should have a very light color that turns translucent, not transparent, when they are cold. Brown stocks are a deep amber or brown because of the preliminary roasting of the bones. Vegetable essences will vary in color according to type.

Aroma. The aroma should be appealing but not overly pungent. When a stock is reboiled for a flavor check, it should be checked for sour smells and musty or "off" odors or taste.

Clarity. Most stocks, with the exception of vegetable essences and fish fumet, should be almost crystal clear when hot. This is achieved by maintaining a proper simmer, never allowing the stock to boil continuously, and also by skimming the surface. Skimming removes impurities that are trapped by the coagulated albumen that rises to the top.

If the stock must be absolutely clear, it is possible to clarify it by combining 1 gallon of cold stock with four beaten egg whites, then bringing the stock to a simmer. The egg whites, which will trap the impurities, are then skimmed away. This procedure should be used only when absolutely necessary, however, because it will weaken the flavor by trapping some of the elements that contribute to that flavor.

SUMMARY

A stock of excellent quality, although it may require up to eight hours of cooking time, actually represents significant savings. It allows meat and vegetable scraps and trimmings to be used in an efficient manner. It is rarely as expensive as prepared bases. Most important, stocks produced in the kitchen are usually superior in quality to most commercially prepared bases.

Included here are a number of recipes for a variety of stocks. Before using these, however, the basic technique should be learned. It is critical to understand what constitutes mise en place and to know how to evaluate a product in terms of its own quality standards. All of these lessons will be emphasized again and again throughout this book.

Game Bird Stock

Yield: 1 gallon (3.75 liters)

Bones from game birds (duck, pheasant, goose, and so forth)	8 pounds	3.75 kilograms
Cold water	6 quarts	5.75 liters
Mirepoix	1 pound	450 grams
Standard sachet d'épices	1	1
Salt	to taste	to taste

1. Rinse the bones; blanch them if they have been frozen.
2. Combine the bones and water.
3. Bring them slowly to a boil.
4. Skim the surface, as necessary.
5. Simmer the stock for 2 to 3 hours.
6. Add the mirepoix and sachet d'épices (and salt, if used); simmer an additional 1 to 2 hours.
7. Strain, cool, and store properly.

White Veal Stock

Yield: 1 gallon (3.75 liters)

Veal bones, cut into 3-inch lengths	8 pounds	3.75 kilograms
Cold water or remouillage	6 quarts	5.75 liters
Mirepoix	1 pound	450 grams
Standard sachet d'épices	1	1
Salt (optional)	to taste	to taste

1. Rinse the bones; blanch them if they are frozen.
2. Combine bones and water.
3. Bring slowly to a boil.
4. Skim the surface, as necessary.
5. Simmer the stock for 5 hours.
6. Add the mirepoix and sachet d'épices (and salt, if used); simmer an additional 1 to 2 hours.
7. Strain, cool, and store properly.

Fish Stock

Yield: 1 gallon (3.75 liters)

Fish bones or crustacean shells	11 pounds	5 kilograms
Cold water	6 quarts	5.75 liters
Mirepoix	1 pound	450 grams
Mushroom trimmings (optional)	10 ounces	280 grams
Salt (optional)	to taste	to taste

1. Combine all ingredients.
2. Bring the mixture slowly to a simmer.
3. Skim the surface, as necessary.
4. Simmer for 30 to 40 minutes.
5. Strain, cool, and store properly.

VARIATION

Replace 1 quart of cold water with an equal amount of dry white wine. Use white mirepoix.

Brown Veal Stock

Yield: 1 gallon (3.75 liters)

Veal bones, including knuckles and trim	8 pounds	3.75 kilograms
Oil	as needed	as needed
Cold water or remouillage	6 quarts	5.75 liters
Mirepoix	1 pound	450 grams
Tomato puree or paste	4 to 6 ounces	120 to 175 grams
Standard sachet d'épices	1	1
Salt (optional)	to taste	to taste

1. Rinse the bones and dry them well.
2. Brown the bones.
3. Combine the bones and water.
4. Bring slowly to a boil.
5. Simmer for 5 hours, skimming the surface as necessary.
6. Brown the mirepoix and tomato puree. Add to the stock; deglaze the pan and add to the stock. Add sachet d'épices (and salt, if used).
7. Simmer an additional 1 to 2 hours.
8. Strain, cool, and store properly.

VARIATIONS

Brown Duck Stock (Jus de Canard): Replace the veal bones with an equal weight of duck bones and lean trim. If desired, add one or more of the following herbs or spices to the standard sachet d'épices: rosemary, caraway seed, tarragon stems, sage.

Brown Lamb Stock (Jus d'Agneau): Replace the veal bones with an equal weight of lamb bones and lean trim. If desired, add one or more of the following herbs or spices to the standard sachet d'épices: mint stems, juniper berries, cumin seed, caraway seed, rosemary.

Brown Pork Stock (Jus de Porc): Replace the veal bones with an equal weight of pork bones and lean trim. If desired, add one or more of the following herbs or spices to the standard sachet d'épices: red pepper flakes, caraway seeds, oregano stems, mustard seeds.

Brown Game Stock (Jus de Gibier): Replace the veal bones with an equal weight of venison bones and lean trim, or rabbit bones and lean trim, depending upon intended applications. Include fennel seeds and/or juniper berries in standard sachet d'épices, if desired.

Shrimp Stock

Yield: 2 quarts (2 liters)

Shrimp shells	10 pounds	4.5 kilograms
Oil	as needed	as needed
Water	2 quarts	2 liters
Mirepoix	8 ounces	225 grams
Standard sachet d'épices	1	1
White wine	4 ounces	115 grams
Tomato paste	2 ounces	55 grams

1. Sauté the shrimp shells in oil.

2. Add the mirepoix and continue to sauté.

3. Add tomato paste and pincé.

4. Add water and seasonings and simmer for 10 minutes.

5. Strain, cool, and store properly.

VARIATION

Lobster Stock: Replace the shrimp shells with an equal amount of lobster shells.

Glace de Viande

Yield: varies

Brown veal stock or remouillage	1 quart	1 liter

1. Place the stock or remouillage in a heavy gauge pot over moderate heat.
2. Bring to a simmer and let reduce until volume is halved, then transfer to a smaller pot.
3. Continue to reduce, transferring to successively smaller pots until very thick and syrupy.

SUBSTITUTIONS

Glace de Volaille: Substitute chicken stock for brown veal stock.

Glace de Poisson: Substitute fish stock for brown veal stock.

Vegetable Stock

Yield: 1 gallon (3.75 liters)

Vegetable oil	2 ounces	55 grams
Onions, sliced	4 ounces	115 grams
Leeks, green and white parts, chopped	4 ounces	115 grams
Celery, chopped	2 ounces	55 grams
Green cabbage, chopped	2 ounces	55 grams
Carrots, chopped	2 ounces	55 grams
Turnips, chopped	2 ounces	55 grams
Tomato, chopped	2 ounces	55 grams
Garlic cloves, crushed	2 to 3	2 to 3
Water	6 pints	4.25 liters
Standard sachet d'épices plus 1 teaspoon (5 milliliters) of fennel seeds and 2 to 3 whole cloves	1	1

1. Heat the oil.
2. Add the vegetables and sweat them for 3 to 5 minutes.
3. Add water and sachet d'épices and simmer for 30 to 40 minutes.
4. Strain, cool, and store properly.

Remouillage

Yield: 1 gallon (3.75 liters)

Bones reserved from preparing stock	8 pounds	3.75 kilograms
Cold water	8 quarts	6.75 liters
Mirepoix	1 pound	450 grams
Standard sachet d'épices	1	1

1. Combine all ingredients, and simmer for approximately 5 to 6 hours.

2. Strain, cool and store properly.

NOTE: Remouillage will not have the same depth of body or flavor as normal stock.

Fish Fumet

Yield: 1 gallon (3.75 liters)

Oil	as needed	as needed
Fish bones or crustacean shells	11 pounds	5 kilograms
Mirepoix	1 pound	450 grams
Mushroom trimmings	10 ounces	280 grams
Cold water	5 quarts	4.75 liters
Dry white wine	1 quart	1 liter
Standard sachet d'épices	1	1
Salt (optional)	to taste	to taste

1. Heat the oil; add the bones and mirepoix.

2. Sweat the bones and mirepoix.

3. Add water, wine, and sachet d'épices (and salt if used); bring to a simmer.

4. Simmer for 35 to 40 minutes, skimming the surface as necessary.

5. Strain, cool, and store properly.

VARIATION

White mirepoix may be used, if desired.

Court Bouillon

Yield: 1 gallon (3.75 liters)

Water	5 quarts	4.75 liters
Vinegar	1 cup	240 milliliters
Salt	2 ounces	55 grams
Carrots, sliced	12 ounces	340 grams
Onions, sliced	1 pound	455 grams
Thyme leaves, dried	pinch	pinch
Bay leaves	3	3
Parsley stems	1 bunch	1 bunch
Peppercorns	½ ounce	15 grams

1. Combine all ingredients except the peppercorns.
2. Simmer for 50 minutes.
3. Add the peppercorns and simmer for an additional 10 minutes.
4. Strain, cool, and store properly.

VARIATIONS

Court Bouillon with White Wine: Replace half of the water with an equal amount of dry white wine. Omit the vinegar. Carrots may be eliminated, if desired.

Court Bouillon with Red Wine: Replace half of the water with an equal amount of dry red wine. Omit the vinegar.

Estouffade

Yield: 1 gallon (3.75 liters)

Unsmoked ham knuckle	1	1
Veal bones	4 pounds	2 kilograms
Beef bones	4 pounds	2 kilograms
Water	6 quarts	5.5 liters
Mirepoix	1 pound	450 grams
Tomato puree or paste	8 to 10 ounces	225 to 280 grams
Standard sachet d'épices	1	1
Salt (optional)	to taste	to taste

1. Rinse the bones and dry them well.
2. Brown the veal and beef bones.
3. Combine the bones and water.
4. Bring the mixture slowly to a boil.
5. Simmer for 5 hours, skimming the surface as necessary.
6. Brown the mirepoix and tomato puree. Add to the stock; deglaze the pan and add to the stock. Add sachet d'épices (and salt, if used).
7. Simmer an additional 3 hours.
8. Strain, cool, and store properly.

Soups

Soups have evolved greatly over time. Today's most robust soups would seem refined compared with the thick slabs of bread dampened with broth that were the original "soupes." Confusion can arise, however, when the modern versions of soups are given names that reflect the older renditions. For example, a bisque was originally a soup made from game birds, which was thickened with fried croutons. Today it may be either a soup made from crustaceans and thickened with rice or roux or one thickened with a vegetable puree. What they have in common with early bisques is a special texture: thick, creamy, and slightly grainy.

This chapter continues the introduction of basic techniques used in many kitchen stations—sweating, straining, pureeing, and finishing with cream, butter, or a liaison. The chef's ability to evaluate the flavors, textures, and colors of foods being prepared for service are all called upon when preparing soups.

KINDS OF SOUPS

This chapter divides soups into two categories: clear soups and thick soups. These distinctions are based on the basic preparation methods and/or the characteristics of the finished soup. Within these divisions are included methods and recipes for representative examples. No attempt was made to rename all the soups found on menus or in recipe books. Before these categories are discussed, an overview of the soup-making process is provided.

INGREDIENTS

The best soups, obviously, are made from the best available ingredients.

Major flavoring components. If this is a meat, it should be highly flavorful and mature. Cuts from the neck, hocks (or shank), or short ribs are preferred for soups based on beef or the meat of other large animals. Stewing hens provide the best meat for chicken-based soups. Fish or shellfish should be perfectly fresh. Vegetables should be well-flavored and fresh, especially when they provide the dominant flavor of a soup.

Aromatics. Aromatics add an extra flavor dimension. Spices and herbs are added to soups to increase flavor, and, frequently, to reduce or eliminate the use of salt. Mirepoix is often used, although it is not essential to all soups. Sachet d'épices or bouquet garni are included in virtually all soups. As with stocks, the sachet or bouquet garni should be removed and discarded as soon as it has contributed sufficient flavor. Preparation of these aromatic combinations is discussed in Chapter 14, "Mise en Place."

Liquid. Quality stock forms the basis of most soups, but water, fumets, vegetable essences, fruit and vegetable juices, and milk may also be used.

PREPARATION AND SERVICE

The following are general guidelines that pertain to most soups.

Cooking

Most soups are cooked at a gentle simmer, just long enough to develop a good flavor and the appropriate body. Vegetables may be added in a staggered manner, according to their cooking times. The soup should be stirred from time to time to prevent starchy ingredients from sticking to the bottom of the pot. Throughout the cooking process, a skimmer or ladle should be used to remove any scum or foam so that the best flavor, texture, and appearance is obtained.

The chef should also taste the soup frequently as it cooks, and when the flavor is fully developed and all of the ingredients are tender, it may be finished or garnished and served right away, or it may be properly cooled and stored. Although some soups may develop a more rounded, mellow flavor if served the day after they are prepared, no soup benefits from hours on the stove. Not only will the flavor become dull and flat, the nutritive value will be greatly decreased.

Finishing and Garnishing

Some soups may be prepared to a specific point and then cooled and stored, using the same techniques appropriate for cooling and storing stocks. The following considerations are important.

• Clear soups should be garnished just before service to prevent them from becoming cloudy and to keep the garnish fresh. Vegetables, for example, should not be overcooked. Some garnishes are added, portion by portion, just prior to service. In other cases, such as for banquet service, the garnish may be added to the entire quantity.

• Cream soups should have the cream added just prior to service for two reasons: The soup will have a fresher flavor, and its shelf life will be greater. Cream should be brought to a boil first to check freshness and to prevent it from lowering the soup's temperature.

• Many soup bases should be brought back to a full boil before finishing; however, soups that have already been finished with cream, sour cream, butter, or a liaison should not be allowed to come all the way up to a boil (see "Reheating," below).

• Final seasoning adjustments should be made after the soup is finished. The seasoning should always be checked just prior to service.

Reheating

If soup has been prepared in advance, only the amount needed for a particular service period should be reheated.

• Clear soups should be brought just up to a boil. Seasoning and consistency should be checked and the appropriate garnishes added before serving.

• Thick   soups,   especially

creams, purees, and bisques, should be reheated gently. A thin layer of water or stock should be put in a heavy-gauge pot before adding the soup. The chef should begin reheating the soup over low heat, stirring it frequently until it softens slightly. Then the heat can be increased slightly and the soup may be brought to a simmer. Seasoning and consistency should be checked and any garnishes added just before serving.

• In order to reheat soup in the microwave oven, the soup must be placed in a microwave-safe bowl and covered with plastic wrap. It should be heated for about 1 minute at high power, then stirred to distribute the heat evenly and returned to the microwave until the soup is very hot.

Adjusting Consistency

Thick soups, especially those made with starchy vegetables or dried beans, may continue to thicken during cooking and storage. As a general rule, purees, creams, and bisques should be about as thick as heavy cream and liquid enough to pour from a ladle into a bowl. The following steps may be taken to adjust consistency.

• For a soup that has become too thick, water or an appropriately flavored stock or broth may be added in small amounts until the proper consistency is reached. The seasoning should be rechecked before serving.

• For a soup that is too thin, a small amount of diluted cornstarch or arrowroot may be added. The soup should be at a simmer or slow boil when the starch is added. It should be stirred continuously and should continue simmering for 2 or 3 minutes.

Adjusting Flavor and Seasoning

• Meat or poultry glaze may be added to bolster a weak broth or consommé flavor; however, this will affect the clarity.

• Chopped fresh herbs; a few drops of lemon juice, Tabasco sauce, or Worcestershire sauce; or grated citrus rind may be added to brighten a soup's flavor. These items should be added a little at a time and the seasoning carefully checked after each addition.

• Salt and pepper to taste may be added just prior to service, when the soup is at the correct temperature.

Degreasing

Some soups, especially broth-based ones, may be prepared in advance, and cooled and refrigerated properly. It is then easy for the chef to remove the fat that will congeal on the surface before he or she reheats the soup. If the soup must be served just after it is prepared, as much surface fat as possible should be skimmed off with a shallow ladle or skimmer. Clear soups may be blotted with strips of unwaxed brown butcher paper to remove any traces of fat before serving. The strips should be floated on the surface and then carefully lifted off. Consommés should be completely fat-free. Broths and clear vegetable soups characteristically have some droplets of fat on the surface.

Garnishing

Garnishes can accomplish many things. They may provide contrasts of texture and flavor; they may introduce a complementary or contrasting flavor. They may also provide additional or contrasting color. Garnishes should be added just prior to service. If garnishes such as custards or quenelles are prepared in advance, they should be properly cooled and stored separately.

Serving

Hot soups should be served very hot; and the thinner the soup, the more important this is. Consommés and broths lose their heat rapidly, so they should be nearly at a boil before they are ladled into heated soup plates or cups. Cold soups should be thoroughly chilled and served in chilled cups, bowls, or glasses. Figure 16-1 shows the proper service setup for a banquet.

CLEAR SOUPS

Broth

There are a number of similarities between stocks and broths. In fact, the techniques for both are identical: The meats may be seared and then are slowly simmered along with various vegetables, spices, and herbs to produce a liquid that is clear and flavorful with some body and a golden to amber-brown color.

The major distinction between broths and stocks is that broths are intended to be served "as is," whereas stocks are a base preparation used in the production of other dishes. Because they are based on meats rather than bones, broths have a more pronounced flavor. For a doubly rich flavor, broths may be prepared with stock as the liquid.

If a broth's cooking speed is carefully regulated so that it is never more than an even, gentle simmer and if the surface is skimmed as necessary, a broth can be as clear, full-bodied, and rich as any consommé, without needing a secondary clarification. The meats

16-1

Efficient banquet setup for soup: Bowls or cups are arranged on the outside of a tray, with plates in the center. A pitcher makes serving the soup simple.

fish in a pot; add cold water or stock to cover by about 2 inches.

2. Slowly bring the liquid to a boil.

3. Skim the surface as needed throughout preparation.

4. Establish an even simmer.

5. Add the mirepoix and sachet d'épices or bouquet garni at the appropriate point.

6. Allow the proper cooking time. A broth should be tasted occasionally as it cooks. When the major flavoring ingredients are fork-tender and the broth is adequately flavored, it is finished. Although it is not possible to give exact cooking times, approximations are provided here for various major flavoring ingredients. The approximate cooking times are:

- for beef, veal, game, or chicken: 2 to 3 hours
- for fish: 30 to 45 minutes
- for vegetables: 30 minutes to 1 hour

7. Check the flavor as the broth develops; remove and discard the sachet d'épices or bouquet garni when the proper flavor extraction is attained.

8. Strain, cool, and store the broth, following the procedures outlined for stock in Chapter 15.

9. To reheat, bring to a full boil, adjust the seasoning, and serve in heated cups or bowls with appropriate garnish.

For a quick summary of broth preparation, refer to the abbreviated method for broth.

Evaluating Quality

A good broth should be clear, rich-tasting, and aromatic, and should have a distinct flavor of the major ingredient. The color will vary by type but will range from a pale gold to a deep amber in most cases.

or poultry used to prepare a broth should be cooked until fork-tender, as for simmered or braised meats (see Chapter 20, "Moist-heat Cooking," and Chapter 21, "Combination Cooking Methods"). This assures a full flavor extraction.

Frequently, the meats or fowl used to prepare broths can be appropriate for other preparations, if they are cooked until fully tender but no longer. The meat can be julienned or diced to use as a garnish, along with vegetables that have been cooked separately, or it can be served as a second course to follow the soup, to name just two options.

Mise en Place

1. Major flavoring ingredient. Cut the meat or poultry into the proper size and tie or truss it as needed. Brown the meat, if necessary.

2. Aromatics. Chop the mirepoix into a medium dice and prepare the sachet d'épices or bouquet garni.

3. Liquid. Have cold stock or water available.

4. Prepare the garnish according to the recipe.

Method

1. Place the meat, poultry, or

Beef Broth

Yield: 2½ gallons (9.5 liters)

Beef hind shank, sliced 2 inches thick	16 pounds	7.25 kilograms
Cold water	2½ gallons	9.5 liters
Mirepoix, caramelized	2 pounds	910 grams
Tomatoes, cored and chopped coarse	1 pound	455 grams
Standard sachet d'épices, plus garlic	1	1
Salt	to taste	to taste

1. Bring the beef shank and water to a simmer, skim the surface, and simmer very gently for 2 hours.
2. Add the mirepoix and tomatoes and simmer for ½ hour.
3. Add the sachet d'épices and simmer for an additional ½ hour.
4. Degrease, remove the beef shank, and strain thoroughly.
5. Season with salt to taste.
6. Bring to service temperature.
7. Adjust the seasoning with salt and pepper to taste and garnish as desired (see Variations, below).

VARIATIONS

Beef Broth with Garden Vegetables: Garnish each portion with fine-diced, blanched vegetables (carrots, celery, leeks, peas, turnips) and diced, cooked beef.

Beef Broth with Barley: Garnish with diced, cooked vegetables and 1 tablespoon of cooked barley per portion.

Beef Broth with Spätzli : Garnish with plain, herbed, or spinach spätzli.

Lamb Broth with Barley and Vegetables: Replace the beef shank with an equal weight of lamb shanks; make broth as above. Garnish as for beef broth with barley, including diced, cooked lamb meat.

Broths should not feel like water on the tongue; they should have a discernible body.

There are problems that can occur. These problems, which will interfere with the taste of a broth, may affect its richness, fullness, or depth.

Weak flavor. If the proper ratio of flavoring ingredient to liquid has not been observed, the broth will have a weak taste. Another cause of this problem is inadequate cooking time.

Sour, off, or musty flavor. A broth may develop a sour, off, or musty flavor if the soup is allowed to boil, if it is not properly skimmed during preparation, or if it is cooled and/or stored improperly.

Cloudy broth. Boiling a broth will result in a cloudy product. The temperature should be adjusted during cooking and a gentle simmer established. A cloudy broth can be clarified with egg whites, but a secondary clarification can rob the broth of flavor.

Insufficient body. Broths that lack body may not have been simmered long enough. Another possibility is that the meats chosen for the broths were not chosen from well-exercised portions of the animal, such as the shank or neck, or from select mature fowls.

Consommés

Consommé is a strong, clear broth or stock of the best quality that has been enriched by simmering gently with a combination of lean chopped meat (beef, chicken, or fish, for example), egg whites, mirepoix, herbs and spices, and an acidic ingredient (such as tomatoes, wine, or lemon juice). This combination is known as a clarification because as it cooks, it traps particles that might make the broth appear cloudy. A consommé should be crystal-clear, completely fat-free, and amber to brown in color, with a good body.

The cold broth is blended with the clarification and the mixture is then cooked over moderate heat and stirred frequently until it just comes to a boil. As the stock heats, the meat and egg white proteins coagulate and rise to the surface, forming a "raft." While forming, the raft traps any impurities that might cloud the finished consommé.

In addition to clarifying the consommé, the raft ingredients provide clarity, flavor, and body. A further boost to both flavor and color may come from oignon brûlé, a halved onion that has been charred on a flat-top or open burner. It is combined with the cold broth and clarification at the beginning of the cooking time.

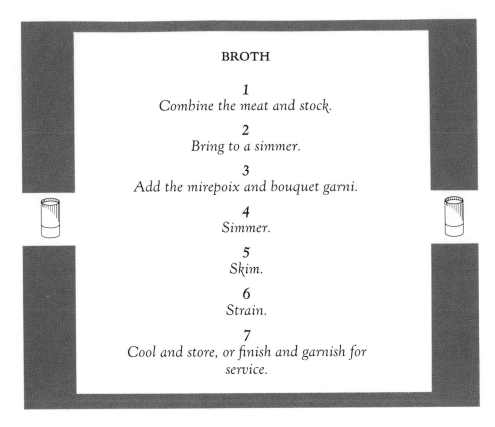

BROTH

1
Combine the meat and stock.

2
Bring to a simmer.

3
Add the mirepoix and bouquet garni.

4
Simmer.

5
Skim.

6
Strain.

7
Cool and store, or finish and garnish for service.

Chilling a prepared consommé makes it easy to lift away the congealed surface fat. Strips of unwaxed butcher paper may be used to blot the surface and remove any traces of fat from hot consommés.

There are many possible garnishes for a consommé. Almost without exception, they are prepared separately and heated in a small amount of stock, broth, or consommé. The garnish will, therefore, not overcook and will not cloud the consommé.

Mise en place

1. Clarification. Grind the meat, chicken, or fish, if necessary. Cut the mirepoix into an appropriate size (fine dice or julienne); some chefs prefer to simply grind it along with the meat or fish. Combine the ground meat or fish, mirepoix, egg white, herbs and spices, and acid component (tomato puree for beef,

poultry, or game; lemon or wine for fish).

2. Stock or broth. Have all or a portion of the stock or broth chilled. If the consommé must be prepared quickly, the majority of the stock may be heated.

3. Oignon brûlé. This is optional. The method outlined in Chapter 14, "Mise en Place," should be followed. Oignon brûlé is used for beef, poultry, and game consommés.

4. Garnish. It may be advisable to prepare the garnish just prior to service when possible. Consult specific recipes for guidance.

Method

1. In a pot, blend cold stock or broth with the clarification and add the oignon brûlé, if required. If time is short, or if there is only a small amount of cold stock available, a small quantity of cold stock

can be added to the clarification and mixed well. It is then possible to add the hot stock to the "tempered" clarification and to continue with the method. There will be no difference in the consommé's quality.

2. Bring the mixture slowly to a boil, stirring frequently.

3. Establish an even simmer; do not stir once the raft has formed.

4. Pierce the raft to allow steam to escape and in order to observe the cooking speed. Many small bubbles should be rising to the surface of the broth or stock. The raft should not sink; if it begins to drop, increase the heat slightly. Some chefs baste the raft to prevent it from breaking up.

5. Cook for approximately 1½ hours. (This is a rough estimate.) By the end of this time, the raft should begin to sink slightly.

6. Ladle the consommé out; strain it through a cheesecloth-lined chinois. If a spigoted pot is used, place the chinois beneath the spigot and drain the consommé out.

7. Check the seasoning. Cool, store, and degrease the consommé, following the procedures outlined for stock in Chapter 15.

Figure 16-2 shows various steps in this method.

Preparation for Service

1. Lift away all congealed fat.

2. Bring the consommé back to a boil.

3. Check the surface for any remaining fat and use butcher paper to blot the surface.

4. Adjust the seasoning with salt. Kosher salt is preferable because it doesn't cause clouding. If pepper is needed, use a small amount of cayenne or finely ground white pepper.

5. Add the appropriate garnish to the cup or bowl and ladle hot

Chicken Consommé

(1) The stock and the clarification are thoroughly blended.

(2) The clarification begins to coagulate into the raft.

Yield: 2 gallons (7.5 liters)

Oignon brûlé	4	4
Mirepoix (carrots, turnips, leeks, celeriac, parsnips, parsley stems)	2 pounds	910 grams
Ground chicken	6 pounds	2.75 kilograms
Egg whites, beaten until slightly frothy	20	20
Tomato concassée	24 ounces	680 grams
Standard sachet d'épices, plus 1 clove and 2 allspice berries	1	1
Chicken stock, cold	2½ gallons	9.5 liters
Kosher salt	as needed	as needed

1. Combine the oignon brûlé, mirepoix, meat, tomatoes, and egg whites. Mix well.

2. Add stock and mix well.

3. Bring to a slow simmer. Stir frequently until a raft forms.

4. Add the sachet d'épices and simmer for 1½ hours or until appropriate flavor is achieved.

5. Strain; adjust the seasoning with the salt and garnish as desired (see Variations on the following page).

(continued)

(3) The consommé is breaking through the raft. An onion brûlé gives additional color and flavor.

(4) The raft has risen to the top.

(5) The finished consommé.

VARIATIONS FOR CHICKEN CONSOMMÉ

Chicken Consommé with Julienned Vegetables: Garnish each portion with blanched, julienned leeks, carrots, celery, and potatoes; include a fine julienne of cooked chicken breast, if desired.

Chicken Consommé Paysanne: Garnish each portion with blanched paysanne-cut leeks, turnips, carrots, celery, and potatoes.

Chicken Consommé with Quenelles: Garnish with small quenelles made of chicken mousseline forcemeat.

Chicken Consommé with Garden Vegetables: Garnish with fresh peas, tomato concassé, and other garden vegetables cut into brunoise, if desired.

CONSOMMÉ

1
Combine the ground meat, mirepoix, seasonings, tomato product, oignon brûlée, and egg white.

2
Incorporate the stock.

3
Bring to a boil.

4
Stir frequently.

5
Simmer.

6
Do not stir after the raft has formed.

7
Break a hole in the raft.

8
Simmer until the consommé has developed flavor, body, and color.

9
Strain.

10
Cool and store, or finish and garnish for service.

consommé over it. If necessary, heat the garnish separately in a small amount of stock or consommé. Delicate garnishes such as royales or a chiffonade of fresh herbs will be properly heated by the consommé. Dense garnishes, such as diced root vegetables, should be heated separately.

For a quick summary of consommé preparation, refer to the abbreviated method for consommé.

Evaluating Quality

A good consommé should be perfectly clear, rich-tasting, and aromatic, and should have a distinct flavor of the major ingredient. The color will vary by type, but will range from golden to deep amber in most cases. Consommés of excellent quality will have a distinct body that can be discerned in the mouth.

The taste of consommé should be rich, full, and deep. As with broth, there are problems that can affect these characteristics.

Sour, off, or musty flavor. The soup may develop a sour, off, or musty flavor if it is allowed to boil, if the ingredients are not perfectly fresh and of the best quality, or if it is not properly cooled and stored.

Flavor of auxiliary ingredients dominate. The mirepoix, tomato product, and any herbs and spices used in preparation should act as grace notes, contributing only subtle flavors. If the consommé tastes strongly of an ingredient other than the major one, the proper ratio of mirepoix and other aromatics to the major flavoring ingredients (stock and ground meat) has not been observed.

Cloudy consommé. A cloudy consommé is most often the result of boiling the soup. The temperature should be adjusted during cooking and a gentle simmer established. Consommés can be clarified a second time by combining one gallon of cold consommé with no more than four beaten egg whites. The consommé is then brought slowly to a boil. As the egg whites coagulate, the impurities will be trapped. However, this emergency measure tends to remove not only the impurities, but some flavor as well.

Weak body. Consommés that lack body may not have been based on the best-quality stocks or broths. Although the raft will reinforce the body as well as the flavor, the base should always be made as carefully as possible.

Clear Vegetable Soups

Clear vegetable soups are based on clear broth or stock. The vegetables are cut into an appropriate and uniform size and the soup is simmered until all ingredients are tender. Meats, grains, and pastas are frequently included to give additional body. Vegetable soups may also be made from a single vegetable, as for example in onion soup. Clear vegetable soups should have a full flavor and be somewhat thicker than broths. Because additional ingredients are cooked directly in the broth, the soups will lack the clarity of either broth or consommé.

Croutons are a common garnish, and they may be an integral part of the preparation, as in onion soup.

Mise en Place

1. Major flavoring ingredients. Trim, peel, and cut vegetables as required by type and recipe. Trim and cut meats, poultry, or fish (other than those used purely as a garnish). Rinse, soak, or sort grains, legumes, and pastas as required by type and recipe.

2. Liquid. Have stock or broth and other liquids available, as appropriate, including water, vegetable essences or juices, and wines.

3. Aromatics. Prepare sachet d'épices or bouquet garni as required by the recipe.

4. Garnish is an optional component.

American Bounty Vegetable Soup

Yield: 2 gallons (7.5 liters)

Leeks, white and light green parts only	6 ounces	170 grams
Onions, ¼-inch dice	1 ounce	30 grams
Carrots, ¼-inch dice	8 ounces	225 grams
Celery, ¼-inch dice	8 ounces	225 grams
Clarified butter	as needed	as needed
Garlic cloves, minced	2 to 3	2 to 3
Beef broth	1½ gallons	5.5 liters
Standard sachet d'épices	1	1
Turnips, ¼-inch dice	8 ounces	225 grams
Cabbage, chiffonade	8 ounces	225 grams
Potatoes, ¼-inch dice	10 ounces	285 grams
Tomato concassé	8 ounces	225 grams
Lima beans	8 ounces	225 grams
Corn	8 ounces	225 grams

1. Sweat the leeks, onions, carrots, and celery in clarified butter.

2. Add garlic and sauté until aroma is apparent.

3. Add the beef broth, sachet d'épices, and turnips. Simmer for approximately 10 minutes.

4. Add the cabbage. Simmer for 10 more minutes.

5. Add the potatoes and continue to simmer for another 10 minutes of cooking.

6. Add the tomato concassé, lima beans, and corn. Simmer until all the vegetables are tender.

7. Adjust the seasoning with salt, pepper, and nutmeg.

8. Garnish each serving with chopped parsley and serve with a cheese crouton.

NOTE: The ratio of vegetables to broth is approximately 4 to 4½ pounds of vegetables to 1 gallon of broth.

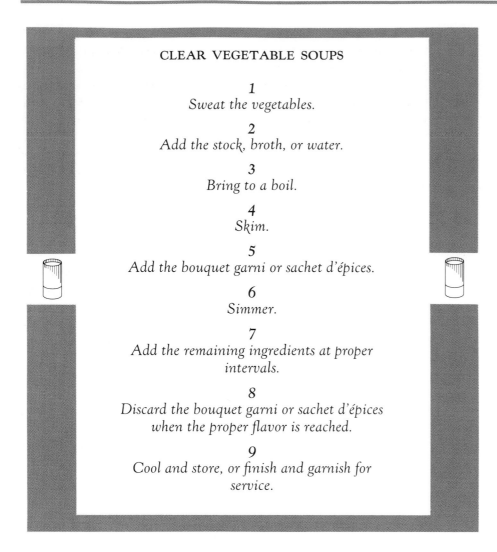

CLEAR VEGETABLE SOUPS

1
Sweat the vegetables.

2
Add the stock, broth, or water.

3
Bring to a boil.

4
Skim.

5
Add the bouquet garni or sachet d'épices.

6
Simmer.

7
Add the remaining ingredients at proper intervals.

8
Discard the bouquet garni or sachet d'épices when the proper flavor is reached.

9
Cool and store, or finish and garnish for service.

Method

1. Sweat the vegetables in a small amount of oil, butter, rendered fat (chicken, lard, or salt pork, for example), or stock until they begin to release their juices. Note that some vegetables, such as broccoli florets, asparagus tips, and other delicate types, are not generally allowed to sweat.

2. Add the stock, broth, or water. If the stock has been heated separately, the cooking time will be reduced. This is not, however, an essential step.

3. Bring the mixture slowly to a boil.

4. Skim the surface as needed throughout preparation.

5. Establish an even simmer.

6. Add any remaining vegetables, meats, or grains in a staggered manner, according to cooking times. Starchy items such as grains or pasta are frequently prepared separately and added as a finishing ingredient.

7. Add the sachet d'épices or bouquet garni 30 to 45 minutes before the end of the cooking time.

8. Cook until all ingredients are fully cooked and tender and the soup's flavor is developed. The flavor of some vegetable soups will improve if the soup is allowed to rest under refrigeration for 24 hours.

9. Check the flavor as the soup develops; remove and discard the sachet d'épices or bouquet garni when the proper flavor extraction is reached.

10. Cook, store, and degrease the soup following the guidelines given for stock in Chapter 15.

Preparation for Service

1. Bring the soup to a boil.
2. Adjust the seasoning to taste.
3. Add the appropriate garnish.

Refer to the abbreviated method for a quick summary of clear vegetable soup preparation.

Evaluating Quality

These soups will not be as clear as either broth or consommé. The flavor should reflect the vegetables used and should be well-balanced, whether from a single vegetable, as in onion soup, or from a blend of many vegetables. Unlike clear, strained soups, the vegetables are part of the soup itself and will give it texture and body. When vegetables (especially green ones) are properly cooked, their colors will stay clear, with no graying.

Harsh flavor. If the flavor is too harsh, the soup was probably not cooked long enough.

Inappropriate color. If the soup appears muddy or gray, the vegetables have probably been overcooked. If pastas or grains have been cooked directly in the soup, they may have been overcooked to the point that they have begun to break down. Ideally, the vegetables should be added to the soup in such a manner that they will cook fully but will not overcook.

THICK SOUPS

Cream Soups

According to classic definitions, a cream soup is based on a béchamel sauce—milk thickened with roux —and is finished with heavy cream. A velouté is based on a light velouté sauce—a stock thickened with roux—and is finished with a liaison of heavy cream and egg yolks. Contemporary menu writers no longer draw a distinction between the two, and in modern kitchens chefs frequently substitute a velouté base for the béchamel in cream soups. The béchamel-based cream soup, however, is still used. True velouté soups are infrequently prepared in professional kitchens, because the addition of a liaison makes the soup difficult to hold.

The major flavoring ingredient for cream soups is simmered in the velouté until it is tender. The solids are strained out and, in some cases, pureed and returned to the soup. Straining is important for all cream soups, because a velvety-smooth texture is critical. The soup should have the thickness of heavy cream. Garnish is usually included just prior to service. The garnish is customarily diced meat or vegetables that reflect the major flavoring ingredient. For example, cream of asparagus soup may be garnished with asparagus tips.

Many cream soups may be served cold. The soup base should be thoroughly chilled before finishing with cream, sour cream, or other ingredients. The seasoning should be checked carefully before the soup is served, because cold foods generally require more seasoning than foods served hot. It may also be necessary to thin a cold soup, as it tends to become thicker when chilled.

Cream of vegetable soups follow one of two methods, depending upon the nature of the vegetables used as the major flavoring ingredients. Hard, aromatic vegetables, such as root vegetables and squashes, are allowed to sweat along with onions, celery, and leeks before the stock is added; softer vegetables, such as leafy, green vegetables or green peas, are added at the same time as the stock and allowed to simmer until they are soft enough to puree easily.

Mise en Place

1. Major flavoring ingredients. Trim, peel, and cut vegetables according to type and recipe. Well-flavored stock should be available for soups where stock acts as both the major flavoring ingredient (cream of chicken soup, for example) and the liquid.

2. Aromatics. Chop the mirepoix into a medium dice and prepare the sachet d'épices or bouquet garni.

3. Liquid. Have stock or milk available or prepare a light velouté (see Chapter 17, "Sauces").

4. Thickening agent. An additional thickening agent is not necessary if velouté is used as the liquid. If used, a thickening agent may be incorporated in one of three ways:

- A blond roux may be prepared separately (see Chapter 14, "Mise en Place") and cooled to room temperature.
- An appropriate amount of flour may be used, as outlined in the method below.
- An appropriate amount of arrowroot or cornstarch can be diluted in cold water or stock.

5. Finishing ingredients. These include heated heavy cream or whole, unsalted butter, which should be added just prior to service.

6. Garnishes. Optional garnishes include julienned or diced pieces of the major flavoring ingredient or a complementary ingredient, croutons or fresh herbs, or other suggestions specified by the particular recipe.

Method

1. Sweat aromatic vegetables and hard vegetables (if they are the major flavoring ingredient) in oil, butter, or a small amount of stock until the vegetables begin to release their juices.

2. Add flour; mix well and cook over moderate heat. This forms the roux. (A prepared and cooled roux may be added to the simmering stock. See the note at the end of this method.)

3. Add the appropriate liquid, which should be colder than the roux for the best results. Add the liquid gradually and work out all lumps before adding more. Bring to a boil, then establish a gentle simmer. (The appropriate liquid may also be a prepared velouté, in which case step 2 can be eliminated.)

4. Add the soft vegetables used as the major flavoring ingredient at this point, along with the sachet d'épices or bouquet garni.

5. Cook for approximately 1½ hours. Skim the surface as needed and stir frequently to prevent scorching. The cooking time is important: The soup must be simmered long enough to allow the roux's starchy taste to cook out.

6. Check the flavor as the soup develops; remove and discard the sachet d'épices or bouquet garni when the proper flavor extraction is reached.

7. Strain the soup, reserving the liquid.

8. For vegetable cream soups, puree the solids and return them to the pot. Gradually reincorporate the liquid until the correct consistency is achieved.

9. Strain vegetable soups again through a fine sieve or cheesecloth.

10. Cool and store the soup as for stocks (see Chapter 15).

Note: When working with a prepared roux, sweat the aromatic vegetables in a small amount of butter, oil, or stock, and add the stock. Bring the stock to a boil. Add roux to the boiling stock in the proper ratio for the correct consistency. When combining roux with a liquid, the chef should make sure that one component is cooler than the other, to prevent lumping.

Preparation for Service

1. Slowly reheat the soup over low heat until it is softened.

2. Bring it to a full boil.

3. Add hot heavy cream and do not allow the soup to return to a boil.

4. Make any necessary adjustments in consistency or flavor.

5. Serve in heated bowls or cups.

6. Garnish individual portions; be sure that the garnish is heated, if necessary.

Refer to the abbreviated method for a quick summary of cream soup preparation.

Evaluating Quality

Cream soups should have the approximate body, consistency, and texture of heavy cream, which means they should be perfectly smooth and somewhat thick. The

Cream of Broccoli Soup

Yield: 2 gallons (7.5 liters)

Onions	1 pound	455 grams
Celery	4 ounces	115 grams
Leeks	4 ounces	115 grams
Broccoli stems	3½ pounds	1.5 kilograms
Butter	4 ounces	115 grams
Chicken stock	2 quarts	2 liters
Chicken velouté	1 gallon	3.75 liters
Cream	2 quarts	2 liters
Broccoli florets	1 ounce per serving	30 grams per serving

1. Sweat the onions, celery, leeks, and broccoli stems in butter.

2. Add the stock and cook until tender.

3. Puree the mixture until it is completely smooth. Add to the velouté and simmer slowly for 10 minutes.

4. Adjust the seasoning with salt and pepper to taste.

5. Add hot cream.

6. Strain through either cheesecloth or chinoise.

7. Garnish to order with broccoli florets before serving.

flavor should be that of the major flavoring ingredient and should not taste too strongly of heavy cream. The color will vary, depending upon the major flavoring ingredient. In all cases, it will be relatively pale.

Consistency too thick. It is uncommon for a cream soup to be too thin; more often, the soup becomes overly thick during cooking and storage. The soup can be thinned with water or stock until the correct consistency is achieved. Do not thin cream soups with more heavy cream, because it can mask the main flavor.

Sour or off flavors. These soups have a brief shelf life once the cream has been added. To extend storage time, be sure that the base is properly chilled and stored and then finish only the amount needed for a single service period. Check cream soups carefully for any souring or off odors. Once a soup begins to curdle or taste sour, it cannot be salvaged.

Starchy taste. The cooking time is important. The soup must be simmered long enough to allow the roux's starchy taste to cook out.

Scorched taste. Using moderate cooking heat and heavy-gauge pots, and stirring cream soups as they cook, will prevent scorching and promote the development of a clear flavor. If the soup does begin to scorch, it should be immediately transferred to a cool, clean pot and

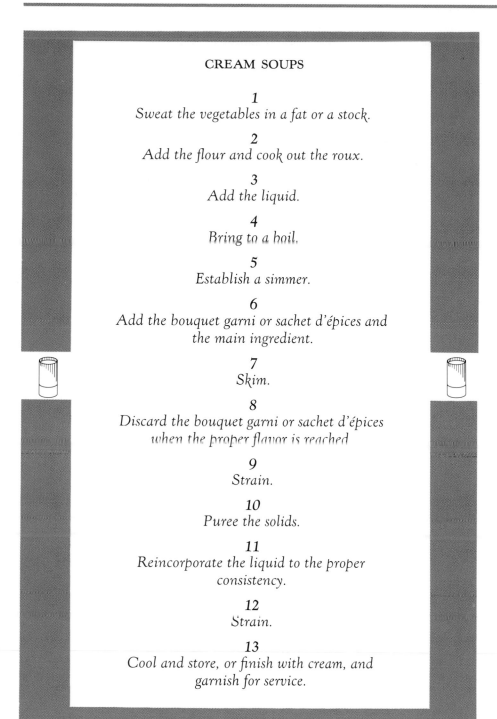

CREAM SOUPS

1
Sweat the vegetables in a fat or a stock.

2
Add the flour and cook out the roux.

3
Add the liquid.

4
Bring to a boil.

5
Establish a simmer.

6
Add the bouquet garni or sachet d'épices and the main ingredient.

7
Skim.

8
Discard the bouquet garni or sachet d'épices when the proper flavor is reached

9
Strain.

10
Puree the solids.

11
Reincorporate the liquid to the proper consistency.

12
Strain.

13
Cool and store, or finish with cream, and garnish for service.

food processor is used, the chef may need to add a small amount of the liquid to expedite the pureeing process.

Once the solids are pureed to a fine paste, they should be returned to the pot. The reserved liquid should be added gradually until the proper consistency is achieved. The soup should be thick but liquid enough to pour from a ladle into a bowl. Some of the solids may be left whole and returned for textural interest after the proper consistency has been reached. Any leftover liquid may be saved to use for braising vegetables or meats or as a base for another soup.

Croutons or small dices of a complementary vegetable or meat are common garnishes. Although it is not necessary, finishing ingredients such as cream or milk are used sometimes. Note: At that point, the distinction between purees and creams becomes blurred, and it is often up to the menu writer to determine how a soup will be designated.

Mise en Place

1. Major flavoring ingredient. Prepare, as necessary, according to recipe. For example, soak the beans, peel and slice the potatoes, etc.

2. Aromatics. Chop the mirepoix into a medium dice and prepare a sachet d'épices or bouquet garni.

3. Liquid. Have stock or water available.

4. A garnish may be prepared, if called for by the recipe.

Method

1. Sweat the aromatic vegetables and, if appropriate, the main flavoring ingredient.

the flavor checked. If the soup does not taste scorched, the process may be continued.

Puree Soups

Puree soups are slightly thicker than cream soups and have a somewhat coarser texture. They are based on dried peas, lentils, or beans, or on starchy vegetables such as potatoes, carrots, and squashes.

In order to assure the proper consistency, the major flavoring ingredients and aromatics are strained out of the cooked soup and pureed separately by running them through a food mill, rubbing them through a drum sieve, or using a blender, food processor, or vertical chopping machine. If a blender or

2. Add the liquid and bring to a full boil; establish a gentle simmer.

3. Add the main flavoring ingredient, if it has not previously been added.

4. Simmer until all the ingredients are soft enough to puree easily.

5. Add the sachet d'épices or bouquet garni approximately 1 hour before the end of the cooking time.

6. Check the flavor as the soup develops; remove and discard the sachet d'épices or bouquet garni when the proper flavor extraction is reached.

7. Strain, reserving the liquid. Remove and discard the bouquet garni or sachet d'épices if this has not yet been done.

8. Puree the solids and return them to the pot.

9. Gradually reincorporate the liquid until the soup reaches the proper consistency.

10. Cool and store as for stock (see Chapter 15).

Preparation for Service

1. Soften the soup over low heat.

2. Bring it to a full boil.

3. Make any necessary adjustments in consistency or flavor.

4. Serve in heated cups or bowls.

5. Garnish individual portions; be sure that the garnish is heated, if necessary.

For a quick summary of puree soup preparation, refer to the abbreviated method for puree soups.

Evaluating Quality

Puree soups are somewhat thicker and have a slightly coarser texture than the other thick soups; however, they should still be liquid

Puree of Black Bean

Yield: 1 gallon (3.75 liters)

Black beans, dried	2 pounds	910 grams
Bacon fat	4 ounces	115 grams
Onions, medium dice	2 pounds	910 grams
Chicken stock	3 quarts	3 liters
Standard sachet d'épices	1	1
Ham hocks	2	2
Dry sherry	4 to 6 ounces	114 to 170 grams
Allspice, ground (optional)	to taste	to taste

1. Soak the beans overnight in enough cold water to cover them.

2. Heat bacon fat in a soup pot; add the onions and sweat until translucent.

3. Add beans, stock, sachet d'épices, and ham hocks.

4. Simmer the mixture until the beans are very tender.

5. Remove half of the beans and puree.

6. Combine the whole beans with the puree.

7. Finish with sherry and allspice.

8. Adjust the seasoning with salt and pepper to taste.

9. Garnish at the time of service with 2 teaspoons (20 grams) of sour cream, 1 teaspoon (10 grams) of tomato concassé, and 1 teaspoon (10 grams) of minced scallions.

enough to pour easily from a ladle into a bowl. The flavor should clearly reflect the major ingredient. The color will vary greatly according to the flavoring ingredient used.

Consistency too thick. Soups that have become too thick can be thinned with stock or water after they have returned to a boil. It is rare for puree soups to be too thin.

Uneven texture. The proper texture is more coarse than that of a cream soup, but still basically smooth. Proper pureeing in a food mill, vertical chopping machine, or food processor is important. Add-

ing a small amount of liquid to the solids when they are pureed will help to assure a smooth quality. The soup should also be strained through a chinois to assure an even texture.

Scorched taste. Because most puree soups are fairly starchy, they should be stirred frequently during cooking to prevent scorching. Employing a moderate cooking heat and heavy-gauge pots will also help to prevent scorching. If the soup does begin to scorch, it should be immediately transferred to a cool, clean pot and the flavor should be checked. If the soup does not taste

are usually garnished with small pieces of the appropriate shellfish or vegetable.

Recipes for bisques may vary at many points. For instance, some chefs still prefer to prepare bisques with rice that has been cooked separately until it falls apart. It is then pureed and added to the soup base until the desired consistency is achieved. Other chefs may adhere to an older method of drying the crustacean shells thoroughly and then pulverizing them to a powder. The method outlined here is but one of a number of equally suitable techniques.

A vegetable-based bisque is prepared in the same manner as a puree soup. If the vegetable does not contain enough starch to act as a thickener, rice may be used to provide additional thickness. After the vegetables are tender, they are pureed and the liquid is reincorporated into the soup. The consistency and texture should be the same as that of a shellfish bisque.

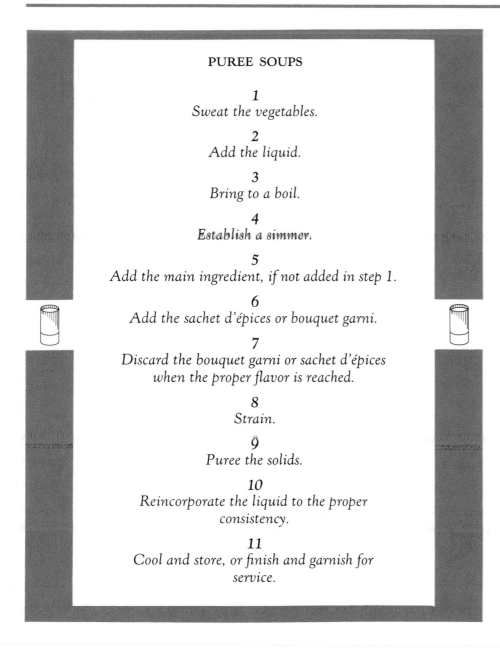

PUREE SOUPS

1
Sweat the vegetables.

2
Add the liquid.

3
Bring to a boil.

4
Establish a simmer.

5
Add the main ingredient, if not added in step 1.

6
Add the sachet d'épices or bouquet garni.

7
Discard the bouquet garni or sachet d'épices when the proper flavor is reached.

8
Strain.

9
Puree the solids.

10
Reincorporate the liquid to the proper consistency.

11
Cool and store, or finish and garnish for service.

Mise en Place

1. Major flavoring ingredient. Rinse crustacean shells and, if necessary, coarsely chop them.

2. Aromatics. Chop the mirepoix into a medium dice and prepare sachet d'épices or bouquet garni.

3. Liquids. Have a fish stock or fish fumet available.

4. Thickening agent. Rice or roux are both acceptable as thickeners.

5. Finishing ingredients. These include heated heavy cream or a liaison, if required by the recipe. The liaison must be tempered with a small amount of the hot soup before being added.

6. Optional components. Have tomato paste or tomato puree, and brandy and/or wine available, if

scorched, the process may be continued.

Separation of liquids and solids. Some liquid may separate out and rise to the top during storage. Fully reheating and stirring the soup well before service will remedy this problem.

Bisques

Bisques, traditionally based on such crustaceans as shrimp, lobster, or crayfish, share characteristics with both purees and cream

soups. A base flavoring ingredient, usually a crustacean, is simmered in stock or a fish fumet, along with aromatic vegetables. Although rice is a classic thickener, contemporary renditions rely on a roux for better texture and stability. The crustacean shells are pureed with the other ingredients before straining to add flavor, thickness, and color. Heavy cream is used as a finisher.

The texture is slightly grainy. Bisques should have about the same thickness as cream soups and

called for by the recipe. Prepare the garnish according to the recipe.

Method

1. Sear the shells in oil, butter, or a small amount of stock until they turn a bright red or pink.

2. Add the mirepoix and allow it to sweat.

3. Add the tomato product, if necessary. Cook until the tomato lightly caramelizes (a process known as *pincé*).

4. Add the alcohol, if required, and reduce until the mixture is nearly dry (known as *au sec*). Add the stock and sachet d'épices or bouquet garni. Bring to a simmer.

5. Simmer for approximately 1 hour; skim the surface as necessary.

6. Check the flavor as the soup develops; remove and discard the bouquet garni or sachet d'épices when the proper flavor extraction is reached.

7. Strain through a chinois, pressing the solids well to extract the liquid. Reserve the liquid.

8. Puree the solids and return them to the pot.

9. Reincorporate the liquid until the proper consistency is achieved.

10. Strain through a fine sieve or cheesecloth.

11. Cool and store as for stocks (see Chapter 15).

Preparation for Service

1. Heat the soup over low heat until softened.

2. Bring it back to a boil.

3. Add hot heavy cream or temper a liaison and add it to the bisque.

4. Adjust the seasoning and consistency, if necessary.

5. Serve in heated cups or bowls and garnish according to the rec-

Shrimp Bisque

Yield: 2 gallons (7.5 liters)

Shrimp shells	1 pound	455 grams
Onions, minced	1 pound	455 grams
Butter	3 ounces	85 grams
Garlic, minced	2 cloves	2 cloves
Paprika	2 tablespoons	14 grams
Tomato paste	3 tablespoons	45 milliliters
Brandy	8 ounces	240 milliliters
Fish velouté (made with fish or shrimp stock)	1½ gallons	5.5 liters
Heavy cream, hot	5 cups	1.25 liters
Shrimp, peeled and deveined	1 pound, 10 ounces	735 grams
Sherry	6 ounces	180 milliliters

1. Sauté the shrimp shells and onions in butter.

2. Add the garlic.

3. Add the paprika and tomato paste. Pincé.

4. Add the brandy and deglaze.

5. Add the fish velouté. Simmer for 45 minutes and strain.

6. Add the heavy cream.

7. Dice the shrimp, sauté, and add to the soup.

8. Add the sherry.

9. Season to taste with Old Bay seasoning, salt, Tabasco sauce, and Worcestershire sauce.

ipe. If necessary, heat the garnish first in a small amount of stock.

For a quick summary of bisque preparation, refer to the abbreviated method for bisques.

Evaluating Quality

A bisque should reflect the flavor of the particular crustacean. The cream or liaison is added to round out and mellow the soup, but it should not mask the shellfish flavor. Bisques are slightly grainy, with a consistency similar to heavy cream. The color should be a pale pink or red. Bisques based on ingredients other than shellfish should have the same characteristics as puree soups.

Consistency too thick. Bisques may thicken during storage. If this happens, the soup may be thinned with additional appropriate stock or fumet, not with heavy cream. Too much heavy cream will disguise the flavor.

Weak flavor. If a weak flavor occurs, the correct ratio of major flavoring ingredient to liquid has not

BISQUES

1

Sear the crustacean shells in a fat or stock.

2

Add the mirepoix and sweat.

3

Add the tomato product and pincé.

4

Add the alcohol, if using, and reduce au sec.

5

Add the stock and sachet d'épices or bouquet garni.

6

Incorporate the roux.

7

Simmer.

8

Skim.

9

Discard the bouquet garni or sachet d'épices when the proper flavor is reached.

10

Strain.

11

Puree the solids.

12

Reincorporate the liquid to the proper consistency.

13

Strain.

14

Cool and store, or finish and garnish for service.

pureed solids and the liquid have been recombined.

Thick Vegetable and Special Soups

These are based on stocks, broth, milk, or vegetable or fruit juices. They may be thickened with a roux, as in some of the gumbos and chowders, or by adding a specific thickening ingredient, such as okra, gumbo filé, potatoes, or other root vegetables. In some classic cookbooks, these soups are referred to as "specialty" or "national" soups.

There are no general definitions or methods that will work for all of these soups at all times. The basic preparation methods share similarities with those for other soups such as clear soups, purees, bisques, and creams. The previously outlined techniques are applied as indicated in the recipes for these various soups. A brief and general definition for some of these soups follows.

Thick vegetable soups, such as chowders and gumbos, are made with a base of broth, milk, or water, thickened by a roux or by one or more of the soup's ingredients; chowders almost invariably contain potatoes; minestrone contains beans and pasta; gumbos are made with a dark roux, okra, and/or gumbo filé; in a garbure, some or all of the ingredients are pureed, or starchy ingredients may be included so that the finished soup will, therefore, have more body than a clear vegetable soup.

Cold Soups

Cold soups may be prepared in a variety of ways. Some, such as vichyssoise, are simply cream soups that are served cold. Others, such as chilled cantaloupe soup or

been observed, or the soup was not simmered long enough.

Dominant rice flavor. If the proper ratio of rice to liquid has not been observed, the soup may taste too strongly of rice. Use only enough rice to adequately thicken the soup.

Uneven texture. Proper pureeing and straining are essential. The solids must be thoroughly pureed and the soup strained again once the

gazpacho, are based on a puree of raw or cooked ingredients that has been brought to the correct consistency by adding a liquid such as a fruit or vegetable juice. The chef should refer to the recipe for a cold soup for guidance on its particular preparation method.

SUMMARY

Soup is often the first dish a restaurant's guest will be served. A well-prepared soup will make a positive initial impression. Soups should always be carefully presented—hot soups hot and cold soups cold—in serving dishes that have been properly heated or chilled. Soups are not difficult to make; the techniques are straightforward, but the options for major flavoring ingredients and garnishes are many.

Not only are quality soups an easy way to please guests, they also allow the kitchen staff to make efficient use of trimmings and leftovers. They are thus important profit-makers for any foodservice establishment.

Chicken Broth

Yield: 2½ gallons (9.5 liters)

Chicken, washed (2 to 3 each)	10 pounds	4.5 kilograms
Water, cold	2½ gallons	9.5 liters
Mirepoix	1 pound	455 grams
Standard sachet d'épices	1	1

Garnish

Chicken, poached, julienne	2 pounds	910 grams
Carrots, julienne, blanched	8 ounces	225 grams
Celery, julienne, blanched	8 ounces	225 grams
Leeks (white only), julienne, blanched	8 ounces	225 grams

1. Bring the chicken and water to simmer, skim, and simmer for 2 hours.
2. Add the mirepoix and simmer for ½ hour.
3. Add sachet d'épices and allow to simmer for an additional half hour.
4. Degrease, remove the chicken and sachet, and strain.
5. Season to taste with salt.
6. Bring the broth to service temperature.
7. Adjust the seasoning with salt and pepper to taste.
8. Garnish and return the broth to a boil before service.

VARIATIONS

Turkey Broth: Replace the chicken with an equal weight of turkey.

Chicken Broth with Julienned Vegetables: Garnish each portion with blanched, julienned leeks, celery, carrots, and julienned, cooked chicken.

Turkey Broth with Quenelles: Make small quenelles from a turkey mousseline forcemeat (see the recipe in Chapter 28, "Charcuterie and Garde-manger").

Chicken Broth with Rice: Garnish with 1 tablespoon of cooked rice.

Chicken Broth with Noodles: Garnish with cooked egg noodles.

Fish Consommé

Yield: 1 gallon (3.75 liters)

Fish, whiting or pike, ground	3 pounds	1.35 kilograms
Egg whites	8	8
Leeks, rough julienne	4 ounces	115 grams
Celery, rough julienne	4 ounces	115 grams
Parsley stems	4 ounces	115 grams
Dry white wine	2 cups	480 milliliters
Lemon juice	2 lemons	2 lemons
Fish stock	1¼ gallon	4.75 liters
Standard sachet d'épices	1	1

1. Mix the fish and egg whites together.
2. Add the leeks, celery, parsley stems, wine, lemon juice, and stock. Mix well.
3. Bring the mixture to a slow simmer, stirring frequently until a raft forms.
4. Add the sachet d'épices and simmer for 45 minutes, or until the appropriate flavor and clarity are achieved.
5. Strain; adjust the seasoning with salt and white pepper to taste.

VARIATIONS

Fish Consommé with Seafood and Fresh Dill: Garnish with small diced, cooked seafood (shrimp, lobster, crab, scallops) and chopped, fresh dill.

Fish Consommé with Quenelles: Garnish each portion with small quenelles made from fish mousseline forcemeat (see Chapter 28, "Charcuterie and Garde-manger").

Beef Consommé

Yield: 2 gallons (7.5 liters)

Oignon brûlé	4	4
Mirepoix (carrots, turnips, leeks, celeriac, parsnips, parsley stems)	2 pounds	910 grams
Ground beef	6 pounds	2.75 kilograms
Egg whites, beaten until slightly frothy	20	20
Tomato concassé	24 ounces	680 grams
Standard sachet d'épices, plus 1 clove and 2 allspice berries	1	1
White beef stock, cold	2½ gallons	9.5 liters

1. Combine the oignon brûlé, mirepoix, meat, tomatoes, and egg whites. Mix well.

2. Add the stock and mix well.

3. Bring mixture to a slow simmer. Stir frequently until a raft forms.

4. Add the sachet d'épices and simmer for 1½ hours, or until the appropriate flavor is achieved.

5. Strain; adjust the seasoning with kosher salt as needed.

VARIATIONS

Beef Consommé Julienne: Garnish with a julienne of vegetables, blanched until tender.

Beef Consommé Paysanne: Garnish with paysanne-cut vegetables, blanched until tender.

Beef Consommé Printanière: Garnish with tourné vegetables, blanched until tender.

Beef Consommé with Wild Mushrooms: Garnish with sliced wild mushrooms that have been sautéed quickly in hot butter.

Onion Soup

Yield: 1 gallon (3.75 liters)

Onions, sliced thin	3 pounds	1.35 kilograms
Butter, clarified	2 ounces	60 grams
Brown beef stock	1 gallon	3.75 liters
Calvados or applejack (optional)	4 ounces	120 milliliters

1. Sauté the onions in clarified butter until browned. Add a little stock, if necessary, to prevent burning.

2. Deglaze the pan with the Calvados; add the stock.

3. Simmer until the onions are tender and the soup is properly flavored.

4. Adjust the seasoning with salt and pepper to taste.

5. Garnish each portion with a crouton. Top generously with grated Gruyère or Emmenthaler and brown under a salamander or broiler or bake in a moderate oven until lightly browned.

Amish-style Chicken Corn Soup

Yield: 2½ gallons (9.5 liters)

Stewing hens, quartered	2	2
Standard sachet d'épices	1	1
Chicken stock	2½ gallons	9.5 liters
Mirepoix	1½ pounds	680 grams
Saffron threads, crushed	1 tablespoon	7 grams

Garnish, per order

Chicken meat, reserved, diced	1 tablespoon	15 grams
Whole-kernel corn, cooked	1 tablespoon	15 grams
Celery, small dice, cooked	1 tablespoon	15 grams
Parsley, chopped	1 teaspoon	5 grams
Egg noodles, cooked	1 ounce	30 grams

1. Combine the hens, sachet d'épices, and stock. Simmer for 1½ hours, skimming as necessary.

2. Add the mirepoix and saffron and simmer for an additional 1½ hours.

3. Remove the chickens, let stand until they are cool enough to handle, then remove the meat and dice.

4. Strain the broth.

5. Bring the soup to service temperature.

6. Add the garnish and adjust the seasoning with salt and pepper to taste.

NOTE: The amount of garnish may be varied to suit preference.

Watercress Soup

Yield: 1 gallon (3.75 liters)

Watercress	4 bunches	4 bunches
Butter	as needed	as needed
Leeks, sliced	3	3
Onion, medium, chopped	1	1
White beef stock	1 gallon	3.75 liters
Potatoes, sliced thin	2 pounds	910 grams

1. Clean and puree the watercress. Reserve it.

2. Sweat the leeks and onions in butter.

3. Add the stock and bring it to a boil.

4. Add the potatoes and simmer them until they are tender.

5. Puree the soup. Adjust the seasoning with salt and pepper to taste.

6. Garnish the soup with watercress sprigs.

Sweet Potato Soup

Yield: 2 quarts (2 liters)

Chicken stock	1 quart	1 liter
Garlic, minced	1 teaspoon	3 grams
Celery, medium dice	3 ounces	85 grams
Onion, fine dice	3 ounces	85 grams
Leeks, fine dice	3 ounces	85 grams
Sweet potatoes, medium dice	1½ pounds	680 grams
Cinnamon stick	½	½
Nutmeg, freshly ground	¼ teaspoon	500 milligrams
Maple syrup	1 ounce	30 milliliters
Salt	1 teaspoon	5 grams
Evaporated skim milk	12 ounces	360 milliliters

Garnish

Heavy cream, whipped to stiff peaks	¼ cup	60 milliliters
Currants, dried	2 tablespoons	20 grams
Almonds, toasted	2 tablespoons	15 grams

1. Sweat the garlic in 2 tablespoons (30 milliliters) of stock. Add the celery, onions, and leeks and sauté them until the onions are translucent.

2. Add the sweet potatoes and remaining chicken stock. Bring the liquid to a boil, reduce the heat, and simmer the soup until the potatoes are tender.

3. Puree the soup in a processor or blender until it is smooth. Return it to the soup pot. Add the remaining ingredients. Return the soup to a boil.

4. Thin the soup with stock or water, if necessary. Remove and discard the cinnamon stick.

5. Serve the soup in heated cups or bowls. Garnish it with the heavy cream, currants, and almonds.

Waterzooi (Chicken Soup)

Yield: 1 gallon (3.75 liters)

Chickens, whole	3¾ pounds	1.7 kilograms
Chicken stock	1 gallon	3.75 liters
Sachet d'Épices	1 each	1 each
Flour	7 ounces	200 grams
Butter	9 ounces	255 grams
Salt	to taste	to taste
Pepper, white	to taste	to taste
Butter, melted	3 ounces	85 grams
Carrots, allumette	5 ounces	140 grams
Celery root, allumette	5 ounces	140 grams
Turnips, allumette	3 ounces	85 grams
Potatoes, allumette	8 ounces	225 grams
Leeks, white only, allumette	4 ounces	115 grams
Egg yolks	3	3
Half-and-half	22 ounces	660 milliliters
Parsley, fresh, chopped	5½ ounces	155 grams

1. Combine the chicken, stock, and sachet d'épices. Bring the mixture to a boil. Simmer it for 45 minutes, skimming if necessary. Remove the chicken.

2. Strain the stock and keep it hot.

3. Remove the chicken meat from the bones and dice it.

4. Combine the butter and flour to make a roux.

5. Stir in the reserved broth. Simmer the mixture for 1 hour. Adjust the seasoning with the salt and pepper and reserve the mixture.

6. Sweat the vegetables in butter until they are tender.

7. Combine the egg yolks and half-and-half. Temper the liaison with the hot velouté. Add the liaison to the velouté with the vegetables and reserved chicken meat.

8. Bring the soup to serving temperature. Serve, garnished with parsley.

Cheddar Cheese Soup

Yield: 1 gallon (3.75 liters)

White mirepoix	12 ounces	340 grams
Butter	4 ounces	115 grams
Garlic, minced	1 ounce	30 grams
Flour	4 ounces	115 grams
Chicken stock	1 gallon	3.75 liters
Cheddar cheese, grated	2 pounds	910 grams
Heavy cream	1 pint	480 milliliters
Green pepper, blanched, julienne	4 ounces	115 grams
Red pepper, blanched, julienne	4 ounces	115 grams
Dry mustard	½ ounce	15 grams
White wine, dry	1 ounce	30 milliliters
Tabasco sauce	to taste	to taste
Worcestershire sauce	to taste	to taste

1. Sweat the mirepoix in the butter until it is tender.

2. Add the garlic and sweat briefly.

3. Add the flour; stir it in to make a roux. Cook out the roux for 5 minutes.

4. Add the stock and simmer the mixture for 45 minutes.

5. Add the cheddar cheese and continue to heat the soup gently until the cheese melts.

6. Add the heavy cream and heat the soup just to a simmer. Do not boil it.

7. Add the peppers to the soup.

8. Add the dry mustard and wine; adjust the seasoning with Tabasco and Worcestershire sauces and salt and pepper.

Minnesota Wild Rice Soup

Yield: 1½ quarts (1.5 liters)

Butter	½ ounce	15 grams
Leeks, fine dice	3 ounces	85 grams
Carrot, fine dice	1 ounce	30 grams
Celery, fine dice	1 ounce	30 grams
Flour	1 tablespoon	7 grams
Chicken stock	5 cups	1.2 liters
Wild rice	⅓ cup	80 grams
Skim milk, evaporated	¾ cup	180 milliliters
Salt	¼ teaspoon	1.5 grams
Chives, minced	4 teaspoons	13 grams
Parsley, chopped	1 teaspoon	3 grams
Sherry, dry	4 teaspoons	15 grams

1. Heat the butter in a 2- to 3-quart saucepan over medium heat. Add the leeks, carrots, and celery and sweat them.

2. Add the flour and stir it in well to make a roux. Cook the roux gently over low heat for approximately 3 minutes, stirring constantly.

3. Add the chicken stock gradually, whipping well with each addition to eliminate lumps. Bring it to a simmer.

4. Add the wild rice, evaporated skim milk, and salt. Continue to simmer the soup until the rice is done.

5. Garnish the soup with chives and parsley immediately before serving. Add the sherry, and serve the soup immediately.

Cream of Chicken Soup

Yield: 2½ gallons (9.5 liters)

Onions, medium dice	1 pound	455 grams
Celery, medium dice	8 ounces	225 grams
Carrots, medium dice	8 ounces	225 grams
Butter	1 pound	455 grams
Flour	12 ounces	340 grams
Chicken stock, hot	2 gallons	7.5 liters
Bay leaf	1	1
Milk, hot	2 quarts	2 liters
Light cream, hot	1 quart	1 liter
Chicken breast, cooked, fine dice	½ ounce per serving	15 grams per serving

1. Sauté the onions, celery, and carrots in butter until tender.

2. Add the flour and cook out the roux for 8 to 10 minutes.

3. Add the stock gradually, stirring until thickened and smooth.

4. Add the bay leaf and simmer for 30 minutes.

5. Bring the soup to a boil and pass it through a food mill. Pass it through a china cap, if necessary.

6. Add the milk and cream.

7. Adjust the seasoning with salt and pepper to taste.

8. Garnish the soup with finely diced chicken meat.

Bergen Fish Soup

Yield: 1 gallon (3.75 liters)

Butter, melted	7 ounces	200 grams
Flour	9 ounces	255 grams
Fish fumet	1 gallon	3.75 liters
Butter	4 ounces	115 grams
Carrots, medium dice	6 ounces	170 grams
Parsnips, medium dice	6 ounces	170 grams
Turnips, medium dice	6 ounces	170 grams
Leeks, medium dice	6 ounces	170 grams
Potatoes, medium dice	12 ounces	340 grams
Sour cream	20 ounces	565 grams
Egg yolks	5	5
Dill, fresh, chopped	5 tablespoons	12 grams
Parsley, fresh, chopped	3 tablespoons	7 grams
Cod or haddock, diced	2 pounds	910 grams

1. Combine the melted butter and flour and cook to a light roux.

2. Add the fish fumet gradually to make a velouté. Bring it to a simmer. Simmer the velouté for 1 hour and reserve it.

3. Sweat the vegetables in the butter until they are tender.

4. Add the reserved velouté.

5. Combine the sour cream, egg yolks, dill, and parsley. Temper the liaison with hot velouté. Combine it with the remaining velouté. Bring the mixture just to a simmer.

6. Add the fish. Remove the soup from the heat and allow the fish to finish cooking in the hot broth for about 10 minutes.

Puree of Lentils

Yield: 2½ gallons (9.5 liters)

Lentils	2½ pounds	1.15 kilograms
White beef stock	9 quarts	8.5 liters
Slab bacon, medium dice	12 ounces	340 grams
Carrots, medium dice	8 ounces	225 grams
Onions, medium dice	1 pound	455 grams
Sachet d'épices	1	1
Whole butter	6 ounces	170 grams
Salt	to taste	to taste
Croutons, fried in butter	as needed	as needed
Chervil, chopped	1 bunch	1 bunch

1. Combine the lentils, beef stock, and bacon. Bring the mixture to a simmer and skim it.
2. Add the carrots and onions; simmer for 45 minutes.
3. Add the sachet d'épices and simmer for another half hour.
4. Strain the mixture. Reserve the stock; discard the sachet d'épices.
5. Puree the solids and add the reserved stock to achieve the proper consistency.
6. Monté au beurre.
7. Adjust the seasoning with salt and pepper to taste. Garnish with croutons and chervil.

Senate Bean Soup

Yield: 1 gallon (3.75 liters)

Navy beans	1 pound	455 grams
Chicken stock, to make 1 gallon when added to bean liquid	2 quarts (as needed)	2 liters (as needed)
Ham hock, smoked	1	1
Onion, diced	1	1
Carrot, diced	8 ounces	225 grams
Celery, diced	8 ounces	225 grams
Garlic cloves, minced	2	2
Oignon piqué	1	1
Chef potatoes, large dice	3	3
Tabasco sauce	to taste	to taste

1. Soak the beans overnight.

2. Combine the beans, soaking liquid, stock, and ham hock and cook for 1 hour.

3. Sweat the onion, carrots, and celery for 4 to 5 minutes, or until the onions are translucent. Add the garlic; sauté it until an aroma is apparent.

4. Add the beans, stock mixture, and ham hock to the vegetables.

5. Add the oignon piqué and potatoes and simmer until the beans and potatoes are tender.

6. Remove the oignon piqué and ham hock. Dice the ham and reserve it.

7. Puree half of the soup. Recombine the puree and reserved ham with the soup.

8. Adjust the seasoning with the Tabasco sauce and with salt and pepper to taste.

Summer-style Lentil Soup

Yield: 2 quarts (2 liters)

Butter	5 teaspoons	25 grams
Onion, diced	3 ounces	85 grams
Leeks, small dice	3 ounces	85 grams
Garlic, minced	1 teaspoon	5 grams
Tomato paste	1 ounce	30 grams
Vinegar	1 tablespoon	15 milliliters
Carrots, small dice	⅓ cup	80 grams
Celery, small dice	⅓ cup	80 grams
Lentils	1½ quarts	190 grams
Chicken stock	6 cups	1.5 liters
Bay leaf	½	½
Thyme, fresh	1 sprig	1 sprig
Caraway seeds	½ teaspoon	1 gram
Lemon peel	3 strips	3 strips
Salt	½ teaspoon	3 grams
Pepper, white	⅛ teaspoon	300 milligrams

1. Heat the butter in a soup pot over medium heat. Sweat the onion, leeks, and garlic in the butter.

2. Add the tomato paste; pincé.

3. Deglaze the pan with the vinegar.

4. Add the carrots, celery, lentils, chicken stock, bay leaf, thyme, caraway seed, and lemon peel. Stir the soup well and bring it to a simmer. Simmer it for 1 hour or until the lentils are very tender.

5. Remove and discard the bay leaf and lemon peel. Adjust the seasoning with the salt and pepper. Serve the soup in heated soup plates or cups.

Potato Kale Soup (Caldo Verde)

Yield: 2 gallons (7.5 liters)

White mirepoix	1 pound	455 grams
Olive oil	4 ounces	115 grams
Potatoes, cut in chunks	7 pounds	3 kilograms
White stock	5 quarts	4.75 liters
Ham hocks	3	3
Bay leaves	3	3
Salt	to taste	to taste
Kale, fresh, julienne	1 pound	455 grams
Chorizo, sliced	8 ounces	225 grams

1. Sweat the mirepoix in oil.
2. Add the potatoes, stock, ham hocks, bay leaves, and salt; simmer until the potatoes and ham hocks are tender.
3. Remove the ham hocks and cut the ham into a fine dice; reserve.
4. Puree the soup. Return the diced ham and pureed soup to the pot. Simmer for 30 minutes.
5. Add the kale and chorizo and simmer for 5 minutes.
6. Adjust the seasoning with salt and pepper to taste.

Puree of Cauliflower

Yield: 1 gallon (3.75 liters)

Cauliflower	3 pounds	2 kilograms
Potatoes	1 pound	450 grams
Onions, chopped	6 ounces	170 grams
Leeks, chopped	6 ounces	170 grams
Celery, chopped	3 ounces	85 grams
Chicken stock	3 quarts	3 liters
Standard sachet d'épices	1	1
Milk, boiling	1 quart	1 liter
Butter, whole, chilled (optional)	10 ounces	285 grams
Parmesan cheese, freshly grated	as needed	as needed

1. Combine the cauliflower, potatoes, onions, leeks, celery, and 8 ounces (240 milliliters) of stock and smother until the vegetables begin to soften.

2. Add the remainder of the hot stock and the sachet d'épices. Simmer the soup until all ingredients are very tender.

3. Drain, reserving the liquid, and puree the vegetables until smooth.

4. Combine the puree with enough soup liquid to correct the consistency.

5. Add the hot milk and adjust the seasoning with salt and pepper to taste.

6. Finish the soup by whipping in the butter, if desired.

7. Garnish with the parmesan cheese.

VARIATIONS

Puree of Carrot Soup: Replace the cauliflower with an equal weight of carrots, cut into a medium dice.

Puree of Celery Soup: Replace the cauliflower with an equal weight of celery root, cut into a large dice.

Puree of Split Pea

Yield: 2½ gallons (9.5 liters)

Bacon, finely chopped	1 pound	455 grams
Oil, vegetable	2 ounces	60 grams
Onion, chopped	1½ pounds	680 grams
Celery, chopped	8 ounces	225 grams
Garlic, chopped	1 tablespoon	15 milliliters
All-purpose flour	6 ounces	170 grams
Chicken stock	2½ gallons	9.5 liters
Split green peas, washed and picked over	2½ pounds	1.15 kilograms
Ham hocks	3 pounds	1.25 kilograms
Bay leaves	4	4
Croutons	as needed	as needed

1. Render the bacon in the oil.

2. Add the onions and celery and sauté until the onions become transparent.

3. Add the garlic and sauté until an aroma develops; do not brown.

4. Add the flour to make a roux and cook out.

5. Add the stock and bring to a simmer.

6. Add the split peas and ham hocks and allow the soup to simmer for 1½ hours.

7. Add the bay leaves and simmer for another half hour.

(continued)

8. Remove the ham hocks; shock. Discard the bay leaves.

9. Clean the ham hocks; chop the meat and return it to the soup.

10. Adjust the seasoning with salt and pepper to taste.

11. Garnish at service with croutons that have been finely diced and fried in butter.

VARIATION

Yellow Split Pea Soup: Replace green split peas with yellow split peas.

Pumpkin Bisque

Yield: 1 gallon (3.75 liters)

Garlic, chopped	1 tablespoon	15 milliliters
Celery, medium dice	5 ounces	140 grams
Onion, medium dice	6 ounces	170 grams
Leeks, white only, medium dice	3 ounces	85 grams
Butter, unsalted	1 ounce	30 grams
Pumpkin flesh	5 ounces	140 grams
Chicken stock	1 gallon	3.75 liters
Ginger, grated	1 teaspoon	5 milliliters
White wine	2 ounces	60 milliliters
Salt	to taste	to taste
Nutmeg, ground (optional)	1 teaspoon	5 milliliters

1. Sauté the garlic, celery, onions, and leeks in butter.

2. Add the pumpkin and stock and simmer until all the vegetables are tender.

3. Puree the solids with enough liquid to achieve the desired consistency.

4. Steep the ginger in the wine. Strain.

5. Add the wine to the soup, season with salt and nutmeg, and finish with a dollop of whipped heavy cream.

Manhattan-style Clam Chowder

Yield: 1 gallon (3.75 liters)

Chowder clams, washed	60	60
Water	1 gallon	3.75 liters
Potatoes, medium dice	2 pounds	910 grams
Salt pork, minced to a paste	7 ounces	200 grams
Onions, medium dice	20 ounces	570 grams
Carrots, medium dice	8 ounces	225 grams
Celery, peeled, medium dice	8 ounces	225 grams
Leeks, white only, medium dice	8 ounces	225 grams
Green pepper, medium dice	8 ounces	225 grams
Garlic, mashed to paste	1 tablespoon	15 milliliters
Tomato concassé	3½ pints	1.5 liters
Standard sachet d'épices, with 1 sprig fresh or 2 teaspoons dried oregano	1	1

1. Steam the clams in water in a covered pot until they open.
2. Pick, chop, and reserve the clams. Strain and reserve the clam broth.
3. Cook the potatoes in the clam broth. Strain and reserve the broth.
4. Render the salt pork in the soup pot.
5. Sweat the onions, carrots, celery, leeks, and green peppers in the rendered salt pork.
6. Add the garlic; sauté until an aroma is apparent.
7. Add the tomato concassé and sachet d'épices; simmer for 30 minutes.
8. Remove the sachet d'épices and discard.
9. Degrease the soup. Add the potatoes and clams.
10. Adjust the seasoning to taste with salt, white pepper, and Tabasco and Worcestershire sauces.

Corn Chowder

Yield: 1 gallon (3.75 liters)

Potatoes, small dice	2 pounds	910 grams
Chicken broth	1 quart	950 milliliters
Salt pork, ground	6 ounces	170 grams
Onions, small dice	6 ounces	170 grams
Celery, peeled, small dice	6 ounces	170 grams
Green pepper, small dice	4 ounces	115 grams
Red pepper, small dice	4 ounces	115 grams
Flour	12 ounces	340 grams
Corn, pureed	2 cups	480 milliliters
Corn, whole kernel	4 cups	950 milliliters
Bay leaf	1	1
Heavy cream	1 pint	480 milliliters
Milk	1 pint	480 milliliters

1. Cook the potatoes in the broth until they are tender. Drain; reserve the broth and potatoes separately.
2. Render the salt pork.
3. Sweat the onions, celery, and peppers in the rendered salt pork.
4. Add the flour and cook to make a blond roux.
5. Add the pureed corn to the roux.
6. Add the reserved chicken stock to the roux in stages.
7. Add the whole corn and bay leaf and simmer until it is tender.
8. Combine the heavy cream and milk; temper and add to the soup.
9. Remove the bay leaf.
10. Add the potatoes.
11. Adjust the seasoning with salt, white pepper, and Tabasco and Worcestershire sauces.

Corn and Crab Chowder

Yield: 1 quart (1 liter)

Butter	2 teaspoons	10 grams
Scallions, split and diced	2 medium	2 medium
Skim milk	1 pint	480 milliliters
Chicken stock	1 pint	480 milliliters
Corn, fresh, cut from cob	9 ounces	250 grams
Russet potatoes, peeled and diced	2 medium	2 medium
Skim milk, evaporated	6 ounces	180 milliliters
Thyme, fresh	1 sprig	1 sprig
Black peppercorns, crushed	¼ teaspoon	1.5 grams
Salt	¼ teaspoon	.5 gram
Backfin crabmeat, well-cleaned	3½ ounces	100 grams
Parsley, fresh, chopped	½ tablespoon	5 grams

1. Heat the butter in the soup pot. Add the scallions and sauté them until they are tender.

2. Add the skim milk, stock, corn, potatoes, evaporated skim milk, thyme, pepper, and salt. Simmer the soup until the potatoes are tender.

3. Remove the soup from the heat. Remove and discard the thyme. Stir in the crabmeat and parsley.

NOTE: If the soup is to be held for later service, allow it to cool to room temperature before adding the crabmeat and parsley. Refrigerate it and then reheat it in a microwave oven for individual servings.

New England-style Clam Chowder

Yield: Yield: 1 gallon (3.75 liters)

Chowder clams, washed	90	90
Water	2 quarts	2 liters
Potatoes, ¼-inch dice	20 ounces	570 grams
Salt pork, minced to a paste	8 ounces	225 grams
Onions, minced	1 pound	455 grams
Flour	5 ounces	145 grams
Milk	40 ounces	1.25 liters
Heavy cream	8 ounces	240 milliliters

(continued)

1. Steam the clams in water in a covered pot until they open.

2. Strain the broth through a filter or cheesecloth and reserve it.

3. Pick, chop, and reserve the clams.

4. Cook the potatoes in the clam broth until they are tender. Reserve the potatoes and broth separately.

5. Render the salt pork in the soup pot; add the onions and sweat until they are translucent.

6. Add the flour; cook to make a blond roux.

7. Add reserved broth gradually and incorporate it completely, working out any lumps that might form.

8. Simmer for 40 minutes, skimming the surface as necessary.

9. Scald the milk and cream and add them to the soup.

10. Add the reserved clams and potatoes.

11. Adjust the seasoning to taste with salt, white pepper, and Tabasco and Worcestershire sauces.

Minestrone

Yield: 1 gallon (3.75 liters)

Salt pork	2 ounces	55 grams
Olive oil	2 ounces	55 grams
Onions, paysanne	1 pound	455 grams
Celery, paysanne	8 ounces	225 grams
Carrots, paysanne	8 ounces	225 grams
Green peppers, paysanne	8 ounces	225 grams
Cabbage, chiffonade	8 ounces	225 grams
Garlic cloves, minced	3	3
Tomato concassé	1 pound	455 grams
Chicken stock	1 gallon	3.75 liters
Chickpeas, cooked	4 ounces	115 grams
Black-eyed peas, cooked	6 ounces	170 grams
Ditalini pasta, cooked	6 ounces	170 grams
Parmesan cheese, grated	to taste	to taste

1. Render the salt pork in the oil. Do not brown.

2. Add the onions, celery, carrots, peppers, cabbage, and garlic and sweat until the onions are translucent.

3. Add the tomato concassé and stock.

4. Simmer until the vegetables are tender. Do not overcook them.

5. Add the chickpeas, black-eyed peas, and ditalini. Simmer the soup until all ingredients are tender.

6. Adjust the seasoning with salt and pepper to taste.

7. Garnish with grated parmesan cheese just prior to service.

Seafood Minestrone

Yield: 2 quarts (2 liters)

White wine	⅓ cup	80 milliliters
Mussels, cleaned and debearded	16	16
Fish stock	1½ quarts (or as needed)	1½ liters
Olive oil	2 teaspoons	10 milliliters
Bacon slices, chopped	2	2
Garlic, minced	1 tablespoon	15 grams
Leeks, small dice	5 ounces	140 grams
Onion, small dice	3 ounces	85 grams
Celery, small dice	1½ ounces	40 grams
Tomato paste	2 ounces	60 grams
Salt	½ teaspoon	3 grams
Rosemary, dried leaves	½ teaspoon	500 milligrams
Thyme, dried leaves	½ teaspoon	500 milligrams
Pepper	⅛ teaspoon	1 gram
Bay leaf, small	1	1
Lemon	1 slice	1 slice
Dry kidney beans, soaked	2 ounces	60 grams
Arborio rice	3 ounces	85 grams
Tomato concassé	1½ cups	270 grams
Shrimp, peeled, deveined, and chopped	2 ounces	60 grams

(continued)

1. Heat the wine over high heat in a saucepan with a tight-fitting lid. Add the mussels. Cover the pan and steam the mussels just until the shells open.

2. Remove the mussels from their shells; reserve them.

3. Strain the steaming liquid through cheesecloth. Add enough fish stock to equal 2 quarts (2 liters). Reserve the liquid.

4. Heat the oil in a soup pot. Add the bacon and cook it until it is limp and translucent. Do not brown it. Add the garlic, leeks, onion, and celery. Sauté the vegetables until the onion is translucent.

5. Add the tomato paste and sauté it.

6. Add the remaining ingredients (except the mussels and shrimp) and the reserved fish stock. Bring the liquid to a boil; reduce the heat and simmer the soup until the beans and rice are tender.

7. Add the mussels and shrimp. Remove the soup from the heat immediately. Serve it in heated bowls garnished with ½ teaspoon (7 milliliters) of pesto.

Philadelphia Pepperpot Soup

Yield: 1 gallon (3.75 liters)

Mirepoix, medium dice	1 pound	455 grams
Butter (or beef fat reserved from skimming stock)	as needed	as needed
White beef broth	1 gallon	3.75 liters
Honeycomb tripe, small dice	1 pound	455 grams
Veal shank meat, small dice	4 ounces	115 grams
Potatoes, medium dice	8 ounces	55 grams
Green pepper, medium dice	2 ounces	60 grams
Standard sachet d'épices	1	1
Spätzle	1 ounce per portion	28 grams per portion

1. Caramelize the mirepoix in the butter or beef fat.

2. Add the beef broth, tripe, and veal shank. Simmer for 1 hour.

3. Add the potatoes, green pepper, and sachet d'épices. Simmer the mixture until the vegetables are tender and the soup is adequately flavored. Degrease it if necessary. Remove the sachet d'épices and discard it.

4. Prepare the spätzle according to the recipe (see note below). Using a spätzle press or colander, push the spätzle into the simmering soup. Simmer the spätzle until it floats to the top, about 3 to 5 minutes.

NOTE: Refer to Chapter 25 for the recipe for Spätzle.

Louisiana Chicken and Shrimp Gumbo

Yield: 1 gallon (3.75 liters)

Andouille sausage, chopped	3 ounces	85 grams
Chicken meat, lean, chopped	5 ounces	140 grams
Green pepper, chopped	5 ounces	140 grams
Celery, chopped	5 ounces	140 grams
Jalapeños, chopped	½ ounce	15 grams
Scallions, split and cut on bias	4 ounces	115 grams
Garlic, chopped	½ ounce	15 grams
Okra, sliced	5 ounces	140 grams
Tomato concassé	8 ounces	225 grams
Chicken stock	13 cups	3 liters
Carolina rice, cooked	5 ounces	140 grams
All-purpose flour, baked to dark brown	5 ounces	140 grams
Filé powder	1 tablespoon	15 milliliters
Oregano	1 teaspoon	5 milliliters
Bay leaves	2	2
Thyme, dried leaves	½ teaspoon	2.5 milliliters
Black pepper	¼ teaspoon	1.25 milliliters
Dry basil	½ teaspoon	2.5 milliliters
Onion powder	1 teaspoon	5 milliliters
Shrimp, chopped	4 ounces	115 grams

1. Sauté the Andouille sausage and add the chicken.
2. Add the green pepper, celery, jalapeños, scallions, garlic, okra, and concassé and sauté lightly.
3. Add the stock and rice.
4. Add the flour and filé, stirring to work out any lumps.
5. Add the seasonings; simmer for a half hour.
6. Add the shrimp and simmer for 2 minutes.
7. Adjust the seasoning to taste with salt and pepper.

Borscht

Yield: 1 gallon (3.75 liters)

Beets, whole, skin on	2 pounds	910 grams
White stock	1 gallon	3.75 liters
Leeks, julienne	4 ounces	115 grams
Cabbage, julienne	3 ounces	85 grams
Onion, julienne	3 ounces	85 grams
Celery, julienne	3 ounces	85 grams
Sachet d'épices with fennel seeds	1	1
Brisket of beef, cooked, julienne	1 pound	455 grams
Breast of duck, cooked, julienne	1	1
Red wine vinegar	to taste	to taste

Garnish (per serving)

Sour cream	2 teaspoons	20 grams
Dill sprigs, fresh	pinch	pinch

1. Cook the beets in half of the stock until they are tender. Drain and reserve the liquid.
2. Sweat the remaining vegetables until the onions are translucent.
3. Add the remaining stock and sachet d'épices and simmer until the vegetables are tender.
4. Peel the cooked beets and cut into a julienne.
5. Add the beets and reserved cooking liquid to the simmering vegetables.
6. Degrease the soup.
7. Add the beef and duck.
8. Add the vinegar and adjust the seasoning with salt and pepper to taste.
9. Garnish each serving with the sour cream and dill.

Goulash Soup

Yield: 1 gallon (3.75 liters)

Bacon, chopped	5½ ounces	155 grams
Onion, diced	1 pound	455 grams
Beef shank or chuck, small dice	2½ pounds	1.15 kilograms
Garlic cloves, minced	5	5
Hungarian paprika	2 ounces	60 grams
Flour	2½ tablespoons	18 grams
Tomato paste	5½ tablespoons	80 milliliters
Brown stock	1 gallon	3.75 liters

Sachet d'Épices

Caraway seeds	½ teaspoon	2 grams
Bay leaf	1	1
Marjoram	½ teaspoon	2 grams
Potatoes, medium dice	1 pound	455 grams

1. Render the bacon over low heat. Remove it from the pot.
2. Raise the heat to medium. Add the onions and sauté them until they are light brown.
3. Add the beef and paprika and sauté the mixture briefly.
4. Add the flour and tomato paste and stir them in well.
5. Add the stock and sachet d'épices. Bring the mixture to a simmer. Simmer it for 45 to 60 minutes, until the beef is nearly cooked.
6. Add the potatoes and continue simmering the soup until they are tender.
7. Adjust the seasoning to taste with salt and pepper on the day of service.

NOTE: The soup has a better flavor if it is served the second day.

Gazpacho

Yield: 1 gallon (3.75 liters)

Tomato concassé	2½ pounds	1 kilogram
Onions, diced	8 ounces	225 grams
Red pepper, diced	8 ounces	225 grams
Cucumber, seeded, diced	12 ounces	340 grams
Garlic, minced	1 ounce	30 grams
Red wine vinegar	1 ounce	30 milliliters
Lemon juice	1 ounce	30 milliliters
Olive oil	1 ounce	30 grams
Lime juice	1 tablespoon	15 milliliters
Salt	to taste	to taste
Tabasco sauce	to taste	to taste
Tomato juice	1 quart	950 milliliters
Consommé	as needed	as needed

Garnish

Tomato, peeled, seeded, small dice	1 cup	240 milliliters
Red and green peppers, small dice	1 cup	240 milliliters
Cucumber, small dice	1 cup	240 milliliters
Scallions, sliced thin	1 cup	240 milliliters
Croutons, small, fried in olive oil and butter, scented with garlic	as needed	as needed

1. Puree all the ingredients except the tomato juice, consommé, and garnish.
2. Adjust the consistency and flavor with the tomato juice and consommé.
3. Add the garnish; chill thoroughly.
4. Adjust the seasoning with salt and pepper to taste.

Chilled Red Plum Soup

Yield: 1 gallon (3.75 liters)

Red plums, pitted, chopped	5 pounds	2.25 kilograms
Apple juice	as needed	as needed

Sachet d'Épices

Ginger, fresh, large slices	2	2
Cinnamon stick	1	1
Allspice, grains	8 to 10	8 to 10
Black peppercorns	6 to 8	6 to 8
Honey	4 ounces	115 grams
Arrowroot	as needed	as needed
Lemon juice	to taste	to taste

Garnish per serving

Sour cream	2 teaspoons	20 grams
Almonds, slivered, toasted	½ teaspoon	3 grams

1. Simmer the plums in the apple juice (to cover), along with the sachet d'épices and the honey, until the plums are tender. Discard the sachet d'épices.

2. Puree the soup until it is very smooth. Strain, if desired.

3. Return the soup to a simmer.

4. Thicken with diluted arrowroot.

5. Adjust the flavor with the lemon juice.

6. Chill the soup thoroughly.

7. At service, garnish each portion with sour cream and toasted, slivered almonds.

Hudson Valley Apple Soup

Yield: 1 gallon (3.75 liters)

Golden Delicious apples, medium, quartered	16	16
White wine	24 ounces	720 milliliters
Apple juice	8 ounces	240 milliliters
Sugar	8 ounces	225 grams
Cinnamon stick	1	1
Ginger, fresh, large slices	3	3
Beef stock	1 cup	240 milliliters
Sour cream	1 cup	240 milliliters
Heavy cream	1 cup	240 milliliters
Lemon juice, fresh	as needed	as needed

1. Combine the apples, wine, apple juice, sugar, cinnamon, and ginger; bring the mixture to a boil.
2. Simmer the mixture until the apples are tender.
3. Remove the cinnamon and ginger.
4. Puree the mixture through a food mill or sieve.
5. Add the stock, sour cream, and heavy cream to the apple puree. Stir to combine.
6. Chill the soup thoroughly.
7. Adjust the seasoning with a few drops of lemon juice.

Chilled Fruited Yogurt Soup

Yield: 1 gallon (3.75 liters)

Yogurt, plain	1 quart	950 milliliters
Peaches, ripe, sliced, peeled	4	4
Bananas, ripe	4	4
Apple juice	1½ quarts	1.5 liters
Lemon juice	1 lemon	1 lemon
Honey	4 tablespoons	60 milliliters
Orange juice concentrate	4 tablespoons	60 milliliters
Nutmeg, ground	2 teaspoons	10 milliliters
Allspice, ground	5 to 6 grains	5 to 6 grains
Peach brandy	2 ounces	60 milliliters

1. Puree all the ingredients in a food processor until they are very smooth.

2. Chill the puree thoroughly.

3. At service, garnish each portion with a pinch of toasted coconut and one mint leaf.

Chapter 17

Sauces

**S**auces are often considered one of the greatest tests of a chef's skill. Whether they are classics, such as sauce suprême, or contemporary, such as red pepper coulis, good sauces demand the highest technical expertise. The successful pairing of a sauce with a food demonstrates an understanding of the food and an ability to judge and evaluate a dish's flavors, textures, and colors.

In this chapter, the grand sauces, contemporary sauces, and modern sauce-making techniques will be explained and evaluated. Cold sauces are covered in Chapter 27, and dessert sauces are covered in Chapter 33.

Understanding the nuances of pairing a particular sauce with a food is something that develops throughout a chef's career, as lessons are learned about how and why certain combinations have become enduring classics. Uncovering the principles behind these pairings will form the foundation for developing a sensitivity to sauces in particular and the skill and artistry of cooking in general.

CATEGORIES

Because sauces are made in different ways and serve different purposes, depending on when and how they are used, they are grouped in rough categories: grand sauces and contemporary sauces. These categories form a framework for understanding sauces in terms of both technique and application.

USES

Sauces are not just an afterthought —they serve a particular function in a dish's composition. It is in learning to understand why a certain sauce will or will not work with a particular dish that the process of developing culinary judgment begins.

Certain sauce combinations endure because the composition is well-balanced in all areas: taste, texture, and eye appeal. Once these functions are understood, it is possible to expand one's understanding of what a sauce is and why one particular combination of sauce and meat works while the same sauce is not as effective when served with a different meat.

Most sauces serve more than one purpose. A sauce that adds a counterpoint flavor may also introduce textural and visual appeal. Sauces generally serve the following purposes:

Introduce complementary or counterpoint flavors. Some examples of sauces that are classically combined with particular foods will help to illustrate this point.

Sauce suprême is made by reducing a chicken velouté with chicken stock and finishing it with cream. Correctly made, this ivory-colored sauce has a deep chicken flavor and a velvety texture. When served with chicken meat, the sauce's color and flavor complement the delicate chicken and help to intensify the meat's flavor. The addition of cream to the sauce serves to "round out" the flavors.

Sauce Robert, on the other hand, is traditionally paired with pork to introduce a counterpoint flavor. The sharpness of the mustard and cornichons tends to cut the meat's richness and introduces a contrast that is pleasing, but not startling, to the palate. This pungent, flavorful sauce brings out the pork's flavor but might overwhelm a more delicate meat, such as veal.

Add moisture or succulence. This is an important consideration when working with naturally lean foods, such as poultry or fish, or with cooking techniques that tend to have a drying effect, such as grilling or sautéing. For this reason, grilled steaks are commonly served with a compound butter or with a butter-emulsion sauce such as a béarnaise. The same rationale applies to serving beurre blanc with lean white fish that has been shallow-poached.

Add visual interest. One of the ways a sauce can enhance a dish's appearance is to add luster and sheen. Lightly coating a sautéed medallion of lamb with a jus lié gives the lamb a glossy finish that gives the entire plate more eye-appeal. Pooling a red pepper coulis beneath a grilled swordfish steak gives a dish a degree of visual excitement by adding an element of color.

Adjust flavors. A sauce that includes a flavor complementary to a food brings out the flavor of that food. For example, a sauce flavored with tarragon will bring out the mild sweetness of poultry. A pungent sauce made with green peppercorns serves to highlight beef's flavors, deepening and enriching the overall taste.

Add texture. Many sauces receive a final garnish that adds texture. For example, chicken chasseur is enhanced by a sauce finished with tomatoes and mushrooms. Conversely, a smooth sauce may be used to contrast with a meat that has a distinct texture.

PROPER SELECTION

The variety of flavors and textures available allows the chef to choose a sauce that makes the best possible sense for the dish being prepared. Here are some of the points to consider when selecting the appropriate sauce.

The sauce should be suitable for the style of service. In a banquet setting, or for any situation where large quantities of food must be served rapidly and at their flavor peak, it is usually best to rely on the traditional grand sauces or a contemporary sauce that shares some of the same characteristics. One of a grand sauce's fundamental benefits is that it may be prepared in advance and held in large quantities at the correct temperature. In an à la carte kitchen, this advantage is less important.

The sauce should be suitable for the main ingredient's cooking technique. A cooking technique that produces flavorful drippings *(fond)*, such as roasting or sautéing, should logically be paired with a sauce that makes use of those drippings.

Beurre blancs are suitable for foods that have been shallow-poached, because the cooking liquid *(cuisson)* can become a part of the sauce instead of being discarded.

The sauce's flavor should be appropriate for the flavor of the food with which it is paired. Make sure the flavor of the sauce does not overpower the main ingredient flavor and vice versa. Although a delicate cream sauce complements the flavor of Dover sole, it would be overwhelmed by the flavor of grilled tuna steak. By the same token, a sauce flavored by rosemary would completely overpower a delicate fish but nicely complements lamb.

THE GRAND SAUCES

The grand sauces—demi-glace, velouté, béchamel, tomato, and hollandaise—were once referred to as the mother sauces, to indicate that from these basic sauces many others were created (see Figure 17-1). Although they may not be relied upon as heavily as in years past, the grand sauces are still important in a contemporary kitchen.

There is some dispute as to how many grand sauces exist. Some argue that because hollandaise cannot be made in advance in a large quantity and stored, and cannot be used to prepare a variety of derivative sauces, it does not qualify. It is included here, however, because the basic technique for preparing hollandaise or a béarnaise does yield a number of variations.

The first sauce to be covered is seldom served by itself as a sauce; however, it is an essential component of demi-glace.

Sauce Espagnole (Brown Sauce)

The classic method of preparing a brown sauce, as written by Carême, is a lengthy and involved process that calls for Bayonne ham, veal, and partridges. The contem-

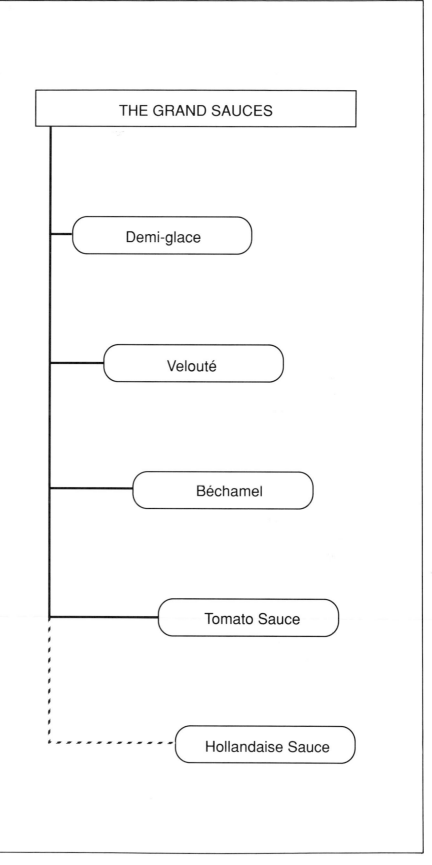

17-1

The family tree of grand sauces.

porary version has been greatly simplified and the cooking time reduced.

Mise en Place

1. Brown veal stock or estouffade should be available.
2. Cut the mirepoix into large dice.
3. Tomato puree should be available.
4. Prepare the brown roux, or have available.

Method

1. Sweat the mirepoix until juices are released and onions are translucent. Add the tomato puree and sauté until caramelized.
2. Add brown roux to the mirepoix and gradually incorporate the veal stock or estouffade. (Remember that the roux should be hotter than the stock.) Work out all lumps.
3. Simmer the sauce for approximately 2½ to 3 hours, skimming the surface throughout the cooking time.
4. Strain the sauce, and use at this point or cool for later use. Refer to proper cooling techniques in Chapter 3, "Sanitation and Safety."

Demi-Glace

It is important to learn the procedure for making a *demi-glace*, a highly flavored, glossy sauce, even though in contemporary kitchens a jus de veau lié is often used in its place. The name "demi-glace" translates literally as "half-glaze."

There are a number of derivatives based on demi-glace that have an important place in the chef's repertoire (see Fig. 17-2). Figure 17-3 shows a demi-glace. Note the color, body, and consistency of the sauce in this figure.

Sauce Espagnole (Brown Sauce)

Yield: 2 quarts (2 liters)

Mirepoix	8 ounces	240 milliliters
Vegetable oil, hot	2 ounces	60 milliliters
Tomato paste	2 ounces	60 milliliters
Brown stock, hot	5 pints	2.5 liters
Pale roux	6 ounces	170 grams
Standard sachet d'épices	1	1

1. Brown the onions from the mirepoix in the hot oil; add the remainder of the mirepoix and continue to brown.
2. Add the tomato paste; pincé.
3. Add the brown stock; bring up to a simmer.
4. Whip the roux into the stock. Return to a simmer and add the sachet d'épices.
5. Simmer for approximately 1 hour; skim the surface as necessary.
6. Strain through a cheesecloth.

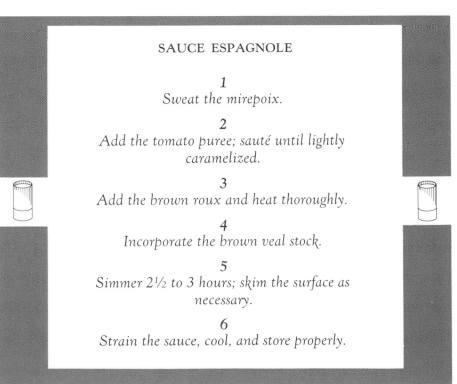

SAUCE ESPAGNOLE

1
Sweat the mirepoix.

2
Add the tomato puree; sauté until lightly caramelized.

3
Add the brown roux and heat thoroughly.

4
Incorporate the brown veal stock.

5
Simmer 2½ to 3 hours; skim the surface as necessary.

6
Strain the sauce, cool, and store properly.

Mise en Place

1. Have brown veal stock *(fond de veau brun)* or estouffade available.

2. Have sauce espagnole available.

Method

1. Combine equal parts of the brown veal stock and sauce espagnole.

2. Bring to a boil and reduce the heat slightly to maintain a simmer.

3. Pull the pot slightly off the center of the heat source to encourage any impurities and fat to collect on one side of the pot.

4. Simmer until the sauce is reduced to half its original volume. Transfer the sauce to successively smaller pots as the volume reduces, to prevent a strong caramel flavor in the finished sauce.

5. Skim as necessary throughout preparation.

6. Strain, using either the wringing or milking techniques (see Figs. 17-4 and 17-5), and use immediately or cool and store.

Refer to the short form for preparing demi-glace for easy reference.

17-3
An example of demi-glace.

Evaluating Quality

A demi-glace of excellent quality will have several characteristics. Demi-glace should have a full, rich flavor. Because the sauce is based on brown veal stock, the flavor should be that of roasted veal. The aromatics, mirepoix, and tomatoes used in the base preparations should not overpower the main flavor.

Demi-glace should have a deep brown color. When properly simmered, skimmed, and reduced, demi-glace is translucent and highly glossy. Because of the reduction and also the use of roux in the sauce espagnol, demi-glace has a noticeable body, although it should never feel gluey or overly tacky in the mouth. It is at the correct consistency when it will evenly coat the back of a spoon (a condition known as *nappé*). The initial roasting of bones, trimmings, and mirepoix will give the finished sauce a pleasant roasted or caramel aroma, readily discernible when the sauce is heated.

Holding

To prevent a skin from forming on demi-glace, a layer of clarified butter may be used to protect the sauce from contact with air.

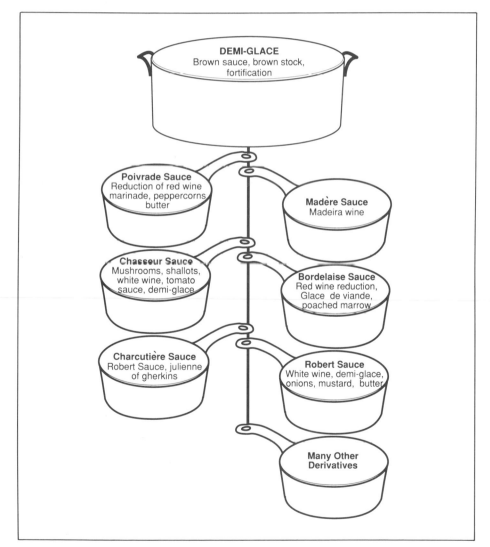

17-2
Demi-glace and its derivatives.

Demi-glace

Yield: 1 quart (1 liter)

Brown stock	1 quart	1 liter
Sauce Espagnole	1 quart	1 liter

1. Reduce the brown stock by one-third.

2. Add the sauce espagnole; continue to reduce to 1 quart. Skim the surface as necessary.

3. Strain the sauce.

NOTE: Demi-glace may be finished with 2 to 3 ounces of meat glaze (glace de viande), if available.

(1) The cheesecloth should be rinsed first in hot and then cool water to remove any stray fibers. Drape it over a bowl, making sure that the cheesecloth extends completely beyond the rim. Pour the sauce into the lined bowl.

VARIATION

Marchand de Vin Sauce: Reduce 8 ounces (240 milliliters) of dry red wine and 1 ounce (30 grams) chopped shallots until syrupy. Strain this reduction and add it to the demi-glace.

(2) Two people, one working on either side of the bowl, should now gather up the cheesecloth edges, each twisting in an opposite direction from the other, expelling the sauce into the bowl below.

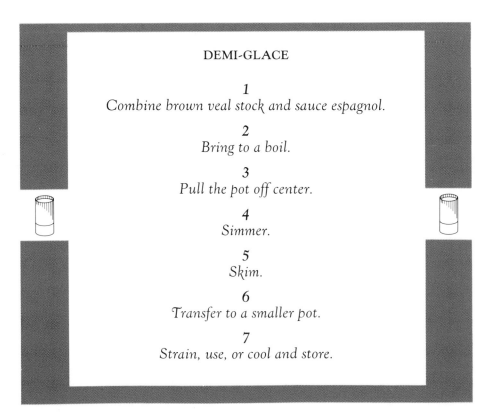

DEMI-GLACE

1
Combine brown veal stock and sauce espagnol.

2
Bring to a boil.

3
Pull the pot off center.

4
Simmer.

5
Skim.

6
Transfer to a smaller pot.

7
Strain, use, or cool and store.

(3) Continue until all of the sauce has been wrung from the cheesecloth. The sauce is now fully strained and ready to be used or cooled for later use.

17-5 THE MILKING METHOD FOR STRAINING SAUCES

(1) Drape the properly rinsed and wrung-out cheesecloth over a pot or bowl. Pour the sauce into the lined pot. Two people should hold on to the corners of the cloth, as shown. Wrapping the ends around the finger should help to keep it firmly grasped.

(2) Alternately lift one corner at a time. The other corners should be held steady. Notice that the upper left corner has been gently lifted.

(3) The upper right-hand corner has been lifted. Continue, alternating corners, until all of the sauce has strained through the cheesecloth into the container.

Preparing Derivatives

There are a number of recipes for sauces derived from demi-glace included in this chapter. All the flavoring and garnishing ingredients must be properly prepared in each of these recipes. Important steps to remember:

1. Sweat the onions, shallots, and garlic to prevent them from giving the sauce a bitter, sulfurous taste.

2. Cook high-moisture ingredients, such as mushrooms and tomatoes, to reduce moisture and intensify flavors.

3. Pre-reduce heavy cream to shorten cooking time.

4. To *monté au beurre* (often the last step in finishing a demi-glace sauce), gently swirl whole butter into the sauce (see Fig. 17-6). The butter will very lightly emulsify the sauce, giving it a smooth, rich flavor.

Velouté

Velouté is prepared by thickening a white stock with an appropriate amount of pale roux, then simmering it until the roux is completely "cooked out," leaving no starchy taste. Veloutés may be based on veal, chicken, or fish stock. A common application for veloutés in contemporary kitchens is in cream soup preparation. There are a number of derivatives prepared from velouté (see Fig. 17-7). Figure 17-8 shows an example of this sauce. Note the color, body, and consistency of the sauce in this figure.

Mise en Place

1. Stock of an appropriate type: fish, chicken, veal.

2. Pale roux. It is acceptable to use rendered and clarified fresh

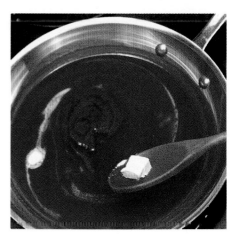

17-6
Monté au beurre.

chicken fat for the roux used to thicken chicken velouté.

For medium consistency, the proper ratio is 12 to 16 ounces of roux to each gallon of stock. For a light velouté used to prepare soup, the ratio is 10 to 12 ounces per gallon; for a heavy velouté to be used as a binder, the ratio is 18 to 20 ounces per gallon.

3. Have mushroom trimmings available, if desired. The proper ratio is 5 ounces per gallon of stock.

4. Have optional aromatics (standard sachet d'épices or flavored as desired) available.

Method

1. Bring the stock to a simmer. Gradually whip in the roux. Either the stock should be hotter than the roux, or the roux should be hotter than the stock, to help prevent lumps from forming.

2. Bring to a full boil, then reduce the heat to establish a simmer.

3. Pull the pot slightly off the center of the heat source to encourage any impurities and fat to collect on the side of the pot.

4. Skim the surface as necessary throughout the cooking time.

5. Stir frequently to prevent scorching.

6. Simmer for at least 30 minutes (some chefs prefer to simmer up to 1 hour). Fig. 17-9 shows velouté at the proper consistency for use as a sauce. It is at the correct thickness when it will evenly coat the back of a spoon, a condition known as "nappé."

7. Strain the sauce through a chinois lined with cheesecloth.

8. Finish and garnish according to desired use, or cool and store properly.

For a quick summary of velouté preparation, refer to the abbreviated method.

Evaluating Quality

When properly prepared, velouté should meet several criteria. The flavor of a velouté should reflect the stock used in its preparation: white veal, which will be nearly neutral in flavor; chicken; or fish. There should be no flour taste if the sauce has been allowed to simmer for a sufficient time. Veloutés should be

(1) The sauce.

(2) Strain the sauce through a china cap to remove any large lumps, herbs, or other items. A ladle should be used to push the sauce through the cap.

Velouté

Yield: 1 quart (1 liter)

White stock (veal, chicken, or fish)	1 quart	1 liter
Pale roux	4 ounces	115 grams

1. Bring the stock to a boil.

2. Whip the roux into the stock; work out all the lumps.

3. Simmer for 30 to 40 minutes, skimming the surface as necessary.

4. Strain the sauce and adjust the seasoning with salt and pepper to taste.

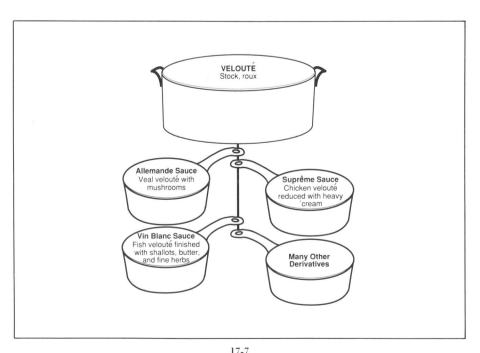

17-7

Velouté and its derivatives.

17-9

Velouté at the proper consistency.

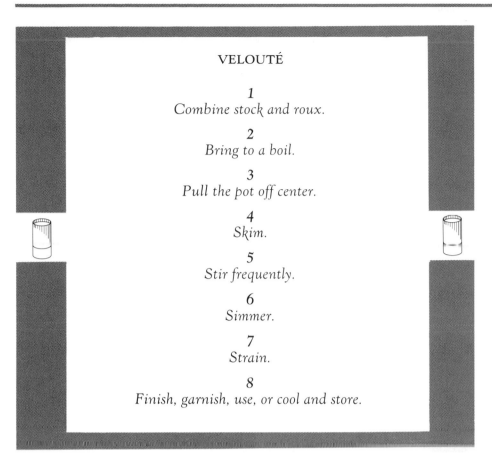

VELOUTÉ

1
Combine stock and roux.

2
Bring to a boil.

3
Pull the pot off center.

4
Skim.

5
Stir frequently.

6
Simmer.

7
Strain.

8
Finish, garnish, use, or cool and store.

Béchamel

Béchamel is a white sauce made by thickening milk with a white roux and simmering it with aromatics. Originally, béchamel called for an amount of lean veal; however, modern practice rarely includes it. Although its importance as a grand sauce has diminished somewhat, béchamel and its derivatives are still important in the contemporary kitchen (see Fig. 17-10). Figure 17-11 provides an example of a béchamel. Note the color, body, and consistency.

Mise en Place

1. Milk.

2. White roux, prepared with butter or oil as the fat.

3. Aromatics: sweated, minced onion, a sprig of fresh thyme, a bay leaf, nutmeg to taste; or an onion

pale in color, almost ivory. There should be no hint of gray.

Although a velouté will never be transparent, it should be translucent. Through proper cooking and skimming, any impurities in either the stock or the roux will be removed. The finished sauce should be lustrous, with a definite sheen. Velouté should be perfectly smooth, with absolutely no graininess. Proper skimming and straining will assure a correct texture. The sauce should have a noticeable body, thick enough to coat the back of a spoon (nappé), yet still quite liquid. Although a heavy velouté does have applications in the kitchen, such a texture is not appropriate for a velouté to be used as a sauce. The aroma of a velouté should be that of the base stock. The roux will impart a slight hint of nuttiness, but this should in no way overpower the stock's aroma.

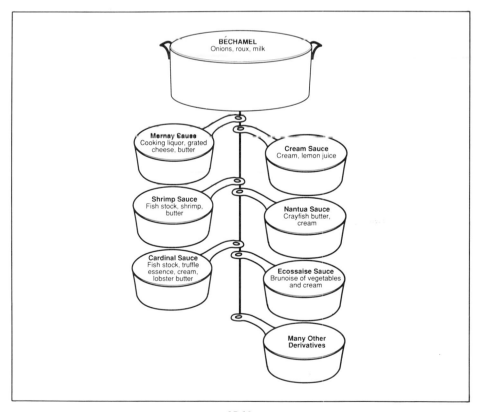

17-10

Béchamel and its derivatives.

Mise en Place

1. Unsalted butter, melted or clarified and warm.

2. Egg yolks.

3. Reduction: vinegar, salt, and crushed peppercorns should be combined and reduced to sec.

4. Water: cold, required to cool the reduction; hot and cold water to adjust the sauce's consistency or temperature, if necessary.

5. Fresh lemon juice.

Method

1. Make the reduction and add a small amount of water to cool it. Transfer the reduction (strained, if desired) to a stainless-steel bowl.

2. Add egg yolks to the reduction and blend with a whip.

3. Place the bowl over a pot of simmering water (a bain-marie).

4. Continue to whip the egg yolks over barely simmering water until they are thickened and frothy. They should be warm, not hot enough to scramble.

5. Have the butter warm (the same temperature as the egg yolks) and add it gradually in a thin stream, whipping constantly. Drape a clean side towel between the bottom of the bain-marie and the bowl to steady it as the butter is added. Continue adding butter and whipping until the sauce is thickened and all the butter is incorporated. Figure 17-15 shows the steps of preparation.

6. Strain the sauce at this point, if necessary, through rinsed and wrung-out cheesecloth. Use the wringing technique demonstrated in the method for demi-glace in this chapter. Step 5 of Figure 17-15 shows hollandaise at the correct consistency; Figure 17-16 is a broken hollandaise, which has a curdled, oily appearance.

17-15 PREPARATION STEPS FOR HOLLANDAISE

(1) Egg yolk in a bowl with refreshed reduction.

(2) Hold the bowl over simmering water; whip constantly as the egg yolks cook.

(3) A clean side towel is used to steady the bowl while the butter is incorporated.

(4) Butter is added in a thin stream while the chef is whipping constantly.

7. Adjust the seasoning of the sauce by adding lemon juice in small increments. Adjust the consistency, if necessary, by adding a small amount of warm water.

Refer to the abbreviated method for a quick summary of preparing hollandaise.

Holding

Hollandaise should not be held directly in a steam table or other area where it could become hot enough to break. Hold it warm over a warm

(5) Hollandaise at the proper consistency. Note the ribbons left in the sauce by the whip.

17-16
A broken hollandaise.

(not boiling) water bath or in a vacuum bottle.

Evaluating Quality

The following evaluations on flavor, color, clarity, texture, aroma, and consistency are for a basic hollandaise, with indications given when the variations will differ in quality.

When the components are combined in the proper ratio, the sauce's flavor will be predominantly that of butter. The egg yolks contribute a great deal of flavor as well. The reduction ingredients (vinegar and peppercorns, for instance) give the sauce a balanced taste, as do the lemon juice and any additional seasonings. Hollandaise should be a pale lemon color. Variations may have slightly different colors. Sauce choron, for instance, contains tomato puree, which will give the finished sauce a pale-orange color.

Hollandaise and its variations are opaque, but the sauce should have a luster and should not appear oily. The basic sauce and its variations should have a buttery-smooth texture. A grainy texture indicates that the egg yolks have overcooked and begun to scramble.

The sauce should have the aroma of good butter. For this reason, some chefs like to use melted rather than clarified butter so they can incorporate a small amount of the milk solids. Hollandaise should have a light consistency, in no way resembling the thicker consistency of mayonnaise. When correctly prepared, hollandaise is almost frothy. Figure 17-17 shows hollandaise with asparagus, a classic combination.

Hollandaise Sauce

Yield: 1½ pints (720 milliliters)

Cider vinegar	1 ounce	30 milliliters
Mignonette peppercorns	¼ teaspoon	½ gram
Water	2 ounces	60 milliliters
Egg yolks	4 to 6	4 to 6
Clarified butter, warm	1 pint	480 milliliters
Lemon juice	1 tablespoon	15 milliliters

1. Combine the vinegar and peppercorns; reduce until sec.

2. Add water to the reduction. (The reduction may be strained at this point, if desired.)

3. Add the reduction to the egg yolks. Whip over simmering water until the yolks ribbon.

4. Gradually add the warm clarified butter, whipping constantly.

5. Add the lemon juice, and adjust the seasoning to taste with salt and pepper.

6. Strain through a cheesecloth, if desired.

VARIATIONS

Sauce Mousseline: Fold 1 part whipped cream into 4 parts hollandaise.

Royal Glacage: Fold together 1 part whipped cream, 1 part velouté, and 1 part hollandaise. Coat the item and glaze under a salamander.

Sauce Bigarade: Finish the hollandaise with the zest and juice from a blood orange.

Special Problem-solving Techniques

Curdled appearance. If the sauce develops a curdled appearance, it may mean that the butter is being added too rapidly for the egg yolks to absorb it. The sauce should be whipped until it appears smooth before more butter is added.

Scrambling of egg yolks. If the sauce becomes too hot, the egg yolks will begin to scramble. To correct the problem, the sauce should be removed from the heat and allowed to cool. It should be

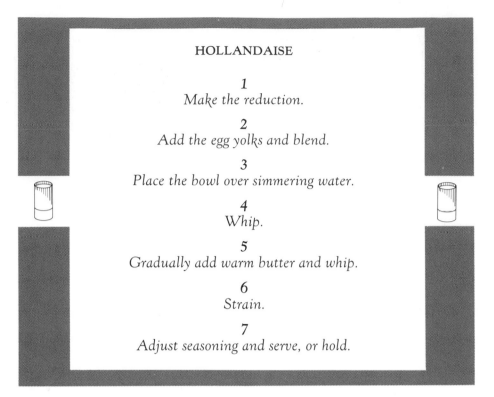

HOLLANDAISE

1
Make the reduction.

2
Add the egg yolks and blend.

3
Place the bowl over simmering water.

4
Whip.

5
Gradually add warm butter and whip.

6
Strain.

7
Adjust seasoning and serve, or hold.

17-17
Hollandaise used to "nappé" asparagus.

whipped constantly, or a small amount of cold water should be added and the sauce whipped until it is smooth. If this does not correct the problem, it may be necessary to incorporate the broken sauce into fresh egg yolks, after which it must be strained.

CONTEMPORARY SAUCES

The broad category of contemporary sauces includes jus lié, beurre blanc, coulis, compound butters, and a variety of miscellaneous sauces, such as relishes, salsas, and compotes. The primary factors distinguishing contemporary sauces from the grand sauces are the following:

• They usually take less time to prepare and are more likely to be specifically tailored to a given food or technique.
• Some sauces—jus lié, for instance—are updated versions of grand sauces.
• Contemporary sauces tend to be lighter in color and body than the grand sauces. They are more likely to rely on emulsions, reductions, and modified starches for thickening, instead of on roux.

Jus Lié

Jus lié, frequently referred to simply as "jus," is a thickened sauce made from stock (usually brown veal stock, although other stocks may be used). It is used in the preparation of many other sauces. Although similar to a demi-glace in appearance and use, jus lié requires less cooking time because it contains a modified starch (arrowroot, for example) as a thickener. It also has a greater degree of clarity, translucence, and sheen.

Jus lié is often used to deglaze pans to create sauces that are specifically tailored to sautés or roasts. Another way in which jus lié can be varied is to introduce the flavor of a special spice or herb. For example, sprigs of rosemary may be added to the jus lié as it develops. Figure 17-18 shows an example of jus lié. Note the color, body, and consistency.

Mise en Place

1. Bones and trimmings from appropriate meats or poultry.

2. Mirepoix, cut into a medium or small dice.

3. Tomato puree for veal and game jus lié.

4. Stock of appropriate flavor: brown veal stock for *jus de veau*; chicken for *jus de volaille* or *jus de canard*, lamb or veal for *jus d'agneau*, and so on.

5. Arrowroot or cornstarch diluted in equal amounts of cold stock, wine, or water.

6. Optional components: A variety of table wines or fortified wines may be used to flavor or finish the jus lié. Standard sachet d'épices or bouquet garni and additional herbs and spices may be included, if desired.

Method

1. Brown the trimmings, mirepoix, and tomato product.

2. Deglaze the pan with the stock or wine.

3. Add the remaining stock and sachet d'épices or bouquet garni; bring to a boil.

4. Reduce the heat to a simmer and cook approximately 2 hours or more; simmer until a good flavor has developed.

5. Skim the surface as needed throughout preparation.

6. Add the diluted arrowroot or cornstarch; use a whip to combine thoroughly, and simmer for 2 to 3 minutes.

7. Strain the sauce through a fine chinois. Press the solids well to extract all flavor.

8. Finish and/or garnish for use at this point or cool and store it.

For a quick summary of the preparation of jus lié, refer to the abbreviated method.

17-18
An example of jus lié.

Jus de Veau Lié

Yield: 2 quarts (2 liters)

Brown veal stock	2½ quarts	2.5 liters
Veal bones and trim, browned	2 pounds	910 grams
Mirepoix, browned	8 ounces	225 grams
Standard sachet d'épices	1	1
Arrowroot or cornstarch, diluted in cold water or dry wine	½ ounce or as needed	14 grams

1. Combine all the ingredients except the arrowroot and bring to a simmer.

2. Simmer for a minimum of approximately 2½ to 3 hours, skimming the surface as necessary, to extract full body and flavor from the bones and trim.

3. Strain the sauce, pressing well. Return the strained sauce to the heat and bring to a full boil. Add enough diluted arrowroot or cornstarch to thicken the sauce to coat the back of a wooden spoon.

VARIATIONS

Jus de Volaille Lié: Replace the brown veal stock with a brown chicken stock and replace the veal bones and trim with an equal weight of chicken bones and trim.

Jus de Canard Lié: Replace the brown veal stock with a brown duck stock, and replace the veal bones and trim with an equal weight of duck bones and trim.

Jus d'Agneau Lié: Replace the brown veal stock with a brown lamb stock, and replace the veal bones and trim with an equal weight of lamb bones and trim.

Jus de Gibier Lié: Replace the brown veal stock with a brown venison stock, and replace the veal bones and trim with an equal weight of venison bones and trim.

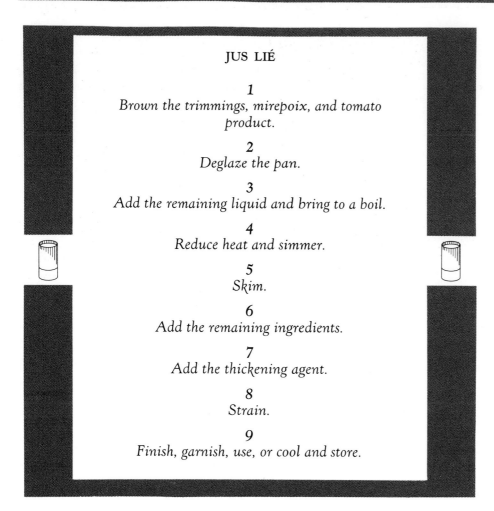

JUS LIÉ

1
Brown the trimmings, mirepoix, and tomato product.

2
Deglaze the pan.

3
Add the remaining liquid and bring to a boil.

4
Reduce heat and simmer.

5
Skim.

6
Add the remaining ingredients.

7
Add the thickening agent.

8
Strain.

9
Finish, garnish, use, or cool and store.

Evaluating Quality

The characteristics important to evaluating quality include flavor, color, body, and texture. Jus lié should have a rich, full flavor of the major ingredient. Jus de veau should taste like roasted veal (from the browning of the meat trimmings and bones); jus de volaille should taste like chicken; jus de poisson should taste like fish; and so on. There should be no evidence of scorching. Aromatic and other flavoring ingredients should contribute to the aroma flavor, giving it a good balance.

The color of a jus lié will vary, depending on the major flavoring ingredient. Colors range from amber or golden (jus de volaille) to a rich brown (jus de veau). Jus liés should not be as dark as a demi-glace. A jus lié should have a definite body, similar to that of a demi-glace, thick enough to coat the back of a wooden spoon. The texture should be smooth and light. A gluey or tacky texture is an indication that the sauce has been allowed to reduce too much or that too much starch has been used.

Beurre Blanc

Beurre blanc is a sauce in which butter forms an emulsion with a reduction. Traditionally, the reduction consists of the cooking liquid *(cuisson)* used to prepare shallow-poached dishes, but it is also possible to prepare a reduction separately. Although beurre blanc is a fragile sauce, adding a small amount of heavy cream can help to stabilize it so that it may be held during a service period. The procedure for holding beurre blanc is the same as that for hollandaise.

Mise en Place

1. Reduction: a combination of an acid (such as vinegar), wine or citrus juice, shallots, and peppercorns may be used, or the poaching liquid, which includes an acid. Additional flavoring ingredients may be included in the reduction; for instance, chopped fresh herbs, tomatoes, saffron, green peppercorns, or other ingredients. See the specific recipes.

2. Unsalted butter, cut into small pieces and kept cold.

3. Optional components include cream, which may be pre-reduced. Use discretion when including cream in a beurre blanc, because it will mask the butter flavor. Garnish is another optional component. Examples are purees of vegetables or herbs, citrus zest, grated ginger root, and a chiffonade of fresh herbs. Mise en place is shown in Figure 17-19. Note that the butter is cut into small pieces.

Method

1. The reduction should be hot enough so that steam rises from the surface but not so hot that there is any boiling action. If desired, add reduced heavy cream at this point to stabilize the sauce.

2. Gradually incorporate the butter. Keep the pan in motion, swirling it over low heat and simultaneously whipping the butter into the sauce. An emulsion will form and will give the sauce the proper consistency (see Fig. 17-20).

3. Continue to incorporate the butter until the sauce is appropriately thickened and light in color.

17-19
Mise en place for beurre blanc.

17-20
Whipping butter into beurre blanc.

4. Add any additional or optional ingredients. The sauce is now ready for service. It may be held in a warm place for short periods of time or in a vacuum bottle, as for hollandaise.

Refer to the abbreviated method for a quick summary of the preparation of beurre blanc.

Evaluating Quality

As with the other sauces, quality is evaluated on the basis of several characteristics. The flavor of beurre blanc is of whole butter, with piquant accents from the reduction. The finishing and/or garnishing ingredients will also influence the flavor. If cream is included, it should not have a dominant flavor. The color should be creamy, although garnishes of herbs, purees, and other ingredients may change the color. The sauce should have a distinct sheen.

The body should be light. If the sauce is too thin, it probably does not contain enough butter. Conversely, a beurre blanc that is too thick includes too much butter or cream. The texture should be frothy, and the sauce should not leave an oily or greasy feeling in the mouth.

Special Problem-solving Techniques

The sauce appears to be breaking. This is an indication that the sauce has become too hot. Remove the pot from the heat immediately and place it on a cool surface, such as a stainless-steel worktable. Continue to whip the cool butter in, keeping both the pan and the sauce in motion. When the sauce loses its oily appearance and dulls slightly, place the pan over low heat and continue to work in the butter.

Lemon Beurre Blanc

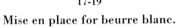

Yield: 1 quart (1 liter)

Shallots, minced	4 ounces	115 grams
White wine	8 ounces	225 milliliters
Lemon juice	3 ounces	90 milliliters
Cider vinegar	3 ounces	90 milliliters
Heavy cream	1 pint	480 milliliters
Unsalted butter, softened	1½ pounds	680 grams

1. Combine the shallots, wine, lemon juice, and vinegar. Reduce until sec.

2. Add the heavy cream and reduce slightly.

3. Gradually whisk in the butter.

4. Adjust the seasoning to taste with salt and pepper.

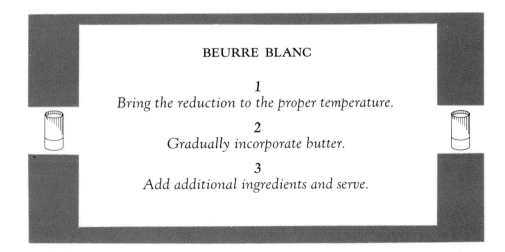

BEURRE BLANC

1
Bring the reduction to the proper temperature.

2
Gradually incorporate butter.

3
Add additional ingredients and serve.

The sauce becomes too thick. This means that the sauce may not be warm enough, generally an indication that the butter is being added too quickly. Do not add additional butter until the sauce has warmed and become less thick.

Compound Butters

These flavored butters may be considered as a kind of sauce used to finish grilled or broiled meats, fish, poultry, game, pastas, or even other sauces. Boiled or steamed vegetables may be tossed in compound butter just before service. Compound butters may be flavored with a wide variety of ingredients, including herbs, nuts, citrus zest, garlic, shallots, ginger, and vegetables.

Mise en Place

1. Whole unsalted butter, softened to room temperature.
2. Appropriate flavoring ingredients, prepared according to type (chop herbs, render bacon, puree and reduce tomatoes, and so on—refer to specific recipes).

Method

1. Prepare the flavoring agents by type or according to individual recipes.
2. Incorporate the flavoring agents into the softened butter by hand, or with a mixer or food processor.
3. Roll the butter into a cylinder in parchment paper (as shown in Fig. 17-21) or pipe it into individual rosettes (as shown in Fig. 17-22).
4. Thoroughly chill the butter before service. Slice chilled cylinders into medallions at the time of service (see step 3 of Fig. 17-21).
5. Serve or freeze for use at a later time. Be sure that the butter

17-21 ROLLING BUTTER INTO A CYLINDER

(1)

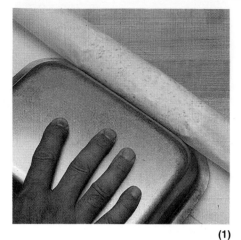
(2)

(3)

(1) Using the edge of a pan to tighten compound butter into an even cylinder.

(2) Twisting ends of the parchment paper.

(3) Slicing the chilled compound butter for service.

Maître d'Hôtel Butter

Yield: 14 ounces (420 milliliters)

Butter, softened	12 ounces	340 grams
Parsley, finely chopped	½ bunch	½ bunch
Fresh lemon juice	2½ tablespoons	37 milliliters
Salt	to taste	to taste
Pepper	to taste	to taste

1. Combine all the ingredients.
2. Pipe into rosettes, using a pastry bag, or roll in parchment paper.
3. Refrigerate until needed.

17-22 PIPING COMPOUND BUTTER

(1) Filling a pastry bag properly.

(2) Piping butter rosettes.

Broccoli Coulis

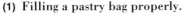

Yield: 2 quarts (2 liters)

Broccoli, sliced	2 bunches	2 bunches
Stock, hot	1 quart	1 liter
Onion, minced	3 ounces	85 grams
Shallot, minced	1	1
Heavy cream, reduced	4 ounces	115 milliliters
Whole butter	2 ounces	60 grams

1. Steam or boil the broccoli until it is very tender.

2. Puree the broccoli in a food mill, blender, or processor until smooth. Add a small amount of the stock, if necessary.

3. Sauté the onion and shallot in oil until they are tender and translucent. Do not brown. Add the pureed broccoli and the remaining stock, and simmer until the flavor and consistency are properly developed.

4. Add the reduced heavy cream and butter, and adjust the seasoning to taste with salt and pepper.

VARIATIONS

Parsley Sauce: Blanch 4 bunches of parsley in boiling water, refresh in cold water, then puree. Proceed with the recipe.

Sorrel Sauce: Blanch 3 bunches of sorrel in boiling water, refresh in cold water, then puree. Proceed with the recipe.

Watercress Sauce: Blanch 4 bunches of watercress in boiling water, refresh in cold water, then puree. Proceed with the recipe.

is wrapped well, labeled, and dated.

Coulis

Before the codification of sauces into the grand sauces and their derivatives, any sauce would most likely have gone by the name of coulis. Certain soups were also known as coulis, especially those based on game and game birds.

Today, coulis generally indicates a sauce that is essentially a puree of a vegetable, such as red peppers, broccoli, or tomatoes. A coulis may be finished with cream or butter. Refer to specific recipes for ingredients and method. Figure 17-23 shows a broccoli coulis. Note the color, body, and consistency.

Miscellaneous Sauces

Several other preparations can be considered sauces because they add moisture, flavor and textural interest, and color to the foods with which they are paired. These include relishes, salsas, compotes, and even beds of vegetables and grains. Various techniques are used to prepare the following miscellaneous sauces.

Cold vinaigrettes and mayonnaise may be used as a sauce for hot sautéed items or as a marinade.

17-23
An example of a coulis.

These sauces are covered in Chapter 27, "Hors d'Oeuvre, Appetizers, and Salads."

Another cold sauce, salsa, may be used as a sauce for hot foods. Because the vegetables in salsa generally are not cooked, it is considered a "raw" sauce. Relishes and compotes based on fruits and/or vegetables may be served hot or cold. An example is a confit of red onion, consisting of onions stewed in butter and finished with a small amount of honey and vinegar. Another example is a dried-fruit compote, composed of dried fruits stewed in wine, stock, or a combination of the two.

Rice and other grains, such as bulgur and barley, are prepared by the pilaf method and used as a bed for other foods. Rice may also be prepared by the risotto method and used in place of a traditional sauce. Beans and other dried legumes, such as lentils, may be stewed and served in lieu of a standard sauce.

These foods are covered in Chapter 24, "Cooking Grains and Legumes."

SUMMARY

Understanding the uses for both grand sauces and contemporary sauces and mastering the preparation techniques are fundamental aspects of a chef's training. Although the pairing of certain foods with certain sauces calls for good judgment, the technical skills needed in sauce making are of basic importance. No matter how effectively or cleverly sauces and foods are joined, a scorched or broken sauce is unacceptable. Understanding ingredients is also necessary. Unless a sauce contains ingredients of the highest quality, it will not have the best possible flavor.

Piquant Sauce

Yield: approximately 1 quart (1 liter)

Chablis	12 ounces	360 milliliters
Cider vinegar	6 ounces	180 milliliters
Shallots, minced	1½ ounces	45 grams
Demi-glace or jus lié	1 quart	1 liter
Cornichons	2 ounces	60 grams
Capers	1 tablespoon	8 grams
Tarragon, fresh, chopped	1 teaspoon	5 grams
Chervil, fresh, chopped	1 teaspoon	5 grams
Parsley, fresh, chopped	1 teaspoon	5 grams
Unsalted butter, in small pieces	2 ounces	60 grams

1. Reduce the chablis, vinegar, and shallots by three-quarters.
2. Add the demi-glace or jus lié and reduce to nappé.
3. Add the remaining ingredients, adjust the seasoning to taste with salt and pepper, and monté au beurre.

Robert Sauce

Yield: 1 pint (480 milliliters)

Onion, diced fine	2 ounces	60 grams
Butter, clarified	1 ounce	30 milliliters
Dry white wine	8 ounces	240 milliliters
Demi-glace or jus de veau	1 pint	480 milliliters
Dry mustard (dissolved in warm water)	1 teaspoon	2 grams
Unsalted butter	1 ounce	30 grams

1. Sauté the onions in the butter until they are lightly caramelized.
2. Add the wine and reduce to 2 ounces.
3. Add the demi-glace or jus de veau; reduce to nappé and remove from heat.
4. Add the dissolved mustard; strain the sauce. Adjust the seasoning to taste with salt and pepper.
5. Monté au beurre.

NOTE: For Sauce Charcutière, add 2 to 3 cornichons cut in a short julienne.

Mushroom Sauce

Yield: 1 quart (1 liter)

Shallots, minced	2 ounces	60 grams
Butter, clarified	1 ounce	30 milliliters
Mushroom trimmings	8 ounces	225 grams
Thyme, fresh	2 sprigs	2 sprigs
Bay leaf, crumbled	1	1
Mignonette of pepper	8	8
Burgundy	4 ounces	120 milliliters
Demi-glace or jus de veau	1 quart	1 liter
Mushrooms, thickly sliced and sautéed in clarified butter	12 ounces	340 grams

1. Sauté the shallots in the clarified butter until they are translucent.
2. Add the mushroom trimmings and sauté until moisture is released.
3. Add the thyme, bay leaf, pepper, and burgundy; reduce by half.
4. Add the demi-glace; reduce to nappé.
5. Degrease the sauce and strain.
6. Add the sautéed mushrooms; adjust the seasoning with salt and pepper to taste.

Marsala Sauce

Yield: 1 quart (1 liter)

Demi-glace	1 quart	1 liter
Shallots, minced	3 tablespoons	40 grams
Mignonette of peppercorns	12	12
Marsala	2 to 3 ounces	60 to 90 milliliters

1. Combine the demi-glace, shallots, and peppercorns.
2. Simmer the mixture until it is reduced to nappé.
3. Strain the sauce.
4. Add the marsala and return to a simmer. Adjust the seasoning to taste with salt and pepper.

Fines Herbes Sauce

Yield: 1 quart (1 liter)

Dry white wine	10 ounces	300 milliliters
Parsley stems	6	6
Chervil, dried	1½ tablespoons	5 grams
Tarragon, dried	1½ tablespoons	5 grams
Shallots, minced	1 ounce	30 grams
Demi-glace	1 quart	1 liter
Lemon juice, fresh	1 teaspoon	5 milliliters
Fine herbs, chopped (per portion)	1 teaspoon	750 milligrams
Butter (per portion)	¼ ounce	7 grams

1. Reduce the wine, parsley stems, chervil, tarragon, and shallots by half.

2. Add the demi-glace; reduce to nappé.

3. Add the lemon juice and strain the sauce.

4. At service, adjust the seasoning to taste, add the fine herbs, and monté au beurre

NOTE: For a tarragon sauce, use only dried tarragon in the initial reduction, and add chopped, fresh tarragon leaves at service.

Sauce Perigeaux

Yield: 1 quart (1 liter)

Madeira sauce	1 quart	1 liter
Truffles, chopped	2 ounces	60 grams
Truffle essence	3 ounces	90 milliliters

Combine all of the ingredients and simmer the mixture until the correct consistency is achieved. Adjust the seasoning with salt and pepper to taste.

Sauce Bordelaise

Yield: 1 pint (480 milliliters)

Shallots, minced	1 ounce	30 grams
Thyme, fresh	1 sprig	1 sprig
Bay leaf	1	1
Mignonette pepper	½ teaspoon	1 gram
Red wine	1 quart	1 liter
Demi-glace	1 quart	1 liter
Marrow, poached, diced (per portion)	¼ ounce	7 grams
Lemon juice, fresh	to taste	to taste
Meat glaze	to taste	to taste
Whole butter (per portion), cold	¼ ounce	7 grams

1. Combine the shallots, thyme, bay leaf, pepper, and red wine; reduce the mixture to 1 cup.

2. Add the demi-glace; reduce to nappé. Strain the sauce.

3. Finish the sauce with the bone marrow, lemon juice, and meat glaze. Adjust the seasoning to taste and monté au beurre.

Sauce Madeira

Yield: 1 pint (480 milliliters)

Shallots, minced	1 tablespoon	15 grams
Thyme, fresh	1 sprig	1 sprig
Bay leaf	1	1
Black peppercorns, cracked	6	6
Burgundy	4 ounces	120 milliliters
Dry madeira	4 ounces	120 milliliters
Demi-glace	1 pint	480 milliliters
Unsalted butter, small pieces, cold	1 ounce	30 grams

1. Combine the shallots, thyme, bay leaf, peppercorns, burgundy, and madeira. Reduce the mixture to 2 ounces (60 milliliters).

2. Add the demi-glace; reduce to nappé. Strain the sauce.

3. At service, adjust the seasoning with salt and pepper to taste and monté au beurre. Add additional madeira to refresh the flavor, if desired.

Sauce Chasseur

Yield: 1 quart (1 liter)

Butter, clarified	1 ounce	30 milliliters
Olive oil	½ ounce	15 milliliters
Mushrooms, sliced thick	10 ounces	285 grams
Shallots, minced	1 ounce	30 grams
Garlic, minced	1 clove	1 clove
Dry white wine	8 ounces	240 milliliters
Brandy	3 ounces	90 milliliters
Demi-glace	1 quart	1 liter
Tomato concassé	1 pint	480 milliliters
Parsley, fresh, chopped	1 tablespoon	2 grams
Meat glaze	1 ounce	30 grams

1. Heat the butter and olive oil until smoking.
2. Add the mushrooms and sauté them until they are browned.
3. Add the shallots and garlic; sauté them until an aroma is released.
4. Add the wine and brandy; reduce the mixture by half.
5. Add the demi-glace; reduce to nappé.
6. Finish the sauce with the meat glaze and parsley.
7. Adjust the seasoning with salt and pepper to taste.

Sauce Chateaubriand

Yield: 1 pint (480 milliliters)

Chablis	16 ounces	480 milliliters
Shallots, minced	2	2
Thyme, fresh	3 sprigs	3 sprigs
Mushroom trimmings	4 ounces	115 grams
Bay leaf	1	1
Demi-glace or jus de veau	1 pint	480 milliliters
Maître d'hôtel butter, small pieces, chilled	2 ounces	60 grams

1. Combine the chablis, shallots, thyme, mushroom trimmings, and bay leaf and reduce by half.
2. Add the demi-glace or jus and reduce the mixture by half again. Strain the sauce and reserve.
3. At service, adjust the seasoning with salt and pepper to taste and monté au beurre with the maître d'hôtel butter.

Dill Sauce

Yield: 2 quarts (2 liters)

Onions, fine dice	4 ounces	225 grams
Butter, clarified	3 ounces	90 milliliters
Butter, clarified	3 ounces	90 milliliters
Velouté	1½ quarts	1.5 liters
Sour cream	10 ounces	225 grams
Dill, fresh, chopped	3 tablespoons	7 grams

1. Sweat the onions in the butter.
2. Add the velouté and simmer until nappé.
3. At service, add the sour cream and dill. Adjust the seasoning to taste.

Sauce Albufera

Yield: 1 quart (1 liter)

White veal stock	1 quart	1 liter
White roux	4 ounces	115 grams
Chicken stock	1 quart	1 liter
Heavy cream	4 ounces	120 milliliters
Glace de viande	2 ounces	60 grams
Pimiento butter	1 ounce	30 grams

1. Combine the white veal stock and the roux. Cook the mixture until it is smooth and thickened.
2. Add the chicken stock. Reduce the mixture by half. Simmer it for 45 to 60 minutes.
3. Temper the heavy cream with some of the hot sauce. Add the tempered cream to the rest of the sauce.
4. Whip the glace de viande and pimiento butter into the sauce.

Nantua Sauce

Yield: 1 quart (1 liter)

Béchamel or velouté	3 cups	720 milliliters
Heavy cream	1 cup	240 milliliters
Crayfish butter	6 ounces	170 grams

1. Combine the béchamel or velouté with the cream; simmer for 5 minutes.
2. Monté au beurre with the crayfish butter just prior to service.
3. Adjust the seasoning with salt and pepper to taste.

Horseradish Sauce

Yield: 3 pints (1.5 liters)

Horseradish, fresh, grated	5 ounces	140 grams
Vinegar	as needed	as needed
Water	as needed	as needed
Velouté	1 quart	1 liter
Sour cream	1 pint	480 milliliters
Egg yolks	4	4
Sugar	as needed	as needed

1. Hold the grated horseradish in enough vinegar and water to cover it.
2. Bring the velouté to a simmer; let it reduce to nappé.
3. Combine the sour cream and egg yolks. Temper with the velouté, then add to the remainder of the velouté. Return to just below a simmer.
4. Drain and squeeze the horseradish and add it to the sauce. Adjust the seasoning to taste with salt, pepper, vinegar, and sugar.

Suprême Sauce

<u>*Yield: 1 pint (480 milliliters)*</u>

Chicken velouté	1 pint	480 milliliters
Heavy cream, hot	4 ounces	120 milliliters
Mushroom infusion (optional)	2 ounces	60 milliliters
Unsalted butter, whole (optional)	1 ounce	30 grams

1. Combine the velouté and heavy cream. (Add the optional mushroom infusion at this point.) Simmer until nappé.
2. Strain the sauce and adjust the seasoning to taste with salt and pepper.
3. Monté au beurre (optional).

Cream Sauce

<u>*Yield: 1 quart (1 liter)*</u>

Béchamel	1 pint	480 milliliters
Heavy cream, hot	½ cup	120 milliliters

1. Combine the béchamel and heavy cream. Simmer to nappé.
2. Strain the sauce, if desired. Adjust the seasoning with salt and pepper to taste.

Saint Andrew's Red Sauce

<u>*Yield: 1 quart (1 liter)*</u>

Olive oil	¾ ounce	20 grams
Onion, minced	3½ ounces	100 grams
Garlic, minced	2 teaspoons	10 grams
Tomato paste	5½ ounces	155 grams
Red wine	6 ounces	180 milliliters
Plum tomatoes, fresh, flesh only	1 pound, 2 ounces	510 grams
Chicken stock	12 ounces	360 milliliters
Basil, fresh	1 sprig	1 sprig
Thyme, fresh	1 sprig	1 sprig
Bay leaf	1	1
Pepper, fresh, ground	to taste	to taste

1. Heat the olive oil; sauté the onions until they are tender. Add the garlic; sauté it briefly. Add the tomato paste; caramelize it lightly.

2. Add the red wine, tomatoes, stock, basil, thyme, and bay leaf. Simmer the mixture for approximately 45 minutes. Remove and discard the herbs.

3. Run the mixture through a food mill with a coarse plate. Adjust the consistency if necessary.

4. Finish the sauce with the pepper. Cool the sauce and hold it under refrigeration.

NOTE: This dish is a reworking of a classic recipe in order to reduce overall calories, fat, cholesterol, and sodium.

Tomato Sauce (Version 2)

Yield: 1 quart (1 liter)

Onion, brunoise	4 ounces	115 grams
Celery, brunoise	2 ounces	60 grams
Carrot, brunoise	4 ounces	115 grams
Garlic, mashed to a paste	1 teaspoon	4.5 grams
Olive oil	2 ounces	60 milliliters
Butter	1 ounce	30 grams
Tomato concassé	3 pounds	1.35 kilograms
Parsley, fresh, chopped	2 tablespoons	4.5 grams

1. Sweat the onion, celery, carrot, and garlic in the oil and butter until they are lightly browned.

2. Add the tomato concassé; simmer for 45 minutes to 1 hour, until the flavor is fully developed and the correct consistency is reached.

3. Add the parsley, and adjust the seasoning to taste with salt and pepper.

Tomato Sauce (Version 3)

Yield: 1 gallon (3.75 liters)

Olive oil	4 ounces	120 milliliters
Onions, small dice	8 ounces	225 grams
Garlic, minced	4 cloves	4 cloves
Plum tomatoes, whole, pureed, fresh or canned	7 pounds	3 kilograms
Tomato puree	2¼ cups	540 milliliters
Basil leaves, fresh, chopped	½ cup	9 grams

(continued)

1. Sweat the onions in the olive oil until they are translucent.

2. Add the garlic and sauté it until an aroma is apparent.

3. Add the plum tomatoes and tomato puree to the onions.

4. Simmer the mixture to achieve a heavy consistency.

5. Add the basil and adjust the seasoning to taste.

Choron Sauce

Yield: 1 quart (1 liter)

Shallots, chopped	3 tablespoons	43 grams
Black peppercorns, cracked	12	12
Tarragon leaves, dried	3 tablespoons	10.5 grams
Tarragon vinegar	6 ounces	180 milliliters
Water	2 ounces	60 milliliters
White wine	1 ounce	30 milliliters
Egg yolks	9	9
Clarified butter, warm	27 ounces	810 milliliters
Tomato puree	3 tablespoons	45 grams

1. Combine the shallots, peppercorns, dried tarragon, and vinegar. Reduce to sec.

2. Add the water and wine to the reduction; strain.

3. Combine the strained reduction and egg yolks in a stainless-steel bowl. Cook over a bain-marie until the yolks form ribbons.

4. Add the clarified butter gradually, whipping constantly.

5. Add the tomato puree; adjust the seasoning to taste with salt.

Creole Mustard Sauce

Yield: approximately 1 quart (1 liter)

Shallots, minced	8 ounces	225 grams
Cider vinegar	4 ounces	120 milliliters
Peppercorns, cracked	2 teaspoons	4.5 grams
Bay leaves	2	2
Dry white wine	16 ounces	480 milliliters
Heavy cream	16 ounces	480 milliliters
Unsalted butter, softened	2 pounds	910 grams
Dijon-style mustard	to taste	to taste
Zatrain's creole mustard	to taste	to taste
Gulden's mustard	to taste	to taste

1. Combine the shallots, vinegar, peppercorns, bay leaves, and wine. Reduce the mixture to 6 ounces.
2. Add the heavy cream and reduce the mixture by half. Strain the sauce and return it to the heat.
3. Whisk in the butter gradually over low heat.
4. Add the mustards, to taste.

Sauce Palois

Yield: 1 quart (1 liter)

Shallots, chopped	3 tablespoons	40 grams
Black peppercorns, cracked	12	12
Mint sprigs, fresh, chopped	3 tablespoons	7 grams
Cider vinegar	6 ounces	180 milliliters
White wine	1 ounce	30 milliliters
Water	2 ounces	60 milliliters
Egg yolks	9	9
Clarified butter, warm	27 ounces	810 milliliters
Mint leaves, fresh, chiffonade	4 tablespoons	9 grams

(continued)

1. Combine the shallots, peppercorns, mint, and vinegar. Reduce to until syrupy.

2. Add the water and wine to the reduction; strain the reduction into a stainless-steel bowl; then combine it with the egg yolks. Cook the mixture over a bain-marie until the yolks form ribbons when dropped from the whip.

3. Add the clarified butter gradually, whipping constantly until all the butter is incorporated and the sauce is thick.

4. Add the chiffonade of mint; adjust the seasoning to taste with salt and ground pepper.

Béarnaise

Yield: 1 quart (1 liter)

Shallots, chopped	3 tablespoons	43 grams
Black peppercorns, cracked	12	12
Tarragon leaves, dried	3 tablespoons	7 grams
Tarragon vinegar	6 ounces	180 milliliters
White wine	1 ounce	30 milliliters
Water	2 ounces	60 milliliters
Egg yolks	9	9
Clarified butter, warm	27 ounces	810 milliliters
Tarragon leaves, fresh, coarsely chopped	3 tablespoons	7 grams
Chervil leaves, fresh, coarsely chopped	1 tablespoon	2 grams

1. Combine the shallots, peppercorns, dried tarragon, and vinegar. Reduce to sec.

2. Add the wine and water to the reduction; strain.

3. Combine the strained reduction and the egg yolks in a stainless-steel bowl. Cook over a bain-marie until the yolks form ribbons.

4. Add the clarified butter gradually, whipping constantly.

5. Add the chopped tarragon and chervil; adjust the seasoning to taste with salt.

Béarnaise Reduction

Yield: 4 ounces (120 milliliters)

Shallots, chopped	3 tablespoons	45 grams
Peppercorns, cracked	12	12
Tarragon, chopped	¾ ounce	20 grams
Vinegar	6 ounces	180 milliliters
White wine	1 ounce	30 milliliters
Water	2 ounces	60 milliliters

1. Combine the shallots, peppercorns, tarragon, and vinegar in a saucepan. Bring to a simmer, then reduce au sec.

2. Refresh the reduction with white wine and water.

Tarragon Butter

Yield: 1½ pints (720 milliliters)

Shallots, minced	2 ounces	55 grams
Tarragon vinegar	2½ ounces	75 milliliters
Black peppercorns, cracked	15	15
Bay leaves	3	3
White wine	12 ounces	360 milliliters
Heavy cream	1 pint	480 milliliters
Unsalted butter, softened	1½ pounds	680 grams
Tarragon leaves, fresh, chopped	1 teaspoon	5 grams

1. Combine the shallots, vinegar, peppercorns, bay leaves, and wine. Reduce to 2 ounces. Strain.

2. Reduce the cream by half and add it to the reduction.

3. Gradually whisk in the butter over low heat.

4. Add the tarragon leaves.

Mustard-Tarragon Sauce with Green Peppercorns

Yield: approximately 1 quart (1 liter)

Shallots, minced	2 ounces	55 grams
Cider vinegar	1 ounce	30 milliliters
Tarragon leaves, dried	2 tablespoons	7 grams
White wine	8 ounces	240 milliliters
Unsalted butter, cut in pieces	1½ pounds	680 grams
Dijon mustard	4 tablespoons	60 grams
Green peppercorns, drained, crushed	3 tablespoons	21 grams

1. Combine the shallots, vinegar, tarragon, and wine. Reduce to 3 ounces. Strain (optional).
2. Whisk in the butter gradually over low heat.
3. Add the mustard and green peppercorns just before service.
4. Adjust the seasoning with salt and pepper to taste.

Red Pepper Coulis

Yield: 1 quart (1 liter)

Red peppers, chopped	5	5
Olive oil	2 ounces	60 milliliters
Shallots	2 ounces	60 grams
Dry white wine	1 pint	480 milliliters
Chicken stock	1 pint	480 milliliters
Crème fraîche	1 cup	240 milliliters

1. Sweat the peppers in the olive oil until they are tender; remove the peppers and puree. Reserve the oil from the sweated peppers.
2. Sweat the shallots in the reserved oil.
3. Deglaze with wine.
4. Add the stock; reduce by half.
5. Add the crème fraîche; reduce to nappé. Adjust the seasoning with salt and pepper to taste.

Tomato-Basil Coulis

Yield: 1½ cups (360 milliliters)

Olive oil	1 teaspoon	5 grams
Garlic, minced	½ teaspoon	3 grams
Shallots, minced	1 teaspoon	7 grams
Jalapeño chili, minced (optional)	½ teaspoon	3 grams
Tomato paste	¼ cup	60 grams
Tomato concassé	1 cup	170 grams
Chicken stock	½ cup	120 milliliters
Tomatillos, medium dice (optional)	½ cup	90 grams
Basil, fresh, chopped	2 teaspoons	1.5 grams
Cilantro, fresh, chopped	1 teaspoon	750 milligrams
Oregano, fresh, chopped	1 teaspoon	750 milligrams

1. Heat the olive oil in a sauteuse. Add the garlic, shallots, jalapeños, and tomato paste and sauté them.

2. Add the tomato concassé and stock. Simmer for approximately 5 minutes, stirring occasionally.

3. Puree the mixture until it is smooth. Add the remaining ingredients. Reheat before serving, if necessary.

Red Pepper Coulis (Version 2)

Yield: 1 quart (1 liter)

Red peppers, quartered and seeded	8	8
Shallots, minced	4 ounces	115 grams
White wine	9 ounces	270 milliliters
Dry vermouth	3 ounces	90 milliliters
Heavy cream	24 ounces	720 milliliters
Whole unsalted butter, cubed	8 ounces	225 grams

1. Sauté the peppers until they are tender; puree them.

2. Combine the shallots, wine, and vermouth; simmer until the shallots are translucent.

3. Add the red pepper puree to the shallot mixture; reduce the mixture by half.

4. Add the cream and reduce to nappé.

5. Monté au beurre.

6. Adjust the seasoning to taste with salt and pepper.

Shrimp Sauce

Yield: 3 pints (1.5 liters)

Shrimp shells	6 ounces	170 grams
Butter	1 ounce	30 grams
Shallots, minced	4	4
Garlic, minced	1 clove	1 clove
Paprika	1 tablespoon	7 grams
Brandy	2 ounces	60 milliliters
Heavy cream	2 quarts	2 liters
Dry sherry	2 ounces	60 milliliters

1. Sauté the shells in the hot butter until they are red.
2. Add the shallots and garlic; sauté until an aroma is apparent.
3. Add the paprika; pincé.
4. Deglaze with the brandy.
5. Add the heavy cream and reduce to nappé.
6. Strain the sauce. Finish with the sherry and adjust the seasoning.

VARIATION

Lobster Sauce: Substitute 1 lobster, cut for sauté, for the shrimp shells. Reserve the roe and tomalley to finish the sauce.

Pimiento Butter

Yield: 12 ounces (360 milliliters)

Butter, softened	10 ounces	285 grams
Pimientos, minced	3½ ounces	100 grams
Garlic, minced	¼ teaspoon	1 gram
Lemon juice, fresh	1 tablespoon	15 milliliters
Salt	to taste	to taste
Pepper	to taste	to taste

1. Combine all ingredients.
2. Pipe the butter into rosettes, using a pastry bag, or roll in parchment paper.
3. Refrigerate until needed.

Chili Butter

Yield: 1 pound (455 grams)

Chili powder	1 tablespoon	7 grams
Cumin, ground	½ teaspoon	1 gram
Paprika	½ teaspoon	1 gram
Hot chili powder	1 tablespoon	7 grams
Oregano	1 tablespoon	3.5 grams
Worcestershire sauce	½ teaspoon	2.5 milliliters
Tabasco sauce	¼ teaspoon	1 milliliter
Garlic powder	¼ teaspoon	500 milligrams
Onion powder	¼ teaspoon	500 milligrams
Unsalted butter	1 pound	455 grams

1. Heat the chili powder, cumin, and paprika in a dry pan to release their flavors.
2. Combine the heated spices with the remaining ingredients.
3. Pipe the butter into rosettes, using a pastry bag, or roll into a cylinder.
4. Refrigerate until needed.

Shellfish Butter

Yield: 10 ounces (285 grams)

Shallots, minced	4	4
Paprika	1½ tablespoons	10.5 grams
Crustacean shells, coarsely chopped	6 ounces	170 grams
White wine	6 ounces	180 milliliters
Unsalted butter, softened	8 ounces	225 grams

1. Sauté the shallots, paprika, and shells until they are bright red.
2. Deglaze with the wine and reduce to 2 ounces.
3. Whip the butter into the reduction.
4. Strain into a bowl set over an ice bath. Press the shells to extract all the flavor.
5. Whip the butter together once it is cool.
6. Roll into a cylinder; refrigerate.

Scallion Butter

Yield: 12 ounces (360 milliliters)

Butter, softened	10 ounces	285 grams
Scallions, minced	4	4
Garlic, minced	¼ teaspoon	1 gram
Parsley, chopped	1 tablespoon	2 grams
Soy sauce	1 tablespoon	15 milliliters
Lemon juice, fresh	1 tablespoon	15 milliliters
Salt	to taste	to taste
Pepper	to taste	to taste

1. Combine all ingredients.
2. Pipe the butter into rosettes, using a pastry bag, or roll in parchment paper.
3. Refrigerate until needed.

Mustard-Dill Butter

Yield: 12 ounces (340 milliliters)

Butter, softened	10 ounces	285 grams
Dijon mustard	3 tablespoons	45 grams
Dill, fresh, chopped	3 tablespoons	7 grams
Lemon juice, fresh	1 teaspoon	15 milliliters
Shallots, minced, smothered	2 tablespoons	25 grams
Worcestershire sauce	1 tablespoon	15 milliliters
Tabasco sauce	to taste	to taste
Salt	to taste	to taste
Pepper, ground	to taste	to taste

1. Combine all of the ingredients.
2. Pipe the butter into rosettes, using a pastry bag, or roll it in parchment paper.
3. Refrigerate the butter until it is needed.

Salsa Cru

Yield: 1 cup (240 grams)

Plum tomatoes concassé	2	2
Jalapeño chilis, minced	2 teaspoons	10 grams
Red onion, finely diced	3 tablespoons	10 grams
Cilantro, fresh, chopped	2 tablespoons	5 grams
Salt	to taste	to taste
Black pepper, cracked	to taste	to taste

Combine all the ingredients and mix them thoroughly. Chill for approximately 1 hour to blend the flavors.

Red Onion Confit

Yield: 8 ounces (225 grams)

Red onion, julienne	1 cup	170 grams
Butter	1 teaspoon	5 grams
Honey	1 tablespoon	20 grams
Red wine vinegar	¾ ounce	25 grams
Red wine	¾ ounce	25 grams

1. Heat the butter in a sauteuse over high heat. Add the onions and sweat them.

2. Stir in the honey; cook the mixture until the onions are lightly caramelized.

3. Add the vinegar and wine; reduce au sec. Adjust the seasoning to taste with salt and white pepper.

Chapter 18

Dry-heat Cooking
without Fats or Oils

Dry-heat methods are so called because the food is cooked either by a direct application of radiant heat or by indirect heat, contained in a closed environment. No liquid, including stock, is added to either the food or the cooking vessel during the actual cooking time. Any fats or oils added during the cooking process itself are intended to add flavor to the finished dish, and do not act as the cooking medium. The result is a highly flavored exterior and a moist interior. The dry-heat techniques are:

- grilling and broiling
- roasting
- poêléing

Grilling is essentially a quick technique and is used with portion-sized or smaller pieces of meat, poultry, or fish. Roasting and poêléing (also called butter roasting) require longer cooking times because these techniques are most frequently used with large cuts of meat or whole birds or fish.

ESSENTIALS

Two major factors in successfully using dry-heat techniques without fat are selecting the proper cuts of meat, poultry, and fish and knowing how to determine the desired doneness. Because dry heat does not have a tenderizing effect, any food prepared by one of these techniques must be naturally tender or should be prepared in a way that will introduce additional moisture. This can be done using one of the methods, such as barding or marinating, outlined in this chapter.

DIRECT-HEAT TECHNIQUES

Grilling and Broiling

Grilled foods are cooked by radiant heat from a source located below the food. The drippings that might have collected or reduced in a sauté pan are actually reducing directly on the food's surface. The sauce that accompanies a grilled item is prepared separately. Broiling, barbecuing, and pan-broiling are all forms of grilling.

Grilled foods have a smoky, slightly charred flavor resulting from the flaring of the juices and fats that are rendered out as the item cooks. Special woods such as grapevines, mesquite, hickory, or apple are frequently used to introduce a special flavor. Another charactéristic is the crosshatch marks made on the food's surface when it is properly placed on a well-heated grill.

The following terms identify techniques that share several characteristics of grilling, although they may differ in some respects.

Broiling. The heat source is located above the food item. Frequently, delicate items such as lean white fish are first brushed with butter and then placed on a heated sizzler platter before being placed on the rack below the heat source. This is not broiling in the strictest sense of the word; it is actually closer to baking. Items prepared in this manner may still be referred to as "broiled" on a menu.

Barbecuing. This term can cause some confusion. It generally signifies a food that has been basted repeatedly with a barbecue sauce during grilling. It may mean something entirely different when used on a menu, however. For instance, a barbecued beef sandwich may simply be roasted beef that has been thinly sliced and simmered in a barbecue sauce.

Pan-broiling. Foods are cooked on top of the stove in a heavy cast-iron or other warp-resistant metal pan over intense heat. Any fat or juices released during cooking are removed as they accumulate, otherwise the result is a sauté or a stew. Special pans made to simulate a grill's effect may be used. These pans have thick ridges that hold the food up and away from any juices or fat that might collect.

Mise en Place

1. Main item. This should be of relatively even thickness and cut thinly enough to allow it to cook properly without excessive exterior charring. Cut it into the appropriate size and trim away any fat, silverskin, and gristle. Optional procedures to prepare the main item may be used to introduce additional flavor or moisture. Marinate it, if desired or required by the recipe. (Because the food should already be tender, marination is useful primarily for introducing additional flavor. The marinade may be a simple bath of olive oil or a more complex, aromatic mix-

ture.) Stuff the main item, wrap it in caul fat, and thread it on skewers. (If wooden skewers are used, they must be thoroughly soaked in water to prevent the wood from burning.) Add a protective coating of melted butter and bread crumbs, known as *à l'anglaise.* This also gives the item textural interest. Brush the item lightly with oil. Although not essential, brushing foods with a neutral or appropriately flavored oil will help to protect them during cooking.

2. Glaze or barbecue sauce. Have a glaze or barbecue sauce available, if required by the recipe.

3. Hardwood chips or herb stems. Have these available to create aromatic smoke, if desired.

A variety of grilled foods is shown in Figure 18-1.

Method

1. Thoroughly clean and properly heat the grill. The grill racks must be perfectly clean to prevent foods from sticking or charring. Also, mentally dividing the grill or broiler into zones, as shown in Figure 18-2, helps the chef keep track of the items' doneness during a busy service period. The chef should also identify which grill

18-1

A variety of grilled foods.

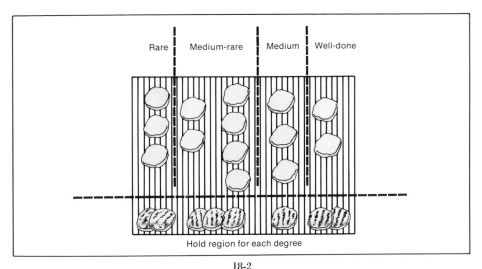

Rare | Medium-rare | Medium | Well-done

Hold region for each degree

18-2

Setting up zones on a grill.

areas tend to be hotter than others, so that items can be moved to hotter or cooler spots as necessary.

2. Place the main item on the grill. When the food comes in contact with the heated grill rack, the rack chars a mark on the food's surface. Point one corner of the item toward one o'clock, as shown in Figure 18-3. After the item has been on the grill for a brief time, rotate it so that the top is pointing toward five o'clock. This will create the crosshatch marks associated with grilling. Crosshatch marks are made on only one side of the item; the unmarked side rests on the surface of the plate. Delicate foods, such as trout and other fish, should be placed on a lightly oiled hand rack for grilling or on a heated sizzler platter for broiling. (Because the heat from the sizzler platter helps to cook the item, it does not have to be turned.)

3. Turn the item once and finish cooking to desired doneness. If necessary, thicker items may be finished in the oven. At this point, some foods should be moved to a cooler area on the grill, or the broiler rack may be adjusted to move the food farther away from the heat.

18-3 MARKING FOODS ON A GRILL

(1) Place the item on a clean, hot, oiled grill.

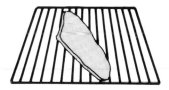

(2) Rotate the item 90 degrees and place it on the grill.

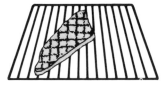

(3) Turn the item and finish cooking on the second side.

4. Adjust the seasoning, if necessary, and serve on heated plates with an appropriate sauce.

For a quick summary, refer to the abbreviated method for grilling.

Determining Doneness

Determining doneness in foods cooked by dry-heat methods is an imprecise science. As the noted chef André Soltner has observed, "One must cook a piece of meat a thousand times before he even begins to understand how it cooks." It is impossible to give exact times for cooking meats, poultry, and fish, because there are so many variables. These guidelines will apply for all the dry-heat techniques, in both this chapter and the following one.

Red meats. Beef, lamb, and some game meats may be cooked to a range of doneness. The chef must be able to accurately determine when a piece of meat has reached the doneness requested by the guest. This can be learned only through experience. The indicators of touch and appearance are inexact but serve as guidelines.

• Touch. Press the meat with the tip of a finger and gauge its resistance. The less well-done a piece of meat is, the softer and more yielding it will feel. This test also applies to sautéed meats (refer to Chapter 19, "Dry-heat Cooking with Fats and Oils"). To practice recognizing the feel of meat cooked to various stages of doneness, hold one hand open, palm up, with the fingers slightly curled. Touch the flesh at the base of the thumb. It will feel soft and yielding. As the fingers are gradually spread open and flat, the flesh will feel increasingly less yielding.

Beef Tenderloin with Scallion Butter

Yield: 1 serving

Beef tenderloin	5 to 8 ounces	140 to 225 grams
Salt	to taste	to taste
Pepper	to taste	to taste
Oil	as needed	as needed
Scallion butter	1 ounce	30 grams

1. Season the tenderloin with the salt and pepper; brush it with the oil.

2. Broil the tenderloin to the desired doneness.

3. Top the tenderloin with a slice of the scallion butter; flash it briefly under a broiler.

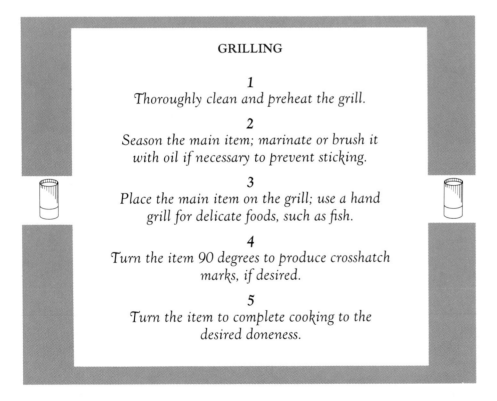

GRILLING

1
Thoroughly clean and preheat the grill.

2
Season the main item; marinate or brush it with oil if necessary to prevent sticking.

3
Place the main item on the grill; use a hand grill for delicate foods, such as fish.

4
Turn the item 90 degrees to produce crosshatch marks, if desired.

5
Turn the item to complete cooking to the desired doneness.

• Appearance. As the meat cooks, the exterior should develop a deep brown color. If the meat appears pale or even gray, it has not been adequately cooked. The juices that run from the meat, although minimal, should be the correct color; the more rare the meat, the "bloodier" the juices should appear.

Appearance is also an important factor in knowing when to turn a piece of meat. When the meat's upper surface begins to appear very moist (there may even be moisture beads), the meat should be turned. Thin pieces may start to change color at the edges when they are ready for turning. The meat's interior gives the most certain determination of doneness.

The photographs in Figure 18-4 clearly demonstrate the changes that meat undergoes at various stages of doneness. Beef cooked "blue" has a very deep maroon color. Beef cooked rare has a very pronounced red interior, but it is no longer maroon. When beef is cooked medium, it has a rosy pink interior and is not quite as juicy. Well-done beef shows no traces of red or pink. Still somewhat moist in appearance, it is no longer juicy.

White meats. Veal, pork, poultry, and some game should be cooked through *(à point)*, but not overcooked. There should be a slight amount of "give" when the meat is pressed with a fingertip. Any juices that run from the meat should show either a "thread of pink" or be nearly colorless. As always, it is best to err on the side of undercooking.

Even thin meat pieces will retain some heat, allowing them to continue to cook after they have been removed from the heat and are being held for completion of the sauce. If the meat is not left slightly underdone, it can end up overcooked by the time it is served.

Fish and shellfish. These are extremely easy to overcook because of their delicacy. Their connective tissues and proteins cook at lower temperatures, so the heat is able to travel rapidly throughout the fish.

The fish should offer only the least bit of resistance when pressed with the fingertip. It bears repeating that it is best to err on the side of undercooking. The traditional

18-4 DEGREES OF DONENESS IN MEATS

(1) Beef cooked "blue."

(2) Beef cooked rare.

(3) Beef cooked medium.

(4) Beef cooked well-done.

wisdom that fish is properly cooked when it flakes easily should be disregarded. Most fish, notably lean white fish, such as flounder or cod, and freshwater fish, such as salmon or trout, will be overcooked if the flesh flakes easily. Other types, such as swordfish, tuna, or shellfish, do not readily flake, so the dictum does not apply at all.

Evaluating Quality

Three things to use as gauges of quality are flavor, appearance, and texture. These foods should have a distinctly smoky flavor, which is enhanced by a certain amount of charring and by the addition to the grill of hardwood or sprigs or stalks of some herbs. This smoky flavor and aroma should not overpower the food's natural flavor, and the charring should not be so extensive that it gives the food a bitter or carbonized taste. Any marinades or glazes should support and not mask the main item's flavor.

The surface of a properly grilled food should appear moist, with the characteristic deep-brown crosshatch marks. The darker the meat, the darker the exterior will be. Broiled foods, especially those that are prepared *à l'anglaise*, should have a golden-brown color. If the surface appears extremely dry or overly dark or charred, the food

may have been overcooked or the heat may have been too intense for the food being cooked.

Grilled foods should have a well-developed crust with a moist and tender interior. If the food has a rubbery or tough texture, it was overcooked or allowed to cook too quickly.

INDIRECT-HEAT METHODS

Roasting

Roasting is a technique that cooks foods by surrounding them with dry air in a closed environment. The air captured in the oven is the cooking medium. The rendered juices are the foundation for sauces prepared while the roast rests.

The original form of roasting—and the oldest form of cookery—is spit-roasting. In this method, foods are cooked by radiant heat given off from a fire or other source. Roasting as it is most commonly practiced today, however, is more similar to baking than it is to spit-roasting. Hot air circulates around the food, and as the outer layers become heated, the food's natural juices turn to steam and penetrate the food more deeply.

The following are terms related to roasting.

Spit-roasting. This technique involves placing the food on a rod that is turned either manually or with a motor. The radiant heat cooks the item in the same manner as grilling or broiling. The constant turning assures that the food cooks evenly and develops a good crust. Spit-roasting may also be done in a specially constructed oven. The tradition of serving roasted and grilled foods on toasted bread or a crouton began when pieces of bread were placed below the cooking food to trap escaping juices. In contemporary kitchens, drip pans are placed under the spit, as shown in Figure 18-5.

Barding. This term is used for meats that have been wrapped in thin sheets of fatback or in caul fat. When barding has been used, the meat will not have a well-developed or flavorful crust, but the interior will be more moist.

Smoke-roasting. This technique is an adaptation of roasting that allows foods to take on the rich, smoky flavor of hardwood chips without undergoing lengthy brining and smoking processes. Basically, the food is placed on a rack over smoldering hardwood chips. The pan is tightly covered, and the main item is roasted in a hot oven to the desired doneness. The setup for smoke-roasting is shown in Figure 18-6.

Jus or jus lié/pan gravy. The sauce made from the accumulated drippings is frequently referred to as au jus. (It should not be confused, however, with the jus discussed in Chapter 17, "Sauces." That jus is used as a base for a variety of sauces and is not a roasting by-product.) When the jus made from drippings is thickened with arrowroot or cornstarch, it is known as jus lié. If a sauce is made with a roux incorporating the fat rendered from a roast, it is usually called pan gravy.

Carryover cooking. This is a term used to describe what happens to a piece of meat or fish after it has been removed from the oven. The roasted item holds a certain amount of heat that will continue to cook the food. The larger the item, the greater the amount of heat it will retain. For example, quail or Cornish hen may show an increase in the internal temperature of 5 to 10°F. A top round of beef's temperature may increase as much as 15°F

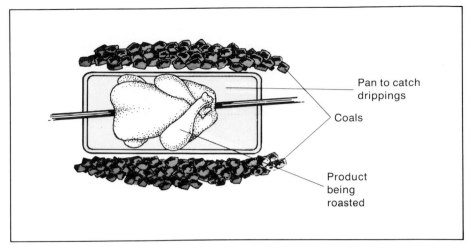

18-5
Setup for spit-roasting.

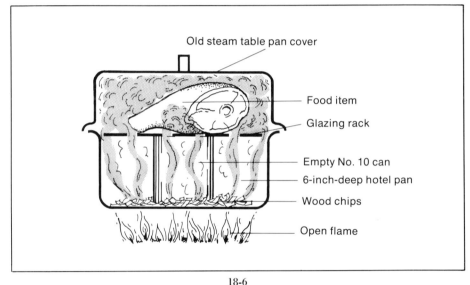

18-6
Setup for smoke-roasting.

and the temperature of a steamship round of beef by up to 20°F. In order to achieve the correct doneness, the main item should be removed from the oven when the internal temperature is *lower* than it should be when served.

Mise en place

1. Main item. Select tender meats from the rib and loin areas for the best results. Certain cuts from the legs of certain animals are also excellent when roasted. Young, tender birds may be

roasted, as may whole fish. Trim the silverskin and excess fat. Because most of the lubrication and tenderness come from the marbling within rather than from the exterior fat, it is generally acceptable to trim away most of the visible fat. This makes subsequent preparation of the jus or pan gravy easier because less fat is left in the roasting pan. There is also less splattering during cooking, which makes the procedure less dangerous and less messy. In some cases, it may be desirable to bard or lard meats to prevent them from drying excessively. Truss the birds or tie the meats.

2. Mirepoix. This is used to flavor the jus, not to provide moisture during the cooking process. It is, therefore, a good idea to add the mirepoix to the pan after the roast has been removed and is resting prior to carving and/or service. Brown the mirepoix in the fat and drippings.

3. Liquid. Have available cognac, wine, water, or stock to deglaze the pan.

4. Base liquid for jus or gravy. Have available jus or stock of the appropriate flavor.

5. Thickeners for gravy or jus lié. Have available: flour to mix with the fat released by the food during roasting; arrowroot or cornstarch diluted in cold liquid; or prepared roux.

6. Optional components. Have available: stuffing or filling; caul fat or fatback for barding; and/or additional aromatics, garnish, or finishing ingredients to be used with the product during roasting or to complete the sauce.

Method

1. Sear the main item, if it is appropriate or desirable.

2. Roast the main item, uncovered, in a hot oven to desired doneness. Some foods will require basting during roasting; some may need to be turned to assure even roasting; some may be placed on a rack so that air can come in contact with the food on all surfaces. The food must roast uncovered. Covering the pan will trap the steam that escapes from the meat. In a closed environment, the food is cooked by steam rather than the hot air's convection. Remove the item at an internal temperature that will allow carryover cooking to bring it to the correct final temperature.

3. Allow the main item to rest before carving it. As foods roast, their juices become concentrated in the item's center. A resting period allows the juices to redistribute evenly throughout the item.

4. Prepare the jus (or see step 5 for the method for pan gravy, if that is desired instead).

- Add the mirepoix to the rendered fat and drippings in the roasting pan (if the drippings are not scorched), either during the last part of the roasting time or after the roast has been removed to rest.
- Place the roasting pan over direct heat and cook until the mirepoix is browned, the fat is clarified, and the drippings are reduced.
- Drain the mirepoix through a strainer. The fat will drain away.
- Return the mirepoix to the roasting pan and deglaze the pan with an appropriate liquid.
- Add the appropriate stock or jus. Simmer, and skim the surface to remove any fat.
- If jus lié is desired, add enough diluted arrowroot or cornstarch to lightly thicken the sauce.
- Strain the jus and adjust the seasoning to taste.
- Garnish or finish the item according to the recipe.

5. Prepare the pan gravy.

- Add the mirepoix to the rendered fat and drippings in the roasting pan (if the drippings are not scorched), either during the last part of the roasting time or after the roast has been removed to rest.
- Place the roasting pan over direct heat and cook until the mirepoix is browned, the fat is

clarified, and the drippings are reduced.

- Pour off the excess fat, leaving only enough to prepare an adequate amount of roux to thicken the gravy.
- Add flour to the roasting pan and stir it well. Cook the roux for a few minutes.
- Add the appropriate stock to the pan. Be sure to add the liquid gradually and stir it continuously to work out all the lumps.
- Simmer the gravy until it is well-flavored and properly thickened.
- Strain the gravy and finish or garnish the main item according to the recipe.

6. Carve the food, if appropriate, and serve it on heated serving platters or on individual plates, accompanied by the jus or pan gravy.

For a quick summary, refer to the abbreviated method for roasting.

Carving

Once the food is properly roasted, the chef's task is not complete. The food must be carved correctly to make the most of the item. Most meats, poultry, and fish are cut into serving-sized portions before they are cooked, although occasionally, it is more appropriate to prepare a large roast or an entire bird. The three items carved in Figures 18-7 through 18-9—a rib roast of beef, a leg of lamb, and a whole duck—should be considered prototypes. For example, because they are similar in structure, a ham would be carved in the same manner as a leg of lamb. Following are carving techniques for three roasted items.

Standing rib roast. This carving method could also be used for a rack of veal.

18-7 CARVING A STANDING RIB ROAST

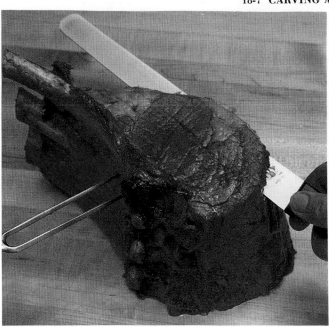

(1) Cut the rib roast using a sharp meat slicer.

(2) Use a knife tip to cut the slice away from the bone.

1. Lay the rib roast on its side. Using a sharp meat slicer, make parallel cuts from the outer edge toward the bones.

2. Use the knife tip to cut the slice of meat away from the bone and serve it (see Fig. 18-7).

Leg of lamb.

1. To steady the leg, hold the shank bone firmly in one hand with a clean side towel. Make parallel cuts from the shank end down to the bone.

2. Continue cutting slices of meat from the leg, cutting away from the bone to make even slices.

3. When the slices become very large, begin to cut the meat at a slight angle, first from the left side, then from the right side, alternating until the leg is entirely sliced (see Fig. 18-8).

Birds. Although a duck is used in Figure 18-9 to demonstrate these carving techniques, they could be applied to any bird.

ROASTING

1
Season, stuff, marinate, bard, or lard the main item, and sear it over direct heat or in a hot oven if desired.

2
Elevate the item in a roasting pan so that hot air can reach all sides.

3
Roast the item uncovered until the desired internal temperature is reached. Be sure to allow for carryover cooking.

4
Add the mirepoix to the roasting pan for pan gravy during the final half hour of roasting time, if desired.

5
Let the roasted item rest before carving.

6
Prepare the pan gravy in the roasting pan.

7
Carve the main item and serve it with the appropriate gravy or sauce.

18-8 CARVING A LEG OF LAMB

(1) Hold the shank bone firmly in one hand and make parallel cuts.

(2) Cut slices of meat from the leg.

(3) When the slices become large, cut the meat at a slight angle.

Standing Rib Roast au Jus with Yorkshire Pudding

Yield: 25 to 30 portions

Beef rib roast, oven-ready	14 pounds	6.35 kilograms
Salt	to taste	to taste
Pepper	to taste	to taste
Mirepoix	8 ounces	225 grams
Brown stock	2 quarts	2 liters
Arrowroot, diluted in cold stock or water	2½ ounces	70 grams

Yorkshire Pudding

Flour	12 ounces	340 grams
Eggs	3 to 6	3 to 6
Milk	30 ounces	890 milliliters
Salt	1 teaspoon	5.5 grams

1. Season the beef with the salt and pepper and roast it to an internal temperature of 130°F (55°C).

2. Add the mirepoix approximately one-half hour before the roast is done and allow it to caramelize.

3. Remove the roast and let it rest for one-half hour.

4. Clarify the fat and reduce the pan drippings. Drain off the fat and reserve it.

5. Deglaze the roasting pan with the stock. Simmer it to reduce.

6. Gradually add the diluted arrowroot until the sauce is lightly thickened.

7. Combine all the ingredients for the Yorkshire pudding. Blend them until they are smooth.

8. Heat the reserved fat and add it to the baking dish. Add the Yorkshire pudding batter. Bake it until it is very puffy. Serve the jus and pudding with the sliced beef.

(4) Alternate sides.

1. Use a knife tip to cut through the skin at the point where the leg meets the breast. Use the tines of a kitchen fork to gently press the leg away from the body. A properly roasted bird's leg will come away easily.

2. Use one kitchen fork to hold the breast steady. Insert another kitchen fork at the joint between the drumstick and the thigh. Pull the leg away from the body. Repeat for the other leg.

3. Cut the leg into two pieces through the joint between the thigh and the drumstick.

4. Cut through the skin on the breast on either side of the breastbone to begin to remove the breast meat.

5. Use the tines of a kitchen fork to gently pull the breast meat away from the rib cage. Make short, smooth strokes with the knife tip to cut the meat cleanly and completely away.

(1) Cut through the skin where the leg meets the breast.

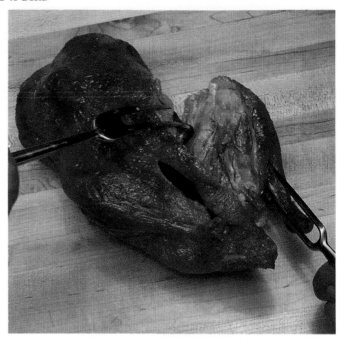

(2) Insert a kitchen fork between the drumstick and the thigh and pull the leg away.

(3) Cut the leg into two pieces through the joint between the thigh and the drumstick.

(4) Cut through the breast's skin on either side of the breastbone to remove the meat.

(5) Use a kitchen fork to gently pull the breast meat away from the rib cage and cut the breast meat completely away with a knife tip.

TABLE 18-1. DONENESS OF MEATS

	Final Internal Temperature
Rare	130–140°F
	55–60°C
Medium	140–150°F
	60–65°C
Well-done*	150–165°F
	65–72°C

* For pork, veal, and poultry.
    Allow a margin of 5 to 12°F for carryover cooking.

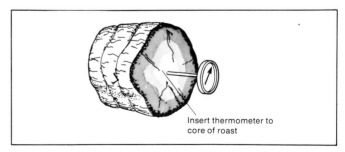

Insert thermometer to core of roast

18-10

Using an instant-reading thermometer.

Determining Doneness

The most reliable method for determining doneness in roasted foods is to use an instant-reading thermometer. The proper use of the thermometer is shown in Figure 18-10. Notice that the stem is inserted into the item's thickest part, away from any bones. It should be inserted at an angle to avoid forcing juices to jet from the meat, which could burn the hands or face. See the chart in Table 18-1, which gives the proper internal temperatures for various roasted foods. Time-temperature charts should be used only as a rough guide for planning purposes.

Some chefs rely on a doneness test that involves using a metal skewer inserted into the food (also at an angle, away from bones, and in the item's thickest portion). The skewer is then held just below the chef's lower lip. The hotter the skewer feels to the lip, the more well-done the item is.

Evaluating Quality

The factors used in evaluating quality are flavor, appearance, and texture. The flavor and aroma of a roasted food should contribute to an overall sensation of fullness, richness, and depth. This is due in part to the nature of the food and in part to the browning process. Roasted foods should have a golden-brown exterior. The color has a direct bearing on the flavor. Items that are too pale lack eye appeal and the depth of flavor associated with properly roasted foods.

A roasted food's texture depends upon the nature of the main item. In general, however, roasted foods should be tender and moist. If left on the food, the skin should be crisp, creating a contrast with the meat's texture.

Poêléing

Poêléing, a technique most often associated with white meats and game birds, is sometimes known as butter-roasting. Meats are allowed to cook in their own juices in a covered vessel on a bed of aromatic vegetables known as a matignon. The matignon then becomes a garnish served as part of the sauce. Jus (see Chapter 17, "Sauces") is often used to prepare a sauce from the pan drippings.

Mise en Place

1. Main item. Veal, capon, and small game are often prepared by this method. The addition of butter, as well as the matignon, furnish additional moisture during cooking. As in other dry-heat techniques, the meats should be trimmed of excess fat, and they are generally tied to help retain their shape and to promote even cooking.

2. Matignon. A matignon is a mirepoix (sometimes referred to as "edible mirepoix") in which the vegetables are peeled and cut into a uniform dice or julienne. Ham is traditionally included.

- Peel and cut the vegetables into a uniform dice or julienne.
- Cut the ham into a dice or julienne of the same size as the vegetables.

3. Butter. Melt whole, unsalted butter.

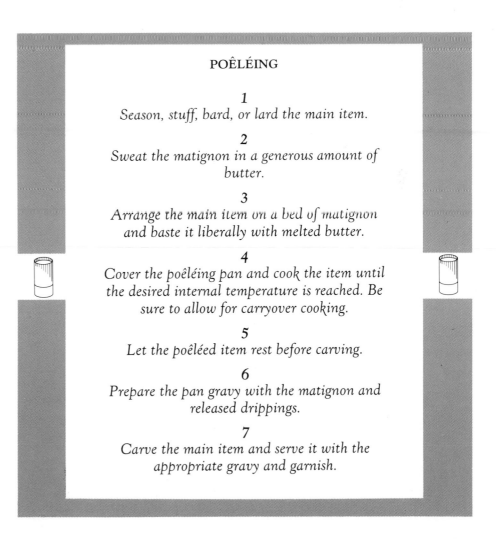

POÊLÉING

1
Season, stuff, bard, or lard the main item.

2
Sweat the matignon in a generous amount of butter.

3
Arrange the main item on a bed of matignon and baste it liberally with melted butter.

4
Cover the poêléing pan and cook the item until the desired internal temperature is reached. Be sure to allow for carryover cooking.

5
Let the poêléed item rest before carving.

6
Prepare the pan gravy with the matignon and released drippings.

7
Carve the main item and serve it with the appropriate gravy and garnish.

4. Optional components. Have available stuffing/filling and/or additional aromatics, garnish, or finishing ingredients to be used with the product during poêléing or to complete the sauce.

Method

1. Heat the oil over high heat in a flame-proof casserole.

2. Cook the main item on all sides in the hot oil, just until the surface begins to turn color. This is known as "seizing." Remove the main item.

3. Add the matignon and butter. Cook them over medium heat, stirring frequently until the onions are translucent.

4. Place the main item on the bed of matignon. Baste it liberally with melted butter.

5. Cover the casserole and place it in a moderate oven. Baste the surface from time to time with butter. If desired, remove the cover during the final cooking stage to allow the surface to brown and develop a crust.

6. When the item has reached the proper internal temperature (allowing an adequate margin for carryover cooking), remove it to a heated platter and allow it to rest before it is carved.

7. Place the casserole over high heat and add the stock or jus. Simmer until it is well-flavored and slightly reduced. Pull the casserole slightly off-center to allow the fat to collect on one side; skim.

8. Thicken the stock or jus with diluted arrowroot or cornstarch. Add any additional ingredients to finish or garnish the sauce. Adjust the seasoning to taste.

9. Slice the main item and arrange it on heated plates. Serve with the sauce.

Poêlé of Capon with Tomatoes and Artichokes

Yield: 10 servings

Capon	one 9-pound bird	one 4-kilogram bird
Salt	to taste	to taste
Pepper	to taste	to taste
Fresh herbs, as available or desired	1 bunch	1 bunch
Matignon	8 ounces	225 grams
Whole butter	as needed	as needed
Chicken stock or jus de volaille	3 pints	1.5 liters
Arrowroot	as needed	as needed
Tomato concassé	8 ounces	225 grams
Artichoke bottoms, poached, sliced	8 ounces	225 grams
Chopped herbs (parsley, chives, chervil, and tarragon)	2 tablespoons each	10 grams each

1. Season the bird with the salt and pepper and stuff the cavity with a bundle of the fresh herbs. Truss the bird.

2. Sweat the matignon in butter. Arrange the capon on the matignon. Brush it liberally with butter. Cover it in a casserole and poêlé the bird in a moderate oven for approximately 2 hours, or until it is fully cooked. Remove the cover during the final half-hour of cooking time to brown the skin.

3. Remove the capon and let it rest before carving it.

4. Place the casserole on direct heat and bring the cuisson to a boil; let it reduce slightly.

5. Add the chicken stock or jus des volaille and bring the mixture to a boil.

6. Dilute the arrowroot and add it to the stock to thicken the stock lightly. Add the tomato concassé, artichoke bottoms, and chopped herbs. Adjust the seasoning to taste. Skim the excess butter from the surface as necessary.

7. Carve the capon and serve it with the sauce.

VARIATIONS

Poêlé of Pheasant: Replace the capon with pheasant. One pheasant is enough for two portions. Adjust the cooking time as necessary. It may be desirable to seize the bird before poêléing.

Poêlé of Rabbit with Prunes: Replace the capon with a rabbit (approximately 3 to 4 pounds); replace the tomatoes and artichokes with diced prunes.

Poêlé of Squab with Fresh Herbs: Replace the capon with squab (1 per serving) and garnish the sauce with chopped, fresh herbs.

For a quick summary, refer to the abbreviated method for poêléing.

Determining Doneness

Unlike roasted items, which may be cooked to various stages of doneness, poêléed items are cooked until just done. For methods of testing, see the previous section on roasting.

Evaluating Quality

As with the other techniques, the important characteristics are flavor, appearance, and texture. Poêléing is often referred to as butter-roasting, and poêléed items should have a definite and pleasing butter taste. Although the flavors of the matignon should also be apparent in the finished dish, they should

not overpower the main item's flavor. Because the food's surface is not browned as deeply as it would be in roasting, the flavor tends to be more delicate.

Removing the cover during the final cooking stage will allow the surface of the poêléed item to brown slightly. In general, however, poêléed items should have a less pronounced color than that of roasted items. The surface should appear moist. Poêléed items should be tender and moist. The surface should develop a slight crust, which offers some contrast in textures.

SUMMARY

Grilling, roasting, and poêléing are used to produce foods that are tender and have a deep flavor. The

crust that forms as a result of most of these techniques contributes to the deep flavor and helps to protect the food. Although dry-heat techniques are notorious for their propensity to dry out foods, this tendency toward dryness will be kept to a minimum if the methods are followed carefully.

Grilled, roasted, and poêléed foods are attractive menu items because, for a variety of reasons, the ingredients most appropriate to these techniques are not commonly prepared at home. Grilling, in particular, is an increasingly popular technique for two versions. The procedure itself is fun for the patron to watch, and, because fat is not added, grilled products tend to have fewer calories than foods prepared in other ways, which makes them appealing to a health-conscious public.

Marinated and Grilled Duck Breast

<u>*Yield: 2 servings*</u>

Duck breast, boned and halved	1	1

Marinade (for 10 servings)

Soy sauce	8 ounces	240 milliliters
Water	8 ounces	240 milliliters
Ginger, fresh, coarsely chopped	1 tablespoon	15 grams
Curing salt	¼ teaspoon	1 gram

1. Trim the duck breast, if necessary, and place it in a hotel pan.
2. Combine all of the ingredients for the marinade and pour the mixture over the duck. Turn the breast to coat it evenly. Let it marinate for several hours or overnight.
3. Cook the duck under a broiler until the fat has rendered and the skin has taken on a mahogany color. The meat should still be extremely rare.
4. At service, slice the breast on the diagonal and finish it on a grill. Brush with marinade during the grilling.

Grilled Canadian Red Perch with Lime Tequila Vinaigrette

<u>*Yield: 1 serving*</u>

Vinaigrette (for 10 servings)

Rice wine vinegar	2 ounces	60 milliliters
Safflower oil	6 ounces	180 milliliters
Lime juice	1 ounce	30 milliliters
Tequila	1 ounce	30 milliliters
Cilantro, fresh, chopped	2 tablespoons	5 grams
Tomato concassé, fine dice	2 ounces	55 grams
Salt	to taste	to taste
Pepper	to taste	to taste
Red snapper fillet, skin attached	5 to 7 ounces	140 to 200 grams
Grapefruit	3 pieces	3 pieces
Avocado	3 slices	3 slices

1. Combine all the ingredients for the vinaigrette and mix them well.

2. Score the skin side of the perch with a sharp knife to create a crosshatch design.

3. At service, place the fish, skin side down, on a sizzler platter. Coat it with 1 ounce (30 milliliters) of the vinaigrette. Place the fish under a broiler and cook it halfway. Turn the fish and finish cooking it, skin side up.

4. Serve the fish with slices of fresh grapefruit and avocado.

Pakistani-style Lamb Patties

Yield: 10 servings

Oil	1 ounce	30 milliliters
Onions, minced	2 ounces	60 grams
Garlic cloves, minced	8	8
Bread crumbs, fresh	2 ounces	60 grams
Lamb, lean ground	3 pounds	1.35 kilograms
Pine nuts, toasted	3 ounces	85 grams
Eggs, beaten	2 or 3	2 or 3
Tahini (sesame paste)	1 ounce	30 grams
Parsley, chopped	3 tablespoons	7 grams
Salt	to taste	to taste
Pepper	to taste	to taste
Coriander, ground	1 teaspoon	2 grams
Cumin, ground	2 tablespoons	15 grams
Fennel, ground	1 teaspoon	2 grams
Ginger, grated	2 tablespoons	25 grams

1. Sauté the onions in hot oil until they are translucent.

2. Add the garlic and sauté it briefly. Remove the mixture from the heat.

3. Soak the bread crumbs in water. Squeeze out any excess moisture.

4. Combine the bread crumbs, onions, and garlic.

5. Add the lamb, pine nuts, beaten eggs, tahini, parsley, salt, pepper, and spices. Mix them together gently but thoroughly.

6. Shape the mixture into patties and chill the patties.

7. Grill or broil the patties to the desired doneness.

Smoked Chicken Breast with Barbecue Sauce

Yield: 1 serving

Chicken suprême	1	1

Marinade (for 10 servings)

Apple cider	1 cup	240 milliliters
Apple-cider vinegar	2 tablespoons	30 milliliters
Shallots, minced	1 tablespoon	15 grams
Garlic, minced	½ teaspoon	2.5 grams
Barbecue sauce	as needed	as needed

1. Place the chicken breast in a pan or shallow bowl. Combine the ingredients for the marinade. Pour the marinade over the breast; let the meat marinate for 1 to 2 hours.

2. Grill the chicken, turning it frequently and basting it occasionally with barbecue sauce, until it is done. Or, pan-smoke the chicken breast until the surface turns light golden, 6 to 7 minutes; then finish it in a moderate oven.

3. Reheat the remaining barbecue sauce and thin it with a little stock, if necessary. Serve the chicken breast with the sauce.

Grilled Chicken Breast with Fennel

Yield: 1 serving

Olive oil	as needed	as needed
Garlic clove, crushed	1	1
Fennel seeds, cracked	⅛ teaspoon	625 milligrams
Salt	to taste	to taste
Pepper	to taste	to taste
Chicken suprême	1	1
Fennel, julienned, cooked	1 ounce	30 grams
Whole butter	as needed	as needed
Shallots, minced	1 teaspoon	5 grams
Pernod	to taste	to taste

1. Combine the olive oil, garlic, fennel seeds, and salt and pepper. Add the chicken and marinate it briefly.

2. Grill the chicken breast, basting it occasionally with marinade, until it is done.

3. Sweat the shallots in the butter. Add the fennel and sauté it until it is heated through.

4. Add a splash of Pernod and season the fennel to taste with salt and pepper.

5. Serve the chicken on a bed of fennel. Garnish it with fennel leaves, if desired.

Smoked Noisettes of Salmon with Horseradish Beurre Blanc

Yield: 1 serving

Salmon fillets, cut into noisettes	two 3-ounce pieces	two 85-gram pieces
Salt	to taste	to taste
Pepper	to taste	to taste
Clarified butter (optional)	as needed	as needed
Basic beurre blanc	2 ounces per serving	60 milliliters per serving
Horseradish, fresh, grated	to taste	to taste
Lemon juice, fresh	to taste	to taste
Parsley, fresh, chopped	1 teaspoon	750 milligrams

1. Season the salmon and brush it with butter, if desired. Place it on a rack or steamer insert.

2. Place hickory, apple, or other hardwood chips in a heavy skillet. Place the skillet over high heat. When the chips are smoking, place the salmon in the skillet and cover it tightly.

3. Finish cooking the salmon in a hot oven for about 8 to 10 minutes.

4. Add the horseradish, lemon juice, and parsley to the beurre blanc. Adjust the seasoning.

5. Nappé the salmon with the sauce.

VARIATION

Smoked Salmon Noisettes with Zucchini "Noodles" and Tomato Coulis: Cut a zucchini into very long juliennes; sauté them until tender. Serve the salmon on the zucchini and pool heated tomato coulis around the salmon.

Broiled Stuffed Lobster

Yield: 2 servings

Lobster	one 1½-pound	one 680-gram

Stuffing

Bread crumbs	1½ ounces	45 grams
Onion, minced	2 ounces	55 grams
Celery, minced	1 ounce	30 grams
Red pepper, minced	¼ ounce	7 grams
Green pepper, minced	¼ ounce	7 grams
Butter	1½ ounces	45 grams

1. Rinse the lobster in cold water. Split it lengthwise without cutting through the back of the shell. Flatten the lobster and remove the stomach and vein.
2. Place the lobster on a grill rack, shell-side up. Grill it until the shell is red. Remove it from the rack.
3. Combine the remaining ingredients and spoon the mixture into the cavity. (Do not place it over the tail meat.)
4. Place the lobster on a sheet pan and finish it in a 400°F (205°C) oven.
5. Crack the claws but leave the meat inside. Serve the lobster with lemon wedges and drawn butter.

VARIATION

Remove the claw meat and mix it with the stuffing before placing it in the cavity. Shrimp or minced fish can also be added. Season the stuffing with Worcestershire sauce and dry sherry.

Broiled Sirloin Strip Steak with Marchand de Vin Sauce

Yield: 1 serving

Strip loin, well-trimmed	5 to 8 ounces	140 to 225 grams
Salt	to taste	to taste
Pepper	to taste	to taste
Oil	as needed	as needed
Marchand de vin sauce	1½ ounces	40 grams
Butter, whole, chilled	1 tablespoon	15 grams

1. Season the strip loin with the salt and pepper; coat it with the oil.

2. Broil the steaks to the desired doneness.

3. Heat the sauce; monté au beurre.

4. Serve the steak with the sauce.

Barbecued Spareribs

Yield: 10 servings

Marinade

Hoisin sauce	1 tablespoon	15 milliliters
Bean sauce	1 tablespoon	15 milliliters
Apple sauce	1 tablespoon	15 milliliters
Catsup	2 tablespoons	30 milliliters
Soy sauce	1 tablespoon	15 milliliters
Rice wine	2 tablespoons	30 milliliters
Peanut oil	1 tablespoon	15 milliliters
Red food coloring (optional)	¼ teaspoon	1 milliliter
Ginger, minced	½ teaspoon	2 grams
Scallion, minced	1	1
Garlic cloves, minced	2	2
Sugar	1 tablespoon	15 grams
Salt	1 teaspoon	5 grams
Pork spareribs, trimmed	1 rack	1 rack
Honey	3 tablespoons	45 milliliters

1. Combine all of the ingredients for the marinade.

2. Score the ribs with a sharp knife. Place the ribs in the marinade. Marinate them for at least 4 hours.

3. Place the ribs in a smoker at 425°F (220°C) for 30 minutes. Reduce the heat to 375°F (190°C). Smoke the ribs for 50 more minutes.

4. Brush the honey on the ribs during the last 5 minutes. Slice the ribs between the bones and serve.

Barbecued Chicken Breast with Black Bean Sauce

Yield: 1 serving

Marinade (for 5 portions)

Apple cider	4 ounces	120 milliliters
Apple cider vinegar	2½ teaspoons	12 milliliters
Shallots, minced	1¼ teaspoons	6 grams
Garlic, minced	¼ teaspoon	500 milligrams
Black peppercorns, cracked	⅛ teaspoon	250 milligrams
Chicken suprême	1	1
Barbecue sauce	as needed	as needed
Black bean sauce	2 ounces	60 milliliters

1. Combine all the ingredients for the marinade in a shallow bowl. Add the chicken; turn to coat it evenly. Marinate the chicken under refrigeration for 1 to 2 hours.
2. Preheat the grill. Add a handful of hardwood chips (hickory or apple, for example) on the coals.
3. Grill the chicken, basting it periodically with the barbecue sauce, until it is cooked through. Turn it every 5 minutes. Serve the chicken on heated plates with heated black bean sauce.

Broiled Chicken with Maître d'Hôtel Butter

Yield: 2 servings

Chicken, broiler, split	1	1
Salt	to taste	to taste
White pepper	to taste	to taste
Oil	as needed	as needed
Maître d'Hôtel butter	2 ounces	60 grams

1. Season the chicken with the salt and white pepper; rub it lightly with the oil.
2. Place the chicken under a broiler; turn it when the skin is browned.
3. Finish the chicken in an oven, if necessary.
4. Plate the chicken and top it with the maître d'hôtel butter; flash it under the broiler.

Grilled Paillards of Chicken with Tarragon Butter

Yield: 1 serving

Chicken breast, boneless, skinless, cut into paillards	5 to 6 ounces	140 to 170 grams
Salt	to taste	to taste
Pepper	to taste	to taste
Lemon juice	as needed	as needed
Oil	1 tablespoon	15 milliliters
Tarragon, fresh, chopped	1 teaspoon	750 milligrams
Tarragon butter	1 tablespoon	15 grams

1. Season the chicken breast with the salt and pepper. Combine the lemon juice, oil, and tarragon and brush the mixture on the chicken.
2. Grill the chicken until it is barely cooked through.
3. Top each paillard with a rosette or slice of the tarragon butter and serve it immediately.

VARIATIONS

Grilled Chicken Sandwich: Serve the chicken on a sliced baguette or club roll. Garnish the sandwich as desired.

Grilled Chicken with Basil and Fresh Mozzarella: Grill the chicken as indicated in the recipe, substituting chopped, fresh basil for the tarragon in the marinade. Top each grilled paillard with a fresh basil leaf and a slice of fresh mozzarella. Place the chicken under a broiler briefly before serving.

Broiled Bluefish à l'Anglaise with Maître d'Hôtel Butter

Yield: 1 serving

Bluefish fillets, skin on	5 to 6 ounces	140 to 170 grams
Salt	to taste	to taste
White pepper	to taste	to taste
Lemon juice	to taste	to taste
Butter, whole, melted	1 tablespoon	15 grams
Oil, vegetable	as needed	as needed
Fresh bread crumbs	1 ounce	30 grams
Maître d'hôtel butter	1 ounce	30 grams

(continued)

1. Season the bluefish fillets with the salt, pepper, and lemon juice.

2. Brush them with the melted butter and dip in the bread crumbs.

3. Place the fillets on an oiled sizzler platter; broil them until they are barely cooked through.

4. Top each fillet with a slice of the maître d'hôtel butter; flash them under a broiler briefly to begin melting the butter.

Broiled Skewered Lamb (Shish Kebab)

Yield: 10 servings

Marinade

Onion, large, fine dice	12 ounces	340 grams
Garlic cloves, chopped	8	8
Lemon juice	6 ounces	180 milliliters
Salt	¼ ounce	7 grams
Coriander, ground	1½ tablespoons	10 grams
Cumin, ground	½ tablespoon	3.5 grams
Oregano, fresh, chopped	½ tablespoon	1 gram
Black pepper	2¼ teaspoons	5 grams
Olive oil	8 ounces	240 milliliters
Lamb, shoulder or leg, 1¼-inch cubes	4 pounds	1.8 kilograms
Pimiento butter	10 ounces	285 grams

1. Combine all the ingredients for the marinade. Add the lamb and marinate it for 2 hours.

2. Thread the lamb onto individual skewers (approximately 6 ounces of meat per skewer).

3. Broil or grill the lamb to a medium doneness. Serve it with 1 ounce (30 grams) of the pimiento butter per portion.

Lamb Chops with Arizona Chili Butter

Yield: 1 serving

Arizona Chili Butter (for 16 servings)

Unsalted butter	1 pound	455 grams
Chili powder	1 tablespoon	7 grams
Cumin	½ teaspoon	1 gram
Paprika	½ tablespoon	3.5 grams
Hot chili powder	1 tablespoon	7 grams
Oregano	1 tablespoon	3.5 grams
Worcestershire sauce	½ tablespoon	7.5 milliliters
Tabasco sauce	¼ teaspoon	1 milliliter
Garlic powder	¼ teaspoon	575 milligrams
Onion powder	¼ teaspoon	575 milligrams
Lamb chops	2 to 3	2 to 3
Salt	to taste	to taste
Pepper	to taste	to taste
Oil	as needed	as needed

1. Combine all the ingredients for the chili butter; roll and chill.

2. Season the chops; brush them lightly with the oil.

3. Grill or broil the chops to the desired doneness.

4. Top each chop with a slice of chili butter; flash the chops under a broiler just before serving.

Bluefish with Creole Mustard Sauce

Yield: 1 serving

Bluefish steaks	5 ounces	140 grams
Oil	as needed	as needed
Creole mustard sauce	2 ounces	60 milliliters

1. Season the bluefish with salt and pepper to taste and brush them with the oil. Place the fish in a hand grill.

2. Grill or broil the fish until they are just cooked.

3. Serve the steaks with the creole mustard sauce.

Sirloin Steak "Star of Texas"

Yield: 1 order

Bread Crumb Topping (for 10 orders)

Garlic cloves, minced	2	2
Parsley, chopped	½ ounce	15 grams
Bread crumbs	6 ounces	170 grams
Butter, melted	6 ounces	170 grams
Salt	to taste	to taste
Pepper	to taste	to taste
Sirloin steaks	7 to 8 ounces	190 to 225 grams
Garlic, minced	1 teaspoon	4 grams
Salt	to taste	to taste
Pepper	to taste	to taste
Vegetable oil	as needed	as needed
Barbecue sauce	as needed	as needed

1. Combine all of the ingredients for the bread crumb topping; blend them well.

2. Rub the steaks with the garlic and season them with the salt and pepper.

3. Brush the steaks with vegetable oil, and broil them until they are rare. Glaze both sides of the steaks with barbecue sauce.

4. Top the steaks with the bread crumb mixture and finish them in a hot oven until they are brown.

Grilled Lamb Chops with Mint Sauce

Yield: 1 serving

Double lamb chops from the rib	2	2
Olive oil	as needed	as needed
Salt	to taste	to taste
Pepper	to taste	to taste
Lamb jus	2 ounces	60 milliliters
Brunoise vegetables (for example, carrot, celery, leek, onion), blanched	2 ounces	55 grams
Mint leaves, fresh, chiffonade	1 tablespoon	2 grams

1. Pound the lamb chops lightly to shape them to an even thickness.

2. Dip the chops in oil seasoned with salt and pepper; grill the chops to the desired doneness. Hold the chops on a sizzler platter.

3. Heat the lamb jus to reduce it slightly. Add the brunoise vegetables and chiffonade of mint. Adjust the seasoning with salt and pepper.

4. Nappé the chops with the sauce and serve.

Grilled Tuna on a Bed of Roasted Peppers with Balsamic Vinegar Sauce

Yield: 1 serving

Sauce (for 10 servings)

Balsamic vinegar	8 ounces	240 milliliters
Fish stock	8 ounces	240 milliliters
Tomato concassé	2 ounces	60 grams
Herbs, chopped (combination of thyme, tarragon, cilantro)	⅔ ounce	20 grams
Arrowroot	as needed	as needed
Enoki mushrooms	2 ounces	60 grams
Tuna	3½ ounces	100 grams
Salt	to taste	to taste
Pepper	to taste	to taste
Red, green, and yellow bell peppers, roasted, peeled, seeded, julienned	1 ounce	30 grams
Spinach linguini, cooked and drained	1½ ounces	45 grams
Whole butter	as needed	as needed

1. Combine the vinegar, stock, tomato concassé, and herbs. Heat the mixture and thicken it lightly with the arrowroot.

2. Add the enoki mushrooms to the sauce.

3. Rub the tuna steaks with the salt and pepper.

4. Grill the steaks to the desired doneness; butterfly them.

5. Sauté the peppers until they are hot.

6. Arrange the tuna steaks on the peppers. Nappé them with the sauce.

7. Toss the spinach linguini with the butter; serve the linguini with the tuna.

Beef Tenderloin with Garlic Glaze

Yield: 1 serving

Garlic Glaze (for 10 servings)

Glace de viande	4 ounces	120 milliliters
Garlic, roasted, pureed	6 ounces	170 grams
Beef tenderloin	5 to 6 ounces	140 to 170 grams
Jus de veau or demi-glace, finished with burgundy, heated	2 ounces	60 milliliters

1. Combine the ingredients for the garlic glaze.
2. Grill the tenderloin briefly on both sides; butterfly it. Season it with salt and pepper to taste.
3. Spread 1 ounce of the garlic glaze on the tenderloin. Gratiné it under a broiler.
4. Serve the tenderloin with the hot burgundy sauce.

Broiled Swordfish with Ginger Scallion Butter

Yield: 1 serving

Swordfish steak	5 to 7 ounces	140 to 200 grams

Marinade

Soy sauce	4 ounces	120 milliliters
Sherry wine	2 ounces	60 milliliters
Garlic, minced	½ teaspoon	2 grams
Ginger, minced	1 tablespoon	15 grams
Scallions, minced	2	2
Sugar	1 teaspoon	5 grams
Lemon juice, fresh	from 1 lemon	from 1 lemon
Ginger scallion butter	1 ounce	30 grams

1. Combine all of the ingredients for the marinade.
2. Marinate the swordfish for 15 minutes.
3. Remove the fish from the marinade and blot it dry.
4. Broil or grill the fish on both sides until it is barely cooked through.
5. Top the fish with the ginger scallion butter.

Broiled Lemon Sole on a Bed of Leeks

Yield: 1 serving

Lemon sole (or other flounder)	5 to 6 ounces	140 to 170 grams
Lemon juice	to taste	to taste
Oil	as needed	as needed
Bread crumbs, fresh	as needed	as needed
Leeks, paysanne or fermière cut	2 ounces	55 grams
Butter	as needed	as needed
Cream	1 ounce	45 milliliters

1. Season the fish with the lemon juice and with salt and pepper to taste. Dip it in the oil and drain it.
2. Dredge the fish in the crumbs; shake off the excess crumbs.
3. Place the fish on a sizzler platter. Broil it until it is cooked through.
4. Stew the leeks in the butter until they are tender. Season them with salt and pepper and finish them with the cream. Serve the fish on a bed of leeks.

Broiled Mackerel with a Compound Butter

Yield: 1 serving

Mackerel	5 to 6 ounces	140 to 170 grams
Lemon	to taste	to taste
Flour	as needed	as needed
Oil or butter	as needed	as needed
Compound butter	1 ounce	30 grams

1. Season the fish with the lemon and with salt and pepper to taste.
2. Brush or dip the fish in oil or butter.
3. Broil the fish in an oiled hand grill until it is just cooked.
4. Before serving, flash the fish under a salamander or broiler; then serve it immediately with the compound butter.

Grilled Swordfish with Pepper Cream Sauce

Yield: 1 serving

Swordfish steak	5 to 6 ounces	140 to 170 grams
Salt	to taste	to taste
Pepper	to taste	to taste
Lemon juice	1 teaspoon	5 milliliters
Oil	1 teaspoon	5 milliliters

Sauce (for 10 servings)

White wine	14 ounces	420 grams
Fish fumet	14 ounces	420 grams
Green peppercorns, drained and mashed	3 tablespoons	30 grams
Black peppercorns, cracked	3 tablespoons	20 grams
White peppercorns, cracked	3 tablespoons	20 grams
Thyme, fresh	1 sprig	1 sprig
Bay leaves	2	2
Heavy cream, reduced	6 ounces	180 milliliters

1. Season the swordfish with the salt and pepper to taste. Brush it with the lemon juice and oil. Boil the fish to the correct doneness at time of service.

2. For the sauce: Combine the wine, fumet, peppercorns, thyme, and bay leaves. Reduce the mixture by half. Remove the thyme and bay leaves. Add the cream and reduce it to the desired consistency. Adjust the seasoning to taste with salt and pepper.

3. Add chives (1 tablespoon or 2 grams per portion) to the sauce immediately prior to service. Pool the sauce on the plate and top it with grilled swordfish.

SUBSTITUTIONS

Salmon with Pepper Cream Sauce: Substitute a 5- to 6-ounce (140- to 170-gram) piece of salmon fillet or salmon steak.

Tuna with Pepper Cream Sauce: Substitute a 5- to 6-ounce (140- to 170-gram) piece of tuna.

Grilled Lamb Chops with Whole Cloves of Garlic

Yield: 1 serving

Garlic cloves, whole	3 to 4	3 to 4
Double lamb chops from rib	2	2
Olive oil, garlic-flavored	as needed	as needed
Salt	to taste	to taste
Pepper	to taste	to taste
Whole butter	1 tablespoon	15 grams
White wine	1 ounce	30 milliliters
Jus d'agneau lié	2 ounces	60 milliliters
Basil, fresh, finely minced	1 tablespoon	2 grams
Tomato concassé	1 ounce	30 grams

1. Blanch the garlic cloves in salted water; shock and peel them. Cook them in three successive changes of water until they are tender (this will remove any bitter taste).

2. Brush the chops with the garlic-flavored oil and season them with the salt and pepper. Broil the chops to the appropriate doneness. Hold them on a sizzler platter.

3. Sauté the blanched garlic cloves in the butter until they are lightly browned. Deglaze the pan with the white wine; reduce to sec.

4. Add the jus d'agneau lié and any juices from the sizzler platter; reduce the mixture lightly.

5. Add the basil and tomato. Monté au beurre. Adjust the seasoning to taste.

6. Nappé the sauce over the chops and serve.

Roast Duckling with Sauce Bigarade

Yield: 2 servings

Duckling	1	1
Salt	to taste	to taste
Pepper	to taste	to taste
Parsley stems	2 to 3	2 to 3
Thyme sprig	1	1
Bay leaf	small piece	small piece

Sauce (for 10 servings)

Sugar	1½ tablespoons	20 grams
Water	1 tablespoon	15 milliliters
Dry white wine	1½ tablespoons	25 milliliters
Cider vinegar	1½ tablespoons	25 milliliters
Orange juice concentrate	2 ounces	60 milliliters
Red currant jelly	2 ounces	60 milliliters
Demi-glace	1 quart	1 liter
Brown stock	1 pint	480 milliliters
Orange zest, julienned, blanched	of 1 orange each	of 1 orange each
Orange segments	of 1 orange each	of 1 orange each

1. Place the duckling, breast side up, on a rack. Season it with salt and pepper. Place the parsley, thyme, and bay leaf pieces in the cavity.

2. Roast the duckling until the juices run barely pink. Remove the duckling from the pan; reserve it.

3. Degrease the pan and reserve the drippings.

4. Cool the duckling, and split and partially debone it. Reserve it.

5. To prepare the sauce: Combine the sugar and water. Caramelize it carefully.

6. Add the wine, vinegar, orange juice concentrate, and currant jelly. Mix them well. Reduce the mixture by half.

7. Add the demi-glace and brown stock and bring it to a boil.

8. Add the pan drippings. Reduce the heat and simmer until the mixture is reduced to 1 quart (1 liter). Strain it through a cheesecloth. Reserve.

9. For each serving, brush the duckling with a small amount of the sauce and reheat it, until it is crisp, in a very hot oven.

10. Reheat approximately 2 ounces (60 milliliters) of sauce per serving and finish it with the blanched orange zest and orange segments. Pool the sauce on a plate and place the duckling on the sauce.

Roast Pheasant with Cranberry-Peppercorn Sauce

Yield: 2 servings

Pheasant	1	1
Salt	to taste	to taste
Pepper	to taste	to taste
Bay leaf	1	1
Thyme sprig	1	1
Mirepoix	10 ounces	285 grams

Sauce (for 10 servings)

Chicken stock	1 quart	1 liter
Red wine	4 ounces	120 milliliters
Black peppercorns, cracked	½ teaspoon	1 gram
Shallots, minced	2 tablespoons	30 grams
Bay leaf, small	1	1
Cranberries	7 ounces	180 grams
Sugar	3 tablespoons	40 grams
Arrowroot, diluted	as needed	as needed
Ruby port	2 tablespoons	30 milliliters
Whole butter	as needed	as needed

1. Trim the pheasant. Season the cavity with the salt, pepper, thyme, and bay leaf. Truss the pheasant.

2. Roast the pheasant on a bed of bones at 450°F (230°C) until its juices run pink. Remove the pheasant and let it rest.

3. Add the mirepoix to the roasting pan and caramelize. Add the chicken stock and simmer until well-flavored. Strain the pheasant jus.

4. Combine the wine, pepper, and shallots and bay leaf; reduce by half and strain.

5. Add the reduction to the pheasant jus, bring it to a boil, and simmer it for 5 minutes.

6. Add the cranberries and sugar. Simmer for 15 minutes.

7. Thicken the sauce with the diluted arrowroot. Remove it from the heat.

8. Finish the sauce with the port.

9. To serve, halve and partially debone the pheasant, brush each half with sauce, and reheat them in a hot oven.

10. Bring the sauce to a boil and finish it with whole butter. Adjust the seasoning to taste. Serve the pheasant on a pool of sauce, 2 ounces (60 milliliters) per serving.

Chicken Legs with Duxelle Stuffing

Yield: 10 servings

Chicken legs, whole	10	10
Clarified butter	2 ounces	55 grams
Shallots, minced	6 ounces	170 grams
Mushrooms, small dice	2 pounds	910 grams
Salt	to taste	to taste
Pepper, white	to taste	to taste
Heavy cream, reduced	1 cup	240 milliliters
Bread crumbs, fresh	8 ounces	225 grams
Butter, melted	as needed	as needed
Suprême sauce, heated	20 ounces	600 milliliters

1. Bone out the chicken legs. Lay the meat flat on parchment paper and fold the paper over the meat. Pound it flat with a mallet and chill it.
2. Sweat the shallots in the clarified butter.
3. Add the mushrooms and sauté them until dry to create a duxelle.
4. Season the duxelle with the salt and pepper.
5. Add the heavy cream to the duxelle.
6. Add the bread crumbs and combine all of the ingredients well.
7. Portion 3 ounces (85 grams) of the stuffing mixture onto each chicken leg. Fold the meat over the stuffing.
8. Brush each chicken piece with melted butter.
9. Roast the legs at 375°F (190°C) until they are done.
10. To serve, pool 2 ounces (60 milliliters) of suprême sauce on a heated plate; place a chicken leg on top of the sauce.

Roast Strip Loin au Jus

Yield: 10 servings

Strip loin, oven-ready	5 pounds	2.25 kilograms
Salt	to taste	to taste
Pepper	to taste	to taste
Mirepoix, coarsely chopped	6 ounces	170 grams
Brown stock or jus de veau, hot	1 quart	1 liter

1. Season the loin with salt and pepper. Begin roasting the loin with the fat side down in a very hot oven. Turn the loin when the fat starts to crackle and reduce the heat to 350°F (175°C).

2. Roast the loin to the desired doneness; remove it from the pan and let it rest for 20 minutes before carving it.

3. Add the mirepoix to the roasting pan and cook it over direct heat until the mirepoix is caramelized, the drippings are reduced, and the fat is clarified.

4. Drain the mirepoix through a colander. Return it to the roasting pan along with the hot stock or jus de veau. Deglaze the roasting pan thoroughly and simmer to achieve a good flavor. Strain the jus de veau.

5. Slice the roast and serve it with the jus de veau.

NOTE: Other sauces may be served if desired. Refer to Chapter 17 for recipes. Possibilities include Chasseur Sauce, Madeira Sauce, and Mushroom Sauce.

Salmon Fillet with Smoked Salmon and Horseradish Crust

Yield: 1 serving

Salmon fillet	3½ ounces	100 grams
Lime juice	as needed	as needed
Shallots, minced	⅛ teaspoon	1 gram
Garlic, minced	⅛ teaspoon	1 gram
Black peppercorns, crushed	⅛ teaspoon	500 milligrams

Crumb Mixture (15 servings)

Butter	2 ounces	60 grams
Shallots, minced	¼ teaspoon	1 gram
Garlic, minced	¼ teaspoon	1 gram
Bread crumbs, fresh	7 ounces	200 grams
Smoked salmon	7 ounces	3 grams
Prepared horseradish	1½ ounces	40 grams

1. Rub the salmon fillet with the lime juice, shallots, garlic, and crushed peppercorns.

2. Sauté the shallots and garlic in the butter until they are aromatic.

3. Combine all of the ingredients for the crumb mixture in a food processor and process them to a fine consistency.

4. Portion 1 ounce (30 grams) of the crumb mixture onto the salmon fillet.

5. Bake the fillet in a medium oven until it is done. Brown it under a salamander, if necessary, to brown the crumbs. Serve the fillet on heated plates.

Tenderloin of Beef with Blue Cheese Herb Crust

Yield: 1 serving

Beef tenderloin, medallion	3 ounces	85 grams

Crumb Mixture (for 10 servings)

White bread crumbs	4 ounces	115 grams
Blue cheese	2¼ ounces	60 grams
Parsley, chopped	½ ounce	15 grams
Chives, chopped	½ ounce	15 grams
Garlic cloves, minced	3	3
White pepper	to taste	to taste
Jus de veau lié	2 ounces	60 milliliters

1. Process the bread, blue cheese, parsley, chives, garlic, and white pepper to a fine crumb.
2. At service, sear the tenderloin in a nonstick pan.
3. Pack ½ ounce (15 grams) of the crumb mixture on top of the medallion. Bake it in a medium oven to the desired doneness. Brown the medallion under a salamander, if necessary. Cut the medallion in half.
4. Heat the jus de veau lié and pool it around the medallion.

Roast Leg of Lamb Boulangère

Yield: 16 servings

Leg of lamb, tied	9 to 10 pounds	4 to 4.5 kilograms
Garlic cloves, slivered	2	2
Potatoes, sliced ⅛-inch thick	4 pounds	1.8 kilograms
Onions, sliced thin	1 pound	455 grams
Brown stock, hot	40 ounces	1.2 liters
Jus d'agneau, heated	40 ounces	1.2 liters

1. Season the lamb with salt and pepper to taste; stud it with the slivered garlic.
2. Layer the sliced potatoes and onions in a rondeau. Season the layers with salt and pepper to taste. Add the stock.
3. Place the lamb on the potatoes. Roast it in a hot oven to an internal temperature of 130 to 135°F (55 to 57°C).
4. Let the leg rest before carving it.
5. Serve the sliced lamb on a bed of potatoes. Nappé it with the hot jus.

Portuguese Stuffed Leg of Lamb
(Pierna de Cordero Pascual Relleno)

Yield: 12 to 14 servings

Leg of lamb, boned (bones reserved)	7 to 8 pounds	3.2 to 3.6 kilograms
Mushrooms, chopped coarse	1 cup	240 milliliters
Lemon juice, fresh	½ ounce	15 milliliters
Olive oil	1 ounce	30 milliliters
Pork, ground	1½ pounds	680 grams
Dry sherry	6 ounces	180 milliliters
Bread crumbs, dry	½ cup	120 milliliters
Egg, whole	1	1
Heavy cream	6 ounces	180 milliliters
Oregano, fresh, chopped	¼ teaspoon	190 milligrams
Basil, fresh, chopped	¼ teaspoon	190 milligrams
Mint, fresh, chopped	½ teaspoon	385 milligrams
Cilantro, fresh, chopped	1 teaspoon	775 milligrams
Mirepoix	6 ounces	170 grams
Brown stock	1½ quarts	1.5 liters
Bay leaves	2	2
Arrowroot	as needed	as needed
Cilantro, chopped	1 tablespoon	2 grams

1. Cut the lamb in half; butterfly, pound, and season each half with salt and pepper to taste.
2. Sprinkle the mushrooms with lemon juice and sauté them in hot oil; let it cool.
3. Combine the ground pork, half of the sherry, the bread crumbs, and eggs in a food processor until they are smooth. Add the herbs and cream and pulse until all are incorporated. Adjust the seasoning to taste. Fold in the mushrooms by hand into the forcemeat.
4. Place the forcemeat on the lamb and roll and tie it with string.
5. Sear the lamb on all sides in hot oil.
6. Brown the bones in a hot oven; add the mirepoix and brown for 10 minutes. more.
7. Deglaze the pan with the remaining sherry and add the brown stock and bay leaves.
8. Add the leg of lamb on a rack (it should not touch the liquid) and glaze it every 10 minutes. Cook to an internal temperature of 150°F (65°C). Remove the lamb and reserve it.
9. Reduce the stock; thicken it with diluted arrowroot and strain. Adjust the seasoning to taste. Add the cilantro to the sauce.
10. Slice the lamb and nappé it with the sauce.

Pork Loin Stuffed with Apples and Prunes

Yield: 10 to 12 servings

Center-cut pork loin, trimmed, rib bones in (bones and trim reserved)	6 pounds	2.72 kilograms
Granny Smith apples, ¼-inch dice	3	3
Pitted prunes, ¼-inch dice	6 ounces	170 grams
Ginger, fresh, grated	½ ounce	15 grams
Vegetable oil	4 ounces	120 milliliters
Mirepoix	8 ounces	225 grams
Red wine	8 ounces	240 milliliters
Brown stock	as needed	as needed
Arrowroot	as needed	as needed

1. Cut a pocket in the eye of the loin.
2. Combine the apples, prunes, and ginger. Season them to taste with salt and pepper. Stuff the loin with the mixture and tie it with a string.
3. Season the loin with salt and pepper and sear it on all sides.
4. Roast the loin to an internal temperature of 150°F (65°C).
5. Meanwhile, brown the bones in a rondeau. Add the mirepoix and brown it; deglaze the rondeau with the red wine. Add the brown stock; simmer it for about 1 hour, until it is reduced and well-flavored.
6. Remove the loin and let it rest for 15 to 20 minutes.
7. Strain the stock. Thicken it with the arrowroot; adjust the seasoning to taste.

Roast Loin of Pork

Yield: 10 servings

Pork loin, bone in	6 pounds	2.75 kilograms
Salt	to taste	to taste
Pepper	to taste	to taste
Rosemary, dried	1 teaspoon	1 gram
Sage, dried	1 teaspoon	1 gram
Mirepoix	12 ounces	340 grams
Bread flour	2 ounces	60 grams
Pork (chicken or beef) stock, hot, strained	1 quart	1 liter

1. Remove the chine bone, leaving the ribs in. Remove the tenderloin for other use.

2. Place the pork in a greased roasting pan; rub the outside with the salt, pepper, and herbs.

3. Place the pork in a preheated 350°F (176°C) oven. Roast it for 1 hour.

4. Turn the loin and add the mirepoix; roast it for 1½ hours. When the meat is done, remove it from the pan and reserve it, covered with a clean, damp towel, in a warm place.

5. Pour about 2 ounces (60 grams) of fat from the roasting pan into a saucepan, and add the flour to make a roux. Cook the roux over low heat for about 10 minutes to brown it lightly.

6. Place the roasting pan on a range. Scrape it to loosen browned drippings. Simmer the stock until the mirepoix is tender, strain it, and bring it to a boil again. Degrease the pan.

7. Add the strained stock to the cooked roux and stir the mixture, until it is thickened and smooth. Strain through a fine china cap and adjust the seasoning to taste. Hold the gravy for service.

8. Slice the meat between the ribs and serve it with 2 ounces (60 milliliters) of gravy poured around the meat.

Roast Duckling with Red Pears, Ginger, and Green Peppercorns

Yield: 2 servings

Duckling	1	1
Parsley stems	2 to 3	2 to 3
Thyme sprig	1	1
Bay leaf	small piece	small piece

Sauce (for 10 servings)

Cider vinegar	2 ounces	60 milliliters
Sugar	2 ounces	55 grams
Red pear puree	3 ounces	85 grams
Duck jus, flavored with ginger	1 quart	1 liter
Green peppercorns	½ teaspoon per order	3 grams per order
Plum brandy	2 teaspoons per order	10 milliliters per order
Whole butter	2 teaspoons per order	9 grams per order

(continued)

1. Season the duckling with salt and pepper to taste. Place herbs in the cavity of the bird.

2. Roast the duckling until its juices run barely pink. Remove the duckling from the oven. Cool, split, and partially debone it. Reserve.

3. Combine the vinegar and sugar; bring the mixture to a boil and cook until it is barely golden.

4. Add the pear puree and duck jus; let the mixture reduce slightly. Adjust the seasoning to taste.

5. Coat the duckling with a small amount of the sauce and reheat it until crisp in a very hot oven.

6. Reheat approximately 2 ounces (60 milliliters) of the sauce per serving and finish it with green peppercorns, plum brandy, and whole butter. Pool the sauce on the plate and top with the duckling.

Roast Tenderloin of Pork with Honey and Thyme

Yield: 10 orders

Pork tenderloin	2½ pounds	1.5 kilograms
Shallots, minced fine	1 tablespoon	15 grams
Garlic, minced fine	½ teaspoon	2 grams
Tomato paste	1 ounce	30 grams
Dijon-style mustard	⅔ ounce	20 grams
Red wine vinegar	1½ ounces	45 milliliters
Honey	1¾ ounces	50 grams
Thyme leaves, fresh, minced	1 teaspoon	1 gram
Black peppercorns, crushed	1 teaspoon	2 grams
Brown stock	22 ounces	660 milliliters
Arrowroot	½ ounce	15 grams

1. Sear the pork in a nonstick pan. Remove it.

2. Add the shallots, garlic, tomato paste, and mustard to the pan. Pincé.

3. Deglaze the pan with the red wine vinegar and honey. Add the thyme and peppercorns.

4. Glaze the tenderloin with the mustard and wine vinegar mixture.

5. Roast the meat in a medium oven until it is done.

6. Deglaze the roasting pan with the brown stock. Add diluted arrowroot; simmer the mixture until it is thickened. Adjust the seasoning to taste with salt and pepper.

7. Slice the pork on a bias. Nappé it with the sauce.

Roast Duckling with Plum Sauce

Yield: 2 servings

Ducklings	one 3-pound bird	one 1.35-kilogram bird
Salt	to taste	to taste
Pepper	to taste	to taste
Parsley sprigs	2	2
Thyme leaves	pinch	pinch
Bay leaf	½	½

Glaze (for 10 servings)

Soy sauce	12 ounces	360 milliliters
Honey	3 ounces	85 grams
Black peppercorns, cracked	5 to 6	5 to 6
Orange zest, grated	from 1 orange	from 1 orange
Ginger root, grated	2 tablespoons	30 grams
Garlic cloves, split	2	2
Cilantro, chopped	1 ounce	30 grams

Gastrique

Cider vinegar	⅓ cup	80 milliliters
Sugar	⅓ cup	80 milliliters
Plum puree (including skins)	4 ounces	115 grams
Jus de canard lié	16 ounces	480 milliliters
Kirsch	to taste	to taste
Salt	to taste	to taste
Pepper	to taste	to taste
Whole butter	as needed	as needed

1. Place the duck, breast up, on a rack. Rub it with the salt and pepper. Place the parsley, thyme, and bay leaf halves in the duck's cavity.

2. Mix together all of the ingredients for the glaze and brush the duckling with it.

3. Roast the duckling in a very hot oven for 15 minutes. Turn the oven down to 350°F (175°C). Roast the duck, brushing it occasionally with more glaze, until it is done. Total roasting time is approximately 1 hour and 15 minutes.

4. Remove the duck and let it rest while completing the sauce.

(continued)

5. Bring the gastrique to a boil; cook it until it is just golden. Add the plum puree and return it to a boil. Add the jus de canard lié, return the mixture to a boil, and simmer to reduce it slightly. Adjust the seasoning with the kirsch and salt and pepper, if necessary. Monté au beurre at service.

6. Split the duck and partially debone the breast. Reheat it in a very hot oven to crisp the skin.

7. Serve the duck (half bird per serving) on a pool of sauce; garnish each dish with sliced plums and mint leaves.

NOTE: After defrosting, the duckling should be kept in the refrigerator overnight, lightly covered, to dry its skin.

Roast Turkey with Chestnut Stuffing

Yield: 12 to 15 servings

Turkey, whole	one 12-pound bird	one 5.5-kilogram bird
Salt	to taste	to taste
Pepper	to taste	to taste

Chestnut Stuffing

Onion, minced	4 ounces	115 grams
Bacon fat	4 ounces	115 grams
Bread cubes, dry	12 ounces	340 grams
Chicken stock, hot	4 ounces	120 milliliters
Egg, beaten	1	1
Parsley, chopped	½ ounce	15 grams
Black pepper	½ teaspoon	1 gram
Sage, fresh, chopped	1 teaspoon	1 gram
Chestnuts, cooked, peeled, chopped	8 ounces	225 grams

1. Season the outside of the turkey with the salt and pepper. Place it on a rack in a roasting pan. Roast it at 425°F (220°C) for 15 minutes. Reduce the heat to 350°F (175°C) and roast the turkey to an internal temperature of 150°F (65°C).

2. Sauté the onion in bacon fat until tender.

3. Combine the bread cubes, chicken stock, and egg and add to the onion.

4. Add the parsley, pepper, sage, and chestnuts. Mix them all well.

5. Place the stuffing in a buttered hotel pan and cover it with parchment paper. Bake the stuffing at 350°F (175°C) for 45 minutes.

6. Let the turkey stand at least 15 minutes before carving it. Serve it with pan gravy and the chestnut stuffing.

Roast Monkfish with Niçoise Olives and Pernod Sauce

Yield: 10 servings

Marinade

Lime juice	2 ounces	60 milliliters
Green peppercorns, mashed	1 tablespoon	5 grams
Tarragon, chopped	1 tablespoon	3 grams
Shallots, minced	1 tablespoon	15 grams
Monkfish, boneless, trimmed of connective tissue	3 pounds, 8 ounces	1,500 grams
Oil	as needed	as needed
Tomato paste	½ ounce	15 grams
Pernod	1 tablespoon	15 milliliters
Beurre blanc	16 ounces	480 milliliters
Niçoise olives, pitted, sliced	1 ounce	30 grams

1. Combine all ingredients for the marinade. Add the monkfish and marinate it for 15 to 30 minutes.
2. Coat a sauté pan with the oil. Heat the pan under a broiler until it is very hot. Sear the monkfish in the hot pan on all sides.
3. Finish in a 350°F (175°C) oven. Remove the monkfish and keep it warm.
4. Pincé the tomato paste in the pan. Deglaze the pan with the Pernod. Add the beurre blanc and olives. Adjust the consistency.
5. Slice the monkfish and fan it on plates. Nappé it with the sauce.

Roast Venison with Mustard Sauce

Yield: 10 servings

Venison roast from loin or leg, boneless, tied	4 pounds	1.8 kilograms
Salt	to taste	to taste
Pepper	to taste	to taste
Jus de veau lié (prepare as for jus de veau, substituting venison stock for veal stock)	20 ounces	600 milliliters
Heavy cream	8 ounces	240 milliliters
Dry white wine	2 ounces	60 milliliters
Creole-style mustard	2 ounces	55 grams

(continued)

1. Season the roast with the salt and pepper. Sear it on all sides.

2. Roast it in a moderate oven to the desired doneness.

3. Let the roast rest for 15 minutes before carving it.

4. To prepare the sauce: Reduce any drippings in the roasting pan and clarify the fat. Pour off the fat.

5. Deglaze the roasting pan with the jus de veau lié; stir it well to release the fond. Pour it into a saucepan.

6. Add the heavy cream; simmer until it has reduced.

7. Whip the wine and mustard into a smooth paste and add it to the sauce. Adjust the seasoning to taste with salt and pepper.

8. Carve the roast; serve each serving with approximately 2 ounces (60 milliliters) of sauce.

VARIATIONS

Roast Venison with Garlic Glaze: Mix together 1 part meat glaze and 2 parts pureed roasted garlic. Spread the glaze on the roast during the final part of roasting. Serve with Mushroom Sauce.

Roast Venison with Sauce Marsala: Serve with Marsala Sauce.

Roast Venison with Tarragon Sauce: Infuse the jus de veau lié with fresh rosemary. Finish the sauce to order with Tarragon Butter.

Breast of Cornish Game Hen, Minnesota Woodsman's Style

Yield: 2 servings

Cornish game hen	1	1
Bacon, minced	½ ounce	15 grams
Butter	1¼ ounces	35 grams
White mushrooms, minced	2 ounces	55 grams
Morels, minced	2 ounces	55 grams
Shallots, finely minced	1 teaspoon	5 grams
Garlic, finely minced	¼ teaspoon	1 gram
Thyme, fresh	1 stem	1 stem
Bay leaf	½	½
Sage, fresh	3 leaves	3 leaves
Madeira	¾ ounce	25 milliliters
Egg white	¾ ounce	25 milliliters
Heavy cream	3½ ounces	105 milliliters

1. Carefully remove the legs from the hen. Remove all meat from the bones. Trim away the skin, tendons, and fat. There should be about ½ pound (225 grams) of leg meat. Cut the meat into a small dice. Hold the meat in the refrigerator until needed.

2. Remove the first two joints from the wing, leaving one wing joint attached to the breast. (The breast should be left on the bone, not split.) Hold it in the refrigerator until needed.

3. Render the bacon in a sauteuse over medium heat.

4. Add ¾ ounce (20 grams) of the butter and melt it. Add the white mushrooms and morels and sauté them.

5. Add the shallots and garlic and sauté until thickened.

6. Add the thyme, bay leaf, sage, and Madeira. Reduce until thickened.

7. Remove the mixture from the sauteuse. Discard the bay leaf, thyme, and sage. Let the mixture cool.

8. Meanwhile, place the chilled leg meat and egg white in a food processor. Process them to a paste (20 to 30 seconds). Scrape down the sides of the bowl. Add the heavy cream and pulse the machine on and off until the cream is just incorporated.

9. Remove the leg meat to a bowl. Fold in the cooled mushroom mixture. Place the mixture in a pastry bag with a plain tip.

10. Loosen the skin from the breast meat. Pipe about 2 ounces (55 grams) of the meat/mushroom mixture between the skin and breast meat on each side of the breast. Smooth out the surface to spread the filling evenly.

11. Place the hen in a baking dish. Brush them lightly with the remaining butter and season them with salt and pepper to taste. Bake them in a preheated 350°F (175°C) oven for 25 minutes.

12. To serve, remove the breast with one joint of the wing from the rib cage. Slice the breast on a slight diagonal into 4 slices. Fan the slices out on a warm plate.

Lamb Chops with Artichokes (Bracioline di Agnello con Carciofi)

Yield: 10 servings

Rib or loin lamb chops (per order)	2 to 3	2 to 3
Marinade		
Olive oil	4 ounces	120 milliliters
Lemon juice	from 2 lemons	from 2 lemons
Soy sauce	2 ounces	60 milliliters
Thyme, fresh, chopped	1 tablespoon	2 grams

(continued)

Artichoke Mixture

Shallots, minced	3 tablespoons	42 grams
Garlic, minced	2 teaspoons	9 grams
Olive oil	2 ounces	60 milliliters
Zucchini, ½-inch julienne	¾ pound	340 grams
Tomato concassé	1 cup	240 milliliters
Artichoke, cooked, leaves and bottoms reserved separately	10	10
Pepperoncini, chopped	1 tablespoon	15 grams

1. Trim the chops. Combine all the ingredients for the marinade. Add the chops and marinate them under refrigeration for 2 to 3 hours.

2. To prepare the artichoke mixture: Sauté the shallots and garlic in the oil. Add the zucchini first, then the tomato concassé and artichokes. Season the mixture with the pepperoncini and with and pepper to taste.

3. Grill or broil the chops to the desired doneness.

4. Serve the chops on a bed of the artichoke mixture. Garnish them with artichoke leaves.

Breast of Chicken with Oyster Stuffing

Yield: 1 serving

Chicken suprême	1	1

Stuffing (for 4 servings)

Butter	2 teaspoons	10 grams
Scallion, finely diced	1 medium	20 grams
Red pepper, finely diced	4 tablespoons	20 grams
Green pepper, finely diced	4 tablespoons	20 grams
Celery, finely diced	4 tablespoons	20 grams
Shucked oysters, juices reserved	8	8
Corn bread	2 ounces	60 grams
Egg white	1	20 grams

Sauce

Tomato paste	2 teaspoons	8 grams
Roasted garlic, minced to a paste	2 teaspoons	8 grams
Red wine	1½ ounces	45 milliliters
Brown stock	¾ cup	180 milliliters
Heavy cream	2 tablespoons	30 milliliters
Arrowroot, diluted in small amount of cold water or stock	1 teaspoon	3 grams

1. Cut a pocket in each chicken breast from the wing end.

2. Heat the butter in a sauteuse. Add the scallions, red and green pepper, and celery and sweat them. Remove them from the heat and let them cool.

3. Heat the liquor from oysters separately. Add the oysters, and poach them gently for about 1 minute, just until the edges begin to curl. Remove the oysters from the liquor and cool them. Reserve the oyster liquor. Cut the oysters into 3 pieces each.

4. Crumble the corn bread and moisten it with the oyster liquor. Allow the mix to cool to room temperature. Add cooled oysters and vegetables; season the mixture with pepper.

5. Use one quarter of the oyster stuffing for each suprême, stuffing loosely into the pockets.

6. Bake the chicken breasts at 350°F (175°C) until the juices from the breast run clear when pierced with a skewer.

7. To prepare the sauce: Combine the tomato paste and garlic paste in a saucepan over high heat; sauté them briefly to caramelize.

8. Add the red wine and stir until the sauce is smooth; reduce it.

9. Add the brown stock and reduce it.

10. Add the heavy cream. Continue to simmer the sauce. Thicken the sauce with the diluted arrowroot and simmer for an additional 2 to 3 minutes.

11. To serve the chicken, remove and discard the skin. Add any pan juices to the sauce. Slice the breasts into medallions and place them on warm plates, nappé with the sauce, and serve immediately.

Chapter 19

Dry-heat Cooking with Fats and Oils

All of the cooking techniques presented in this chapter rely on a fat or oil to act as the cooking medium. As the amount of oil is altered in relation to the quantity of food being cooked, different effects are achieved. The techniques using a fat or oil are:

- sautéing
- stir-frying
- panfrying
- deep-frying

Sautéing and stir-frying use only a small amount of oil, resulting in a well-developed flavor. Panfrying and deep-frying use a proportionately larger amount of oil and a coated product; the result is an interesting combination of flavors and textures.

The techniques described in this chapter all take a brief amount of time, use high heat, and require tender, portion-size or smaller pieces of meat, poultry, or fish. They are considered dry-heat methods because no liquid (stock or water) is added during the cooking time. Although oils pour at room temperature and might seem to be liquid, they function differently than liquids such as stock, milk, and water.

TECHNIQUES USING A SMALL AMOUNT OF OIL

Sautéing

Because sautéing is a rapid technique and does not have the tenderizing effect of some of the moist-heat methods, the food to be sautéed must be naturally tender. This technique cooks food rapidly in a small amount of fat over relatively high heat. The juices released during cooking form the base for a sauce made in the same pan and served with the sautéed item.

The sauce serves three purposes: it captures the food's flavor that is lost during cooking; it introduces additional flavor (an important factor because tender foods have a delicate flavor); and it adds moisture, which counteracts the dryness resulting from the sautéing process.

Stir-frying, generally associated with Asian styles of cooking and successfully borrowed by innovative Western chefs, shares many similarities with sautéing. Foods to be stir-fried are customarily cut into small pieces and cooked rapidly in a small amount of oil.

Mise en Place

1. Main item. Cut the main item into an appropriate size. Trim away the fat, silverskin, and gristle. For poultry suprême and fillets of fish, remove the skin and bones. Pound or butterfly the meats to achieve an even thickness. Dust the item with flour. This is generally recommended for meat cut into strips (émincé) and for chicken and fish. One particular application of sautéing, *à la meunière*, requires dusted meats. Dusting is optional otherwise, and many chefs feel that it is not always desirable.

2. Cooking medium. The cooking medium must be able to reach relatively high temperatures without breaking down or smoking. Have available clarified butter, neutral-flavored oil, olive oil, or rendered fats such as bacon, goose fat, or lard.

3. Liquid for deglazing. Have available wine, stock, cognac or liqueur, fortified wine, or water.

4. Liquid base for the sauce. Have available jus lié of the appropriate flavor, meat glaze, or vegetable coulis or purees.

5. Optional components. Some possibilities to have available are aromatics to flavor the sauce, such as shallots, garlic, peppercorns, or spices; finishing ingredients, such as whole butter, heavy cream (may be reduced), crème fraîche, liaison, fresh herbs, and compound butters; and garnishing ingredients, such as wild or domestic mushrooms, capers, cornichons, or julienned meats, depending upon the recipe.

See Figure 19-1 for a sauté mise en place, in this case for Chicken Sauté Provençal.

Method

1. Heat a small amount of the cooking medium in an appropriate-size sauté pan over high heat. The cooking medium lubricates the pan and prevents the food from sticking. It also does assist in even heat transfer from the pan to the item.

19-1

Mise en place for Chicken Sauté Provençal.

Red meats and/or very thin meat pieces will require the fat to be at, or nearly at, the smoking point. Less intense heat is required for white meats, fish, and shellfish. The pan and the cooking medium must reach the correct temperature before the main item is added so that a good crust will form on the food's exterior.

2. Season the main item, if desired.

3. Add the main item to the pan in a single layer. It is important that the pan be of an appropriate size, to avoid overcrowding. If too much is put in the pan, the pan's temperature will drop quickly and a good seal will not form on the food. Without this seal, juices are rapidly released and the result is more a stew than a sauté. Equally important, the pan must not be too large. This can cause the drippings to scorch, rendering them unsuitable for the sauce. Figure 19-2 shows the proper relationship between the pan size, the main item, and the amount of cooking medium used.

4. Let the main item sauté undisturbed on the first side until the proper color develops on the bottom. Place the skin side in the pan first. The side that sautés first will generally have the best appearance. Very thin pieces of meat are generally cooked completely on top of the stove, over high heat. Larger cuts, or meats that must be cooked through (veal, chicken, and pork, for example), may need to have the heat beneath them lowered slightly or may need to be finished in the oven, either in the sauté pan or in a second pan.

5. Remove the main item and add aromatics and garnish items that require some cooking time, such as shallots, garlic, mushrooms, or tomato concassé. This step must not be overlooked, be-

19-2 RELATION OF PAN SIZE, MAIN ITEM, AND AMOUNT OF COOKING MEDIUM

(1) The correct amount of fat in the pan for sautéing.

(2) The correct amount of product in the pan. The chicken breast, shown here, has been lightly floured.

cause juices released into the sauce by these ingredients could cause it to taste bitter or to be overly thin. Shallots and garlic, especially, will impart a harsh flavor if they are not first cooked in butter.

6. Deglaze the pan by adding a small amount of an appropriate liquid, according to the recipe. Stir the mixture to loosen all the drippings (or fond) and allow them to reduce until they are syrupy.

7. Add jus of the proper flavor or any other base liquid for the sauce. Allow the sauce to simmer until the proper flavor and consistency are reached.

8. Add pre-reduced heavy cream, if indicated, as well as ingredients that need only to be heated in the sauce, such as fresh herbs, mustard, peppercorns, and capers. Final adjustments to the sauce's flavor are made at this point. Ingredients such as fortified wines, citrus juices, zest, and salt and pepper are frequently used. Any garnish indicated by the recipe is also added. The sautéed item may need to be returned to the sauce at this point to be reheated briefly and coated thoroughly with the sauce.

9. Finish the sauce with butter, if indicated. If the product was returned to the sauce for reheating, remove it again and place it on a heated plate or serving dish before adding the butter.

10. Season the food, if necessary, and serve it immediately on heated plates.

Steps in the sauté method are shown in Figure 19-3. For a quick summary, refer to the abbreviated method for sautéing.

Determining Doneness

Determining doneness in sautéed foods is an imprecise science. In the following guidelines, cooking times for various meats, poultry, and fish are noticeably absent.

Although it would be helpful to indicate that a strip loin steak, for example, will be cooked to medium rare in 6 to 7 minutes, such an instruction ignores some crucial factors: the intensity of the heat beneath the pan, the pan's material, the number of meat pieces in the pan, how well aged the meat is, the conditions under which the meat was raised and/or harvested,

(1) Turn the chicken when the first side is properly browned. Note that the skin side is placed in the pan first.

(2) The fond.

SAUTÉING

1
Sauté the item on both sides in a hot pan and hot oil until it is properly browned.

2
Remove the main item and finish it in an oven, if necessary.

3
Deglaze the pan.

4
Add the liquid for the sauce.

5
Reduce the sauce.

6
Add the finishing ingredients (except butter), if appropriate.

7
Adjust the seasoning to taste.

8
Return the main item to the pan to reheat it, if necessary.

9
Monté au beurre, if desired.

(3) Deglazing the pan. The shallots have been allowed to cook until they are translucent for the best flavor.

(4) The garnish is added to the pan.

(5) The sautéed chicken is returned to the sauce to reheat.

Chicken Sauté Provençal

<u>Yield:</u> *1 serving*

Chicken suprême	1	1
Salt	to taste	to taste
Pepper	to taste	to taste
Flour	as needed	as needed
Vegetable oil	as needed	as needed
Whole butter	½ ounce	15 grams
Garlic, minced	1 teaspoon	8 grams
Chablis	1½ ounces	45 milliliters
Tomato concassé	3 ounces	100 grams
Black olives, sliced or julienne	2	2
Anchovy fillet, mashed to a paste	⅓	⅓
Fresh basil leaf, chiffonade	1	1

1. Season the chicken suprême with the salt and pepper. Dredge it lightly with the flour, shaking off any excess.

2. Heat the vegetable oil in a sauté pan and sauté the chicken breast until it is golden brown and cooked through. Remove the breast from the pan and keep it warm.

3. Pour off any excess fat from the sauté pan, and add the butter. Return the pan to the heat. Add the garlic to the melted butter and sauté it briefly.

4. Deglaze the pan with the chablis, stirring well to release all of the drippings. Add the tomato concassé, olives, and anchovy paste. Bring this mixture to a simmer and cook it for a few minutes or until the flavor is developed.

5. Return the chicken breast along with any released juices to the sauté pan and toss it to coat the chicken with the sauce.

6. Serve the chicken with the sauce on a heated plate.

and so on. In general, the thinner and more delicate the piece of meat, the more quickly it will cook. For further information, review the section on determining doneness for grilled meats in Chapter 18.

Evaluating Quality

The following evaluations are for the quality of the sautéed item, not the sauce that accompanies it. Sauces should be evaluated using the standards established for specific sauces in Chapter 17. The three things to use as a gauge of quality are flavor, color, and texture. The object of sautéing is to produce a flavorful exterior, resulting from proper browning, which serves to intensify the food's flavor. Weak flavor indicates that the food

was sautéed at an overly low temperature or that the pan was too crowded.

The proper color depends upon the product. Red meats and game should have a deep-brown exterior. White meats, such as veal, pork, and poultry, should have a golden or amber exterior. Lean white fish will be pale gold when sautéed as skinless fillets, whereas steaks of firm fish, such as tuna, will take on a darker color. In all cases, the item should not be extremely pale or gray. Improper color is an indication that incorrect pan size or improper heat levels were used.

Only naturally tender foods should be sautéed, and after sautéing the product should remain tender and moist. Excessive dryness is a signal that the food was allowed to overcook, that it was cooked too far in advance and held too long, or that it was sautéed at a temperature higher than necessary.

Stir-frying

Because items to be stir-fried are cut into small pieces, which acts as a means of tenderizing the food, the food does not need to be as naturally tender as for sautés, where it is left in portion-size pieces. The foods should be relatively tender, however, and all bits of fat, gristle, or silverskin must be removed for the best results.

Mise en Place

1. Main item(s). A variety of foods may be combined in this technique (meat and vegetables, poultry and fish, and so on), but whatever the main item is, it should be carefully trimmed and cut into regular pieces. Cut the main item into an appropriate size and shape, generally thin strips. Marinate it

briefly, if required by the recipe. Pat it dry before adding it to the cooking oil.

2. Cooking medium. The oil should be able to withstand rather high temperatures without breaking down or smoking excessively. Peanut oil, because of its flavor and its high smoking point, is traditionally used.

3. Liquid for the sauce. A variety of liquids may be used. The ratio of liquid to main item is generally lower than it is for a sauce prepared for a sautéed item. Have available fortified wine, soy sauce, meat glaze, or other liquids.

4. Optional components. These may include aromatics, such as finely minced or chopped herbs, spices, citrus zest, mushrooms, or other aromatics as required by type and by recipe; vegetable garnishes such as vegetables cut into thin juliennes, dices, or on the bias, for quick cooking; or thickeners. It is often advisable to very lightly thicken the sauce for a stir-fried dish. The thickener is diluted with a small amount of liquid and added at the last moment. It should not affect the flavor. Have available diluted arrowroot, cornstarch, or rice flour.

Method

1. Heat the peanut oil or other cooking oil in a wok or large sauté pan.

2. Add the main item to the hot oil. The temperature must be very high and the main item must be as dry as possible. This will help lessen splattering that can occur when water comes in contact with hot oil. It will also allow a crust to form on the main item, which intensifies the food's flavor and gives it a good color.

3. Keep the food in constant motion by stirring, lifting, and tossing.

4. Cook for a short amount of time over high heat.

5. Add any aromatics required by the recipe at the appropriate point (longest-cooking in first, shortest-cooking in last). Continue to stir-fry until all of the components are properly cooked and very hot.

6. Add the liquid for the sauce and any necessary thickener. Cook until the liquid comes to a simmer so that the correct flavor is achieved and the sauce is properly thickened.

7. Serve the food immediately on heated plates.

For a quick summary, refer to the abbreviated method for stir-frying.

Determining Doneness

Stir-fried foods should not appear raw and should have an appropriate color, according to type. The texture should be moist and tender.

Evaluating Quality

The characteristics of properly prepared stir-fried foods are basically the same as those of sautéed foods. Refer to the section on evaluating quality for sautéed foods, above.

TECHNIQUES USING MORE OIL

Panfrying

Although this technique shares similarities with sautéing, it has some important differences. Whereas a sautéed item is often lightly dusted with flour and quickly cooked over high heat in a small amount of oil, a panfried food is usually coated with batter or breaded and cooked in a larger amount of oil over less intense heat. The product is cooked more by the oil's heat than by direct contact with the pan.

In panfrying, the hot oil seals the food's coated surface and thereby locks the natural juices inside in-

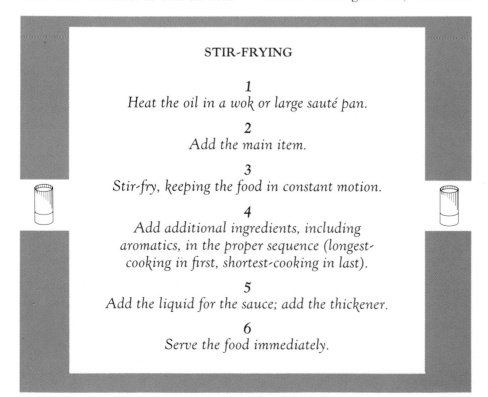

STIR-FRYING

1
Heat the oil in a wok or large sauté pan.

2
Add the main item.

3
Stir-fry, keeping the food in constant motion.

4
Add additional ingredients, including aromatics, in the proper sequence (longest-cooking in first, shortest-cooking in last).

5
Add the liquid for the sauce; add the thickener.

6
Serve the food immediately.

stead of releasing them. Because no juices are released and a larger amount of oil is involved, any accompanying sauce is made separately.

Mise en Place

1. Main item. Cut the main item into an appropriate size. Trim away any fat, silverskin, and gristle. Remove the skin and bones for poultry suprêmes and fillets of fish, if necessary or desired. Pound the chicken, veal, pork, or beef to an even thickness.

2. Standard breading procedure setup or batter.

3. Cooking medium. (The fat or oil should be able to reach a high temperature without breaking down or smoking.) Have available clarified butter (usually used in combination with oil), neutral-flavored oil, olive oil, or rendered fats such as bacon, goose fat, or lard.

4. Optional components. Have available, if desired or called for by the recipe, fillings, stuffings, or sauce.

Figure 19-4 shows a mise en place for panfried, breaded cutlets.

Method

1. Add the filling, if required by the recipe. Some items are butterflied and stuffed. Others may have a pocket cut into them. Do not add too much stuffing because most stuffings will expand during cooking.

2. Complete the standard breading procedure one hour in advance of cooking and chill the breaded item to allow the coating to firm and dry (see Fig. 19-5). Do not stack the breaded items or let them touch each other, or they will become sticky and mat together.

19-4

Mise en place for panfried breaded cutlets

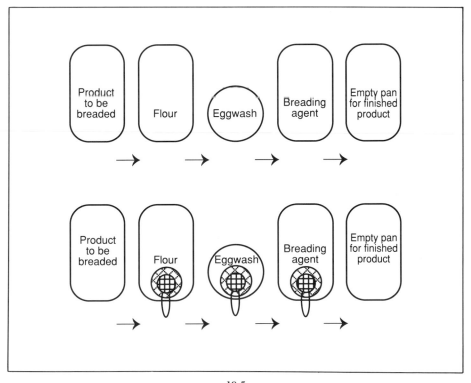

19-5

Standard breading procedures.

- Dry the main item well.
- Hold the main item in the left hand (for a right-handed person) and dip it in flour. Shake off any excess.
- Still using the left hand, transfer the main item to the egg wash. With the right hand, turn the item to coat it evenly.
- Again using the right hand, transfer the egg-washed item to the bread crumbs. With the left hand, press the crumbs evenly over the surface and remove the item to a holding tray. (If left-handed, use opposite hands and reverse the workflow described above.)

3. Heat the cooking medium in a sautoir of an appropriate size over medium-high heat. In general, the cooking medium should come one-quarter to one-half the way up the sides of the food; the thinner the main item, the less oil is required. Figure 19-6 illustrates the proper relationship of pan size to the main item and the amount of oil used. The pan and the cooking medium must reach the correct temperature before the product is added, so that a good crust forms on the food's exterior. When a faint haze or slight shimmer is noticeable, the cooking medium is hot enough.

4. Add the main item to the pan in a single layer, making sure that the pieces do not touch one another. The pan must be large enough to avoid overcrowding. If the pan is crowded, the oil's temperature will drop quickly and a good seal will not form. If this happens, the food may absorb the oil and the breading can become soggy or even fall away in places.

5. Allow the main item to panfry on the first side until the breading is well-browned. Keep the pieces in motion, either by gently

Breaded Veal Cutlet Gruyère

Yield: 1 serving

Veal cutlet, breaded	5 to 6 ounces	140 to 170 grams
Vegetable oil	as needed	as needed
Tomato slices, thin	2 or 3	2 or 3
Swiss cheese slice	1	1
Parsley, chopped	as needed	as needed
Mushroom sauce	2 ounces	60 milliliters

1. Panfry the breaded veal cutlet in the oil until it is golden brown on both sides. Place the cutlet on a sizzler platter. Arrange the tomato slices on the cutlet; cover these with a slice of cheese.

2. Place the cutlet under a broiler to melt and lightly brown the cheese.

3. Sprinkle the cutlet with the parsley and serve it with the mushroom sauce.

swirling the pan or by moving the pieces with tongs. (Forks are not used for this purpose—or in any other dry-heat method—because they can pierce the food and cause the release of valuable juices.) A layer of cooking fat should lie between the product and the pan. The food is then turned once and cooked to the appropriate degree of doneness.

19-6

Proper amount of cooking fat for panfrying.

Thin pieces of meat are generally cooked completely on top of the stove over moderate heat. Larger cuts or meats that must be cooked through, such as veal and chicken, may need additional cooking over low heat once they have browned or may need finishing in the oven, uncovered.

6. Briefly drain the food on absorbent paper toweling, season it, if necessary, and serve it on heated plates with the appropriate sauce.

Figure 19-7 shows two steps in the panfrying method. For a quick summary, refer to the abbreviated method of panfrying.

Determining Doneness

As is true for sautéed foods, it is difficult to give precise instructions for determining doneness in pan-fried foods, for the same reasons. All panfried foods are to be cooked through (*à point*). In general, the thinner and more delicate the meat, the more quickly it will cook.

19-7 TWO STEPS IN THE PANFRYING METHOD

PANFRYING

1
Heat the cooking medium.

2
Add the main item (usually breaded or batter-coated) to the pan in a single layer.

3
Panfry the food on the first side until it is well-browned.

4
Turn the item and cook it to the desired doneness.

5
Remove the main item and finish it in an oven, if necessary.

6
Drain the item on absorbent paper.

7
Season and serve it with the appropriate sauce and garnish.

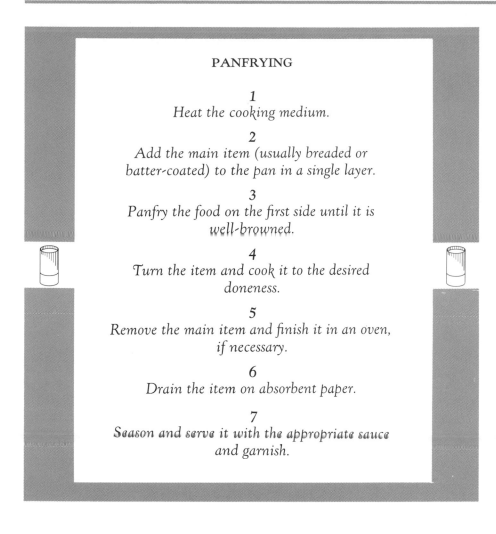

(1) The main ingredient in a single layer in the pan.

(2) Properly browned panfried cutlets.

Meats. Panfried items may be held for a short time before service, and even thin pieces will retain enough heat to continue cooking after they have been removed from the pan. It is thus best to err on the side of undercooking. The following indicators are inexact but serve as guidelines. The outside of the panfried item should be evenly golden, with a firm crust. A slight amount of "give" should occur when the meat is pressed with a fingertip. Any running juices should show either a "thread of pink" or be nearly colorless.

Fish and shellfish. Avoid overcooking fish and shellfish, which are more delicate than animal meats. Their connective tissues and proteins cook at a lower temperature, so the heat is able to travel rapidly through the fish.

The fish should offer only a small amount of resistance when pressed with the fingertip, and it is best to err on the side of undercooking.

Evaluating Quality

The important evaluation characteristics are flavor, color, and texture. The object of panfrying is to produce a flavorful exterior with a crisp, brown crust, which acts as a barrier to retain juices and flavor. Because the product itself is not browned, the flavor will be different than if the item had been sautéed.

The proper color depends upon the type of item, the breading that is used, and, to a certain extent, the item's thickness. The color of relatively thin and delicate meats (fish, shellfish, and poultry) should be golden to amber. Thicker pieces may take on a deeper color resulting from the longer cooking time. In all cases, the product should not be extremely pale. As with sautéing, an improper color indicates that improper heat levels or the incorrect pan size were used.

Only naturally tender foods should be panfried, and, after cooking, the product should still be tender and moist. Excessive dryness means the food was allowed to overcook, was cooked too far in advance and held too long, or was cooked at a temperature higher than required.

Deep-frying

In this technique, foods are cooked by being completely submerged in hot fat. (Significantly greater amounts of fat are used than for either sautéing or panfrying.) The food is almost always given a coating—a standard breading, a batter such as a tempura or beer batter, or, in some instances, simply a flour coating. The coating acts as a barrier between the fat and the product and also contributes flavor and texture contrast.

As with the other dry-heat methods that use cooking fats and oils, the foods must be naturally tender and of a shape and size that allow them to cook quickly without becoming tough or dry. Poultry and fish are the most commonly selected foods for deep-frying. In some cases, cooked meats are made into croquettes and then deep-fried.

There are several specific terms related to deep-frying.

Swimming method. Foods are gently dropped in hot oil, fall to the bottom of the fryer, and are allowed to "swim" to the surface. They may be gently turned once they reach the surface, to allow them to brown evenly. They are then removed with a skimmer. This method is most often used for batter-coated foods (see Fig. 19-8).

Basket method. The foods are placed in a basket that is lowered into the hot oil, and then they are lifted out in the basket once properly cooked. This method is generally used for breaded items (see Fig. 19-9).

Double-basket method. Certain types of food, in order to develop a good crust, need to be fully submerged in hot oil for a fairly long time. Foods that would tend to rise to the surface too rapidly are

19-8 THE SWIMMING METHOD FOR DEEP-FRYING

Use for items coated with batter.

19-9 THE BASKET METHOD FOR DEEP-FRYING

Use for breaded items.

placed in a basket, which is lowered into the hot oil, and are then held under the oil's surface by the bottom of a second basket.

Recovery time. This measures the amount of time it takes the oil to return to the correct temperature after a product has been cooked. The food absorbs some of the heat, causing the oil's temperature to drop. The more food items in the oil, the lower the temperature drops and the longer the recovery time.

Smoking point. This is the temperature at which fats and oils begin to smoke, indicating that the fat has begun to break down. The higher a particular fat's smoking point, the higher the temperature at which it is safe to cook with that oil. For further information, refer to the section on oils in Chapter 10, "Nonperishable Goods Identification."

Blanching. This means giving foods a preliminary cooking at a lower temperature, followed by finishing at the time of service at a higher temperature. During the initial cooking, the food cooks evenly but the crust does not brown completely. In finishing, the food is re-

heated to develop the proper color. This procedure is especially useful when it is not possible to cook a food, such as fried chicken, immediately prior to service in a reasonable amount of time.

Fat and Oil Selection and Maintenance

Both fats and oils may be used as a cooking medium for deep-frying, although vegetable oil is most commonly used. Fats and oils differ in specific properties but are all basically the same compound and contain a combination of fatty acids, flavor, and glycerin. In general, a neutral flavor and color and a high smoking point (around 425°F/218°C) are the most important considerations in choosing an oil for deep-frying.

In deep-frying, several things, in addition to selecting the proper oil, will help prolong the product's life. Follow these 10 steps:

1. Store oils in a cool, dry area and keep them away from strong lights, which leach vitamin A.

2. Use a high-quality oil.

3. Prevent the oil from coming in contact with copper, brass, or bronze, because these metals hasten breakdown.

4. When frying moist items, dry them as thoroughly as possible before placing them in oil, because water breaks down the oil and lowers the smoking point.

5. Do not salt products over the pan because salt breaks down the oil.

6. Fry items at the proper temperature. Do not overheat the oil.

7. Turn off the fryer after using it and cover when it is not used for long periods of time.

8. Constantly remove any small particles (such as loose bits of breading or batter) from the oil during use.

9. Filter the kettle's entire contents after each shift, if possible, or at least once a day. After the oil has been properly filtered, replace 20 percent of the original volume with fresh oil, to extend the life of the entire amount.

10. Discard the oil if it becomes rancid, smokes below 350°F (176°C), or foams excessively. As oil is used, it will darken; if it is a great deal darker than when it was fresh, it will brown the food too rapidly. The food may appear properly cooked but actually be underdone.

Mise en Place

1. Main item. Remove any bones. Bones are usually removed because they slow down the cooking process. Cut the item into the appropriate size. Foods should be fairly thin, with a uniform size and shape so that they can cook rapidly and evenly. Remove the skin (especially from fish), as desired or as indicated in the recipe. Remove any gristle, fat, and silverskin or any inedible shells. Cut the food into chunks or fingers, or butterfly and pound it, depending upon the food and the desired result.

2. Coating. Breading may be done up to one hour in advance of deep-frying and chilled to allow the breading to firm. For best quality, batter or plain flour should be applied immediately before cooking. Have available the ingredients for a standard breading, batter or tempura, or flour.

3. Cooking medium. The cooking medium must be able to reach a high temperature without smoking or breaking down. Have available a neutral-flavored oil with a high smoking point. A rendered fat, such as lard, maybe used to create a special flavor or effect, as in certain regional dishes; for example, southern fried chicken.

4. Optional components. This is often a stuffing. A classic example is chicken Kiev, in which the meat is butterflied and pounded to increase its surface area. The appropriate filling, a garlic butter, is encased completely by rolling and folding the meat around the filling. The item is then coated and deep-fried.

Figure 19-10 shows the mise en place for a breaded, deep-fried shrimp.

Method

1. Heat the cooking fat to the proper temperature. If a food is added to oil that is too cool, the food's surface will not form a proper seal and the food will become soggy and greasy. In addition, water from the food is released into the oil, shortening the oil's life.

2. Add the main item to the hot cooking fat in the proper manner. Use the swimming method for items coated with batter and the basket method for items coated with standard breading.

19-10
Mise en place for breaded, deep-fried shrimp.

3. Turn the items during frying, if necessary. Items coated with batter must be turned because the batter will frequently cause the food to float at the surface, with part of the food above the oil level. To ensure even browning, turn the food using tongs or a kitchen fork, being careful not to pierce the item.

4. Remove the items from the oil as soon as they are fully cooked (see "Determining Doneness") and blot them on absorbent paper toweling. They may be seasoned with salt at this point. They must not be suspended over the fryer when they are salted, because salt contributes to the oil's breakdown.

5. Serve the food immediately on heated plates, with the appropriate sauce.

For a quick summary, refer to the abbreviated method for deep-frying.

Determining Doneness

Most deep-fried foods are done when the items have risen to the oil's surface and their exteriors are evenly brown. In some cases, it may be necessary to finish fried foods, uncovered, in a hot oven. This is not ideal, because the food's natural juices begin to leak out, resulting in a soggy coating. Foods served very hot, directly from the frying kettle, have a better, less greasy taste.

Evaluating Quality

As with the other methods in this chapter, the important characteristics are flavor, color, and texture. Deep-fried foods should taste like the food item being prepared, not like the oil used (or like other foods previously fried in the oil). If the food tastes heavy, oily, or strongly of another food, the oil was not hot

Deep-fried Breaded Shrimp

Yield: 1 serving

Shrimp, peeled and deveined	4 ounces	120 grams
Flour	as needed	as needed
Egg wash	as needed	as needed
Fresh white bread crumbs	as needed	as needed
Salt	to taste	to taste
Rémoulade sauce or tartar sauce	1½ ounces	45 grams

1. Bread the shrimp according to the standard breading procedure: First, dip them into the flour and shake off any excess. Then, coat the shrimp with the egg wash. Finally, evenly coat the shrimp with the breadcrumbs.

2. Place the shrimp in a fryer basket and lower them into a deep fryer set at 375°F (190°C).

3. Deep-fry the shrimp until they are evenly brown and thoroughly cooked. Lift the basket and allow the excess oil to drain back into the fryer. Drain the shrimp very briefly on absorbent toweling, and season them to taste with salt as desired.

4. Serve the shrimp on a heated plate with rémoulade or tartar sauce, or as desired.

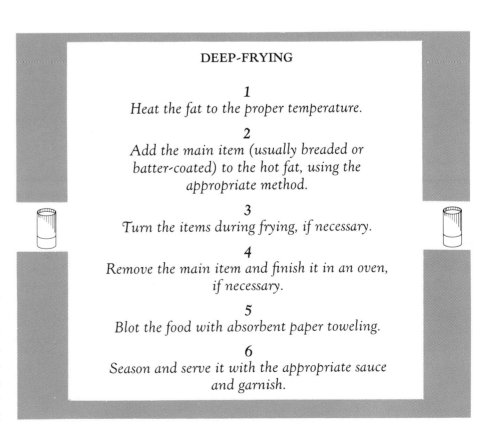

DEEP-FRYING

1
Heat the fat to the proper temperature.

2
Add the main item (usually breaded or batter-coated) to the hot fat, using the appropriate method.

3
Turn the items during frying, if necessary.

4
Remove the main item and finish it in an oven, if necessary.

5
Blot the food with absorbent paper toweling.

6
Season and serve it with the appropriate sauce and garnish.

Shrimp Tempura with Dipping Sauce

Yield: 1 serving

Shrimp, peeled and deveined	4 ounces	120 grams
Salt	to taste	to taste
Pepper	to taste	to taste

Tempura Batter (for 10 servings)

Cold water	1 cup	240 milliliters
All-purpose flour	4½ ounces	130 grams
Cornstarch	2 ounces	60 grams
Sesame oil	2 tablespoons	30 grams
Egg yolk	1	1

Dipping Sauce (for 10 servings)

Daikon, minced	½ cup	120 grams
Cold water	½ cup	120 milliliters
Soy sauce	¼ cup	60 milliliters
Shin mirin	1 tablespoon	15 milliliters
Katsuo dashi	1 tablespoon	5 grams
Wasabi powder	1 teaspoon	3 grams

1. Season the shrimp with the salt and pepper and pat them dry with absorbent toweling.

2. Mix the ingredients for the tempura batter, making sure that the mixture stays very cold.

3. Mix all of the ingredients for the dipping sauce and chill the mixture until it is needed for service.

4. Heat the oil in the fryer to 350°F (175°C). Dip each shrimp into the batter and drop it carefully into the hot oil. Deep-fry the shrimp until they are golden brown and puffy. Turn them if necessary for even color.

5. Remove the shrimp from the oil with a spider and drain them briefly on absorbent toweling. Serve them at once with the dipping sauce.

enough, the oil was too old, or a strongly flavored food such as fish was fried in the same oil.

With the exception of tempura, which will be light gold in color, most deep-fried foods should have a strong golden color. Overly pale items have been undercooked, cooked in oil that was not hot enough, coated too thickly, or cooked in a crowded fryer.

A properly deep-fried food's texture is moist and tender on the interior, with a crisp, delicate crust. If the crust has become soggy, the food may have been held too long after cooking or, again, the oil was not at the correct temperature. Another possibility is that the coating was applied too heavily.

SUMMARY

In dry-heat cooking with fats and oils, it is extremely important to select the proper cuts, shapes, and sizes of meats and to be adept at determining doneness—a skill acquired through experience. The chef should also thoroughly understand the role of the cooking medium. In sautéing, for example, the medium contributes flavor as well as pan lubrication, whereas in pan-frying and deep-frying, the flavor of the cooking oil is less important than its cooking properties.

Understanding how these techniques work and how they actually cook the food makes it clear that the reason for choosing a particular technique for a food depends on the desired result.

Chicken Breast with Ham and Sherry

<u>*Yield: 1 serving*</u>

Chicken suprême	1	1
Salt	to taste	to taste
Olive oil	as needed	as needed
Garlic, mashed	½ teaspoon	2 grams
Onions, julienned	1 ounce	30 grams
Red pepper, peeled, julienned	1 ounce	30 grams
Green pepper, peeled, julienned	1 ounce	30 grams
Ham julienned	¾ ounce	20 grams
Tomato, peeled, julienned	¾ ounce	20 grams
Olives, ripe, pitted and sliced	4	4
Dry sherry	½ ounce	12 milliliters
Chicken stock	2 ounces	60 milliliters
Thyme and marjoram, fresh, chopped	¼ teaspoon	200 milligrams
Arrowroot, diluted in cold water	as needed	as needed

1. Dry the suprême and season it with the salt.
2. Sauté the chicken in the oil until it is just cooked through. Remove and keep it warm.
3. In the same oil, sauté the onions, garlic, and peppers. Add the ham, tomatoes, and olives; deglaze with the sherry.
4. Add the stock; bring it to a boil and adjust the seasoning with the thyme and marjoram.
5. Add the diluted arrowroot to thicken the sauce. Serve the sauce over the chicken.

Calf's Liver Berlin Style

<u>*Yield: 1 serving*</u>

Calf's liver slices, trimmed	5 to 6 ounces	140 to 170 grams
Flour	as needed	as needed
Salt	to taste	to taste
Pepper	to taste	to taste
Clarified butter	as needed	as needed
Onion, sliced	2 ounces	55 grams
Apple slice, ½-inch thick	1	1
Jus de veau lié, heated	1½ ounces	45 milliliters

1. Season the flour with the salt and pepper and dust the liver slices with it.

2. Sauté the liver in the clarified butter until it is medium (slightly pink).

3. Sauté the onion separately in the butter until it is golden brown.

4. Sauté the apple slice in the butter until it is cooked but still firm.

5. Plate the liver, onion, and apple slices in layers. Serve with heated jus de veau lié.

Pork Cutlets with Wild Mushrooms and Crabmeat

Yield: 1 serving

Pork cutlet	4 to 5 ounces	115 to 140 grams
Salt	to taste	to taste
Pepper	to taste	to taste
Clarified butter	1 ounce	30 grams
White wine	2 ounces	60 milliliters
Heavy cream, reduced	as needed	as needed
Whole butter	1 ounce	30 grams
Wild mushrooms, cut in uniform size	1 to 2 ounces	30 to 55 grams
Crabmeat	1 ounce	30 grams
Herbs, fresh (as available)	½ teaspoon	380 milligrams

1. Season the cutlets with the salt and pepper.

2. Heat the clarified butter. Add the cutlets and sauté them until they are nearly cooked through. Remove them from the pan and keep them warm.

3. Deglaze the pan with the wine and reduce.

4. Add the reduced heavy cream and reduce the sauce to nappé.

5. In a separate pan, sauté the mushrooms in the whole butter until they are tender.

6. Add the crabmeat and fresh herbs and heat them through.

7. Place the crabmeat mixture on top of the cutlets.

8. Add any accumulated drippings to the sauce.

9. Reheat the sauce and pool it on a warm plate. Serve the cutlets on the pool of sauce.

Pork with Apricots, Currants, and Pine Nuts

Yield: 1 serving

Pork scallops, pounded thin	three 2-ounce pieces	three 55-gram pieces
Flour	as needed	as needed
Clarified butter or oil	as needed	as needed
Brandy	1 tablespoon	15 milliliters
Jus de veau lié, heated	2 ounces	60 milliliters
Dried apricots, diced, soaked in brandy	¼ ounce	7 grams
Dried currants, soaked in brandy	¼ ounce	7 grams
Pine nuts, roasted	1 tablespoon	7 grams

1. Lightly flour the pork scallops and sauté them in clarified butter or oil until they are browned on both sides. Finish them in an oven.

2. Deglaze the pan with the brandy and reduce au sec.

3. Add the jus de veau lié, apricots, and currants. Simmer the sauce to achieve the correct consistency. Add the pine nuts and adjust the seasoning with salt and pepper to taste.

4. Return the pork to the sauce to reheat it; add any accumulated drippings as well.

5. Serve the pork on heated plates and nappé with the sauce.

Pork Medallions with Red Onion Confit

Yield: 1 serving

Pork medallions	two 2-ounce pieces	two 55-gram pieces
Sherry vinegar	1 teaspoon	5 milliliters
Jus de veau lié	2 ounces	60 milliliters
Red onion confit	2 ounces	60 grams

1. Sear the medallions in a sauté pan on both sides and finish them in the oven.

2. Combine the vinegar and jus de veau lié in a saucepan; bring to a quick boil. Remove from the heat.

3. Deglaze the sauté pan with the vinegar and jus de veau lié. Bring it to a boil. Keep it warm or reheat at time of service.

4. Place the warm red onion confit onto the center of a heated serving platter or plate. Pour the sauce around the confit and place two medallions on the plate.

Chicken Suprêmes "Marechal"

Yield: 1 serving

Chicken breast, boneless and skinless	1	1
Salt	to taste	to taste
Pepper	to taste	to taste
Flour	as needed	as needed
Egg wash	as needed	as needed
Bread crumbs	as needed	as needed
Vegetable oil	as needed	as needed
Sauce suprême, heated	2 ounces	60 milliliters
White asparagus tips, cooked	3	3
Truffles, sliced	1	1

1. Trim the breast and pound it lightly to an even thickness. Season the chicken breast with the salt and pepper and put it through the standard breading procedure.

2. Panfry the breast in hot oil. If necessary, finish it in the oven.

3. Reheat the sauce, as needed, to order; garnish the chicken with asparagus tips and a truffle slice.

Sautéed Chicken with Tarragon Sauce

Yield: 1 serving

Chicken suprême	1	1
Salt	to taste	to taste
Pepper	to taste	to taste
Flour	as needed	as needed
Clarified butter	as needed	as needed
Shallots, minced	½ teaspoon	2.5 grams
Chablis	1 ounce	30 milliliters
Tarragon sauce	1½ ounces	45 milliliters
Tarragon leaves, fresh, coarsely chopped	pinch	pinch
Whole butter	⅓ ounce	9 grams

(continued)

1. Season the chicken and dredge it in the flour.

2. Sauté the chicken in the clarified butter until it is golden. Finish it in the oven.

3. Degrease the sauté pan.

4. Add the shallots and sweat them. Do not brown them.

5. Deglaze the pan with the chablis and reduce to sec.

6. Add the tarragon sauce; simmer it.

7. Add the chopped tarragon; finish the sauce with the whole butter.

8. Serve the sauce with the chicken.

Blackened Beef with Corn and Pepper Sauce

Yield: 4 servings

Sauce

Corn on the cob, husks on	2 ears	2 ears
Olive oil	2 teaspoons	10 milliliters
Onion, large dice	½ cup	80 grams
Tomato paste	2 tablespoons	30 grams
Red wine	⅔ cup	160 milliliters
Beef stock	2½ cups	600 milliliters
Bay leaf	1	1
Thyme, small sprig	1	1
Butter	1 tablespoon	15 grams
Green pepper, fine dice	½ cup	50 grams
Red pepper, fine dice	½ cup	50 grams
Jalapeño chili, diced	½ teaspoon	2 grams
Garlic cloves, minced	2	2
Shallots, minced	3 tablespoons	40 grams
Turmeric	¼ teaspoon	500 milligrams
Curry powder	¼ teaspoon	500 milligrams
Beef tenderloin	1 pound	455 grams
Curry powder	½ teaspoon	1 gram
Fennel seed	2 teaspoons	750 milligrams
Cayenne pepper	pinch	pinch

1. Dampen the corn husks and roast the corn in a 375°F (190°C) oven for 15 minutes. Remove the corn from the oven. Shuck the ears, slice the kernels from the cob with a knife, and reserve them.

2. Grill the cobs over hot coals until they are evenly browned and reserve them.

3. Sauté the onions in the olive oil until they are caramelized. Add the tomato paste and sauté. Add the wine; reduce au sec.

4. Add the stock, bay leaf, thyme, and grilled cobs. Simmer until the sauce is reduced by one-quarter. Strain the sauce and reserve it.

5. Return the pan to medium heat and melt the butter. Add the peppers, reserved corn kernels, chili, garlic, shallots, turmeric, and curry. Sauté the mixture until the peppers are tender.

6. Return the strained sauce to the pan and simmer it until all the vegetables are tender.

7. Slice the beef tenderloin into 4 medallions. Season each medallion with a mixture of the curry powder, fennel seeds, and cayenne. Grill the beef over hot coals to the desired doneness. Pool the hot corn-and-pepper sauce on heated plates and top each serving with a medallion.

Noisettes of Lamb Judic

Yield: 1 serving

Vegetable oil	as needed	as needed
Lamb noisettes, cut from the loin or leg	two 2½ to 3 ounces	two 70 to 85 grams
Salt	to taste	to taste
Black pepper, coarse	to taste	to taste
Dry white wine	2 teaspoons	10 milliliters
Jus d'agneau, heated	2 ounces	60 milliliters
Whole butter	2 teaspoons	9 grams

1. Season the noisettes with the salt and pepper. Sauté them over high heat for 2 minutes on each side in the oil. Remove the lamb from the pan and keep it warm on a rack.

2. Deglaze the pan with the wine. Add the jus d'agneau and reduce the sauce.

3. Finish the sauce with the whole butter and adjust the seasoning.

4. Serve the sauce over the lamb.

NOTE: A traditional garnish consists of braised lettuce, château potatoes, and tomatoes stuffed with mushroom duxelle.

Sautéed Veal Scallopini with Sauce Zingara

Yield: 1 serving

Veal scallopini, cut from the leg	5 to 6 ounces	140 to 170 grams
Flour (optional)	as needed	as needed
Clarified butter	as needed	as needed

Sauce (for 10 servings)

Olive oil	¾ ounce	23 milliliters
Onions, chopped	2 ounces	55 grams
Garlic clove, minced	1	1
Tomato concassé	12 ounces	340 grams
Tomato paste	1 ounce	30 grams
Demi-glace, heated	1 quart	1 liter
Tarragon, fresh, chopped	½ teaspoon	380 milligrams
Ham, julienned	3 ounces	85 grams
Tongue, julienned	3 ounces	85 grams
Mushroom, julienned	1 cup	240 milliliters
Truffle, julienned	¼ cup	60 milliliters

1. Season the veal, dredge it with flour (optional), and sauté it in the clarified butter at service. Remove the veal and keep it warm.

2. Add the olive oil and sauté the onions until they are transparent.

3. Add the garlic and sauté it until it is aromatic.

4. Add the tomato concassé and paste; pincé.

5. Add the demi-glace; reduce to a sauce consistency. Puree and strain the sauce.

6. Add the tarragon, ham, tongue, mushroom, and truffle. Bring the sauce to a simmer and adjust the seasonings.

7. Serve approximately 2 ounces of sauce per serving.

VARIATIONS

Sautéed Veal Scallopini, Sauce Champignon: Serve the veal with 2 ounces of Mushroom Sauce.

Sautéed Veal Scallopini with Zucchini Noodles and Red Pepper Coulis: Serve the veal on a nest of zucchini cut into long julienne; pool Red Pepper Coulis around the veal.

Veal Scallopini Shaker Village

Yield: *1 serving*

Veal scallopini, cut from the leg, pounded thin	5 to 6 ounces	140 to 170 grams
Salt	to taste	to taste
Pepper	to taste	to taste
Flour	as needed	as needed
Clarified butter	as needed	as needed
Shallots, minced	1 teaspoon	4.5 grams
White wine	1½ ounces	45 milliliters
Jus de veau lié, heated	2 ounces	60 milliliters
Herbs, fresh, minced	1 tablespoon	2 grams
Tomato concassé	2 ounces	60 milliliters
Whole butter	¼ ounce	7 grams

1. Dry the veal and season it with salt and pepper.
2. Sauté the veal in the clarified butter until it is golden brown on both sides. Remove it from the pan and keep it warm.
3. Degrease the pan. Add the shallots and sauté them briefly.
4. Deglaze the pan with the wine.
5. Add the jus de veau lié and herbs; reduce to nappé consistency.
6. Add the tomatoes and heat them through.
7. Finish the sauce with the whole butter and adjust the seasoning to taste.

Trout Amandine

Yield: *1 serving*

Trout fillet	4 to 5 ounces	115 to 140 grams
Salt	to taste	to taste
Pepper	to taste	to taste
Milk (optional)	as needed	as needed
Flour	as needed	as needed
Clarified butter	as needed	as needed
Whole butter	½ ounce	15 grams
Almonds, slivered	½ ounce	15 grams
Lemon juice	1 tablespoon	15 milliliters
Parsley, chopped	2 teaspoons	1.5 grams

(continued)

1. Season the trout with the salt and pepper.

2. Dip the fish in the milk and dredge it in the flour.

3. Sauté the trout in the clarified butter until it is cooked through. Remove it and keep it warm.

4. Pour off the excess butter. Add the whole butter and let it brown slightly.

5. Add the almonds and brown them.

6. Add the lemon juice and parsley.

7. Nappé the sauce over the trout.

Sautéed Salmon with Zucchini "Noodles" and Red Pepper Coulis

Yield: 1 serving

Marinade (for 10 servings)

Lime juice, fresh	2 tablespoons	30 milliliters
Black peppercorns, cracked	10	10
Shallots, minced fine	2 teaspoons	9 grams
Garlic, minced fine	1 teaspoon	4.5 grams
Salmon fillet	3 ounces	85 grams
Flour	as needed	as needed
Butter or oil	as needed	as needed
Zucchini, seeded, julienned fine	½ cup	120 milliliters
Red pepper coulis	2 ounces	60 milliliters

1. Combine all of the ingredients for the marinade. Marinate the salmon at room temperature for 25 to 30 minutes.

2. Dredge the salmon in the flour and sauté it in the butter or oil until it is barely cooked through. Remove it and keep it warm.

3. Add the zucchini to the skillet and sauté it until it is very hot.

4. Heat the red pepper coulis. Pool the warm coulis on heated dinner plates.

5. Arrange the zucchini in a nest in the center of the plate. Place the salmon fillet in the nest and garnish it with fresh basil.

Chicken Suprême with Fine Herb Sauce

Yield: 1 serving

Chicken suprême	1	1
Salt	to taste	to taste
Pepper	to taste	to taste
Flour (optional)	as needed	as needed
Clarified butter	as needed	as needed
Shallots, fine dice	1 teaspoon	4.5 grams
Dry white wine	2 ounces	60 milliliters
Chicken stock	2 ounces	60 milliliters
Glace de volaille	1 tablespoon	15 milliliters
Cream	1 ounce	30 milliliters
Parsley, tarragon, and chervil, fresh, chopped fine	1 teaspoon	780 milligrams

1. Dry and season the chicken breast. Dredge it in flour, if desired.
2. Sauté the chicken in the clarified butter until it is almost cooked through. Remove it and keep it warm.
3. Degrease the pan. Add the shallots and sauté them until they are translucent.
4. Deglaze the pan with the wine; reduce the sauce au sec.
5. Add the stock and glace de volaille.
6. Add the cream; reduce the sauce to nappé.
7. Add the herbs and adjust the sauce's consistency. Serve the sauce over the chicken.

Breast of Chicken Chardonnay

Yield: 1 serving

Chicken suprême	1	1
Salt	to taste	to taste
Pepper	to taste	to taste
Flour	as needed	as needed
Clarified butter	as needed	as needed
Mushrooms, sliced	1 to 2 ounces	30 to 55 grams
Chardonnay wine	1 to 2 ounces	30 to 60 milliliters
Chicken stock, reduced	2 ounces	60 milliliters
Heavy cream	1 ounce	30 milliliters
Mustard seeds	¼ teaspoon	580 milligrams
Leeks, cut into triangles, blanched	2 ounces	55 grams

(continued)

1. Dry the chicken, season it with salt and pepper, and dredge it in flour.
2. Sauté the chicken in the clarified butter until it is done. Remove the chicken and keep it warm.
3. Sauté the mushrooms in the same pan.
4. Deglaze the pan with the wine; add the stock and reduce it by half.
5. Add the heavy cream and reduce the sauce by half.
6. Add the mustard seeds and reduce to nappé.
7. Add the leeks and heat them through. Serve the sauce over the chicken.

Swiss-style Shredded Veal

Yield: 10 servings

Veal top round or tender leg cut	2½ pounds	1.15 kilograms
Salt	to taste	to taste
Flour	as needed	as needed
Vegetable oil	as needed	as needed
Shallots, chopped	3 ounces	85 grams
Mushrooms, sliced	5 ounces	140 grams
White wine	10 ounces	300 milliliters
Demi-glace	10 ounces	300 milliliters
Heavy cream	4 ounces	120 milliliters
Brandy	1 ounce	30 milliliters
Lemon juice	to taste	to taste
Salt	to taste	to taste
Pepper	to taste	to taste

1. Cut the veal meat into thin émincé or shreds.
2. Salt the sliced veal and dust it with flour.
3. Heat the oil in a heavy skillet to the smoking point. Add the veal and sauté it until it is lightly browned but do not overcook it. Remove it and keep warm.
4. Add the shallots and mushrooms and sauté them lightly.
5. Deglaze the pan with the white wine.
6. Add the demi-glace, heavy cream, and any accumulated meat juices to the pan. Reduce the sauce to a creamy consistency.
7. Add the brandy, lemon juice, salt, and pepper. Return the meat to the pan with the sauce. Heat it through but do not boil it.

Beef Tournedos Sauté à la Niçoise

Yield: 1 serving

Beef tenderloin	5 to 6 ounces	140 to 170 grams
Clarified butter	as needed	as needed
Garlic, minced	1 teaspoon	5 grams
Tomato concassé	2 ounces	55 grams
Demi-glace	2 ounces	60 milliliters
Tarragon, fresh, chopped	1 teaspoon	1 gram

1. Sauté the beef in the clarified butter to the desired doneness. Keep the beef warm.
2. Sauté the garlic in clarified butter to release its aroma.
3. Add the tomato concassé and demi-glace. Let the mixture reduce slightly.
4. Add the tarragon and adjust the seasoning with salt and pepper to taste.
5. Portion the sauce onto the tournedos.

VARIATIONS

Tournedos of Beef with Virginia Bacon, Pearl Onions, and Grapes: Sauté the beef and reserve it. Degrease the pan. Add 1½ ounces (45 grams) of blanched, smoked Virginia bacon lardons and sauté them until they are crisp. Degrease the pan again, if necessary; add 3 or 4 pearl onions and sauté them. Deglaze the pan with red wine and reduce it. Add 6 to 8 peeled grapes and 2 ounces (60 milliliters) of fond de veau lié. Monté au beurre. Adjust the seasoning. Add a few drops of brandy and accumulated meat juices. Nappé the tournedos with the sauce.

Medallions of Beef with Marchand de Vin Sauce: Sweat 1 teaspoon (5 milliliters) of shallots in whole butter. Add 4 ounces (120 milliliters) of red wine and ¼ ounce (7.5 milliliters) of jus de veau lié. Reduce the sauce by two-thirds. Monté au beurre. Incorporate any accumulated meat juices. Nappé the medallions with the sauce.

Medallions of Beef with Mustard Hollandaise: Finish 2 ounces (60 milliliters) of Hollandaise Sauce (see the recipe in Chapter 17) with mustard to taste. Use Dijon-style, Creole, or a combination of prepared mustards. Nappé the medallions with the sauce.

Medallions of Beef with Two Sauces: Prepare Marchand de Vin (see the recipe in Chapter 17) and mustard hollandaise. Nappé one side of the medallion with the hollandaise. Then nappé the other side with the Marchand de Vin. The heavier hollandaise will form a dividing line.

Sautéed Veal Scallopine with Tomato Sauce

<u>*Yield:* 1 serving</u>

Veal scallopine, cut from the leg, pounded thin	5 to 6 ounces	140 to 170 grams
Salt	to taste	to taste
White pepper	to taste	to taste
Flour	as needed	as needed
Clarified butter	as needed	as needed
Chablis	1 ounce	30 milliliters
Tomato sauce	2 ounces	60 milliliters
Whole butter	¼ ounce	7 grams

1. Dry the veal and season it with the salt and pepper; dredge it in the flour, and shake off the excess.
2. Sauté the veal in the butter until it is golden brown on both sides.
3. Remove the veal and keep it warm.
4. Degrease the pan; deglaze it with wine.
5. Add the tomato sauce and bring it to a simmer.
6. Monté au beurre to finish.

Calf's Liver with Bacon Cream Sauce

<u>*Yield:* 1 serving</u>

Bacon Cream Sauce (for 10 orders)

Bacon, medium dice	1¼ pounds	570 grams
Onions, chopped fine	10 ounces	285 grams
Heavy cream	40 ounces	1.2 liters
Calf's liver	5 to 8 ounces	140 to 225 grams
Salt	to taste	to taste
Pepper	to taste	to taste
Oil (or rendered bacon fat)	as needed	as needed

1. Sauté the bacon until it is crisp; remove and drain it. Strain the bacon grease and reserve the fat.

2. Sauté the onions in the strained bacon fat until they are lightly browned, drain the excess fat, and add the cooked bacon.

3. Add the heavy cream and reduce to sauce consistency. Keep the sauce hot until needed.

4. Season the liver with the salt and pepper.

5. Sauté the liver in the oil or rendered bacon fat until it is medium-rare and browned on both sides.

6. Serve the liver with 2 ounces (60 grams) of bacon cream sauce per serving.

Trout à la Meunière

Yield: 1 serving

Trout, pan-dressed	8 ounces	225 grams
Salt	as needed	as needed
Pepper	as needed	as needed
Flour	as needed	as needed
Clarified butter or oil	as needed	as needed
Whole butter	1 tablespoon	15 grams
Lemon juice, fresh	to taste	to taste
Parsley, chopped	½ teaspoon	380 milligrams

1. Season the fish with the salt and pepper and dredge it in the flour.

2. Heat the clarified butter in a sauteuse.

3. Add the fish and sauté it until it is lightly browned. Remove it and finish it in an oven, if necessary. Keep it warm.

4. Remove the excess fat from the pan. Add the whole butter and cook it to beurre noisette.

5. Add the lemon juice and parsley and swirl it to lightly emulsify it.

6. Nappé the sauce over the fish.

VARIATIONS

Red Snapper with Pecans: Substitute 5 ounces (140 grams) of red snapper fillet for the trout. Add ¼ ounce (7 grams) of chopped pecans to the beurre noisette. Then add lemon juice and parsley.

Red Snapper with Tomatoes, Cucumber, and Fennel: Substitute 5 ounces (140 grams) of red snapper fillet for the trout. Add 1 ounce (30 grams) of peeled, seeded, and diced cucumbers and 1 ounce (30 grams) of diced, blanched fennel to the browned butter. Omit the lemon juice. Garnish the fish with chopped fennel leaves.

Flounder Sautéed with Almonds: Substitute flounder for the trout. Proceed as in the main recipe. Add ¼ ounce (7 grams) of sliced, blanched almonds to the beurre noisette. Finish the sauce with lemon juice and parsley.

Fisherman's Platter

<u>Yield:</u> *1 serving*

Fish, cut in goujonettes	2 ounces	55 grams
Oysters, shucked	2	2
Clams, shucked	2	2
Shrimp, peeled, de-veined, butterflied	2	2
Sea scallops	1 ounce	30 grams
Salt	to taste	to taste
Pepper	to taste	to taste
Lemon juice	to taste	to taste
Standard breading	as needed	as needed
Tartar sauce	1½ ounces	45 milliliters

1. Season the fish and shellfish with the salt, pepper, and lemon juice.
2. Bread the fish and shellfish.
3. Panfry them until they are cooked through.
4. Drain the fish and shellfish briefly on absorbent paper.
5. Serve the fish immediately with the tartar sauce.

Clam Fritters

<u>Yield:</u> *10 servings*

Flour	7 ounces	200 grams
Baking powder	1 tablespoon	8 grams
Salt	¼ teaspoon	1 gram
White pepper	⅛ teaspoon	300 milligrams
Clams, drained, juice reserved, chopped fine	10 ounces	285 grams
Reserved clam juice	6 ounces	180 milliliters
Milk	4 ounces	120 milliliters

1. Combine all the dry ingredients.
2. Combine all the wet ingredients (including the chopped clams).
3. Combine the wet and dry ingredients.
4. Drop the mixture by spoonfuls (one-third of a serving spoon) into 375°F (190°C) oil.
5. Fry the fritters until they are golden brown. Serve them with tartar sauce, rémoulade sauce, or other mayonnaise-based sauces.

Deep-fried Flounder with Rémoulade Sauce

Yield: 1 serving

Flounder fillet, cut into goujonettes	4 to 5 ounces	115 to 140 grams
Salt	to taste	to taste
Pepper	to taste	to taste
Lemon juice	to taste	to taste
Flour	as needed	as needed
Egg wash	as needed	as needed
Bread crumbs	as needed	as needed
Rémoulade sauce	2 ounces	60 milliliters

1. Season the fish with the salt, pepper, and lemon juice.
2. Bread the fish using the standard breading procedure.
3. Deep-fry the fish at 350°F (175°C) until it is golden brown.
4. Drain it well on absorbent paper.
5. Serve the fish with the rémoulade sauce.

Basic Beer Batter

Yield: approximately 1 pint (480 milliliters)

All-purpose flour	5 ounces	140 grams
Baking powder	2 tablespoons	24 grams
Sugar	1 tablespoon	15 grams
Salt	1 teaspoon	5 grams
White pepper	¼ teaspoon	500 milligrams
Beer	12 ounces	360 milliliters

1. Sift together all the dry ingredients.
2. Add the beer and mix until smooth.
3. The batter is now ready to use at this point to coat shrimp, clams, oysters, chicken, and other items.

Chapter 20

Moist-heat Cooking

Once man was able to produce cooking vessels of clay or metal that were both watertight and able to withstand direct heat, foods could be prepared by methods other than roasting them over a fire. Moist-heat techniques have traditionally been a frugal way to prepare foods. Often an entire meal—meats, fish, vegetables, and grains—is prepared in a single pot.

The classic dishes of many cuisines—the New England boiled dinner and the French pot-au-feu, for example—capitalize on the fact that in addition to producing a moist, tender, and delicately flavored food, these techniques also produce a good quantity of a rich, deeply flavored broth. This broth can be served as a separate course or can form the basis for a sauce. Moist-heat techniques offer the chef the opportunity to present healthful and appealing dishes with a range of flavors, textures, and appearances not available through other methods.

The moist-heat techniques are:

• steaming
• en papillote
• shallow poaching
• poaching and simmering

DIFFERENCES FROM DRY-HEAT COOKING

Moist-heat cooking methods are used to produce flavorful dishes by cooking the main item in a liquid bath. The amount of liquid varies from one technique to another. Unlike dry-heat methods, moist-heat cookery does not form a seal on the food as an initial step in the cooking process. Without this seal, a certain amount of flavor is transferred from the food into the cooking liquid. For this reason, it is important either to hold the flavor and juices in the food during cooking (by wrapping the main item with lettuce or other coverings prior to cooking as discussed in this chapter) or to recapture the flavor by serving it as part of the finished dish.

STEAMING TECHNIQUES

Steaming

This method cooks the food by surrounding it with a vapor bath. Relatively little flavor and moisture are lost, but it is advisable to protect the food in some way during cooking by wrapping or coating it. For example, fish may be wrapped in lettuce leaves or corn husks. The liquid used in steaming often includes herbs, spices, and other aromatics, and these flavors are transferred from the steam to the food during cooking.

Foods are placed in a closed vessel, and are above and not touching the liquid. As the liquid comes to a boil, some of it will turn into steam. When the steam comes in contact with the food's surface, the vapor's heat is transferred to the food. Steam circulating around the food provides an even, moist environment, which allows the food to retain most of its natural juices.

If an aromatic liquid such as stock, beer, or tea is used or if aromatic ingredients are added to the liquid to make a court bouillon, some flavor transfer from the steam to the food may occur. A flavorful liquid may be served as a broth or it may be further reduced and used as a sauce base.

Steamed foods generally contain a greater proportion of nutrients, because water-soluble nutrients are not drawn out of the food as readily. Properly steamed foods do not generally lose much of their original volume, and they are exceptionally moist and tender.

Mise en Place

1. Main item. Items to be steamed should be naturally tender and of a size and shape that will allow them to cook in a short amount of time. Cut the main item into the appropriate sizes. Remove the skin and bones from fish to prepare fillets. Remove the skin and bones of poultry and game birds, if necessary or desired. Score whole fish (make shallow cuts at regular intervals), if desired, to promote even cooking and flavor penetration. Leave shellfish in the shells, unless otherwise indicated (scallops are customarily removed from the shell, for example).

2. Steaming liquid. Any liquid may be used for steaming. To produce a flavorful finished dish, however, the liquid itself should be aromatic or additional ingredients such as herbs, spices, citrus rind, or vegetables should be added to it. Have available water, stock, beer, wine, or court bouillon.

3. Optional components. Have available stuffings or fillings, according to the recipe. Have available lettuce leaves, seaweed, corn husks, or leek strips to wrap food in, for the purpose of retaining the

natural juices or introducing additional flavor.

The mise en place for Moules Marinière is shown in Figure 20-1.

Method

1. Bring the liquid to a full boil in a covered vessel. Because the steam is trapped in a covered cooking vessel, a small amount of pressure will build up. Enough liquid should be used to assure that the food will cook completely without requiring the addition of more liquid during cooking. When the chef is opening the pot to add the main item, he or she should take care to avoid a burn by removing the lid so that the steam will vent away from the face and hands.

2. Add the main item to the steamer on a rack in a single layer. To ensure even cooking, foods should be placed in a single layer, not touching one another, so that the steam can circulate completely. More than one layer of food may be cooked at a time in a tiered steamer. Foods may be placed on plates or in shallow dishes on the rack in order to collect any juices that might escape.

3. Replace the lid and allow the steam to build up again. It is a good idea to adjust the heat to maintain even, moderate heat. Even if the liquid is only at a simmer, it can still produce steam, and rapid boiling will cause the liquid to cook away too quickly. Once the food is in the steamer and the cover has been replaced, the chef should avoid removing the lid unnecessarily, because the steam can dissipate rapidly, causing cooking to slow down.

4. Steam the main item to the correct doneness.

5. Serve the food immediately on heated plates with an appropriate sauce, as desired or as indicated by the recipe.

For a quick summary, refer to the abbreviated method for steaming.

Determining Doneness

Steamed foods should be cooked until they are just done but not overcooked, because they can easily become rubbery and dry. Any juices from the food should be nearly colorless. The flesh of fish and shellfish will lose its translucency when properly cooked, taking on a nearly opaque appearance. The shells of molluscs (mussels, clams, oysters) will open when properly cooked and the edges of the flesh should curl. Crustaceans (shrimp, crab, and lobster) should have a bright pink or red color. Poultry should take on an evenly opaque appearance and the flesh should offer little resistance when pressed with a fingertip.

Evaluating Quality

The factors to consider in evaluating quality are flavor, appearance, and texture. Because no initial browning of the food occurs as in a dry-heat technique, the flavor of steamed foods is delicate. Any aromatics used during cooking should be appropriate to the food's flavor and should not be so intense as to overwhelm it.

Steamed foods are usually pale because they do not receive an initial browning. The surface should appear quite moist. Fish, especially salmon, should not have deposits of white albumin on the flesh, which indicate that a fish has been overcooked and/or cooked too quickly.

Steamed foods should be moist and plump. Food suitable for this

20-1
Mise en place for Moules Marinière.

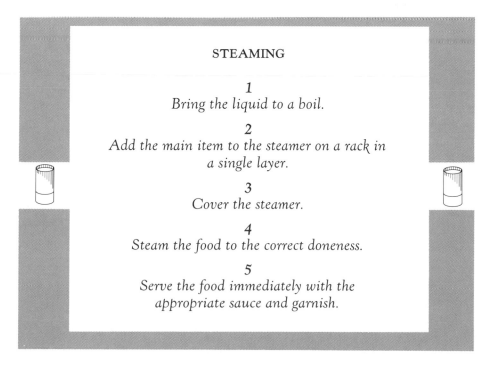

STEAMING

1
Bring the liquid to a boil.

2
Add the main item to the steamer on a rack in a single layer.

3
Cover the steamer.

4
Steam the food to the correct doneness.

5
Serve the food immediately with the appropriate sauce and garnish.

Moules Marinière

Yield: 10 servings (4 mussels each)

Mussels, scrubbed and debearded	40	40
Dry white wine	12 ounces	360 milliliters
Shallots, minced	4 ounces	115 grams
Bay leaf	1	1
Black pepper	½ teaspoon	1 gram
Thyme, fresh	1 sprig	1 sprig
Garlic cloves, minced	6	6
Butter, softened	4 to 6 ounces	115 to 170 grams
Parsley, chopped	3 tablespoons	2.5 grams
Chives, chopped	1 tablespoon	750 milligrams

1. Combine the mussels, wine, shallots, bay leaf, pepper, thyme, parsley, and garlic in a shallow pot. Steam them over moderate heat until the mussels open. Strain off all the liquid and reserve it.

2. Reduce the cooking liquid by two-thirds. Remove and discard the thyme.

3. Monté au beurre, gradually whipping in the butter. Add the parsley and chives.

4. Arrange the mussels in a heated bowl or platter; pour the sauce over the mussels and serve.

technique is naturally tender, and if not overcooked, it will remain tender. There should be no hint of rubberiness or dryness.

En Papillote

In this variation of steaming, the main item and accompanying ingredients are encased in parchment paper and cooked in a hot oven. The main item rests on a bed of herbs, vegetables, or sauce and the combination of these ingredients and the natural juices serves as the sauce. The steam created by the food's natural juices cooks the food. As the steam volume increases, the paper puffs up.

Mise en Place

1. Main item. See information on the main item under "Steaming," in the previous section. In addition, there is an optional first step. Sear thicker meat cuts in advance to ensure that they will be adequately cooked during the relatively short cooking times associated with this technique and to provide additional color and flavor.

2. Parchment paper. The paper must be nonabsorbent so that it will not fall apart during cooking.

3. Optional components. Vegetables provide additional moisture and steam. They also add color, flavor, and texture. Cut the vegetables into a fine julienne or dice. Sweat or blanch the vegetables, if necessary, to ensure that they will cook in the same amount of time as the main item. Prepare herbs and spices according to type. Some herbs may be left in sprigs; others are cut into a chiffonade or minced. Have available a prepared sauce, reduced heavy cream, wine, or citrus juices.

The mise en place for Fillet of Red Snapper en Papillote is shown in Figure 20-2.

Method

1. Cut the parchment paper into a heart shape large enough to hold the main item on one half of the heart, with a 1½-inch margin of paper all the way around. Oil or butter the paper on both sides to prevent it from burning.

2. Place a bed of aromatics, vegetables, or sauce on one half of the heart and top it with the main item.

3. Fold the empty half of the heart over the main item and fold and crimp the edges of the paper to form a tight seal.

4. Place the bag on a preheated sizzler platter and put it in a very hot oven.

20-2

Mise en place for Red Snapper en Papillote.

5. Bake the food until the bag is highly puffy and the paper is browned. The oven temperature may need to be carefully monitored since delicate foods such as fish fillets can be overcooked quickly at a high temperature. A thicker cut may be best if cooked slowly at a moderate temperature and "puffed" in a very hot oven.

Figure 20-3 demonstrates various steps in this method. For a quick summary, refer to the abbreviated method for en papillote.

Determining Doneness

Foods prepared en papillote should be cooked until they are just done.

This is difficult to gauge without experience, since the chef cannot apply the senses of sight and touch in determining doneness. If the item has been cut to the correct size or if it has been partially cooked before being placed en papillote, it should be done when the bag is very puffy and the paper is brown.

Evaluating Quality

Foods that have been properly prepared en papillote will demonstrate the same characteristics of flavor, appearance, and texture as other steamed foods (see the previous section on "Steaming").

Fillet of Red Snapper en Papillote

Yield: 1 serving

Red snapper fillet, skinless	6 ounces	170 grams
Butter	1 ounce	30 grams
Salt	to taste	to taste
Pepper	to taste	to taste
Fish velouté	2 ounces	60 milliliters
White wine	1 ounce	30 milliliters
Shallots, minced	½ teaspoon	2 grams
Scallions, sliced	½ ounce	15 grams
Mushrooms, sliced	½ ounce	15 grams

1. Cut the parchment in a heart shape large enough to enclose the fillet.

2. Heat a sauté pan. Add the butter. Season the fillet with the salt and pepper and sear it briefly on the flesh side only. Remove it from the pan.

3. Place the velouté on one side of the parchment heart. Place the fish on top. Sprinkle it with the wine, shallots, and scallions. Top it with shingled, sliced mushrooms.

4. Fold the paper over and seal the sides tightly.

5. Place the bag on a hot, buttered sizzler platter. Shake it to prevent burning.

6. Finish the fish in a hot oven for 5 to 8 minutes. Serve it immediately.

SUBMERSION TECHNIQUES

Shallow Poaching

This method cooks foods using a combination of steam and a liquid bath: The food is partially submerged in a liquid that often contains an acid, such as wine or lemon juice, and aromatics, such as shallots and herbs. The cooking vessel is covered to capture some of the steam released by the liquid during cooking; the captured steam cooks the portion of the food not directly in the liquid.

In shallow poaching, a significant amount of flavor is transferred between the food and the liquid. In order to retain the flavor released into the liquid, the liquid is reduced and used as a sauce base. The acid in the cooking liquid makes it easier for butter to be emulsified in the sauce, thus a beurre blanc is often the sauce of choice. Like sautéing and grilling, this is an à la minute technique suited to foods that are cut into portion-size or smaller pieces.

Mise en Place

1. Main item. As previously noted, items to be shallow-poached should be naturally tender and of a size and shape that will allow them to cook in a short time. Remove the skin and bones from poultry and game birds to make them into suprêmes. Remove the skin and bones from fish to prepare fillets. The fillets may be rolled or folded to form *paupiettes*. The "meat" side of the fish should show on the exterior. Remove shellfish from its shell, if desired.

2. Cooking liquid. The liquid should contribute flavor to the food as well as to the sauce prepared from the cooking liquid. Have available stock, combined with wine, vinegar, and/or citrus juice.

20-3 STEPS IN THE EN PAPILLOTE METHOD

(1)

(2)

(3)

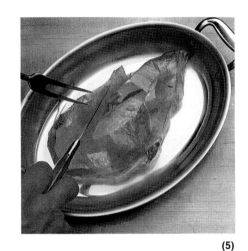

(4)

(5)

(1) Cut the parchment "heart" for en papillote.

(2) Brush the parchment with oil or clarified butter.

(3) Place the salmon on a bed of vegetables on one side of the heart.

(4) Make the folds along the edge to crimp the paper closed.

(5) The finished dish.

3. Aromatics. Cut shallots into a fine dice and allow them to sweat in butter in order to cook out their sulfurous flavor in the raw stage. Cut other vegetables to an appropriate size. A julienne or fine dice is most often indicated, to allow the vegetables to cook completely. Have available herbs, citrus zest, and other ingredients, according to the desired result.

4. Optional components. Have butter available for a beurre blanc. Cut the butter into pieces and keep them cool until the sauce is actually being made. Have available chopped or minced herbs for a garnish, and vegetable purees, tomato concassé, and citrus zest, as required by recipe, for a sauce.

EN PAPILLOTE

1
Cut parchment paper into a heart shape of the appropriate size and butter or oil it.

2
Place a bed of aromatics, vegetables, or sauce on one half of the paper, then top the bed with the main item.

3
Fold the paper in half; fold and crimp the edges.

4
Place the paper packet on a hot sizzler platter.

5
Bake the packet until it is puffed and browned.

6
Plate the packet and serve it immediately.

The mise en place for Poached Sole Vin Blanc is shown in Figure 20-4.

Method

1. Add a quantity of whole butter or stock to the pan. This will act as the cooking medium to smother the aromatic ingredients.

2. Make a bed of aromatic ingredients. Smother chopped shallots and julienned vegetables until tender and make them into a bed on the bottom of the sauteuse. This bed will elevate the food item so that it will cook evenly and not stick to the pan.

3. Add the main item and the cooking liquid. The liquid's level should be no higher than halfway up the item; generally, less liquid is required. If too much is used, either a great deal of time will be needed for it to reduce properly or only part of it will be usable in the sauce. This is undesirable and could result in a flavor loss in both the main item and the sauce.

4. Bring the liquid to a bare simmer over direct heat. Do not allow the liquid to boil, because it could cause the delicate flesh of fish to break apart or poultry and game suprêmes to toughen.

5. Lightly cover the sauteuse with parchment paper. It is not necessary or even desirable to cover the pan tightly. Cooking speed is difficult to monitor, and it is easy for the item to overcook or become tough if it is too tightly covered.

6. Finish cooking the main item either over direct heat or in a moderate oven. Acceptable results can be achieved by finishing the cooking over direct heat; however, the heat in an oven, which is more even and gentle, is preferable. In addition, finishing shallow poaching in the oven makes burner space available for other purposes.

7. Remove the main item to a holding dish and moisten it with a small amount of the cooking liquid. Cover the item and keep it warm while completing the sauce.

8. Reduce the cooking liquid to a syrupy consistency and prepare a beurre blanc or other sauce, as desired.

9. Serve the food immediately on heated plates with the sauce.

For a quick summary, refer to the abbreviated method for shallow poaching.

Determining Doneness

Shallow-poached foods should be cooked until they are just done. Fish and shellfish should appear opaque; the flesh of oysters, clams, and mussels should show curling on the edges. Poultry and game suprêmes will also appear opaque and should offer slight resistance when pressed with a fingertip.

Evaluating Quality

The factors to consider are flavor, appearance, and texture. Shallow-poached foods should reflect both the flavor of the main item and the cooking liquid's ingredients. Because acid and aromatic ingredients are included, the flavor should be "bright." The beurre blanc or other sauce should add a rich, complementary flavor.

It is not possible to make a single statement about the appearance of shallow-poached foods, because

20-4

Mise en place for Poached Sole Vin Blanc.

20-5
Mise en place for Poached Salmon Darnes.

would be difficult and dangerous to lift a large pot full of hot liquid off the stove and into the oven.

4. Carefully remove the main item to a holding container and moisten it with some of the liquid to prevent it from drying out while the sauce is being prepared.

5. Cut or slice the main item, as necessary, and serve it immediately on heated plates with the appropriate sauce.

For a quick summary, refer to the abbreviated method for poaching and simmering.

Determining Doneness

Poached and simmered foods should not be overcooked. Most fish should appear nearly opaque in all areas, particularly near the backbone. Shellfish such as lobster and shrimp should turn a bright pink or red; the shells of molluscs (clams, mussels, oysters) should

3. Maintain the proper cooking speed throughout the poaching or simmering process. Make sure the liquid does not boil. The temperature should be checked periodically with an instant-reading thermometer and the heat adjusted as necessary.

If a cover is used on a fish poacher, the cooking speed must be monitored. Covering a pot has the effect of creating pressure, which allows the liquid's temperature to become higher. As is true for shallow-poached items, it is sometimes desirable to complete poaching or simmering in the oven, once the proper cooking temperature has been reached over direct heat. Common sense will indicate which items can be placed in the oven and which should remain on top of the stove. For instance, it

POACHING AND SIMMERING

1
Bring the cooking liquid to a simmer.

2
Add the main item, using a rack if necessary. Be sure the item is fully submerged.

3
Cover the food, if directed by the recipe.

4
Finish the food over direct heat or in an oven.

5
Remove the main item, moisten it, and keep it warm while preparing a sauce, or cool it in liquid, as appropriate.

6
Cut or slice the main item and serve it with the appropriate sauce and garnish.

Poached Salmon Darnes

Yield: 10 servings

Salmon darnes	ten 6-ounce pieces	ten 200-gram pieces
Court bouillon	as needed	as needed
Bouquet garni	1	1
Lemon slices	2 to 3	2 to 3
Sauce (see note below)	1 to 2 ounces per serving	30 to 55 grams per serving

1. Trim the salmon darnes; be sure to remove all the bones. Place them on a fish poacher rack.

2. Bring the court bouillon, bouquet garni, and lemon slices to a bare simmer.

3. Lower the salmon into the court bouillon. Monitor the cooking speed carefully.

4. Cook the salmon just until it is barely cooked through; the flesh should still hold together.

5. Remove the darnes from the court bouillon and blot them briefly, if necessary. Serve them on heated plates with the desired sauce.

NOTE: A few suggested sauces: Broccoli Coulis, Lemon Beurre Blanc, or Mousseline Sauce.

open and the flesh should begin to curl at the edges.

Poultry and meats should be fork-tender, which means the meat should slide easily from a kitchen fork. Juices that run from the poultry at the point where the thigh meets the breast or from the thickest part of a piece of meat should be nearly clear or have a slight pink blush.

If a poached or simmered item is to be served cold, it should be slightly undercooked. The pot should be removed from the heat and the food allowed to cool in the poaching liquid. The liquid will retain some heat, which will complete the cooking process. Cool the liquid in a cold or ice-water bath to prevent bacterial growth. Once it has reached room temperature, the item may be removed for any fur-

ther preparation. The liquid is customarily used in a sauce or as the basis of another dish.

Evaluating Quality

As with the other methods in this chapter, the important factors are flavor, appearance, and texture. Items that have been poached or simmered should have a clean, pure flavor. Any aromatic ingredients should either bolster or complement the main item's flavor. If the food was cooked at an overly high temperature, there will be a significant flavor loss from the food to the liquid; the same is true of items that have been prepared in too much liquid.

Poached or simmered items should have an appropriate but generally light color. Poultry, es-

pecially breast meat, should be almost white. Fish should be opaque, with a delicate color appropriate to the type. For example, turbot should be very white; salmon should be a delicate pink or orange-pink color. However, there should be no deposits of white albumin on the flesh. Meats should be beige, light brown, or, in the case of white meats such as veal, an ivory color, but never gray. Proper tying or trussing of the item will ensure that its natural shape is preserved. Holding the item correctly once the cooking time is complete is also an important factor in preventing the food from breaking apart.

As noted throughout the discussion of this technique, the aim of poaching and simmering is to produce foods that are moist and extremely tender. Any stringiness, dryness, rubberiness, or excessive flaking indicates that the item may have been cooked for too long or at too high a temperature. If the item is not tender or is chewy, it may not have been allowed to cook sufficiently.

SUMMARY

Moist-heat techniques result in products that have a distinctly different flavor, texture, and appearance from those prepared with dry-heat methods. Instead of having a rich color and flavor, steamed, shallow-poached, poached, and simmered foods are generally pale in color and have a delicate flavor. With the exception of simmering, these techniques require the use of naturally tender meat, poultry, or fish; all moist-heat techniques require a flavorful liquid. Careful monitoring of cooking temperatures and times and the ability to determine doneness are critical to a mastery of moist-heat methods.

Marinated Mackerel in White Wine

<u>*Yield: 20 appetizer servings*</u>

Whole mackerel, fresh, drawn, head removed	3 pounds	1.35 kilograms

Marinade

Dry chablis	1 quart	1 liter
Carrots, sliced thin	2 ounces	55 grams
Onions, sliced thin	2 ounces	55 grams
Salt	½ ounce	15 grams
Thyme, fresh	1 sprig	1 sprig
Bay leaves	4	4
Whole peppercorns	¼ teaspoon	350 milligrams
Parsley stems	¼ ounce	7 grams

1. Trim the fish, rinse it to remove all traces of blood. Drain it well.
2. Combine all of the ingredients for the marinade. Bring it to a boil and simmer it, covered, for 45 minutes.
3. Place the mackerel in a poaching vessel. Pour the hot marinade over the fish; poach it slowly (190°F/88°C) for 8 to 10 minutes. Remove the pan from the heat; cool it in the poaching liquid. Chill it well.
4. Serve the fish chilled.

Poached Tenderloin with Green Peppercorn Sabayon

<u>*Yield: 10 servings*</u>

Beef tenderloin, trimmed and tied	3 pounds	1.35 kilograms
Beef consommé	3 quarts	3 liters
Bouquet garni (use desired fresh herbs, leeks, celery)	1	1
Dry white wine	2 ounces	60 milliliters
Egg yolks	3	3
Green peppercorns, crushed	2 ounces	55 grams
Salt	to taste	to taste

1. Season the beef well.

2. Bring the consommé to a simmer in a rondeau.

3. Add the tenderloin and bouquet garni. Poach the tenderloin until it reaches an internal temperature of 125 to 130°F (51°C). Remove the tenderloin from the consommé and keep it warm.

4. At the time of service, slice the tenderloin.

5. Combine 3 ounces of cooking liquid with the egg yolks in a stainless-steel bowl. Add the wine.

6. Cook the yolks, whipping them constantly, until they are thick and foamy. Add the green peppercorns and adjust the seasoning with the salt.

7. Serve the sauce with the sliced tenderloin.

Poule-au-Pot (Chicken with Vegetables)

Yield: 2 servings

Whole chicken, trimmed	2½ pounds	1.15 kilograms
Chicken stock or broth	as needed	as needed
Bouquet garni	1	1

Vegetable Garnish (per portion)

Carrots, tourné or batonnet	2	2
Pearl onions	2	2
Celery, tourné or batonnet	2	2
Parsnips, tourné or batonnet	2	2
Peas, fresh or frozen	1 tablespoon	20 grams
Fennel, batonnet	2	2
Mushrooms (shiitake, enoki, or domestic), sliced if desired	1 to 2	1 to 2
Salt	to taste	to taste
Pepper	to taste	to taste
Herbs, chopped, fresh (optional)	to taste	to taste

1. Truss the chicken.

2. Cover the chicken with cold stock. Bring the stock to a simmer. Add the bouquet garni. Poach the chicken until it is tender and cooked through. Skim the surface, as necessary, throughout the poaching period.

3. Cook the vegetables separately until they are tender. Refresh and hold them.

4. At service, portion the chicken and serve it with the broth and vegetables reheated in the broth. Add the salt, pepper, and chopped, fresh herbs, if desired.

Seafood Poached in a Saffron Broth with Fennel

Yield: 10 servings

Fish consommé	2 quarts	2 liters
Saffron, crushed	1 teaspoon	1.5 grams
Standard sachet d'épices	1	1
Pernod	4 ounces	120 milliliters
White wine	4 ounces	120 milliliters
Fennel, julienned	1 pound	455 grams
Tomato concassé	1 pound	455 grams
Assorted seafood, cleaned and cut into large dice	4 to 5 ounces per portion	115 to 140 grams per portion

1. Combine the consommé, saffron, sachet d'épices, Pernod, wine, fennel, and tomato concassé; simmer the liquid until the fennel is barely tender and the broth is well-flavored.

2. At the time of service, heat to a bare simmer 8 ounces (240 milliliters) of the broth per serving. Add the seafood and poach it until it is just cooked through. Serve the fish in heated soup bowls.

NOTE: A variety of seafood may be used, including shrimp, monkfish, squid, shark, scallops, lobster, and so forth.

Poached Salmon with Hollandaise

Yield: 1 serving

Court bouillon	as needed	as needed
Salmon, cut into scallops, tranche, or steak	5 ounces	140 grams
Hollandaise sauce	¾ ounce	22 grams

1. Heat the poaching liquid to 165°F (74°C). Place the salmon in the liquid.

2. Keep the liquid at a simmer; do not boil it. Poach the fish for 4 to 5 minutes for scallops, 8 to 10 minutes for tranches, or 10 to 12 minutes for steak.

3. Remove the fish from the liquid and drain it.

4. Nappé the fish with the sauce.

NOTE: Other warm emulsified sauces, such as Beurre Blanc, may also be used.

Cioppino

Yield: 10 servings

Olive oil	3 ounces	75 milliliters
Onion, finely diced	6 ounces	170 grams
Scallions, diced	2 bunches	2 bunches
Green pepper, diced	2	2
Fennel, diced	5 ounces	140 grams
Garlic, minced	5 cloves	5 cloves
Tomato concassé	4 pounds	1.8 kilograms
Tomato puree	8 ounces	225 grams
Dry white wine	8 ounces	240 milliliters
Bay leaves	2	2
Black peppercorns, crushed	to taste	to taste
Salt	to taste	to taste
Cherrystone clams	20	20
Crab, disjointed	3	3
Shrimp, peeled, de-veined	20	20
Swordfish, diced	2½ pounds	1.15 kilograms
Basil, fresh, chopped	3 tablespoons	7 grams
Garlic-flavored croutons	10	10

1. Heat the oil in a soup pot. Add the onions, scallions, peppers, and fennel. Sauté them until the onions are translucent.

2. Add the garlic and sauté it until an aroma is apparent.

3. Add the tomato concassé, tomato puree, white wine, and bay leaves. Cover the pot and simmer the mixture slowly for about 45 minutes. Add a small amount of water, if necessary.

4. Add the pepper and salt to taste. Remove and discard the bay leaves.

5. Add the whole clams and crab. Simmer them for about 10 minutes. Add the shrimp and swordfish; simmer them until the fish is just cooked through.

6. Add the chopped basil; adjust the seasoning to taste. Ladle the cioppino into heated bowls and garnish each bowl with a crouton.

New England Boiled Dinner

Yield: 25 servings

Corned beef brisket	1	1
Beef tongue	4 to 5 pounds	1.8 to 2.25 kilograms
White stock, cold	1 gallon (or as needed)	3.75 liters (or as needed)
Standard sachet d'épices	1	1

Vegetable Garnish (per serving)

Potatoes, red bliss	2	2
Green cabbage wedges	2	2
Onions, pearl or boiling	2	2
Carrots, tourné	2	2
Parsnips, tourné	2	2
Rutabaga, tourné	2	2
Beets, tourné	2	2
Green beans, cut in 2-inch lengths	1 ounce	30 grams

Sauce (per serving)

Béchamel	2 ounces	60 grams
Heavy cream	½ ounce	15 milliliters
Horseradish	to taste	to taste

1. Place the beef and tongue in a pot with enough cold stock to cover them. Bring the stock to a slow simmer.

2. Add the sachet d'épices; continue to simmer the liquid gently for approximately 3 hours or until the meats are very tender. Remove the meats; keep them warm and moist.

3. Cook the vegetables separately in the stock or reserved cooking liquid.

4. Combine the ingredients for the sauce and heat the mixture.

5. Slice the meats and serve them with the vegetables and sauce.

Boiled Lobster

Yield: 1 serving

Lobster	1	1
Drawn butter	as needed	as needed
Lemon	as needed	as needed
Parsley sprigs (optional)	as needed	as needed

1. Plunge the live lobsters, headfirst, into a large pot of boiling, salted water.

2. When the water returns to a boil, simmer the lobster for 6 to 8 minutes (for a 1-pound lobster). Larger lobsters may take up to 20 minutes, depending on their weight. Do not overcook it or the meat will toughen.

3. For cold boiled lobster or when lobster meat will be removed from the shell for another use, cool the cooked lobster in cold running water. (This step makes handling easier and prevents further cooking.)

4. For hot boiled lobster, serve it immediately with lemon wedges and drawn butter.

DIRECTIONS FOR CRACKING A LOBSTER

Disjoint the claws, and crack and/or remove a portion of the shell for the guest's convenience

Split the body from head to tail all the way through the shell and remove the stomach and intestinal vein; or break the tail carapace (body), split it in half lengthwise, and remove the intestinal vein.

Pull the shell from the remainder of the body section and remove the stomach. Then reassemble the body section and place it head-up in the center of a platter or plate Arrange the claws and tail sections around the body.

Chapter *21*

Combination Cooking Methods

Combination cooking methods are so called because they apply both dry heat and moist heat to the main item. The two major combination techniques are:

- braising
- stewing

Because they require less tender (and less expensive) main ingredients than à la minute techniques, braises and stews are often referred to as "peasant" dishes. These dishes traditionally have had a robust, hearty flavor and are often thought of as "winter meals"; however, with some modification, braising and stewing techniques have valid applications year-round. The customary heavy foods are being replaced with poultry, fish, and shellfish, which can be faster to prepare, lighter in flavor and color, and appropriate to most contemporary menus. There are numerous examples of dishes that combine two or more distinct cooking methods, such as the coulibiac of salmon shown at left. The salmon steams inside the pastry as the dish bakes.

COMBINATION METHOD USES

Combination methods are most often considered appropriate for foods that are flavorful but that are too tough to be successfully prepared by any of the à la minute techniques. However, tender foods also can be braised or stewed successfully. Tender foods will require less cooking liquid, a lower temperature, and a shorter cooking time.

The first step for most combination methods is to sear the main item. The item then completes the cooking process in the presence of a liquid, which may be simply the juices released from the food, which are already present, or a liquid that is added to the pot. Because the cooking vessel is covered during most of the cooking time, these liquids turn to steam and the food cooks by simmering and steaming.

Braising

In braising, the item is first seared in hot oil and then slowly cooked in a liquid medium. This technique is considered appropriate for foods that are portion-sized or larger, or cuts from more exercised areas of large animals, mature whole birds, or large fish. Relatively little liquid (stock or jus) is used in relation to the main item's volume. A bed of mirepoix, which lifts the main item away from the pot bottom, also introduces additional moisture and flavor.

One of braising's benefits is that less tender cuts of meat become tender as the moist heat gently penetrates the meat and causes tough connective tissues to soften. Another bonus is that any flavor from the item is released into the cooking liquid, and becomes the accompanying sauce; thus, virtually all flavor and nutrients are retained.

This does not mean that tender foods, even delicate fish and shellfish, cannot be braised. To properly braise these kinds of foods, the chef must use less cooking liquid, and must cook the food at a lower temperature and for a shorter time.

The first step for most braises is to sear the main item in a small amount of hot fat. This develops the proper flavor and color and is done in a rondeau or brazier over direct heat on the stove top. Mirepoix is then allowed to lightly brown or sweat in the same pot and the cooking liquid is added and brought to a simmer. Once these steps are completed, the pot is usually covered and placed in a moderate oven.

Braising in the oven tends to result in a better product without danger of causing the food to scorch from prolonged contact with a pot in direct contact with an open flame. Air is a less efficient conductor than metal—the result is a gentler transfer of heat. There is also less chance of inadvertently overcooking (and thereby toughening) the item. Finally, burner space is kept open for other needs.

If all the braising is to be done on the stove top, certain precautions must be taken. The cooking speed must be carefully regulated because the liquid can easily become too hot. If this happens, the portion of the main item covered by the liquid will cook more quickly than any exposed areas and could become tough or stringy. Scorching will also be a problem.

The following is a partial listing of braising techniques and specific names for braised dishes of various types and nationalities.

Daube. A daube is a braise customarily made from red meats, often beef, and includes red wine. The main item is often marinated before braising. The name is derived from the French pot used to prepare a daube, the *daubière*, which has an indentation in the lid to hold hot pieces of charcoal.

Estouffade. This is a French term used to refer to the braising method and the dish itself.

Pot roast. This common American term for braising is also the name of a traditional braised dish.

Swissing. This is a braising technique often associated with portion-size meat cuts. The main item is repeatedly dredged in flour and pounded to tenderize the flesh (Swiss steak, for example).

Mise en Place

1. Main item. Foods to be braised are traditionally more mature, less tender, and more flavorful than foods prepared by dry-heat and moist-heat techniques. Tender foods, especially fish, should be cooked the minimum amount of time necessary to achieve the best flavor. Trim away all fat, silverskin, and gristle on the main item. Marinate and stuff red meats, if desired. Truss poultry. Marinate and/or stuff the item if desired. Stuff whole fish with an aromatic filling and then wrap it in lettuce leaves or other coverings to help maintain shape and prevent it from breaking apart during cooking, if desired. Dredge the main item in flour. This will help to thicken the sauce during cooking.

2. Mirepoix. A mirepoix used in braising should be peeled if it is to be pureed and used in the sauce. Cut the vegetables into an appropriate size, depending on the cooking time required for the main item.

3. Liquid. Have available a well-flavored stock or jus appropriate to the main item's flavor.

4. Aromatics. Prepare a sachet d'épices or bouquet garni, including spices, herbs, and other aromatic ingredients, as desired or required by the recipe.

5. Optional components.

- Pork product. Braised items often include some sort of pork product. Have available ham, bacon, or salt pork. Blanch these to remove excess salt, if necessary.
- Tomatoes. Tomatoes, frequently included in braised dishes, act as a tenderizer to break down the tough tissues of less tender meats and also give the finished dish additional flavor and color. Have available tomato puree, tomato concassé, or tomato paste.
- Other vegetables. Vegetable garnishes may be added for color, flavor, and texture to the dish as it braises. They should be added in a timely fashion, so that they will finish cooking at the same time as the main item. Prepare the vegetables as required by type.
- Thickener. Various thickeners may be used to prepare a sauce from the braising liquid: Dilute arrowroot or cornstarch in a cold liquid and add it to the sauce at the end of the cooking time; prepare a roux and add it to the braised item at the start of the cooking time; or puree the mirepoix and return it to the sauce.
- Garnishes. Many different garnishes are commonly used with braised items. Have available a garnish, according to the recipe.

Figure 21-1 shows the mise en place for a braised item, Yankee pot roast.

Method

1. Sear the main item in hot oil. This initial searing helps the item develop color and flavor. White meat and poultry should be seared only to the point at which the skin begins to turn color. Red meats should be seared to a deep brown color. Fish may not require an initial searing.

2. Remove the main item and add the mirepoix. For white meats, fish, poultry, and game birds, sweat the mirepoix until the onions are translucent. For red meats and large game, sweat until the onions are golden-brown. If a roux is being used as a sauce thickener, it may be added at this point.

21-1
Mise en place for Yankee Pot Roast.

3. Place the main item on the bed of mirepoix in the pot. The mirepoix furnishes both moisture and flavor. It also elevates the main item somewhat from the pot bottom and helps to prevent it from sticking.

4. Add the appropriate amount of liquid. There should be just enough liquid to keep the main item moistened throughout the cooking time and to produce an adequate amount of sauce to serve with the finished dish. The more tender the product, the less liquid will be required, because the cooking time will be shorter and there will be less opportunity for the liquid to reduce properly. In general, the liquid should cover the main item only by one-third (see Fig. 21-2).

5. Bring the liquid to a simmer over direct heat.

6. Cover the pot and place it in a moderate oven. The more tender the item, the lower the oven's temperature should be. Covering the pot allows the steam to condense on the lid and fall back onto the main item, moistening the food's exposed surfaces. The main item should be turned from time to time during cooking to keep all surfaces evenly moistened with the braising liquid.

7. Add the sachet d'épices or bouquet garni and vegetable garnish at the appropriate times, to assure proper flavor extraction and cooking.

8. Remove the lid during the final portion of the cooking time. This will cause the braising liquid to reduce adequately so that the sauce will have the

21-2

The correct ratio of braising medium to meat.

Yankee Pot Roast

Yield: 10 servings

Beef (cross-cut rib, bottom round, eye of round)	4 pounds	1.8 kilograms
Salt	to taste	to taste
Pepper	to taste	to taste
Oil	as needed	as needed
Mirepoix	1 pound	450 grams
Flour	2 ounces	60 grams
Tomato puree	6 ounces	170 grams
Red wine	8 ounces	240 milliliters
Brown stock	2½ quarts	2.5 liters
Standard sachet d'épices	1	1

1. Trim the beef and season it with the salt and pepper.
2. Sear the beef in hot oil; remove it and keep it warm.
3. Add the mirepoix; sauté it until it is browned.
4. Add the flour; cook it out for 3 to 4 minutes.
5. Add the tomato puree and pincé.
6. Place the beef on a bed of mirepoix.
7. Add the wine, stock, and sachet d'épices. Bring the liquid to a simmer. Cover the pan and braise the beef until it is fork-tender.
8. Remove the beef and keep it warm. Degrease the sauce and strain it. Simmer the sauce to reduce it, if necessary. Adjust the seasoning with salt and pepper to taste.
9. Slice the beef and serve it with the sauce.

VARIATION

Pot Roast with Root Vegetables: Tourné a variety of vegetables such as carrots, turnips, rutabaga, parsnips, and potatoes. Cook them separately until they are tender. Reheat them in the sauce.

proper consistency and flavor. Also, if the main item is turned frequently after the lid has been removed and is thus exposed to hot air, a glaze will form on its surface, providing a glossy sheen and a good flavor.

9. Remove the main item from the braising liquid when it is fork-tender. (See the information that follows on determining doneness.)

10. Place the pot over direct heat and continue to reduce the sauce to develop its flavor, body, and consistency. This additional reduction fortifies the sauce's flavor and provides an opportunity to skim away any surface fat. Add additional garnish or finishing ingredients at this point, as appropriate.

11. Strain the sauce. The mirepoix that is strained out may be either discarded or pureed and returned to the sauce. The sachet d'épices or bouquet garni should be discarded. Return the sauce to the heat and bring it to a boil. Add diluted arrowroot or cornstarch to lightly thicken the sauce, if desired. Add any final finishing or garnishing ingredients. Adjust the seasoning with salt and pepper.

12. Carve or slice the main item and serve it on heated plates with the sauce and an appropriate garnish.

For a quick summary, refer to the abbreviated method for braising.

Determining Doneness

Properly cooked braised foods are fork-tender. This means that they will slide easily from a kitchen fork inserted at the food's thickest part.

Evaluating Quality

The factors for evaluating quality are flavor, appearance, and texture. Braised foods should have an intense flavor as the result of long, gentle cooking. The main item's

BRAISING

1
Sear the main item on all sides in hot oil.

2
Remove the main item.

3
Add the mirepoix and sweat it.

4
Add the roux, if it is being used.

5
Return the main item to the bed of mirepoix in the pot.

6
Add the liquid.

7
Bring it to a simmer over direct heat.

8
Cover; finish the item in an oven until it is fork-tender.

9
Add the sachet d'épices or bouquet garni and garnishes at the appropriate times.

10
Remove the main item and keep it warm.

11
To prepare the sauce: Strain, reduce, thicken, and garnish it as desired.

12
Slice or carve the main item and serve it with a sauce and an appropriate garnish.

natural juices, along with the braising liquid, become concentrated, providing both a depth of flavor and a full-bodied sauce. If a braised food does not have a robust flavor, it may have been undercooked or perhaps was allowed to braise at an overly high temperature for an insufficient time. Another possibility is that the main item was not seared properly, with inadequate time allowed for browning the product before liquids were introduced. Finally, if the lid was not removed from the pot during the final stage of cooking, the sauce may not have reduced properly and a glaze may not have been allowed to form on the main item's surface.

Braised foods should have a deep color appropriate to the type of food. They should retain their natural shape, although a significant amount of volume is lost during cooking. To maintain the proper shape throughout the cooking time, the main item should be trussed or tied. It is also important to maintain the proper cooking speed.

Braised foods should be extremely tender, almost to the point at which they can be cut with a fork. They should not, however, fall into shreds; this would indicate that the main item has been overcooked.

Stewing

Stewing, similar to braising, can use the same meat cuts, but the main item is cut into bite-size pieces. The amount of liquid used in relation to the amount of the item varies from one style of preparation to another. Some stews call for very little additional liquid; others may call for proportionately more liquid than main item. A stew's components do not differ to any substantial degree from those of a braise.

The technique for stewing is also nearly identical to that for braising, although a few optional steps in stewing allow the cook to vary the results. For example, initial blanching of the main item, instead of searing, results in a pale, almost ivory-colored stew. Because the main item is cut into small pieces, the cooking time for stewing is shorter than for braising.

The following is a partial listing of stews of various types and nationalities.

Blanquette. This white stew is traditionally made from white meats (veal or chicken) or lamb, and is garnished with mushrooms and pearl onions. The sauce is always white and is finished with a liaison of egg yolks and heavy cream.

Bouillabaisse. This is a Mediterranean-style fish stew combining a variety of fish and shellfish.

Fricassée. Fricassée is a white stew, often made from veal, poultry, or small game (rabbit, for example).

Goulash (gulyas). This stew originated in Hungary and is made from beef, veal, or poultry, seasoned and colored with paprika, and generally served with potatoes and dumplings.

Navarin. This is a stew traditionally prepared from mutton or lamb, with a garnish of root vegetables, onions, and peas. The name probably derives from the French word for turnips, *navets*, which are the principle garnish.

Ragout. A French term for stew, this literally translates as "restores the appetite."

Matelote. This is a special type of fish stew, typically prepared with eel, although other fish may be used. Other fish stews that are served as main courses include bouillabaisse, cioppino, and bourride.

Mise en Place

Review the mise en place for braising. The difference between these techniques is that the main item is cut into small pieces, generally no larger than bite-size. In addition, stews are frequently prepared from naturally tender foods such as poultry or fish.

The essential components for stews are the same as for braising; however, the proportion of liquid to main product changes slightly. This is illustrated in the mise en place for a stew called Veal Blanquette (see Fig. 21-3).

Veal Blanquette

Yield: 10 servings

Breast of veal, boned, cut in a large dice	4 pounds	1.8 kilograms
Cold water	as needed	as needed
White beef stock	2 quarts	2 liters
Standard sachet d'épices	1	1
Roux	3 to 4 ounces	85 to 115 grams
Mushrooms	1½ pounds	680 grams
Butter	1 ounce	30 grams
Lemon juice	to taste	to taste
Egg yolks	2	2
Heavy cream	8 ounces	240 milliliters
Pearl onions, blanched	20	20

1. Cover the veal with cold water and blanch it. Drain and rinse the veal.

2. Combine the veal with the stock; simmer the veal until it is tender, about 1½ hours. Add the sachet d'épices during the final half-hour of cooking time.

3. Combine the roux with the cooking liquid; simmer the mixture until it is thickened.

4. Stew the mushrooms in butter until they are tender. Add the lemon juice and reserve the mushrooms.

5. At service, heat the blanquette to just below a boil. Combine the egg yolks and cream for a liaison. Temper the mixture and add it to the blanquette. Simmer the sauce until it is thickened, but do not boil it.

6. Add the mushrooms and pearl onions. Adjust the seasoning with salt and pepper to taste.

21-3
Mise en place for Veal Blanquette.

Method

1. Sear the main item in hot oil or blanch it by placing it in a pot of cold stock or water and bringing the liquid to a boil. Searing the main item assists in developing color and flavor.

In order to develop a good color, the main item should not be added to the pot in quantities so large that the pieces are touching one another. If they are touching, the pan's temperature will be lowered significantly, hindering proper

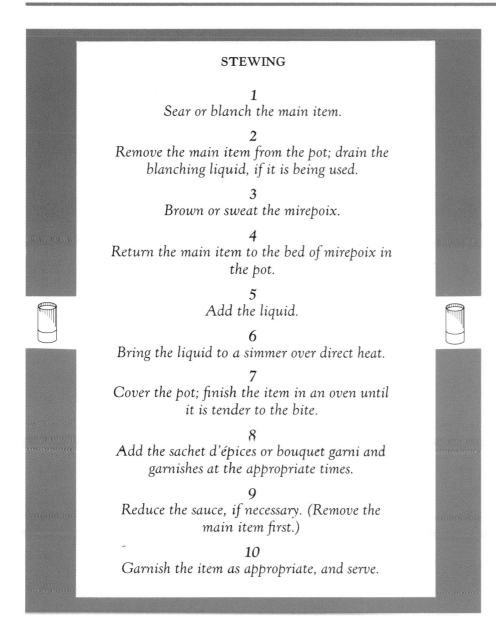

STEWING

1

Sear or blanch the main item.

2

*Remove the main item from the pot; drain the
blanching liquid, if it is being used.*

3

Brown or sweat the mirepoix.

4

*Return the main item to the bed of mirepoix in
the pot.*

5

Add the liquid.

6

Bring the liquid to a simmer over direct heat.

7

*Cover the pot; finish the item in an oven until
it is tender to the bite.*

8

*Add the sachet d'épices or bouquet garni and
garnishes at the appropriate times.*

9

*Reduce the sauce, if necessary. (Remove the
main item first.)*

10

Garnish the item as appropriate, and serve.

ing on the main item's natural juices to provide moisture. This is especially true for stews made from naturally tender foods such as fish or shellfish. Other stews may include proportionately more liquid than main item. See the specific recipes for guidance.

4. Cover the pot and place it in a moderate oven, or cook it over direct heat on the stove top.

5. Add the aromatics and vegetable garnish, if necessary or desired, at the appropriate time to assure proper cooking and extraction of flavor.

6. Stew the food until a piece of the main item is tender to the bite.

7. See step 11 under "Method" in the section on braising for information on finishing the sauce.

8. Serve the stew on heated plates with the sauce and the appropriate garnish.

For a quick summary, refer to the abbreviated method for stewing.

Determining Doneness

Because the main item is cut into small pieces, it is possible and advisable to test for doneness by biting into the food rather than applying the fork-tender test.

Evaluating Quality

See the guidelines under "Evaluating Quality" for braised foods.

SUMMARY

The result of a properly prepared braise or stew is a dish of complexity and flavor concentration that is simply not possible with other cooking techniques. The sauce also has exceptional body, because of the

coloring. Instead, the item should be seared in batches, and each batch should be removed when it has developed a good color. The main item is generally dredged in flour prior to searing, to assist in lightly thickening the cooking liquid.

Blanching also improves the color and flavor of the finished stew. In addition, skimming the surface of the blanching liquid removes any impurities that could give the stew a gray color or off flavor. Once the boil is reached, drain the main item.

2. Remove the main item from the pot and add the mirepoix. Lightly brown the mirepoix, or, for stews that should remain pale in color, sweat it until the vegetables begin to release their juices and become translucent.

3. Return the main item to the mirepoix bed in the pot; add the appropriate cooking liquid and bring it to a simmer. Some stews call for only a small amount of liquid, rely-

slow cooking needed to dissolve the main item's tough connective tissues. The proteins and other nutrients "lost" from the main item into the cooking liquid are not lost to the dish itself.

Braising and stewing may be thought of as "peasant" techniques, often associated with regional, home-style cooking. The successful use of these techniques depends, as do all cookery methods, on the proper choice of main ingredients and careful attention to the proper application of technique throughout each step of preparation and service. Contemporary renditions of classic dishes, such as a navarin made with lobster instead of mutton, are clear examples that no cooking technique need become outmoded.

Savory Swiss Steak

Yield: 10 servings

Beef bottom round, trimmed	ten 5-ounce steaks	ten 140-gram steaks
Flour	3 ounces	85 grams
Salt	to taste	to taste
Pepper	to taste	to taste
Oil	as needed	as needed

Seasoned Stock

Beef stock	5 quarts	4.75 liters
Tomato puree	8 ounces	240 milliliters
Soy sauce	5 ounces	150 milliliters
Black pepper	1 teaspoon	2 grams
Whole cloves	6	6
Bay leaves	2	2
Thyme sprig	1	1
Savory stem	1	1
Onions, small dice	1 pound	455 grams
Garlic cloves, crushed	2	2
Celery, small dice	½ pound	225 grams
Oil	as needed	as needed
Flour	12 ounces	340 grams
Salt	to taste	to taste

1. Season the flour with the salt and pepper and dredge the steaks; shake off any excess flour.

2. Heat ⅛-inch of oil in a skillet. Add the steaks and brown them on both sides. Remove the steaks to a brazier or roasting pan.

3. Combine all of the ingredients for the stock and simmer it for 20 minutes.

4. Sauté the onions, garlic, and celery in the oil in a saucepot until the vegetables are tender.

5. Add the flour and cook it to make a light brown roux.

6. Strain the hot stock and add it gradually to the roux, stirring it until it is thickened and smooth. Adjust the seasoning with salt, if desired, and pour the sauce over the steaks.

7. Braise the steaks at 350°F (175°C) until they are tender, about 2 hours.

Estouffade of Beef (Beef Stew)

Yield: 10 servings

Beef shank or chuck, cut into 1½-inch cubes	4 pounds	1.8 kilograms
Salt	to taste	to taste
Pepper	to taste	to taste
Oil	as needed	as needed
Mirepoix	1 pound	450 grams
Tomato paste	1 ounce	30 grams
Flour	2½ ounces	70 grams
Brown veal stock	1 quart	1 liter
Standard sachet d'épices	1	1

Garnish

Peas	4 ounces	115 grams
Carrots, tourné	20	20
Celery, tourné	20	20
Turnips, tourné	20	20
Pearl onions	10	10

1. Season the beef with the salt and pepper and sear it in hot oil. Remove and reserve it.
2. Add the mirepoix and let the onions brown. Add the tomato paste and pincé.
3. Place the mirepoix and tomato paste in a cheesecloth sachet.
4. Add the flour to the oil in the pan used to sear the meat. Cook out the roux.
5. Add one-third of the stock; whip out the lumps and bring it to a simmer. Add the remaining stock and return it to a simmer. Add the beef and mirepoix sachet.
6. Return it to a simmer; add the standard sachet d'épices.
7. Cover the food and braise it in an oven until the meat is very tender.
8. Cook the vegetables for the garnish separately until they are tender; reserve them.
9. Degrease the stew; discard the sachet.
10. Adjust the seasoning with salt and pepper to taste; reheat the vegetable garnish. Serve the stew garnished with the vegetables.

Choucroute

Yield: 20 servings

Onions, sliced	10 ounces	285 grams
Garlic, minced	1 ounce	30 grams
Granny Smith apples, peeled, ¼-inch dice	2	2
Goose fat, lard, or shortening	6 ounces	170 grams
Sauerkraut, prepared	2½ pounds	1.15 kilograms
Chicken stock	1 pint	480 milliliters
White wine	8 ounces	240 milliliters
Sachet d'épices plus 6 juniper berries	1	1
Carrot, whole	1	1
Pork loin, smoked	5 pounds	2.25 kilograms
Garlic pork sausages (optional)	2½ pounds	1.15 kilograms
Salt	to taste	to taste
Pepper	to taste	to taste
Idaho (or other high-starch) potatoes, finely grated	1 to 2	1 to 2

1. Sauté the onions, garlic, and apples in the hot fat without browning them.
2. If the sauerkraut is very salty, rinse it in several changes of water and squeeze it dry. Add the sauerkraut to the onions, garlic, and apples.
3. Add the chicken stock, wine, sachet d'épices, and carrot and stir.
4. Place the pork loin on top of the sauerkraut, cover the pan, and braise the meat for approximately 45 minutes.
5. Prick the skins of the sausages in 5 or 6 places and add them to the pan with the sauerkraut. Cover the pan and cook the pork loin and sausages until they reach 150°F (65°C) in internal temperature, approximately 15 to 20 minutes.
6. Remove the carrot, sachet d'épices, pork loin, and sausages. Season the sauerkraut with the salt and pepper.
7. Add the grated potato to the sauerkraut and cook it for 2 minutes to bind it.
8. Slice the pork loin and sausages and serve them on a bed of sauerkraut. Serve the boiled potatoes on the side.

Chicken Fricassée

Yield: 10 servings

Chicken, disjointed	7 pounds	3.2 kilograms
Salt	to taste	to taste
Pepper	to taste	to taste
Oil	4 ounces	115 grams
Spanish onions, diced	1 pound	450 grams
Garlic cloves, minced	2	2
Flour	2 ounces	60 grams
Dry white wine	8 ounces	240 milliliters
Chicken broth	16 ounces	480 milliliters
Bay leaves	2	2
Thyme	1 teaspoon	1 gram
Heavy cream	8 ounces	240 milliliters
Carrots, diced, blanched	1 pound	450 grams
Leeks, diced, blanched	1 pound	450 grams
Water, salted, boiling	as needed	as needed

1. Season the chicken with the salt and pepper. Sauté the chicken in oil for 1 minute without browning it.

2. Scatter the onions and garlic over the chicken. Cook the chicken, turning it often, for 5 minutes.

3. Sprinkle the flour over the chicken, turning it to coat evenly. Cook the chicken for 5 minutes.

4. Deglaze the pan with the wine.

5. Add the chicken broth, bay leaves, and thyme. Cover the pan and braise the chicken until it is fork-tender, about 30 minutes.

6. To finish, add the heavy cream and vegetables to the chicken. Simmer the chicken about 2 minutes and serve it with rice pilaf.

NOTE: Refer to Chapter 24 for the recipe for Rice Pilaf.

Mole Poblano

Yield: 10 servings

Onion, fine dice	8 ounces	225 grams
Olive oil	4 ounces	120 milliliters
Garlic cloves, mashed	6	6
Green pepper, fine dice	8 ounces	225 grams
Jalapeño peppers, chopped fine	10	10
Almonds, blanched, chopped	1 ounce	30 grams
Chili powder	2 ounces	60 grams
Anise seeds	1 teaspoon	2.5 grams
Ginger, fresh, grated	1 tablespoon	14 grams
Cinnamon, ground	½ teaspoon	500 milligrams
Thyme, dried leaves	½ teaspoon	1 gram
Tomato concassé	1 pound	450 grams
Chicken stock	1 pint	480 milliliters
Peanut butter	4 tablespoons	60 milliliters
Chicken breasts, boneless	10	10
Mexican chocolate, chopped	3 to 4 ounces	85 to 115 grams
Sesame seeds, toasted	2 tablespoons	14 grams

1. Brown the onions; add the garlic, peppers, and almonds and sauté them for a few minutes.

2. Add the seasonings and sauté the mixture briefly. Add the tomato concassé.

3. Deglaze the pan with the stock and add the peanut butter.

4. Sear the chicken and place it in a braising pan. Add the sauce and bring it to a boil. Cover the pan and braise the chicken in a moderate oven until it is tender. Remove the chicken and keep it warm.

5. Adjust the consistency of the sauce, add the chocolate, and adjust the seasoning with salt and pepper to taste.

6. Pour the sauce over the chicken and reheat it in the oven. Garnish it with the toasted sesame seeds.

Sauerbraten

Yield: 10 servings

Marinade

Dry red wine	8 ounces	240 milliliters
Red wine vinegar	8 ounces	240 milliliters
Water	2 quarts	2 liters
Onion, sliced	2	2
Black peppercorns	8	8
Juniper berries	10	10
Bay leaves	2	2
Cloves	2	2
Beef knuckles, split and tied	5 pounds	2.25 kilograms
Salt	2 teaspoons	10 grams
Vegetable oil	3 ounces	90 milliliters
Mirepoix, diced	1 pound	450 grams
Tomato paste	4 ounces	115 grams
Flour	2 ounces	60 grams
Brown stock	3 quarts	2.85 liters
Gingersnap cookies, pulverized	3 ounces	85 grams

1. Combine all the ingredients for the marinade and bring the mixture to a boil. Cool it to room temperature.

2. Season the beef with salt and place it in the marinade; marinate it under refrigeration for 3 to 5 days, turning it twice per day.

3. Remove the meat from the marinade. Strain and reserve the marinade; reserve the onions and herbs separately.

4. Bring the strained marinade to a boil and skim off the scum.

5. Heat the oil in a brazier. Add the meat and sear it on all sides. Remove the meat and reserve it.

6. Add the mirepoix and reserved onions and herbs from the marinade. Let them brown lightly.

7. Add the tomato paste and pincé.

8. Deglaze the pan with the marinade and reduce the liquid.

9. Add the flour and combine the mixture thoroughly.

10. Add the brown stock and whip out any lumps. Return the meat to the pan, cover it and simmer until tender.

11. Remove the meat and reduce the sauce.

12. Add the gingersnaps and cook the sauce for 10 minutes, until the gingersnaps dissolve. Strain the sauce through cheesecloth.

NOTE: Sauerbraten is traditionally served with dumplings or boiled potatoes and braised red cabbage (see the recipes in Chapter 22).

Braised Lamb Shanks

Yield: 10 servings

Lamb shank, well-trimmed	10 pounds	4.5 kilograms
Salt	to taste	to taste
Black pepper, freshly ground	to taste	to taste
Oil	as needed	as needed
Mirepoix	1 pound	450 grams
Garlic cloves, minced	3	3
Tomato paste	1 ounce	30 grams
Dry white wine (optional)	1 pint	480 milliliters
Brown sauce (or half brown sauce, half brown stock)	2 quarts	2 liters
Standard sachet d'épices	1	1

1. Season the lamb with the salt and pepper. Sear it in hot oil on all sides and remove it.

2. Add the mirepoix to the same oil and caramelize it.

3. Add the garlic, tomato paste, and wine and reduce the sauce.

4. Add the brown sauce and reduce it slightly.

5. Add the lamb shanks and sachet d'épices and adjust the seasoning with salt and pepper to taste. Cover the pan and braise the lamb until it is fork-tender, about 1¼ hours.

6. Remove the lamb shanks. Strain the sauce, degrease it, and return the meat to the sauce.

VARIATIONS

Lamb Shanks "Pontchartrain": Serve the lamb shanks with Creole Vegetables (see Chapter 24, "Cooking Grains and Legumes").

Lamb Shanks Printanière: Garnish the lamb with tournéed carrots, turnips, potatoes, glazed pearl onions, peas, and green beans. The vegetables and lamb should be prepared separately.

Couscous

Yield: 10 servings

Olive oil	3 ounces	90 milliliters
Lamb, shoulder or leg, cut in 1-inch cubes	2 pounds	910 grams
Onion, diced	8 ounces	225 grams
Garlic cloves, chopped	8	8
Saffron threads	pinch	pinch
Ginger, grated	1 tablespoon	14 grams
Cloves, ground	dash	dash
Cumin, ground	3 tablespoons	21 grams
Coriander, ground	1 teaspoon	2.5 grams
Nutmeg	½ teaspoon	1 gram
Turmeric	3 tablespoons	20 grams
Bay leaves	2	2
Salt	to taste	to taste
Chicken or lamb stock	1 quart	1 liter
Carrots, 1-inch dice	8 ounces	225 grams
Turnips, 1-inch dice	4 ounces	115 grams
Chicken legs	4	4
Couscous	1 pound	450 grams
Zucchini, 1-inch dice	8 ounces	225 grams
Green pepper, 1-inch dice	8 ounces	225 grams
Chickpeas, cooked	½ cup	120 milliliters
Tomatoes, peeled, wedges	1 pound	450 grams
Artichoke bottoms, quarters	10	10
Lima beans, cooked	2 ounces	60 grams
Arabic white truffles, sliced (if available)	4 ounces	115 grams

Garnish

Almonds, sliced and toasted	6 ounces	170 grams
Raisins, washed, or currants	6 ounces	170 grams
Harissa sauce (hot sauce), diluted with 1 ounce water	1 ounce	30 milliliters
Parsley, chopped	as needed	as needed

1. In the lower pan of a couscoussière, sauté the lamb with the onion, garlic, and spices in the olive oil. Cover with the stock and simmer until the lamb is nearly cooked.

2. Add the carrots, turnips, and chicken legs.

3. Wash and soak the couscous in warm water for 1½ minutes and place it in the top pan of the couscoussière.

4. Steam the couscous over the simmering stew for 20 minutes.

5. Remove the top pan and mix the salt into the couscous.

6. Add the zucchini and green peppers to the lower pan and cook the stew for 4 minutes.

7. Add the chickpeas, tomatoes, artichoke bottoms, lima beans, and truffles and return the stew to a boil. Adjust the seasonings to taste.

8. Mound the couscous on a heated plate or platter and place the meat stew in the center of the mound. Serve the garnishes separately.

Chili

Yield: 10 servings

Beef shank, diced	4 pounds	1.8 kilograms
Salt	to taste	to taste
Pepper	to taste	to taste
Onion, minced	8 ounces	225 grams
Oil	as needed	as needed
Garlic cloves, minced to a paste	3	3
Chili powder, mild	1 ounce	30 grams
Cumin, ground	1 ounce	30 grams
Tomato puree	3 ounces	85 grams
Demi-glace	4 ounces	120 milliliters
Tomato concassé	1½ pounds	680 grams

1. Season the beef with the salt and pepper.

2. Sweat the onions in hot oil.

3. Add the garlic and cook it until an aroma is apparent.

4. Add the meat. Sauté it until lightly seared.

5. Add the spices, tomato puree, and demi-glace. Mix them together with the meat.

6. Bring the chili to a simmer; cover the pan and braise the meat in a moderate oven until it is very tender to the bite.

7. Add the tomato concassé; heat the chili thoroughly. Adjust the seasoning with salt and pepper to taste.

Paella

Yield: 10 servings

Chicken legs, cut into thighs and drumsticks	10	10
Olive oil	3 ounces	90 milliliters
Garlic, chopped	1 ounce	30 grams
Onion, 1-inch dice	8 ounces	225 grams
Red pepper, 1-inch dice	8 ounces	225 grams
Green pepper, 1-inch dice	8 ounces	225 grams
Rice, converted	1½ pounds	680 grams
Saffron, crushed	1 teaspoon	1.5 grams
Salt	to taste	to taste
Chicken stock, hot	24 ounces	720 milliliters
Clams, fresh, cleaned	30	30
Mussels, fresh, cleaned	30	30
Shrimp, 21 to 25 count, peeled and de-veined	30	30
Chorizo, cooked and sliced	8 ounces	225 grams
Tomato concassé, 1-inch dice	8 ounces	225 grams
Niçoise (black) olives, pitted	6 ounces	170 grams
Picholine (green) olives, pitted	6 ounces	170 grams
Scallions, sliced	4 ounces	225 grams

1. Brown the chicken legs in the olive oil. Transfer the chicken to a baking pan; reserve the oil. Place the chicken in a 375°F (190°C) oven and roast it until it is done.

2. Sauté the vegetables in the reserved oil.

3. Add the rice and season the mixture with saffron and salt.

4. Add the stock and bring the mixture to a boil. Cover the pan and place it in a 400°F (205°C) oven; cook the rice mixture for 8 minutes.

5. Place the clams and mussels on top of the rice. Replace the cover and return the pan to the oven for 4 minutes.

6. Add the shrimp, chorizo, and tomato concassé. Return the pan to the oven and cook the paella until the shrimp is cooked through and all ingredients are very hot.

7. Garnish the paella with the olives and scallions.

Stewed Rabbit with Prunes

Yield: 10 servings

Rabbit, skinned and dressed	3	3
Flour	6 ounces	170 grams
Lard	2 ounces	55 grams
Shallots, minced	2 ounces	55 grams
Mirepoix, fine dice	1½ pounds	680 grams
Dry white wine	24 ounces	720 milliliters
Espagnole sauce	1½ quarts	1.5 liters
Salt	to taste	to taste
Pepper	to taste	to taste
Thyme, fresh	1 sprig	1 sprig
Bay leaf	2	2
Arrowroot, diluted	as needed	as needed
Prunes, pitted	40	40
Red currant jelly	6 ounces	170 grams

1. Clean the rabbits thoroughly. Remove all sinews and tendons. Cut the rabbits into 7 pieces. Reserve the trim meat and bones.

2. Dredge the rabbit pieces in the flour. Shake off the excess.

3. Sauté the rabbit in hot lard in a brazier until it is light brown. Remove it and keep it warm.

4. Add the shallots and mirepoix to the pot along with the reserved trim meat and bones. Sauté them briefly.

5. Add the wine, Espagnole sauce, salt, pepper, and spices with the reserved rabbit. Bring the mixture to a boil.

6. Cover the pot and braise the rabbit in a 350°F (175°C) oven until it is tender. Remove the rabbit to a clean pan.

7. Strain and skim the sauce.

8. Adjust the sauce consistency with the diluted arrowroot. Pour the sauce over the rabbit.

9. Add the prunes and currant jelly and simmer the sauce for 5 minutes. Adjust the seasoning to taste. Serve the rabbit with the sauce.

Cassoulet

<u>*Yield:* 12 servings</u>

Confit

Kosher salt	4 tablespoons	60 grams
Curing salt	¼ teaspoon	4 grams
Black pepper	¼ teaspoon	2 grams
Juniper berries, crushed	2	2
Bay leaf, crushed	1	1
Garlic, chopped	½ tablespoon	7 grams
Duck, cut in 6 pieces	one 6-pound bird	one 2.72-kilogram bird
Duck fat, rendered	as needed	as needed

Bean Stew

Navy beans, dried	2 pounds	910 grams
Chicken stock	3 quarts	2.85 liters
Slab bacon	1 pound	450 grams
Garlic sausage	1 pound	450 grams
Onions medium, whole	2	2
Garlic, chopped	1 ounce	30 grams
Bouquet garni	1	1

Meat Stew

Pork loin, cut in 2-inch cubes	1½ pounds	680 grams
Lamb, shoulder or leg, cut in 2-inch cubes	1½ pounds	680 grams
Olive oil	3 ounces	90 milliliters
Salt	to taste	to taste
White mirepoix	1 pound	450 grams
Garlic, chopped	1 ounce	30 grams
Dry white wine	8 ounces	240 milliliters
Tomato concassé, ¼-inch dice	2 pounds	910 grams
Sachet d'épices	1	1
Demi-glace	1 quart	1 liter
Brown stock	8 ounces	240 milliliters
Bread crumbs, fresh	2 cups	480 milliliters
Parsley, fresh, chopped	½ cup	18 grams

1. To prepare the confit: Mix all the seasonings, coat the duck with the mixture, and place it in a container with a weighted lid. Press the duck for 72 hours under refrigeration.

2. Brush off the excess seasoning mixture and stew the meat in the duck fat until it is very tender.

3. When ready to use the confit, scrape away any excess fat and broil the duck on a rack until the skin is crisp. Debone and slice the duck.

4. Clean and sort the beans for the bean stew. Bring the chicken stock to a boil, drop in the beans, and cook them for 2 minutes. Remove them from the heat and let them stand for 1 hour.

5. Add the bacon to the beans, return them to a boil, and cook them for 30 minutes.

6. Add the sausage, onions, garlic, and bouquet garni; return the mixture to a boil and cook it until the sausage reaches 150°F (65°C) internal temperature and the bacon is fork-tender.

7. Remove the sausage, bacon, and bouquet garni.

8. Cook the beans until they are tender. Strain the beans and reserve; reduce the stock.

9. Sear the pork and lamb in hot olive oil until they are brown. Remove and reserve them.

10. Degrease the pan and sauté the white mirepoix. Add the garlic and salt.

11. Deglaze the pan with the white wine.

12. Add the tomato concassé, sachet d'épices, demi-glace, and brown stock. Bring the sauce to a boil and pour it over the meat.

13. Cover the pan and braise the meat in an oven at 375°F (190°C) until the beans are quite tender.

14. Remove the meat and reduce the sauce. Adjust the seasoning and strain the sauce. Add it to the stew for flavor.

15. Peel the sausage and slice it.

16. Cut the bacon in ¼-inch slices.

17. Place the sausage, bacon, pork, and lamb in a casserole. Cover the meat with half of the beans, then the duck confit, and then the remaining beans.

18. Pour the sauce over all and sprinkle it with the breadcrumbs and parsley.

19. Bake the cassoulet in a moderate oven until it is heated through and a good crust has formed.

Shrimp Jambalaya

Yield: 10 servings

Salt pork	6 ounces	170 grams
Onion, diced	6 ounces	170 grams
Green peppers, diced	6 ounces	170 grams
Red peppers, diced	6 ounces	170 grams
Ham, diced	8 ounces	225 grams
Garlic, minced	5 cloves	5 cloves
Rice, long-grain	8 ounces	225 grams
Salt	2 teaspoons	10 grams
Hot pepper sauce	to taste	to taste
Coriander seed	1 teaspoon	2 grams
Fish stock	3 pints	1.5 liters
Chickpeas, cooked, drained	8 ounces	225 grams
Olives, ripe, pitted	3 ounces	85 grams
Tomato concassé	8	8
Shrimp, peeled, de-veined	2½ pounds	1.15 kilograms
Okra, whole	20	20
Cilantro or parsley, fresh, chopped	3 tablespoons	7 grams

1. Render the salt pork until it is lightly browned.
2. Add the onions, peppers, ham, and garlic; cook them over high heat until an aroma is apparent.
3. Add the rice; cook until the rice is coated with the rendered fat. (It should appear shiny.) Add the salt, hot pepper sauce, coriander, and stock. Bring the mixture to a boil.
4. Add the chickpeas, olives, and tomato concassé. Cover the pot and cook the mixture over low heat for 20 minutes, or until the rice is nearly tender.
5. Add the shrimp; cover the pot again and cook the jambalaya until the shrimp are barely cooked through.
6. Sauté the okra quickly and add it to the jambalaya. Serve.

Seafood Newburg, St. Andrew's Style

Yield: 4 servings

Scallops	5 ounces	140 grams
Lobsters, blanched	two 1-pound lobsters	two 450-gram lobsters
Shrimp, shelled and de-veined, shells reserved	6 ounces	170 grams
Olive oil	1 teaspoon	5 milliliters
Shallots, chopped	1 tablespoon	15 grams
Tomato paste	2 teaspoons	10 grams
Fish stock	28 ounces	840 milliliters
Brandy	3 tablespoons	45 milliliters
Arrowroot	3½ teaspoons	20 grams
Evaporated skim milk	⅓ cup	90 milliliters
Butter	3½ teaspoons	18 grams
Sherry	⅓ cup	90 milliliters

1. Remove and discard the muscle tabs from the scallops.

2. Remove and reserve the meat from the lobster tail and claws; reserve the shells.

3. Heat the olive oil over high heat in a large skillet. Add the shallots and sauté them until they are translucent, stirring constantly. Add the tomato paste; sauté the mixture for another minute, stirring constantly. Add the fish stock and simmer.

4. Add the lobster and shrimp shells. Reduce the heat to medium. Cover the skillet and sweat the shells for 5 to 6 minutes. Stir once or twice to prevent sticking. Remove the cover. Add the brandy and stir well; reduce the mixture.

5. Strain the liquid through a sieve or a cheesecloth lined colander, pressing the solids well. Return the strained liquid to a skillet over high heat.

6. Dilute the arrowroot with the evaporated milk and add it to the skillet. Simmer the sauce for 2 to 3 minutes, or until it is thickened.

7. Heat the butter over high heat in a skillet. Add the scallops, lobster, and shrimp. Sauté them until they are just cooked.

8. Add the sauce to the seafood and simmer it for 5 minutes. Finish the sauce with the sherry and serve the seafood in heated soup plates.

NOTE: This dish is a reworking of a classic recipe in order to reduce overall calories, fat, cholesterol, and sodium.

Calamares Rellenos (Stuffed Squid)

Yield: 10 servings

Squid, cleaned	ten 8-ounce squid	ten 225-gram squid
Ham, chopped fine	10 ounces	285 grams
Stuffed olives, chopped	30	30
Tomato concassé	8 ounces	225 grams
Salt	to taste	to taste
Pepper	to taste	to taste
Parsley, fresh, chopped	2 tablespoons	4.5 grams
Olive oil	3 ounces	90 milliliters
Onion, chopped	8 ounces	225 grams
Garlic cloves, minced	6	6
White wine	8 ounces	240 milliliters
Tomato sauce	1 pint	480 milliliters
Flour	as needed	as needed
Cilantro, chopped	1 ounce	30 grams

1. Remove the squid tentacles. Reserve half the tentacles (leaving them whole). Finely chop the remaining tentacles and mix them with the ham, olives, tomato concassé, salt, pepper, and parsley. Stuff each squid three-quarters full with this mixture, close the ends, and secure them with toothpicks.

2. Sauté the onion and garlic in the olive oil until they are soft. Place the squid on top of the onion mixture.

3. Add the wine and bring the mixture to a boil.

4. Pour the tomato sauce over the squid and braise it in a moderate oven until it reaches an internal temperature of 140°F (60°C).

5. Flour and fry the reserved tentacles to be used as a garnish.

6. Serve the calamari sprinkled with the cilantro.

Irish Stew

Yield: 10 servings

Lamb shoulder, cut in 1½-inch cubes	4 pounds	1.8 kilograms
White stock	1½ quarts	1.5 liters
Mirepoix	4 ounces	115 grams
Potatoes, peeled, cut into large chunks	1 pound	450 grams
Sachet d'épices: bay, thyme, peppercorns, parsley	1	1
Salt	to taste	to taste
White pepper	to taste	to taste

Garnish (pre-cooked separately, then combined)

Carrots, batonnet	20	20
Turnips, batonnet	20	20
Celery, batonnet	20	20
Pearl onions	20	20

1. Combine the lamb, stock, mirepoix, and potatoes.

2. Bring the stock to a simmer and skim the surface.

3. Add the sachet d'épices, cover the pan, and stew the meat in a moderate oven or over low heat until it is tender to the bite.

4. Degrease the pan; remove and discard the sachet d'épices; remove the potatoes and reserve them.

5. Puree the potatoes in a food mill or ricer.

6. Place the puree in a large bowl and thin it with the braising liquid to the desired consistency (a lightly thickened sauce).

7. Reduce any remaining broth to glace consistency and add to the puree.

8. Combine the broth with the lamb; season to taste with the salt and white pepper.

9. Garnish the lamb stew with the heated vegetables. Serve with parslied tournéed potatoes.

Polish Stuffed Cabbage

Yield: 10 servings

Savoy cabbage	2	2
Veal, cubed	12 ounces	340 grams
Pork, cubed	12 ounces	340 grams
Beef, cubed	12 ounces	340 grams
Onions, diced, sautéed, and cooled	10 ounces	285 grams
Cream	8 ounces	240 milliliters
Eggs, whole	3	3
Salt	to taste	to taste
Pepper	to taste	to taste
Nutmeg, ground	to taste	to taste
Bread crumbs, dry	1½ cups	360 milliliters
Mirepoix, sliced thin	6 ounces	170 grams
Bay leaf	1	1
Beef stock, hot	1 quart	1 liter
Bacon	10 slices	10 slices
Demi-glace, heated	1 pint	480 milliliters

1. Separate the cabbage into leaves; blanch and cool them.

2. Combine the meat, onions, cream, and eggs. Season them with the salt, pepper, and nutmeg and mix them well.

3. Run the mixture through a grinder twice.

4. Add the bread crumbs to the ground meat mixture.

5. Remove the large vein from each cabbage leaf. Place the meat in the center of each leaf and roll them up.

6. Place the cabbage rolls on top of the mirepoix and bay leaf. Add the hot stock and place the sliced bacon on top of the cabbage rolls.

7. Braise the cabbage rolls in a 350°F (175°C) oven, basting occasionally, to an internal temperature of 150°F (65°C).

8. Remove the cabbage rolls and keep them warm. Degrease the sauce; add the demi-glace and let the sauce reduce to the correct consistency and flavor. Adjust the seasoning with salt and pepper to taste.

Chicken Enchiladas

Yield: 10 servings

Olive oil	2 ounces	60 milliliters
Onion, minced	4 ounces	115 grams
Garlic cloves, minced	6	6
Flour	1 tablespoon	7 grams
Chili powder	2 tablespoons	15 grams
Salt	1½ teaspoons	8 grams
Allspice berries	3 to 4	3 to 4
Cumin, ground	2 tablespoons	15 grams
Thyme leaves	½ teaspoon	380 milligrams
Red and green bell peppers, julienned	8 ounces	225 grams
Vinegar	1 tablespoon	15 milliliters
Pimientos, julienned	7 ounces	200 grams
Ham trimmings	2 ounces	55 grams
Tomato paste	2 ounces	55 grams
Chicken stock	as needed	as needed
Chicken meat, cooked, cut in émincé	20 ounces	565 grams
Flour tortillas	20	20
Monterey Jack cheese, grated	4 ounces	115 grams

1. Sauté the onion in the olive oil until it is translucent. Add the garlic and sauté it briefly.

2. Combine the flour and spices. Stir them into the onion and garlic and cook the mixture for 1 minute.

3. Combine the peppers, vinegar, pimientos, ham trimmings, and tomato paste. Add the mixture to the sauce. Simmer the sauce until it is thick. Adjust the consistency with chicken stock if necessary.

4. Dip the tortillas in the sauce to coat them evenly. Portion the chicken onto the tortillas. Fold or roll them.

5. Place the enchiladas in a baking dish. Cover them with more of the sauce. Sprinkle the cheese on top. Bake the enchiladas at 350°F (175°C) until they are bubbly.

Matambre (Argentine Braised Stuffed Flank Steak)

<u>*Yield: 10 servings*</u>

Beef flank steaks, trimmed	3	3

Marinade

Garlic cloves, mashed	4	4
Cilantro, chopped	2 tablespoons	4.5 grams
Basil, chopped	2 tablespoons	4.5 grams
Olive oil	1 pint	480 milliliters
Red wine vinegar	1 cup	240 milliliters
Salt	to taste	to taste
Pepper	to taste	to taste

Stuffing

Bread crumbs, fresh	8 ounces	225 grams
Eggs, hard-boiled, chopped	3	3
Sweet corn kernels	6 ounces	170 grams
Spinach	1 pound	455 grams
Carrots, peeled and cut lengthwise	3	3
Onions, sliced	4 ounces	115 grams
Cilantro	1 ounce	30 grams
Salt	to taste	to taste
Pepper	to taste	to taste
Olive oil	4 ounces	120 milliliters
Red wine	10 ounces	300 milliliters
Demi-glace	1 quart	1 liter
Brown stock	1 quart	1 liter
Sachet d'épices with oregano	1	1

1. Butterfly the steak, slitting it horizontally in the direction of the grain.
2. Combine all of the ingredients for the marinade. Add the meat and marinate it under refrigeration for 24 hours. Drain the meat and dry it.
3. Mix the bread and eggs, sprinkle them over the meat, and top it with the spinach.
4. Boil the carrots until they are al dente. Cool them and place them on top of the spinach.
5. Spinkle the onions, cilantro, and salt and pepper on top.
6. Roll the flank steak in jelly-roll fashion and tie it with butcher's twine.

7. Brown the steak rolls evenly in hot oil.

8. Deglaze the pan with the wine. Add the demi-glace, stock, and sachet d'épices and braise the meat until it is fork-tender.

9. Reduce the sauce, adjust the seasoning, and strain it.

10. Slice the steak rolls crosswise. Serve them with the sauce.

Pork in Orange-and-Lemon Sauce with Sweet Potatoes

Yield: 20 servings

Marinade

Cider vinegar	2 cups	480 milliliters
Annatto seeds, crushed fine	3 tablespoons	21 grams
Cumin, ground	2 tablespoons	14 grams
Garlic, chopped	2 tablespoons	28 grams
Salt	1 tablespoon	17 grams
Black pepper, fresh, ground	1 teaspoon	2 grams
Pork loin, lean, cut in 1-inch cubes	3½ pounds	1.6 kilograms
Olive oil	4 ounces	120 milliliters
White stock	3 pints	1.5 liters
Orange juice, fresh	24 ounces	720 milliliters
Lemon juice, fresh	2 ounces	60 milliliters
Arrowroot	as needed	as needed
Salt	to taste	to taste
Pepper	to taste	to taste
Sweet potatoes, parcooked	5	5

1. Combine all of the ingredients for the marinade. Add the pork and marinate it overnight.

2. Remove the pork and dry it; reserve the marinade.

3. Brown the pork in the olive oil. Degrease the pan.

4. Add the reserved marinade and white stock. Bring it to a boil and simmer until the meat is tender.

5. Add the orange and lemon juices, bring the mixture to a simmer, and cook it for 3 minutes.

6. Adjust the consistency and seasoning with the arrowroot and salt and pepper.

7. Slice the sweet potatoes ¼-inch thick; reheat them. Arrange the potatoes on a plate and serve the pork and sauce over them.

Beef Goulash

Yield: 10 servings

Onions, sliced or diced	2 pounds	910 grams
Lard or oil	2 ounces	60 grams
White vinegar	1 ounce	30 milliliters
Hungarian paprika	4 tablespoons	28 grams
Marjoram, powdered	1 teaspoon	1 gram
Garlic cloves, minced	3	3
Lemon zest	1 teaspoon	4.5 grams
Salt	to taste	to taste
White beef stock	1 quart	1 liter
Tomato paste	4 ounces	115 grams
Beef shank, cut in large cubes	5 pounds	2.25 kilograms

1. Sauté the onions in the lard or oil until they are brown.
2. Add the vinegar, spices, garlic, lemon zest, and salt and mix them well.
3. Add the stock and tomato paste and bring the mixture to a boil.
4. Add the beef shank, cover the pan, and simmer it until it is tender, approximately 1½ hours.

Osso Buco Milanese

Yield: 10 servings

Veal shank pieces	10	10
Salt	to taste	to taste
Pepper	to taste	to taste
Flour	as needed	as needed
Oil	as needed	as needed
Dry white wine	8 ounces	240 milliliters
Tomato paste	6 ounces	170 grams
Brown veal stock	2 quarts	2 liters

Gremolada

Garlic clove, minced	1	1
Lemon zest, grated	of 1	of 1
Italian parsley, fresh, chopped	1 tablespoon	2.5 grams
Anchovy fillets, chopped	10	10

1. Season the meat with the salt and pepper, dredge it in the flour, and sear it on all sides in hot oil.

2. Degrease the pan and deglaze it with the wine; reduce the wine by three-quarters.

3. Add the tomato paste and stock and return the meat to the pan.

4. Cover the pan and braise the meat until it is fork-tender, approximately 1¼ to 1½ hours. Remove the meat to a hotel pan and keep it hot.

5. Reduce the sauce to the proper thickness and flavor.

6. Combine all of the ingredients for the gremolada.

7. Serve the meat with the sauce and gremolada.

Chicken Cacciatore

Yield: 2 servings

Chicken, fryer	1	1
Flour	1 ounce	30 grams
Salt	to taste	to taste
Pepper	to taste	to taste
Olive oil	as needed	as needed
Onion, medium dice	2 ounces	60 grams
Dry white wine	1 ounce	30 milliliters
Demi-glace	4 ounces	120 milliliters
Mushrooms, sliced	3 ounces	35 grams
Tomato concassé	5 ounces	140 grams
Garlic cloves, minced	1	1
Lemon zest, grated	¼ teaspoon	1 gram

1. Clean and disjoint the chickens.

2. Season the chicken with the salt and pepper and dredge it in the flour.

3. Sauté the chicken in the olive oil until it is lightly browned. Remove and reserve it.

4. Sauté the onion in the same oil.

5. Deglaze the pan with the wine and reduce the liquid.

6. Add the demi-glace and reduce the sauce as desired.

7. Add the mushrooms, tomato concassé, garlic, lemon zest, and salt and pepper to taste; stir the mixture well.

8. Cover and braise until the chicken is done. Split the chicken in half and partially debone it. Serve one half per order, coated with the sauce.

Part Seven

Cooking Methods for Vegetables, Potatoes, Grains and Legumes, and Pasta and Dumplings

The foods covered in this section are all enjoying a position of greater importance on the contemporary menu. Vegetables are no longer side dishes to be tolerated because they are "good for you." Potatoes were once fattening starches to be avoided but are now desirable additions to a healthy diet. Grains and legumes have new prominence as an important protein source without the drawbacks of fat and cholesterol and are available in countless variations for side dishes and main courses. The recent popularity of pasta shows no sign of diminishing. In countless shapes, sizes, colors, and flavors, filled and unfilled, it is the foundation for appetizers, entrées, and salads.

The preparation techniques are, in many cases, variations of those used for meats, poultry, and fish. Vegetables, for example, may be boiled, roasted, stir-fried, or grilled in much the same way as meats are. In all cases, careful selection of raw materials and attention to cooking technique and the determination of doneness can make the difference between a dish that is merely mediocre and one that is superior.

Chapter 22

Vegetable Cookery

Vegetables are far more important in contemporary menu planning than simply as a side dish meant to "fill up" a plate. They add visual and textural interest, but their primary importance is to round out and balance a meal's nutritional content. As eating habits continue to change, reflecting an increasing awareness of the links between diet and health, vegetables are becoming more important. This chapter will cover the various cooking techniques for vegetables (potatoes will be covered separately in the following chapter). These techniques will be evaluated in terms of how they affect the color, nutrient retention, flavor, and texture of the vegetable. Purchasing vegetables that are at the peak of quality, observing proper storage and handling standards, and meticulous attention to the actual cooking process are vital to producing a vegetable dish that will appeal to the guest.

GENERAL GUIDELINES

Each vegetable cookery technique produces specific and characteristic results. For example, stir-frying, microwaving, and steaming are often preferred for cooking vegetables that should have a crisp texture and bright color. Boiled vegetables are generally more tender and moist. Baking a vegetable produces a texture that is fluffy, mealy, and dry, with a special "roasted" flavor.

One way to broaden the repertoire of vegetable dishes is to pair a technique with a particular vegetable with which it is not ordinarily associated. For instance, cucumbers, most commonly considered a vegetable to be eaten raw, also may be steamed, sautéed, or even braised. The flavor, texture, and color differences can be quite interesting. Acorn squash does not always have to be baked and glazed with honey; it can be stewed, braised, or prepared in a savory custard. Vegetable cookery can escape the boundaries of "standard" preparations or even personal dislikes.

However, the best overall quality is generally assured by rapidly cooking vegetables and serving them as soon as possible after a desirable doneness is reached. This is a basic rule. Certain principles of vegetable cookery cannot be too strongly emphasized. Correct procedures for purchasing, handling, preparing, and holding techniques will be reinforced throughout this chapter.

Purchasing

In order to produce the best dishes, the chef must begin with products of excellent quality. Review the information in Chapter 8, "Fruit, Vegetable, and Fresh Herb Identi-

fication." The chef must be able to evaluate vegetables to determine their freshness and quality.

Ideally, the market should serve as the chef's guide. There is no excuse for buying woody broccoli or mealy tomatoes. It is almost always possible to find a better alternative than relying on "standard" vegetable dishes made with less-than-standard ingredients. There are times of the year when the available selection may become slim. Rather than relying on very expensive imported vegetables, the chef should have the freedom and confidence to use those vegetables that are in season to prepare creative and satisfying dishes.

Proper Handling

Once any vegetable has been harvested, it begins to change. Sometimes the change is dramatic and rapid, as is the case for sweet corn or peas—they begin to lose quality, flavor, and texture almost from the moment they are picked. Root vegetables, on the other hand, last over the winter because they lose quality relatively slowly. Review information regarding storage for vegetables in Chapter 8, "Fruit, Vegetable, and Fresh Herb Identification."

Many vegetables may require some sort of advance "prep" before they are cooked. To preserve the

22-1 PEELING WITH A VARIETY OF TOOLS

(1) Scraping a carrot with a paring knife.

(2) Peeling a carrot with a rotary or swivel-bladed peeler.

(3) Peeling a rutabaga with a chef's knife.

(4) Using a paring knife to loosen fibrous skins. The broccoli stem is being peeled after florets have been trimmed away.

best quality, these steps should be performed as close as possible to cooking time. Vegetable cuts should be uniform in size, first, to assure that they will cook evenly, and second, to give them a neat, attractive appearance.

Preliminary Preparation

Peeling

Vegetables are peeled in a variety of ways, as shown in Figure 22-1. Not all vegetables will require peeling before cooking, but when it is necessary, the chef should use a tool that will evenly and neatly remove the skin without removing too much of the valuable flesh. Rotary peelers are used for thin-skinned vegetables such as carrots, celery, and asparagus. An alternative tool is a paring knife, which is simply scraped across the vegetable's surface to remove a thin layer. Thick-skinned vegetables, such as rutabagas or winter squash, are peeled by cutting away the skin with a chef's knife. Fibrous or tough skins can be removed from broccoli, fennel, and similar vegetables by using a paring knife to trim away the skin; often it can then be pulled away after the initial cut.

Cleaning Leeks

Leeks are especially prone to catching large amounts of grit and sand between their layers. Any grit should be completely removed by thoroughly rinsing leeks under running water, as demonstrated in Figure 22-2. First, the leaves should be trimmed to remove the very tough green portion. The roots should be trimmed, with enough of the root left intact to hold the layers together. This will make it easier to cut the leek later. Then water should be run over the leek, while the chef pulls the layers back so that all of the grit can be flushed out.

Seeding and Cutting Peppers

A special technique is required when working with sweet peppers to achieve an absolutely even julienne, as shown in Figure 22-3. The pepper's top and bottom are trimmed away. These scraps can be used to prepare coulis or can be finely diced or minced to use in other preparations, such as soups, stuffings, or fillings. Then the seeds and ribs are removed. If necessary, the pepper can be filleted to even the thickness of the flesh and to remove the waxy skin. The prepared pepper is then easy to cut into a julienne, batonnet, or other cut.

Chili peppers hold most of their heat in the seeds and ribs. To avoid burning the skin or other sensitive tissues, especially around the eyes, the chef should be sure to wear rubber gloves when working with very hot peppers, such as the jalapeños shown in Figure 22-4. The trimmed and cleaned chili can then

22-3 CUTTING SWEET PEPPERS INTO JULIENNE

(1)

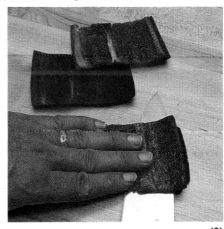

(2)

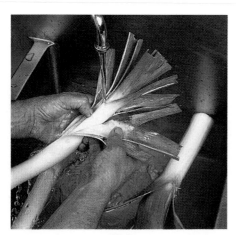

22-2

Rinsing leeks under cold running water.

(3)

(1) Removing the seeds and ribs from the pepper.

(2) Filleting the pepper to achieve an even thickness.

(3) Cutting the pepper into julienne.

be julienned or diced. One word of caution: Be sure to thoroughly clean and rinse hands, knives, and all work surfaces after cutting chilies.

Stringing Peas and Beans

Snow peas, sugar snap peas, and snap beans usually have a tough string that should be removed before they are cooked and served. This is an easy but time-consuming task. There aren't any special tools to speed the process, as Figure 22-5 shows. The stem end of the pea or bean is snapped and pulled downward toward the tail. The string will pull away easily. The fresher the pea or bean, the easier this process is. This is a very important preparation technique, as it is quite possible for a guest to choke on a tough string.

Preparing Artichokes

Artichokes require some special attention before cooking, as demonstrated in Figure 22-6. There are two areas of concern. First, artichokes have sharp barbs on the ends of their leaves that must be removed. Second, they have a tendency to discolor when exposed to air. The barbs are simply snipped away with kitchen scissors. An artichoke's color is kept a pale green by tying a slice of lemon onto the cut surface. Tying artichokes has a secondary benefit—it prevents them from falling apart during cooking and gives this vegetable a neat, compact shape.

Working with Corn on the Cob

The traditional American way to serve corn is simply boiled, steamed, or roasted on the cob, then swathed in butter. To prepare other corn dishes, such as creamed

22-4

Removing the seeds from a jalapeño chili.

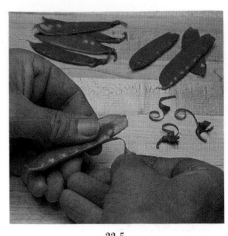

22-5

Removing the string from snow peas.

22-6 PREPARING ARTICHOKES

(1) Cutting away the tip and stem ends with a chef's knife.

(2) Snipping the barbs from the ends of the leaves.

corn or corncakes, it is necessary to remove the kernels as well as the milk, shown in Figure 22-7. First, the kernels are scored with a knife to begin to release their juices, or milk, as it is known. Then, the kernels are sliced away and the cob is finally scraped to express all of the milk.

Determining Doneness and Evaluating Quality

Vegetables are cooked to produce flavor, texture, and color changes,

(3) Tying the lemon in place to prevent discoloration of the cut surface.

22-7 REMOVING THE KERNELS AND MILK FROM CORN ON THE COB

(1) Scoring the rows of kernels.

(2) Cutting the kernels away . . .

(3) . . . or scraping out the milk.

which make the vegetable easier to chew and digest and improve taste and appearance. Various specific techniques are detailed following this general discussion. The success or failure of these preparations depends on cooking the vegetable just to the point of correct doneness. The proper standards of and tests for doneness are discussed here. There are distinct differences in how tender a vegetable should be when it is properly cooked. Preferences regarding the correct doneness of certain vegetables may vary from one part of the country to another and from one vegetable to another. In order to correctly determine doneness, the chef should understand the following:

• The natural characteristics of the vegetable: Some vegetables should always retain some "bite" (fully cooked but still firm), whereas others will not be sufficiently cooked until they are quite tender.

• The normal standard of quality for a particular technique: For example, stir-frying will generally result in a very crisp texture, whereas baking or braising produces very tender vegetables.

• Regional or cultural preferences regarding doneness: In the South, vegetables are cooked until very tender, often over a long period of time. In Oriental cuisines, vegetables are cooked rapidly so that they retain most of their texture.

• The characteristics of a particular vegetable when properly cooked: Winter squash is usually cooked until very tender, whereas green beans, snow peas, and broccoli are usually cooked so that they will retain a significant degree of "bite."

The following tests should be applied, bearing in mind the style of cookery, the vegetable itself, and the desired result.

Check the appearance. The vegetable's appearance can often act as a guide to determining doneness. Blanched and stir-fried vegetables should have a vivid color. Spinach, for instance, should be an intense green and have wilted leaves. Sautéed onions become translucent and eventually take on a golden-brown color. The three stages of caramelization of onions are shown in Figure 22-8.

Check the texture. Experience is the best guide. Vegetables that are properly cooked should have the correct degree of bite. Carrots should be tender, but not mushy. Asparagus should be slightly softened, but still firm enough to hold together. Turnips and rutabagas should be quite soft, but should still hold their shape. The best test is to bite into a piece of the vegetable. Vegetables to be pureed should be soft enough to mash easily. To check doneness in vegetables to be pureed, pierce the vegetable with the point of a knife or the tines of a

22-8

Stages in caramelization of onions: Translucent *(top),* golden *(bottom left),* and browned *(bottom right).*

kitchen fork. If they are easy to insert, the vegetable is properly cooked.

Vegetables that have been properly cooked, overcooked, and undercooked are shown in Figure 22-9. Note that green vegetables will demonstrate a marked visual difference from one stage of doneness to the next, whereas white and orange vegetables display very little color change from one stage of doneness to the next. Instead, the texture must be checked.

22-9 DETERMINING DONENESS

(1) Cauliflower, raw *(top)*, properly cooked *(bottom left)*, and overcooked *(bottom right)*.

(2) Carrots, raw *(top)*, properly cooked *(middle)*, and overcooked *(bottom)*.

(3) Broccoli, raw *(top)*, properly cooked *(bottom left)*, and overcooked *(bottom right)*.

(4) Red cabbage, raw *(top)*, properly cooked *(bottom left)*, and overcooked *(bottom right)*.

Holding

Ideally, vegetables should be cooked and then served immediately. In reality, it may be necessary to hold vegetables for a short time, especially for banquet service. Whenever possible, however, avoid holding vegetables either in steam tables or directly in water for extended periods of time.

Boiled or steamed vegetables are generally refreshed in cold water immediately after they are properly cooked, thoroughly drained, and then held in hotel pans, covered and refrigerated until they are required. Starchy vegetables that can readily absorb water (winter squash and turnips, for example) should be well-drained and spread out in a single layer at room temperature to allow them to briefly dry. Baked or roasted vegetables should be held, uncovered, in a warm oven or holding drawer. Braised or stewed vegetables, unlike most vegetables, will withstand being held in stainless-steel bain-maries or hotel pans, loosely covered, in a steam table.

An example of holding vegetables is shown in Figure 22-10.

Proper Reheating

Vegetables can be reheated in simmering stock or water, in a microwave oven, or by sautéing.

In simmering stock or water. The vegetables should be placed in a sieve or perforated basket and lowered into a pot of simmering stock or water just long enough to heat them through. They are then drained and immediately dressed as appropriate with butter, sauce, etc.

In the microwave. Vegetables should be evenly spaced on a flat, round, or oval plate or other micro-

22-10
Holding vegetables properly for service.

wave-safe container. (This technique is generally best for small amounts.) They should be reheated on the highest power setting for the shortest possible time and dressed immediately, as desired, and served.

By finishing in butter, cream, or a sauce. A small amount of butter, cream, or sauce may be heated in a sauté pan and the vegetable added until it is heated through. It should be tossed repeatedly during the heating.

Special Concerns

Another important aim of vegetable cookery is to produce dishes that retain the greatest nutritive value, the best color, and the freshest, most appealing flavor. Outlined

next are some of the factors that affect nutrient, color, and flavor retention in cooked vegetables.

Color Retention

A vegetable's color is determined by the pigments it contains. Although most vegetables contain more than one pigment, the overall color is determined by the one that is predominant. The various plant pigments will react differently in the presence of heat, acids, metals, water, and fat.

Table 22-1 lists the effects of water, overcooking, and a vegetable's age on a vegetable's color during boiling. The strategies to reduce or eliminate color loss during cooking will be explained in succeeding sections outlining specific cooking techniques.

Generally speaking, the best color is retained when vegetables are cooked for as short a time as possible. Overcooked or improperly cooked vegetables take on unappealing dull or gray colors. In many cases, this indicates that the vegetable has been robbed not only of its color, but also of nutrients, texture, and flavor.

Nutrient Retention

There is no way to retain all of a vegetable's nutrients during cooking. The major culprits in nutrient

TABLE 22-1.
COMMON PROBLEMS AND THEIR CAUSES: BOILING VEGETABLES

	Not Enough Water	Water Not at a Boil	Acids in Water	Vegetables Old or Immature	Overcooked or Held Too Long
Inappropriate color	•		•	•	•
Soft texture				•	•
Undercooked	•	•			
Dull flavor	•	•		•	•
Strong flavor	•			•	•

loss are heat, air, water, and enzymes. In trying to minimize this loss, the chef must balance practical concerns with nutritional ones.

To minimize the loss of nutrients:

1. Avoid holding vegetables in liquid before or after cooking.

2. Rinse, trim, peel, and cut vegetables as close as possible to cooking time.

3. Cook vegetables as quickly as possible, in as little liquid as possible.

4. Cook vegetables as close to service time as possible.

5. When feasible, steam or microwave vegetables, or bake them whole, in their skins.

Flavor Retention

Any vegetable's flavor changes once the vegetable is cooked. In some cases the change is subtle, in others it is more pronounced. The degree of change will depend on both the type of vegetable and the technique used.

The compounds in vegetables responsible for their characteristic flavors and odors are as readily affected by heat, water, and enzymes as the nutrients. Overcooking tends to give some vegetables (especially members of the cabbage family) a strong flavor. Other vegetables may become flat or dull.

Holding a vegetable in water either prior to or after cooking will rob it of most of its flavor along with leaching out nutrients and making it unacceptably soggy. Prolonged heat exposure also tends to worsen the flavor, resulting in either inappropriately bland or strong flavors.

COOKING TECHNIQUES

There is no single "perfect" vegetable cookery method. The chef must make a decision based on how the dish should taste and appear. The size and shape of the cut (if any), as well as whether moist heat or dry heat is applied, will have a great influence on the cooked vegetable's texture, color, appearance, and flavor.

Vegetables are best when they are:

• Cooked for the shortest possible amount of time
• Cooked in the least possible amount of liquid
• Cooked as close to service as possible

Boiling

It is difficult to think of any vegetable that cannot be boiled. Even though many people tend to think of boiled vegetables as bland or boring, boiling is of great importance in vegetable cookery. Whether one is thinking of tiny sweet peas to be bathed in whole butter, fresh sweet corn to be served on the cob, or slender spring asparagus, these vegetable dishes are all appealing, fresh, and flavorful when properly boiled and served.

This technique's applications go much further than simply boiling up a pot of vegetables that will be doused with butter and served. Boiling also forms the basis for such fundamental operations as blanching and parcooking.

Blanching. This step is important for several reasons—to make skins easy to remove, to eliminate or reduce strong odors or flavors, to "set" the color of vegetables to be served cold, or as the first step in other cooking techniques.

Parcooking/parboiling. This is done to partially cook vegetables to be used in other preparations such as braises, grills, or gratins.

To achieve the proper color and flavor in various vegetables, be sure to follow guidelines given in the method section.

Mise en Place

1. Vegetable. Rinse the vegetable throroughly and scrub it, if necessary, to remove surface dirt. Trim and peel the vegetable, as appropriate, immediately prior to cooking. If vegetables are to be cooked whole, choose those of a similar size, shape, and diameter to assure even cooking. If the vegetable is to be cut prior to boiling, make sure that the cuts are uniform in size and shape to promote even cooking and good appearance. Cut the vegetable immediately prior to boiling and avoid holding it in water.

2. Liquid. Water is the most commonly used liquid. However, other liquids may be appropriate, depending upon the desired flavor of the finished dish. Various stocks, court bouillons, and, in some cases, milk may be used. Add salt to the water, if desired. There should only be enough salt to make its taste barely apparent. Bring the liquid to a rolling boil. Covering the pot will cause the liquid to boil more rapidly.

3. Optional components. Seasonings and aromatics may be added to the cooking liquid or they may be combined with the vegetable once it is boiled. Ingredients, especially acidic ingredients such as citrus juice or zest, wine, or vinegar, should be added to the cooking liquid of certain vegetables (white vegetables, beets, and red cabbage) to help maintain the best color. Other ingredients, such as herbs, spices, and additional vegetables added for flavor, are added according to the desired result. Boiled vegetables often are tossed with fresh herbs or freshly ground spices just before they are served.

Butter, cream, and sauces may be combined with the vegetable while it is still hot or they may be added as it reheats just prior to service (see "Sautéing").

Method

1. Bring the liquid to a full boil. The amount required will vary, depending upon the vegetable and the length of cooking time. In general, there should be enough water to hold the vegetables comfortably, without excessive crowding (see Fig. 22-11). Add any seasonings, acids, and/or aromatic ingredients that are appropriate to the liquid at this point.

2. Add the vegetables to the boiling liquid. Add them in small enough batches so that the liquid's temperature does not drop dramatically. Return the cover to the pot for the best color in red cabbage, beets, and white vegetables (cauliflower, for example) to retain acids that help to set color in these vegetables. It is acceptable to cover the pot while boiling orange and yellow vegetables (carrots and squash, for example).

If preparing a green vegetable that will cook rapidly, such as peas or spinach, the lid may be returned to the pot to help shorten cooking time. Denser green vegetables, such as broccoli, should be boiled uncovered, at least for the first two to three minutes, to allow natural acids to escape. These acids could cause the vegetable's color to turn a dull olive- or yellow-green.

3. Cook the vegetables to the desired doneness.

4. Drain the vegetable thoroughly in a colander or sieve. At

22-11

The proper relation of water to vegetables for boiling.

Boiled Carrots

Yield: 10 servings

Carrots, peeled, trimmed, and cut into even pieces	2 pounds	910 grams
Water, boiling, salted	2 to 3 quarts	2 to 3 liters

1. Add the carrots to the boiling water. If necessary, return the cover to the pot to allow the water to return to a boil as quickly as possible.

2. Boil the carrots for 4 to 7 minutes (depending upon the thickness of the cut). Remove them from the boiling water (lift them out with a skimmer or spider if the water is to be reused).

3. If the carrots are to be served cold, place them in an ice water bath to stop the cooking process.

NOTE: Follow the same procedure to boil other vegetables. Vegetables may be boiled whole; in that case the skin is often left on the vegetable.

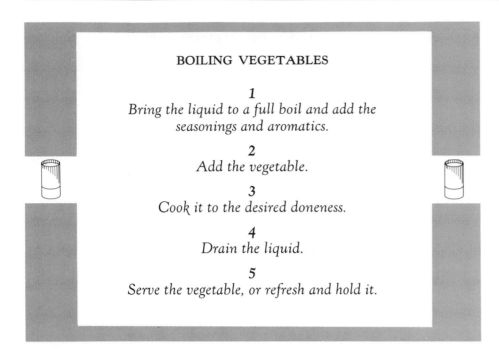

BOILING VEGETABLES

1

*Bring the liquid to a full boil and add the
seasonings and aromatics.*

2

Add the vegetable.

3

Cook it to the desired doneness.

4

Drain the liquid.

5

Serve the vegetable, or refresh and hold it.

the vegetables will take to cook—
the more delicate the vegetable,
the less liquid will be required.

3. Optional components. It is
often appropriate to add aromatics
such as spices, herbs, citrus zest,
and additional vegetables to the
steaming liquid to produce specific
flavors. Salt, pepper, and other
seasonings may be combined with
the vegetable once it is steamed.
The steamed vegetable may be
combined with butter, some oils
(including olive and walnut), heavy
cream, or a sauce while the vegetable is still hot, or these items may
be used just prior to service as a
medium for reheating vegetables.

this point the vegetable may either
be served as is; combined with butter, fresh herbs, spices or other aromatics, or sauces; refreshed to
hold for later service; or used in
other vegetable preparations such
as braises, gratins, grills, or purees.

For a quick summary, refer to
the abbreviated method for boiling
vegetables. Refer also to "General
Guidelines" for a discussion of determining doneness and evaluating
quality, earlier in this chapter.

Steaming and "Pan-steaming"

Steaming is an efficient and practical way to prepare vegetables for à
la minute service, especially those
that are naturally tender or thin, or
have been cut into small, uniform
pieces. This is one of the gentler
cooking techniques for vegetables.
Because the vegetables are cooked
in a vapor bath and are not in direct
contact with water, fewer of the vitamins and minerals will be lost
though prolonged direct contact
with a liquid.

Steaming may be used to fully
cook vegetables or to blanch or parcook them. (See the explanation of
parcooking under "Boiling.") The
effects of steaming are similar to
those of boiling, and any vegetable
that can be boiled can also be
steamed.

Pan-steaming is actually a combination of steaming and boiling.
The vegetable is placed in a layer
in a pot. The amount of water or
other liquid that is then added will
vary according to the size, cut, and
density of the vegetable. Turnips
and carrots, for example, would require more water for pan-steaming
or boiling than would spinach or
peas. The pot is then covered so
that the steam trapped in the pot
cooks the vegetables by both boiling and steaming.

Mise en Place

1. Main ingredient. Preparation
is the same as for boiling.

2. Liquid. Although the most
commonly used liquid is water, a
flavorful stock or court bouillon is
also appropriate. The amount required will depend upon how long

Method

1. In the bottom of a steamer,
bring the liquid to a full boil, with
the lid on the pot. Add any additional seasonings or aromatics to
the liquid as it comes to a boil to
help release their flavors.

2. Add the vegetables to the
steamer in a single layer so that the
steam can circulate freely. This
will shorten cooking and result in
better flavor, color, and nutrient retention. (A steamer, set up and
ready to cook, is shown in Fig. 22-
12. Vegetables arranged in the
steamer are shown in Fig. 22-13.)
For pan-steaming, add the vegetables to the pot, working in batches
(see Fig. 22-14).

3. Return the lid to the steamer
or pot and steam the vegetables to
the desired doneness. The appropriate degree of doneness is determined by how the particular
vegetable will be handled once it is
steamed. Vegetables may be
blanched, parcooked, or fully
cooked.

4. Remove the vegetables from
the steamer. Serve them at once or
hold and refresh them if necessary.
Once the appropriate doneness is

Steamed Broccoli

22-12
A steamer ready to cook.

Yield: 10 servings

Broccoli, trimmed and peeled	2 pounds	910 grams
Water	1 inch	2.5 centimeters
Salt	to taste	to taste
Pepper	to taste	to taste

1. Arrange the broccoli on a steamer rack so that the pieces are not crowded.

2. Bring the water to a full boil in the bottom of the steamer.

3. Add the broccoli to the steamer, replace the lid, and steam the vegetable for 5 to 7 minutes, or until it is just tender. Season the broccoli with salt and pepper to taste.

NOTE: Steamed broccoli may also be served after tossing it with whole butter or a compound butter, or served with a meunière butter, or hollandaise, or polonaise sauce (melted butter, breadcrumbs, chopped eggs, salt, pepper, parsley, and a dash of lemon).

SUBSTITUTION

Cauliflower may be substituted for the broccoli. It should be steamed for 10 minutes. Instead of a hollandaise, substitute a mornay butter.

22-13
Cauliflower, properly arranged for the most efficient cooking.

STEAMING VEGETABLES

1
Bring the liquid to a full boil and add the seasonings and aromatics.

2
Add the vegetable to the steamer in a single layer.

3
Steam the vegetable to the desired doneness.

4
Serve the vegetable or refresh and hold it.

22-14
Pan-steaming peas in a small amount of water.

reached, the vegetable may be served immediately. The vegetable may be handled in any of the same ways that boiled vegetables are.

For a quick summary, refer to the abbreviated method for steaming vegetables. Refer also to "General Guidelines" for a discussion of determining doneness and evaluating quality, earlier in this chapter.

Microwaving

Microwaving, essentially a moist-heat cooking method, works by causing a food's molecules to vibrate; this friction generates heat. That heat causes a food's natural liquids to "steam" the item.

Vegetables may be cooked in two ways in a microwave oven. In the first method, they are placed in an appropriate container with a small amount of liquid and covered; the added liquid turns to steam and cooks the vegetable. In the second, used for dense vegetables, the vegetable is left whole, with skin or peel intact, and steamed using its own moisture, held in by the skin.

Microwave ovens are also frequently used just before service to reheat vegetables that were prepared by other techniques. This is an extremely useful application, because the vegetable can be reheated rapidly with little loss of color, nutrients, or texture.

Mise en Place

1. Main item. Prepare the vegetable according to the type and desired result. For vegetables to be combined with a small amount of liquid: Rinse, peel, trim, and cut the vegetable into even pieces, as necessary. Arrange the pieces on a shallow platter or dish; they should be evenly spread over the surface. For vegetables to be cooked whole,

such as squashes or beets, rinse them well and pierce the skin in two or three places to allow the steam to escape.

2. Liquid. There should be only enough liquid to produce steam during the relatively short cooking time required by the microwave process. No additional liquid is needed for vegetables that will be left whole. Have available water, stock, or juices, as desired or appropriate.

3. Optional components. Vegetables that are cooked with additional liquid are often combined with various seasonings and aromatics before they are microwaved. Vegetables microwaved whole are combined with aromatics and seasonings after they have been cooked. Have available spices, fresh herbs, citrus zest, or additional vegetables. Finishing in-

gredients may include butter, certain oils, heavy cream, or a sauce.

Method

1. Place the vegetable on a suitable dish or plate, as shown in Figure 22-15. Add any liquid, if necessary, and cover the dish tightly, if necessary. If plastic wrap is used, it should be punctured to allow steam to vent.

2. Place the dish in a microwave oven. Cook the vegetable at the highest power setting for the appropriate amount of time. It may be necessary to stir, turn, or rearrange some vegetables to assure even cooking. There will be some carry-over cooking because the heat produced within the vegetable itself is responsible for the cooking.

3. Serve the vegetable with the appropriate finishing ingredients or

22-15

The proper arrangement of vegetables for microwave cooking or reheating.

Ratatouille (Microwave Method)

Yield: 10 servings

Garlic, minced	⅓ ounce	10 grams
Olive oil	1 ounce	30 milliliters
Shallots, minced	½ ounce	15 grams
Red onion, small dice	3½ ounces	100 grams
Tomato paste	1 ounce	30 grams
Yellow squash, seeded, small dice	3½ ounces	100 grams
Zucchini, seeded, small dice	8 ounces	225 grams
Green pepper, small dice	3 ounces	85 grams
Red pepper, small dice	3 ounces	85 grams
Eggplant, peeled, medium dice	6 ounces	170 grams
Salt	½ teaspoon	3 grams
White pepper	½ teaspoon	1 gram
Basil, chopped	2 tablespoons	4.5 grams

1. Sauté the garlic in the heated olive oil. Add the shallots and sauté them until they are soft.

2. Add the red onion and sauté it until it is soft.

3. Add the tomato paste and sauté the mixture briefly.

4. Combine the sautéed mixture with the remaining ingredients.

5. At service time, cook the ratatouille by order in a microwave, as needed.

MICROWAVING VEGETABLES

1
Place the vegetable on a suitable dish or plate and cover it.

2
Place it in a microwave oven and cook it to the desired doneness.

3
Serve the vegetable, or refresh and hold it.

sauces; vegetables cooked whole are ready to be used in a secondary technique.

For a quick summary, refer to the abbreviated method for microwaving vegetables. Refer also to "General Guidelines" for a discussion of determining doneness and evaluating quality as well as reheating, earlier in this chapter.

Roasting/Baking

This technique should not be confused with other techniques that cook vegetables in an oven, such as in braised dishes and gratins. To some extent, roasting or baking vegetables involves the same principles applied to roasting meats: The vegetable is generally left whole or cut into large pieces, no additional liquid is used, and the moisture already present in the vegetable carries the heat from the exterior to the interior.

Roasting or baking is best suited to vegetables that have thick skins which will protect the interior from drying or scorching. Examples include various winter squashes and eggplant.

This method is also frequently used to prepare vegetables that might otherwise be difficult to peel, such as sweet bell peppers that will be used in a puree. The aim is to create a special flavor and texture. Browning produces the expected "roasted" flavor. The absence of added liquid means that the vegetable should have a dry, fluffy texture.

Mise en Place

1. Vegetable. Rinse, peel, trim, and cut the vegetable, as necessary. To assure even cooking, vegetables should be cut into pieces of uniform size and shape. Pierce the

skin, if necessary; heavy-skinned vegetables, such as acorn squash, beets, or turnips, would need to have their skins pierced. This allows the steam that builds up during cooking to escape. Rub the skin with oil to prevent excessive drying and scorching.

2. Optional components. A marinade can influence flavor and give additional protection to the vegetable as it cooks in the dry heat. Rub or coat the surface of the vegetable with seasonings or aromatics such as salt, pepper, or garlic cloves, as appropriate. Have available finishing ingredients such as whole or compound butter, reduced heavy cream, or a sauce prepared separately, as desired or according to the particular recipe.

Method

1. Place the prepared vegetable in a hot or moderate oven. The oven's temperature will depend upon the vegetable's size and density. The longer the roasting time—also determined by the vegetable's size, the diameter of its cut, and its density—the lower the temperature should be. Vegetables may be roasted on sheet pans or in hotel pans, or, in some cases, directly on the oven rack, which allows the hot air to circulate readily.

2. Roast the vegetable to the desired doneness. Generally, vegetables are thoroughly roasted when they can be easily pierced with the tip of a knife or a kitchen fork. Vegetables should be rotated as they roast to promote even cooking, because most ovens will have hot spots. The placement of other items in the oven could also cause uneven cooking.

3. Serve the vegetable immediately on heated plates with the appropriate finishing ingredients; hold it, covered, in a warm place;

Baked Acorn Squash with Cranberry-Orange Compote

Yield: 12 servings

Acorn squashes	3 small	3 small
Butter, melted	6 ounces	170 grams
Brown sugar, honey, or maple syrup	4 ounces	115 grams
Salt	to taste	to taste
Pepper	to taste	to taste
Compote		
Cranberries	1 pound	450 grams
Orange juice	6 ounces	180 milliliters
Water	as needed	as needed
Sugar	as needed	as needed
Orange zest, blanched	2 ounces	60 grams

1. Cut the squash into quarters and remove the seeds.

2. Combine the butter and brown sugar. Brush the glaze on the squash. Season the squash with the salt and pepper. Reserve any excess butter and sugar.

3. Bake the squash quarters in a moderate oven until they are tender. Baste them periodically with the reserved butter and sugar mixture.

4. Combine the cranberries, orange juice, and water, as needed, to barely cover the berries. Add sugar to taste. Simmer the berries over medium heat until they are softened and thickened. Add the orange zest.

5. To serve, spoon the hot cranberry mixture over the squash.

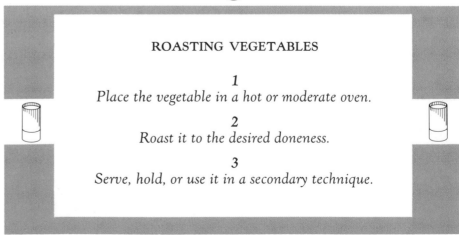

ROASTING VEGETABLES

1
Place the vegetable in a hot or moderate oven.

2
Roast it to the desired doneness.

3
Serve, hold, or use it in a secondary technique.

or use it in a secondary cooking technique. If the vegetable is to be pureed, it should be pureed while it is still hot (see the section on pureeing in this chapter).

For a quick summary, refer to the abbreviated method for roasting vegetables. Refer also to "General Guidelines" for a discussion of determining doneness and evaluating quality earlier in this chapter.

Sautéing and Stir-frying

Some vegetables are sautéed or stir-fried from their raw state. Examples of such vegetables include mushrooms, summer squashes, and onions. Denser vegetables such as green beans, carrots, and brussels sprouts need to be fully or partially cooked by boiling, steaming, microwaving, or roasting before they are sautéed or stir-fried.

Cooked vegetables are sautéed prior to service for the purpose of reheating the vegetable, not to create a browned exterior. This is known as "finishing in butter." Finishing may also be accomplished by using small amounts of stock, cream, and some sauces. The process of sautéing vegetables is shown in Figure 22-16.

Glazing is another finishing technique. A small amount of honey, sugar, or maple syrup is added to the vegetable as it reheats. The sugars liquefy, coating the vegetable evenly to give it some sheen and a sweet flavor. (There is a second way to "glaze" vegetables: The prepared vegetable may be cooked in a lightly sweetened liquid, which is allowed to reduce, coating the vegetable with a glaze.) Glazing is shown in Figure 22-17.

Mise en Place

1. Vegetable. Rinse, peel, trim, and cut the raw vegetable, if re-

22-16

Sautéing or finishing vegetables in butter.

quired. Partially or wholly cook the vegetable by boiling, steaming, roasting, or microwaving it, if necessary. This is especially important for vegetable "mixtures." Each vegetable should be cooked separately in advance, and then reheated and mixed only at the time of service.

2. Cooking medium. Have available whole or clarified butter. Because sautéing vegetables does not require the high temperatures necessary for sautéing meats or fish, whole butter is acceptable. If an oil is used, the oil's flavor should complement that of the vegetable. For example, virgin olive oil may be

best suited to a stir-fry of zucchini and red peppers. Have available other ingredients, such as stock, vegetable or fruit juices, wine, heavy cream, or sauces. Use only enough of these to lightly coat the vegetable and to act as insulation between the vegetable and the pan.

3. Optional components. Have available seasonings and aromatics such as salt, pepper, and/or lemon juice to adjust or heighten the flavor. Finely mince or chop fresh herbs and add them at the last moment. Small amounts of ingredients that contain a high sugar concentration may be added to vegetables, generally near the end of the cooking time, to act as a glaze, giving additional flavor, sheen, and a golden color. Have available honey, sugar, maple syrup, or fruit juice.

Method

1. Heat the pan; add the cooking medium and heat it.

2. Add the vegetable. If more than one type is being used, as in a stir-fry, the vegetables should be added in the proper sequence, beginning with those with the longest cooking times, to assure that all components complete their cooking times at the same point.

22-17 GLAZING VEGETABLES

(1) Adding ingredients (honey used here) to carrots for a glaze.

(2) Properly glazed carrots.

Glazed Carrots

Yield: 10 servings

Butter	3 ounces	85 grams
Carrots, cut oblique, batonnet, or sliced	24 ounces	680 grams
Sugar (optional)	2 tablespoons	30 grams
Salt	pinch	pinch
White pepper	pinch	pinch
Chicken stock	12 ounces	360 milliliters

1. Melt the butter and add the carrots.

2. Cover the pan and lightly sweat the carrots.

3. Add the sugar, salt, pepper, and stock.

4. Cook, covered, at low heat until the carrots are almost done.

5. Remove the cover and allow the liquid to reduce to a glaze.

NOTE: If the carrots are done before a glaze is formed, remove them with a slotted spoon and reduce the liquid. Return the carrots to the pan to finish the process.

SAUTÉING AND STIR-FRYING VEGETABLES

1
Heat the pan; add the cooking medium and heat it.

2
Add the vegetable.

3
Sauté the vegetable, keeping it in motion.

4
Add the aromatics, seasonings, or glaze and heat thoroughly.

5
Serve the vegetable immediately.

---

3. Keep the vegetable in motion in the pan and sauté it only until it is very hot and tender to the bite.

4. Add any aromatics, seasonings, or ingredients for a glaze. Heat them thoroughly.

5. Serve the vegetable immediately on heated plates.

For a quick summary, refer to the abbreviated method for sautéing and stir-frying vegetables. Refer also to "General Guidelines" for a discussion of determining doneness and evaluating quality, earlier in this chapter.

Panfrying

Panfrying is similar to sautéing; the main difference is that in panfrying, the amount of oil used as a cooking medium is greater than that for sautéing. Also, any sauce served with panfried vegetables is made separately. In some cases, the main item is breaded or coated with flour or a batter. Thick or dense vegetables, such as rutabagas or carrots, that require lengthy cooking times may need to be parcooked first by boiling or steaming. Vegetables that are prepared as fritters or croquettes are also panfried. The proper ratio of cooking

22-18
Zucchini slices being panfried.

fat to product is shown in Figure 22-18.

Mise en Place

1. Vegetable. Prepare the vegetable according to the type and the desired result. Peel, trim, rinse, and cut the vegetable into even slices, as necessary. Wholly or partially cook the vegetable, if necessary. Bread it with a standard breading, or coat it with flour or batter.

2. Cooking medium. As is true for panfried meats or fish, the cooking fat or oil must be able to reach a high temperature without breaking down or smoking during the cooking process.

3. Optional components. Aromatics and seasonings may be added to the vegetable before or after cooking or they may be included in the breading or batter if appropriate. Have available salt and pepper, minced fresh herbs, grated cheeses, ground nuts, or mixtures with spices or seeds (such as sesame or mustard). In addition, the recipe may call for finishing ingredients, such as a compound butter, sauce, relish, or salsa.

Method

1. Heat the cooking medium in a heavy-gauge skillet, rondeau, or brazier.

2. Add the main item carefully. For the best color and rapid cooking, avoid crowding the vegetables in the pan.

3. Cook the item over moderate to high heat until the vegetable's exterior is lightly browned and crisp and the interior is tender to the bite and very hot. The shorter the necessary cooking time, the higher the heat may be.

4. Blot the vegetable briefly on absorbent paper toweling.

Panfried Zucchini

Yield: 10 servings

Zucchini, trimmed and sliced	2 pounds	910 grams
Basic frying batter	1 pint or as needed	480 milliliters or as needed
Oil (olive, vegetable, peanut, or other neutral oil)	as needed	as needed
Salt	to taste	to taste
Pepper	to taste	to taste
Sauce	1 to 2 ounces per portion	30 to 60 grams per portion

1. Evenly coat the zucchini slices or sticks with batter and add them to a hot oiled pan in a single layer. Do not crowd them.

2. Panfry the zucchini on the first side for approximately 1 minute, or until it is golden brown. Turn and complete the cooking on the second side.

3. Remove the zucchini from the hot oil and blot it briefly on absorbent paper toweling.

4. Season the slices with the salt and pepper.

NOTE: Possible sauces include Tomato-Basil Coulis, Red Pepper Coulis, or Lemon-Parsley Compound Butter.

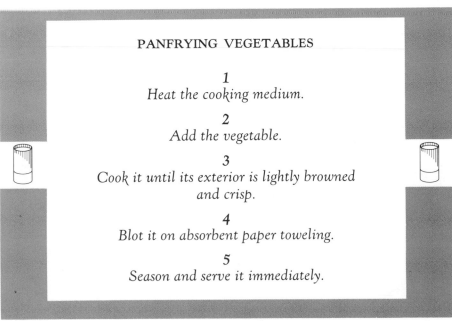

PANFRYING VEGETABLES

1
Heat the cooking medium.

2
Add the vegetable.

3
Cook it until its exterior is lightly browned and crisp.

4
Blot it on absorbent paper toweling.

5
Season and serve it immediately.

5. Season it with salt and pepper, if desired, and serve it immediately on heated plates. Serve the vegetable with a compound butter, a sauce, or a relish or salsa, as desired or appropriate.

For a quick summary, refer to the abbreviated method for panfrying vegetables. Refer also to "General Guidelines" for a discussion of determining doneness and evaluating quality, earlier in this chapter.

Deep-frying

Few vegetables are deep-fried in their raw state; most are either wholly or partially cooked by boiling, steaming, microwaving, or baking. Tempura batter is often used to coat vegetables that will be deep-fried (see Fig. 22-19). Croquettes are also commonly deep-fried—they are prepared by making an appareil that includes minced vegetables or a puree,

Vegetable Tempura

Yield: 1 serving

Vegetables, assorted, cut into small pieces	3 to 4 ounces per portion	85 to 115 grams per portion
Tempura batter, chilled	as needed	as needed
Dipping sauce, as desired	1 to 2 ounces per portion	30 to 55 grams per portion

1. Blot the vegetables dry before coating them with batter.

2. Coat the vegetables evenly with the batter. The batter should not be too thick.

3. Deep-fry the vegetables by the swimming method until the batter is golden brown and puffy. Remove them from the fryer with a spider and blot them briefly on absorbent toweling.

4. Serve the vegetables with a dipping sauce (honey-mustard or soy sauce, or sesame and ginger, for example).

NOTE: For the tempura, use bell peppers, mushrooms, summer squash, red onions, and scallions, and blanched broccoli, cauliflower, and carrots.

22-19 VEGETABLE TEMPURA

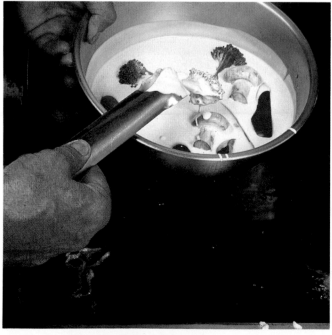

(1) Coating the vegetable with batter.

(2) Removing the finished vegetables with a spider.

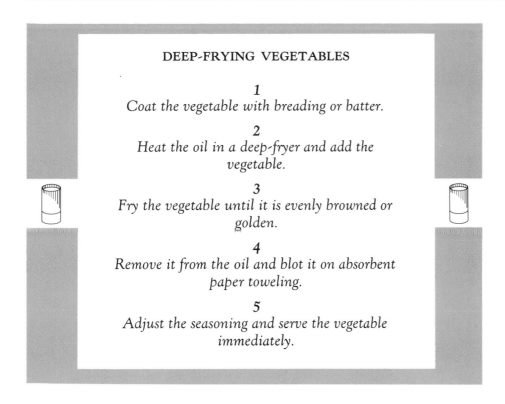

DEEP-FRYING VEGETABLES

1
Coat the vegetable with breading or batter.

2
Heat the oil in a deep-fryer and add the vegetable.

3
Fry the vegetable until it is evenly browned or golden.

4
Remove it from the oil and blot it on absorbent paper toweling.

5
Adjust the seasoning and serve the vegetable immediately.

which is then coated with a standard breading. Potatoes, the most commonly deep-fried vegetable, are covered in a later chapter.

Mise en Place

1. Vegetable. Prepare the vegetable according to the type and desired result. Peel, trim, rinse, and cut the vegetable, as necessary. Wholly or partially cook the vegetable, as necessary. Mince or puree the vegetable, as necessary.

2. Coating. For the best results, coat the vegetable with breading or batter just before cooking it. Have available ingredients for a standard breading or a prepared batter.

3. Cooking medium. The cooking medium must be able to reach a high temperature without smoking or breaking down. Have available oil with a neutral flavor heated to the proper temperature.

4. Optional components. These may include aromatics and seasonings and/or finishing ingredients. See "Mise en Place" in the section

on panfrying vegetables for suggestions.

Method

1. Heat the oil in a deep-fryer to approximately 350°F (176°C).

2. Fry the vegetable until it is evenly browned or golden in color. Most vegetables will float to the surface when they are properly cooked if the oil has been properly maintained and is at the correct temperature.

3. Remove the vegetable from the deep-fryer and blot it briefly on absorbent paper toweling.

4. Adjust the seasoning and serve the vegetable immediately on heated plates, with a compound butter, sauce, or relish or salsa, as desired or appropriate.

For a quick summary, refer to the abbreviated method for deep-frying vegetables. Refer also to "General Guidelines" for a discussion of determining doneness and evaluating quality, earlier in this chapter.

Grilling and Broiling

Some vegetables can be grilled or broiled from the raw state; others may require preliminary cooking or marination in an oil-based bath to assure thorough cooking. Vegetables that hold up well when subjected to a grill's intense heat include eggplant, mushrooms, onions, summer squashes, and peppers. Broiled vegetables bring to mind preparations such as stuffed tomatoes or zucchini.

Mise en Place

1. Vegetable. Vegetables may be raw or may be prepared partially or completely. Prepare the vegetable according to the type and desired result. Rinse, trim, peel, and cut it in appropriate, even pieces. Thread it on a skewer, if appropriate.

2. Optional components.

Grilled vegetables. A marinade or oil may be used to provide both lubrication and additional flavor. The vegetable may be either raw or partially or wholly cooked prior to marination. Have available an oil-based marinade or plain oil, according to the recipe or desired result. Aromatics and seasonings may be added to the vegetable prior to cooking, or after cooking and immediately prior to service. Have available salt and pepper, citrus zest, minced fresh herbs, or spices.

Broiled vegetables. The core or seeds of some vegetables may be removed and the cavity then filled with an appropriate filling, as in the case of broiled stuffed tomatoes. A topping often is added before the vegetable is broiled. Have available duxelles, a forcemeat, or another stuffing, as desired or according to the recipe. Have available bread crumbs, butter, and cheese for a

Grilled Vegetables

Yield: 10 servings

Vegetables, assorted, according to season (leeks, fennel, sweet peppers, summer squash, etc.)	4 ounces total per portion	115 grams

Marinade

Oil	3 parts	3 parts
Soy sauce	1 part	1 part
Lemon juice	to taste	to taste
Garlic	1 tablespoon	15 grams
Fennel seeds	½ teaspoon	1 gram
Salt	to taste	to taste
Pepper	to taste	to taste

1. Slice the vegetables into pieces thick enough to withstand the grill's heat. If necessary, parcook or blanch the vegetables prior to grilling them.
2. Combine all the ingredients for the marinade. Coat the vegetables evenly with the marinade. Let any excess drain completely away from the vegetables.
3. Place the vegetables on a hot grill; grill them on both sides (the time will vary depending upon the type of vegetable and the thickness of the cut), turning once to create crosshatch marks, if desired.
4. Turn the vegetables once and complete the cooking on the second side.

topping, as desired or according to the recipe. If a marinade has been used, it may also be served as a sauce with the cooked vegetable. Other possible sauces include salsa, soy sauce, a jus-based sauce, reduced heavy cream, butter sauces, or cream sauce.

Method

1. Thoroughly heat the grill or broiler.
2. Place the prepared vegetable directly on a rack. If there is a danger that the vegetable might stick easily to the rack, it may be set on a sizzler platter or in a hand-grill. To create crosshatch marks on grilled vegetables, place the vegetable so that the top points to 11 o'clock, then turn it after a few minutes so that the top points to 1 o'clock.
3. Grill or broil the vegetable until it is heated through and tender. Baste it with a marinade or oil during the cooking time, if appropriate. Turn grilled vegetables once during cooking. (Do not turn broiled vegetables.) Broiled vegetables should have a browned top; grilled vegetables should be lightly browned on both sides, with well-browned crosshatch marks.

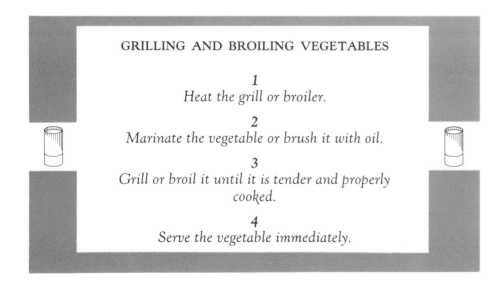

GRILLING AND BROILING VEGETABLES

1
Heat the grill or broiler.

2
Marinate the vegetable or brush it with oil.

3
Grill or broil it until it is tender and properly cooked.

4
Serve the vegetable immediately.

22-20

Grilled vegetables.

A variety of grilled vegetables are shown in Figure 22-20. For a quick summary, refer to the abbreviated method for grilling and broiling vegetables. Refer also to "General Guidelines" for a discussion of determining doneness and evaluating quality, earlier in this chapter.

Stewing and Braising

Vegetable stews and braises, such as ratatouille and peas bonne femme, are excellent ways to retain the vitamins and minerals lost from the vegetable into the cooking liquid, because the liquid is served as part of the dish. The distinction between a vegetable stew and a braise is the same as for meats: The vegetables in a stew are customarily cut into small pieces, whereas those in a braise are in large pieces or are left whole. Stewed or braised vegetables literally cook in their own juices. Occasionally, the beurre manié, arrowroot, or cornstarch will be added to the juices to give the dish more substance and to improve its appearance. The thickened sauce lightly coats the vegetable, providing an attractive sheen.

Mise en Place

1. Vegetable(s). Vegetable stews and braises are often composed of more than one kind of vegetable. Prepare the vegetables according to the type and the desired result. Peel, trim, rinse, and cut the vegetables, as necessary. Blanch them to remove bitter flavors or to aid in removing peels.

2. Cooking medium. The stewing process often begins with searing or sweating the main item in fat or oil to develop its flavor. The particular fat or oil chosen should have a good flavor appropriate to the dish. For example, olive oil is a good choice for a ratatouille, whereas butter is better for stewed mushrooms. Vegetables that will not release a significant amount of liquid as they cook may need additional liquid, such as stock, fumets, juices, or water.

3. Optional components. It may be desirable to add a thickener to bind the juices and other liquids. Dilute arrowroot or cornstarch in a small amount of cold liquid or prepare a beurre manié. Have available seasonings and aromatics such as salt and pepper, shallots, garlic, minced fresh herbs, spices, mirepoix, or matignon; a pork product such as salt pork, bacon, or ham; or an acid such as vinegar, citrus zest or juice, or wine. The acid should be added near the end of the cooking time to avoid toughening the vegetable.

Various finishing ingredients may be added to give a vegetable stew a rich flavor, some sheen, and a smooth texture. Have available reduced heavy cream, a cream sauce, a liaison, or whole butter.

A vegetable stew or braise may be garnished as desired or appropriate. Have available such ingredients as diced roasted peppers, bread crumbs and cheese (to create a gratin), chopped, hard-cooked eggs, or toasted nuts.

Method

1. Heat the oil or a small amount of stock.

2. Add the appropriate seasonings or aromatics and the main item. If aromatics such as garlic, shallots, or mirepoix are used, allow them to sweat before adding the main ingredient. Cook these ingredients over gentle heat with the lid on to encourage them to release their juices.

3. Add the liquid, if appropri-

French-style Peas

Yield: 10 servings

Pearl onions	2 ounces	60 grams
Peas	1¼ pounds	570 grams
Butter, fresh	2 ounces	60 grams
Lettuce (Boston or Romaine), shredded	¾ pound	340 grams
Chicken broth	4 ounces	120 milliliters
Salt	to taste	to taste
Pepper	to taste	to taste
Beurre manié	as needed	as needed

1. Smother the pearl onions in the fresh butter without browning them.

2. Add the peas, lettuce, and broth. Season the broth to taste with the salt and pepper.

3. Cook the mixture quickly, covered, for a few minutes.

4. Add the beurre manié gradually in small pieces until the mixture is thickened.

Braised Lettuce

Yield: 10 servings

Romaine lettuce, trimmed and cleaned	2½ heads	2½ heads
Onion, diced	5 ounces	140 grams
Carrots, sliced thin	5 ounces	140 grams
Butter	2½ ounces	70 grams
Brown stock	10 ounces	300 milliliters
Bacon strips	10	10

1. Blanch the lettuce briefly. Shock it in cold water and reserve it.

2. Combine the onion, carrots, butter, and brown stock and place the mixture in a baking dish. Simmer it for 5 minutes.

3. Quarter the romaine lengthwise. Squeeze it to remove any excess water. Remove the cores and roll each quarter "cigar"-fashion.

4. Wrap the bacon strips around each roll. Place the rolls in the reserved liquid.

5. Adjust the seasoning with salt and pepper to taste. Braise the lettuce, covered, in a 350°F (175°C) oven until the bacon is completely cooked. Brown the bacon under a salamander or broiler before serving.

STEWING AND BRAISING VEGETABLES

1
Heat the oil or stock.

2
Smother the vegetable and seasonings or aromatics.

3
Add the liquid, bring it to a simmer, and cook the vegetable.

4
Add the remaining vegetables and aromatics.

5
Cook the stew or braise until the vegetables are tender.

6
Adjust the seasoning and finish the dish according to the recipe.

7
Serve the vegetable or hold it

ate, and bring it to a simmer. Cook the vegetable over low heat or in a moderate oven.

4. Introduce additional vegetables and aromatics in the proper sequence so that all components complete their cooking times at the same point.

5. Cook the stew or braise until the vegetables are tender; then add a thickener and/or finishing ingredients, if appropriate. It may be necessary to strain out the vegetables before adding the thickener to the liquid. If that is the case, return the vegetable to the sauce once it is properly thickened or finished.

6. Adjust the seasoning as necessary.

7. Finish the dish with the ingredients for a gratin, if desired, and glaze it under a salamander or broiler.

8. Serve it immediately on heated plates.

Stewed and braised vegetables can be held for a longer time than other vegetables without losing significant quality. Hold them, loosely covered, in a steam table.

For a quick summary, refer to the abbreviated method for stewing and braising vegetables. Refer also to "General Guidelines" for a discussion of determining doneness and evaluating quality, earlier in this chapter.

Pureeing

Pureed vegetables may be served as is or they may be used in other preparations, such as timbales, custards, or soufflés. They may also be used as ingredients in other dishes once they are properly pureed. For example, a watercress puree may be used to flavor a sauce; a red pepper puree may be used as a pasta ingredient.

Parsnip and Pear Puree

Yield: 10 servings

Parsnips, peeled, boiled until tender	1½ pounds	680 grams
Pears, peeled, boiled until tender	2	2
Heavy cream, heated	3 to 4 ounces	85 to 115 grams
Salt	to taste	to taste
White pepper	to taste	to taste

1. All the ingredients should be very hot. Push the parsnips and pears through a fine sieve or Foley mill.

2. Add the hot heavy cream gradually and blend the mixture to a smooth, light puree. Season the puree with salt and ground white pepper to taste.

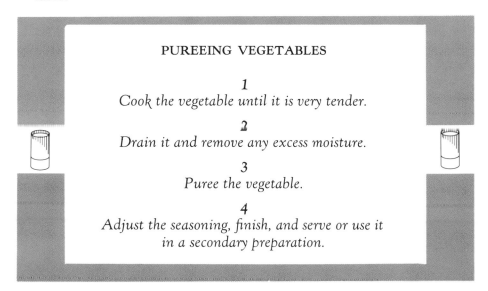

PUREEING VEGETABLES

1
Cook the vegetable until it is very tender.

2
Drain it and remove any excess moisture.

3
Puree the vegetable.

4
Adjust the seasoning, finish, and serve or use it in a secondary preparation.

Whatever the intended use, the vegetable must be cooked until it is tender enough to puree easily, by either pushing it through a sieve or food mill or pureeing it in a vertical chopping machine (VCM), food processor, or blender. Depending upon the desired smoothness of the finished puree, it may be advisable to sieve purees that have been made in the VCM or food processor.

Mise en Place

1. Vegetable. The vegetable may first need to be fully cooked, drained, and dried. Some vegetables, such as spinach, cucumbers, and tomatoes, are occasionally pureed from the raw state.

2. Optional components. These include aromatics and seasonings and finishing ingredients. Have available salt and pepper, minced fresh herbs, spices, or citrus juice or zest. Finishing ingredients should be added gradually to the pureed vegetable to assure the proper consistency. Have available whole butter or heavy cream.

Method

1. Boil, steam, roast, or microwave the vegetable until it is extremely tender.

2. If the vegetable has been cooked in water, drain it well and remove any excess moisture by either spreading it on a sheet tray and placing the tray in a warm oven to dry or wringing the vegetable in cheesecloth.

3. Puree the vegetable by pushing it through a sieve or food mill or by pureeing it in a food processor, blender, or VCM. The puree's consistency is determined by its intended use. For a smooth, light feel, a puree prepared in a food processor or VCM should be strained a second time through a fine sieve or chinois. The puree may be used in another preparation at this point.

4. Adjust the seasoning; finish the puree and serve it immediately on heated plates. Finishing ingredients should be added gradually until the desired consistency and flavor are reached. Note that the pureed vegetable and heavy cream or other liquids should be at the same temperature; butter should be soft but not melted.

For a quick summary, refer to the abbreviated method for pureeing vegetables. Refer also to "General Guidelines" for a discussion of determining doneness and evaluating quality, earlier in this chapter.

SUMMARY

Vegetable cookery is a true test of the chef's ability to coordinate technique and raw materials to achieve special flavor and color effects. Proper vegetable cookery calls upon several skills: the ability to purchase foods wisely and to store and handle them properly once purchased; a mastery of the proper techniques for assembling a good mise en place—cleaning, cutting, and trimming; and the ability

Belgian Endive à la Meunière

Yield: 10 servings

Belgian endive, blanched	10	10
Water	as needed	as needed
Salt	1 ounce	30 grams
Sugar	1 ounce	30 grams
Lemon juice	1 ounce	30 milliliters
Milk	4 ounces	120 milliliters
Flour	4 ounces	115 grams
Butter, clarified	4 ounces	115 grams
Lemon juice	1 ounce	30 milliliters
Parsley, chopped	1 tablespoon	2 grams

1. Blanch the endive in water flavored with salt, sugar, and lemon juice and drain it thoroughly.

2. Pare the endive cores with a sharp knife and flatten each head slightly.

3. Dip the endive in milk.

4. Dredge the endive in flour; shake off any excess.

5. Sauté the endive in the clarified butter until it is crisp and brown. Finish it in a moderate oven, if necessary. Remove it from the pan.

6. Deglaze the pan with 1 ounce of lemon juice.

7. Add the parsley and swirl it. Pour the pan liquid over the endive or return the endive to the pan to coat.

Spinach Pancakes

Yield: 20 servings

Milk	12 ounces	360 milliliters
Butter, melted	1 ounce	30 grams
Flour	5 ounces	140 grams
Eggs	4	4
Sugar	to taste	to taste
Spinach, steamed and chopped, squeezed dry	1 pound	455 grams
Nutmeg (optional)	to taste	to taste

1. Combine the milk, butter, flour, eggs, and sugar to form a batter.
2. Add the spinach and season the batter with salt, pepper, and nutmeg to taste.
3. Sauté the pancakes on a griddle or in plättar pans until done. Serve them immediately.

Italian-style Spinach

Yield: 10 servings

Bacon, pancetta, or prosciutto, chopped	3 slices	3 slices
Olive oil	1 ounce	30 milliliters
Onion, fine dice	1 ounce	30 grams
Garlic, minced	2 cloves	2 cloves
Leaf spinach, stems removed	3 pounds	1.3 kilograms
Salt	to taste	to taste
Parmesan cheese, grated	to taste	to taste
Black pepper	to taste	to taste

1. Sauté the bacon in the olive oil.
2. Add the onion, garlic, and spinach; sauté the spinach until it is limp.
3. Season the spinach with the salt, nutmeg, Parmesan, and pepper and serve immediately.

Macédoine of Vegetables

Yield: 10 servings

Mushrooms, large dice	2 ounces	55 grams
Shallots, minced	2 tablespoons	30 grams
Butter	as needed	as needed
Onion, large dice	2 ounces	55 grams
Celery, large dice	4 ounces	115 grams
Zucchini, large dice	6 ounces	170 grams
Yellow squash, large dice	6 ounces	170 grams
Carrot, large dice, parcooked	6 ounces	170 grams
Turnip, large dice, parcooked	6 ounces	170 grams
Rutabaga, large dice, parcooked	6 ounces	170 grams
Red pepper, small dice	2 ounces	55 grams
Chives, tarragon, and basil, fresh, chopped	to taste	to taste

1. Sauté the mushrooms and shallots in the butter until their moisture is reduced.
2. Add the onion and celery and sauté them until the onions are translucent.
3. Add the zucchini and yellow squash and sauté them until they are tender.
4. Add the remaining vegetables. Sauté them until they are heated through and tender.
5. Add the herbs; toss them to mix. Adjust the seasoning with salt and pepper to taste. Serve.

Glazed Beets

Yield: 10 servings

Beets, fresh, tops trimmed to 2 inches	2 pounds	910 grams
Butter	2 ounces	60 grams
Vinegar, distilled, or lemon juice	1 tablespoon	15 milliliters
Sugar, honey, or maple syrup	2 ounces	60 grams

1. Boil the beets in their skins until they are tender.
2. Peel and cut them into allumette.
3. Melt the butter; add the vinegar, sugar, and beets.
4. Cook the beets over high heat until they are glazed.
5. Adjust the seasoning with salt and pepper to taste.

Braised Red Cabbage

Yield: 10 servings

Onions, diced	4 ounces	115 grams
Green apples, diced	8 ounces	225 grams
Fat (vegetable oil or rendered bacon fat)	1½ ounces	45 grams
Water	8 ounces	240 milliliters
Red wine	3½ ounces	100 milliliters
Red wine vinegar	3½ ounces	100 milliliters
Granulated sugar	1 ounce	30 grams
Red currant jelly	2 ounces	60 grams
Red cabbage, cut in fine strips	2 pounds	910 grams
Cinnamon stick	1	1
Cloves	1	1
Bay leaf	1	1
Juniper berries	2 to 3	2 to 3
Arrowroot	½ teaspoon	1.5 grams

1. Slowly sweat the onions and apples in the oil or bacon fat.

2. Add the liquid ingredients, the sugar, and the jelly. Check the flavor; it should be tart and strong.

3. Add the cabbage and seasonings. Cover the pan and braise the mixture until the apples are tender, checking occasionally to make sure the liquid does not completely evaporate.

4. When the cabbage and apples are cooked, mix the arrowroot with cold water or wine. Use this to thicken the cooking liquid slightly if necessary. Adjust the seasoning with salt and pepper to taste.

Glazed Zucchini

Yield: 10 servings

Zucchini	2 pounds	910 grams
Salt pork, ground	2 ounces	55 grams
Whole butter	1 ounce	30 grams

1. Trim the ends from the zucchini; cut them as desired (tourné, batonnet, rounds).
2. Render the salt pork in a sauté pan. Add the whole butter and melt it.
3. Add the zucchini and toss it until it is heated through and glazed.
4. Adjust the seasoning with salt and pepper to taste.

Carrots and Salsify with Cream

Yield: 10 servings

Carrots, batonnet	1 pound	455 grams
Salsify, batonnet	1 pound	455 grams
Whole butter	2 ounces	55 grams
Sugar	½ ounce	15 grams
Cream sauce	3 ounces	90 milliliters

1. Blanch the carrots and salsify separately. (To blanch salsify, add lemon juice and flour to water for *en blanc* to keep the salsify white.)
2. Drain and reserve the vegetables.
3. Heat the butter and sugar; add the carrots and salsify and cook them until they are glazed.
4. Add the cream sauce and toss the vegetables to reheat and coat them thoroughly.
5. Adjust the seasoning with salt and pepper to taste.

Viennese-style Green Peas

Yield: 10 servings

Butter, melted	2 ounces	60 grams
Flour	1 ounce	30 grams
White beef stock, hot	12 ounces	360 milliliters
Sugar	to taste	to taste
Salt	to taste	to taste
Pepper	to taste	to taste
Green peas, fresh or frozen	1¾ pounds	800 grams
Parsley, chopped	1 tablespoon	2 grams

1. Heat the butter. Add the flour and cook it out to form a light roux.
2. Add the hot beef stock. Stir the mixture well and simmer it for 10 minutes.
3. Add the sugar, salt, and pepper.
4. Add the peas and bring the mixture to a boil.
5. Stir in the parsley.

Broccoli Mousse

Yield: 10 servings

Broccoli, cooked until tender, pureed	1 pound	455 grams
Whole eggs	4	4
Egg yolk	1	1
Heavy cream	2 to 3 ounces	55 to 85 grams
Cream cheese, softened	4 ounces	115 grams
Salt	to taste	to taste
Pepper	to taste	to taste

1. Combine all of the ingredients until they are smooth. Do not overmix them.
2. Place the mixture in buttered 2-ounce (60-milliliter) timbales in a pan and cover them with buttered parchment.
3. Bake them in a water bath until a skewer inserted near the center of a timbale comes out clean.
4. Remove and keep them warm. Unmold them and serve. The broccoli mousse may be served with a variety of sauces.

(continued)

VARIATIONS

Red Pepper Mousse: Replace the broccoli with pureed roasted red peppers.

Beet Mousse: Replace the broccoli with pureed cooked beets. Flavor them with orange zest and a small amount of orange juice concentrate to taste, if desired.

Green Beans with Bacon, Shallots, and Mushrooms

Yield: 10 servings

Green beans, trimmed	2½ pounds	1.15 kilograms
Bacon, julienned	4 ounces	115 grams
Shallots, minced	1 ounce	30 grams
Mushrooms, sliced	8 ounces	225 grams

1. Blanch, shock, and reserve the green beans.
2. Sauté the bacon until it is crisp. Drain it on absorbent paper toweling and reserve the fat.
3. Sauté the shallots in the bacon fat.
4. Add the mushrooms and sauté them.
5. Add the green beans and sauté them to the desired doneness. Sprinkle them with the reserved bacon.

Gingered Snow Peas and Yellow Squash

Yield: 8 servings

Snow peas	1 pound	455 grams
Yellow squash	8 ounces	225 grams
Ginger, fresh, chopped	1 teaspoon	2.5 grams
Shallots, chopped	1 tablespoon	15 grams
Garlic, chopped	1 teaspoon	2 grams
Chicken stock	¾ cup	180 grams
Chives, fresh, chopped	2 tablespoons	20 grams
White pepper	¼ teaspoon	0.5 gram

1. Remove the stem end and strings from the snow peas. Rinse them well. Slice off the stem end of the squash. Rinse it well and cut it into a medium dice.

2. Combine the vegetables with the ginger, shallots, garlic, stock, and chives.

3. Steam the vegetables until they are tender, about 2 to 3 minutes.

4. Season to taste with the pepper.

Green Beans with Walnuts

Yield: 4 servings

Green beans, split lengthwise	10 ounces	280 grams
Chicken stock, hot	2 tablespoons	30 milliliters
Shallots, minced	2 teaspoons	9 grams
Garlic	1 teaspoon	5 grams
Walnut oil	½ tablespoon	7 milliliters
Walnuts, chopped	2 tablespoons	16 grams
Chives, sliced	2 teaspoons	6 grams

1. Place the green beans in a sauté pan with the hot stock. Top them with the shallots, garlic, walnut oil, walnuts, and chives.

2. Cover and pan-steam the beans for approximately 3 minutes or until they are tender.

Potato Cookery

The potato may be one of the most versatile foods. It is found in nearly every menu category as the main component of appetizers, soups, entrées, and side dishes; it is also an important ingredient in such preparations as soufflés, pancakes, and breads.

In this chapter, the various techniques for preparing and presenting potatoes will be examined. Each technique produces a markedly different texture, flavor, and appearance. In addition, different potato varieties will produce different results. Knowing the natural characteristics of different potatoes and the ways in which particular techniques can either enhance or detract from these characteristics is important to any chef.

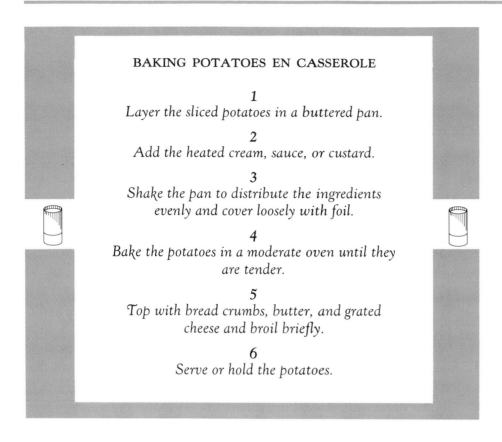

BAKING POTATOES EN CASSEROLE

1
Layer the sliced potatoes in a buttered pan.

2
Add the heated cream, sauce, or custard.

3
Shake the pan to distribute the ingredients evenly and cover loosely with foil.

4
Bake the potatoes in a moderate oven until they are tender.

5
Top with bread crumbs, butter, and grated cheese and broil briefly.

6
Serve or hold the potatoes.

COOKING IN FAT

Sautéing

This technique may be referred to interchangeably as sautéing or pan-frying, depending on the recipe one is reading. There is no difference in the end product. For the best results, choose all-purpose or chef's potatoes. They have a good balance of moisture and starch, which will tend to produce dishes with the best texture and appearance.

Mise en Place

1. Potato. Scrub and peel the potatoes, and remove the eyes. Cut the potatoes into even slices, dice, julienne, tourné, or balls. If the potatoes are peeled and cut in advance, be sure to hold them submerged in liquid until it is time to cook them. Drain and thoroughly dry them on absorbent toweling immediately before sautéing. Potatoes that are wet will cause the cooking fat to splatter. To shorten the cooking time, partially or fully cook the potatoes in advance by steaming or boiling. Drain and dry them as directed in the section on boiling.

2. Cooking fat. A variety of cooking fats and oils may be used, singly or in combination, to achieve an appropriate flavor in the finished dish. Have available clarified butter, vegetable oil, olive oil, or rendered duck, goose, or bacon fat.

3. Seasoning. Have available salt and pepper to season the potatoes after cooking, prior to service.

4. Optional components. A wide range of herbs, spices, vegetables, and meats can be combined with potatoes to produce a dish with a special appearance, flavor, or color. The ingredients listed here are examples; refer to the specific recipes for their appropriate use. Have available diced sweet peppers, diced bacon or ham, meat glaze, chopped fresh herbs, corn kernels (fresh or frozen), or sliced mushrooms.

The following finishing ingredients may be added to the potatoes during the actual cooking process or after they have been cooked until tender: heated cream, melted butter, heated sour cream, or grated cheese.

Method

1. Add the potatoes to the hot fat. Do not overcrowd the pan. (The arrangement for Potatoes Anna is shown in Fig. 23-2.) There should be enough cooking fat to coat the pan generously, to prevent the potatoes from sticking and falling apart as they cook. The potatoes should not be "floating" in the fat, however. The fat must be very hot, so that a crust will begin to develop immediately. This crust assures the proper color, flavor, and texture and also helps prevent the potato from absorbing too much fat.

2. Allow the potatoes to begin to form a golden skin.

3. Stir the potatoes or shake the pan occasionally as the potatoes cook.

4. Sauté the potatoes until they are tender. In general, garnishes or finishing ingredients should be added when the potatoes have almost finished cooking.

5. Follow the instructions in the next section for determining doneness, holding, and serving.

See Figure 23-3 for the step-by-step preparation of roësti potatoes, and refer to the abbreviated method for sautéing potatoes for quick reference.

Potatoes Anna

23-2

Placing potatoes Anna in a pan. (A finished dish is shown in the background.)

Yield: 10 servings

Potatoes, long yellow	2½ pounds	1.6 kilograms
Salt	to taste	to taste
Pepper	to taste	to taste
Butter, clarified	as needed	as needed

1. Peel the potatoes and trim them into uniform cylinders. Cut the cylinders into thin slices.

2. Arrange the sliced potatoes in layers in a buttered sautoir. Season each layer with salt and pepper and sprinkle them with clarified butter.

3. Cover the potatoes and begin cooking them on the stove top until the bottoms are browned. Turn the potato cake and brown the other side. Place it in a hot oven and cook until tender, about 30 to 35 minutes in all.

4. Drain off the excess butter and turn out the potato cake onto a platter. Slice it into portions.

23-3 PREPARING ROËSTI POTATOES

(1) Grated potatoes are formed into an even cake.

(2) Turning the cake over by first sliding it onto a plate.

(3) Covering the cake with the skillet, inverted, as shown here.

(4) Flipping the cake and pan over simultaneously.

(5) Sliding the finished roësti onto a plate.

(6) The finished dish.

Roësti Potatoes

Yield: 10 servings

Potatoes, russet	3 pounds	1.35 kilograms
Butter, clarified	as needed	as needed
Salt	to taste	to taste
Pepper	to taste	to taste
Whole butter	as needed	as needed

1. Parcook the potatoes until they are slightly underdone. Cool and store them under refrigeration until needed.

2. Peel and coarsely grate the potatoes.

3. Heat a well-seasoned sauté pan and add a small amount of the clarified butter.

4. Place the potatoes in the heated pan with the remaining clarified butter. Season them with the salt and pepper, and dot the outside edge with whole butter.

5. Cook the potatoes until they are golden brown and form a cake. Turn the entire cake, dot the edge with whole butter, and cook the other side until it is golden brown and heated through.

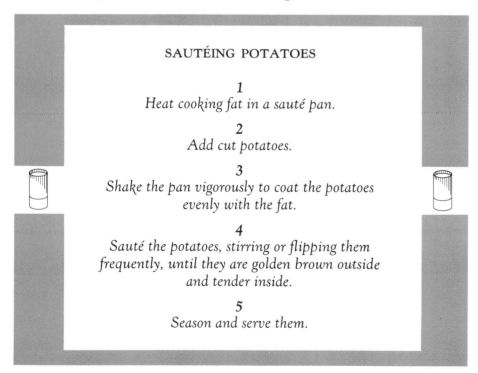

SAUTÉING POTATOES

1
Heat cooking fat in a sauté pan.

2
Add cut potatoes.

3
Shake the pan vigorously to coat the potatoes evenly with the fat.

4
Sauté the potatoes, stirring or flipping them frequently, until they are golden brown outside and tender inside.

5
Season and serve them.

Determining Doneness and Evaluating Quality

Sautéed potatoes should have a crisp, evenly browned exterior and a tender interior. They should not be greasy. The best way to test for doneness is to bite into a piece; it should be very tender.

Holding

For the best flavor and texture, sautéed potatoes should be served immediately after they are cooked.

Deep-frying

French fries, game chips, and steak fries, as well as waffle-cut, matchstick, and soufflé potatoes, are all examples of deep-frying. In order to achieve excellent quality, the steps outlined in this technique must be followed closely. Russet potatoes are preferred because of their high-starch and low-moisture content.

Blanching

Most deep-fried potatoes prepared from the raw state are first blanched in oil heated to approximately 325°F (162°C) until they are tender and almost translucent. They are then drained thoroughly and held until just before service, when they are finished in oil at approximately 375°F (190°C).

Blanching assures that the finished potato will have the proper color, texture, and flavor, and that it will be thoroughly cooked without being greasy or scorched. It is especially important to blanch soufflé potatoes so that they will puff adequately. Potatoes cut very thinly (matchstick potatoes or game chips, for example) can usually be cooked in a single step, without being blanched. Deep-fried potatoes, such as lorette, croquette, and dauphinoise potatoes, which are made from a pureed appareil, are discussed separately.

Mise en Place

1. Potato. Scrub and peel the potatoes, and remove the eyes. Cut the potatoes into even slices, julienne, batonnet, or other cuts. If the potatoes are peeled and cut in

advance of cooking, be sure to hold them submerged in water. Rinse the potatoes in several changes of cold water, if indicated, and drain and dry them thoroughly to prevent splattering when they are added to the oil.

Rinsing the potatoes in several changes of cold water will remove the surface starch. Potatoes that are to be deep-fried for such preparations as straw or matchstick potatoes should be rinsed so they won't clump together as they cook. Potatoes used for deep-fried potato nests (see Fig. 23-4) and cakes need the cohesiveness provided by the surface starch and should not be rinsed.

2. Oil. A neutral flavored oil should be heated to the proper temperature, according to the type of potatoes being prepared. Have available a neutral-flavored oil with a high smoking point.

3. Seasonings. Deep-fried potatoes are customarily seasoned with salt prior to service.

Method

1. Blanch raw potatoes in oil heated to the proper temperature. After blanching, drain the potatoes

23-4

Lining a mold for deep-fried potato nests. (A finished nest is shown in the background.)

on absorbent toweling and hold them, covered and under refrigeration, until just prior to service.

2. Lower the potatoes into oil heated to the proper temperature (350 to 375°F/176 to 190°C).

3. Deep-fry the potatoes until they are done, following the instructions for determining doneness in the next section.

4. Remove the potatoes from the oil and let the oil drain back into the automatic fryer or pot.

5. Drain the potatoes well on absorbent toweling and season them with salt.

For quick reference, refer to the abbreviated method for deep-frying potatoes.

Potato Nest

Yield: 1 nest

Potatoes, Idaho, grated	3 ounces	85 grams

1. Grate the potatoes immediately before preparing the potato nest. Do not rinse them in cold water.

2. Arrange the grated potatoes in the bottom of a basket. Fit a second basket in place.

3. Deep-fry the potatoes in 350°F (176°C) oil until they are crisp, brown, and thoroughly cooked. Drain them briefly.

4. Use the nest as a container for soufflé potatoes or other items, as desired.

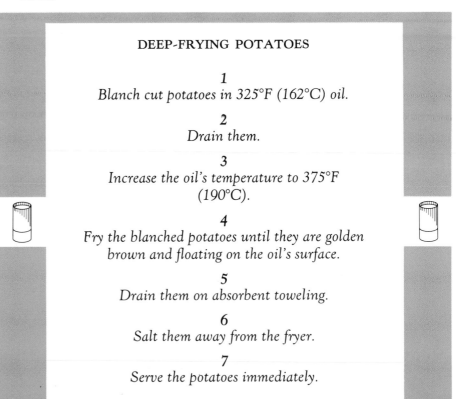

DEEP-FRYING POTATOES

1
Blanch cut potatoes in 325°F (162°C) oil.

2
Drain them.

3
Increase the oil's temperature to 375°F (190°C).

4
Fry the blanched potatoes until they are golden brown and floating on the oil's surface.

5
Drain them on absorbent toweling.

6
Salt them away from the fryer.

7
Serve the potatoes immediately.

Determining Doneness and Evaluating Quality

To check for doneness in a potato preparation, bite into one of the pieces. Very thin potatoes, such as game chips, gaufrette (waffle-cut) potatoes, and soufflé potatoes, should be extremely crisp, almost to the point at which they will shatter when bitten into. Thick-cut potatoes should have a crisp exterior and a tender, fluffy interior.

Soufflé potatoes are done when they are golden-brown and puffed. This technique is never 100 percent foolproof, and inevitably some of the soufflé potatoes will deflate. For the best results, use potatoes with a high starch content and an extremely low moisture content. (See Fig. 23-5 for steps in the preparation of soufflé potatoes.)

In order to avoid a transfer of flavors, fats used for deep-frying potatoes should be used only for potatoes.

Holding

Deep-fried potatoes cannot be held successfully and must be served immediately after cooking. Potatoes that have only been blanched in hot oil, however, may be held (covered) under refrigeration for up to several hours before finishing the cooking process. After deep-fried potatoes are drained briefly on paper toweling, they should be seasoned with salt and served immediately. A variety of condiments—catsup and malt vinegar are the most common—may be served with them.

Pureeing

A potato to be pureed is first cooked by boiling, steaming, or baking in its skin. After it is pureed, it may be combined with ingredients such as butter, eggs, cream, vegetable purees, or pâte à choux, or it may be served simply whipped or mashed.

Mise en Place

1. Potato. Have available boiled or steamed potatoes, drained or dried and still very hot.

2. Optional components. A number of ingredients may be added to the pureed potatoes. They should all be properly prepared, whether heated to the same temperature as the puree or at room temperature, grated, or beaten, as necessary. Refer to the specific recipes.

Method

1. Push hot drained and dried potatoes through a sieve, ricer, or food mill. For the best results, the equipment should be heated as well. Do not use a blender or food processor. The texture of the potato will be broken down irreparably, resulting in a soupy and sticky product that will not hold its shape. When working with large quantities of potatoes, it may be appropriate to run them through a grinder directly into a mixer's bowl.

2. Add the seasonings, purees, finishing ingredients, grated cheese, or pâte à choux to the puree, as desired or according to the recipe. Be sure that they are at room temperature or heated, as appropriate.

3. Using a wooden spoon or a mixer with a paddle attachment, quickly work the puree until it is smooth and all ingredients are blended. Do not overwork, because this will break down the potatoes, giving the puree a heavy, sticky consistency.

4. Pipe the potatoes into the desired shapes (see Fig. 23-6). The method for deep-fried purees is discussed below.

23-5 PREPARING SOUFFLÉ POTATOES

(1) Properly shaped potatoes swimming in hot oil.

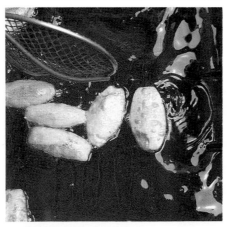

(2) Potatoes have puffed.

(3) Finished potatoes being removed with a spider.

For quick reference, refer to the abbreviated method for pureeing potatoes.

Determining Doneness and Evaluating Quality

The proper doneness depends directly upon the doneness of the steamed, boiled, or baked potatoes that are used as the puree's base. A potato puree should be smooth, light in texture, and able to hold its shape when dropped from a spoon.

Holding

Whipped or mashed potatoes may be held for service over a hot-water bath (bain-marie) or in a steam table. Purees to be used in dishes that are subsequently baked, sautéed, or deep-fried may be held under refrigeration for up to several hours before completion of the cooking. Once the final cooking is completed, they should be served immediately.

Method for Deep-frying Purees

1. Shape the potato puree: Pipe a lorette potato appareil (duchesse potatoes with pâte à choux) onto

23-6

Duchesse appareil piped onto a sheet pan.

Duchesse Potatoes

Yield: 1 pound

Potatoes, peeled, quartered	1 pound	455 grams
Egg yolks	2	2
Butter, softened	3 tablespoons	85 grams
Salt	to taste	to taste
Pepper	to taste	to taste
Nutmeg	to taste	to taste

1. Cook the potatoes in boiling, salted water until they are just tender.

2. Drain and dry the potatoes; keeping them hot, and puree them.

3. Mix in the egg yolks and add the butter and seasonings.

PUREEING POTATOES

1
Cook the potatoes until they are tender by boiling, steaming, or baking them.

2
Dry steamed or boiled potatoes on a sheet pan in a moderate oven.

3
Puree the potatoes through a ricer, food mill, or sieve.

4
Add eggs, heated milk or cream, or softened butter, as needed.

5
Adjust the seasoning to taste.

6
Serve or hold the potatoes.

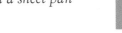

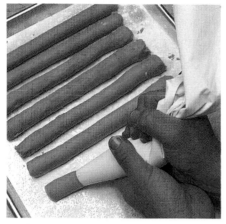

(1) Piping croquette potatoes onto a lightly floured sheet pan.

(2) Cutting the croquettes into pieces, and rolling with flour and dried bread crumbs. Rolled croquettes *(left foreground)*, coated with bread crumbs *(middle)*, and properly fried *(back)*.

(3) Lowering the croquettes into hot oil.

(4) The potatoes dropping below the surface.

(5) The potatoes rising to the surface.

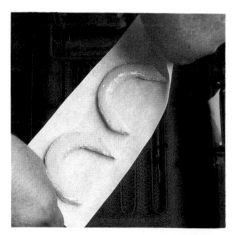

(1) Piping the mixture onto strips of parchment.

(2) Lowering the lorettes carefully into hot oil.

(3) Removing the finished potatoes with a spider.

Croquette Potatoes

Yield: 18 to 20 servings

Potatoes, Idaho or russet	2 pounds	910 grams
Butter, softened	1 ounce	30 grams
Egg yolks	3	3
Salt	to taste	to taste
Pepper	to taste	to taste
Standard breading	as needed	as needed

1. Cook the potatoes until they are very tender. Drain and dry them.
2. Puree the potatoes while they are very hot.
3. Add the butter and egg yolks, mixing them well, and season the appareil with salt and pepper.
4. Shape the croquettes as required.
5. Bread the croquettes and deep-fry them in 375°F (190°C) oil until they are golden brown. Serve them immediately.

Lorette Potatoes

Yield: 10 servings

Potatoes, baking, peeled, quartered	2 pounds	910 grams
Butter, soft	2½ ounces	70 grams
Eggs, beaten	2	2
Nutmeg	pinch	pinch
Salt	to taste	to taste
Pepper	to taste	to taste
Pâte à choux, room temperature	20 ounces	565 grams
Oil or frying fat	as needed	as needed

1. Cook the potatoes in boiling, salted water until they are tender. Drain and dry them; keep them hot. Puree.
2. Add the butter, eggs, nutmeg, salt, and pepper to the potatoes and mix them in well.
3. Mix in the pâte à choux.
4. Pipe the mixture into the desired shapes on strips of parchment paper. Deep-fry the lorettes until they are golden.

NOTE: Refer to Chapter 14 for the recipe for Pâte à Choux.

strips of parchment paper. A number of shapes are possible. Hold them on the strips until ready to deep-fry. A second option is to bread potato croquettes by piping them out or shaping them directly onto a sheet pan coated with flour. Roll them in the flour to coat them evenly. Cut the potatoes into pieces of the desired length. Transfer them to a sheet tray lined with bread crumbs and coat them evenly. Hold them on the crumb-lined sheet pans at room temperature until ready to deep-fry.

2. Add the potatoes to heated oil (375°F/190°C). For lorette potatoes, hold one end of the parchment paper strip. Lower the other end into the oil. Gently pull away the paper as the potato lifts off the paper. Breaded croquettes should be lowered into the hot oil with a basket.

3. Deep-fry the potatoes to the appropriate golden-brown color. Remove them with a spider if they were fried by the swimming method. Use the double-basket method for croquette potatoes to assure an even browning. Two different methods are shown in Figures 23-7 and 23-8: preparing croquette potatoes and preparing lorette potatoes.

SUMMARY

The potato has broad appeal not only because its flavor is well-appreciated, but also because it can be prepared in numerous ways.

As shown in this chapter, a wide range of preparation techniques can be applied to produce a number of preparations with special flavors, textures, and appearances. This flexibility allows the chef considerable latitude in developing the overall plate presentation.

Glazed Sweet Potatoes

Yield: 10 servings

Sweet potatoes	3 pounds	1.35 kilograms
Pineapple, fresh, chunks	8 ounces	225 grams
Lemon juice	of 1 lemon	of 1 lemon
Sugar	8 ounces	225 grams
Cinnamon	1 teaspoon	1.5 grams
Butter	2 ounces	60 grams

1. Bake the sweet potatoes in a moderate oven until they are tender.

2. Combine all the remaining ingredients in a saucepan and bring them to a boil. Simmer the mixture until it is thick.

3. Peel the potatoes and cut them into large chunks. Pour the glaze over them and toss to coat them lightly.

Baked Stuffed Potatoes

Yield: 10 servings

Potatoes, Idaho	10	10
Butter, softened	2 ounces	60 grams
Salt	to taste	to taste
Pepper	to taste	to taste
Egg yolk	1	1
Light cream or milk, hot	as needed	as needed
Paprika	as needed	as needed
Butter	as needed	as needed

1. Bake the potatoes until they are tender.

2. Remove the tops of the potatoes by slicing them lengthwise.

3. Scoop out the potato pulp.

4. Rice the pulp and mix it with the butter, salt, and pepper.

5. Work in the egg yolk and hot cream or milk.

6. Pipe the potato mixture back into the shells.

7. Sprinkle the potatoes with paprika and butter. Return them to the oven until they are heated through and lightly browned on top.

Potatoes Jackson: Add 2 ounces (60 grams) of grated Parmesan cheese to the potato mixture.

Potatoes Georgette: Add nutmeg and 2 ounces (60 grams) of chopped chives to the potato mixture.

Potatoes Hashed in Cream

Yield: 10 servings

Potatoes, peeled, quartered	3 pounds	1.35 kilograms
Light cream, heated	3 cups	720 milliliters
Salt	to taste	to taste
Pepper	to taste	to taste

1. Parcook the potatoes in boiling, salted water.

2. Drain them well and cut them into a small dice.

3. Combine the potatoes and the heated cream. Simmer the potatoes until they are completely cooked and the cream is thickened. Season them to taste with the salt and pepper.

Sweet Potatoes Baked in Cider with Currants and Cinnamon

Yield: 10 servings

Sweet potatoes, peeled and sliced thin	2½ pounds	1.15 kilograms
Whole butter	2 ounces	55 grams
Shallots, minced	1 ounce	30 grams
Apple or pear cider	8 ounces	225 grams
Currants, dried	2 ounces	60 grams
Cinnamon, ground	1 teaspoon	2 grams
Salt	to taste	to taste
Pepper	to taste	to taste

1. Shingle the sweet potato slices in a well-buttered casserole or gratin dish. Sprinkle them with the shallots. Add the cider; there should be enough to thoroughly moisten the potatoes.

2. Add the currants and cinnamon. Cover the dish loosely with aluminum foil and bake the potatoes until they are very tender. Season them with salt and pepper. Serve them immediately.

Chapter 24

Cooking Grains and Legumes

Once thought of as "peasant food," grains and legumes are now appreciated for their healthful qualities and are taking an increasingly prominent position in the average diet. It is not just their excellent food value that makes them appealing. Chefs' rediscovery of traditional dishes based on grains, legumes, or a combination of the two have turned what might once have been considered stodgy, starchy dishes into favorite menu items. Grains that were once seldom seen, such as barley, millet, and brown rice, are now appreciated for their special flavors and textures. Newly available grains such as quinoa and amaranth are opening up new options. The same is true of legumes; dishes that incorporate black beans, stews of black-eyed and yellow-eyed peas, and lentils in a number of guises have become a familiar sight on the menu. This chapter will focus on the various ways to prepare and present grains and legumes.

CHARACTERISTICS

Grains

Grains, which are actually the fruit of a grass, have a pleasant taste, are inexpensive and readily available, and provide a valuable and concentrated source of nutrients and fiber. Although grains differ in appearance from other fruits, such as apples and pears, their botanical composition is quite similar.

Culinary grains commonly undergo some degree of processing (milling) before they reach the kitchen. The milling process either strips away or scores the bran and may also remove the kernel's germ. In addition to refining, milling may also break the grain into small pieces or grind it into a meal.

There are various levels of preliminary processing. For example, brown rice that reaches the kitchen has undergone little refining; white rice, on the other hand, has been stripped of its bran and may be polished or converted as well. Dried corn may be left whole (a form known as hominy), cracked to produce grits, or made into cornmeal or flour.

The grain's most nutrient-rich part is the endosperm, which serves as a storage facility for the carbohydrates, vitamins, and minerals, and for some of the proteins and oils used by the plant for growing and regeneration. Even if the germ and the bran are removed, the endosperm itself is still a potent energy source.

The techniques covered here are for cooking the major culinary grains—rice, barley, bulgur wheat, couscous, cornmeal, and certain grains used as side dishes. Additional grains are covered in Chapter 10, "Nonperishable Goods Identification."

Legumes

Legumes are seeds that grow in pods. These seeds can be used in the kitchen fresh or dried. When fresh, they are treated as vegetables. In the dried form they are known collectively as legumes. Lima beans, for example, can be treated as a vegetable in their fresh state and as a legume when dried.

Like grains, legumes are a potent nutrient source, though they have a higher protein content than most grains. Dishes that combine grains and legumes, such as the traditional southern Hoppin' John (black-eyed peas and rice) contain a particularly effective balance of essential nutrients, providing not only the necessary proteins but also an impressive amount of complex carbohydrates, dietary fiber, vitamins, and minerals.

The purpose of cooking both grains and legumes is threefold. First it is done to change their texture enough to make them easy to chew. Second, cooking develops an acceptable flavor. Finally, cooking grains and legumes deactivates various naturally present substances that have unpleasant or even harmful effects on humans by directly or indirectly causing vitamin deficiencies. Grains may be cooked using any of several methods; legumes, however, are always boiled. Figure 24-1 shows raw, properly cooked, and overcooked chickpeas.

24-1

The stages in cooking a legume. Uncooked chickpeas *(top)*; properly cooked chickpeas *(bottom left)*—plump, moist, and tender to the bite with the skin still firmly attached; overcooked chickpeas *(bottom right)*, with the skin starting to separate from the bean.

GENERAL GUIDELINES

Storing

Grains and legumes should be stored in a dry area, away from moisture, light, and excessive heat. It may be necessary to store whole grains (those with the bran left intact) under refrigeration, because the amount of oil present in the bran and germ could cause the grain to become rancid.

Legumes must be kept in dry storage because molds can develop quickly under damp conditions. Legumes will take longer to cook as they become older. For additional information on purchasing and storing grains and legumes, consult Chapter 10, "Nonperishable Goods Identification."

Sorting and Rinsing

Itp is important to rinse unmilled or whole grains and virtually all legumes, because a certain amount of dust often clings to the surface. Occasionally a few stones will be mixed in with the legumes, so they should be carefully sorted out and removed prior to rinsing.

Grains or legumes should be placed in a large colander or sieve and rinsed well with cold running water to remove any dust or foreign particles. Then they should be put in a large pot with cold water. Any grains or legumes that float on the surface are overly dry for culinary or nutritional purposes and should be removed and discarded. Milled grains, especially enriched, converted, and polished rices, need not be rinsed.

Soaking

Soaking is not essential in the advance preparation of grains and legumes, although it is helpful in shortening the cooking time. Whole grains such as scotch barley and buckwheat benefit from soaking because prolonged exposure to water tends to soften the outer layer (bran). Couscous is also customarily soaked briefly in tepid water, prior to being steamed. Bulgur wheat to be used in stuffings or salads is "cooked" by soaking the grain in a large quantity of boiling water for several minutes, until the grain softens enough to be chewed easily. (Refer to Table 24-1 for more information on soaking times.)

Legumes' tough seed coats do not absorb water quickly (and in some cases may not become significantly softer even after cooking), the only way for water to enter the bean is through a small opening called the hilum, where the legume was attached to the pod. Legumes that require more than two hours of cooking time benefit from soaking overnight in enough cold water to

TABLE 24-1. COOKING RATIOS AND TIMES FOR SELECTED GRAINS

Type	Ratio of Grain to Liquid (Cups)	Approximate Yield (Cups)*	Cooking Time
Barley, pearled	1:2	4	35 to 45 minutes
Barley groats	1:2½	4	50 minutes to 1 hour
Buckwheat groats (Kasha)	1:1½ to 2	2	12 to 20 minutes
Couscous**	—	1½ to 2	20 to 25 minutes
Hominy, whole***	1:2½	3	2½ to 3 hours
Hominy grits	1:4	3	25 minutes
Millet	1:2	3	30 to 35 minutes
Oat groats	1:2	2	45 minutes to 1 hour
Polenta	1:3 to 3½	3	35 to 45 minutes
Rice, Arborio (risotto)	1:3	3	20 to 30 minutes
Rice, basmati	1:1½	3	25 minutes
Rice, converted	1:1¾	4	25 to 30 minutes
Rice, Long-grain, brown	1:3	4	40 minutes
Rice, Long-grain, white	1:1½ to 1¾	3	18 to 20 minutes
Rice, Short-grain, brown	1:2½	4	35 to 40 minutes
Rice, Short-grain, white	1:1 to 1½	3	20 to 30 minutes
Rice, wild	1:3	4	30 to 45 minutes
Rice, wild, pecan	1:1¾	4	20 minutes
Wheat berries	1:3	2	1 hour
Wheat, bulgur, soaked†	1:4	2	2 hours
Wheat, bulgur, pilaf†	1:2½	2	15 to 20 minutes
Wheat, cracked	1:2	3	20 minutes

* From 1 cup of uncooked grain.
** Grain should be soaked briefly in tepid water and then drained before it is steamed.
*** Grain should be soaked overnight in cold water and then drained before it is cooked.
† Grain may be cooked by covering it with boiling water and soaking it for 2 hours or cooking it by the pilaf method.

24-3 PREPARING COUSCOUS

(1) Mise en place, including ingredients for the stew.

(2) The grain in the upper tier of the couscoussière.

(3) Fluffing the couscous with a fork.

Couscous

Yield: 10 servings

Couscous	1 pound	450 grams
Warm water or stew	as needed	as needed
Salt	to taste	to taste
Olive oil	as needed	as needed

1. Soak the couscous for about 5 minutes in enough warm water to cover, then drain it in a colander.

2. Set the colander over a pot of simmering water or stew; cover the pot and let the couscous steam for 3 to 4 minutes. Uncover the pot and stir the couscous with a fork to break up any lumps. (Rinse the couscous at this point if it is not the precooked variety, and continue to steam it for another 5 minutes.)

3. Fluff the couscous with a fork, and season it to taste with the salt. Drizzle a small amount of olive oil over the couscous, if desired.

STEAMING GRAINS

1
Place the grain over simmering or boiling liquid.

2
Steam the grain until tender.

3
Adjust the seasoning to taste and serve or hold the item.

---

abbreviated method for steaming grains.

Pilaf Method

There is no consensus on the origin of the word *pilaf*; however, it has come to mean a grain dish in which the grain is first heated in a pan, either dry or in an oil, and then combined with hot liquid. The grain is cooked, covered, in the oven or on the stove top. In this dish the grains tend to remain sep- arate, with a nutty flavor caused by the initial toasting or "parching" of the grain, and with a slightly firmer texture than grains prepared by boiling.

Mise en Place

1. Main ingredient. See "Mise en Place" for boiling, previously.

2. Cooking fat or oil. Often a neutral-flavored oil is used; however, a cooking fat that will contrib- ute a flavor of its own, such as

butter or rendered goose fat, is also appropriate.

3. Liquid. Stock is generally preferred. Bringing the liquid to a boil in a separate pot before adding it to the grain helps to shorten the total cooking time. To give rice a particular flavor and/or color, vegetable or fruit juice or a vegetable coulis may be substituted for up to half of the liquid. If the juice is acidic (tomato juice, for instance), the cooking time may need to be increased by as much as 15 to 20 minutes.

4. Onion. A member of the onion family, such as finely diced or minced onions, shallots, scallions, or leeks, is required.

5. Optional components. In addition to onions, bay leaf and thyme are commonly used for flavor. Other herbs and spices may also be added. Have available bay leaves, thyme, saffron, curry powder, tarragon, basil, or other herbs and spices.

Additional vegetables may be allowed to sweat along with the onion. Refer to the recipes for the appropriate times to add other ingredients such as mushrooms, pine nuts, or currants. Citrus juices, wine, and vinegar may be added at the last minute to adjust the seasoning. Have available: finely diced carrots, mushrooms, bell peppers, and/or celery; chopped nuts or dried fruits; and/or citrus juices, wine, or vinegar.

Method

1. Heat the cooking fat or oil in a heavy-gauge pot.

2. Add the minced onions and other aromatic vegetables and sweat them until they are translucent.

3. Add the grains and sauté them, stirring frequently, until they are coated with oil and heated through. Heating the grain in hot fat or oil begins to gelatinize the starches. This encourages the grains to remain separate after they are cooked.

4. Add the heated liquid.

5. Bring the liquid to a simmer, stirring the grain once or twice to prevent it from sticking to the pot bottom.

6. Add herbs and spices to the pilaf according to recipe, cover the pot, and place it in a moderate oven.

7. Cook the grains until they are tender, but not soft or mushy, and will separate readily. Use a fork to separate the grains and release the steam.

8. Adjust the seasoning to taste and serve the pilaf on heated plates.

The preparation of a rice pilaf is shown in Figure 24-4. For a quick summary of the pilaf method, refer to the abbreviated method.

Determining Doneness and Evaluating Quality

Test a few grains by biting into them. They should be tender but with a noticeable texture. In addition, the individual grains should separate easily. The cooking times listed in Table 24-1 are only a guide.

Pilafs that have been overcooked will have a "pasty" flavor; the individual grains may be mushy or soggy and will clump together. Grains that have been inadequately cooked or in an insufficient amount of liquid will be crunchy.

Rice Pilaf

Yield: 6 servings

Onion, diced	1 ounce	30 grams
Butter	½ ounce	15 grams
White rice, long-grain	1 cup	240 milliliters
Stock, seasoned, hot	2 cups	480 milliliters
Bay leaf	1	1
Salt	to taste	to taste
Pepper	to taste	to taste

1. Sweat the onion in the butter.

2. Add the rice and stir it to coat with the butter.

3. Add the hot stock and seasonings.

4. Bring the liquid to a boil. Cover the pot and transfer it to a moderate oven and simmer it for 18 to 20 minutes until the liquid is absorbed and the rice is tender.

VARIATION

Leek Pilaf: Sweat ¾ cup (180 grams) of minced leeks along with the onions in the first step of the recipe.

(1) Mise en place.

(2) Sweating the onions in butter.

(3) Sautéing the rice.

(4)

(4) Adding the stock.

(5) Adding the aromatics and covering the pot.

(5)

(6) The properly cooked pilaf. There is no free liquid in the bottom of the pot.

(7) Separating the grains with a fork.

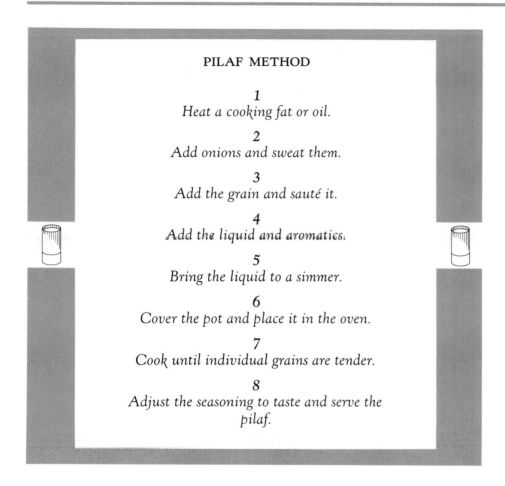

PILAF METHOD

1
Heat a cooking fat or oil.

2
Add onions and sweat them.

3
Add the grain and sauté it.

4
Add the liquid and aromatics.

5
Bring the liquid to a simmer.

6
Cover the pot and place it in the oven.

7
Cook until individual grains are tender.

8
Adjust the seasoning to taste and serve the pilaf.

and herbs may also be added as optional components. Finely mince leeks, shallots, or yellow or white onions.

4. Cooking fat or oil. Butter is the fat of choice, because it contributes a sweet, rich flavor. Other fats and oils, especially olive oil, may be used as desired or appropriate.

5. Optional components. Various herbs and spices, especially saffron, are frequently added during cooking to provide additional color and flavor. Various wines may be added during the final cooking stage. The wine should not be added initially, because its acids will prevent the rice from softening correctly.

Good-quality grating cheese, such as Parmesan or Romano, should be added as close to service time as possible to assure the best flavor. Various meats, fish, poultry, and vegetables are possible garnishes. Refer to the specific recipes for ingredients and preparation.

Risotto Method

This method is customarily limited to a special short-grain rice—arborio. The rice is stirred constantly as small amounts of hot liquid are added and absorbed by the grain. The rice's starch is released gradually during the cooking process, producing a creamy texture. Although other rices, including long-grain varieties, are sometimes used in a risotto, the finished dish's quality is not the same. The best risotto has an almost porridge-like consistency, with each grain retaining a distinct bite. Onions and grated cheese are often included, and vegetables, meats, or fish may be added to create a risotto that can be served as an appetizer or main course.

Although risotto's preparation is relatively lengthy and requires con-

stant attention, there are ways to streamline the process, making it suitable for restaurant service.

Mise en Place

1. Main ingredient. Arborio rice (a short-grain polished rice) is preferred, although it is possible to use either short- or long-grain varieties of white and brown rice. The cooking time will be longer for brown rice and the amount of liquid required may be greater.

2. Liquid. Good-quality stock should be at a simmer. This is done to reduce the cooking time and also aids somewhat in speeding the rice's liquid absorption.

3. Onion. A member of the onion family should be included. Other aromatic vegetables, spices,

Method

1. Heat the cooking fat or oil.
2. Add the onion and other aromatics, as desired or necessary, and sweat the onions until they are translucent. A wide variety of aromatic vegetables in addition to onions or leeks, including carrots, celery, and mushrooms, may also be included. They should be chopped and allowed sufficient time to sweat in the hot butter or oil to fully develop their flavor. In some risottos, a puree of cooked onion may be used.

Saffron is often called for and should be stirred into the hot oil or butter to release its flavor and color. Other spices, either left whole or ground, may be added at this point as well.

3. Add the rice and cook it in the fat or oil until it is well-coated and slightly "parched."

4. Add the simmering liquid in parts. Generally, no more than one-third of the cooking liquid is added at any time. The dish is stirred constantly to avoid scorching and is allowed to cook until the rice has absorbed the liquid. The next portion of liquid is then added and the mixture is once again stirred until the liquid is absorbed. This continues until all of the liquid has been added and the risotto appears creamy. If the wine is part of the liquid to be used, it should be added last. Again, the risotto is stirred until the wine is absorbed.

Although the best risotto is prepared from start to finish just prior to service, it is possible to partially cook the dish in advance. To do this, remove the risotto from the heat after the second part of the liquid has been absorbed. Spread the risotto in a sheet pan and hold it until it is needed for service. At that point, complete the cooking and finishing, a portion at a time, as needed. Add the final third of the hot liquid, allow it to be absorbed, and finish the dish as instructed below.

5. Add the grated cheese or other garnish. Stir the cheese or garnish into the risotto and continue to cook it briefly until it is heated through. (Some garnish ingredients may be added early in the cooking process so that they fully cook along with the risotto. Others may be cooked separately and added.)

6. Add the fresh herbs, adjust the seasoning to taste, and serve the risotto on heated plates.

This method is demonstrated in Figure 24-5. For a quick summary, refer to the abbreviated method for risotto.

Basic Risotto

Yield: 6 servings

Onion, diced	1 ounce	30 grams
Butter	½ ounce	15 grams
Arborio rice	1 cup	240 milliliters
Chicken stock, hot	2½ to 3 cups	600 to 720 milliliters
Salt	to taste	to taste
Pepper	to taste	to taste

1. Sweat the onion in the butter.

2. Add the rice and mix it thoroughly with the butter. Cook it, stirring, until a toasted aroma develops.

3. Add the liquid in several additions, stirring the rice frequently. Cook the risotto until the rice is al dente and most of the liquid is absorbed. The texture should be creamy.

VARIATIONS

Add grated, fresh Parmesan cheese to taste just before serving the risotto.

Replace one-quarter of the chicken stock with dry white wine. Add it as the final liquid addition.

Garnish the risotto with fresh peas for *risi e bisi.*

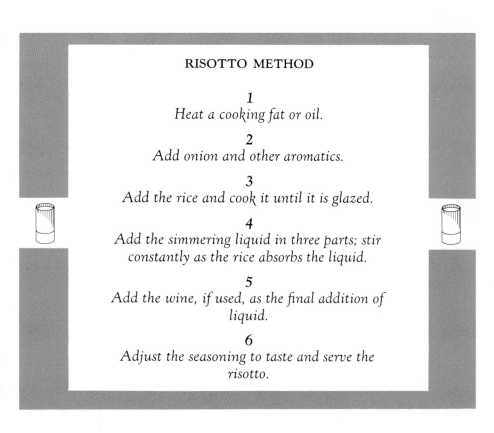

RISOTTO METHOD

1
Heat a cooking fat or oil.

2
Add onion and other aromatics.

3
Add the rice and cook it until it is glazed.

4
Add the simmering liquid in three parts; stir constantly as the rice absorbs the liquid.

5
Add the wine, if used, as the final addition of liquid.

6
Adjust the seasoning to taste and serve the risotto.

24-5 PREPARING RISOTTO

(1) Mise en place, including several optional components: wild mushrooms, diced peppers, herbs, and grated cheese.

(2) Sweating the onions in butter.

(3) Parching the rice by sautéing.

(4) Gradually adding the hot stock.

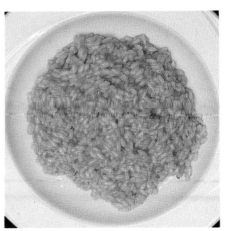

(5) The stock is almost completely absorbed before more is added.

(6) The finished risotto. The individual grains are still visible but the dish looks creamy.

Determining Doneness and Evaluating Quality

Risotto is properly cooked when it has absorbed the required amount of liquid (based on the proper ratio of liquid to grain) and has developed a creamy, almost porridge-like consistency. Each grain should still have a distinct bite. If it is overcooked, the risotto will be sticky. Risottos that have been cooked over high heat or too rapidly will neither develop the proper consistency nor be adequately cooked.

SUMMARY

It might seem strange to most of the world that Americans are just beginning to "rediscover" the goodness of rice, beans, wheat, corn, peas, and lentils. In the United States, these foods were, until only recently, considered peasant fare or—even less glamorous—animal fodder. The enlightened chef is well aware that these foods are nutritionally superior and offer a range of special flavors, textures, and colors that can be used to great effect.

As grains and legumes continue to gain culinary acceptance, more familiar grains such as rice can be replaced with others such as barley, millet, or couscous to give a slightly different flavor and a fresh look to a dish. The innovative use of beans, lentils, and dried peas has brought them into the foreground as adventurous cooks look to ethnic dishes as inspiration for their own creations.

Polenta with Parmesan Cheese

Yield: 24 servings

Shallots, chopped fine	1 ounce	30 grams
Garlic, chopped fine	2 tablespoons	25 grams
Butter	½ pound	225 grams
Chicken stock	3 quarts	2.85 liters
Cornmeal, yellow	24 ounces	680 grams
Egg yolks	3	3
Parmesan cheese, grated	½ cup	120 milliliters
Salt	to taste	to taste
Pepper	to taste	to taste

1. Sauté the shallots and garlic in the butter until they are translucent.

2. Add the stock and bring it to a boil.

3. Add the cornmeal in a stream, stirring constantly until it has all been added. Simmer the mixture for 45 minutes, stirring often; when done, it should pull away from the sides of the pot.

4. Remove the pot from the heat and blend in the egg yolks, cheese, and seasonings.

5. Pour the polenta onto a greased half-size sheet pan and refrigerate it until it is cool and firm.

6. Cut it into the desired shape.

7. Panfry the polenta until it is golden brown on both sides.

Wild Rice Pilaf

Yield: 6 servings

Onion, diced	1 ounce	30 grams
Butter	½ ounce	15 grams
Wild rice	1 cup	240 milliliters
Chicken stock	2½ to 3 cups	600 to 720 milliliters
Salt	to taste	to taste
Pepper	to taste	to taste

1. Sweat the onions in the butter.

2. Add the rice and sauté it briefly.

3. Add the stock and seasonings. Bring the liquid to a simmer.

4. Cover the pot and finish the pilaf in a 350°F (176°C) oven. Drain off the excess liquid if necessary. The cooking time is 45 to 50 minutes.

SUBSTITUTION

Brown Rice Pilaf: Substitute brown rice for the wild rice.

Risotto with Assorted Seafood

Yield: 6 servings

Basic Risotto, prepared with fish stock	1 recipe	1 recipe
Combination of seafood: shrimp, scallops, mussels, and crayfish, shelled and cleaned	24 ounces	675 grams
Parsley, fresh, minced	1 ounce	30 grams
Whole butter	3 ounces	85 grams
Parmesan cheese, grated	3 ounces	85 grams

1. Prepare the risotto according to the directions in the basic recipe.

2. Add the shellfish when the final addition of stock or wine has been almost completely absorbed.

3. Stir in the parsley and butter. Finish it with the parmesan cheese. Serve the risotto immediately.

NOTE: Refer to the recipe for Basic Risotto, earlier in this chapter.

Risotto with Mussels

Yield: 6 servings

Basic risotto, prepared with fish stock	1 recipe	1 recipe
Mussels, cleaned, debearded, and lightly steamed	2 to 3 pounds	1 to 1.35 kilograms
Parsley, fresh, minced	1 ounce	30 grams
Whole butter	3 ounces	85 grams

1. Prepare the risotto according to the directions in the basic recipe.

2. Add the mussels, removed from their shells, when the final addition of stock or wine has been completely absorbed.

3. Stir in the parsley and butter. Serve the risotto immediately.

NOTE: Refer to the recipe for Basic Risotto, earlier in this chapter.

Risotto with Asparagus Tips

Yield: 6 servings

Basic Risotto, prepared with vegetable stock	1 recipe	1 recipe
Asparagus tips, peeled and blanched	24 ounces	675 grams
Parsley, fresh, minced	1 ounce	30 grams
Whole butter	3 ounces	85 grams
Parmesan cheese, grated	3 ounces	85 grams

1. Prepare the risotto according to the directions in the basic recipe.

2. Add the asparagus tips when the final addition of stock or wine has been almost completely absorbed.

3. Stir in the parsley and butter. Finish the risotto with the parmesan cheese and serve it immediately.

NOTE: Refer to the recipe for Basic Risotto, earlier in this chapter.

Rice Croquettes

Yield: 20 servings

Béchamel

Butter	4 ounces	115 grams
Bread flour	4 ounces	115 grams
Milk	24 ounces	720 milliliters
Onion, chopped	2 ounces	60 grams
Saffron	pinch	pinch
Butter	1 ounce	30 grams
Rice	8 ounces	225 grams
Stock, hot	1 quart	1 liter
Parmesan cheese, freshly grated	6 ounces	170 grams
Egg yolks	6	6
Egg wash	as needed	as needed
Bread crumbs, dry	4 parts	4 parts
Cornmeal, yellow	1 part	1 part
Vegetable oil	as needed	as needed

1. Make a thick béchamel sauce: Heat the butter. Add the flour and cook the mixture to make a blond roux. Add the milk and stir it in vigorously, working out any lumps. Simmer the sauce to cook out any floury taste.
2. Sauté the onions and saffron in the butter. Add the rice and sauté it until it is coated. Add the stock and bring it to a simmer.
3. Cover the rice and cook it in the oven until it is tender. Stir in the parmesan cheese.
4. Bind the rice with the béchamel. Allow the mixture to cool slightly and add the egg yolks.
5. Pour the mixture onto a buttered, parchment-lined sheet pan.
6. Place a sheet of plastic wrap over the mixture and press it out to an even thickness.
7. Refrigerate it overnight.
8. Cut the rice into the desired shapes.
9. Bread the croquettes with a mixture of the bread crumbs and cornmeal, using the standard breading procedure.
10. Deep-fry the croquettes in oil heated to 350°F (175°C) until they are golden.

Braised Lentils with Eggplant and Mushrooms

Yield: 10 servings

Lentils, green or brown	12 ounces	340 grams
Water or stock	as needed	as needed
Olive oil	1 ounce	30 milliliters
Garlic, minced	2 cloves	2 cloves
Onion, diced	1	1
Eggplant, large dice	1	1
Mushrooms, sliced or quartered	4 ounces	115 grams
Cinnamon, ground	½ teaspoon	1 gram
Turmeric, ground	½ teaspoon	1 gram
Lemon zest	1 piece to taste	1 piece to taste
Salt	to taste	to taste
Pepper	to taste	to taste

Gratin

Bread crumbs, fresh	4 ounces	115 grams
Butter, melted	2 ounces	60 grams

1. Cook the lentils, in enough water or stock to cover them by 1 inch (2.5 centimeters), until they are tender (about 30 to 40 minutes). Drain the lentils, reserving the cooking liquid.

2. Heat the oil in a rondeau. Add the garlic and onion; cook them until they are lightly browned.

3. Add the eggplant, stirring to coat it evenly with oil. Add the mushrooms, spices, and lemon zest. Cook the mixture until the mushrooms begin to release their juices.

4. Add the lentils and enough cooking liquid to moisten them well. Cover the rondeau and place it in a moderate oven (350°F/175°C). Braise the mixture for 30 minutes or until the eggplant is completely tender. Adjust the seasoning to taste.

5. Combine the bread crumbs with the butter and place it on top of the lentils. Return the rondeau to a hot oven until a crust has developed and browned evenly. (This may be done by individual portions in gratin dishes, if desired.)

Stewed Garbanzo Beans with Tomato, Zucchini, and Cilantro

Yield: 10 servings

Garbanzo beans, dried	12 ounces	340 grams
Water	as needed	as needed
Olive oil	1 ounce	30 milliliters
Garlic, minced	1 clove	1 clove
Zucchini, diced	2	2
Tomato concassé	4 ounces	115 grams
Cilantro, fresh, chopped	1 ounce	30 grams
Salt	to taste	to taste
Pepper	to taste	to taste
Lime juice, fresh	to taste	to taste

1. Presoak the beans by the long or quick method.

2. Cook the beans in plenty of water until they are tender enough to mash, about 2 hours.

3. Heat the olive oil in a sauteuse. Add the garlic and cook it until an aroma is apparent.

4. Add the zucchini and tomato concassé. Sauté the vegetables until they are tender and heated through.

5. Add the garbanzo beans to the sauteuse, along with enough cooking liquid to keep them moist. Stew them until they are heated through. Add cilantro and adjust the seasoning to taste with the salt, pepper, and lemon juice.

VARIATION

Garbanzo Salad: Cook the beans and drain them as above. Combine them with a lime–olive oil vinaigrette. Add a variety of vegetables, including tomatoes, zucchini, cucumbers, grated carrots, and grated radishes.

Refried Beans

Yield: 20 servings

Pinto beans, soaked overnight in water to cover	30 ounces	850 grams
Stock, seasoned	as needed	as needed
Onions, chopped fine	8 ounces	225 grams
Garlic cloves	3	3
Bacon fat or lard	6 ounces	170 grams
Tomato concassé	3	3
Salt	to taste	to taste
Pepper	to taste	to taste
Cumin	to taste	to taste
Chili powder	to taste	to taste
Monterey Jack cheese, grated (per serving)	½ ounce	15 grams

1. Cook the beans in the seasoned stock until they are very soft.
2. Sauté the onions and garlic in the bacon fat, add the tomato concassé, and cook the mixture for 2 minutes.
3. Add the cooked beans and continue to cook the mixture, mashing the beans with a spoon.
4. Season the beans to taste with the salt, pepper, cumin, and chili powder.
5. Top the beans with grated jack cheese before serving, and heat them briefly under a salamander or broiler.

Hoppin' John

Yield: 10 servings

Black-eyed peas	8 ounces	225 grams
Bacon, large dice	4 ounces	115 grams
Onion, diced	4 ounces	115 grams
Garlic, minced	2 cloves	2 cloves
Red pepper flakes	½ teaspoon	2 grams
Rice, long-grain	8 ounces	225 grams
Chicken stock	1 quart	1 liter
Sweet bell peppers, diced	4 ounces	115 grams
Bay leaf	1	1
Thyme, fresh	1 sprig	1 sprig
Salt	to taste	to taste
Pepper	to taste	to taste

1. Simmer the black-eyed peas in enough water to cover them by 2 inches (5 centimeters) until they are just tender. Drain and reserve them.

2. Render the bacon in a pot. Remove the crisped bacon; drain and reserve it. Pour off all but 2 to 3 tablespoons of the bacon fat.

3. Add the onion, garlic, and red pepper flakes. Sauté them until they are translucent. Add the rice and stir it until it is coated.

4. Add the stock and the black-eyed peas and bring the mixture to a simmer. Add the peppers, bay leaf, and thyme. Cover the pot and cook the mixture in an oven until the beans and rice are thoroughly cooked.

5. Remove the pot from the oven. Return the bacon to the dish, and season it to taste with the salt and pepper.

Black Beans with Peppers and Chorizo

Yield: 10 servings

Black beans, dried, soaked overnight	12 ounces	340 grams
Water or stock	as needed	as needed
Oil	2 ounces	60 milliliters
Bacon strips, minced	2	2
Onion, diced	1	1
Garlic, minced	2 cloves	2 cloves
Chorizo, sliced	4 ounces	115 grams
Red pepper, diced	1	1
Green pepper, diced	1	1
Scallions, sliced thin	1 bunch	1 bunch
Salt	to taste	to taste
Pepper	to taste	to taste
Basil, oregano, and cilantro, fresh, chopped	to taste	to taste

1. Cook the beans in enough stock or water to cover them for about 90 minutes, or until they are tender to the bite. Reserve them in their cooking liquid.

2. Heat the oil and add the bacon. Cook the bacon until it is rendered. Add the onion and garlic, and sauté them until they are lightly browned.

3. Add the chorizo and red and green peppers; sauté them until the peppers are tender.

4. Add the drained, cooked beans and enough cooking liquid to keep them moist (the consistency should be that of a thick stew). Simmer the beans until all the flavors are developed and all the ingredients are heated through.

5. Add the scallions, salt, pepper, and fresh herbs to adjust the seasoning. Serve the beans with sour cream, if desired.

Chapter *25*

Cooking Pasta and Dumplings

The immense popularity of pastas and dumplings is not at all surprising. Nutritious and highly versatile, these foods are an important element of most cuisines. They are based on ingredients that are inexpensive and easy to store: flours, meals, and eggs. They adapt well to a number of uses and can be found on contemporary menus as appetizers, entrées, salads, and even desserts.

This chapter will discuss how to prepare, roll, cut, and shape fresh pasta (also known as egg-noodle dough), as well as how to work with dried pastas and noodles. Also included will be preparation of a variety of dumplings, including simmered dumplings, such as the ones used for the classic American chicken and dumplings, and steamed and fried dumplings, such as dim sum.

BASICS

Pastas and dumplings are prepared from a dough or batter that always includes a starchy ingredient—such as flour, meal, or potatoes—and a liquid. Additional ingredients, such as eggs, spices and herbs, baking soda or baking powder, yeast, and seasonings, may be added to change the dish's shape, color, texture, and flavor.

The formula for fresh pasta may be thought of as the "base" recipe to produce a stiff dough that can be stretched, rolled into thin sheets, and then cut into the desired shape. Changing the ratio of flour to liquid or introducing other ingredients into the formula will produce doughs and batters that are handled and cooked differently from fresh dough. For example, the amount of liquid can be increased to create a soft batter for spätzli dumplings. This batter is dropped through a sieve or spätzli maker into simmering liquid. Adding a leavener will produce a soft batter that can be used for larger dumplings with a breadlike texture that are simmered in a stew or other liquid.

Pasta

Dried and fresh noodles are both included in the general category of pasta. Pasta may be prepared fresh on the premises or purchased as either fresh or dried noodles. There are advantages to both fresh and dried pastas. Fresh pasta allows the chef freedom to create dishes with special flavors, colors, shapes, or fillings; however, it has a limited shelf life. Dried pasta can be held in dry storage almost indefinitely. When cooked, fresh and dried pasta differ noticeably in texture. Fresh pasta generally is more tender, whereas dried pasta has a more definite "bite." The chef should select the kind of pasta that best suits the dish being prepared.

With the exception of the information under the headings for cooking and serving pasta, most of the information in this section applies to making fresh pasta.

Mise en Place

1. Flour. Because flour provides the structure of pasta, it is important to choose one that has the necessary qualities for making the best possible dough. All-purpose flours can be used successfully for most fresh pasta; however, replacing all or part of the flour with semolina or bread flour (see Chapter 10, "Nonperishable Goods Identification") will yield a dough that is easier to roll out and that will have a better "bite" after it is cooked.

Whole-wheat flour, cornmeal, rye flour, ground legumes (chickpeas, for instance), and other special flours and meals can be used to prepare various pastas and noodles. To ensure the proper texture, some all-purpose white flour may need to be incorporated as well. Experimentation is often the best way to determine how to use special flours. Refer to the recipes for guidance on flours, ratios, and substitutions.

2. Water. Water is the liquid most often used for making pasta. It is especially important to add the proper amount of liquid. Doughs that are too dry or too moist are difficult to roll out.

3. Eggs. An optional ingredient, eggs are frequently included in fresh pasta to provide richness and color. Different formulas may specify the use of either whole eggs, yolks, or whites.

4. Oil. Have available an oil of a neutral flavor. This is optional; it is often called for in doughs used for filled pastas because it helps the dough to adhere better during cutting and filling.

5. Seasonings, flavorings, and colorings. Several ingredients may be added to fresh pasta dough to change its color, flavor, or texture. Black peppercorn pasta, for example, has a pronounced flavor and texture. Spinach pasta, on the other hand, will have a bright green color but not necessarily a strong "spinach" flavor. The ingredients listed here are among the more common additions, although there are a number of other possibilities. If the ingredients contain high moisture levels, it may be necessary to adjust the basic formula by using additional flour or less water.

- Vegetables. Vegetables used for flavor or color, especially those with a high moisture content, must be "dried" as much as possible before they are added to the dough. Spinach is chopped and squeezed to remove its moisture; peppers and tomatoes are often sautéed both to remove moisture and to concentrate flavor.
- Fresh herbs. Fresh herbs generally need only to be chopped or finely minced.
- Saffron. Saffron is often used to impart a golden color as well as a subtle flavor. It should be diluted or steeped in hot water before being added to the dough. The threads are often ground before being steeped.

Step 1 of Figure 25-1 shows the proper ratio of ingredients for a basic pasta dough. Table 25-1 is a table of ratios for basic pasta dough and several variations.

25-1 PREPARING FRESH PASTA DOUGH

(1) Mise en place.

(2) Placing beaten eggs in a well in the center of the flour.

(3) Incorporating the flour into the eggs.

(4) Adjusting the consistency with additional liquid.

(5) Kneading the dough on a lightly floured surface.

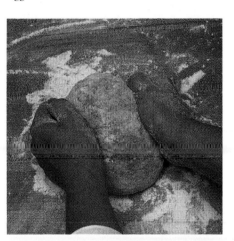

(6) The pasta at the correct consistency.

Basic Pasta Dough

Yield: 1½ pounds (680 grams)

Pasta flour	1 pound	450 grams
Eggs	5 to 6	5 to 6
Salt	pinch	pinch

1. Combine all the ingredients in a large bowl and knead the mixture until it is smooth.
2. Cover the dough and allow it to rest for 30 minutes.

VARIATIONS

Spinach Pasta: Add 6 ounces (170 grams) of raw, pureed spinach.

Tomato Pasta: Add 8 ounces (225 grams) of tomato paste.

Mixing Methods

Pasta dough can be mixed by hand or machine. For small batches, it may be just as efficient to mix and knead the dough manually. Large batches, on the other hand, can be made much more rapidly by using a machine. The following guidelines should be followed.

1. Observe the correct ratios, as given in specific recipes.

2. Add the minimum amount of liquid at first. If the dough seems too stiff or dry, or if it cannot be formed into a ball, add very small amounts of water until a workable consistency is reached.

3. Allow the dough time to relax. This will make it easier to roll out.

The three basic ways to mix pasta dough are by hand, in a food processor, or with an electric mixer.

1. Mixing by hand.

- Combine the dry ingredients on a clean work surface and make a well in the center.
- Place the liquid, eggs, flavoring ingredients, and oil in the well.
- Working as rapidly as possible, gradually incorporate the flour into the liquid ingredients until a loose mass is formed.
- Knead the dough vigorously until it becomes smooth and elastic.
- Allow the dough to rest, covered with plastic wrap, for approximately 1 hour before rolling it out by hand or machine.

2. Mixing in a food processor.

- Place all the ingredients in the bowl of a food processor fitted with a steel blade.
- Process the ingredients until they are blended and the dough resembles a coarse meal. To test for the proper consistency, pinch a small amount of the dough. If it does not clump together easily, it is too dry. Add a small amount of water, process the dough again briefly, and check it again. If the dough is too wet, it will form a ball that rides on top of the blade. Add a small amount of flour and process the dough again briefly.
- Remove the dough from the

TABLE 25-1. RATIOS FOR FRESH PASTA VARIATIONS*

Pasta Type	Additional Ingredients/Adjustments
Basic Egg Pasta	water or flour as needed
Spinach Pasta	6 ounces (170 grams) pureed, raw spinach; flour as needed
Saffron Pasta	2 to 4 teaspoons (3 to 6 grams) pulverized saffron (mix with the eggs)
Citrus Pasta	4 teaspoons (10 grams) finely grated lemon or orange zest; 2 tablespoons (30 milliliters) citrus juice; flour as needed
Herb/Spice Pasta	4 to 8 tablespoons (10 to 20 grams) chopped fresh herbs or 2 to 4 teaspoons (1 to 3 grams) ground spices (add to the eggs)
Black Pepper Pasta	2 to 4 teaspoons (10 to 20 grams) coarsely cracked black peppercorns (add to the eggs); flour as needed
Red Pepper Pasta	⅔ cup (160 milliliters) pureed, roasted red pepper (add to the eggs); flour as needed
Tomato Pasta	4 tablespoons (60 grams) tomato paste (add to the eggs); flour as needed
Pumpkin, Carrot, or Beet Pasta	6 ounces (170 grams) pureed, cooked pumpkin, carrots, or beets, sautéed gently to remove excess moisture, then cooled (add to the eggs); flour as needed
Wild Rice Pasta	¾ cup (180 milliliters) cooked, pureed wild rice; water as needed

* Yield = 1½ pounds (680 grams). Each pasta type requires 1 pound (455 grams) of flour, 5 to 6 eggs, and a pinch of salt.

MIXING PASTA DOUGH BY HAND

1
Mound all the dry ingredients on a work surface and make a well in the center.

2
Combine all the wet ingredients and pour them into the well.

3
Working rapidly, pull the dry ingredients into the wet ingredients, mixing them together to form a rough dough.

4
Knead the dough until it is smooth, and let it rest before rolling it out.

processor and gather it into a ball. The dough should feel slightly moist but not tacky.

- Allow the dough to rest for at least 1 hour before rolling it out by hand or machine.

3. Mixing with an electric mixer.

- Place all the ingredients in the work bowl of the mixer.
- Using a dough hook, blend the ingredients at medium speed until the dough forms a smooth ball that pulls cleanly away from the bowl.
- Allow the dough to rest for at least 1 hour before rolling it out by hand or machine.

For summaries of these methods, refer to the abbreviated methods for mixing pasta dough.

Evaluating Quality

Depending on the finished product for which the dough is to be used, different characteristics are desirable. For example, some filled pastas may require a dough that is slightly more moist than that used for flat pastas such as fettuccine and linguine. It is important that the dough be able to adhere to itself when filled so that none of the filling will escape as the pasta is cooked.

In general, pasta dough should be smooth, fairly elastic, and just slightly moist to the touch. If the dough is either tacky (from excess moisture) or crumbly (too dry), it will be difficult to roll out properly. Experience is the best guide for determining when the proper consistency has been reached.

Rolling

After the dough has been allowed to rest, it can be rolled into sheets,

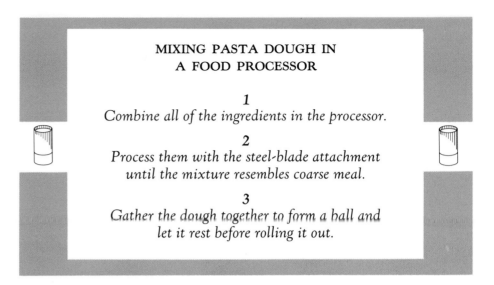

MIXING PASTA DOUGH IN
A FOOD PROCESSOR

1
Combine all of the ingredients in the processor.

2
Process them with the steel-blade attachment until the mixture resembles coarse meal.

3
Gather the dough together to form a ball and let it rest before rolling it out.

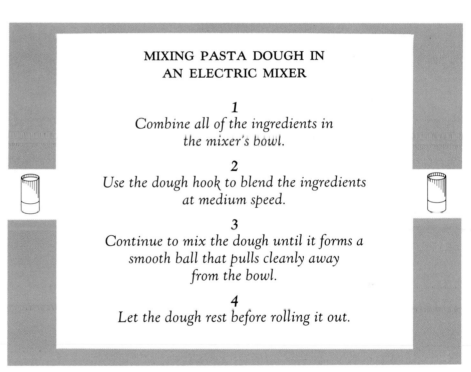

MIXING PASTA DOUGH IN
AN ELECTRIC MIXER

1
Combine all of the ingredients in the mixer's bowl.

2
Use the dough hook to blend the ingredients at medium speed.

3
Continue to mix the dough until it forms a smooth ball that pulls cleanly away from the bowl.

4
Let the dough rest before rolling it out.

either by hand or by machine. The resting stage is particularly important if the dough is to be rolled by hand; if the dough is not sufficiently "relaxed," it will be difficult to roll into thin sheets.

Tube pastas such as elbow macaroni or ziti are made by forcing the dough through a special die in an extruding pasta maker. The following directions are for making pasta sheets.

1. Rolling by machine. Different machines will have different methods of operation. The guidelines below are intended for use with a two-roller hand-operated machine.

- Working with a reasonable amount of dough (the amount will vary, depending on the width of the particular machine), and with the rollers set at the widest opening, begin

ROLLING PASTA DOUGH WITH A MACHINE

1

Break off a piece of pasta and flatten it into an oval or rectangle about the width of the opening in the machine.

2

Set the gauge at the widest opening and roll the pasta through the machine.

3

Fold the dough in thirds, like a letter, and roll it through the machine again. Repeat this step two or three times without changing the opening of the rollers.

4

Set the rollers at the next narrowest opening and roll the sheet through the machine. Repeat this step, setting the gauge at progressively smaller openings until the desired thickness is reached.

(1) Running the dough through the machine at the widest setting, then folding it in thirds.

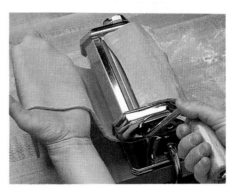

(2) Rolling the pasta through successively smaller settings.

(3) Dusting the pasta with flour.

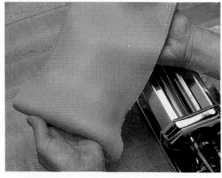

(4) Properly rolled pasta.

to guide the dough through the machine.

- Fold the sheet in thirds, like a letter, and run it through the rollers again. Repeat this step two or three times, folding the dough into thirds each time. If necessary, dust the dough with flour to keep it from sticking to the rollers.

- Continue to roll the pasta through the machine, setting the rollers at a narrower setting each time, until the sheet of pasta is the desired thickness. If necessary, lightly dust the sheets with flour to prevent them from sticking or tearing. Figure 25-2 demonstrates the steps in rolling pasta by machine.

- Allow the pasta to dry before cutting it. The dough should feel smooth and not at all tacky. Ideally, the pasta sheets should be draped to

dry in such a way that air can reach both sides at once. The sheets should not be over-dried, because the dough can become brittle and difficult to cut.

- Cut the pasta as desired, by hand or using attachments for the machine (see Figs. 25-3 and 25-4).

Refer to the abbreviated method for rolling pasta dough by machine for a quick summary.

2. Rolling by hand.

- Flatten a manageable amount of dough (about the size of an orange) on a clean work surface dusted with flour. Using a rolling pin, work from the center of the dough to the edges with a back-and-forth motion, rolling and stretching the dough.

- Continue rolling, turning the dough occasionally and dust-

25-3
Cutting pasta by machine.

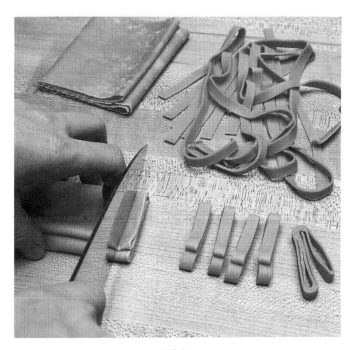

25-4
Cutting pasta by hand.

ROLLING PASTA DOUGH BY HAND

1
*Break off a piece of the dough and flatten it
with a rolling pin.*

2
*Use a back-and-forth stretching motion to roll
the pasta into an evenly thin piece.*

3
*Let the sheet of pasta dry until the surface is
no longer tacky to the touch.*

4
*Use a sharp knife or rotary blade to cut the
pasta into the desired shapes.*

ing it with flour to prevent
sticking and tearing, until the
sheet is the desired thickness.
• Cut or shape the pasta as for
pasta rolled by machine.

For a quick summary of the
method, refer to the abbreviated
summary for rolling pasta dough by
hand.

Holding Prior to Cooking

Fresh pasta can be held under refrigeration for a day or two. If the
pasta is cut in long strands, it
should be sprinkled with cornmeal
or semolina to keep the strands
from sticking together. Hold the
pasta on trays lined with plastic,
and cover it with plastic as well.

If fresh pastas are to be stored
for more than two days, they can
be allowed to dry in a warm, dry
area and then may be held, well-
wrapped, in a cool, dry spot in the
same manner as commercially prepared dried pastas. Fresh pasta,
especially filled pastas such as tortellini and ravioli, may be frozen
successfully.

Cooking

Fresh pasta cooks very quickly;
therefore, in order to avoid a soft or
mushy finished product, it is important to pay attention as it cooks so
that it can be drained as soon as it
is properly done. The pasta should
be tender but have a discernible
texture, known as *al dente* (which
is Italian for "to the tooth"). Because fresh pasta cooks so rapidly,
it may be feasible to cook the
amount needed to order for taste
far superior to fresh pasta cooked
in advance, with a noticeable difference in flavor and texture.

Special pasta cookers, which resemble deep-fryers, are available.
The pasta is placed in a wire basket

with a handle and dropped into boiling or simmering water. Once the pasta is properly cooked, the basket is lifted out of the water, allowing the pasta to drain.

The following steps are appropriate for cooking both fresh and dried pastas. The only difference is the amount of cooking time involved; dried pasta will take considerably longer to cook.

1. Bring a large amount of water to a rolling boil. The ratio of water to pasta is 8:1; use 4 quarts of water for 1 pound of pasta. Add salt to the water, if desired.

2. Add the pasta and stir it to separate the strands or shapes.

3. For filled pastas, reduce the heat to a simmer to keep them from breaking apart or bursting open.

4. Cook the pasta until it is al dente. See "Determining Doneness" for additional information.

5. Drain the pasta in a colander (unless a pasta cooker is being used) and serve it immediately with the appropriate sauce or garnish.

6. To hold the pasta, rinse it thoroughly with cold water and toss it with a small amount of oil to keep the strands from clumping together.

7. To reheat the pasta, place it in a wire basket and lower it into a pot of simmering water for a few minutes. Remove the basket from the water, finish the pasta with the appropriate sauce or garnish, and serve it immediately on heated plates or serving dishes.

For quick reference, use the abbreviated method for cooking pasta.

Determining Doneness and Evaluating Quality

Fresh pasta cooks rapidly, which makes it easy to overcook. Be sure

Basic Boiled Pasta

Yield: 10 servings

Water	4 quarts	4 liters
Salt	to taste	to taste
Pasta, dry	1 pound	450 grams

1. Bring the water and the salt to a rolling boil in a large pot.

2. Add the pasta to the water and stir it well to separate the strands. Let the pasta cook until it is tender but not soft. Fresh pastas may cook in less than 3 minutes; dried pastas may take up to 8 minutes or longer, depending upon the size and shape of the noodle.

3. Drain the pasta at once. Add any desired sauce or garnish at this point, according to the specific recipe. If the pasta is to be held, plunge it into an ice-water bath to stop the cooking. Drain it immediately and drizzle a small amount of vegetable oil over the pasta and toss it to prevent it from sticking together.

NOTE: If cooking fresh pasta, use 1½ pounds (680 grams) to yield 10 servings.

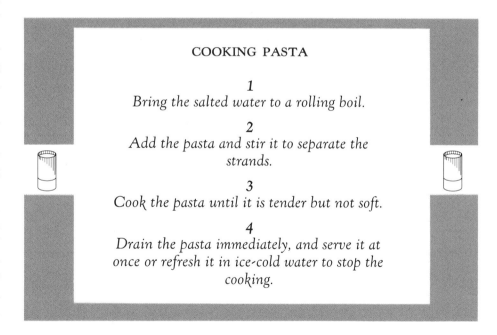

COOKING PASTA

1
Bring the salted water to a rolling boil.

2
Add the pasta and stir it to separate the strands.

3
Cook the pasta until it is tender but not soft.

4
Drain the pasta immediately, and serve it at once or refresh it in ice-cold water to stop the cooking.

to cook both fresh and dried pastas only to the point of al dente. To test it for doneness, bite into a strand. It should be tender but have a definite "bite."

Dried pasta takes longer to cook, but it is equally important that it not be cooked too long. Dried pasta may be checked for doneness by either biting into or breaking a strand. There should be only a faint core of white in the strand's center.

Pairing with Sauces

Sauces are customarily selected to suit a particular type of pasta. Long, flat pastas such as fettucine or linguine are generally served with smooth, light sauces such as cream sauces, vegetable coulis, or butter-and-cheese combinations that coat the strands evenly. Tube pastas, such as elbow macaroni or ziti, and twisted pastas, such as fusilli, are normally paired with more heavily textured sauces (a meat sauce or one with a garnish of fresh vegetables) because these shapes are able to trap the sauce.

A pasta's flavor is also an important consideration when choosing a sauce. The delicate flavor of fresh pasta is most successfully paired with a light cream or butter-based sauce. Heartier sauces, such as those that include meats, are usually combined with dried pastas.

Filled pastas require only a very light sauce, because the filling provides a certain amount of flavor and moisture. A sauce that will overwhelm the flavor of the filling is inappropriate.

Serving

Pasta dishes are suited to a number of different service styles. The speed and ease of preparing pasta makes it a good choice for à la carte restaurants; in fact, some restaurant kitchens include a separate pasta station on the hot-food line. When properly prepared, handled, and held, pasta can also be used for banquet and buffet service. Both the pasta and the accompanying sauces can be prepared in advance.

À la carte service. Cook or reheat the pasta as close to service time as possible. Because pasta loses heat rapidly, be sure to heat the bowls or plates on which it is to be served and serve it immediately.

Banquet service. Use bowls or deep platters so that the pasta can be mounded to help conserve heat.

Once again, be sure to heat the serving pieces.

Buffet service. Fully preheat the steam table or heat lamps before placing the pasta on the buffet line. Cook, reheat, and/or finish the pasta as close to serving time as possible. Choose a hotel pan deep enough to contain the pasta comfortably, but not so large that the pasta is spread out in a thin layer, as it will lose heat and moisture rapidly. Even in a steam table, heat is lost rapidly.

There is a limit to the length of time pasta dishes can be held successfully for buffet service. Holding them over heat for too long can cause the sauce to dry out and the pasta to begin to lose its texture.

Dumplings

Although the term "dumpling" may mean something very specific to an individual or a particular ethnic group, it actually is a very broad category. Some dumplings are based on doughs and batters, others on ingredients ranging from bread to pureed potatoes. The popular Chinese dim sum, including steamed yeast doughs and fried egg rolls, is yet another category. Dumplings may be cooked in a variety of ways, according to type. They may be simmered in liquid, steamed, poached, baked, panfried, or deep-fried.

Mise en Place

It is difficult to outline a standard mise en place because a variety of ingredients can be used, depending on what sort of dumpling is being prepared. See the recipes included in this chapter for specific instructions. The guidelines given here are for simmered or poached dumplings.

1. Measure and sift the ingredients and allow sufficient time for the batter to "rest" according to the specific recipe.

2. Be sure to have the stock, water, or other cooking liquid, according to the recipe used, at a simmer. Liquid that is boiling rapidly could cause the dumplings to fall apart.

3. Be sure to have the appropriate equipment on hand to shape, drain, and finish cooking the dumplings. These tools may include a pastry bag fitted with a large, plain tube, or a pair of spoons, for shaping the dumplings; a colander, slotted spoon, or spider, to lift the dumplings from the liquid and drain them; a gratin dish or hotel pan to hold the dumplings as they finish cooking; and appropriate serving dishes.

4. Many dumplings are finished with a sauce (cream sauce, duxelles, and tomato sauce are examples). Be sure the sauce has been prepared before the dumplings are cooked and have it at the proper temperature for serving.

Method for Poaching

Many dumplings are initially cooked by poaching, as described in this method. Once poached, they may be finished in a variety of ways, including panfrying, baking in a sauce, or broiling.

1. Have the liquid at a simmer. Some dumplings are cooked directly in a stew or soup; others are cooked separately and used as a garnish or finished in another appropriate manner.

2. Lower the shaped dumplings into the simmering liquid. Large dumplings may be tied in cheesecloth (following the procedure used in making a galantine—see chapter 28, "Charcuterie and Garde-manger"), poached, and then untied. In some cases, these dumplings are sliced and then panfried (see the recipe for bread dumplings).

Other dumplings (cream-puff pastry dumplings, for example) are piped out directly into the simmering liquid or are shaped with two spoons and dropped into the liquid, as for the gnocchi shown in Figure 25-5. Dumplings that are sufficiently firm may be rolled into ropes and sliced into pieces. Dumplings made from a pourable batter, such as spätzli, are allowed to drop through a colander or a special spätzli machine into the simmering liquid. Three ways to shape spätzli are shown in Figure 25-6.

3. Cook the dumplings to the desired doneness. The time may range from 1 to 2 minutes for very small dumplings, such as spätzli, up to 20 or 30 minutes for a large bread dumpling. Refer to the particular recipe for specific guidelines.

4. Finish the dumplings as necessary or desired. If a dumpling is to be served as a garnish in a stew or soup, no finishing is necessary. Poached dumplings may be sautéed or panfried in butter and finished with a variety of herbs, spices, and grated cheeses, or they may be baked in a sauce.

Determining Doneness and Evaluating Quality

The cooking time for any dumpling will vary, depending upon the batter's stiffness, the dumpling's diameter, and the liquid's temperature. The only truly reliable way to test for doneness is to break into one of the dumplings to be sure it

does not have a doughy uncooked interior. A properly cooked dumpling should have an appropriate texture and flavor according to its type.

Holding and Serving

Some dumplings may be prepared in advance and held; others should be served immediately. Spätzli, bread dumplings, and gnocchi may be held. Stewed and deep-fried dumplings are best when served immediately.

Gnocchi di Semolina Gratinati

Yield: approximately 30 gnocchi

Milk	5 pints	2.4 liters
Butter	4 ounces	115 grams
Salt	1 tablespoon	15 grams
Semolina	2 cups	480 milliliters
Egg yolks, beaten	4	4
Parmesan cheese, fresh grated	1½ cups	360 milliliters

1. Combine the milk, butter, and salt in a pot and bring the mixture to a boil.

2. Pour in the semolina in a steady stream, stirring it constantly to avoid lumps. Return the liquid to a boil.

3. Cover the pot and bake it in an oven for 20 to 25 minutes at 325°F (165°C).

4. Add the egg yolks and the parmesan cheese.

5. Shape the gnocchi mixture into quenelles or spread it on a sheet pan to a thickness of ½ inch. Cool it completely and cut it as desired.

6. At service, place the gnocchi in a buttered dish. Sprinkle them generously with parmesan and melted butter and brown them under a salamander or broiler.

25-5

Shaping semolina gnocchi with two serving spoons.

25-6 THREE METHODS FOR SHAPING SPÄTZLI

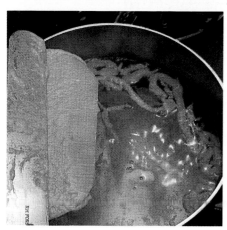

(1) Pushing narrow "strips" of batter into the simmering water with a palette knife.

(2) Using a spätzli machine.

(3) Using a second style of machine to press the batter through holes in the bottom.

Spätzli Dough

Yield: 10 servings

Eggs	2	2
Milk	3 ounces	90 milliliters
Salt	to taste	to taste
Pepper	to taste	to taste
Nutmeg	to taste	to taste
Flour	6 ounces	170 grams

1. Combine the eggs, milk, and seasonings and mix them well in a large bowl.

2. Work in the flour by hand.

3. Let the dough rest for 10 minutes.

4. Using a spätzli machine (or other shaping technique), drop the dough into a large pot of boiling, salted water. Simmer it until it is done.

5. Remove the spätzli with a spider, shock it in cold water, and drain it well.

6. Sauté the spätzli in whole butter and serve.

SUMMARY

Pasta has become such a familiar food that it is hard to remember that spaghetti seemed exotic to many people in this country not so many years ago. Today, the number of different shapes, the increasing sophistication on the part of the consumer, and the imaginative use of sauces and other ingredients have made dishes that include pasta among the most popular on any menu. Both dumplings and pastas are prepared from staple ingredients and have, by themselves, an unobtrusive flavor. The use of special sauces, fillings, and seasonings allows the chef the freedom to apply "color" in the form of flavor freely.

Chorizo-filled Pasta with Tomato-Basil Coulis and Salsa Cru

Yield: *4 entree or 8 appetizer servings*

Filling

Lean pork, 1-inch cubes	2 ounces	60 grams
Rice, cooked	2 tablespoons	35 grams
Jalapeño chilies, minced	1 teaspoon	5 grams
Garlic, minced	2 cloves	2 cloves
Chorizo, chopped	1 ounce	30 grams
Salt	¼ teaspoon	1 gram
Oregano, fresh	¼ teaspoon	250 milligrams
Cider vinegar	½ teaspoon	3 milliliters
Chili powder	¼ teaspoon	600 milligrams
Cayenne pepper	⅛ teaspoon	300 milligrams
Pasta dough	8 ounces	225 grams
Tomato-basil Coulis	8 ounces	240 milliliters
Salsa Cru	2 ounces	60 grams

1. Place the pork and rice in a food processor using the steel blade; blend the mixture until it is smooth.

2. Add the remaining ingredients for the filling and pulse the machine on and off until the ingredients are just combined. Remove the filling from the processor and refrigerate it.

3. Roll the pasta into thin sheets. Cut the sheets into sixteen 3-inch (7.5-centimeter) circles. Keep the dough circles covered until they are ready to be filled.

4. Brush the pasta circles lightly with water. Place 1 teaspoon (5 milliliters) of the filling on each pasta circle. Fold the circles in half and crimp the edges with the tines of a fork to seal them.

5. Add the ravioli to boiling water and simmer them for approximately 5 minutes.

6. Pool ¼ cup (60 milliliters) of the tomato-basil coulis on each of four heated plates. Place 4 ravioli on the coulis. Garnish the pasta with 1 tablespoon (15 milliliters) of salsa.

NOTE: This dish is a reworking of a classic recipe in order to reduce overall calories, fat, cholesterol, and sodium.

Shrimp with Curried Pasta

Yield: 1 serving

Shrimp, peeled, de-veined, and butterflied	3 ounces	85 grams
Salt	to taste	to taste
Pepper	to taste	to taste
Oil	as needed	as needed
Whole butter	1 tablespoon	15 grams
Shallots	1 tablespoon	15 grams
Brandy	½ ounce	15 milliliters
Fish fumet	2 ounces	60 milliliters
Reduced heavy cream	1 ounce	30 milliliters
Shellfish butter	1 tablespoon	15 grams
Scallions, sliced on the bias	1 tablespoon	15 grams
Fresh pasta (linguini, fettucini, etc.), flavored with curry, cooked al dente	3 ounces	85 grams

1. Season the shrimp to taste with salt and pepper.

2. Sauté the seasoned shrimp in the hot oil. Remove them from the pan.

3. Add the whole butter and shallots to the oil; cook the shallots until they are translucent.

4. Add the brandy to deglaze the pan; reduce the liquid.

5. Add the fumet and heavy cream; let the mixture reduce until it lightly coats the back of a spoon.

6. Finish the sauce with the lobster butter. Return the shrimp to the pan and add the scallions. Adjust the seasoning if necessary.

7. Serve the shrimp on a bed of drained, heated pasta.

VARIATION

Shrimp and Scallops: Replace half of the shrimp with sea scallops. If the scallops are very large, slice them horizontally.

Pasta alla Carbonara

Yield: 4 to 6 servings

Butter	2 ounces	60 grams
Ham, cooked, julienne	¾ pound	340 grams
Mushrooms, sliced	¼ pound	115 grams
Salt	to taste	to taste
Pepper	to taste	to taste
Egg	1	1
Light cream	1¼ cups	600 milliliters
Pasta (spaghetti, flat noodles, or other), cooked al dente	1 pound	450 grams
Parsley, chopped	as needed	as needed

1. Melt the butter in a sauteuse and add the ham. Sauté the ham until it is hot.

2. Add the mushrooms and sauté them. Season them to taste with the salt and pepper.

3. Beat the egg thoroughly and stir in the light cream.

4. Add the cream mixture and reheated, drained pasta to the ham and mushrooms; cook the mixture gently, stirring constantly, until the sauce is heated through. Do not allow the mixture to overheat, or it will curdle.

5. Pour the sauce over the pasta and serve it immediately, sprinkled with the chopped parsley.

Lobster Tortellini with Ginger Sauce

Yield: 4 entrée or 8 appetizer servings

Filling

Lobsters, blanched, shelled, and cleaned	four 1-pound	four 450-gram
Egg white, lightly beaten	1 tablespoon	15 milliliters
Heavy cream	1 tablespoon	15 milliliters
Shallots, minced, smothered	1 teaspoon	4.5 grams
Garlic, minced, smothered	1 teaspoon	4.5 grams
Chives, minced	½ teaspoon	375 milligrams

Pasta

Saffron threads, crushed	¼ teaspoon	500 milligrams
Boiling water	2 tablespoons	30 milliliters
Egg white	1	1
Semolina flour	6 to 8 ounces	170 to 225 grams

Ginger Sauce

Shallots, minced	1 teaspoon	4 grams
Ginger, minced	1 teaspoon	4 grams
Lime juice, fresh	1 tablespoon	15 milliliters
Dry white wine	2 tablespoons	30 milliliters
Fish stock	¾ cup	180 milliliters
Arrowroot	1 teaspoon	3 grams
Skim milk, evaporated	¼ cup	60 milliliters
Heavy cream	2 tablespoons	30 milliliters

1. Reserve the lobster claw meat, intact, for a garnish. Chop the remaining lobster meat coarsely; puree it to a coarse paste in a food processor.

2. Add the egg white and cream; process the mixture to a fine paste.

3. Add the shallots, garlic, and chives. Pulse the machine on and off a few times to incorporate them into the lobster paste.

4. Infuse the saffron in the boiling water; drain it and reserve the water.

5. Add the saffron water and egg white to the flour. Knead the mixture until it is smooth. Let the dough rest for 1 hour.

6. Roll out the dough into thin sheets and cut it into squares.

7. Place one teaspoon of the lobster filling on each square. Fold the squares into tortellini.

8. Cook the tortellini in boiling water; drain and reserve them.

9. Combine the shallots, ginger, lime juice, and wine in a saucepan. Reduce the mixture over medium heat until it is syrupy.

10. Add the fish stock; bring the mixture to a simmer.

11. Dissolve the arrowroot in the evaporated milk. Add this mixture to the sauce, and simmer the sauce until it is lightly thickened.

12. Add the heavy cream. Simmer the sauce for 2 more minutes and strain it.

13. Reheat the tortellini and lobster claws. Serve the tortellini in shallow bowls. Ladle the sauce over pasta and garnish each portion with lime zest and a lobster claw(s).

NOTE: This dish is a reworking of a classic recipe in order to reduce overall calories, fat, cholesterol, and sodium.

Lasagne di Carnevale Napolitana

<u>*Yield: 12 servings*</u>

Lasagne noodles	12 ounces	340 grams
Sweet Italian sausage	12 ounces	340 grams
Cheese Filling		
Ricotta cheese	1 pound	450 grams
Parmesan cheese, freshly grated	4 ounces	115 grams
Salt	to taste	to taste
Pepper, freshly ground	to taste	to taste
Nutmeg	to taste	to taste
Eggs	4	4
Parsley, chopped fine	4 tablespoons	9 grams
Tomato sauce with meat (recipe follows)	1 quart	1 liter
Mozzarella cheese, sliced thin or shredded	12 ounces	340 grams
Parmesan cheese, freshly grated	4 ounces	115 grams

1. Cook the noodles in boiling salted water until al dente. Drain and rinse them with cold water.

2. Cook the sausage in boiling water until it is done. Remove it from the water.

3. Remove the casing from the sausage and slice the meat thin.

4. Combine all the ingredients for the cheese filling and mix them well.

5. Spread a thin layer of the tomato sauce in a large baking dish.

6. Layer the ingredients: Begin with a layer of the lasagne noodles, arranged so that there is an overlap of about 3 inches at the sides of the pan.

7. Follow the noodles with a layer of the cheese filling (about ¼-inch thick), then a layer of the sausage, a layer of the sauce, a thin layer of the mozzarella, and a sprinkle of the parmesan.

8. Continue layering the ingredients in this manner until they are all used up, finishing with a layer of noodles.

9. Fold the overhanging noodles over the top of the lasagne. Cover the lasagne with the remaining meat sauce and top it with the remaining parmesan cheese.

10. Place the lasagne in a preheated 375°F (190°C) oven and bake it for 15 minutes.

11. Reduce the heat to 325°F (165°C). Bake the lasagne for another 45 minutes. If the top browns too quickly, cover it lightly with aluminum foil. The top should be a light golden brown.

12. Remove the lasagne from the oven and let it stand for 30 to 45 minutes before serving.

Tomato Sauce with Meat (for Lasagne di Carnevale Napolitana)

Yield: approximately 2 quarts (2 liters)

Olive oil	2 tablespoons	30 milliliters
Garlic cloves, minced	2	2
Onion, minced	3 ounces	85 grams
Chuck, ground (or combination of ground veal and chuck)	2½ pounds	115 kilograms
Tomato puree	1 quart	1 liter
Tomato paste	1½ ounces	45 grams
Salt	to taste	to taste
Pepper, freshly ground	to taste	to taste
Basil, fresh, chopped	1 tablespoon	2 grams
Oregano, fresh, chopped	1 tablespoon	2 grams
Thyme, fresh, chopped	1 tablespoon	2 grams
Heavy cream, hot	6 to 8 ounces	180 to 250 grams

1. Heat the olive oil in a large skillet

2. Add the garlic and onion and sauté them until the onions are tender and light brown.

3. Add the ground meat. Sauté the mixture, stirring it with a wooden spoon to break up any lumps, until the meat is browned, about 5 minutes.

4. Add the tomato puree and 2 tablespoons (30 milliliters) of the tomato paste. Mix well.

5. Season the sauce to taste with the salt and pepper. Add the herbs.

6. Degrease the sauce if necessary.

7. Finish the sauce with the heavy cream.

Gnocchi Piedmontese

Yield: 10 to 12 servings

Potatoes, peeled	2 pounds	910 grams
Butter	1 ounce	30 grams
Egg yolks	2	2
Whole eggs	2	2
Pasta flour	as needed	as needed
Salt	to taste	to taste
Pepper	to taste	to taste
Nutmeg	to taste	to taste
Whole butter	as needed	as needed
Parmesan, grated	5 tablespoons	60 grams
Parsley, chopped	3 tablespoons	10 grams

1. Peel and cook the potatoes. Rice them and add the butter, yolks, and eggs. Mix them well.

2. Incorporate the flour slowly while mixing until a stiff dough is formed.

3. Roll out the dough and cut the pasta into the desired shapes.

4. Cook it in boiling salted water for 5 to 6 minutes.

5. Serve the gnocchi tossed with the butter, cheese, and chopped parsley.

Spring Rolls

Yield: approximately 20 portions

Oil	½ ounce	15 grams
Ginger, minced	2 teaspoons	6 grams
Scallions, chopped	1 ounce	30 grams
Pork butt, shredded or ground	1 pound	450 grams
Shrimp, peeled, de-veined, chopped	1 pound	450 grams
Bamboo shoots, shredded	3 ounces	85 grams
Black fungus, soaked, chopped	½ ounce	15 grams
Chinese cabbage, shredded	12 ounces	340 grams
Bean sprouts	½ pound	225 grams
Mushrooms, thinly sliced	4 ounces	115 grams
Scallion greens, sliced	3 ounces	85 grams
Salt	to taste	to taste
White pepper	to taste	to taste
Dark soy sauce	1 ounce	30 milliliters
Sesame oil	½ ounce	15 milliliters
Cornstarch	½ ounce	15 grams
Spring roll wrappers	2 packages	2 packages
Flour	1½ ounces	45 grams
Water	2 ounces	60 milliliters

1. Heat the oil. Add the ginger, scallions, and pork. Stir-fry the mixture until the pork is done.

2. Add the shrimp, bamboo shoots, and black fungus and continue to stir-fry the mixture.

3. Add the cabbage, bean sprouts, mushrooms, and scallion greens and continue to stir-fry the mixture.

4. When the vegetables are cooked, add the salt, pepper, soy sauce, and sesame oil and mix them in well.

5. Drain off the liquid if necessary. Add the cornstarch mixed with cold water. Remove from the heat.

6. Mix the flour and water to form a smooth paste.

7. Place 1 heaping tablespoon of the filling in the center of each spring roll wrapper. Roll the wrappers, sealing the edges with the flour paste.

8. Deep-fry the spring rolls in 375°F (190°C) hot oil, or panfry them over medium heat, until they are golden brown. Serve them at once.

Spinach and Cheese Spätzli

Yield: 10 to 12 servings

Eggs	8	8
Salt	to taste	to taste
Pepper	to taste	to taste
Nutmeg	to taste	to taste
Sapsago cheese, grated	1½ ounces	45 grams
Spinach, washed and chopped fine, squeezed dry	1½ pounds	680 grams
Flour	2 pounds	910 grams
Milk	as needed	as needed

1. Combine the eggs, seasonings, cheese, and spinach. Mix them well.

2. Work in the flour by hand and adjust the consistency with the milk to form a smooth batter.

3. Using a spätzli machine (or other shaping technique), drop the dough into a large pot of boiling salted water. Simmer the spätzli until they are done.

4. Remove the spätzli with a spider, shock them in cold water, and drain them well.

5. Before serving, sauté the spätzli in whole butter.

Bread Dumplings

Yield: approximately 40 to 50 dumplings

Ingredient	US	Metric
Onions, fine dice	8 ounces	225 grams
Butter	4 ounces	115 grams
Rolls, hard, stale, small dice	2 pounds	910 grams
Flour	8 ounces	225 grams
Milk	2 cups	480 milliliters
Eggs	10	10
Parsley, fresh, chopped	1 ounce	30 grams
Salt	to taste	to taste
White pepper, ground	to taste	to taste
Nutmeg, ground (optional)	to taste	to taste

1. Sauté the onions in the butter until they are lightly browned; cool them.

2. Combine the diced rolls, flour, and sautéed onion in a large bowl.

3. Combine the milk, eggs, and seasonings separately in another bowl.

4. Pour the liquid mixture into the dry mixture and blend them together lightly. Let the mixture rest for 30 minutes, covered. Add additional egg-and-milk mixture if the bread is very dry.

5. Shape the mixture into 2-inch dumplings by hand.

6. Poach the dumplings in boiling salted water for 15 minutes. Store them in the same water.

NOTE: If the bread is not at least one day old and dried, the egg and milk amounts may need to be adjusted. It is important for the bread mixture to be moist but not soggy.

Chinese Dumplings (Fried or Boiled)

<u>*Yield*</u>*: approximately 20 dumplings*

Dough

Flour	1 pound	450 grams
Hot water	8 ounces	240 milliliters

Filling

Pork, ground	12 ounces	340 grams
Chinese cabbage, chopped	8 ounces	225 grams
Scallions, chopped	2 ounces	60 grams
Ginger, minced	1 teaspoon	7 grams
Soy sauce	½ ounce	15 milliliters
Sesame oil	½ ounce	15 milliliters
Egg white	1	1
Salt	to taste	to taste
White pepper	to taste	to taste

1. Mix the flour and water. Let the dough set for 30 minutes. Divide the dough into ½-ounce portions and roll it out into thin circles for individual dumpling skins.

2. Combine all the filling ingredients. Mix them well. Check the consistency and seasoning of the filling by sautéing a small amount.

3. Place 1 tablespoon (15 milliliters) of filling on each dumpling skin and seal the edges tightly.

4. Cook the dumplings in boiling water until they are cooked through, about 8 minutes. Or, panfry the dumplings on one side only until they are golden brown and cooked through. Serve them immediately.

Wontons (Boiled or Fried)

Yield: approximately 20 wontons

Wonton wrappers (thin)	20 pieces	20 pieces
Egg whites	2	2
Filling for Chinese dumplings	one-half recipe	one-half recipe

1. Combine all the ingredients for the filling. Mix them well. Check the consistency and seasoning.
2. Place ½ teaspoon of the filling in the center of each wonton wrapper. Fold the wrappers, sealing them with the egg white.
3. Cook the wontons in boiling soup or stock until they are done, about 2 minutes. Or, deep-fry them in hot oil. Serve boiled wontons in soup or with Oriental dipping sauce. Serve fried wontons with duck sauce and/or hot Chinese mustard.

NOTE: For the filling, see the recipe for Chinese Dumplings.

Biscuit Dumplings (for Stew)

Yield: approximately 30 dumplings

Cake flour	1 pound	450 grams
Baking powder	4 teaspoons	11 grams
Salt	1 teaspoon	5 grams
Milk	1 pint	480 milliliters
Parsley, chopped (optional)	2 tablespoons	4.5 grams

1. Sift together all the dry ingredients.
2. Add the milk and mix it in lightly. Do not overmix. The consistency should be slightly softer than biscuit dough.
3. Drop 1-ounce (30-gram) portions from a spoon about 1 inch apart into the simmering sauce or stew. Cover the pot and cook the dumplings for 20 to 25 minutes.

Part Eight

Pantry Cookery and Garde-manger

T he items covered in this section were traditionally prepared in a separate kitchen or part of the kitchen known as the "cold kitchen." Today, however, the boundaries have blurred; the techniques and skills used elsewhere are also used for many garde-manger items. Although the portion sizes and styles of presentation may vary, the cooking fundamentals remain the same.

Contemporary trends and innovative uses of ingredients are reflected in all of this section's chapters. For the making of salads, new varieties of greens, oils, vinegars, and other ingredients are discussed.

Standard breakfast offerings are revitalized with the use of grains, meals, and vegetables to make them healthier and more appealing. Appetizers offer the chef an opportunity to combine ingredients, flavors, and textures to please patrons who might prefer to choose a selection of appetizers instead of a traditional multi-course meal.

Chapter 26

Breakfast and Egg Cookery

Many restaurants are discovering breakfast's potential for dramatically increasing profits. Two factors, in particular, have encouraged this trend—the lower costs of breakfast items compared to those required for lunch and dinner, and the opportunity to practice that often overlooked culinary art of total utilization. A wide variety of meats, vegetables, and grains can be used to garnish or flavor such egg dishes as scrambled eggs, quiches, and soufflés.

Breakfast cookery involves competencies in egg cookery, including "boiled" eggs, fried eggs, scrambled eggs, omelets, poached eggs, and soufflés; breakfast meats, breads, and beverages.

The title of this chapter may be unnecessarily limiting. Although they are indeed "breakfast" foods, a great many of these preparations have an important role in other meals. Quiches, crêpes, and omelets are all found on luncheon and supper menus. By the same token, the breakfast and brunch menu often draws freely from foods that are generally considered more appropriate for dinner.

26-2 THE ROLLED OMELET

(1) Pouring eggs into the heated pan.

(2) The eggs are beginning to coagulate.

(3) The eggs are almost completely set but are still moist.

(4) Tilting the pan to start to "roll" the omelet and using a fork to help the omelet roll.

Method for Flat Omelets

Flat omelets may be made either as individual portions or in larger quantities. For the latter, use large skillets or, for buffet service, hotel pans.

1. Prepare the eggs as for rolled omelets.

2. Heat a properly oiled or buttered skillet or hotel pan over direct heat. Generally, garnish ingredients are added to the pan first in order to properly cook and heat them. For instance, onions or peppers are allowed to sauté until they are tender. Cooked potatoes or pastas are allowed to heat through.

3. Add the egg mixture and

26-2 THE ROLLED OMELET *(continued)*

(5) Jarring the handle to loosen the omelet from the pan.

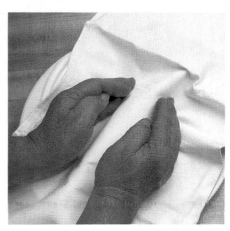

(6) Tilting the omelet out onto a heated plate.

(7) Using a clean cloth to mold the omelet into a neat oval.

(8) Rubbing the surface with whole butter.

allow it to cook over gentle heat, without stirring, until the edges of the omelet appear set.

4. Place the pan or skillet in a hot oven. The cooking time will vary, depending on the size and depth of the skillet and on the recipe yield.

5. Cook the eggs until they are fully set. The omelet will appear slightly puffy. Additional garnish ingredients, such as grated cheese, may be used to top the omelet; these are added a few minutes before it is done. To test the omelet for doneness, insert a skewer near its center. It should come away

ROLLED OMELET

1
Blend the eggs, adding any liquid and seasonings.

2
Pour or ladle the egg mixture into a heated and oiled pan.

3
Swirl the pan over the heat, stirring and scraping the eggs simultaneously, until curds begin to form.

4
Add a filling, if desired.

5
Cook the omelet until it is set.

6
Roll the omelet, completely encasing the filling, out of the pan directly onto a heated plate. Shape it, using a clean towel, if necessary.

7
If a filling was not added in step 4, the omelet's top may be slit and a filling spooned into the pocket.

8
Rub the surface with butter, if desired.

Frittata/Farmer-style Omelet

Yield: 4 servings

Lean bacon, diced, or butter or oil	6 ounces or as needed	170 grams or as needed
Onion, minced	4 ounces	15 grams
Potatoes, cooked, diced	4 ounces	15 grams
Eggs	8	8
Salt	to taste	to taste
Pepper, freshly ground	to taste	to taste

1. Cook the bacon in a skillet until it is crisp, or heat the oil in a skillet.

2. Add the onions and sauté them for 1 minute.

3. Add the potatoes and sauté them until they are lightly browned.

4. Meanwhile, beat the eggs with the salt and pepper. Pour them over the ingredients in the skillet and stir gently.

5. Reduce the heat to low, cover the skillet, and cook until the eggs are nearly set.

6. Remove the cover and place the skillet under a broiler to brown the eggs lightly. Cut the frittata into wedges and serve it immediately, or cool and serve it at room temperature.

NOTE: Many of the suggested fillings for basic omelets may be used.

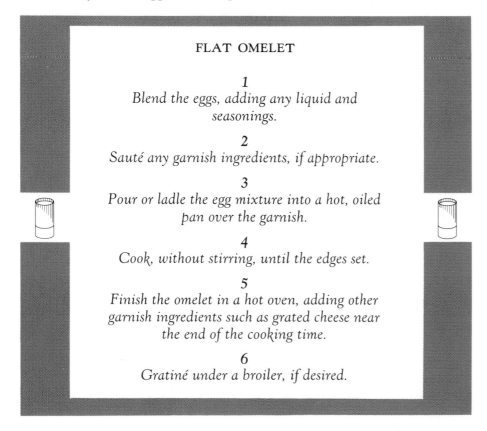

FLAT OMELET

1
Blend the eggs, adding any liquid and seasonings.

2
Sauté any garnish ingredients, if appropriate.

3
Pour or ladle the egg mixture into a hot, oiled pan over the garnish.

4
Cook, without stirring, until the edges set.

5
Finish the omelet in a hot oven, adding other garnish ingredients such as grated cheese near the end of the cooking time.

6
Gratiné under a broiler, if desired.

clean. If desired, the omelet may be lightly browned under a broiler or salamander.

The abbreviated method for the flat omelet serves as an easy reference.

Method for Souffléed or Puffy Omelets

Like a soufflé, these omelets have a light, fluffy texture that is achieved by incorporating air into the eggs. This is done either by whipping whole eggs until they are very frothy or by reserving part of the whites to make a meringue that is folded into the remainder of the beaten eggs.

1. Whip the eggs until they are very frothy or separate the eggs and blend the yolks until they are smooth. Whip the egg whites to a soft peak and fold them into the yolks. Any seasonings or garnish ingredients (for example, cooked, chopped spinach) may be added to the beaten eggs.

2. Thoroughly heat a buttered or oiled skillet or hotel pan over moderate heat.

3. Add the egg mixture and cook it on the stove top until the edges and the bottom are set. The heat should be carefully regulated. The idea is simply to set the eggs; they should not take on a brown color.

4. Place the skillet or pan in a hot oven to complete the cooking. Again, the cooking time will vary according to the size and depth of the skillet and the recipe yield. Test the omelet for doneness by inserting a skewer into its center; it should come away clean. The omelet should puff during the cooking time. It should be served immediately after removal from the oven

Souffléed Omelet

Yield: 1 serving

Eggs	3	3
Cheddar cheese, grated	½ ounce	15 grams
Chives, fresh, minced	1 teaspoon	750 milliliters
Salt	to taste	to taste
Pepper	to taste	to taste
Butter, clarified, or oil	as needed	as needed

1. Separate the eggs. Beat the yolks and season them to taste.

2. Add the grated cheese and chives to the beaten yolks.

3. Beat the egg whites to medium peaks and fold them into the yolks.

4. Pour the batter into a preheated, well-oiled skillet. When the sides and bottom have set, finish the omelet in a hot oven until it is fully set but not dry. Serve it immediately.

NOTE: Souffléed omelets may be prepared using variations for the traditional omelet.

SOUFFLÉED OMELET

1
Whip the eggs until they are very frothy or separate the eggs and blend the yolks until they are smooth; whip the whites to a soft peak and fold them into the yolks. Add any seasonings and garnish ingredients at this time.

2
Pour or ladle the egg mixture into a heated and oiled pan.

3
Cook until the edges and bottom are set.

4
Finish in a hot oven.

---

so it is not flat when it arrives at the table.

Refer to the abbreviated method for the souffléed omelet for quick reference.

Quiches

A quiche is a custard baked in a crust. Quiches are popular at breakfast, brunch, and lunch and are a creative way of using a wide variety of foods. Classic quiches include Lorraine (made with bacon and cheese), Florentine (made with spinach), and seafood.

Especially effective for increasing interest in the breakfast or lunch menu, quiches have low food costs and high customer appeal. Although it may have become something of a cliché, the quiche remains a popular and well-received menu item.

Method

1. Blend the eggs with milk or cream to make a smooth mixture. The usual ratio for a quiche calls for 6 to 8 eggs per quart of liquid.

2. Add appropriate seasonings and garnish ingredients to the egg mixture, or add the garnish to the prepared crust in a layer.

3. Pour the egg mixture into the prepared, filled crust.

4. Bake the quiche in a moderate oven until the custard is set. To test it for doneness, insert a knife tip into the center; it should come away clean.

5. Let the quiche set for a few moments before serving it. Quiche is generally served while it is still hot or quite warm. It may, however, be prepared in advance, cooled and refrigerated, and briefly reheated in a microwave or conventional oven prior to service.

Leek and Tomato Quiche

Yield: 8 appetizer or 6 entrée servings

Scallions, white only, sliced thin	1 bunch	1 bunch
Leeks, white and light green parts, sliced thin	1½ cups	250 grams
Butter or oil	as needed	as needed
Tomato concassé	1½ cups	350 grams
Salt	to taste	to taste
Cayenne pepper	to taste	to taste
Heavy cream	1½ cups	360 milliliters
Eggs	3	3
Cheese, grated (Monterey Jack, Gruyère, cheddar)	3½ ounces	100 grams
Herbs, fresh, minced (tarragon, basil, or other)	2 tablespoons	5 grams
9-inch pastry crust, partially baked	1	1

1. Sauté the scallions and leeks in butter or oil until they are translucent.

2. Add the tomato concassé and sauté it until the liquid evaporates. Season with salt and cayenne pepper.

3. Whisk together the heavy cream and eggs. Stir in the cheese and season it with the herbs, and more salt and cayenne.

4. Spoon the filling mixture into the crust. Add the custard mixture gradually, stirring it with a fork to distribute the filling ingredients evenly.

5. Set the quiche pan on a baking dish and bake it in a 350°F (175°C) oven until a knife blade inserted in the quiche's center comes out clean, about 40 to 45 minutes. Serve the quiche hot or at room temperature.

NOTE: Refer to the variations on basic quiche at the end of this chapter.

Savory and Dessert Soufflés

Soufflés, like omelets and quiches, are not strictly for breakfast; in fact, they are more typically part of the luncheon or even the dinner menu, where small soufflés often appear as hot appetizers or desserts.

Although not inappropriate for breakfast, soufflés are seldom served then. The main reason is time. Most people think of breakfast as a quick meal, and soufflés must be prepared to order. A common rule in the kitchen is that "the customer waits for the soufflé; the soufflé does not wait for the customer." Thus, tradition and common sense have relegated soufflés to more leisurely meals served later in the day.

The basic procedure calls for adding beaten egg whites to a base. Beaten egg yolks are used as a base for a souffléed omelet; a heavy béchamel with the incorporation of additional egg yolks is the base for most savory soufflés. The base may be flavored or garnished in a variety of ways: with grated cheese, chopped spinach, or pesto, for example. Dessert soufflés may require either pastry cream or pureed fruit as a base.

The preparation of the base and a soufflé's assembly are not of themselves difficult procedures. The tricky part is timing. The kitchen staff and the front of the house must communicate well, to assure that the guest receives the soufflé while it is still puffy and hot.

A variety of sauces may be served with these dishes. Cheese sauce (also made from a béchamel base), vegetable ragouts or coulis, or tomato sauces are appropriate for savory soufflés; custard sauces and fruit purees are often used for dessert soufflés.

Method

1. Prepare a base. Use either a heavy béchamel (see the recipe in Chapter 17, "Sauces"), a pastry cream, or a fruit puree (see Chapter 33, "Dessert Sauces, Creams, and Frozen and Fruit Desserts"). The base should be at room temperature or else worked with a wooden spoon until it has softened.

2. Add the flavoring, which should also be at room temperature.

3. Whip the egg whites to a soft peak. Avoid overbeating the whites. Stiff egg whites will expand

Basic Savory Soufflé (Cheese)

<u>Yield</u>: *4 servings: one 1-quart (1-liter) soufflé or 4 individual soufflés*

Butter	4 tablespoons	60 grams
Flour	5 tablespoons	35 grams
Milk	2 cups	480 milliliters
Egg yolks	6	6
Butter	as needed	as needed
Parmesan, grated	1 ounce	30 grams
Emmenthaler or Gruyère, grated	2½ ounces	75 grams
Salt	to taste	to taste
Pepper, freshly ground	to taste	to taste
Nutmeg	to taste	to taste
Egg whites, at room temperature	4	4

1. Prepare a light roux with the butter and flour.

2. Gradually add the milk, whipping out any lumps after each addition. Simmer the mixture for 15 minutes, stirring it frequently. Remove the sauce from the heat.

3. Beat the egg yolks in a small bowl. Temper the yolks with hot sauce, and add them to the sauce. Reserve the base in a large bowl. (Soufflé base may be prepared up to this point and refrigerated or frozen for later use.)

4. Butter a 1-quart (1-liter) soufflé dish or four individual dishes. Sprinkle the sides and bottom with some of the Parmesan. Tap the dish(es) on the counter to shake off any excess cheese; reserve the remaining Parmesan.

5. Stir in the Emmenthaler or Gruyère, salt, pepper, and nutmeg into the reserved soufflé base.

6. Whip the egg whites to semi-stiff peaks. Fold the whites into the base, half at a time.

7. Spoon the soufflé batter into the prepared molds to within ½ inch (1.5 centimeters) of the rim. Wipe the rim carefully to remove any batter. Tap the soufflés gently on the counter to settle the batter.

8. Sprinkle the soufflé tops with the remaining Parmesan.

9. Place the soufflés in the bottom third of a preheated 425°F (220°C) oven and bake them until they are puffy and a skewer inserted in their centers comes out relatively clean (14 to 18 minutes for individual soufflés, 30 to 35 minutes for a single large soufflé).

NOTE: Refer to the variations on the basic savory soufflé at the end of this chapter.

a great deal in the oven's heat, but the trapped air escapes readily, resulting in a flat or fallen soufflé. Soft peaks will produce the proper rise, texture, and structure in the finished soufflé.

Use the egg yolks to prepare the base, or save them for another recipe (hollandaise or mayonnaise, for example).

4. Incorporate the egg whites in thirds. This procedure will help retain the maximum volume. The first addition of egg whites lightens the base and makes it ready for the subsequent additions.

5. Fill the prepared molds quickly. Wipe the rims and outside of the mold clean. To prepare the molds, butter them lightly and thoroughly, dusting the sides and bottom with grated Parmesan cheese for savory soufflés or with sugar for dessert soufflés.

6. Place the soufflés immediately in a hot oven.

For even cooking and a good rise, place the molds on a sheet pan with a little water. The rack should be in the oven's center.

7. Do not disturb the soufflés as they bake. The temperature drop when an oven door is opened could be enough to affect the soufflé. Check individual savory and dessert soufflés made with a béchamel or pastry cream base after 16 to 18 minutes. Fruit soufflés made with only a fruit puree and egg whites should be checked after 10 to 12 minutes.

8. Serve the soufflé immediately. Any accompanying sauce should be hot and ready in a dish. If desired, dessert soufflés may be dusted with powdered sugar. The server should be standing by with a tray, underliner plates, and the sauce, ready to serve the soufflés as soon as they come from the oven.

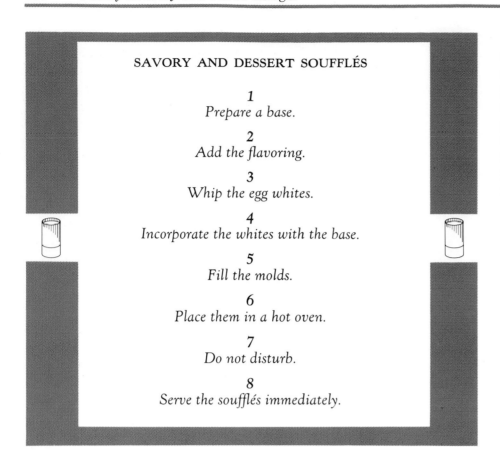

SAVORY AND DESSERT SOUFFLÉS

1
Prepare a base.

2
Add the flavoring.

3
Whip the egg whites.

4
Incorporate the whites with the base.

5
Fill the molds.

6
Place them in a hot oven.

7
Do not disturb.

8
Serve the soufflés immediately.

For easy reference, check the abbreviated method for savory and dessert soufflés.

OTHER BREAKFAST FOODS

Pancakes, Crêpes, Waffles, and French Toast

Although this discussion may seem to deal with only four simple products, the chef and the breakfast cook can exercise a great deal of freedom in garnishing and serving these foods. Pancakes are traditionally thought of as plain, slightly sweetened fried cakes served with syrup or jam. There is no good reason why a pancake cannot become a savory dish, rather than a sweet one, by garnishing the batter differently. For example, a cornmeal pancake could be garnished by folding diced ham and potatoes into the batter, and a salsa or sour cream served as a topping. Crêpes are used to prepare such classic dessert dishes as Crêpes Suzette, but there is no reason that they cannot be filled with seafood in a spicy sauce and used as an appetizer or luncheon entrée. A cheese filling, that is sweetened and garnished with currants or raisins can be used to prepare a blintz, topped with a compote of berries.

The batters for pancakes, crêpes, waffles, and French toast are simple to make and many recipes can be prepared up to one day ahead of time and held in the refrigerator. Crêpes can also be fully prepared in advance and successfully frozen with minimal quality loss.

Pancake batter may be cooked on a griddle or in a skillet. Crêpes are generally prepared in special pans. Waffles require the use of a special waffle iron. French toast is perhaps the simplest of these batter types. It consists of sliced bread that is dipped in an uncooked custard and then quickly "fried" in a skillet or on a griddle.

Mise en Place

1. Flour or meal. Sift and measure the flour according to the recipe. Flours and meals are the basis of most batters; though for French toast, this is not the case. A variety of flours can be used in batters, from all-purpose white flour to pastry flour, graham flour to corn meal, buckwheat flour to rye flour.

2. Liquid. Have available water, milk, cream, or cultured milks. These ingredients should usually be at room temperature.

3. Eggs. Have available beaten eggs, either whole or whites only. Eggs are frequently required in these batters. The egg may simply be added to enrich the batter, or it may be used to provide some leavening.

4. Leaveners. Additional leaveners are sometimes required in a particular recipe. These should be properly measured, and sifted along with the flour or meal.

5. Optional components. Flavoring ingredients and garnishes can run the gamut from fresh fruits and berries to nuts. Other examples might include a variety of herbs, seeds, spices, chocolate, vegetables, and even meat.

Method

1. Prepare all ingredients for the batter and blend them together until the mixture is smooth. The batter should be of an appropriate

Basic Pancakes

Yield: 10 servings

Flour, all-purpose	6 cups	680 grams
Salt	1 tablespoon	15 grams
Sugar	6 ounces	170 grams
Baking soda	1 tablespoon	10 grams
Baking powder	2 tablespoons	25 grams
Milk or buttermilk	3 pints	1.5 liters
Eggs, lightly beaten	6	6
Butter, melted	3 ounces	75 grams
Vegetable oil	as needed	as needed

1. Sift together the flour, salt, sugar, baking soda, and baking powder into a large mixing bowl.

2. In a separate bowl, whisk together the milk, eggs, and melted butter.

3. Add the wet ingredients to the dry. Stir with a wooden spoon to combine. (The batter will be slightly lumpy.)

4. Brush a griddle or skillet lightly with the oil; heat the oil until it is moderately hot.

5. Drop the batter onto the griddle, using a 2 ounce (60 milliliter) ladle, leaving about 1 inch of space between pancakes.

6. Cook the pancakes until the undersides are brown, the edges begin to dry, and bubbles begin to break the surface of the batter, about 3 to 5 minutes.

7. Turn the pancakes and cook them until the second side is brown. Repeat using the remaining batter.

8. Serve the pancakes immediately or keep them warm, uncovered, in a slow oven. (Do not hold the pancakes longer than 30 minutes, or they will become tough.)

VARIATIONS

Whole-grain Pancakes: Replace ¾ cup (85 grams) of the flour with whole-wheat flour, buckwheat flour, oatmeal, or a combination of whole-grain flours.

Berry Pancakes: Increase the sugar to 12 ounces (340 grams) and add 12 ounces (340 grams) of berries (fresh, or frozen and drained).

Johnny Cakes: Substitute cornmeal for half of the flour.

Cottage Cheese Pancakes: Add 3 cups of very well-drained cottage cheese to the mixed batter.

Souffléed Pancakes: Separate the eggs; add the yolks to the batter. Whip the egg whites to a medium peak and fold them into the batter just before cooking.

consistency. For some pancakes, the batter may be about as thick as a cake batter. Crêpe batter should be quite thin—more like heavy cream. French toast batter should also be smooth and thin.

In general, if the batter contains either baking powder or beaten egg whites, it must be used at once. Other batters can usually be held for one to two days under refrigeration.

2. Let the batter rest, if necessary, and strain it if appropriate. Crêpe batters are very often strained to assure a smooth, tender finished product.

3. Thoroughly heat the pan, griddle, or waffle iron.

4. Add enough oil or butter to prevent the batter from sticking. Nonstick pans are especially helpful in producing uniform, golden pancakes and crêpes. These pans also reduce or eliminate the need for additional oil or butter.

5. Pour or drop an appropriate amount of batter—usually about 2 ounces—into the heated pan, griddle, or waffle iron. (For French toast, dip the sliced bread into the batter and place it in the heated oil.)

6. Turn the pancakes, crêpes, or French toast; complete the cooking.

Pancakes are ready to turn when small air bubbles burst open on the cakes' upper surface. Crêpes should be turned when the edges appear cooked. An offset spatula or palette knife can be used to turn pancakes and crêpes; crêpes are also very often "flipped" in the same manner as fried eggs. A waffle iron will cook both sides of the waffle at once. Check for doneness after the waffles have cooked for approximately 2 minutes.

7. Serve the item while it is still very hot. Add the appropriate garnishes, fillings, or sauces. Crêpes

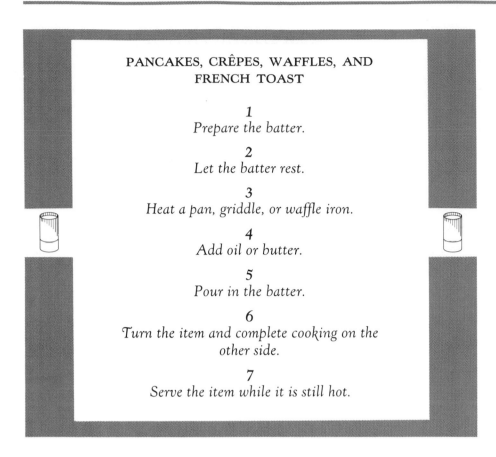

PANCAKES, CRÊPES, WAFFLES, AND
FRENCH TOAST

1
Prepare the batter.

2
Let the batter rest.

3
Heat a pan, griddle, or waffle iron.

4
Add oil or butter.

5
Pour in the batter.

6
*Turn the item and complete cooking on the
other side.*

7
Serve the item while it is still hot.

may be held for later use, if desired.

The abbreviated method for pancakes, crêpes, waffles, and French toast is provided for easy reference.

Determining Doneness and Evaluating Quality

Waffles, pancakes, and French toast should have a golden-brown exterior and a moist, tender interior. Most pancakes and waffles will cook in 2 to 4 minutes, depending upon their thickness. Crêpes cook very quickly, usually in less than a minute, and generally do not take on as deep a brown color as waffles or pancakes. The side of the pancake or crêpe that cooked first will have a better appearance. This side should be facing up on the plate.

Cereals

Cereals, both hot and cold, are among the most nutritious offerings on a breakfast menu. A wide variety of cold cereals is available, many featuring oat bran and/or low sodium and sugar content for the benefit of health-conscious individuals. An especially popular example is granola, a mixture of grains (customarily including oats and wheat berries), nuts, dried fruits, coconut, and a sweetener (usually honey). The mixture is baked in the oven until it is toasted and crunchy. For children, manufacturers continue to offer sugar-coated cereals in novel shapes.

Oatmeal, cream of wheat or rice, and cornmeal mush are all typical hot cereals. Whole-grain dishes, such as rice pilaf, bulgur, or buckwheat groats, are also finding more acceptance as breakfast dishes. Grits and cornmeal mush are tradi-

tional Southern breakfast foods. The methods for preparing these grain dishes are covered in Chapter 24, "Cooking Grains and Legumes."

Method for Hot Cereals

1. Have the liquid (milk or water is most commonly used) at a simmer.

2. Add the cereal in a stream, stirring it constantly.

3. Simmer the mixture until it is thickened.

4. Serve it immediately, garnished or flavored as desired.

Determining Doneness and Evaluating Quality

Hot cereals are done when they are thick and the grains are tender. It is important to use the proper ratio of liquid to cereal. Cooked cereals should not be so thin that they appear watery; on the other hand, they should not be so thick that they hold their shape when dropped from a spoon. Remember that cereals will continue to thicken in a steam table. Hot cereals should have a pleasant, nutty flavor and be free of lumps.

Meats, Fish, and Potatoes
Bacon, Sausage, Ham, and Scrapple

Bacon may be baked in a hot oven or cooked on a griddle or in a skillet. In some cases, it may be appropriate to cook it in a microwave oven. It is never proper to deep-fry bacon, however. Although this will not harm the bacon, the frying fat will break down rapidly.

Bacon should be cooked until crisp, and properly drained to remove any excess grease. Rendered drippings may be saved and used as a cooking medium for other dishes. Every effort should be made to assure that bacon is very hot when it is served. Cold bacon has an unpleasant, greasy feel in the mouth. Bacon may be partially cooked, or "blanched," in the oven or on a griddle and then held. It can be finished as needed, either in small batches for buffet service or to order for à la carte operations.

Sausage may be grilled, baked, or fried on a griddle or in a skillet. Small breakfast links are cooked and served whole. Larger sausages, such as kielbasa, may be sliced and fried. Take care to insure that sausage is thoroughly cooked, properly drained, and served hot. For additional suggestions and methods of sausage preparation, see Chapter 28, "Charcuterie and Garde-manger."

Ham is another popular breakfast meat. It can be panbroiled, cooked on a griddle, or baked. Canadian bacon and fully cooked ham can be served cold as well as hot. The purpose of grilling or broiling is simply to heat the meat through.

Scrapple is a cross between cornmeal mush and sausage. Ground pork and seasonings are mixed with cornmeal mush and poured into a loaf mold. Once the loaf is cold, it can be sliced. The scrapple slices are slowly panfried (it takes about 10 minutes to properly panfry a ⅜-inch-thick slice). Scrapple should have a dark-brown exterior and a creamy, moist interior.

Steaks

Breakfast steaks (ham steaks and beef steaks) are generally smaller than those served for lunch or dinner. They may be grilled or sautéed until heated through and properly cooked. They are often served with a simple "gravy" prepared by de-

Red Flannel Hash

Yield: 10 servings

Butter	2 ounces	60 grams
Onions, minced	6 ounces	170 grams
Bell peppers, minced	4 ounces	115 grams
Corned beef, cooked, minced or ground	1 pound	450 grams
Chef's potatoes, cooked, grated	8 ounces	225 grams
Beets, cooked, peeled, grated	8 ounces	225 grams
Green onions, minced	4 ounces	115 grams
Parsley, fresh, chopped	1 ounce	30 grams
Thyme leaves, fresh, chopped	1 tablespoon	3 grams
Salt	to taste	to taste
Pepper, ground	to taste	to taste
Vegetable oil	as needed	as needed

1. Heat the butter over medium heat in a sauté pan. Add the onions and peppers and cook them until they are translucent. Remove the vegetables from the pan and place them in a large bowl.

2. Combine all the remaining ingredients with the cooked onions and peppers (except for the vegetable oil) and mix them until they are evenly combined.

3. Heat the oil in a griswold over high heat. Add the hash mixture and press it into an even layer in the pan. Turn the heat down; cook the hash until a good crust has formed on the bottom.

4. Turn the hash and cook it until a crust has formed on the second side and the hash is thoroughly heated. Cut the hash into wedges and serve it at once.

NOTE: An optional cooking method is to combine the ingredients and place them into an oiled hotel pan. The hash can be cooked in a hot oven until it is heated through and a crust has formed on the top. This is a convenient way to prepare hash for buffet service.

glazing the pan used to sauté the steak.

Hash

This humble mixture of chopped meats, potatoes, and onions is an excellent vehicle for total utilization. The ratio of meat to vegetables is not an exact one, and the chef or breakfast cook can include a wide variety of additional vegetables—corn, carrots, peppers, or beets, for example—to give the dish color and flavor. Hash is most traditionally panfried in cast-iron skillets (griswolds), but it can also be made in hotel pans in larger batches for buffet service. The traditional way to serve hash is topped with a fried or poached egg.

Method for Hash

1. Combine chopped, minced, or ground cooked meat with grated or minced onions and potatoes. Add other ingredients and seasonings as desired.

2. Thoroughly heat the skillet and add enough oil to prevent the hash from sticking.

3. Add the hash mixture. Let it cook on the first side until a crust forms on the bottom. Note: If the hash is being prepared in a hotel pan, oil the pan, add the hash in an even layer, and bake it in a moderate oven until it is thoroughly heated.

4. Turn the hash, disturbing the crust as little as possible.

5. Continue to cook the hash until a crust develops on the second side.

6. Serve the hash at once with appropriate garnishes or hold it, hot, for service.

Fish

Breakfast menus often include various kinds of fish. Among the most popular are smoked salmon or trout, lox, and kippered herring. Techniques for smoking and pickling fish are covered in Chapter 28, "Charcuterie and Garde-manger." Dishes based on salt cod, such as fishcakes and kedgeree, are also possible breakfast items.

Potatoes

Potatoes have an honored place on the breakfast menu. Among the most popular potato preparations are home fries, hash browns, Lyonnaise potatoes, and O'Brien potatoes. See Chapter 23, "Potato Cookery," for methods and recipes.

Fruits

A selection of fruits, left whole, peeled, sliced, or sectioned, is often offered for breakfast and brunch. Tropical fruits such as mangoes, papayas, star fruit, and special melons greatly expand the standard repertoire. Compotes of cooked fruits, fresh or dried, may also be offered.

Breads

Muffins, quick breads, bagels, English muffins, and toast are all traditional breakfast items. Croissants and Danish pastries are also popular. Many of these items are covered in the baking and pastry section of this book.

Butter toasted bread, bagels, and muffins while they are hot, whether they are on a buffet line or being held in the kitchen for short periods during à la carte service.

Beverages

Traditional breakfast beverages come immediately to mind: coffee, tea, hot chocolate, various juices. Other, less obvious choices include "blender" drinks based on milk, yogurt, or whole fruits.

Coffee

Coffee is an extract made by combining hot water (190°F/88°C) with ground coffee. As the water runs through the coffee (and very often through some sort of filtering device), the ground coffee's flavor and essential oils are "leached" into the water. Coffee preparation techniques are known variously as "brewing," "perking," and "dripping."

With a great number of coffee makers available to both restaurants and homes, and the increasing demand for consumer good coffee—both regular and decaffeinated—this area should be of great concern to chefs. It is an easy and cost-effective way to make a good opening impression at breakfast or to leave the lunch or dinner guest with a pleasant memory.

Whatever the type of equipment used, it must be scrupulously clean. The manufacturer's directions regarding care and maintenance should be followed.

Coffees should be selected based on suiting a particular establishment's needs. It is unreasonable to assume that every operation will be able or willing to grind beans before brewing each pot; however, the closer roasting and grinding is done to brewing time, the better, whether it is done by a purveyor or in the restaurant. Different purveyors' samples should be tasted on a continuing basis, to make sure the freshest possible product is obtained.

Brewed coffee does not hold well for more than 45 minutes to an hour, unless it is held in a vacuum container. Contact with heat (a hot plate or a large electric percolator) can cause the coffee to break down.

Tea

The process of making tea involves creating an infusion. The tea is combined with boiling water and allowed to steep until a beverage with the proper flavor is achieved. The "spent" leaves are generally removed from the pot.

Tea should be prepared with boiling water in order to have a full body and flavor and should then be served immediately. A great many teas are available, in different blends and styles, either loose or in bags. "Herbal" teas, more accurately known as *tisanes*, are increasingly popular.

Hot Chocolate

Hot chocolate may be prepared from powdered mixes that are blended with hot milk or water. Although it is difficult to hold hot chocolate, especially when it is made with milk (a skin forms on the surface), individual packets of dried cocoa, made-to-order, alleviate this problem.

Juices

Review the information on juices in Chapter 10, "Nonperishable Goods Identification." The choice of fresh, frozen, or canned juices depends on the restaurant's needs.

SUMMARY

Until quite recently, breakfast was a fairly standard meal of "eggs any style, choice of juice, choice of bacon or sausage, potatoes, toast, and coffee." Whether the patron is motivated by health and nutrition concerns or by the patterns of modern life that make breakfast a convenient time for meeting business colleagues or friends, this meal has taken on a whole new look. Brunch, too, has become an established part of the weekly routine for many people.

Hard Boiled Eggs

Yield: 1 serving

Eggs   2 | 2

1. Place the eggs in a pot. Fill the pot with enough cold water to cover the eggs.

2. Bring the water to a light boil and immediately lower the temperature to a simmer. Begin timing at this point. Cook small eggs for 12 minutes, medium eggs for 13 minutes, large eggs for 14 to 15 minutes, and extra-large eggs for 15 minutes.

3. Cool the eggs in cold water.

Soft-Cooked Eggs

Yield: 1 serving

Eggs   2 | 2

1. If the eggs are used directly from the refrigerator, temper them in warm water before cooking them.

2. Place the eggs in boiling water. Time the cooking from the point that the boiling resumes. For coddled eggs in the shell, cook for 2 to 5 minutes. For soft eggs in a glass, cook for 4 minutes. For soft eggs, cook for 5 minutes.

3. Shock the eggs in cold water for 2 to 3 seconds. Serve them warm. Serve the coddled eggs in the shell in an egg stand; peel the soft eggs and arrange them as for poached eggs.

NOTE: Coddled eggs may also be prepared by submerging tempered eggs (or eggs cracked into ceramic egg coddlers) in simmering water, covering the pot and removing it from the heat, and allowing the eggs to stand. Soft-cooked eggs take 3 to 4 minutes; medium-cooked eggs take 5 to 7 minutes. Eggs cooked in coddlers may take slightly longer.

Deviled Eggs

Yield: 12 egg halves

Eggs, hard-cooked, cooled and peeled	6	6
Mayonnaise	3 ounces	75 grams
Mustard, prepared	2 teaspoons	10 grams
Salt	to taste	to taste
Pepper	to taste	to taste

1. Slice the eggs in half lengthwise. Separate the yolks from the whites. Reserve the whites separately.

2. Rub the yolks through a sieve into a bowl or food processor. Add the mayonnaise, mustard, salt, and pepper. Mix or process the ingredients into a smooth paste.

3. Pipe (using a star tip) or spoon the yolk mixture into the cavities of the egg whites.

NOTE: The eggs may be separated and the filling mixed in advance, but if they are not to be served immediately, the whites and yolks should be held separately until as close as possible to service. Garnishes may include chopped parsley, snipped chives, sliced scallion tops, dill sprigs, pimiento strips, chopped olives, caviar, or shredded carrots. Spices may include toasted cumin seeds (ground after toasting), oregano, cayenne, or crushed red pepper flakes.

VARIATIONS

Deviled Eggs with Tomato: Add tomato concassé (1 small) to the yolk mixture. Add a small amount of fresh or dried herbs (basil, oregano, sage, thyme) and/or ½ teaspoon (2 grams) of minced garlic or shallots to the tomatoes as they sauté, if desired.

Deviled Eggs with Greens: Add 1 teaspoon (5 grams) per yolk of blanched, pureed spinach, watercress, sorrel, lettuce, or other greens to the yolk mixture.

Deviled Eggs with Vegetables: Add small dice of cooked, raw, and/or marinated vegetables, such as celery, carrot, red onion, peppers, fennel, mushrooms (wild or cultivated), tomato, green beans, peas, corn, eggplant.

Deviled Eggs with Peppers: Puree roasted sweet bell peppers (red or green), pimientos, and/or hot chilies. Add approximately ⅓ cup of puree (hot chilies to taste) per 6 yolks.

Deviled Eggs with Cheese: Add up to ¼ cup (25 grams) of grated hard cheese or 2 ounces (55 grams) of soft cheese. Puree the filling well in a food processor.

Deviled Eggs with Fish or Shellfish: Add approximately 4 ounces (115 grams) of finely diced fish or shellfish (also any vegetables desired; see above) to the yolk mixture. Or, make a paste of fish by pureeing it with butter, mayonnaise, or heavy cream. Use smoked fish (especially small pieces or trimmings), shrimp, fresh cooked or canned tuna, salmon, crab, or lobster.

For all or part of the mayonnaise substitute softened butter or compound butter, sour cream, pureed cottage cheese, softened cream cheese, yogurt, or crème fraîche.

27-3 RED PEPPER MOUSSE

(1)

(2)

(3)

(4)

(5)

(1) Mise en place.

(2) Pushing the red pepper puree through a drum sieve.

(3) Adding heavy cream to the puree with the machine running.

(4) Folding whipped heavy cream into the mousse.

(5) The finished mousse.

and hotel kitchens. Far from being a simple thing that can be thrown together with any lettuce available, this course deserves the same sort of scrupulous attention to detail, preparation, and presentation as any other item worthy of a top-quality operation.

Table 8-5 in Chapter 8, "Fruit, Vegetable, and Fresh Herb Identification," gives the characteristics of a variety of salad greens, from the mild to the bitter. The range of acceptable greens for use in a salad has expanded and includes some herbs and edible flowers. It is essential to keep in mind the individual flavors, textures, and colors of lettuces and other greens in order to produce a well-balanced, pleasing salad.

Other important considerations are impeccably clean greens, proper temperature, and a proper ratio of dressing to greens.

Preparing Greens

The following guidelines should be kept in mind when preparing or using greens:

• Hold greens under refrigeration until they are to be prepared and served. Clean them as close to serving time as possible.
• Clean all greens scrupulously to remove all traces of sand, grit, and insects. Figure 27-4 shows how to remove a core from head lettuce before it is cleaned. Then, in Figure 27-5, the proper method for

cleaning lettuces is demonstrated. The entire head is repeatedly dipped in and out of the water. Figure 27-6 shows the correct sequence for cleaning loose-leaved greens (spinach is shown). Greens must not be bruised or roughly handled during rinsing. They should not be soaked to remove sand and grit, because they tend to absorb water. Instead, the leaves should be plunged into cold water and then lifted out, so that the sand remains in the water, not in the crevices of the leaves.

This step may have to be repeated several times in order to completely clean the leaves. Spinach leaves, for instance, provide a perfect place for sand and grit to catch. The procedure should be re-

27-4 PREPARING LETTUCE

(1) Loosening the core.

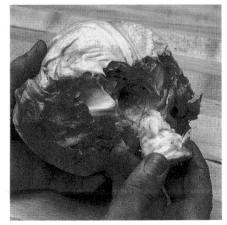

(2) Removing the core.

27-5 CLEANING LETTUCE

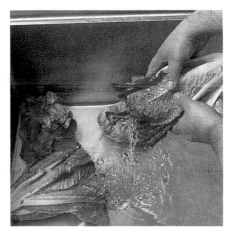

(1) Dipping the lettuce in and out of water.

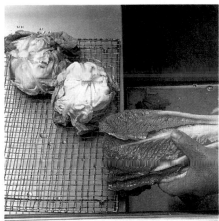

(2) Draining the lettuce.

(3) Removing the stems from the leaves.

27-6 CLEANING SPINACH

(1) Rinsing.

(2) Draining.

(3) Removing the stems.

peated as often as is necessary, until the rinse water shows no evidence of even a few particles of sand or dirt.

• Dry the greens as thoroughly as possible after rinsing. This may be done by allowing them to drain thoroughly, blotting them on absorbent cloth or paper toweling, or spinning them in a greens dryer (salad spinner). With this equipment, the greens are placed in a perforated basket and then spun rapidly, as in a centrifuge, to drive the water away from the leaves.

• Place the greens on plastic sheet trays that have been covered with plastic wrap. Cover them loosely, first with lightly dampened paper toweling and then plastic wrap. Once the greens are rinsed and dried, they may be held under refrigeration for a few hours—the extent of an entire service period—or, if they are of a sturdy variety, such as iceberg or romaine, through an entire day.

• Remove any tough stems or wilted spots with a sharp knife or by tearing them away (see step 3 of Fig. 27-6). If a knife is used, be sure that it is very sharp, to avoid bruising the leaves. Tearing is preferred for more delicate greens, but, again, it is important not to bruise the leaf.

Greens that are ready for service should be in pieces that are easy to pick up with a fork and in general should not be so large that the guest is required to cut them with a knife. Usually, a piece of lettuce should be about the size of half of a dollar bill.

• Dress greens with the appropriate salad dressing as close to service time as possible (see Fig. 27-7). Use only enough dressing to coat the greens lightly; there should not be a pool of dressing at the bottom of the salad bowl or plate (see Fig. 27-8). The generally accepted ratio of dressing to greens is ⅓ fluid ounce of dressing per 1 ounce of greens. Toss the greens lightly until all of the salad components are evenly coated.

For à la carte service, house salads may be assembled and held on sheet trays. The salad dressing is placed in a spray bottle. The salads may then be sprayed with dressing at the time of service and lifted with an offset spatula onto chilled salad plates (see Fig. 27-9).

Mesclun Salad

Yield: 1 quart (1 liter)

Dressing

Safflower oil	24 ounces	720 milliliters
Rice-wine vinegar	8 ounces	240 milliliters
Granny Smith apple, peeled, minced	3 ounces	85 grams
Curry powder	2 tablespoons	15 grams
Shallots, minced	2	2
Salt	to taste	to taste
Pepper	to taste	to taste

By Portion

Assorted baby greens such as frisée, oak leaf, and green leaf	3 to 4 ounces	85 to 115 grams
Goat's cheese, aged, sliced, at room temperature	3 slices	3 slices
Sesame seeds, toasted	as needed	as needed
Poppy seeds	as needed	as needed
Peppers, roasted, julienne	3 to 4 strips	3 to 4 strips
Almonds, toasted	3	3

1. Combine all of the ingredients for the dressing and mix them well.

2. Combine the greens with approximately 1 ounce of dressing and toss them to coat. Place on a salad plate.

3. Garnish the salad as follows: Dip 1 slice of the goat's cheese in the sesame seeds and 1 slice in the poppy seeds, and leave 1 slice plain. Place them on the salad. Add the roasted peppers and toasted almonds.

27-7

Tossing salad to coat with a dressing.

27-8

Adding dressing to a salad.

27-9

Assembled salads, ready to be sprayed with dressing.

Mixed Green Salad

Yield: 10 servings

Mixed greens (romaine, bibb, Boston, red leaf, green leaf, etc.), rinsed, trimmed, and torn into bite-sized pieces	20 to 30 ounces	60 to 85 grams
Vinaigrette or other dressing	5 to 10 ounces	150 to 300 grams

1. Mix the lettuces and keep them well chilled until they are ready for service.

2. Place the amount of lettuce required by a portion (2 to 3 ounces/60 to 85 grams per portion) in a mixing bowl.

3. Add sufficient dressing to lightly coat the leaves. Toss the salad gently to coat it evenly.

4. Mound the lettuces on chilled salad plates and garnish them as desired with 5 to 10 ounces (150 to 300 grams) of sliced cucumbers, radishes, carrots, tomatoes, peppers, etc.

Special Salads

On contemporary menus the term "salad" is used to categorize many more preparations than the green salad. In addition to filling a spot between major courses, salads are taking on increased "substance" and may be served as one of those major courses. Salads that incorporate meats or cheese may be served as appetizers or entrées, for example, and fruit salads are often served as a breakfast or luncheon item.

Warm salads are enjoying increasing popularity and may be positioned as either a first course or a main course. Examples include a warm foie gras salad, a salad of grilled chicken on a bed of greens, or a combination of greens and other vegetables. The warm temperature is particularly suited to certain meats and cheeses as it highlights particular subtle flavors.

Some salads associated with luncheon menus, such as tuna or chicken salad, may also be used as fillings for sandwiches or as stuffings for such vegetables as tomatoes or peppers.

DRESSINGS

Selecting and/or creating an appropriate dressing for a particular salad is an area where personal preference and a sense of style and creativity can come into play. The guiding principle is: The dressing should always be prepared with the proper ratios, to provide a correct balance between acidity and oil. When a dressing does not have a sharp bite, a bitter edge, or an oily feel in the mouth, the balance is correct.

Vinaigrettes are generally most suitable for contemporary menus. They coat the ingredients lightly but evenly. They also require less oil per salad, which makes them a desirable alternative to high-calorie, high-fat, high-cholesterol dressings made with a mayonnaise base. Although emulsified, creamy dressings do still have a role, they too are taking on a much lighter, thinner texture and are more similar to vinaigrettes than they used to be.

In all cases, the dressing's flavor should be appropriate to the salad ingredients, because the dressing serves to pull all the flavors together. Delicate dressings should be used with delicately flavored greens and more robust dressings with more strongly flavored greens.

The weight and coating capabilities of different dressings should also be considered. Emulsified vinaigrette dressings and light mayonnaise dressings, which are thicker than vinaigrettes, tend to coat the ingredients more heavily. They are good general-purpose dressings and are especially effective for salads that include heavier ingredients such as grains, pastas, meats, or fish. Mayonnaise and mayonnaise-based dressings will provide even greater binding.

Vinaigrette Dressings

It has been said that the proper vinaigrette is made by using oil like a wealthy man, using vinegar like a miser, and whipping them together like a madman.

The generally accepted ratio is approximately three parts oil to one part vinegar (citrus juice may replace all or part of the vinegar). This ratio will vary according to the

Basic Vinaigrette

Yield: 2 quarts (2 liters)

Oil (such as vegetable, peanut, extra-virgin olive, sesame, or safflower)	3 pints	1.5 liters
Vinegar (such as red or white wine, tarragon, or cider)	1 pint	500 milliliters
Salt	to taste	to taste
Pepper, freshly ground	to taste	to taste
Dry mustard (optional)	1 teaspoon	3 grams
Fresh herbs, chopped (optional)	4 tablespoons	10 grams
Sugar (optional)	to taste	to taste

1. Combine all of the ingredients and whip them until they are thoroughly blended.

2. Taste the vinaigrette and adjust the seasoning to taste with additional salt, pepper, or sugar.

VARIATION

Balsamic and Citrus Vinaigrette: Use 4 ounces (120 milliliters) of balsamic vinegar and 4 ounces (120 milliliters) of a citrus juice (lemon or lime) to replace 1 pint (0.5 liter) of vinegar.

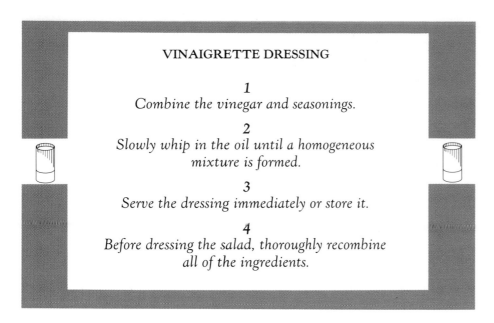

VINAIGRETTE DRESSING

1
Combine the vinegar and seasonings.

2
Slowly whip in the oil until a homogeneous mixture is formed.

3
Serve the dressing immediately or store it.

4
Before dressing the salad, thoroughly recombine all of the ingredients.

acidity and strength of the particular vinegar or citrus juice. For this reason, the vinaigrette should be tasted carefully to determine if the proper balance between vinegar and oil has been reached. It may be necessary to use slightly more oil, even as much as four parts oil to one part vinegar, if the vinegar has an exceedingly sharp or strong flavor. Tarragon and balsamic vinegars, for example, should be used with discretion.

Strongly flavored oils, especially virgin olive oils and nut oils, contribute a great deal of their own flavor, which is part of the reason for using them in salad dressings. The vinegar should not mask this special flavor.

It may sometimes be appropriate to blend a flavorful oil with a neutral oil, in order to introduce a special flavor without making the vinaigrette too intense for the particular salad. For additional information on specific oils and vinegars, see Chapter 10, "Nonperishable Goods Identification."

Vinaigrettes are temporary emulsions. They will stay blended for only a short time, although certainly long enough to go from the kitchen to the guest. As the dressing is allowed to stand, the oil and vinegar will gradually separate. It is, therefore, always a good idea to remix the ingredients before serving the vinaigrette. Otherwise, the balance of flavors will be lost, and a given portion could be dressed primarily with oil or primarily with vinegar. This commonly happens in many restaurants, because it is too easy to just dip a ladle of vinaigrette out of a bain-marie without taking the time to properly blend the ingredients each time.

Adding ingredients such as sugar or mustard to a vinaigrette can make the emulsion a little more stable, but the difference is minimal. The major reason to add any ingredient is to add a special flavor.

For optimum flavor, it is advisable to make all salad dressings in quantities that will last no more than three days.

Method

1. Combine the vinegar with salt, pepper, spices, herbs, mustard, and/or other seasonings.

2. Slowly whip in the oil until a homogeneous mixture is formed.

3. Serve the dressing at once or store it. Vinaigrettes that contain any foods that might spoil or become infected (sour cream, yogurt, or eggs, for example) should be stored under refrigeration. Let the vinaigrette return to room temperature before serving it.

Other vinaigrettes may be stored at room temperature, under the conditions appropriate for storing oils (see Chapter 10, "Nonperishable Goods Identification").

4. Before dressing the salad, thoroughly recombine all of the ingredients.

For easy reference, refer to the abbreviated method for vinaigrette dressing.

Emulsified Vinaigrette and Light Mayonnaise

These dressings have essentially the same ratio of major ingredients (oil to vinegar or to citrus juice) as vinaigrettes. The main differences are that they also contain egg yolks and are blended in a slightly different manner. The yolks' emulsifying abilities produce a thicker dressing that will not separate as readily into its individual components.

Method

1. Beat the egg yolks until they are frothy. It may be desirable to add a small amount of water to provide a lighter consistency in the finished dressing.

2. Add a small amount of the vinegar or lemon juice, as required by the recipe.

3. Gradually incorporate the oil into the egg yolks, whipping the dressing constantly.

4. Add the remainder of the vinegar or lemon juice when approximately two-thirds of the oil has been added. Blend it in well.

5. Gradually incorporate the remainder of the oil and additional seasonings or flavoring ingredients, as desired.

6. Serve the dressing at once or store it under refrigeration.

For a quick summary, refer to the abbreviated method for emulsified vinaigrette.

Mayonnaise

Mayonnaise is the most stable of the basic salad dressings. It contains a higher ratio of oil to vinegar and a greater quantity of egg yolks than is required for an emulsified vinaigrette.

A good mayonnaise is creamy and, in general, pale ivory in color. It should be thick but not enough to hold its own shape firmly (if dropped from a spoon, the mayonnaise should spread slightly). The flavor should be balanced, with enough acid to prevent the dressing from being bland but not so much that the distinct flavor of the vinegar or lemon juice is noticeable.

Mustard is often added to mayonnaise for flavor, not because of any effect that the mustard might have on the dressing's stability. For best results, have all the ingredients at the same temperature—room temperature—before preparation begins.

Method

1. Beat the egg yolks with a small amount of water until they are frothy.

2. Gradually incorporate the oil, beating constantly. The mixture should become quite thick.

3. Add a small amount of vinegar and/or lemon juice as the mayonnaise begins to take on a stiff consistency.

Anchovy-Caper Mayonnaise

Yield: 1 pint (500 milliliters)

Mayonnaise, made with olive oil	1 pint	450 grams
Lemon juice, fresh	2 ounces	60 grams
Mustard, Dijon-style	2 teaspoons	20 grams
Shallots, minced	2	2
Parsley, fresh, chopped	1 ounce	30 grams
Capers, drained, minced	½ ounce	15 grams
Anchovy fillets, minced	3	3
Salt	to taste	to taste
Pepper	to taste	to taste

1. Combine all of the ingredients and mix them well.

2. Refrigerate the mayonnaise until service time; stir it to recombine the ingredients.

NOTE: Refer to the recipe for Basic Mayonnaise, later in this chapter.

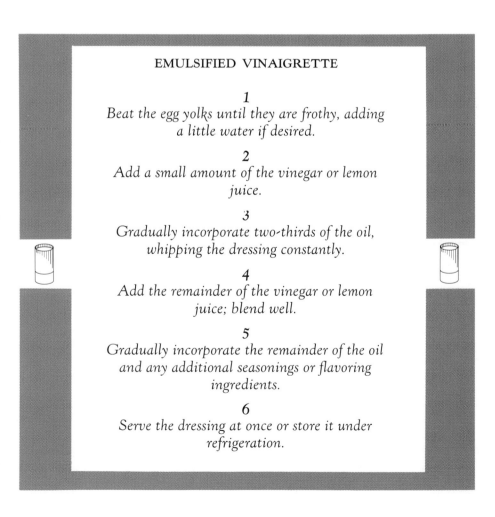

EMULSIFIED VINAIGRETTE

1
Beat the egg yolks until they are frothy, adding a little water if desired.

2
Add a small amount of the vinegar or lemon juice.

3
Gradually incorporate two-thirds of the oil, whipping the dressing constantly.

4
Add the remainder of the vinegar or lemon juice; blend well.

5
Gradually incorporate the remainder of the oil and any additional seasonings or flavoring ingredients.

6
Serve the dressing at once or store it under refrigeration.

Basic Mayonnaise

Yield: 1½ pints (750 milliliters)

Egg yolks	2	2
Wine vinegar	½ ounce	45 grams
Water	½ ounce	45 grams
Dry mustard	1 teaspoon	5 grams
Oil (such as vegetable, olive, or peanut, as desired to achieve flavor)	1 pint	450 grams
Salt	to taste	to taste
Pepper	to taste	to taste
Lemon juice, fresh	to taste	to taste

1. Combine the yolks, vinegar, water, and mustard in a bowl. Mix them well with a balloon whip until the mixture is slightly foamy.
2. Gradually add the oil in a thin stream, constantly beating with the whip, until the oil is incorporated and the mayonnaise is thick.
3. Adjust the flavor with salt, pepper, and lemon juice.
4. Refrigerate the mayonnaise immediately.

MAYONNAISE

1
Beat the egg yolks with a small amount of water until they are frothy.

2
Gradually incorporate the oil, beating constantly.

3
Add a small amount of vinegar and/or lemon juice as the mayonnaise begins to stiffen.

4
Add any additional seasonings or flavoring ingredients.

5
Serve the dressing at once or store it under refrigeration.

4. Add additional seasonings or flavoring ingredients, as desired or according to the recipe.
5. Serve the mayonnaise at once or store it under refrigeration.

For a quick summary, refer to the abbreviated method for mayonnaise.

Other Dressings and Cold Sauces

Many dressings may be made by combining the basic dressings previously described with additional ingredients or by replacing the traditional ingredients with something else. A number of other variations or derivatives are covered in the recipes included at the end of this chapter.

SUMMARY

There are no unimportant parts of any meal. The same attention that is paid to producing a perfectly roasted bird or grilled steak must also be applied to the preparation and service of hors d'oeuvre, appetizers, and salads. These dishes draw freely from all kitchen areas, all foods stocked in the kitchen, and all cooking techniques available to the chef. This results in smaller, but no less important, versions of the same foods that may be featured elsewhere on the menu in larger portions. The same concerns with absolute freshness, respect for seasonality, and a general, commonsense understanding of the appropriateness of an item, a garnish, and a style of presentation still apply.

Melon and Prosciutto

Yield: 1 serving

Melon, ripe, sliced thin	3 slices	3 slices
Prosciutto, sliced thin	1 ounce	30 grams
Lime wedge	1	1

1. Chill the melon until ready to serve. Place it on chilled plates.

2. Drape the prosciutto over the melon and serve with the lime wedge.

NOTE: Serve melon and prosciutto with figs, when they are in season. Be sure the fruit is perfectly ripe.

Salmon Gratin

Yield: 10 servings

Salmon fillet, pounded thin	ten 3-ounce pieces	ten 85-gram pieces
Salt	to taste	to taste
Pepper	to taste	to taste
Dill, fresh, chopped	4 tablespoons	10 grams
Fish stock, hot	6 ounces	180 milliliters
Yogurt, plain	12 ounces	340 grams
Heavy cream, whipped	6 ounces	170 grams
Egg yolks, lightly beaten	2	2

1. Season the salmon and rub it with the salt, pepper, and dill.

2. Combine the hot stock with the yogurt to temper the yogurt.

3. Fold the egg yolks into the whipped heavy cream. Fold the yogurt mixture into the cream mixture.

4. At service, place the salmon on an oven-proof plate and coat it with the cream mixture. Bake in 450°F (230°C) oven until the salmon is barely cooked through (3 to 4 minutes). Glaze it under a salamander or broiler, if desired.

5. Serve it immediately.

Seviche of Scallops

Yield: 16 servings

Sea scallops, muscle tab removed, sliced thin	2 pounds	910 grams
Tomato concassé	14 ounces	400 grams
Lemon or lime juice, fresh-squeezed	7 ounces	200 grams
Red onion, thin rings	3½ ounces	100 grams
Scallions, bias-cut	3 ounces	85 grams
Olive oil	2 ounces	60 milliliters
Jalapeños, fine dice or julienne	½ ounce	15 grams
Garlic, mashed to a paste	1 teaspoon	5 grams
Cilantro, fresh, chopped	6 tablespoons	15 grams

1. Combine all of the ingredients. Marinate the scallops for a minimum of 4 hours to a maximum of 12 hours before service.

2. Serve the seviche with sliced tomatoes and guacamole on chilled plates.

Guacamole

Yield: 1 pound (450 grams)

Avocado, flesh only	2	2
Scallions, minced	2	40 grams
Lime juice, fresh	1 tablespoon	20 grams
Jalapeño, minced	1 teaspoon	6 grams
Garlic, mashed to a paste	½ teaspoon	4 grams

1. Combine all of the ingredients and mash them to a relatively smooth paste with a fork.

2. Serve the guacamole immediately or refrigerate it.

Marinated Salmon with Lime and Olive Oil Vinaigrette

Yield: 1½ cups (360 milliliters) of marinade

Olive oil, extra virgin	1 cup	240 milliliters
Lime juice	from 2 limes	from 2 limes
Lemon juice	from 1 lemon	from 1 lemon
Wine vinegar	1 ounce	30 milliliters
Shallots, minced	3 tablespoons	40 grams
Peppercorns, pink, cracked	2 tablespoons	15 grams
Salt	to taste	to taste
Pepper	to taste	to taste
Chardonnay	2 cups	480 milliliters
Chives, chopped	½ cup	18 grams
Salmon fillet, thinly sliced (per portion)	2 ounces	60 grams

1. Combine all the ingredients.
2. Marinate the salmon under refrigeration for 15 minutes before serving.

Hummis bi Tahini (Chickpea and Sesame Dip)

Yield: 1 pound (450 grams)

Chickpeas, cooked, drained	12 ounces	170 grams
Lemon juice	2 to 3 ounces	55 to 85 grams
Garlic, minced	2 cloves	2 cloves
Tahini (sesame paste)	2 ounces	55 grams
Olive oil	1 ounce	30 grams
Salt	to taste	to taste
Pepper	to taste	to taste

1. Combine all of the ingredients in a food processor and puree them to a very smooth consistency. Adjust the seasoning to taste with additional lemon juice, garlic, salt, and pepper, as needed.
2. To serve the hummus, place it in earthenware crocks or bowls. Drizzle it with additional olive oil and serve it with pita bread, along with sliced peppers and other fresh crudités.

Caviar in New Potatoes with Dilled Crème Fraîche

Yield: 10 servings

New potatoes, 1 inch in diameter	20	20
Whole butter	2 ounces	60 grams
Crème fraîche	5 ounces	140 grams
Dill, fresh, chopped	1 ounce	30 grams
Caviar	20 teaspoons	100 grams
Chives, sliced	as needed	as needed

1. Bake the potatoes until they are very soft; split them in half. Scoop out the flesh and work the butter into it.

2. Return the mashed potatoes to their shells. Combine the crème fraîche and the dill, and top the potatoes with it. Place ½ teaspoon of the caviar on each potato half. (Serve 4 halves per portion.)

3. Sprinkle the potatoes with fresh chives and serve.

VARIATION

Three Caviars on Game Chips with Crème Fraîche: Make game chips by slicing Idaho potatoes very thin. Deep-fry 6 slices per portion. Top each slice with a dollop of crème fraîche and place three different caviars on top of the crème fraîche. Garnish the potatoes with chopped chives or chopped dill.

Marinated Roasted Peppers

Yield: 8 servings

Peppers (different colors), roasted, peeled, seeded, and halved	12 total	12 total
Olive oil, virgin	8 ounces	240 milliliters
Garlic, finely minced	1 clove	1 clove
Salt	to taste	to taste
Pepper	to taste	to taste
Balsamic vinegar	2 ounces	60 milliliters
Basil leaves, fresh, chiffonade	¼ cup	10 grams
Parmesan, thinly sliced	12 slices	12 slices

1. Place the roasted peppers in an earthenware container.

2. Combine all the remaining ingredients, except for the cheese. Pour the marinade over the peppers and let them marinate overnight under refrigeration.

3. At service, arrange three pepper halves on plates, alternating colors. Garnish them with the fresh chiffonade of basil and the Parmesan.

Stuffed Mushrooms with a Gratin Forcemeat

Yield: 10 servings

Mushrooms, large	40	40
Butter, clarified	as needed	as needed
Shallots	1	1
Garlic	1 clove	1 clove
Port wine	1 ounce	30 milliliters
Chicken livers	8 ounces	225 grams
Rosemary leaves, fresh, chopped	2 teaspoons	2 grams
Salt	to taste	to taste
Pepper	to taste	to taste
Parsley, fresh, minced	1 tablespoon	3 grams

1. Wipe the mushrooms clean, and remove the stems. Chop the stems coarsely. Reserve each cap separately.

2. Heat the butter and sauté the shallots and garlic until they are translucent. Deglaze the pan with the wine. Add the chopped mushroom stems and sauté them until they are dry.

3. Sauté the chicken livers in the pan (add more clarified butter, if necessary) until they are seared on all sides. Puree the livers in a food processor. Add the salt, pepper, and rosemary.

4. Pipe the mixture into the mushroom caps. Heat 4 caps per portion in a hot oven at the time the mushrooms are ordered. Sprinkle them with additional wine and chopped parsley.

Santa Fe–style Black-bean Cakes with Sautéed Crab and Corn

Yield: 10 servings

Black beans, dried, soaked overnight	12 ounces	340 grams
Ham hock, smoked	1	1
Bouquet Garni		
Peppercorns	6 to 8	6 to 8
Rosemary, fresh	1 sprig	1 sprig
Thyme, fresh	1 sprig	1 sprig
Parsley stems	3 to 4	3 to 4
Garlic, whole cloves	5	5
Onion, minced	1	1
Chicken stock	as needed	as needed
Whole eggs	2	2
Cake flour	1 ounce	30 grams
Butter, clarified, or olive oil	as needed	as needed
Crabmeat, picked	10 ounces	285 grams
Corn kernels	10 ounces	285 grams
Cilantro, chopped	3 tablespoons	7 grams
Salt	to taste	to taste
Pepper	to taste	to taste
Salsa	1 pound	450 grams

1. Simmer the beans, ham hock, bouquet garni, and onion, in enough chicken stock to cover by about 3 inches (7.5 centimeters). Simmer for 1½ hours, or until the beans are tender. Drain off the liquid and discard the bouquet garni.

2. Puree the beans to a chunky paste. Stir in the eggs and flour. Adjust the seasoning with salt and pepper. Form the mixture into cakes.

3. Sauté the crabmeat and corn in the clarified butter until they are hot. Adjust the seasoning and add the chopped cilantro. Keep warm.

4. Sauté the bean cakes in butter or oil until they are heated through. Serve the cakes on a pool of salsa and top them with the crabmeat and corn mixture.

Gorgonzola Custards

Yield: 6 servings

Butter	as needed	as needed
Onion, minced	4 ounces	115 grams
Half-and-half or cream	12 ounces	360 milliliters
Eggs	4	4
Gorgonzola or other blue-veined cheese, crumbled	3 ounces	85 grams
Salt	to taste	to taste
Pepper	to taste	to taste

1. Sauté the onions in the butter until they are translucent. Cool them.

2. Combine the onions, half-and-half, eggs, and Gorgonzola in a mixing bowl. Season to taste.

3. Spoon the custard into buttered ½-cup (120-milliliter) ramekins.

4. Bake the custards in a bain-marie in a preheated 350°F (175°C) oven until a knife blade inserted in their centers comes out clean. Serve the custards hot or at room temperature, either unmolded or in ramekins.

Vitello Tonnato

Yield: 16 servings

Leg of veal, boneless, tied, roasted, cooled	2 pounds	910 grams
Tuna, canned, drained	7 ounces	200 grams
Anchovy fillets	6	6
Onion, finely diced	2 ounces	55 grams
Carrots, finely diced	2 ounces	55 grams
Dry white wine	4 to 5 ounces	120 to 160 milliliters
White-wine vinegar	2 ounces	60 milliliters
Water	3 ounces	85 grams
Olive oil	as needed	as needed
Egg yolks, hard-cooked, sieved	2	2
Capers, drained, chopped	1 tablespoon	15 grams

1. Slice the veal thinly, about 2 ounces (55 grams) per serving.

2. Combine the tuna, anchovies or anchovy fillets, onion, carrots, wine, vinegar, and water in a food processor. Process them to a relatively smooth paste.

3. Arrange the sliced veal on chilled plates. Nappé it with the tuna sauce and drizzle with olive oil. Garnish the veal with the egg yolks and capers.

Warm Iowa Blue Cheese Mousse

Yield: 6 servings

Blue cheese, room temperature	6 ounces	170 grams
Cream cheese, room temperature	4 ounces	115 grams
Pepper	to taste	to taste
Eggs, whole	6	6
Heavy cream	14 ounces	420 milliliters
Chives, fresh, sliced	1 ounce	30 grams
Salt	to taste	to taste
Pepper	to taste	to taste
Grapes, seedless	24	24

1. Combine 4 ounces (115 grams) of the blue cheese (reserve the remainder for the garnish), the cream cheese, and pepper in a food processor until the mixture is very smooth.

2. Add the eggs, 4 ounces (120 milliliters) of the heavy cream, and half of the chives. Pulse the processor on and off until the ingredients are just blended. Place the mixture in buttered 2-ounce (60-milliliter) timbale molds and cover the molds with buttered parchment paper.

3. Bake the mousse in a bain-marie until a knife inserted near the timbales' centers comes away clean.

4. Reduce the remaining cream by half and season it to taste with the salt and pepper. Add the remaining chives and grapes to the cream immediately before service.

5. Unmold the mousse and nappé it with the sauce. Garnish with the reserved blue cheese.

SUBSTITUTION

The blue cheese may be replaced with one of the following cheeses: fresh or aged goat's cheese, Boursin, Brillat-Savarin, Camembert, or Brie.

Smoked Salmon Mousse Barquettes

Yield: 10 servings

Fish velouté	6 ounces	170 grams
Salmon, smoked, diced	5 ounces	140 grams
Aspic gelée, softened	1 ounce	30 grams
Pepper	to taste	to taste
Heavy cream, whipped	4 ounces	115 grams
Pre-baked barquettes, made from pâte brisée	10	10

1. Combine the velouté and smoked salmon in a food processor. Process the ingredients to a smooth consistency.

2. Add the aspic gelée while the processor is running, incorporating it into the salmon mixture. Adjust the seasoning to taste.

3. Remove the salmon mixture from the processor and fold in the whipped cream. Pipe the mixture into the barquettes and chill it to a firm mousse.

Grilled Shiitake Mushrooms

Yield: 10 servings

Shiitake mushrooms, caps only	2¼ pounds	1 kilogram
Olive oil	1 cup	240 milliliters
Basil leaves, fresh, minced	4 tablespoons	10 grams
Garlic, mashed to a paste	2 cloves	2 cloves
Salt	to taste	to taste
Pepper	to taste	to taste
Tomato concassé, fine dice	10 ounces	285 grams

1. Remove the woody stems from the mushrooms. Wipe the caps clean, if necessary.

2. Combine the olive oil, basil, garlic, salt, and pepper.

3. Dip the mushrooms into the olive oil mixture. Grill them for about 30 seconds per side.

4. Place the mushrooms on heated plates (3 to 4 caps per portion) and drizzle them with some of the olive oil mixture. Surround them with the fresh tomato concassé.

Broiled Shrimp with Garlic and Aromatics

Yield: 10 servings

Bread crumbs, dry	8 ounces	225 grams
Garlic, minced	10 cloves	10 cloves
Parsley, flat-leaf, chopped	¼ cup	10 grams
Oregano, chopped	¼ cup	10 grams
Butter, melted	12 ounces	340 grams
Salt	to taste	to taste
Pepper	to taste	to taste
Shrimp, peeled (tail intact) and butterflied	30	30

1. Combine the bread crumbs, garlic, parsley, oregano, and 8 ounces (225 grams) of the butter. Adjust the seasoning to taste with the salt and pepper.

2. Arrange the shrimp on a gratin dish (3 per portion) and brush them with the remaining melted butter.

3. Place 1 to 2 teaspoons of the bread crumb mixture on the shrimp and broil them under a salamander until they are very hot and cooked through. Serve.

Broccoli and Cheddar Fritters

Yield: 10 servings

Flour, all-purpose, sifted	12 ounces	340 grams
Whole eggs	4	4
Milk	12 ounces	340 grams
Baking powder	1½ tablespoons	15 grams
Salt	1 teaspoon	5 grams
Worcestershire sauce	to taste	to taste
Tabasco	to taste	to taste
Broccoli florets, cooked	1 pound	455 grams
Sharp cheddar cheese, coarsely grated	8 ounces	225 grams

1. Combine the flour, eggs, milk, baking powder, salt, Worcestershire, and Tabasco. Mix them into a smooth batter.

2. Fold in the broccoli and cheese. Drop the mixture by spoonfuls into 350°F (175°C) oil. Deep-fry the fritters until they are uniformly brown; turn them, if necessary, during frying.

3. Remove the fritters with a spider and drain them briefly on absorbent toweling. Serve them immediately.

Oysters Diamond Jim Brady

Yield: 1 serving

Oysters, fresh	5	5
Tomato concassé	1 tablespoon	15 grams
Whole butter	½ ounce	15 grams
Shallots, minced	1 teaspoon	5 grams
Crème fraîche	as needed	as needed
Pernod	dash	dash
Royal glaçage	1 to 2 ounces	30 to 60 grams
Salt	to taste	to taste
Pepper	to taste	to taste

1. Rinse and shuck the oysters, to order. Reserve the oyster liquor to flavor the royal glaçage.

2. Heat the tomato concassé and butter; add the shallots and sauté them until they are tender and the liquid is reduced. Add a small amount of the crème fraîche to bind the mixture. Add the Pernod, salt, and pepper to taste.

3. Place the tomato mixture in the deep half of the oyster shell. Top it with an oyster and nappé it with the flavored royal glaçage.

4. Gratiné the oysters under a broiler. The oysters' edges should be lightly curled.

Clams Casino

Yield: 10 servings

Bacon, diced	4 ounces	115 grams
Onions, minced	4 ounces	115 grams
Green peppers, minced	3 ounces	85 grams
Red pepper, minced	3 ounces	85 grams
Salt	to taste	to taste
Pepper	to taste	to taste
Worcestershire sauce	to taste	to taste
Butter, softened	1 pound	450 grams
Topneck clams	4 to 6 per serving	4 to 6 per serving
Bacon, whole strips, blanched, quartered	1 per portion	1 per portion

1. Render the diced bacon until it is crisp. Add the onions and peppers and sauté them until they are tender. Remove them from the heat and allow them to cool.

2. Combine the onion and pepper mixture with the salt, pepper, Worcestershire, and butter. Blend all ingredients until they are evenly mixed.

3. Open the clams to order and loosen the meat from the shells. Top each clam with about 1 teaspoon (5 grams) of butter and a piece of blanched bacon. Broil the clams until the bacon is crisp, and serve them immediately.

Fennel and Chorizo Strudel

Yield: 10 servings

Butter, melted	5 ounces	140 grams
Shallots, minced	2	2
Chorizo, sliced thin	4 ounces	115 grams
Fennel, fresh, diced	8 ounces	225 grams
Tarragon leaves, minced	2 tablespoons	5 grams
Egg, whole	1	1
Bread crumbs, dry	as needed	as needed
Salt	to taste	to taste
Pepper	to taste	to taste
Phyllo dough, thawed	6 sheets	6 sheets

1. Heat about ½ ounce (15 grams) of the butter in a sauteuse. Add the shallots and sauté them until they are translucent.

2. Add the chorizo and allow some of the fat to render. Add the fennel and cook it until it is tender. Process all of the ingredients to a coarse paste in a food processor.

3. Add the tarragon leaves, egg, and enough bread crumbs to lightly bind the mixture. Adjust the seasoning to taste.

4. Brush each sheet of phyllo with butter, sprinkle with bread crumbs, and top with another sheet. Repeat the process; when three sheets are stacked, place half of the chorizo-fennel mixture down the center of the dough and roll up the sheets. Brush the top with butter. Repeat with the remaining dough and filling. Chill them well, and score the top on the diagonal to divide the strudels into 10 sections.

5. Bake the strudels at 400°F (205°C) until they are browned. Slice and serve two slices per portion.

Cheese-filled Risotto Croquettes with Tomato Sauce

Yield: 10 servings

Prepared risotto	2 pounds	910 grams
Heavy cream	2 ounces	60 milliliters
Parmesan cheese, grated	2 ounces	55 grams
Egg yolks	2	2
Mozzarella or Fontina cheese, cut into 20 cubes	10 ounces	285 grams
Standard breading	as needed	as needed
Tomato sauce	20 ounces	570 grams

1. Combine the risotto with a liaison of the cream, Parmesan, and egg yolks.

2. Form the mixture into croquettes wrapped around the cubed cheese (about 1½ ounces/45 grams of risotto per croquette).

3. Put the croquettes through the standard breading procedure. Chill them thoroughly before panfrying or deep-frying them.

4. Fry, to order, two croquettes per portion until they are evenly browned. Serve them on a pool of heated tomato sauce (2 ounces/55 grams per portion).

Apple, Carrot, and Raisin Salad

Yield: 10 servings

Raisins	2 ounces	55 grams
Orange juice	4 ounces	120 milliliters
Carrots, shredded	1 pound	455 grams
Golden Delicious apples, shredded	1 pound	455 grams
Horseradish, shredded	1 ounce	30 grams
Vegetable oil	3 ounces	90 milliliters
Salt	to taste	to taste
Pepper	to taste	to taste

1. Combine the raisins and orange juice; let the raisins become plump. Drain the fruit and reserve the orange juice.

2. Combine the raisins, carrots, apples, and horseradish.

3. Beat together the reserved orange juice, oil, salt, and pepper. Add the dressing to the shredded carrots and combine until all ingredients are thoroughly coated.

European-style Potato Salad

Yield: 10 servings

Potatoes, boiled until tender	3 pounds	1.35 kilograms
Onions, finely diced	5 ounces	140 grams
Vinegar	3 ounces	90 milliliters
Meat broth	8 ounces	240 milliliters
Mustard, prepared	to taste	to taste
Salt	to taste	to taste
Pepper	to taste	to taste
Sugar	to taste	to taste
Oil	3 ounces	90 milliliters
Parsley or chives, chopped	1 tablespoon	2 grams

1. Peel and slice the potatoes.
2. Combine the onions, vinegar, and broth. Bring the mixture to a boil. Add the mustard, salt, pepper, and sugar, to taste.
3. Add the oil to the dressing.
4. Immediately pour the dressing over the potatoes.
5. Sprinkle the potato salad with the parsley or chives and serve it at room temperature.

Spinach, Avocado, and Grapefruit Salad

Yield: 10 servings

Avocados, ripe, sliced	3 to 4	3 to 4
Grapefruit, sectioned	4	4
Spinach, cleaned, stems removed	2 pounds	910 grams
Balsamic and citrus vinaigrette	as needed	as needed

1. Toss together the avocados and grapefruit (this will prevent the avocado from browning).
2. Toss the spinach leaves with the vinaigrette; use only enough dressing to coat the leaves very lightly.
3. Arrange the spinach on chilled plates. Top it with the avocados and grapefruit.
4. Drizzle additional dressing on the avocado mixture.

NOTE: Refer to the recipe for Balsamic and Citrus Vinaigrette, a variation of Basic Vinaigrette, earlier in this chapter.

Chapter 28

Charcuterie and Garde-manger

In its strictest interpretation, the term *charcuterie* refers to items made from the pig. These include sausages, smoked hams, bacon, pâtés, terrines, and head cheeses. Translated from the French, the word literally means "cooked flesh." Garde-manger refers to the kitchen's pantry or larder section, where foods were kept cold. Various preparations completed in this "cold kitchen" came to be known as part of the garde-manger repertoire. Over time, because of the similarities in their products, the seemingly separate areas of charcuterie and garde-manger have become closely joined.

In this chapter, the various responsibilities of the garde-manger and charcuterie kitchen areas and the types of items they produce will be covered. Also discussed will be fundamental techniques for preparing a variety of forcemeats and using them for sausages, terrines, pâtés, and galantines and the proper methods for brining, curing, and smoking meats and fish.

BACKGROUND

The history of charcuterie extends back to the workers' guilds at the end of the Middle Ages, when the *charcutières* were granted a charter allowing them to sell products from the pig, including cooked items.

Since those times, the role of the *charcutière* has expanded greatly. Sausages, pâtés, and terrines today are made from a wide range of ingredients, including poultry, fish, shellfish, and vegetables. In contemporary kitchens, especially large ones, there may still be a separate area for the preparation and production of charcuterie and garde-manger items. Smaller kitchens may rely on outside purveyors for some or all of these products or may incorporate their production into other kitchen areas.

Historically, charcuterie and garde-manger products provided a way of preserving meat over the winter by using spices and herbs, smoking, and curing with salt. Now that refrigeration is available, the flavoring is somewhat lighter and less fat is used, but the result should still be a rich, well-flavored product.

One of the basic components of charcuterie and garde-manger items is a preparation known as a forcemeat. In the following sections, five distinct forcemeat styles are explained and a variety of items prepared from forcemeats are also discussed.

FORCEMEATS

A forcemeat is a lean meat and fat emulsion that is established when the ingredients are forced through a sieve or grinder. Depending on the grinding and emulsifying methods and the intended use, the forcemeat can have a smooth consistency or be heavily textured and coarse. The result must not be just a mixture but an emulsion, so that it will hold together properly when sliced and have a rich and pleasant taste and feel in the mouth.

Basic Preparation Guidelines

1. Maintain proper sanitation and temperature at all times. All necessary ingredients and tools used in preparing any forcemeat must be scrupulously clean and well-chilled at all times. If the forcemeat is to be a true emulsion, it must be kept quite cold throughout its preparation so that the proteins and fats can combine properly. Ingredients should be refrigerated until they are ready to be used and, if necessary, held over

a container of ice to keep the temperatures low during actual preparation.

Maintaining the correct temperature is important for more than the proper formation of an emulsion. These foods are often highly susceptible to contamination. Pork, poultry, seafood, and dairy products can begin to lose their quality and safety rapidly when they rise above 40°F (4°C). If the forcemeat seems to be approaching room temperature, it is too warm. Work should be stopped and all ingredients and equipment refrigerated. Work may be resumed only after everything is below 40°F (4°C) once more.

2. Grind foods properly. This technique is known as progressive grinding. For most forcemeats, one of the first steps is to grind the meats and fat together. The following procedures should be observed:

- Cut all solid foods into dice or strips that will fit easily through the grinder's feed tube.
- Do not force the foods through the feed tube with a tamper. If they are the correct size, they will be drawn easily by the worm.
- Be sure that the blade is sharp. Meats should be cut cleanly, never mangled or mashed, as they pass through the grinder.
- For all but very delicate meats (fish or some types of organ meats, for example), begin with a die that has large or medium openings. Continue to grind through progressively smaller dies until the correct consistency is achieved. Remember to chill ingredients and equipment between successive grindings.
- When using a food processor to finish grinding the meat, be sure that the meat is not overprocessed.
- Push forcemeats that are properly ground, whether through a meat grinder or in a food processor, through a sieve (tamis) for the smoothest possible texture.

Types

Forcemeats may be used for quenelles, sausages, pâtés, terrines, and galantines or to prepare stuffings for other items (a salmon forcemeat may be used to fill a paupiette of sole, for example). Each forcemeat style will have a particular texture, as described in the following text.

Straight. This is a forcemeat that combines pork and pork fat with a dominant meat in equal parts, through a process of progressive grinding and emulsification. The meats and fat are cut into strips, seasoned, cured, rested, progressively ground, and then processed with a binder, such as egg.

Country-style. This forcemeat is rather coarse in texture. It is traditionally made from pork and pork fat, with a percentage of liver and other garnish ingredients.

Gratin. In a gratin, some portion of the dominant meat is sautéed and cooled before it is ground. The term *gratin* means "browned" and does not imply that cheese is included in the recipe.

5/4/3. This method combines meat, fat, and seasonings into a very finely textured forcemeat. The basic mixture is five parts meat/four parts fat/three parts ice. This forcemeat is used for frankfurters, bockwurst, and knockwurst.

Mousseline. A very light forcemeat, mousseline is based on white meats (veal or poultry) or fish. The inclusion of cream and eggs gives a mousseline its characteristic light texture and consistency.

Special Preparations
Panada

A panada is an ingredient or mixture used in forcemeats to assist in forming a good emulsion. Its function is to assure that pâtés, terrines, and other items do not fall apart or crumble when sliced. If a panada is required, it should comprise no more than 20 percent of the forcemeat's total volume, not including garnish ingredients.

The type of panada used will vary, depending on the type of meat, fish, or vegetable used as a flavoring. The three types most often called for are bread panada, flour panada, or pâte à choux. Panadas may also be based on rice and potatoes, although these are less frequently used. In some forcemeats, heavy cream or a liaison of heavy cream and eggs may take the place of the previously mentioned panadas.

• Bread panada. Cubed bread is soaked in milk, in an approximate ratio of one part bread to one part milk. The bread cubes and milk are combined and allowed to soak until the bread has absorbed the milk. If necessary, the bread may be squeezed to remove any excess milk before the panada is added to the forcemeat.

• Flour panada. This is essentially a very heavy béchamel. A roux is prepared and milk added, in an approximate ratio of one part roux to one part milk. Three to four egg yolks per pound of béchamel are added. The panada is chilled completely before it is added to the forcemeat.

• Pâte à choux. The recipe and directions for preparing pâte à choux are found in Chapter 14, "Mise en Place." The pâte à choux must be completely chilled before it is added to the forcemeat.

Aspic Gelée

Aspic gelée is a well-seasoned, highly gelatinous, perfectly clarified stock. It is frequently strengthened by adding a quantity of gelatin (either sheets or granular gelatin may be used). The aspic is applied to foods to prevent them from drying out, preserving their moisture and freshness. When properly prepared, aspic should set firmly but still melt in the mouth. The recipe and ratios for aspic are included at the end of this chapter.

Aspic gelée made from white stock will be clear, with practically no color. When the base stock is brown, the result is amber or brown in color. Other colors may be achieved by adding an appropriate spice, herb, or vegetable puree.

Pâté Dough

Pâté dough is by necessity a stronger dough than a normal pie dough, although its preparation technique is identical to that used for more delicate pastry doughs. (Refer to Chapter 32, "Pastry Doughs and Cookies.") Other flours, herbs, ground spices, or lemon zest may be added to change the dough's flavor. Instructions for lining a mold with pâté dough are included in the step-by-step description of preparing a pâté en croûte later in this chapter.

Evaluating Quality

The characteristics to check when evaluating the quality of forcemeats are flavor, appearance, and texture. The dominant meat (including fish, chicken, or vegetable) should be the predominating flavor. Additional ingredients, such as herbs, spices, and various garnishes, should enhance the flavor. Special attention should be paid to the seasoning of products made from forcemeats. They should always be tested for the appropriate seasoning; this is done by making a quenelle and tasting it at the proper serving temperature. Flavors are more pronounced in hot foods; for cold service, it may be necessary to adjust the seasoning.

When properly prepared, forcemeats should retain their shape after cooking and slicing. Garnishes should be appropriate to the dominant meat and should be spread evenly throughout the preparation.

The forcemeat itself should not appear gray, nor should the color from a garnish "bleed" into it.

The final shape will depend on the type of forcemeat, the shape of the mold or casing (if any), and the way in which the product is sliced for service.

If aspic is used as a coating, it should be evenly applied and firm enough to hold its shape, although not rubbery. Pastry dough for pâté en croûte should not be cracked or "checkered." It should have an appealing golden color and be of an even thickness. Pastry garnishes should be of the appropriate size and not excessive in number.

The texture should be appropriate to the type of forcemeat. Smooth forcemeats should be properly sieved to assure that there are no "strings." Textured forcemeats, such as country-style pâté, should not crumble when sliced. All forcemeats should be well-emulsified and free from gristle and sinew.

Straight Forcemeat

Mise en Place

This is a basic forcemeat that can be used to prepare a variety of items, including sausages, pâtés, terrines, and galantines, illustrated later in this chapter.

1. Dominant meat. This need not necessarily mean pork, veal, beef, lamb, or game; it could be poultry, fish, shellfish, or even vegetables. The ratio of dominant meat to other ingredients will vary, depending upon the desired result (see the specific recipes). Cut the meat into cubes or strips. Combine it with spices and/or a marinade, if desired; see the recipes. Chill it.

2. Fat. Pork fat is traditionally used, but in the case of delicately flavored forcemeats heavy cream may be more appropriate. Cut the fat into cubes or strips and chill it.

3. Binders. Different forms of binders can be used, depending on the type of forcemeat. In some cases, the proteins naturally present in the dominant meat may be sufficient to bind the forcemeat so that it will slice well after it is cooked. In other cases, it may be necessary to add a panada, additional eggs, or sometimes both.

4. Seasonings and flavoring ingredients. Forcemeats, especially those to be served cold, should have a full flavor. Salt, in addition to providing flavor, also helps extend the shelf life of some products. Curing salt, a special compound that combines salt with sodium nitrite, is often used to produce a particular effect in forcemeats. This preservative is responsible for the pink color of many sausages and other cured meats. It is most often required

Pheasant Pâté (Straight-method Forcemeat)

Yield: *approximately 2 pounds (900 grams)*

Pheasant legs, meat only, diced	10 ounces	285 grams
Lean pork, diced	10 ounces	285 grams
Pork fat, diced	10 ounces	285 grams
Whole eggs	2	2
Shallots, minced, sweated, cooled	2 ounces	60 grams
Salt	¾ ounce	20 grams
White pepper	¼ ounce	7 grams
Pâté spice or other spice blend	pinch	pinch
Curing salt (optional)	¼ teaspoon	1 gram

1. Grind the pheasant meat, pork, and pork fat through the coarse die of a grinder, then again through a finer die.

2. Place the ground meats and fat in the chilled bowl of a food processor and add all of the remaining ingredients. Process the forcemeat until it is smooth and well-emulsified.

3. Make a test quenelle to check for seasoning and consistency. Use the forcemeat as desired for a variety of charcuterie and garde-manger items. Keep it well-chilled at all times.

VARIATIONS

Rabbit Forcemeat: Replace the pheasant meat with lean, diced rabbit meat. If desired, reserve the loin meat and cut it into dice or julienne for a garnish. Marinate the loin meat in a small amount of brandy. Garnish the forcemeat with chopped nuts, mushrooms, or sweated vegetables for additional color and flavor, as desired.

Venison Forcemeat: Replace the pheasant meat with lean, diced venison. Use lean meat from the loin as a garnish, as described for rabbit forcemeat, above.

when the forcemeat is to undergo smoking after it has been prepared.

5. Optional components. These include garnishes and aspic. A variety of garnishes may be included to provide additional texture, flavor, or color. The choices include diced meats (usually the same as the dominant meat), vegetables (dices, purees, juliennes), herbs and spices, nuts, and dried fruits. Aspic is often used to coat charcuterie items. Although aspic adds visual appeal by giving a sheen and luster, its basic function is to protect the product from moisture loss during storage.

Method

1. Have all ingredients and equipment at the correct temperature, under 40°F (4°C).

2. Cut the meats and fat into a dice or strips. Combine the dominant meat and garnish ingredients with a marinade and refrigerate them.

3. Run the meats and fat through a meat grinder, using a die with large openings (coarse die). Hold the ingredients over ice or refrigerate them.

4. Grind the meats and fat a second time, using a die with medium openings. This will produce a forcemeat that has a moderately coarse texture. Again, hold the ingredients over ice or refrigerate them.

5. Place the ground meat in a food processor and add the panada. Process the mixture to a smooth consistency.

6. Gently fold the garnish into the forcemeat by hand, working over ice. The forcemeat is now ready to use for a variety of applications.

Figure 28-1 demonstrates steps in this method. For a quick summary, refer to the abbreviated method for straight forcemeat.

28-1 METHOD FOR STRAIGHT FORCEMEAT

(1) Mise en place.

(2) Marinating the meats and fat.

(3) First stage: grinding through a coarse die.

(4) Second stage: grinding through a medium die.

(5) Third stage: grinding with the egg in a food processor.

(6) Adding the garnish.

Country-style Forcemeat

Mise en Place

For a description of essential and optional components, refer to the mise en place for straight forcemeat.

Method

1. Prepare all meats, fat, and garnish ingredients as indicated by the recipe. Cut the meats and fat into dice or strips. Marinate the ingredients if desired or appropriate. Keep them chilled at all times.

2. Grind the meats once through a coarse die and again through a medium die, and hold over ice or keep them refrigerated.

3. Push the liver through a sieve (tamis) to remove all sinews, membranes, and fibers.

4. Gently work the sieved liver and panada into the ground meats and fat by hand. Do this over ice to keep all ingredients at the correct temperature. Any garnish should be added at this time.

The forcemeat is now ready to be used in a variety of applications. See the recipes at the end of this chapter for guidance. Figure 28-2 demonstrates steps in this method. For a quick summary, refer to the abbreviated method for country-style forcemeat.

Gratin Forcemeat

Mise en Place

The livers are an important component of this style of forcemeat. Review the information regarding the mise en place for the straight method for additional information.

Method

1. When preparing a gratin forcemeat, sear the livers first to give it the proper flavor. Allow the

STRAIGHT FORCEMEAT

1
Prepare the meats, fat, and garnish ingredients; chill well.

2
Cut the meats and fat into strips or dice. Marinate them as required. Keep them chilled at all times.

3
Grind the meats and fat twice, using first a coarse and then a medium die. Refrigerate or hold the mixture over ice.

4
Combine the ground meat with the panada in a food processor; process the mixture until it is smooth.

5
Fold in the garnish by hand, working over ice.

COUNTRY-STYLE FORCEMEAT

1
Prepare the meats, fat, and garnish ingredients as directed in the recipe; chill well.

2
Cut the meats and fat into strips or dice. Marinate them as required. Keep them chilled at all times.

3
Grind the meats and fat twice, using first a coarse and then a medium die. Refrigerate or hold the mixture over ice.

4
Push the liver through a drum sieve.

5
Gently work the liver, panada, and garnish ingredients into the ground meats and fat by hand, working over ice.

(1) Mise en place.

(2) Pushing the liver through a drum sieve.

(3)

(4)

(5)

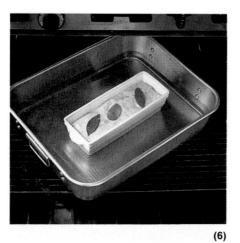

(6)

(7)

(3) Adding the liver and panada (cream and eggs) to the ground meat.

(4) Filling a lined mold.

(5) Folding the fatback overhang.

(6) Cooking in a bain-marie.

(7) Adding aspic to the cooled pâté.

28-3 METHOD FOR
GRATIN FORCEMEAT

(1) Mise en place.

GRATIN FORCEMEAT

1
Sear the livers and cool them completely.

2
Cut the other meats and fat into strips or dice.

3
Grind the meats, livers, and fat twice, using first a coarse and then a medium die. Refrigerate or hold the mixture over ice.

4
Stir the panada into the ground meats, working over ice.

(2) Cooking chicken livers with spices and aromatics.

(3) Adding cream to the ground meats while working over ice.

livers to cool completely before proceeding with the method.

2. Grind the other meats (cut into dice or strips of the appropriate size), pork fat, and cooked livers first through a coarse die and then through a medium or fine die. Hold the ground mixture over ice or refrigerate it between grindings.

3. Stir the panada into the ground meats, working over ice. The forcemeat is now ready to be used in a variety of applications. See the specific recipes for guidance.

Figure 28-3 shows the steps in this method. For a quick summary, refer to the abbreviated method for gratin forcemeat. A recipe is included at the end of this chapter.

5/4/3, or Emulsion, Forcemeat

Mise en Place

A typical emulsion forcemeat will always contain five parts meat, four parts fat, and three parts ice, hence the name "5/4/3." Refer to the mise en place for straight forcemeat for

additional information regarding essential and optional components.

Method

1. Cut all meats and fat into dice or strips. Hold the meats and fat separately and keep them very cold.

2. Add a curing mix to the meat only; do not add it to the fat.

3. Grind the meats separately through the fine die once. Place them in the bowl of a chopping machine or a food processor. Add the ice along with the spices and other ingredients and blend the mixture until it reaches 40°F (4°C).

4. Grind the fat through a fine die. Add this to the meat mixture. Continue to blend the mixture until it reaches a temperature of 58°F (40°C).

5. Make a quenelle to test for binding and taste, and adjust these accordingly. Stuff the mixture into casings and hot-smoke them (see the information later in this chapter about smoking). These sausages are usually smoked only until they have a good color; they must be poached to an internal temperature

(1) Mise en place.

(2) Adding a curing mix.

(3) Grinding the meats through a fine die.

(4) Combining the meats with ice and spices in the bowl of a chopper.

(5) Chopping the meat until it reaches a temperature of 40°F.

(6) Grinding jowl fat through a fine die.

(7) Adding the ground fat to the mixture.

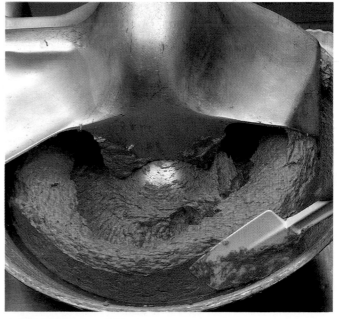

(8) The correct consistency.

673

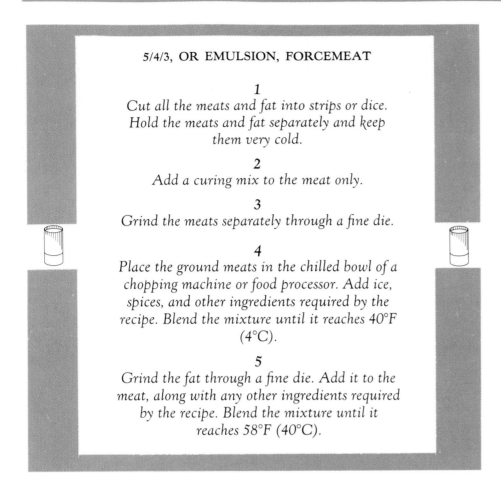

5/4/3, OR EMULSION, FORCEMEAT

1

*Cut all the meats and fat into strips or dice.
Hold the meats and fat separately and keep
them very cold.*

2

Add a curing mix to the meat only.

3

Grind the meats separately through a fine die.

4

*Place the ground meats in the chilled bowl of a
chopping machine or food processor. Add ice,
spices, and other ingredients required by the
recipe. Blend the mixture until it reaches 40°F
(4°C).*

5

*Grind the fat through a fine die. Add it to the
meat, along with any other ingredients required
by the recipe. Blend the mixture until it
reaches 58°F (40°C).*

---

of 155°F (137°C) and then cooled before service.

Figure 28-4 demonstrates the steps in this method. For a quick summary, refer to the abbreviated method for 5/4/3, or emulsion, forcemeat. The recipe for this forcemeat can be found at the end of this chapter.

Mousseline Forcemeat

Mise en Place

Review the information for essential and optional components in the mise en place for straight forcemeat.

Method

1. Cut the meat into dice, and keep it very cold until it is time to prepare the forcemeat.

2. Grind the meat to a paste in a cold food processor. If eggs are included, add them at this time, and pulse the machine on and off to incorporate them into the meat. Do not overwork the meat.

3. With the machine running, add cold heavy cream in a thin stream. Once the cream is incorporated, add aspic gelée in the same manner, if desired or necessary. The forcemeat should be very smooth, but not rubbery.

4. Push the forcemeat through a drum sieve to remove any sinews and membranes that may remain. This assures the correct texture.

5. The forcemeat is ready to be used at this point as a stuffing or to prepare sausages, terrines, or quenelles. See the next section for a description of the preparation of quenelles.

Figure 28-5 shows the steps in this method. For a quick summary, refer to the abbreviated method for mousseline forcemeat.

GARDE-MANGER AND CHARCUTERIE SPECIALTIES

This section includes step-by-step instructions for preparing a number of different items produced in the garde-manger kitchen, including various forcemeat-based preparations such as quenelles, sausages, pâté en croûte, galantines, and items such as daubes and gravad lax.

Quenelles

Quenelles are similar to poached dumplings. A mousseline forcemeat is prepared and then shaped, using one of a variety of methods. Quenelles are an important step when preparing virtually any forcemeat, as testing a quenelle is the way to check a forcemeat's quality before going on to prepare other items. The quenelles may also simply be served either as a garnish for a soup or as an appetizer that may be served with an appropriate sauce.

A richly flavored stock or court bouillon is used as the poaching liquid. Properly prepared quenelles should be light and tender, with a good flavor.

Method

1. Prepare the forcemeat and keep it chilled until it is time to poach the quenelles.
2. Bring the poaching liquid to a simmer. The liquid must not be at a rolling boil; this could cause the quenelles to fall apart as they cook.

(1) Mise en place.

(2) Grinding the chicken in a food processor.

(3) Adding the cream with the machine running.

(4) The correct consistency before pushing the forcemeat through a drum sieve.

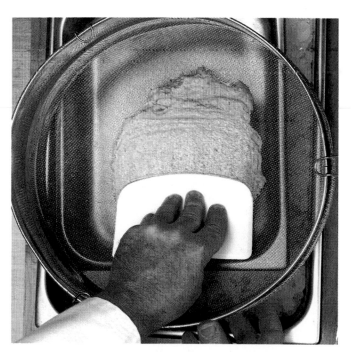

(5) Pushing the forcemeat through a drum sieve.

Chicken Mousseline Forcemeat

Yield: approximately 1¾ pounds (750 grams)

Chicken breast, boneless, cubed	1 pound	450 grams
Whole egg	1	1
Heavy cream, chilled	10 ounces	285 grams
Salt	2 teaspoons	12 grams
Ground white pepper	¼ teaspoon	3 grams
Fresh herbs, chopped (dill, parsley, tarragon, etc., as desired or available)	2 tablespoons	5 grams

1. Grind the chicken through the fine die of a grinder and place it in the chilled bowl of a food processor.

2. Process the chicken with the egg until it is a smooth paste, but do not allow it to exceed 40°F (4°C).

3. Add the heavy cream, salt, pepper, and fresh herbs. Pulse the machine on and off just until the ingredients are blended.

4. Make a test quenelle by poaching it in simmering water or stock to test for consistency and seasoning. Make any necessary adjustments. Keep the forcemeat chilled until ready to use for quenelles, stuffings, or other charcuterie and garde-manger items.

MOUSSELINE FORCEMEAT

1
Cut the meat into dice. Keep it very cold.

2
Grind the meat to a paste in a food processor.

3
If the recipe requires eggs, add them, and pulse the machine on and off to incorporate them into the meat.

4
With the machine running, add cold heavy cream in a thin stream; process the meat just until the cream is incorporated.

5
Add the aspic gelée, if desired or necessary, in the same manner.

6
Push the forcemeat through a drum sieve.

---

3. Shape the quenelles. There are many ways to do this, one of which employs spoons. The spoons are dipped in cold water; an appropriate amount of the forcemeat is scooped up with one of the spoons, and the second spoon is used to smooth and shape the mixture. The quenelle is pushed from the spoon into the poaching medium. Other shaping methods include using ladles or piping the mixture through a plain-tipped pastry bag.

4. Poach the quenelles in barely simmering liquid. The cooking time will vary, depending upon the quenelles' diameter. They should appear completely cooked through when broken open.

5. When making a sample quenelle, be sure to test it at serving temperature (if the forcemeat is to be served cold, let the sample cool completely before tasting it). Make any necessary adjustments in the forcemeat. If it has a rubbery or tough consistency, add heavy cream; if it does not hold together properly, additional panada or egg whites may be necessary. Adjust the seasoning and flavoring ingredients as needed.

Figure 28-6 shows the preparation of quenelles.

28-6

Preparing quenelles from a forcemeat.

Sausages

There are almost countless types of sausages. Each ethnic group and cuisine tends to have its own favorite examples. Sausage meat may be used either in bulk (loose) form or to fill casings, natural or synthetic, which are then usually formed into links.

From this point, they may be used fresh (poached, grilled, fried, or baked), or, if appropriate, they may be dried and smoked or cured. Smoked or cured sausages generally do not require additional cooking. The following method describes the procedure for filling sausage casings using a sausage-stuffing machine. The same general guidelines apply to hand stuffing.

Method

1. Prepare and garnish the forcemeat as desired or required by the recipe used.

2. Rinse the casings thoroughly in tepid water to remove the salt and to make them more pliable.

3. Be sure that all parts of the sausage stuffer that will come in contact with the forcemeat are clean and chilled.

4. Tie a double knot in the casing end. Depending on the type of casing, as well as the type of sausage, the casing may be cut into appropriate lengths.

5. Gather the casing over the nozzle of the sausage stuffer.

6. Support the casing as the forcemeat is expressed through the nozzle and into the casing.

7. If the sausage is to be made into links, use either of the following methods: Press the casing into links at the desired intervals and then twist the link in alternating directions for each link; or, tie the casing with twine at the desired intervals.

28-7 FILLING SAUSAGES AND MAKING LINKS

(1) Filling the casing with forcemeat.

(2) Using the fingers to press the sausage into even links.

(3) Twisting the links to keep them separate (no twine is used here) . . .

(4) . . . or tying the sausages into even links.

8. At this point, fresh sausages may be cooked or stored under refrigeration. Other types of sausage may undergo additional curing, smoking, or drying. (See Figs. 28-7 and 28-8 for the steps in the preparation of sausages and a selection of sausages, including fresh sausages, semi-dry sausages, and cooked and smoked sausages.)

Pâté de Campagne

Traditionally, the mold for a pâté de campagne would be lined with sheets of fatback. Contemporary versions may call for other liners, including romaine leaves, plastic wrap, or leek leaves.

Method

1. Line the mold completely with thin slices of fatback. There should be a 2- to 3-inch overhang on all sides.

2. Add the forcemeat to the lined mold and press it down with a spatula to remove any air pockets.

3. Fold the overhanging fatback onto the top of the pâté to completely encase the forcemeat.

4. Lay various herbs and spices over the top of the pâté, if desired. Cook the pâté in a bain-marie in order to maintain the correct temperature. This will yield a product that is smooth, moist, and flavorful.

28-8 A SELECTION OF SAUSAGES

(1) **Fresh sausages** *(clockwise from top):* Tuscan, hot Italian, Mexican chorizo, and merguez.

(2) **A selection of smoked and cooked sausages.**

(3) **Semi-dry sausages** *(clockwise from top):* salami, Swiss pantli, hard smoked salami, and Lyonwurst (also a hard smoked salami).

5. After the pâté has cooked to the correct internal temperature, allow it to cool to room temperature. Pour off all the fat and liquid that may have collected in the mold. Pour aspic gelée into the mold to fill it to the top. Then chill it completely before slicing.

Pâté en Croute

This is a more elaborate style of pâté in which the mold is lined with a pastry crust. The procedure for lining the mold, baking the pâté, cutting the chimney, and filling the pâté with aspic is explained here.

Method

1. Prepare the forcemeat as necessary, according to the type. Keep the forcemeat and garnish cold until it is time to fill the mold.

2. Prepare the mold. Roll out sheets of dough to approximately ⅛-inch thick. Cut the sheets to fit the mold, using one of two methods:

• Measure the mold's bottom and sides and lightly score the dough. The corners are cut out, and will eventually be pinched together as a seam. An overhang of about 2 inches on the sides and ends of the pâté is necessary. A second piece, known as the cap piece, should be measured out large enough to completely cover the mold's top and extend down into the mold about 2 to 2½ inches.

- Cut the piece to line the mold as a large rectangle. Eventually, the excess will be pinched away, creating a pastry case that is essentially seamless. Cut the cap piece as directed above.

3. Lay the pieces into the mold and press them into place. If a single large rectangle has been used, fit the dough gently into the corners and use a ball of scrap dough to press out any air pockets. If the pieces have been cut to fit, lay them in the mold and press them into place.

4. Use egg wash to "glue" the pastry together in the corners and pinch the seams closed or pinch away the excess in the corners. Save dough scraps to make the chimney and any desired decorations.

5. Line the bottom and sides of the pastry-lined mold with sheets of fatback, thinly sliced prosciutto, or other sliced meats.

6. Garnish the forcemeat as desired, if the garnish has not already been folded in. Add the forcemeat to the lined mold and press out any air pockets with a spatula, smoothing the surface.

7. Fold the fatback, prosciutto, or other sliced meat over the top of the forcemeat. Then fold over the pastry sheets and trim the top layers with scissors so that the edges just meet. Pull the pâté away from the mold's edges with a spatula.

8. Add the cap piece to seal the pâté, and tuck the edges down into the mold. Lightly coat the top pastry layer with egg wash.

9. Cover the pâté with aluminum foil and bake it until it is approximately half done (about 45 minutes). Remove the pâté from the oven and remove the foil.

10. Using round cutters, cut one or two holes in the pastry to allow steam to escape. Cut a ring of pastry to go around the chimney's base. Use aluminum foil bent into a chimney to keep the hole from closing during the final baking. This will allow steam to escape and will prevent the crust from rupturing. Add any decorative pieces, as desired, using egg wash to secure them.

11. Complete the baking in a moderate oven (about 350°F/170°C) to an internal temperature of 150°F (65°C) for meat and 140°F (60°C) for fish and vegetables.

12. Remove the pâté from the oven and let it cool for about 1 hour. Drain away any cooking liquid. Fill the mold with aspic, pouring the liquid through the holes that have been cut in the crust.

13. Chill the pâté thoroughly before slicing and service. Excessive shrinkage or gaps between the pastry and the pâté itself usually means that the pâté has been baked too long or in an oven that was too hot.

Figure 28-9 shows the steps in this method.

28-9 PREPARING A PÂTÉ EN CROÛTE

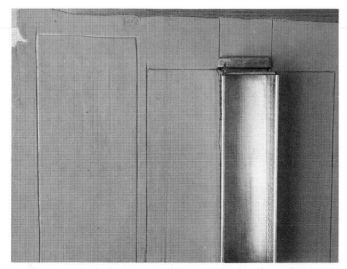

(1) One method for measuring pastry dough to line the mold.

(2) A second method for measuring the dough.

(continued)

(3) Pressing out air pockets with a ball of dough . . .

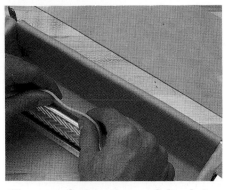

(4) . . . or laying pieces of dough into the mold and forming seams.

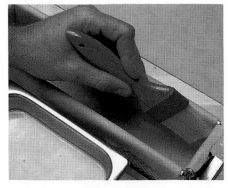

(5) Using egg wash to "glue" the seams closed.

(6) Lining the pastry dough with thin fatback sheets.

(7) Filling the prepared mold.

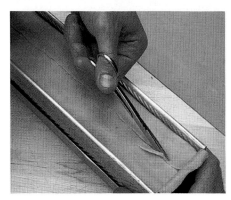

(8) Trimming the excess dough.

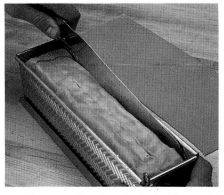

(9) Freeing the dough from the mold sides.

(10) Putting the cap piece in place.

(11) Covering the pâté with foil before the first stage of baking.

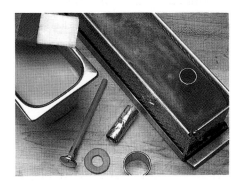

(12) Cutting a hole in the crust.

(13) Filling the cooled pâté with aspic.

(14) The finished pâté.

Terrines

Like pâtés, terrines are loaves of forcemeat baked in a mold. The difference is that terrines are traditionally placed in a covered earthenware mold, called a terrine, and cooked in a hot-water bath. Although pâtés are traditionally unmolded before they are served, terrines would customarily have been served from the mold. The strict interpretation of a terrine has been somewhat modified for contemporary service; they are usually unmolded.

To vary the presentation, the mold can be filled with two forcemeats of different colors—for example, layers of a forcemeat flavored and colored with green herbs could be alternated with layers of a forcemeat flavored and colored with saffron.

Method

1. Prepare a forcemeat as desired or necessary according to the recipe. Chill it until it is time to fill the mold.

2. Prepare any garnishes as desired or necessary. Keep them refrigerated until they are ready to be used.

3. Prepare the mold. Line it first with plastic wrap and then with a "liner" ingredient, of which the following are the most common: thin sheets of fatback, blanched vegetables, blanched romaine leaves, or thin slices of ham or smoked fish.

4. Fill the mold, adding the garnish as described for pâtés.

5. Fold all liners over the mold's surface.

6. Cover the terrine with its lid. If necessary, make a flour paste to seal it.

7. Place the terrine in a roasting pan. Set the pan on the rack of a moderate (about 350°F/175°C) oven. Add enough boiling water to come up nearly to the level of the top of the forcemeat.

8. Bake the terrine to an internal temperature of 150°F (65°C) for meats and 140°F (60°C) for fish. Regulate the temperature of the oven throughout the cooking time. The water temperature should remain at approximately 170 to 180°F (75 to 82°C).

9. Remove the terrine from the bath and allow it to cool. Drain off any cooking liquid. If desired, fill the mold with aspic.

10. Chill the terrine thoroughly before slicing and serving it.

Galantines

The term *galantine* derives from an Old French word, *galin*, meaning "chicken." Originally, galantines were made exclusively from poultry and game birds and were stuffed and tied in the bird's natural shape. Today, however, they are made from a wide range of products, including fish, shellfish, and meats. The skin, if available, is used as a casing to hold the forcemeat.

Method

1. Remove the skin, keeping it as intact as possible: Make an incision through the skin down the middle of the breast and pull the entire skin away from the bird. Use a small knife to help loosen it, if necessary.

2. Bone out the dominant meat, reserving intact any pieces that will be used for garnish. All other meat should be cut into dice or strips of the appropriate size to prepare the forcemeat. The bones and any nonusable trim should be used to prepare a rich stock in which to poach the galantine.

3. Trim the skin to form a large rectangle. Lay out the skin or other casing for the galantine on a large cheesecloth square. Mound the forcemeat down the rectangle's center and position any garnish (the tenderloin or diced, marinated breast meat, for example) as desired. Use the cheesecloth to roll the galantine into a tight cylinder.

4. Tie the ends with butcher's twine and use a strip of cheesecloth to secure it at even intervals in order to maintain the shape of the cylinder.

5. Place the galantine on a perforated rack and then submerge it in a simmering stock. Be sure that the galantine is completely submerged. Maintain the liquid at an even simmer throughout the cooking time—generally 1 to 1½ hours or until an internal temperature of 150°F (65°C) for meats and 140°F (60°C) for fish has been reached.

6. Let the galantine cool in the cooking liquid. (If cheesecloth or plastic wrap has been used, remove the casing.) Rewrap the galantine in fresh plastic wrap, re-roll it to form a tight cylinder, and refrigerate it. Figure 28-10 shows the steps in this method for a chicken galantine.

Smoked and Cured Items

Before they are used in other charcuterie preparations, many foods undergo a cure, usually by allowing the meats to marinate briefly with a curing salt. This is often noted in the recipe as "tinted curing mixture," or TCM. This step gives sausages and other items their pink color. Curing is especially important as the first step for items that are to be smoked.

Curing may be accomplished by using a "dry cure" (dry salts, spices, and herbs) or a brine (a

(1) Mise en place.

(2) Removing the skin in one piece.

(3) Boning out the meat.

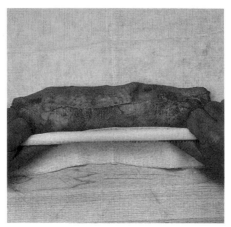

(4) Filling and rolling the galantine.

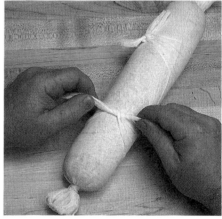

(5) Tying the galantine.

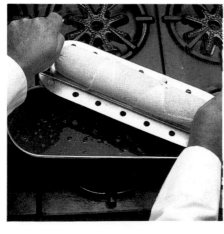

(6)

(7)

(6) Placing the galantine on a rack before poaching it.

(7) The finished, sliced galantine.

682

28-11 A SELECTION OF CHARCUTERIE SPECIALTIES

(1) *Clockwise from top left:* Kielbasi, stuffed derma, jambonneau, head cheese, lieberkaese, rolled pressed pig's head. Kiszka, a polish blood sausage, is in the center.

(2) *Clockwise from top left:* bacon, English bacon, tasso, smoked loin of pork.

combination of water, salt, spices, and other flavorings).

Dry cures are packed around the item to be cured. Instructions for ratios and times used in dry curing are given in specific recipes. In a wet cure, the food is completely immersed in a brine and allowed to cure for a specified amount of time, depending on the nature and size of the item. Again, ratios and times for curing by brine are given in specific recipes. After the food has been properly cured or brined, it is allowed to air-dry, making it more receptive to smoke.

·Smoking flavors foods and preserves their colors. A variety of smoking methods can be used. Even kitchens too small to have a smoker can produce foods with a smoked flavor. The common ways of smoking are cold smoking, hot smoking, and smoke-roasting.

Smoking takes place in an enclosed structure—a smokehouse—where smoke from hardwood chips

(hickory, mesquite, apple) circulates freely and reaches all sides of the product. Depending on the nature of the items, they may be hung from the ceiling or placed on racks. The smokehouse temperature and the time needed for smoking depends on the product's nature and the desired outcome.

Cold smoking is done within a specified temperature range, less than 100°F (37°C). The food should take on a smoky flavor and color but will not be fully cooked during the process. It is usually necessary to complete the cooking of the product before it is served. This method is commonly used for smoked salmon, landjaer, classic French garlic sausage, and all other hard-salami sausage types.

Cold smoking will give the food a smoky flavor and a darker color. Hot smoking, at temperatures above 145°F (63°C), will fully cook the food. Smoke-roasting is not a traditional smoking method, but it

offers a wide range of possibilities for smaller kitchens with no access to a smokehouse. This technique is discussed in Chapter 18, "Dry-heat Cooking without Fats or Oils." A selection of charcuterie items is shown in Figure 28-11.

Gravad Lox

Method

1. Coat trimmed salmon fillets with a dry-cure-and-herb mixture. Wrap them tightly in cheesecloth, place them in a hotel pan, and weight them with heavy cans. Allow the salmon to cure for several hours or days, according to the recipe.

2. Drain away any drippings that have accumulated in the pan and reserve them to make a mayonnaise-style sauce to serve with the gravad lox.

3. Unwrap the salmon and scrape away the cure. Slice the salmon very thinly on the diagonal to serve.

4. Prepare a mayonnaise. (See Chapter 27, "Hors d'Oeuvre, Appetizers, and Salads," for directions on preparation.)

Figure 28-12 shows the steps in this method.

Daube

A daube, when prepared by a *charcutière*, is a cold preparation of a variety of meats, usually including the tongue, head, and feet of veal and/or pork.

Method

1. Gently simmer the meats in an aromatic broth enriched with

28-12 PREPARING GRAVAD LOX

(1)

(2)

(3)

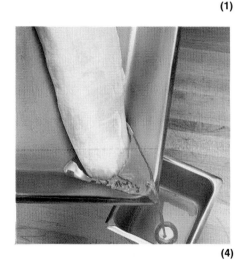
(4)

(5)

(6)

(7)

(1) Coating salmon fillets with a spice mixture.

(2) Wrapping the salmon tightly in cheesecloth.

(3) Placing a weight on the salmon before marinating it.

(4) Draining away the drippings.

(5) Unwrapping the salmon and scraping away the cure.

(6) Slicing the salmon thinly on the diagonal.

(7) Preparing a mayonnaise.

28-13 PREPARING A DAUBE

(1) Simmering the meats.

(2) Lining the mold with plastic wrap.

(3) Filling the mold with meats and aspic.

(4) Sealing by folding back the overhanging plastic wrap.

(5) The finished, sliced daube.

vegetables and herbs. Once the meats are tender, trim and cut them into julienne or dice.

2. Line the mold, usually an earthenware terrine, with plastic wrap. Leave enough overhang to ensure that the mold can be fully sealed.

3. Place the prepared meats, along with the desired herbs and other garnishes, in the mold. An aspic, made by clarifying and enriching the stock used to simmer the meats, is added to completely fill the mold.

4. Fold back the overhanging plastic wrap over the top of the mold to seal the daube, and refrigerate the entire dish until the aspic is firmly set.

5. Once the daube is thoroughly chilled, it is ready to be sliced and served.

Figure 28-13 shows the steps in this method. Refer to the recipe for daube at the end of this chapter.

SUMMARY

This chapter has touched on only a small number of the vast array of items that can be prepared in charcuterie and garde-manger kitchens. Pâtés, sausages, terrines, and galantines allow the chef to make full use of all food items brought into the kitchen, whether as the foundation for a mousseline forcemeat or as the garnish for a pâté.

The change in eating style of most contemporary diners has reduced the emphasis on rich, high-fat terrines and other delicacies. This does not mean that the role of the cold kitchen has been greatly diminished. It simply offers a new challenge to chefs to update classic preparations, making them lighter and more appealing to modern tastes.

Country-style Forcemeat

Yield: approximately 3 pounds (1.36 kilograms)

Pork butt, diced	2½ pounds	1.14 kilograms
Pork liver, cleaned and diced	½ pound	230 grams
Onion, chopped fine	4 ounces	115 grams
Garlic, minced	2 cloves	2 cloves
Fresh parsley, chopped fine	5 sprigs	5 sprigs
Flour	2½ ounces	70 grams
Eggs	2	2
Salt	¾ ounce	20 grams
White pepper	to taste	to taste
Pâté spice	pinch	pinch
Brandy	1 ounce	30 grams
Heavy cream	4 ounces	115 grams
Fatback, sliced thin	as needed	as needed

1. Grind 1 pound (450 grams) of the pork butt with the pork liver, onion, garlic, and parsley through the fine die of a grinder.

2. Grind the remainder of the pork butt through a coarse die. Combine the fine- and coarse-ground meats in a large bowl. Working over an ice bath, stir in the remainder of the ingredients, except the fatback, until they are just blended.

3. Use the fatback to line the desired mold. Bake in a waterbath at 325°F (160°C) to an internal temperature of 150°F (65°C).

Chicken Liver Gratin-style Forcemeat

Yield: approximately 2 pounds (900 grams)

Vegetable oil	as needed	as needed
Chicken livers, cleaned	10 ounces	285 grams
Onions, minced	4 ounces	115 grams
Shallots, minced	2 ounces	60 grams
Bay leaf	1	1
Thyme leaves, dried	1 teaspoon	2 grams
Salt	2 teaspoons	12 grams
Black pepper	¼ teaspoon	3 grams
Lean pork, cubed	10 ounces	285 grams
Pork fat, cubed	10 ounces	285 grams
Whole eggs	2	2
Curing salt (optional)	¼ teaspoon	3 grams

1. Heat a small amount of oil in a sauté pan. Add the livers, onions, shallots, bay leaf, thyme leaves, salt, and pepper. Cook the livers over low heat until they are done, but do not allow them to take on any color.

2. Refrigerate the liver mixture to chill it thoroughly.

3. Grind the liver mixture, lean pork, and pork fat through a coarse die, then again through a medium or fine die.

4. Place the ground meats in the chilled bowl of a food processor. Process them with the eggs and curing salt until a smooth paste is formed.

5. Make a test quenelle to check the forcemeat for consistency and seasoning. Make any necessary adjustments. Keep the forcemeat chilled until it is ready to use for various charcuterie and garde-manger items.

NOTE: A number of herbs and spices may be used to vary the flavor of this forcemeat, according to the discretion of the chef or the needs of a specific recipe.

5/4/3 Forcemeat

Yield: approximately 5¼ pounds (2.5 kilograms)

Pork butt (approximately 25 percent fat), diced	5 pounds	2.25 kilograms
Bratwurst seasoning (below)	2 ounces	55 grams
Ice, shaved	4 ounces	115 grams
Hog or sheep casing, rinsed well	as needed	as needed

Seasoning Mix (for 100 pounds of meat)

Salt	2 pounds	910 grams
White pepper, ground	6 ounces	170 grams
Celery seed, ground	½ ounce	15 grams
Mace, ground	½ ounce	15 grams
Sage, rubbed	1 ounce	30 grams

1. Season the meat with the spices. Mix well.

2. Grind the meat, using a fine die.

3. Place the ground meat in a food processor with a steel blade. Run the machine at low speed (or in pulses), adding the shaved ice. Process the meat until the ice is incorporated, about 20 seconds.

4. Stuff the mixture into the prepared hog or sheep casing. Tie the casing at 4-inch intervals with fine twine.

5. Poach the sausages in 170°F (75°C) water for about 30 minutes. Chill them in ice and water.

Seafood Sausage

Yield: 4 pounds (1.8 kilograms)

White bread, crust trimmed, diced	2½ ounces	70 grams
Egg whites	5	5
Heavy cream	1 pint	480 milliliters
Sole or pike, fillet, cubed and chilled	1½ pounds	680 grams
Ice, crushed	as needed	as needed
Salt	¼ ounce	7 grams
Paprika	½ teaspoon	1 gram
Coriander, ground	½ teaspoon	1 gram
Cayenne pepper	pinch	pinch

Garnish

Bay scallops	8 ounces	225 grams
Shrimp, peeled, deveined, and diced	8 ounces	225 grams
King crab meat, sea legs, or titi shrimp	8 ounces	225 grams
Pistachio nuts or truffles	¼ cup	60 grams
Parsley or chervil, chopped	1 tablespoon	2.5 grams
Pork casing	as needed	as needed

1. Combine the bread, egg whites, and 4 ounces of the heavy cream. Chill the mixture.

2. Place the fish in a food processor with a little ice (¼ cup) and puree it.

3. Add the bread and cream mixture to the fish and mix them well.

4. Add the salt and spices.

5. Gradually incorporate the rest of the heavy cream.

6. Poach a test quenelle to check the seasoning and binding.

7. Fold in the garnish ingredients and stuff the mixture into the pork casing. Tie off the casing into links with twine at 4- to 5-inch intervals.

8. Blanch the sausages in 170°F (75°C) water to an internal temperature of 150°F (65°C). Shock them in ice and refrigerate.

9. Cook the sausages, using the desired method (poach, sauté, grill, etc.).

Smoked Venison Sausage

<u>*Yield: 11 pounds (5 kilograms)*</u>

Venison, diced	7 pounds	3.18 kilograms
Fatback or jowl fat, diced	3 pounds	1.36 kilograms
White pepper, ground	1 tablespoon	7 grams
Ginger	1 teaspoon	2.5 grams
Nutmeg	1 teaspoon	2.5 grams
Curing salt	2 teaspoons	10 grams
Sugar	1 tablespoon	15 grams
Sage	1 teaspoon	2.5 grams
Salt	3½ ounces	100 grams
Water, cold	1 pint	480 milliliters
Sheep casing	as needed	as needed

1. Spread the meat over a sheet pan.
2. Sprinkle the spices over the meat. Incorporate them well.
3. Grind the meat, using a fine die.
4. Mix the meat with a mixer fitted with a paddle attachment for approximately 60 seconds. Add the water while mixing.
5. Stuff the meat into the sheep casing.
6. Tie the casing at 4½-inch intervals.
7. Cold-smoke the sausages to the desired golden color.
8. Cook the sausages, using the desired method.

Breakfast-style Sausage

<u>*Yield: 12 pounds (5.5 kilograms)*</u>

Pork butt, diced	10 pounds	4.5 kilograms
Jowl fat, frozen, diced	2 pounds	900 grams
Salt	⅛ ounce	3.75 grams
Poultry seasoning	pinch	pinch
Dextrose	1/16 ounce	1.5 grams
Ginger	pinch	pinch
Water, very cold	1 pint	480 milliliters
Sheep casing	as needed	as needed

1. Spread the meat and fat over a sheet pan.

2. Mix the spices in a bowl, then sprinkle them over the meat and fat. Incorporate them well.

3. Grind the meat and fat, using a fine die.

4. Mix the meat in a mixer fitted with a paddle attachment for approximately 60 seconds. Add the water while mixing.

5. Make a test patty, panfry it, and taste it to check the seasoning and consistency, which should be adjusted as necessary.

6. Stuff the mixture into the sheep casing.

7. Twist off the casing at approximately 4½-inch intervals.

8. Cook the sausages, using the desired method (panfry, bake, etc.).

Mexican Chorizo

Yield: 12 pounds (5.75 kilograms)

Pork, ground fine	2 pounds	910 grams
Pork, lean, ground coarse	6 pounds	2.72 kilograms
Jowl fat, ground fine	4 pounds	1.8 kilograms
Curing salt	½ ounce	14 grams
Onion powder	½ teaspoon	1 gram
Cumin, ground	8 teaspoons	19 grams
Spanish paprika	7 tablespoons	50 grams
Dextrose	⅔ ounce	30 grams
Cayenne pepper	2½ tablespoons	18 grams
Garlic powder	2 teaspoons	4.5 grams
Red peppers, crushed	1 teaspoon	2.5 grams
Vinegar	2½ ounces	75 milliliters
Milk, nonfat dry	3 ounces	21 grams
Water, cold	6 ounces	180 milliliters
Hog or sheep casing	as needed	as needed

1. Combine all of the ingredients except the water and casing. Mix them together in a mixer fitted with a paddle attachment. Add the water while mixing.

2. Stuff the mixture into the casing. Twist or tie off the casing at 3- to 4-inch intervals.

3. Cook the sausages, using the desired method.

Italian-style Sausage

<u>Yield</u>: *11 pounds (5 kilograms)*

Pork (approximately 25 percent fat, 75 percent lean)	10 pounds	4.5 kilograms
Black pepper, coarse-ground	1 ounce	30 grams
Salt	3 ounces	85 grams
Paprika	¼ ounce	7 grams
Fennel seeds, whole	1½ ounces	45 grams
Water, cold	1 pint	480 milliliters
Hog casing	as needed	as needed

1. Grind the meat, using a fine die.
2. Combine the meat and spices on a sheet pan. Mix them well, using the hands.
3. Mix the meat again, using a mixer fitted with a paddle attachment, for 30 seconds on slow speed. Add the water while mixing.
4. Mix the meat for 30 seconds more on fast speed.
5. Stuff the mixture into the hog casing.
6. Tie the casing at 4½-inch intervals.
7. Cook the sausages using the desired method.

Spicy French-style Apple Sausage

<u>Yield</u>: *5½ pounds (2.5 kilograms)*

Pork butt, chilled, diced	5 pounds	2.25 kilograms
Salt	1 tablespoon	17 grams
Pepper, fresh, ground	2 teaspoons	4.5 grams
Ginger	1 teaspoon	2.5 grams
Allspice	1 teaspoon	2.5 grams
Cloves, ground	1 teaspoon	2.5 grams
Apples, peeled, ⅛-inch dice	1 cup	125 grams
Chablis or other dry white wine	½ cup	120 milliliters
Sheep casing	as needed	as needed

1. Spread the meat over a sheet pan.
2. Mix the spices in a bowl, then sprinkle them over the meat. Incorporate them well.
3. Grind the meat, using a fine die.
4. Add the apples to the meat mixture and combine them with a mixer fitted with a paddle attachment until the mixture is well blended. Add the wine while mixing.
5. Make a test patty, panfry it, and taste it to check the seasoning and consistency, which should be adjusted as necessary.
6. Stuff the mixture into the sheep casing.
7. Twist off the casing at approximately 4-inch intervals.
8. Cook the sausages, using the desired method.

Greek Sausage (Loukanika)

Yield: 8 pounds (3.5 kilograms)

Pork (approximately 40 percent fat), diced	6 pounds	2.75 kilograms
Salt	2 tablespoons	35 grams
Black pepper, ground	2 teaspoons	4.5 grams
Cayenne pepper	½ teaspoon	1 gram
Chili pepper	½ teaspoon	1 gram
Oregano	2 teaspoons	2.5 grams
Thyme	1 teaspoon	1 gram
Allspice, ground	½ teaspoon	1 gram
Parsley, chopped	¼ cup	9 grams
Water, very cold	6 ounces	180 milliliters
Onion, chopped fine	12 ounces	340 grams
Bay leaves, chopped fine	2	2
Caul fat	1½ pounds	680 grams

1. Spread the meat over a sheet pan.
2. Mix the spices in a bowl; then sprinkle them over the meat. Incorporate them well.
3. Grind the meat, using a fine die.
4. Mix in a mixer fitted with a paddle attachment for approximately 60 seconds. Add the water while mixing.
5. Make a test patty and panfry it to check the seasoning.
6. Shape the meat into patties. Wrap the patties in caul fat.
7. Panfry, broil, or bake the patties until they are done.

Chicken and Herb Sausage

Yield: 12¼ pounds (5.75 kilograms)

Chicken, 1-inch dice	5 pounds	1 kilogram
Pork, 1-inch dice	5 pounds	1 kilogram
Salt	3 ounces	85 grams
Jowl fat, diced	1½ pounds	630 grams
Milk, ice cold	18 ounces	500 milliliters
Eggs, cold	7	7
Ginger, ground	½ teaspoon	5 grams
Mace, ground	⅛ teaspoon	1 gram
Cardamom, ground	⅛ teaspoon	1 gram
White pepper, ground	⅛ teaspoon	1 gram
Coriander, ground	⅛ teaspoon	1 gram
Chives, snipped	½ bunch	½ bunch
Parsley, fresh, chopped	½ ounce	15 grams
Lemon zest, grated	from ½ lemon	from ½ lemon
Hot or beef middle casing, rinsed	as needed	as needed

1. Sprinkle the salt over the chicken and pork; toss to coat evenly.
2. Grind the meat, using a medium die. Place it in a freezer.
3. Grind the jowl fat separately, using a medium die. Refrigerate it.
4. When the meat is semi-frozen, place it in a vertical chopping machine.
5. Run the machine for approximately 30 seconds.
6. Mix the eggs and milk. Incorporate them into the meat mixture.
7. Incorporate the fat.
8. Add the spices, herbs, and lemon zest.
9. Use the forcemeat to fill the casings. Twist or tie the filled casings into links.
10. Poach the sausages to an internal temperature of 160°F (70°C).

Andouille Sausage

Yield: 30 pounds (13.5 kilograms)

Pork butt, boned and cubed	25 pounds	11.3 kilograms
Cayenne pepper	2½ ounces	70 grams
Salt	6¼ ounces	175 grams
Curing salt	1¼ teaspoons	7 grams
Thyme, ground	5 teaspoons	6 grams
Mace, ground	1¼ teaspoons	3 grams
Cloves, ground	1¼ teaspoons	3 grams
Allspice, ground	1¼ teaspoons	3 grams
Marjoram	5 teaspoons	6 grams
Onion, chopped	5 pounds	2.25 kilograms
Garlic, minced	5 ounces	140 grams
Sheep casing, rinsed	as needed	as needed

1. Spread the meat over a sheet pan.
2. Mix the spices in a bowl; then sprinkle them over the meat. Incorporate them well.
3. Grind the meat, onions, and garlic using a fine die.
4. Stuff the meat into the sheep casing. Tie or twist it off at 8-inch intervals.
5. Cold-smoke the sausages for 12 to 14 hours.
6. Cook them using the desired method.

Duck Sausage

Yield: 10 pounds (4.5 kilograms)

Shallots, chopped fine	8 ounces	225 grams
Butter	1 ounce	30 grams
Garlic, minced	1 ounce	30 grams
Red wine	24 ounces	720 grams
Duck meat	6 pounds	2.75 kilograms
Fatback	3 pounds	1.36 kilograms
Thyme, fresh, chopped	1 teaspoon	1 gram
Sage, fresh, chopped	2 tablespoons	4 grams
Parsley, fresh, chopped	4 tablespoons	9 grams
Black pepper, coarse ground	1 tablespoon	7 grams
Curing salt	⅜ ounce	10 grams
Salt	2 ounces	60 grams
Dextrose	¾ ounce	20 grams
Sheep casing	as needed	as needed

1. Sauté the shallots in the butter.

2. Add the garlic and red wine; reduce it to sec.

3. Grind the meat and fatback, using a fine die.

4. Combine the meat, fat, shallot/garlic mixture, and spices, and mix them together thoroughly.

5. Stuff the mixture into the sheep casing. Twist or tie it off at 4- to 5-inch intervals.

6. Smoke the sausages lightly.

7. Poach the sausages to an internal temperature of 160°F (70°C).

Garden Terrine St. Andrew's

Yield: 2 terrines

Chicken breast, skinless, boneless, ground	1 pound	455 grams
Egg whites	¼ cup	70 grams
Heavy cream	1 cup	240 milliliters
Salt	1 teaspoon	5.5 grams
Dill, chopped	1 tablespoon	2 grams
Tarragon, chopped	1 tablespoon	2 grams
Basil, chopped	1 tablespoon	2 grams
White pepper, ground	¼ teaspoon	500 milligrams
Carrots, sliced	1 pound	455 grams
Zucchini, de-seeded, natural cut	8 ounces	225 grams
Artichoke bottoms, small pie cuts	8 ounces	225 grams
Shiitake mushrooms, batonnet	8 ounces	225 grams
Red peppers, julienne	1 pound	455 grams
Spinach, deribbed	1 pound	455 grams

1. Place the ground chicken meat, along with the egg whites, in the well-chilled bowl of a food processor. Process them to a fine paste.

2. Add the heavy cream, salt, dill, tarragon, basil, and pepper; process using quick on-off pulses until the ingredients are *just* incorporated. Do not overprocess it. Place the mixture in a bowl and hold it under refrigeration until the vegetables are prepared.

3. Line several baking sheets or large trays with several layers of absorbent toweling.

4. Steam the vegetables until they are tender and cooked through. Place them on lined sheet trays, spread out so that they will cool and the toweling can absorb any excess moisture.

5. Chop the cooled and dried spinach leaves coarsely. Fold all the vegetables gently into the mousseline.

6. Line 2 terrine molds with plastic wrap. Divide the terrine mixture evenly between the two molds. Cover the molds with additional plastic wrap and place them in a prepared bain-marie.

7. Cook the terrines in the bain-marie in a preheated 275°F (135°C) oven to an internal temperature of 140°F (60°C). Remove them from the water bath, and remove the plastic wrap covering. Cool them to room temperature, then refrigerate them overnight before serving.

NOTE: This dish is a reworking of a classic recipe in order to reduce overall calories, fat, cholesterol, and sodium.

Country-style Duck Terrine

Yield: 4 pounds (1.75 kilograms)

Garnish

Duck breast, large dice	½ pound	225 grams
Salt	to taste	to taste
Pepper	to taste	to taste
Curing salt	pinch	pinch
Brandy	3 ounces	90 milliliters
Onion, diced	4 ounces	115 grams
Garlic, chopped	½ tablespoon	5 grams
Butter	1 ounce	30 grams
Tarragon, chopped	1½ tablespoons	4 grams
Parsley, chopped	1½ tablespoons	4 grams
Basil, chopped	1½ tablespoons	4 grams
Fatback, cubed	12 ounces	340 grams
Pork, cubed	8 ounces	225 grams
Duck leg, cubed	1 pound	455 grams
Duck livers or foie gras	8 ounces	225 grams
Salt	1½ tablespoons	25 grams
Curing salt	1¼ teaspoons	7 grams
Pepper, freshly ground	½ teaspoon	1 gram
Egg	1	1
Parsley, chopped	½ cup	18 grams
Pistachios, peeled and chopped coarse	½ cup	120 grams

1. Season the duck breast with the salt, pepper, and curing salt; marinate it in 3 ounces of the brandy and reserve it.

2. Sauté the onion and garlic in the butter. Cool the mixture.

3. Add the herbs and fatback, then freeze the mixture until the fatback is very cold and slightly firmed.

4. Combine the fatback mixture with the pork, duck leg meat, livers, remaining brandy, salt, curing salt, and pepper. Grind the mixture, using a medium die.

5. Combine one-third of the meat mixture with the egg in a food processor. Process it to a smooth consistency.

6. Poach a test quenelle to check the seasoning and binding.

7. Fold in the parsley, pistachios, and marinated duck breast meat.

8. Pack the mixture into a terrine mold that has been coated with barding fat or lined with plastic wrap.

9. Place the terrine in a 140°F (60°C) bain-marie. Bake it in a 250°F (121°C) oven to an internal temperature of 140°F (60°C).

VARIATIONS

Rabbit Terrine: Add 5 mashed and minced juniper berries to the herb mixture. Substitute rabbit leg for the duck. Substitute gin for the brandy. Substitute a rabbit loin and 1 tablespoon (7 grams) of butcher's pepper for the garnish of diced duck breast.

Artichoke Terrine: Double the herb mixture. Substitute chicken livers for the duck. Add an inlay of 10 cooked artichokes. Substitute artichokes in a ½-inch dice for the duck breast garnish.

Venison Terrine: Add 5 mashed and minced juniper berries and the blanched zest of 1½ oranges to the herb mixture. Substitute venison trim for the duck leg. Substitute chestnuts for pistachios. Substitute venison loin for duck breast garnish. Add 1 cup (240 milliliters) of chopped dried fruits.

Galantine of Foie Gras

Yield: 2 pounds (1 kilogram)

Duck livers	1¾ pounds	795 grams
Salt	1 tablespoon	17 grams
Sugar	1 teaspoon	4.5 grams
White pepper	1 teaspoon	2.5 grams
Port	2 ounces	60 milliliters
Armagnac	2 ounces	60 milliliters
Caul fat	as needed	as needed
Chicken stock	1 gallon	3.75 liters
Tarragon stems	4	4

(continued)

1. Soak the livers in cold water for 1 hour.

2. Add warm water to soften the livers.

3. Separate the lobes and carefully split them, removing all the veins.

4. Place the livers in a bowl and add the salt, sugar, pepper, and liquors. Marinate for 12 hours under refrigeration. Turn them after 6 hours.

5. Bring the livers to room temperature; pour off the marinade.

6. Roll the livers in the caul fat into a 2- to 3-inch-diameter galantine. Roll the galantine in cheesecloth and tie it.

7. Add the tarragon stems to the stock. Bring the stock to 160°F (70°C). Add the galantine.

8. Poach the galantine for 20 minutes.

9. Place the entire poaching pan in an ice bath and cool it.

10. Let the galantine rest, refrigerated, for 24 hours before slicing it.

Chicken Galantine

Yield: 5 pounds (2.25 kilograms)

Panada

Eggs	2	2
Brandy	2 to 3 tablespoons	30 to 45 milliliters
Pâté spice	1 teaspoon	2.5 grams
Flour	3 ounces	85 grams
Salt	1 tablespoon	17 grams
White pepper	½ teaspoon	1 gram
Heavy cream	1 cup	240 milliliters
Chicken, boned, wing tips removed, skin removed intact	one, about 3 pounds	one, about 1.36 kilograms
Pork butt, 1-inch cubes, chilled	2 pounds	910 grams
Madeira	6 ounces	180 milliliters
Ham (or cooked tongue), ¼-inch cubes	½ cup	120 milliliters
Truffles or trufflettes, chopped fine	2 tablespoons	30 grams
Pistachio nuts, shelled, poached, peeled, chopped coarse	½ cup	120 milliliters
Stock	as needed	as needed

1. Prepare the panada: Mix the eggs with all of the panada ingredients except the heavy cream.

2. Bring the heavy cream to a boil. Remove it from the heat.

3. Temper the egg mixture with the hot cream. Add the tempered egg mixture to the cream and cook it until it is thickened. Cool the mixture completely.

4. Weigh the leg and thigh meat from the chicken. Add an equal amount of pork butt, or enough for approximately 4 pounds of meat. Grind the chicken leg and thigh meat and pork twice, using a fine die.

5. Cut the chicken breast meat into ½- to ¾-inch cubes. Season it to taste. Marinate the meat in the Madeira under refrigeration.

6. Drain the chicken breast; add the Madeira and panada to the ground meat mixture. Blend well.

7. Fold in the ham, truffles, and pistachios. Mix well.

8. Gently fold in the reserved chicken breast meat.

9. Roll the galantine securely.

10. Poach the galantine, in enough simmering stock to cover it, to an internal temperature of 160°F (70°C).

11. Cool the galantine in the stock in the half hotel pan. Refrigerate it overnight. Remove the galantine from the stock and wrap it in new cheesecloth to firm its texture. To serve the galantine, unwrap and slice it.

NOTE: Refer to the recipe for Pâté Spice, later in this chapter.

Scallop Mousseline Timbales

Yield: 10 servings

Scallops, fresh, cleaned	1 pound	455 grams
Whole butter, diced, chilled	3 ounces	85 grams
Egg whites	3	3
Salt	to taste	to taste
Pepper	to taste	to taste
Nutmeg	to taste	to taste
Heavy cream, cold	12 ounces	360 milliliters
Fresh herbs (as available or desired)	1 cup	35 grams

1. Puree the scallops, butter, egg whites, salt, pepper, and nutmeg in a food processor just until a smooth paste forms.

2. Remove the paste from the bowl to a chilled bowl. Place it over an ice bath.

3. Incorporate the heavy cream and herbs, taking care not to overmix.

4. Place the mixture in buttered timbales and cover them with buttered parchment. Bake the timbales in a water bath until an internal temperature of 130 to 135°F (55 to 57°C) is reached. Remove them from the water bath.

VARIATIONS

Saffron Scallop Mousseline: Add 2 teaspoons (10 milliliters) of saffron extraction (steep the threads in white wine). Be sure to thoroughly chill the wine before adding it to the mousseline.

Seafood Mousseline: Add small dice of shellfish to the mixture before placing it in the timbales; a good ratio is approximately 4 ounces (115 grams) of garnish to one recipe.

Scallop Timbale Sampler with Saffron-cream Sauce

Yield: 10 servings

Saffron Cream

Fish fumet	8 ounces	240 milliliters
White wine	8 ounces	240 milliliters
Shallots	½ ounce	15 grams
Heavy cream, reduced	8 ounces	240 milliliters
Saffron, crushed	1 teaspoon	1.5 grams
Scallop mousseline (see the recipe in this chapter)	1 recipe	1 recipe
Fines herbes, chopped	⅓ ounce	9 grams
Tomato flesh, fine dice	2 ounces	55 grams
Shrimp, cooked, fine dice	2 ounces	55 grams

1. To make the saffron cream: Combine the fumet, wine, and shallots and reduce the mixture by half. Bring the heavy cream and saffron to a simmer; reduce them by half. Combine both reductions; simmer to nappé. Let the mixture cool.

2. Divide the basic mousseline mixture into three equal parts. Add the fines herbes to one portion; add the tomato and shrimp to the second; add 1 ounce (30 milliliters) of saffron cream to the third.

3. Layer each flavor of scallop mousseline in 10 small timbales.

4. Cover the timbales with buttered parchment and bake them in a water bath until a skewer inserted near the center of a serving comes out clean.

5. To serve, pool heated saffron cream on heated plates. Unmold one of each type of mousseline onto each plate. Garnish with asparagus tips and morels if desired.

Tripe à la Mode de Caën

Yield: 6 *pounds* (2.75 *kilograms*)

Onions, chopped coarse	1 pound	455 grams
Carrots, diced	1 pound	455 grams
Leeks, white only, sliced thin	2	2
Butter	4 ounces	115 grams
Tripe, blanched, cut into 1½-inch squares	5½ pounds	2.5 kilograms
Salt	to taste	to taste

Bouquet Garni

Parsley	5 ounces	140 grams
Thyme, fresh	1 sprig	1 sprig

Sachet d'Épices

Peppercorns, crushed	10	10
Garlic cloves, crushed	3	3
Bay leaf	1	1

Hard cider or dry white wine	1 ounce	30 milliliters
Veal stock	as needed	as needed
Calf's feet, cut in 4 pieces	2	2
Applejack	2 jiggers	2 jiggers

1. Sweat the onions, carrots, and leeks in the butter for 5 minutes.
2. Add the tripe, salt, bouquet garni, sachet d'épices, cider, and 1 to 1½ pints of stock. Bring the stock to a boil and cook it over direct heat.
3. Cover the pot and cook it in a 350°F (175°C) oven for 10 hours. Check it periodically and add more liquid if necessary.
4. Remove the bouquet garni and sachet d'épices.
5. Drain the tripe; reserve the liquid.
6. Reduce the liquid by one-third.
7. Bone the calf's feet. Dice the meat and add it, with the tripe, to the reduced liquid.
8. Adjust the seasoning to taste.
9. Finish with the applejack.

NOTE: This dish is typically served hot with boiled potatoes.

Cold Beef Daube

Yield: 6 pounds (2.7 kilograms)

Oxtail, cut into 4 pieces	1	1
Beef tongue	1	1
Pig's head or short ribs	½ or 5 pounds	½ or 2.25 kilograms
Beef stock	2 gallons	7.5 liters

Sachet d'Épices

Leek tops	1 pound	455 grams
Mirepoix	1 pound	455 grams
Juniper berries, cracked	10	10
Garlic heads	4	4
Bay leaf	3	3
Thyme	4 sprigs	4 sprigs
Mushroom stems	6 ounces	170 grams
Peppercorns	12	12
Parsley stems	16	16
Parsley, chopped	½ cup	16 grams
Shallots, chopped	½ cup	16 grams
Chives, chopped	½ cup	16 grams

1. Combine all of the ingredients (preparing the sachet d'épices separately) and simmer them for 2 hours. Remove the tongue and simmer for 2 more hours.

2. Remove all of the ingredients from the stock. Reserve the meats.

3. Reduce the stock to ½ gallon. Adjust the seasoning to taste and strain the stock.

4. Julienne the tongue. Dice the tail and head meat.

5. Return all the meat to the stock. Bring the liquid to a boil.

6. Pour the daube into prepared molds. Refrigerate it for 24 hours before slicing it.

Gravad Lox

Yield: Two salmon fillets

Kosher salt	7 ounces	200 grams
Brown sugar	1 pound	455 grams
Peppercorns, white, cracked	¾ ounce	20 grams
Dill, freshly chopped	2 bunches	2 bunches
Lemon juice	juice of 2	juice of 2
Olive oil	1 ounce	30 grams
Brandy	¾ ounce	15 milliliters
Salmon fillets	2	2

1. Combine the salt, sugar, peppercorns, and dill to make the dry cure.
2. Combine the lemon juice, olive oil, and brandy. Brush this mixture on the salmon fillets.
3. Pack the cure evenly on the salmon fillets and wrap them tightly.
4. Place the wrapped fillets in a pan and weight them. Refrigerate and let the salmon marinate for 2 to 3 days.
5. Unwrap the salmon and scrape off the cure.
6. Slice the salmon thinly on the bias to serve it.

Cooked Brine

Yield: 1 gallon (3.75 liters)

Water	1 gallon	3.75 liters
Salt	1 pound	455 grams
Curing salt	3 ounces	85 grams
Dextrose	30 ounces	850 grams
Sachet d'épices, including pickling spice	1	1

1. Combine all of the ingredients.
2. Boil the liquid for approximately 3 minutes.
3. Cool the brine and chill it before using it.

Liquid Brine for Pork, Chicken, and Tuna

Yield: 1 gallon (3.75 liters)

Water	1 gallon	3.75 liters
Kosher salt	½ pound	225 grams
Curing salt	1 ounce	30 grams
Sugar	½ cup	110 grams
Pickling spice	2 tablespoons	15 grams
Garlic cloves, crushed	3	3

1. Combine all of the ingredients.

2. Boil, cool, and strain the brine. Refrigerate it until it is needed.

Pâté Dough

Yield: 4 pounds (1.8 kilograms)

Bread flour, sifted	2½ pounds	1.15 kilograms
Powdered milk (optional)	2½ ounces	70 grams
Baking powder	½ ounce	15 grams
Salt	1 ounce	28 grams
Shortening	7 ounces	200 grams
Butter	5 ounces	150 grams
Water	9 ounces	255 grams
Eggs	3	3
Lemon juice or vinegar	1 ounce	30 grams

1. Combine the flour, powdered milk, baking powder, and salt in a food processor. Mix the ingredients well, until the mixture resembles a coarse meal.

2. Transfer the mixture to a mixer bowl. Incorporate the shortening, butter, water, eggs, and lemon juice with a dough hook. If the dough seems too dry, add up to 1 ounce (30 grams) of additional water.

3. Let the dough rest for 1 hour before rolling it out.

NOTE: The flavor of this dough can be varied by adding ground spices and herbs, lemon zest, or grated cheese. Rye or whole wheat flour, or cornmeal, may be used to replace up to ⅓ of the bread flour for a different flavor, texture, and appearance.

Pâté Spice

Yield: 14¾ ounces (425 grams)

White peppercorns	1½ ounces	45 grams
Coriander, ground	3 ounces	85 grams
Thyme	1¾ ounces	50 grams
Basil	1¾ ounces	50 grams
Cloves	3 ounces	85 grams
Nutmeg	1½ ounces	45 grams
Bay leaf	½ ounce	15 grams
Mace	¾ ounce	20 grams
Cèpes (mushrooms), dry	1 ounce	30 grams

Combine all of the ingredients and grind them, using a mortar or blender.

Country-style Pâté Spice

Yield: 4½ ounces (133 grams)

Green peppercorns, dry	1½ ounces	45 grams
Pimientos, dry	⅓ ounce	9 grams
Mace	⅓ ounce	9 grams
Hungarian paprika	¾ ounce	20 grams
Coriander, ground	⅓ ounce	9 grams
Thyme	⅓ ounce	9 grams
Rosemary	¼ ounce	7 grams
Basil	⅓ ounce	9 grams
Marjoram	⅛ ounce	3.5 grams
Cloves	⅛ ounce	3.5 grams
Bay leaf	⅓ ounce	9 grams

Combine all of the ingredients and grind them, using a mortar or blender.

Aspic Gelée

Yield: 10 quarts (9.5 liters)

Small veal bones	9 pounds	4 kilograms
Small beef bones	2 pounds	900 grams
Calves' feet, split	4	4
Pork skin	10 ounces	285 grams
Water, cold	10 quarts	9.5 liters
Salt	¾ ounce	20 grams
Carrots, large dice	7 ounces	200 grams
Onions, large dice	7 ounces	200 grams
Leeks, white part only, large dice	7 ounces	200 grams
Celery	4 ounces	115 grams
Bouquet garni	1	1

1. Combine the veal and beef bones, calves' feet, pork skin, water, and salt. Bring to a boil and skim. Simmer for at least 10 hours, skimming often.

2. Brown the carrots, onions, leeks, and celery lightly in the oven or over direct heat. Add the vegetables to the simmering bones along with the bouquet garni and simmer for an additional 2 hours.

3. Strain the aspic carefully through a cheesecloth and chill. Check the strength of the gelatin after the stock is completely cooled. Remove all fat from the aspic before using.

4. Add additional gelatin to the stock in the ratio of ½ to 1 ounce (15 to 30 grams) per quart of stock.

NOTE: Before adding additional gelatin, check this aspic gelée carefully to see if it will coat or slice as desired.

GELATIN-TO-STOCK RATIOS FOR ASPIC GELÉE

Delicate Gel: Add 2 ounces of gelatin per gallon of stock (for binding individual portions of food that will not be sliced).

Coating Gel: Add 4 ounces of gelatin per gallon of stock (for edible coatings on charcuterie and garde-manger items, known as "chaud froid").

Sliceable Gel: Add 8 ounces of gelatin per gallon of stock (for molding food in a loaf to be sliced; for example, chilled daubes).

Hard Gel: Add 12 ounces of gelatin per gallon of stock (an underlayer for show items; not intended to be eaten).

Part Nine

Baking and
Pastry

Although baking and pastry can be a specialization in itself, every chef must learn basic procedures and be able to produce, on a regular basis, items such as pie crust, puff pastry, and simple, pleasing desserts.

This section begins with a chapter on baking mise en place, basic information on ingredients, chemical processes, and specific equipment. The importance of accurate ingredient measurement, known as scaling, is stressed.

An attempt has been made here to select techniques of general and basic importance. As in all the techniques in this book, the emphasis is on learning the basic method that will allow the chef to create a variety of products according to individual recipes.

Freshly baked breads and desserts make a good and lasting impression on the guests and contribute significantly to an operation's success.

Chapter 29

Baking Mise en Place

Before covering specific types of baking for such items as yeast doughs, batters, and pastry dough, several basic bakeshop procedures and techniques need to be explained. The function of various ingredients and how they will affect the finished product by giving it a tender "crumb," a well-developed crust, or a very light texture are examined in this chapter. Also included are the six basic functions of ingredients and the techniques of measuring (known as scaling), proper pan preparation, sifting, tempering chocolate, and working a pastry bag. The chef should always bear in mind that baking is a science that is dependent upon exact measurements and the proper handling of ingredients and tools in order to assure the same results consistently.

BASIC INGREDIENTS

Although baking is not a difficult process, understanding the role that a given ingredient will play in the finished product is helpful. Baking ingredients will generally fall into six basic categories of function:

- strengtheners, such as flour and eggs
- shorteners, such as butters and oils
- sweeteners, including a variety of sugars and syrups
- chemical and organic leaveners
- thickeners, such as cornstarch, flour, and eggs
- a number of different flavorings

As this partial list demonstrates, one ingredient may fulfill a number of different functions; for example, eggs and flour can each be found as both a strengthener and a thickener.

Strengtheners

Strengtheners provide stability, ensuring that the baked good does not collapse once it is removed from the oven. For most baked items, the major strengthener is flour, often referred to as the "backbone" of baked goods because it provides the structure or framework.

Flour functions as a strengthener because of its proteins and starches. One of flour's proteins, gluten, is especially important in the production of yeast breads. Gluten develops into long, elastic strands during the mixing and kneading process. Because it is able to stretch without breaking, it traps the gases that result when yeast ferments in the dough, producing a light, even texture in the finished product. The protein in eggs allows them to serve as a strengthener as well. Eggs are used in this way for cakes, such as genoise, angel food, and chiffon, made by the foaming method.

Starches are also important to many baked goods' overall structure. The starch granules first swell in the presence of liquid. Then, as they are heated, they swell even more, trapping liquid or steam within their expanded frame. As heat continues to set the starch into a stable structure, texture is also affected.

Shorteners

Shorteners make baked goods tender and moist. This occurs when the shortener (butter, oil, hydrogenated shortening, or lard) is incorporated into the batter.

The fat tends to surround the flour and other ingredients, breaking the long strands of batter or dough into shorter units—hence the term "shorteners."

The more thoroughly incorporated the fat is, the more it will affect the item's overall texture. Fats that are rubbed or rolled into doughs tend to separate the dough into large layers, creating a flaky texture. When the fat is thoroughly creamed together with sugar so that it can be mixed evenly throughout the batter, the resulting item's texture will be more cake-like.

Fat also helps to retain moisture in the finished product. In addition to the fats and oils commonly considered shorteners, egg yolks, cream, and milk may also fall into this category because they contain a relatively high percentage of fat.

Sweeteners

Sweeteners (sugars, syrups, honey, and molasses) perform other functions in addition to providing flavor. Sugars in any form tend to attract moisture, so baked goods containing sweeteners generally are more moist and tender than unsweetened products. In addition, whether the sugar is simply one present in flour or milk or an added sugar, its presence is required to make yeast function properly.

The caramelization of sugar is responsible for the appealing brown color on the surface of many baked products. Heat applied to the sugar causes this browning reaction. Besides affecting the color, caramelization also gives a product a deep, rich, and complex flavor. An obvious example is the difference in taste between simple syrup, made by dissolving a sugar in water, and a caramel syrup.

Leaveners

Leaveners produce a desirable texture by introducing gas (in this case, carbon dioxide) into the batter or dough. The gas stretches the dough and creates small pockets. There are three types of leaveners: chemical, organic, and physical.

Chemical Leaveners

Baking soda and baking powder are the primary chemical leaveners. In these leaveners, an alkaline ingredient (baking soda or baking powder) interacts with an acid (already present in baking powder, or an ingredient such as buttermilk, sour cream, yogurt, or chocolate). The alkalies and acids produce a gas, carbon dioxide, when combined in the presence of liquid.

As the item is baked, this gas expands, giving the baked goods their characteristic texture, known as "crumb." This process of expansion happens rapidly; hence, many items prepared with chemical leaveners are called "quick breads."

Double-acting baking powder is so-called because a first action occurs in the presence of moisture in the batter and a second action is initiated by the presence of heat. That is, it reacts once when it is mixed with the batter's liquids and again when the batter is placed in a hot oven.

Organic Leaveners

Organic leaveners, or yeasts, are living organisms that feed on sugars, producing alcohol and carbon dioxide. Unlike chemical leaveners, organic leaveners take a substantial amount of time to do their job. The yeast has to grow and reproduce sufficiently to fill the dough with air pockets. For this to take place, the temperature must be controlled carefully. Yeast will not function well below approximately 65 to 70°F (18 to 21°C), and above 110°F (43°C), yeast is destroyed.

Physical Leaveners

The basic physical leavener is steam, which is produced when liquids in a batter or dough are heated. This causes the air pockets to expand. Steam leavening is critical in sponge cakes and soufflés. It also plays a vital role in the production of puff pastry, croissant, and Danish. In the latter, the steam is trapped, causing the layers to separate and rise.

Thickeners

Sauces and puddings can be thickened by using various ingredients, including eggs, gelatin, and starches such as flour, cornstarch, or arrowroot. These thickeners may be used to lightly thicken a mixture, as for a sauce, or to produce an item that is firmly set, such as a Bavarian cream.

The quantity and type of thickener, as well as the amount of stirring or other manipulation, will determine the finished product's properties. For example, if a custard is cooked over direct heat and stirred constantly, the result will be a sauce that pours easily. The same custard cooked in a bain-marie with no stirring at all will set into a firm custard that can be sliced.

Uses

Arrowroot and cornstarch are generally preferred for thickening sauces, puddings, and fillings where a translucent effect is desired. If these thickeners are to be diluted before incorporation with other ingredients, they should be mixed with a small amount of a cool liquid.

Flour is commonly used to thicken items such as *crème pâtisserie*. In order to prevent lumping, the flour and sugar are often stirred together before they are combined with the liquid. Flour-thickened sauces are also often additionally thickened and enriched with eggs. The eggs must be tempered to prevent the sauce from curdling.

Eggs (whole eggs or yolks) may be used either alone or in conjunction with other thickeners. As the egg proteins begin to coagulate, the liquid becomes trapped in the network of set proteins, producing a "nappé" texture, in which the sauce will coat the back of a spoon when the spoon is dipped into the sauce and withdrawn.

Gelatin, when added in the desired amount, can produce light, delicate foams (Bavarian creams, mousses, and stabilized whipped cream, for example) that are firmly set. Such foams will retain a mold's shape and can be sliced. Gelatin is an animal protein found in bones. (It is this protein that causes stock to gel as it cools.) Gelatin powder or sheets are frequently used for a variety of bakeshop items. Before use, gelatin must first be softened (also known as "bloomed") in a cool liquid. Once the gelatin has absorbed the liquid, it is then gently heated to melt the crystals. This is accomplished either by adding the softened gelatin to a hot mixture, such as a hot custard sauce, or by gently heating the gelatin over simmering water.

Flavorings

Flavoring ingredients can range from extracts and essences to chocolate chips and chopped nuts. Dried fruits and fruit purees can also be considered flavorings. In general, flavoring ingredients do not have a great impact on the characteristics of the batter or dough as it is mixed, shaped, and baked. They are not, therefore, covered in detail in this chapter. Specific recipes throughout the book indicate appropriate flavorings.

PREPARATION, COOLING, AND STORING

Scaling

Careful measuring, known as scaling, is more important in baking than in other types of cookery. The most accurate way to measure ingredients is to weigh them. Even liquid ingredients are often, though not always, weighed.

Various scales may be used in the bakeshop, including balance-beam, spring-type, or electronic scales (for descriptions and illustrations, see Chapter 5, "Equipment Identification"). Other measuring tools, including volume measures and measuring spoons, are also required.

Once the batter or dough is mixed, it is scaled once more, to ensure that the proper amount is used for the pan size. Not only does this contribute to the uniformity of products, but it also decreases the possibilities of uneven rising or browning caused by too much or too little dough in the pan.

Sifting Dry Ingredients

Dry ingredients used for most baked goods should be sifted before they are incorporated into the dough or batter. Sifting aerates flour and confectioners' sugar, removing lumps and filtering out any impurities. Leavening ingredients and some flavoring ingredients (cocoa powder, for example) are more evenly distributed after sifting.

Sifting should take place after the ingredients have been properly scaled. They are passed through a sifter onto a sheet of parchment paper. The paper can then be rolled into a cone, making it easier to add the dry ingredients to the batter or dough.

Preparing Pans

A variety of pans are used in the bakeshop. The correct shape and size are important to ensure that the baked item's texture and appearance are correct. If the pan is too large, the item may not rise properly during baking and the edges may quickly become overbaked. Conversely, a pan that is too small will result in items that may not be properly baked through; their appearance will also suffer.

Delicate batters, especially those for sponge cakes, jelly rolls, or cookies that include a high proportion of eggs, sugar, and butter, are baked in pans that have been liberally greased (usually with a hydrogenated shortening or a blend of shortening and flour), lined with parchment paper, and then greased again and dusted with flour.

To coat a pan with flour, shake a handful of flour into the pan and spread it around to coat all surfaces. To release the excess flour and shake it out, rap the pan sharply on a work surface.

Lean doughs, such as pizza dough, hard rolls, and French and Italian breads, are baked in pans that are dusted only with cornmeal. The cornmeal very slightly elevates the dough so that a good crust can form on all surfaces.

Angel food cakes are baked in ungreased tube pans. An exception to the general rule of greasing pans, this is critical in producing tall cakes. The batter must be able to adhere to the pan sides in order to give the cake stability until it is fully baked and cooled.

Selecting and Preparing Ovens

The success of many baked goods depends on baking them at the right temperature and in the appropriate oven. In all cases, the oven should be fully preheated to the correct temperature. A variety of ovens are described in Chapter 5, "Equipment Identification."

Items that will rise during baking, such as vol-au-vents made from puff pastry or éclairs made from pâte à choux, should be prepared in standard ovens. The oven must not be overloaded because the air will not be able to circulate evenly in a crowded space. For even baking and browning in a conventional oven, the racks should be inserted in the oven's center.

Some cakes, muffins, and cookies may be baked in a convection oven, the advantage being that larger batches may be baked in a single load. The forced movement of air allows each item to bake evenly.

Cooling

Once the baked item is completely cooked, it should be removed from the oven and, in most cases, allowed to cool briefly in the baking pan. The item then should be removed from the pan and allowed to cool completely on racks. Placing the item on racks allows air to circulate readily around all surfaces and prevents steam from condensing on the item. Any added moisture could adversely affect the texture.

Storing

Once properly cooled, baked goods can be either served immediately or stored in various ways, depending upon the product. Breads may be stored or sliced. They can be held for a short time on parchment-lined trays or in baskets. For longer storage, items should be wrapped well in plastic wrap. Most items made from yeast doughs can be successfully frozen for longer storage. After thawing, they should be refreshed by reheating before service.

Although the major advantage of baking items fresh is that preservatives are unnecessary, it should be noted that some items will become stale rapidly, especially those made from lean doughs (hard rolls, Italian bread). Reheating these breads before service will refresh them. Microwave ovens, however, are not recommended for this purpose, because they can cause the product to become tough and rubbery. (Richer doughs—Danish, muffins, and some cakes—are not as adversely affected and may be successfully reheated in a microwave.)

Cakes are often prepared in advance and frozen. Ideally, they should not be filled and frosted until just before service, because most frostings and fillings do not stand up well after freezing and thawing. Baked goods thaw rapidly at room temperature. They should always be checked for a good, fresh flavor before they are served. Simple syrup is often brushed on a cake's surface to refresh the flavor and add moisture.

SPECIAL INGREDIENTS AND TOOLS

Fondant and Other Glazes

Fondant is basically a sugar-and-water syrup that has been cooked to the correct temperature, cooled, and worked repeatedly until it is smooth, creamy, opaque, and thick. Although it is made in some bakeshops, good-quality fondant can be purchased from purveyors in quantity.

Fondant may be either rolled into sheets and molded onto the cake or torte or heated and used as a glaze. For the latter use, fondant must be heated to approximately 105°F (40°C) and poured evenly over the product. The product may also be dipped into the fondant. In any form, the fondant provides a protective coating that is especially beneficial for cakes that need to be held or that could dry out easily—petits fours, for example.

Glazes made from preserves or jellies are often brushed onto fresh fruit tarts or tartlets to give the fruit a sheen. The glazes also help to prevent the darkening of fruits that might discolor in the presence of air. The jelly or preserves should be heated gently to a liquid state, and then strained if necessary to remove seeds or fibers. The glaze should be applied lightly with a pastry brush.

Tempered Chocolate

Chocolate contains two distinct types of fat, which melt at different temperatures. In order to ensure that the chocolate will melt smoothly and harden evenly with a good shine, it must be carefully melted in a process known as "tempering." Tempered chocolate is used as a glaze or to prepare decorations.

Method

1. Chop the chocolate coarsely with a chef's knife and place it in a stainless-steel bowl. Place the bowl over very low heat or barely simmering water, making sure that no moisture comes in contact with the chocolate. Stir the chocolate occasionally as it melts to keep it at an even temperature throughout.

2. Continue to heat the chocolate until it reaches a temperature of between 105 to 110°F (40 to 43°C). Use an instant-reading thermometer for the most accurate results.

3. Remove the chocolate from the heat. Add a large piece of chocolate and stir it in until the temperature drops to approximately 87 to 92°F (30 to 33°C). If the chocolate drops below 85°F (29°C) while working with it, it will be necessary to repeat the steps described here to retemper it. If the chocolate scorches or becomes grainy, it can no longer be used. If any moisture comes in contact with the chocolate as it is being tempered, it will "seize." The method for tempering chocolate is illustrated in Figure 29-1.

Working with Tempered Chocolate

Tempered chocolate will coat items with an even layer and then harden into a shiny shell. The item can be either dipped directly into the tempered chocolate with a dipping fork, or placed on a rack over a clean sheet tray and the chocolate poured over it.

Another way to work with tempered chocolate is to pour it onto a marble slab and work it with a spatula until it begins to lose its glossy appearance. Just before it hardens, it can be combed and then cut with sharp cutters or knives to create decorative shapes.

A third alternative is to make a parchment cone and pipe out designs, either using a stencil or piping directly onto a pastry. See the next section on preparing parchment cones.

29-1 TEMPERING CHOCOLATE

(1) Melting coarsely chopped chocolate.

(2) Heating the chocolate.

(3) Cooling the chocolate.

Parchment Cones

Parchment cones are used to decorate pastries with delicate designs of chocolate, fondant, or special piping gels. The proper method for preparing a cone and making a design using a stencil is shown in Figure 29-2.

Method

1. Fold a sheet of parchment paper on the diagonal, slightly overlapping. Do not form a perfect triangle (see step 1 of Fig. 29-2).

2. Hold the uneven corner between the thumb and forefinger of one hand. Use the other thumb and forefinger to make a "pivot point" by holding the parchment at the diagonal's midpoint (see step 2 of Fig. 29-2).

3. Roll the parchment into a funnel shape, keeping the point closed as the paper is rolled. This may require some practice. It is important to keep the paper taut as it is rolled.

4. When the entire triangle has been rolled into a cone, there will be three points at the cone's top. Fold the point on the outside so that it is on the interior of the cone (see step 4 of Fig. 29-2).

5. Hold the cone so that the tip is pointing downward, and fill the cone slightly more than half full. Do not add too much, or it will ooze out of the top. Fold the outer points in toward the cone's center and fold the last corner over the top of the other points, sealing the cone completely.

6. Hold the cone so that the tip is resting on a cutting surface and use a sharp knife to nick away a

small amount of the paper, creating a small opening. The deeper the cut, the larger the opening and, therefore, the lines of piping will be.

7. Secure a stencil to the back of a sheet pan, near the center of the pan. Position a parchment sheet over the stencil so that it can be used as a guide for piping the chocolate. The parchment can then be easily slid to a clean spot once the initial design is completed, until the desired amount of designs have been traced onto the sheet. Use the fingers to gently pinch the top of the cone, expressing the chocolate out through the tip. Use the fingertips of the other hand to steady the cone.

Pastry Bags and Tips

Pastry bags are important throughout the kitchen for a number of different applications. The photographs in Figures 29-3 through 29-5 show how to properly fill, use, and care for a bag, as well as a sample of the various effects that can be created with a few frequently used tips.

Filling and Using

1. Select the desired tip and position it securely in the pastry bag's opening or a coupler.

2. Fold down the bag's top to create a cuff, then transfer the buttercream or other preparation to the bag with a spatula or spoon. Support the bag with the free hand while filling it.

3. Unfold the bag's cuff, and use one hand to gather together and twist the top of the bag. Press on the bag first to expel any air pockets. Once these

(1) Cutting a parchment sheet.

(2) Position for the hands to begin the rolling.

(3) Rolling the cone.

(4) Folding in one of the points.

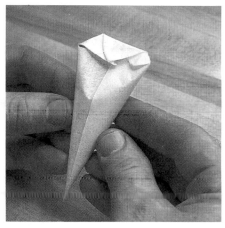

(5) Folding down the remaining points after the cone is filled with chocolate.

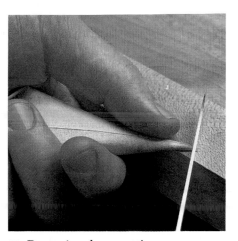

(6) Removing the cone tip.

29-3 USING A PASTRY BAG

(7) Tracing a design.

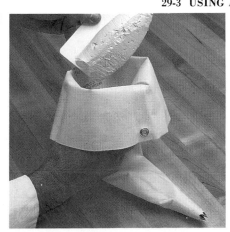

(1) Filling the bag.

(2) Piping out buttercream rosettes.

29-4

Drying the inside of the bag.

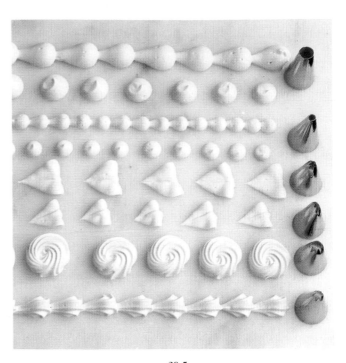

29-5

A sampling of effects created from various tips.

have been removed, the bag is ready to use. With one hand, press the buttercream down and out of the bag. Use the other hand to support and guide the bag. When the design is finished, first release the pressure on the bag, then gently twist the tip while simultaneously lifting it cleanly away from the rosette or other design. This will prevent the formation of tails and threads that could spoil the effect.

4. Remove all the buttercream, etc., from the bag and wash it carefully with warm, soapy water after each use. Turn the bag inside out. Wipe the bag dry with absorbent toweling before storing it to keep it in good condition, safe, and sanitary between uses.

5. Figure 29-5 shows various effects that can be created using a basic pastry tip "starter kit." From the top, rows 1 and 2 show a border design and individual rosettes made with a plain opening. Rows 3 and 4 show the same technique using a plain tip with a smaller opening. Rows 5 and 6 show the effect of two different-sized leaf tips. Rows 7 and 8 show rosettes made with a star tip and a shell border from the same tip. A number of other tips are available.

EQUIPMENT AND DEFINITION

Equipment

In addition to measuring devices and ovens, which were discussed previously, the major category of bak-

ing equipment is pans of various sizes and shapes. Pans are available in several gauges (metal thicknesses). Heavy-gauge pans are usually preferred; some very delicate items, such as wafer-type cookies, may even be baked on doubled pans.

Pans also come with different surfaces. Shiny pans are used for items containing large amounts of sugar and fat, which could burn or scorch easily during cooking. The shiny surface tends to reflect some of the heat away from the pan, slightly slowing down the cooking process. Darker surfaces hold the heat better and are used for items in which a well-developed crust and a deeper color are desirable.

The following is a list of the most frequently used pans for baking.

Cake pans—These are pans with straight sides, available in various sizes (diameters and heights) and shapes (round, square, or rectangular).

Springform pans—These are similar to cake pans, but their sides have springs that can be released in order to remove the cake from the pan more easily. Springform pans are often used for delicate cakes and to mold Bavarian-filled cakes as they chill.

Loose-bottomed tart pans—These shallow, round pans have a removable bottom. The sides may be scalloped or straight and are generally shorter than those of pie pans. Small versions are called tartlet pans.

Pie pans—Round pans with flared sides, pie pans are deeper than tart pans.

Loaf pans—These deep pans are usually rectangular. The sides may be straight or slightly flared. Loaf pans are used for preparing a variety of breads. Pullman loaf pans have lids and produce square loaves.

Muffin tins—These are pans with small, round sections for producing muffins of various sizes.

Tube pans—These deep, round pans have a tube in the center and are used to create a specific effect. Some styles are similar to springform pans, having removable sides. Tube pans are most often used for chiffon and angel food cakes.

Kugelhopf forms—These special tube pans with a fluted design are traditionally used to prepare a sweet, yeast-raised cake flavored with dried fruits and nuts.

Baking Terms

The following list contains terms used to describe baking techniques and baked products. Some of these terms are more fully explained in the text in this and other chapters in the baking section. Refer also to the Glossary at the end of this book.

Baking blind—Partially or fully baking a pie or tart crust before it is filled.

Caramelization—The browning of sugar in the presence of heat.

Creaming—The process of beating sugar and fat together until they are light and fluffy before adding other ingredients. This serves to disperse the sugar and fat throughout a mixture and introduces air.

Crumb—A term used to describe a baked item's texture, which can range from fine to coarse.

Docking—Slashing the top of shaped dough before baking it to allow the top to expand and/or to create a decorative effect.

Folding—The process of gently combining ingredients (especially foams) so as not to release trapped air bubbles.

Formula—Another name for a baking recipe. A formula may include ratios, weights, and/or volumes.

Leavening—The process of introducing air into a baked product through the use of yeast, chemical leaveners, foams, or steam.

Proofing—The second and/or third rising or fermentation stages in the making of yeast breads. Also the initial rising of yeast in warm liquid to create a sponge.

Punching down—Flattening yeast dough after proofing to expel carbon dioxide gas and stabilize the temperature.

Roll-in—Butter worked into a malleable paste and layered into the dough to make flaky pastry such as puff pastry, croissant, and Danish.

Rounding—Forming dough into balls in order to stretch and relax the gluten before shaping the dough.

Sponge—A mixture of yeast, liquid, and a small amount of flour and/or sugar that is allowed to rise in a warm place for the appropriate amount of time.

Turn—One folding and rolling step in the making of rolled-in doughs.

SUMMARY

Baking mise en place has more to do with preparing individual ingredients—measuring or sifting, for example—than with combining ingredients to form appareils, as covered in Chapter 14 on general mise en place. One of the goals of this chapter has been to explain the function of various ingredients. Understanding how such ingredients as flour, eggs, and sugar can affect the texture, flavor, and appearance of a baked item allows the pastry chef the freedom to use basic ratios as a starting point for preparing a wide variety of baked goods.

In addition, the selection and preparation of equipment and the proper handling of the baked product were also included here.

Chapter 30

Yeast Doughs

The earliest breads were nothing like the light, airy breads we know today. Leavened bread did not become possible until the Egyptians, using the wheat that flourished in the fertile Nile River valley, discovered that some of their baked dough seemed to have a different texture.

The Egyptians may not have been sure about what had caused the difference but they were able to continue producing leavened cakes by preserving some of the dough each day to combine with new batches. This is exactly how the American settlers kept their sourdough alive thousands of years later.

Since these early times, we have come to a better understanding of how yeast works and the role that wheat and its gluten play in the creation of light breads. This chapter will cover how to scale (measure) ingredients properly and work with various yeast doughs, from mixing to shaping and baking. (Croissant and Danish doughs, although they are yeast-leavened, are covered in Chapter 32, "Pastry Doughs and Cookies.")

CATEGORIES

Yeast breads are divided into two categories: lean doughs and rich doughs. A lean dough can be produced with only flour, yeast, and water; in fact, that is the formula for a classic French baguette. This dough can be varied by including additional ingredients such as spices, herbs, special flours, and/or dried nuts and fruits. These additions will not greatly change the basic texture.

A rich dough is produced by the addition of shortening or tenderizing ingredients such as sugars or syrups, butter or oil, whole eggs or egg yolks, milk or cream. When these fats are introduced, they will change the bread's overall texture, as well as the way in which the dough is handled.

Lean doughs contain only small amounts of sugar and fat, if any. Breads made from lean dough tend to have a chewier texture, more bite, and a crisp crust. Hard rolls, French- and Italian-style breads, and whole-wheat, rye, and pumpernickel breads are considered lean. By adding small amounts of any of the previously mentioned enriching ingredients, a very lean dough can be made slightly softer to produce items such as dinner rolls or pullman loaves.

Rich doughs should have a cakelike texture after baking. They may be golden in color because of the use of eggs and butter and their crusts are usually very soft. Challah, egg rolls, brioche, Parker House rolls, and cloverleaf rolls are all examples of items made with rich doughs. The doughs are usually softer and a little more difficult to work with during kneading and shaping than lean doughs.

Scaling Ingredients

For all baking, ingredients must be measured properly—a process known as scaling. Unlike home baking, which relies on volume measurement (cups, tablespoons, and teaspoons), in professional baking, ingredients are most often weighed to ensure consistent results.

Yeast

In general, two types of yeast are used in the professional bakeshop: dry (or granulated) yeast and fresh (compressed) yeast. Yeast is an organic leavener, which means that it must be "alive" in order to be effective. The yeast can be killed by overly high temperatures and, conversely, cold temperatures can inhibit the yeast's action.

Dry yeast, in bulk or packets, should be refrigerated. It will keep for several months, which makes it suitable for kitchens that only occasionally make their own bread. Fresh yeast, on the other hand, is quite perishable and can be held under refrigeration for only 7 to 10 days. It may be frozen for longer storage.

Cold yeast should be allowed to return to room temperature before it is used. If there is any doubt about whether or not the yeast is still alive, it should be "proofed" before it is added to the other ingredients. Proofing is accomplished as follows:

1. Combine the yeast with warm liquid and a small amount of flour or sugar.
2. Let the mixture rest at room temperature until a thick surface foam forms.
3. The foam indicates that the yeast is alive and can be used. If there is no foam, the yeast is dead and should be discarded.

Sponge

A sponge should not be confused with a sourdough starter. A sponge is prepared by combining the yeast and liquid with a portion of the flour and allowing it to ferment until the mixture is light and spongy. When the remaining ingredients are added to the sponge, the yeast is distributed evenly throughout the dough. A sponge is often needed to produce a good texture when using flours such as rye or oat that are low in gluten. Once the sponge is formed, the dough is prepared using the straight method.

Sourdough Starter

The traditional sourdough was a simple combination of flour and water that was allowed to stand until the mixture had absorbed wild yeast spores present in the air. Today, it is more common for some percentage of yeast to be added to a sourdough starter to produce a more uniform and reliable starter. The starter is allowed to ferment until it has soured. Part of this starter is used to prepare a dough. The remaining starter is generally replenished, either by adding flour and water or by returning a portion of the newly made dough to the starter.

The type of wild yeast present in the air differs greatly from region to region. San Francisco is famous for its sourdough breads; the "sour" flavor in sourdoughs made in other locations may not be as well-developed.

Mixing—The Straight Dough Method

The primary technique used for mixing yeast doughs is the straight dough method. It is applicable to all types of doughs: lean doughs, rich doughs, and sponge types such as rye and oat. Individual recipes should be consulted for specific directions.

Sourdough Starter

Yield: 6 pounds of starter

Flour, unbleached	2 pounds	900 grams
Water	1 gallon	3.75 liters
Yeast	1 ounce	30 grams

1. Mix all the ingredients thoroughly. Put the mixture in a clean container, cover it with cheesecloth, and place it in an area that is free from drafts and approximately 80°F (35°C).

2. Allow the starter to ferment for approximately 48 hours, or until it has a sour odor and all of the foam has subsided. The starter is ready to be used at this point.

3. To keep the starter alive, feed it every few days with an additional pound of flour and a quart of warm water. As the starter is used in bread, replace the amount of starter used with flour and water, maintaining the ratio of 1 part flour to 2 parts water, by weight.

Mise en Place

1. Flour. Select the appropriate flour for the type of bread being prepared. Yeast doughs made with low-gluten flour (rye, oat, pumpernickel) must include at least some wheat flour, to introduce the necessary gluten for proper rise and texture. Consult the individual recipes. The flour should be carefully scaled. For lean doughs, it is generally not important to sift the flour.

2. Liquid. Have available water or other liquid. The most frequent choice for lean doughs is water. Milk is used for most rich doughs. The liquid should be carefully measured and at the correct temperature.

3. Yeast. Have yeast available, properly weighed and at room temperature. If necessary, proof the yeast in warm water and a small amount of sugar. (Some of the flour may also be incorporated, to create a sponge.) Let the mixture ferment until it is light and foamy.

4. Salt. Salt controls the yeast's activity, and, with the exception of sodium-free breads, it is an essential component. It also helps to give bread the correct texture and flavor.

5. Optional components. These include eggs; butter or oil; sugars, syrups, and honey; nuts, seeds, spices, or herbs; and any additional flavoring ingredients. Weigh the eggs and have them at room temperature for best results. Have butter in the proper state, at room temperature or melted. If melted butter is required by the recipe, allow it to cool slightly so that it will not kill the yeast. Flavoring ingredients may be added as indicated by the recipe or as desired.

Method

This method is shown in Figure 30-1.

1. Place the warm liquid in the bowl of a mixer that is fitted with a dough hook. Add the yeast and mix it thoroughly. If the sponge method is used or if the yeast should be proofed to test its power, combine the yeast with some liquid, some of the flour, and/or a small amount of sugar. Cover the bowl and let the yeast ferment in a warm place until it is frothy.

2. Add all the remaining ingredients except the salt to the yeast mixture. Once all the dry ingredients have been added, add the salt. To prevent it from killing the yeast, the salt should be added as shown in step 2 of Figure 30-1.

3. Mix on low speed until the dough starts to "catch." It should look like a shaggy mass at this point, as can be seen in step 3 of Figure 30-1. Scrape down the bowl's sides and bottom.

4. Increase the mixing speed to medium and continue to knead until the dough develops a smooth appearance and feels springy when touched. Step 4 of Figure 30-1 shows the dough after proper mixing and kneading.

The dough must be properly kneaded. This step ensures full development of the gluten so that the dough stretches to "give" as the yeast produces the gas that causes the bread to rise. If the dough is either under- or overkneaded, it will not rise properly and the finished product will have a coarse texture.

5. Remove the dough to a clean bowl that has been lightly oiled. Rub the dough's surface with oil to keep it from drying out.

6. Cover the dough with plastic wrap or clean cloths and let it rise in a warm area, away from drafts. Step 5 of Figure 30-1 shows the

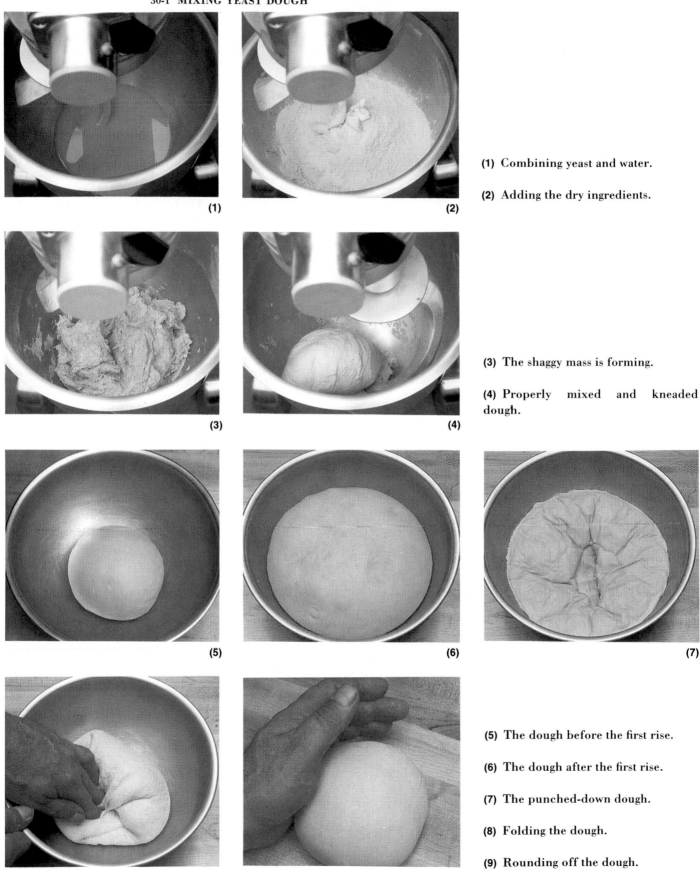

(1) Combining yeast and water.

(2) Adding the dry ingredients.

(3) The shaggy mass is forming.

(4) Properly mixed and kneaded dough.

(5) The dough before the first rise.

(6) The dough after the first rise.

(7) The punched-down dough.

(8) Folding the dough.

(9) Rounding off the dough.

dough before it has risen. Step 6 of Figure 30-1 shows the same dough after it has risen properly. Note the dramatic change in volume. Test the dough to determine if it has risen sufficiently by pressing it with a finger. The indentation should remain; the dough should not spring back in place.

Doughs should be allowed to rise sufficiently so the bread will have the correct texture. Dough that has not risen sufficiently (considered underfermented) will have a coarse texture and will be flat after it is baked. Dough that has risen too much due to overfermentation may have a sour taste, sometimes described as "yeasty" or as tasting like beer.

7. When the dough has risen sufficiently, punch it down. Push the dough down in a few places. This will gently expel the carbon dioxide, even out the overall temperature, and redistribute the yeast evenly. Then, fold the dough over on itself to further expel gases.

8. Remove the dough to a lightly floured workbench.

9. Scale the dough into the appropriate size for rolls, loaves of bread, etc., then shape it as desired or indicated by recipe and place it in prepared pans. Gently round the dough into smooth balls, as shown in step 9 of Figure 30-1.

For a quick summary, refer to the abbreviated method for straight dough.

Shaping Doughs

Properly shaping the dough helps to achieve an attractive appearance; but, more important, proper shaping will ensure that the items bake evenly. After shaping, many products will need to be "docked," meaning that the dough's surface is punctured so that the steam that

builds up inside the product during baking will not cause it to split or rupture. The surface may be simply slashed with a sharp knife. Round loaves may be punctured with a wooden spoon handle.

Shaping dough into loaves is shown in Figure 30-2.

Baguettes and Loaf Breads

The first step is to scale the dough into pieces of the appropriate

weight. Use a flattened fist to punch the dough into a rectangle of an even thickness. This technique is demonstrated in step 1 of Figure 30-2. Once the dough is flattened, fold it in half and flatten it once more. Now grasp both ends of the dough and gently stretch it. Lift the ends up from the cutting board and allow the dough's weight to stretch itself out. Fold the dough in thirds, as shown in step 3 of Figure 30-2. Begin to roll the dough into a cylin-

Basic French Bread

Yield: 10 pounds (4.5 kilograms) of dough

Water, warm	4¼ pounds	2 kilograms
Yeast	2 ounces	60 grams
High-gluten bread flour	5 pounds	2.25 kilograms
Organic wheat flour	1 pound	450 grams
Salt	2 ounces	60 grams

1. Combine the water and yeast in the bowl of an electric mixer, and mix until the yeast is thoroughly dissolved.

2. Add the remaining ingredients and mix the dough on the lowest speed until all of the flour is incorporated.

3. Increase the setting of the mixer to the second speed and mix the dough until it is smooth and very elastic.

4. Remove the dough to an oiled bowl. Cover the dough with a clean cloth and let the dough rise until it has doubled in volume. (The indentation left when the dough is pressed with a finger should remain; the dough should not spring back.)

5. Scale the dough into the appropriate size (this will vary according to the intended product; for example, rolls, loaves, and so forth).

6. Bench proof the dough for approximately 20 minutes, then shape the scaled dough into the desired product.

7. Place the shaped dough onto prepared pans. Let the dough rise again (in a proof box if possible) until it is nearly doubled in volume.

8. Bake the bread at 400°F (200°C) until crust is well developed, golden brown, and bread is baked through (the time will vary depending upon the size of the finished product).

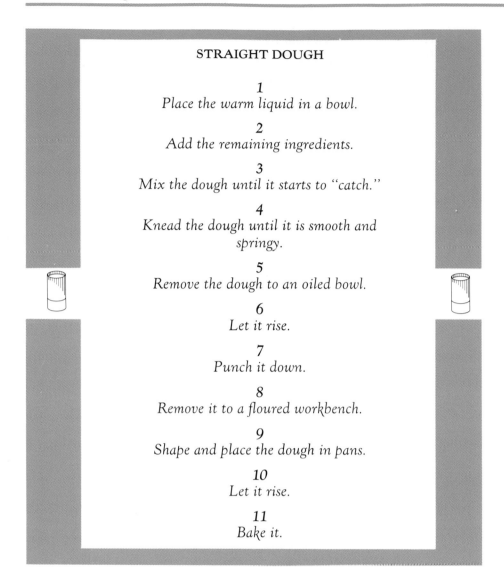

STRAIGHT DOUGH

1
Place the warm liquid in a bowl.

2
Add the remaining ingredients.

3
Mix the dough until it starts to "catch."

4
Knead the dough until it is smooth and springy.

5
Remove the dough to an oiled bowl.

6
Let it rise.

7
Punch it down.

8
Remove it to a floured workbench.

9
Shape and place the dough in pans.

10
Let it rise.

11
Bake it.

der. Use the heel of the palm to firmly seal the seams as the dough is rolled. The dough's tight seams can be easily seen in step 5 of Figure 30-1. The dough is now shaped and ready to be placed in the prepared pan.

The dough is allowed to rise once more, this time in a proof box. The dough will rise to more than double its original volume.

Hard and Club Rolls

Scale the dough into equal-sized pieces. Flatten the dough and begin to roll it into a cylinder as for loaves. Pinch the seam closed. Be sure that the outer layer is stretched wide enough to encase the roll completely. Figure 30-3 shows the dough rolled into a hard roll, or a club roll, as it is also known.

Round Loaves and Rolls

For round loaves, gather the dough into a ball and roll it on a worktable to develop a smooth exterior. Gather up the roll from the under-

side and pinch it to seal the seam. Place it on the pan, the seam side down.

There are a number of ways to shape dinner rolls. One way is to roll each ball of dough into a rope and then "tie" it into various knots. Parker House rolls are named for the hotel in Boston where they were first served. They are formed by flattening a piece of dough, brushing it with butter, and folding it in half. Cloverleaf rolls are made by arranging three small balls of dough in a triangular pattern. Cloverleaf rolls are often prepared in muffin tins.

Proofing and Baking

The way a pan is prepared depends on the type of dough being used. To prepare the pan for lean doughs, either line the pan with parchment paper or dust it with cornmeal (the cornmeal is especially appropriate for free-form loaves—baguettes or round loaves). For doughs that have higher percentages of milk, sugar, and fat, the pan should be greased, lined with parchment paper, or greased and lined. For extremely rich doughs (brioche or challah, for example), both greasing and lining are necessary.

Once the dough is in the pan, it must be allowed to rise a second time; this is known as bench proofing. Some doughs will be allowed to rise in a proof box; some are bench-proofed in steam to produce the correct texture and crust. The dough should not be allowed to rise too much during bench proofing, as it will continue to rise slightly when it is in the oven. This additional rising is known as oven spring.

The dough should then be baked at the appropriate temperature until it is done.

The doneness of baked goods can be determined by examining

(1) Flattening out the dough into a rectangle.

(2) Stretching out the dough.

(1)

(2)

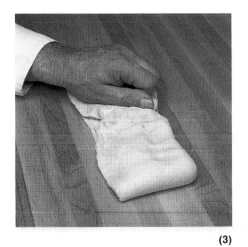
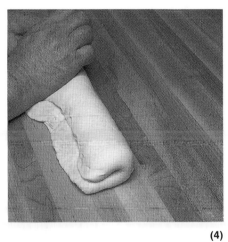

(3) Folding it in thirds.

(4) Rolling it into a cylinder and sealing the seams.

(3)

(4)

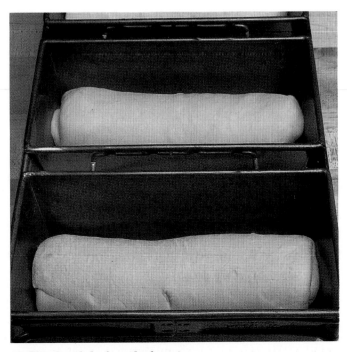

(5) The rolled loaf.

(6) The dough before the last rise.

729

30-3
Shaping hard rolls.

the item; it should have a good color and the appropriate size.

Some products should be baked in steam-generating ovens. This is especially important for such items as hard rolls and French breads, which require a very crisp crust.

Determining Doneness and Evaluating Quality

Yeast doughs are allowed to bake until they have a good aroma and golden to brown color; these are the primary indicators of doneness. Texture and flavor are, of course, also important. Thumping the item to see if it has a hollow sound is not always effective. The interior should have a uniform, dry crumb. Yeast-raised products should not be cut until they have cooled sufficiently. Refer to Table 30-1 for a list of common problems with yeast-raised baked goods and their probable causes.

Baked yeast-raised products should have a golden to deep-brown color and a fully developed crust. The use of special flours, such as rye or graham, will influence the color. Doughs that have been brushed with egg wash or milk will have a more tender and golden crust after baking. Doughs that include butter and eggs should be golden on the inside.

If, after baking, a dough has a pale color, it is either not completely baked or has been baked at too low a temperature.

Products made from yeast doughs should be fairly elastic but still easy to bite into. The higher the proportion of eggs and shorteners, such as butter or milk, the more tender the finished product will be.

The baked item should not taste strongly of yeast; if it does, it is an indication that the dough was not allowed sufficient time to proof before baking or that too much yeast was used. Doughs that do not include a sufficient amount of salt will have a bland flavor.

TABLE 30-1. COMMON PROBLEMS WITH YEAST BREADS AND THEIR PROBABLE CAUSES

Faults	Improper mixing	Insufficient salt	Too much salt	Dough weight too much for pan	Dough weight too light for pan	Insufficient yeast	Dough proofed too much	Dough underproofed	Dough temperature too high	Dough temperature too low	Dough too stiff	Proof box too hot	Green flour	Dough chilled	Too much sugar	Insufficient sugar	Dough too young	Dough too old	Improper molding	Insufficient shortening	Oven temperature too high	Oven temperature too low	Over-baked
Lack of volume	✓		✓	✓	✓	✓								✓			✓	✓			✓		
Too much volume		✓	✓			✓												✓				✓	
Crust color too pale									✓		✓					✓	✓						
Crust color too dark									✓						✓		✓				✓		
Crust blisters												✓					✓	✓	✓				
Shelling of top crust							✓			✓		✓			✓								
Poor keeping qualities		✓					✓		✓						✓			✓			✓	✓	
Poor texture, crumbly							✓				✓						✓	✓				✓	
Crust too thick																✓		✓				✓	✓
Streaky crumb																		✓					
Gray crumb							✓	✓				✓											
Lack of shred							✓										✓	✓					
Coarse grain	✓			✓		✓	✓			✓							✓	✓	✓				
Poor taste and flavor		✓						✓										✓					

Source: *The Baker's Manual*, Revised Third Edition, Joseph P. Amendola. New York: Ahren's Publishing Company, 1972, p. 16.

SUMMARY

Few foods appeal so directly to the guest as bread. Fresh breads and rolls can be an excellent means of creating a good first impression, especially if they have been baked on the premises.

The information in this chapter applies not only to operations that have a separate bakeshop but to those where any baking must be done in the main kitchen. Several factors should be kept in mind when deciding whether or not to bake goods on the premises. The first is the amount of space available—there should be room to accommodate each stage of the process.

Second, there should be adequate and appropriate baking equipment, with enough oven space to avoid "competing" against other kitchen needs.

The baker's work often can be dovetailed with the rest of the kitchen's needs so that there is no overlap. A variety of products do not require the production capabilities of a full-scale bakeshop.

Although baking is meticulous work, requiring careful measuring and proper handling of doughs, the rewards can be significant, especially if quality baked goods are not readily available through a reliable purveyor.

Raisin Pumpernickel Bread

Yield: 10 pounds (4.5 kilograms)

Water	2½ pounds	1.15 kilograms
Coffee, strong, dark	1½ pounds	680 grams
Molasses	8 ounces	225 grams
Cocoa powder	1 ounce	30 grams
Rye flour, organic, coarse	1 pound	450 grams
Wheat flour, 90-percent organic	5 pounds	2.25 kilograms
Yeast	2 ounces	60 grams
Salt	2 ounces	60 grams
Raisins	8 ounces	225 grams

1. Combine the water, coffee, molasses, cocoa powder, rye flour, 1 pound of the wheat flour, and the yeast in the bowl of an electric mixer and mix until thoroughly blended. Allow this sponge to ferment until it is very foamy.

2. Add the remainder of the whole wheat flour, the salt, and the raisins. Mix the dough on the lowest speed until all of the flour is incorporated.

3. Increase the setting of the mixer to the second speed and mix the dough until it is smooth and very elastic.

4. Remove the dough to an oiled bowl. Cover the dough and let it rise until it has doubled in volume. Scale the dough and shape it as desired.

5. Let the dough rise a final time (in a proof box if one is available).

6. Bake the bread at 400°F (200°C). The baking time will vary, depending on the size of the finished product.

Traditional Sourdough Wheat Bread

Yield: 10 pounds (4.5 kilograms)

Water	3 pounds	1.3 kilograms
Sourdough starter	3 pounds	1.3 kilograms
Wheat flour, 90-percent organic	4⅓ pounds	2 kilograms
Salt	1½ pounds	45 grams

1. Combine the water, starter, and flour in the bowl of an electric mixer. Add the salt once all of the ingredients have been blended.

2. Mix the dough on the lowest speed until all of the flour is incorporated.

3. Increase the setting of the mixer to the second speed and mix the dough until it is smooth and very elastic.

4. Remove the dough to an oiled bowl. Cover the dough and let it rise until it has doubled in volume. Scale the dough and shape it as desired.

5. Let the dough rise a final time after placing it on properly prepared pans (in a proof box if one is available).

6. Bake the bread at 400°F (200°C). The baking time will vary, depending on the size of the finished product.

Multigrain Loaf

Yield: 10 pounds (4.5 kilograms)

Water	4 pounds	1.8 kilograms
Yeast	2 ounces	60 grams
Cracked wheat, organic	4 ounces	115 grams
Cracked rye, organic	4 ounces	115 grams
Coarse cornmeal, organic	4 ounces	115 grams
Millet, organic	4 ounces	115 grams
Whole-wheat flour, organic	1 pound	450 grams
Wheat flour, 90-percent organic	4⅓ pounds	2 kilograms
Salt	2 ounces	60 grams

1. Combine the water and yeast in the bowl of an electric mixer, and mix them until the yeast is thoroughly dissolved.

2. Add the remaining ingredients. Mix the dough on the lowest speed until all of the flour is incorporated.

3. Increase the setting of the mixer to the second speed and mix the dough until it is smooth and very elastic.

4. Remove the dough to an oiled bowl. Cover the dough and let it rise until it has doubled in volume. Scale the dough and shape it as desired.

5. Let the dough rise a final time after placing it on properly prepared pans (in a proof box if one is available).

6. Bake the bread at 400°F (200°C). The baking time will vary, depending on the size of the finished product.

Whole Grain Wheat and Rye Bread

Yield: 10 pounds (4.5 kilograms)

Water	4 pounds	1.8 kilograms
Yeast	2 ounces	60 grams
Wheat flour, cracked	4 ounces	115 grams
Rye flour, cracked	4 ounces	115 grams
Whole-wheat flour, organic	10 ounces	285 grams
Wheat flour, 90-percent organic	5 pounds	2.25 kilograms
Salt	2 ounces	50 grams

1. Combine the water and yeast in the bowl of an electric mixer, and mix them until the yeast is thoroughly dissolved.

2. Add the remaining ingredients. Mix the dough on the lowest speed until all of the flour is incorporated.

3. Increase the setting of the mixer to the second speed and mix the dough until it is smooth and very elastic.

4. Remove the dough to an oiled bowl. Cover the dough and let it rise until it has doubled in volume. Scale the dough and shape it as desired.

5. Let the dough rise a final time after placing it on properly prepared pans (in a proof box if one is available).

6. Bake the bread at 400°F (200°C). The baking time will vary, depending on the size of the finished product.

Caraway Rye Bread (Straight Dough Method)

Yield: 10 pounds (4.5 kilograms)

Water	4⅓ pounds	2 kilograms
Yeast	2 ounces	60 grams
Rye flour, coarse	1 pound	450 grams
Wheat flour, 90-percent organic	2½ pounds	1.15 kilograms
White flour, high-gluten	2½ pounds	1.15 kilograms
Salt	2 ounces	60 grams
Caraway seeds	1½ ounces	40 grams

1. Combine the water and yeast in the bowl of an electric mixer, and mix them until the yeast is thoroughly dissolved.
2. Add the remaining ingredients. Mix the dough on the lowest speed until all of the flour is incorporated.
3. Increase the setting of the mixer to the second speed and mix the dough until it is smooth and very elastic.
4. Remove the dough to an oiled bowl. Cover the dough and let it rise until it has doubled in volume. Scale the dough and shape it as desired.
5. Let the dough rise a final time after placing it on properly prepared pans (in a proof box if one is available).
6. Bake the bread at 400°F (200°C). The baking time will vary, depending on the size of the finished product.

Sourdough Caraway Rye Bread

Yield: 10 pounds (4.5 kilograms)

Water	3 pounds	1.36 kilograms
Sourdough starter	3 pounds	1.36 kilograms
Rye flour, coarse	1 pound	450 grams
Wheat flour, 90-percent organic	1¾ pounds	800 grams
White flour, high-gluten	1¾ pounds	800 grams
Salt	2 ounces	60 grams
Caraway seeds	1½ ounces	40 grams

1. Combine the water and the sourdough starter in the bowl of an electric mixer, and mix them until they are thoroughly combined.

2. Add the remaining ingredients. Mix the dough on the lowest speed until all of the flour is incorporated.

3. Increase the setting of the mixer to the second speed and mix the dough until it is smooth and very elastic.

4. Remove the dough to an oiled bowl. Cover the dough and let it rise until it has doubled in volume. Scale the dough and shape it as desired.

5. Let the dough rise a final time after placing it on properly prepared pans (in a proof box if one is available).

6. Bake the bread at 400°F (200°C). The baking time will vary, depending on the size of the finished product.

Brioche

Yield: 12 pounds

Yeast	4 ounces	115 grams
Milk, warm	1 pint	240 milliliters
Flour, bread	5 pounds	2.27 kilograms
Salt	¾ ounce	20 grams
Sugar	12 ounces	340 grams
Eggs	26	26
Butter, softened	3½ pounds	1.6 kilograms

1. Combine the yeast and the milk in a mixing bowl, and blend them together until the yeast is thoroughly dissolved.

2. Add 1 pound of the flour and mix well. Allow this mixture to ferment until a sponge forms.

3. Add the salt, sugar, 18 to 20 of the eggs, and the remainder of the flour to the sponge. Blend in a mixer on the second speed until the dough starts to pull cleanly away from the sides of the bowl.

4. Add the remaining eggs and blend well.

5. Add the butter gradually it has all been incorporated and a smooth, fairly soft dough has formed.

6. Transfer the dough to a clean bowl, cover it, and let it rise until it has doubled in volume. Punch the dough down and refrigerate it overnight.

7. Scale and shape the dough into brioche of the desired size. Let the dough proof once more in prepared pans. Bake the brioche at 350°F (175°C) until the crust is golden and the brioche is baked through. If desired, the dough may be brushed with egg wash before baking.

Chapter 31

Quickbreads, Cakes, and Other Batters

This chapter covers a broad range of products, from soda breads, biscuits, and cornbreads, which have a homestyle appeal, to classic genoise and dessert soufflés, which have a sophisticated delicacy of both flavor and texture. The basic mixing methods for a variety of batters and their formulas are included in this chapter.

Quick breads differ from yeast breads in that they use chemical leaveners rather than organic ones and thus do not require a rising period. Muffins, biscuits, and scones are examples of quick breads that have a place on the breakfast menu as well as in the breadbasket at lunch or dinner. These simple baked items allow the chef to offer homemade breads and cakes without the time needed for yeast doughs. From these uncomplicated items, the chef can learn the skills required for all batters, from elegant tortes and soufflés to homespun puddings and cobblers.

THE BASIC METHODS

There are four basic methods for preparing batters, depending on the product being prepared.

• The straight mix method calls for all ingredients to be combined at once and blended into a batter.
• The creaming method is used to prepare products with more refined crumb and texture—pound cakes, butter cakes, and most drop cookies.
• The "two-stage" method is used to prepare cakes that contain a very high percentage of sugar. The dry ingredients are first blended with all of the shortening and half of the liquid until smooth, then the remaining wet ingredients are gradually added.
• The foaming method, which produces the lightest texture, is used for genoise (sponge cakes), angel food, and chiffon cakes.

These methods require careful measuring, proper temperature control, and the proper application of technique. The following basic techniques and the appropriate formulas will show how the same ingredients combined in different ways can produce different results.

The Straight Mix Method

The reputation of an establishment's breakfast, brunch, lunch, or high tea menu can be made on the basis of the quality of its muffins and quick breads. Various ingredients can be used to flavor or garnish a basic bread, and the recipes included in this chapter can be considered a blueprint for creating additional offerings.

The straight mixing method is used when making such popular items as cornsticks, bran muffins, pumpkin bread, and carrot cake.

Once the basic technique is understood, they are simple to produce, requiring little special equipment.

All ingredients are combined at once in this method and blended into a batter. The important thing to remember is that the batter should not be overworked; unlike yeast doughs, these batters should be mixed as briefly as possible to ensure a light, delicate texture.

Mise en Place

1. Flour. Specific recipes may indicate the use of a number of different flours—for example, unbleached flour, whole wheat flour, pastry flour, or cornmeal—according to the desired result. The flour should be carefully weighed, then properly sifted. It may be necessary to sift all of the dry ingredients together, after the flour has been sifted once, to allow the ingredients to mix quickly without overworking the batter.

2. Liquid. The recipes for batters rely upon a variety of different ingredients to moisten a batter and hold it together. Milk, buttermilk, water, oil, the moisture from vegetables such as zucchini, and other liquids can all be appropriate, according to the recipe. The liquid should be properly measured, either by weight or by volume; both methods of measure will be accurate.

3. Leavener. The leavener for most quickbreads and many other batters is a chemical leavener: either baking soda, baking powder, or a combination of the two. Because the leavener is used in very small amounts, it may be appropriate to measure it by volume rather than by weight; a teaspoon or tablespoon measure may be more accurate than a scale at very small measures. The leavener should be sifted with the flour, the salt, and

any other dry ingredients required by the recipe.

Some batters rely on a physical leavener—beaten egg whites—to provide the proper texture in the finished item. The best volume, a medium peak, is easiest to achieve when the whites are at room temperature before they are beaten. (For additional information regarding the proper way to handle and whip egg whites, refer to Chapter 14, "Mise en Place.") The beaten whites should be folded into the batter immediately, in two or three stages, so that the maximum volume is retained. As soon as the whites are properly incorporated, be sure to scale and pan the batter and bake it to its correct doneness.

4. Shortening ingredients. The amount of shorteners used in a dough will determine its final texture. Refer to the specific recipe for directions to prepare the shortener. In some cases, it may need to be melted and cooled; for others, it should be left cold.

5. Flavoring ingredients. The number and types of flavoring ingredients that can be used in batters is almost limitless: cocoa, chopped nuts, grated vegetables, berries, citrus zest, and spices and herbs, for example. Refer to the specific recipe for information regarding the advanced preparation of these ingredients.

Method

1. Scale all the dry ingredients and sift them. All-purpose flour is commonly used for items prepared by this method, although pastry flour may be used for a more tender, cake-like product. Special flours such as cornmeal, graham flour, or oat flour also may be used.

2. Combine all the liquid ingredients (eggs, milk or buttermilk, oil or butter, for example) in a mixing bowl.

3. Add the dry ingredients to the liquid ingredients.

4. Mix the ingredients by hand or in a mixer with a paddle attachment, just until the dry ingredients are moistened. The appearance and consistency of the batter will differ from product to product. Batters for some items, popovers and crêpes for example, may be thin enough to pour easily; others may be stiff enough to mound slightly, as in any kind of muffin. In any case, they should be easy to stir.

Flavoring ingredients, such as fresh fruit or nuts, should be dusted with flour and then folded gently into the batter once it has been properly mixed. The flour will help suspend the ingredients evenly throughout the batter.

5. Scale off the batter into prepared baking pans. Use paper liners, if available, to line pans and muffin tins, or grease the pans and dust them with flour.

6. Bake the batter at the appropriate temperature until it is baked through. When properly done, the item's surface should spring back when pressed with a fingertip, a skewer inserted near the center should come away clean, and the item should pull away slightly from the pan's edges. Some muffins and quick breads will develop a crack on their upper crust during baking; this should not be considered a fault.

7. Remove the item from the oven, then cool and store it.

For a quick summary, refer to the abbreviated method for straight-mix batters.

Determining Doneness and Evaluating Quality

For all baked goods, the important characteristics are appearance, texture, and flavor. During baking,

Popovers

Yield: 10 servings

Butter	as needed	as needed
Eggs	6	6
Milk	2 cups	480 milliliters
Butter, melted	6 tablespoons	90 grams
Flour, all-purpose, sifted	2 cups	240 grams
Salt	1 teaspoon	5 grams

1. Generously butter ten ½-cup (120-milliliter) ramekins.

2. Whisk together the eggs, milk, and melted butter. Beat them until the mixture is frothy.

3. Combine the flour and salt in a separate bowl. Beat in the liquid gradually. Continue to beat the mixture until it is smooth and well-blended.

4. Spoon the batter into the prepared ramekins; they should be about three-quarters full. Place the ramekins on a sheet pan. Place the pan in a preheated 425°F (220°C) oven; reduce the heat to 375°F (190°C) and bake the popovers, undisturbed, for 50 minutes.

5. Remove the popovers from the oven. For moister popovers, remove them from the ramekins and serve them immediately. For crisp popovers, slit the side of each popover to allow the steam to escape, then return them to the oven until the tops are firm, crisp, and brown, about 10 minutes.

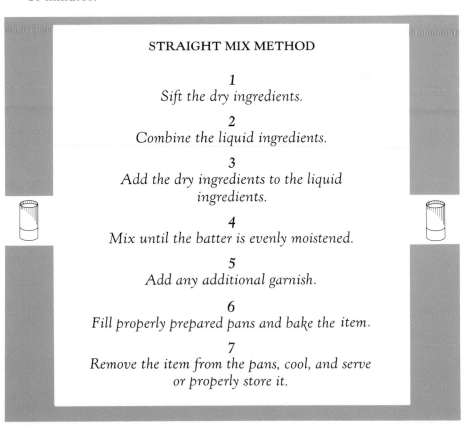

STRAIGHT MIX METHOD

1
Sift the dry ingredients.

2
Combine the liquid ingredients.

3
Add the dry ingredients to the liquid ingredients.

4
Mix until the batter is evenly moistened.

5
Add any additional garnish.

6
Fill properly prepared pans and bake the item.

7
Remove the item from the pans, cool, and serve or properly store it.

muffins and quick breads should rise to create a dome-shaped upper crust. The crust may develop a crack. The edges may become slightly darker than the center, but they should not shrink too far away from the pan's sides.

The texture should be even throughout the product's interior, with a cake-like crumb. Quick breads should be moist but not wet. The flavor should be well-developed and appropriate to the ingredients used. The batter must be properly mixed in order to ensure that there are no leavener or flour pockets.

The Creaming Method

Creaming together fat and sugar produces an exceptionally fine crumb and a dense, rich texture that holds up well and slices evenly. Pound cakes are the primary example of the results of this method. Many cookies are also made by creaming, although the ingredient proportions differ—cakes have less butter and more eggs, whereas cookies usually have greater amounts of butter and sugar.

A leavener, such as baking powder or baking soda, is not always required for pound cake and cookies; however, use of a leavener will result in lighter, less dense products. Refer to the specific recipes for guidelines.

Mise en Place

Refer to the basic mise en place for the straight mix method, earlier in this chapter.

Method

Pound cake is used as an example of the typical creaming method. The method is illustrated in Figure 31-1.

(1)

(2)

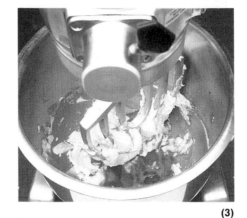
(3)

(4)

(5)

(6)

(7)

(1) The butter and sugar at an early stage.

(2) The properly creamed mixture—smooth and light.

(3) Adding eggs to the butter/sugar mixture.

(4) Proper appearance after the eggs are fully incorporated.

(5) Adding approximately one-third of the dry ingredients.

(6) Adding the liquid ingredients alternately.

(7) The finished batter.

1. Combine the butter and sugar and blend them together until the mixture is smooth, light, and creamy. This can be done in a mixer, using a paddle attachment, as shown in steps 1 and 2 of Figure 31-1. Occasionally scrape down the bowl's sides and bottom. The mixture should be light in both color and texture and relatively smooth. Do not undermix at this stage, because the final texture will depend upon this step.

2. Gradually add the eggs, which should be at room temperature. If they are not, they may cause the mixture to appear curdled, like a broken hollandaise. If this should happen, continue to mix, without adding more eggs, until the mixture looks completely smooth again.

3. Once the eggs are incorporated, add the sifted dry ingredients, alternating with the liquid ingredients, and mix until the batter is very smooth. It is not necessary to divide the dry and liquid ingredients into exact thirds, but they should be added, alternately, to the batter in about three separate operations. The finished batter should be extremely smooth and light, with no trace of lumps, as shown in Figure 31-1. Remember to scrape down the bowl's sides and bottom, as necessary, during mixing.

4. Pour the batter into pans that have been greased and floured or lined with parchment paper. Bake the batter until the cake springs back when pressed lightly with a fingertip and the edges have begun to shrink from the pan's sides.

5. Remove the cake from the oven, and cool and store it.

For a quick summary, refer to the abbreviated method for creamed batters.

Pound Cake

Yield: 1 cake

Sugar, granulated	1 pound	455 grams
Butter	8 ounces	225 grams
Shortening	8 ounces	225 grams
Eggs (may be fortified)	1 pound	455 grams
Flour	1 pound	455 grams
Salt	2 teaspoons	10 grams
Vanilla	to taste	to taste

1. Cream the sugar, butter, and shortening together until they are smooth.

2. Gradually incorporate the eggs.

3. Add the flour, salt, and vanilla. Mix until the batter is smooth. Scrape down the bowl frequently.

4. Scale the batter into a prepared loaf pan. Bake it at 350°F (175°C) until a skewer inserted near the center comes out clean.

CREAMING METHOD

1
Allow the shortening or butter to come to room temperature.

2
Sift the flour, leaveners, and other ingredients as necessary.

3
Cream the butter and sugar until the mixture is light and smooth.

4
Add the eggs and mix them in until the batter is smooth.

5
Add the sifted dry ingredients and liquid ingredients alternately, in thirds.

6
Scale out the batter into prepared pans and bake the item.

7
Remove the item from the pans, cool, and serve or properly store it.

Determining Doneness and Evaluating Quality

For cakes, muffins, and quickbreads made by the creaming method that do not exhibit the following quality characteristics, refer to Table 31-1, "Ordinary Cake Faults and Their Causes." Figure 31-2 shows muffins that were undermixed, properly mixed, and overmixed. The muffin on the left shows poor volume and large air pockets. The middle muffin has risen evenly and has an even grain. The muffin on the left has risen unevenly and when cut open shows visible tunnels.

The crust of these products is usually slightly darker than the interior. The higher proportion of eggs, butter, and sugar causes this browning action. The cake should rise evenly, without a noticeable center hump or dip. Cakes that do not rise adequately may have been either overmixed or undermixed. If the cake has been properly mixed it should not have tunnels or air pockets.

When pressed with a fingertip, the cake should spring back into place. A skewer inserted into the center should come out clean, with no moist particles clinging to it. These cakes should have a moist, delicate, and regular crumb when cut. It is not possible to give specific guidelines regarding the flavor of batters; however, the flavor should always reflect that of the major components and flavoring ingredients.

31-2

Degrees of mix in the batter. Undermixed *(left)*, properly mixed *(center)*, and overmixed *(right)*.

TABLE 31-1. ORDINARY CAKE FAULTS AND THEIR CAUSES

Faults	Improper mixing	Batter too stiff	Too much leavening agent	Not enough leavening agent	Batter too slack	Too much heat	Not enough heat	Excessive sugar	Not enough sugar	Improper type of flour	Too much flour	Not enough flour	Cakes scaled too light	Aged baking powder	Overbaking	Underbaking	Sugar too coarse	Not enough eggs	Fruit not drained properly	Not enough shortening	Unbalanced formula	Batter too warm	Not enough liquid
External																							
Crust too dark						✓		✓															
Cake too small				✓		✓				✓		✓	✓								✓	✓	
Specks on cake																	✓						✓
Shrinkage of cake	✓			✓											✓								
Cake falls during baking											✓					✓							
Cake bursts on top	✓	✓				✓				✓	✓												
Crust too thick							✓																
Internal																							
Coarse and irregular grain	✓	✓	✓			✓												✓			✓		
Dense grain				✓	✓					✓											✓		
Poor flavor			✓																		✓		
Cake tough								✓	✓	✓											✓	✓	✓
Lack of body in quality	✓			✓			✓		✓											✓			
Sinking of fruit			✓		✓					✓									✓			✓	
Poor keeping qualities						✓		✓	✓											✓	✓	✓	

Source: *The Baker's Manual*, Revised Third Edition, Joseph P. Amendola. New York: Ahren's Publishing Company, 1972, p. 53.

The Two-stage Method

This technique is used to prepare what are referred to as "high-ratio cakes." This means that the weight of the sugar given in the recipe is either equal to or greater than the weight of the flour. In order for these cakes to be successfully prepared, it is necessary to use an emulsified shortening.

A high-ratio cake has a tender texture, a fine crumb, and excellent keeping qualities. The sugar acts as a moisturizing agent, and prevents rapid staling and drying.

Mise en Place

Refer to the basic mise en place for the straight mix method, earlier in this chapter.

Method

1. Place all of the sifted dry ingredients in the bowl of a mixer.

2. Add all of the shortening and approximately half of the liquid to the dry ingredients, and mix them using the whip attachment, at a low speed. The batter should be smoothly blended but stiff and fairly thick.

3. Combine the eggs and the remaining liquid ingredients and blend them with a whip to a smooth consistency. Add this mixture to the batter in two or three parts. Mix the batter well between additions and remember to scrape the sides and bottom of the bowl in order to blend the batter smoothly. This process should usually be accomplished in 3 minutes.

4. After all of the wet ingredients have been incorporated, increase the speed of the mixer to medium and mix the batter for another 3 minutes.

5. Scale the batter as desired and place it into prepared pans. Bake the cake at 350°F (175°C).

White Cake

Yield: 22 pounds (10 kilograms) of batter

Flour, cake	6 pounds	2.75 kilograms
Butter	1⅓ pounds	625 grams
Shortening, emulsified, or butter	1⅓ pounds	625 grams
Sugar	7 pounds	3.2 kilograms
Salt	3 ounces	85 grams
Baking powder	6 ounces	170 grams
Vanilla	1 ounce	30 grams
Milk	2 quarts	1.9 liters
Egg whites	1½ quarts	1.4 liters
Eggs, whole	1 pint	480 milliliters

1. Combine the ingredients, using the two-stage mixing method.

2. Scale off the batter into prepared pans.

3. Bake the cake at 375°F (190°C) until it is golden brown and the top springs back when lightly pressed.

NOTE: For yellow cake, reverse the ratio of egg whites to yolks.

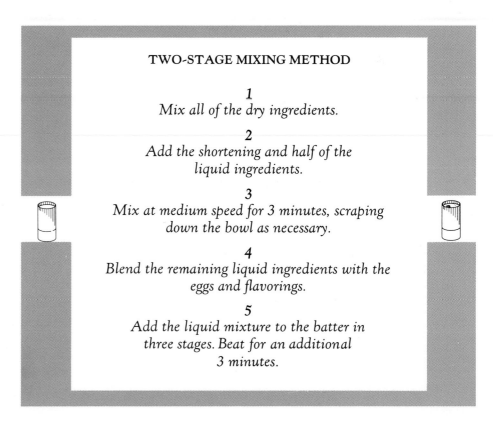

TWO-STAGE MIXING METHOD

1
Mix all of the dry ingredients.

2
Add the shortening and half of the liquid ingredients.

3
Mix at medium speed for 3 minutes, scraping down the bowl as necessary.

4
Blend the remaining liquid ingredients with the eggs and flavorings.

5
Add the liquid mixture to the batter in three stages. Beat for an additional 3 minutes.

746 Baking and Pastry

For a quick summary, refer to the abbreviated method for two-stage batters.

Determining Doneness and Evaluating Quality

These cakes are baked until the surface of the cake springs back when it is lightly pressed with a fingertip. The top crust should be lightly browned, with an even, uncracked surface. The texture and crumb throughout the cake should be quite fine and very even, with no evidence of air pockets or tunnels. When properly prepared and baked, the taste of the cake should reflect the dominant flavoring ingredients (butter, vanilla, or chocolate, for instance).

The Foaming Method

A foam of whole eggs or their yolks or whites provides the structure for genoise, angel food cake, and chiffon cakes, and some special small cakes such as madeleines and langues-de-chat. These extremely delicate cakes are also quite resilient; in some cases, cakes made by this method may be rolled, as in the classic holiday dessert, bûche de Noël.

There are two versions of the foaming method. In one method, used for genoise, the eggs and sugar are heated before they are beaten into a foam. In the other, used for angel food and chiffon cakes, a basic meringue is prepared using egg whites. In the method outlined below, requirements for angel food and chiffon cakes are given as variations of the genoise technique.

The foaming method is also used for preparing meringue, a mixture made of egg whites and sugar beaten until thickened. Recipes for meringue can be found at the end of Chapter 32, "Pastry Doughs and Cookies," along with recipes for other toppings and fillings.

Mise en Place

Refer to the basic mise en place for the straight mix method, earlier in this chapter.

Method

This method is demonstrated in Figure 31-3.

1. Combine the eggs (whole, yolk, or whites) with sugar in a bowl. Place the bowl over a hot water bath and heat it to approximately 100°F (38°C), as shown in step 1 of Figure 31-3. This is done to completely dissolve the sugar, increase the volume, and develop a finer grain. Use a whip to blend together the sugar and eggs.

For angel food and chiffon cakes, especially those made with only egg whites, it may be preferable to omit this stage and start by whipping the whites into a thick foam and then gradually incorporating the sugar.

2. Remove the mixture from the heat and beat it with the whip attachment until the eggs form a stable foam that has tripled in volume. Steps 2 and 3 of Figure 31-3 show the difference in volume. The mixture should form a ribbon as it falls from the whip.

3. Gently fold in the sifted dry ingredients. This can be done by hand, as shown in step 4 of Figure 31-3. Do not overwork the batter at this point, as the foam could start to deflate, resulting in a flat, dense product.

4. If butter or another shortening is required, add it after the dry ingredients have been properly incorporated. These ingredients should be hot to ensure that they are evenly distributed throughout the batter.

5. Immediately pour the batter into pans that have been greased and floured or lined with parchment paper. Bake the batter until the surface springs back when lightly pressed with a fingertip and the cake has begun to shrink from the pan's sides. Step 5 of Figure 31-3 shows properly baked sponge cakes.

Pans for angel food and chiffon cakes should not be greased. For a properly developed structure, these cakes must adhere to the pan's sides.

6. Remove the cake from the oven and let it cool briefly in the pan.

7. Remove it from the pan and let it cool completely on a rack.

Angel food and chiffon cakes should be allowed to cool completely, upside down, in the pan before unmolding so that they retain their full volume.

For a quick summary, refer to the abbreviated method for foamed cakes.

Determining Doneness and Evaluating Quality

The cake should rise evenly during baking. When it is properly baked, it will just begin to shrink away from the pan's sides. When cut, the cake should have no large tunnels or air pockets. Cakes prepared by the foaming method are often more spongy than other cakes, although they do have a discernible crumb. Angel food and chiffon cakes are the most spongy of these types. The limited amount of shortening used gives these cakes a slightly dry texture, which is why they are often moistened with simple syrup. Even though there is a large proportion of eggs in foamed cakes, there should not be a marked egg flavor.

(1)

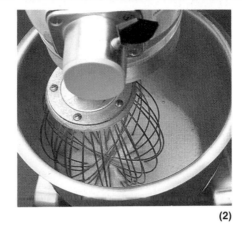
(2)

(3)

(4)

(5)

(1) Using a whip to beat together the eggs and sugar.

(2) Starting to beat the egg/sugar mixture.

(3) The proper volume.

(4) Folding in the dry ingredients.

(5) Properly baked sponge cakes.

Sponge Cake (Genoise)

Yield: Five 10-inch cakes or eight 8-inch cakes

Eggs	30	30
Sugar, granulated	1 pound, 14 ounces	850 grams
Flour, cake	1 pound, 6 ounces	624 grams
Cornstarch	8 ounces	227 grams
Butter, melted and cooled	10 ounces	285 grams
Lemon and/or vanilla extract	as needed	as needed

1. Combine the eggs and sugar. Heat them over a water bath to 100°F (38°C).

2. Whip the mixture until it begins to recede, is very thick, and falls in ribbons.

3. Sift together the flour and cornstarch.

4. Fold the sifted dry ingredients into the egg mixture.

5. Fold the butter and extract into the batter.

6. Scale the batter into prepared pans.

7. Bake at 350°F (175°C) until the cake springs back when pressed.

FOAMING METHOD—GENOISE

1
Sift the flour and other dry ingredients as necessary.

2
Heat the eggs and sugar over a hot-water bath to approximately 100°F (38°C).

3
After removing it from the heat, beat the egg/ sugar mixture until it triples in volume.

4
Fold in the sifted dry ingredients by hand.

5
Add the flavorings, hot butter, and other optional ingredients.

6
Scale out the batter into prepared pans and bake it.

7
Remove the cake from the oven and let it cool briefly in the pan.

METHODS FOR OTHER BATTERS

Biscuits, Scones, and Soda Breads

Although biscuits, scones, and soda breads are quick breads, the technique for preparing their batters is different from the straight mix method. They are made from a stiff batter, almost a dough, which produces a texture slightly chewier than that of the more cake-like muffins and breads described previously. The mixing method accounts for the difference.

Instead of combining all the ingredients at once, a fat such as shortening, butter, or lard is rubbed into the flour until the mixture is mealy in appearance. This can be done by hand or by using a food processor or mixer. The liquid ingredients (eggs and milk or buttermilk) and flavoring ingredients are then added. As with muffins and quick breads, it is important not to overmix.

In some cases, this batter may be *very briefly* kneaded and then rolled out and cut. The dough must not be overworked, as this could cause the finished product to be quite tough.

Once the dough has been mixed and shaped, it may be brushed with an egg wash before being baked, in order to enhance the finished product's appearance. Some scones and biscuits may be cooked on a griddle, although most are baked in an oven.

Mise en Place

Refer to the basic mise en place for the straight mix method, earlier in this chapter.

Method

The method outlined here is for making biscuits.

1. Work the butter or other shortening into the dry ingredients. The butter or shortening should be cold so that it is still solid enough to be worked into the flour without blending the mixture into a smooth dough. This is quite similar to the technique used to prepare pie doughs, discussed in Chapter 32, "Pastry Doughs and Cookies." If the shortening is worked into the flour too thoroughly at this point, the end result will not be as flaky and delicate as desired.

2. Once the shortening is properly worked into the flour (the mixture should resemble coarse meal), add the blended wet ingredients and mix them together just until they begin to cohere. The mixture should not be overworked; vigorous or prolonged mixing will result in a tough product.

3. If necessary, turn the dough out onto a floured work surface and knead it very briefly (refer to the specific recipes).

4. Roll or pat out the dough to an even thickness and cut it into the appropriate shape. (Some biscuits are simply dropped from a spoon onto a baking sheet, requiring no kneading or rolling.)

5. Place the biscuits on baking sheets or pans that have been greased or lined with parchment paper. The closer together the biscuits are placed, the softer and less well-developed their crusts will be.

6. Bake the biscuits at the appropriate temperature until the tops are evenly browned and there is no appearance of moisture on the sides.

7. Remove the biscuits from the oven and cool and store them.

For a quick summary, refer to the abbreviated method for biscuit batters.

Determining Doneness and Evaluating Quality

These products are generally less sweet, and leaner, than quick breads. They should have a delicate texture, which may be either flaky or cake-like, depending on the product being prepared. The crust is often more fully developed than those of quick breads. The flavor is almost impossible to describe except in terms of a specific recipe; for example, scones should have a noticeable and pleasant aroma of good-quality butter.

Steamed Puddings and Dessert Soufflés

Steamed puddings are batters that generally include a high percentage of eggs and sugar and rely on rice, bread, or flour for their structure. These puddings, although slightly similar in texture to soufflés, are less likely to deflate, because of the greater percentage of stabilizers or strengtheners used in the batter. The leavening is usually physical, which means that the steam produced as the batter bakes in a steam bath causes the mixture to lighten. Often, beaten egg whites are folded into the batter, which gives the finished pudding an even lighter texture.

Buttermilk Biscuits

Yield: 12 pounds (5.5 kilograms) of dough

Flour, bread	4½ pounds	2.04 kilograms
Flour, pastry	4½ pounds	2.04 kilograms
Salt	2¼ ounces	60 grams
Baking powder	12 ounces	340 grams
Sugar	1⅓ pounds	625 grams
Eggs, whole	12	12
Buttermilk	1½ pounds	680 grams

1. Sift together the dry ingredients.

2. Combine the eggs and buttermilk.

3. Combine the liquid and dry ingredients. Mix them with an electric mixer fitted with a paddle attachment at medium speed for 5 minutes.

4. Scale the dough into 3-pound presses.

5. Separate the biscuits and place them, six by six, on each tray.

6. Egg wash the biscuits.

7. Bake the biscuits at 400°F (205°C) until they are light-golden.

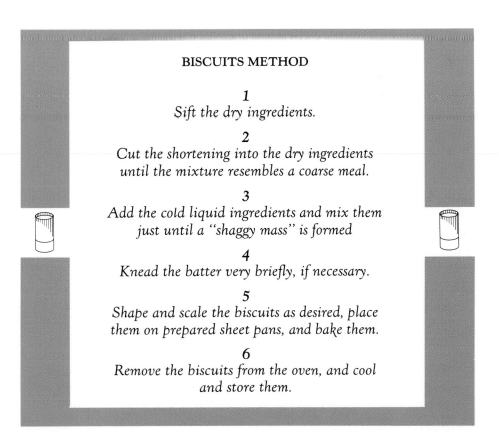

BISCUITS METHOD

1
Sift the dry ingredients.

2
Cut the shortening into the dry ingredients until the mixture resembles a coarse meal.

3
Add the cold liquid ingredients and mix them just until a "shaggy mass" is formed

4
Knead the batter very briefly, if necessary.

5
Shape and scale the biscuits as desired, place them on prepared sheet pans, and bake them.

6
Remove the biscuits from the oven, and cool and store them.

Dessert soufflés rely much more upon egg whites for both leavening and structure than do steamed puddings. Soufflés, therefore, will not be as stable as most steamed puddings. They must be served as soon as they come from the oven. Dessert soufflés may use a base that is similar to pastry cream (see Chapter 33, "Dessert Sauces, Creams, and Frozen and Fruit Desserts"); in some cases, the base may be a fruit puree.

Mise en Place

Refer to the basic mise en place for the straight mix method, earlier in this chapter.

Method

The method described here is for a dessert soufflé and is illustrated in Figure 31-4.

1. Assemble all of the ingredients for the base and prepare it as necessary. Fruits should be poached or sautéed, if necessary, pureed, and, in some cases, strained to remove seeds, fibers, or tough skins. A pastry cream should be prepared for other soufflé types. The base should be at room temperature to make folding in the egg whites easier. Refer to the specific recipes to properly prepare the base for steamed puddings.

2. Prepare the molds. Brush the insides lightly with softened butter. Make sure that all the surfaces are evenly covered. Then, place a generous amount of sugar in each mold and turn it around until all of the surfaces are coated. Pour the excess sugar out of the mold. Rap the mold on the work surface to loosen any additional excess.

3. Add any desired flavoring to the base and incorporate it well. Common flavorings include concentrated citrus juices or purees, cordials and liqueurs, chocolate, or spices.

4. Beat the egg whites to a medium peak. Be sure not to overbeat the egg whites, because that could result in a soufflé that is more likely to fall, or have less volume, and the possibility of the surface cracking during baking is greater.

5. Gently fold the egg whites into the base, blending them evenly. Work carefully to avoid, as much as possible, "deflating" the whites.

6. Fill the molds to the top rims. It may be a good idea to level off the top of the soufflé with a palette knife. Rap the filled mold on a level surface to help remove any air pockets that may have formed. Be sure to use a clean cloth to wipe away any drips from the rim. These drips will create a spot that "drags" the soufflé or pudding, preventing an even rise.

7. Place the soufflés or pudding molds on a sheet pan and add a small amount of water. The water will help create the best cooking environment, assuring that the finished soufflé will have risen evenly, with a well-formed crust.

8. Bake the soufflés or puddings in a very hot oven (400 to 425°F/200 to 220°C) until they have risen and the surfaces are evenly browned. A properly baked soufflé will not "jiggle" excessively, and should have a level, straight top with no cracks. (See step 6 of Fig. 31-4.)

9. Serve the soufflés immediately with the appropriate sauce.

For a quick summary, refer to the abbreviated method for dessert soufflés.

Lemon Soufflé

Yield: 1 individual soufflé

Pastry cream	2 ounces	60 grams
Lemon zest	1 teaspoon	5 grams
Lemon extract	1 teaspoon	12 grams
Softened butter	as needed	as needed
Granulated sugar	as needed	as needed
Egg whites, beaten to stiff peaks	2	2

1. Combine the pastry cream with the lemon zest and extract, and stir until smooth and softened.
2. Prepare the soufflé mold by brushing it with the softened butter and coating it with the granulated sugar.
3. Fold the beaten egg whites into the flavored base in two stages.
4. Pour the soufflé batter into a mold. Place the mold on a sheet pan with a small amount of water and bake it in a 400°F (205°C) oven until the soufflé has risen and its top is well browned. Serve the soufflé at once, dusted with sugar if desired, and with any sauce desired.

(1) Coating the soufflé molds with butter.

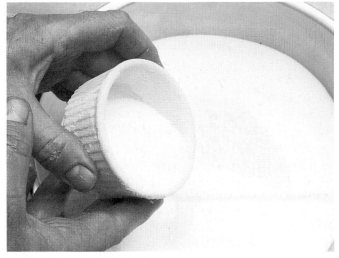

(2) Coating the molds with sugar.

(3) Starting to fold the whites into the base.

(4) The properly mixed soufflé batter.

(5) Adding water to the sheet pan.

(6) The finished soufflés.

DESSERT SOUFFLÉ METHOD

1
Prepare a base according to the recipe and have it at room temperature.

2
Coat the molds with butter and sugar.

3
Add any desired flavoring to the base.

4
Whip the egg whites to a medium peak and fold them into the base.

5
Fill the molds and level the tops.

6
Bake the soufflé on a sheet pan in a hot oven.

7
Serve them immediately, with the appropriate sauce.

Determining Doneness and Evaluating Quality

When properly baked, soufflés and steamed puddings will not wobble when very lightly shaken. The edges of a soufflé should appear cooked, but should still be quite moist. The top should be level and smooth with no cracks. Steamed puddings are more stable and so will appear more fully baked than soufflés. The texture should be very light and airy for both products, and the flavor should not be overwhelmed by the taste of eggs. Most puddings and soufflés are quite sweet, but they should not have a cloying taste.

SUMMARY

It is important to understand and be able to use the four basic techniques for preparing batters: the straight mix method, the two-stage method, the creaming method, and the foaming method. The method used and the ingredient ratios can produce varying results, ranging from moist and dense items such as carrot cake to crisp and light items such as a baked meringue.

The products can be as simple as biscuits or as elaborate as a cake made by combining a genoise with a Bavarian filling and a glaze. No matter how simple or complex the preparation, combining the proper technique with the correct ratios can yield baked goods of high quality.

Warm Chocolate Pudding

Yield: 25 portions

White bread, crust removed	6 ounces	170 grams
Milk	2 to 3 ounces	60 to 85 grams
Butter	12 ounces	340 grams
Confectioner's sugar, sifted	6 ounces	170 grams
Egg yolks	12	12
Chocolate, semi-sweet, melted	8 ounces	225 grams
Hazelnuts, toasted, ground	8 ounces	225 grams
Bread crumbs	8 ounces	225 grams
Vanilla extract	1 ounce	30 grams
Egg whites	20	20
Sugar, granulated	8 ounces	225 grams

1. Soak the white bread in the milk, then squeeze the bread dry and reserve it.

2. Cream together the butter and confectioner's sugar until light.

3. Add the egg yolks slowly and beat the mixture until it is very smooth.

4. Add the melted chocolate, hazelnuts, bread crumbs, and vanilla extract and stir until smooth.

5. Beat the egg whites to medium peaks; then, while still beating, gradually add the granulated sugar to make a meringue.

6. Fold the meringue into the chocolate base.

7. Fill buttered molds three-quarters full with the pudding mixture and bake the pudding in a water bath until it is set.

Pumpkin Bread

Yield: 62 pounds (27 kilograms)

Raisins	9 pounds	4.08 kilograms
Water	7 pounds	3.18 kilograms
Pumpkin	2 No. 10 cans	2 No. 10 cans
Sugar	18 pounds	8.16 kilograms
Whole eggs	6 pounds	2.72 kilograms
Baking soda	3 ounces	85 grams
Salt	4 ounces	114 grams
Cloves	1 ounce	28 grams
Nutmeg	1 ounce	28 grams
Cinnamon	1 ounce	28 grams
Oil	6 pounds	2.72 kilograms
Flour, bread	12 pounds	5.44 kilograms
Flour, pastry	2 pounds	910 grams
Baking powder	5 ounces	140 grams

1. Soak the raisins in the water overnight.
2. Combine the pumpkin, sugar, eggs, baking soda, salt, and spices.
3. Gradually add the oil.
4. Sift together the flours and baking powder.
5. Add and incorporate the flour and baking powder.
6. Add the raisins and soaking liquid. Mix the batter until it is smooth.
7. Scale off the batter (1 pound, 14 ounces/850 grams per loaf) into lined pans. Bake the loaves at 370°F (180°C). Cool them in the liners.

Banana Nut Bread

Yield: *47 pounds (20.5 kilograms)*

Flour, cake	6 pounds	2.75 kilograms
Shortening, emulsified	5 pounds	2.25 kilograms
Orange zest	1 ounce	30 grams
Sugar	10 pounds	4.5 kilograms
Flour, cake	4 pounds	1.8 kilograms
Milk powder	1¼ pounds	570 grams
Salt	5 ounces	140 grams
Baking powder	7½ ounces	215 grams
Bananas, ripe, mashed	10 pounds	4.5 kilograms
Honey	2½ pounds	1.14 kilograms
Eggs, whole	5 pounds	2.25 kilograms
Pecans or walnuts, chopped	2 pounds	910 grams
Vanilla	3 ounces	85 grams

1. Combine the first measure of the cake flour with the shortening and orange zest in an 80-quart (75-liter) mixing bowl; mix them for 2 minutes at medium speed.

2. Add the sugar, remaining flour, milk powder, salt, baking powder, bananas, and honey and mix the batter for 3 minutes on the first speed.

3. Gradually add the eggs.

4. Add the nuts and vanilla.

5. Mix for 5 minutes at medium speed.

6. Scale off the batter into 1-pound, 14-ounce (850-gram) loaves.

7. Bake the bread at 350°F (175°C) for approximately 45 minutes to 1 hour.

Roulade

Yield: 4 to 5 sheets

Eggs	30	30
Sugar, granulated	30 ounces	850 grams
Flour, cake	22 ounces	624 grams
Cornstarch	8 ounces	225 grams
Lemon and/or vanilla	as needed	as needed

1. Combine the eggs and sugar. Heat the mixture over a water bath to 100°F (38°C).

2. Whip the mixture until it begins to recede, is very thick, and falls in ribbons.

3. Sift together the flour and cornstarch.

4. Fold the sifted dry ingredients into the egg mixture.

5. Add the flavoring ingredients.

6. Scale the batter onto parchment-lined sheet pans.

7. Bake the roulade at 350°F (175°C) until the cake springs back when pressed.

8. Turn the roulade out of the sheet pans immediately to stop the cooking. Cover it until ready to use.

Fruitcake

Yield: Twelve 1-pound (455-gram) cakes

Butter	1 pound, 8 ounces	680 grams
Sugar	2 pounds, 4 ounces	1.02 kilograms
Shortening	12 ounces	340 grams
Salt	¼ ounce	7 grams
Lemon rinds, finely grated	2 ounces	60 grams
Eggs	2 pounds, 8 ounces	1.14 kilograms
Flour, bread	1 pound	455 grams
Flour, cake	1 pound	455 grams
Flour, all-purpose	4 ounces	115 grams
Walnuts, chopped	1 pound	455 grams
Fruit mix, candied, diced	1 pound, 8 ounces	680 grams
Raisins, golden	1 pound, 8 ounces	680 grams

1. Cream together the butter, sugar, shortening, salt, and lemon rind for 18 minutes at medium speed.

2. Using a mixer on low speed, gradually incorporate the eggs.

3. Sift together the dry ingredients twice (except for the all-purpose flour) and add them to the batter.

4. Coat the nuts and fruit with the all-purpose flour and add them to the batter. Mix them in just until they are incorporated.

5. Scale off the batter into prepared tins. Bake the fruitcakes at 325°F (165°C) until they are baked through. The cakes should spring back when lightly pressed with a fingertip.

NOTE: An option is to brush the cakes with rum, brandy, or cognac and wrap them in cheesecloth dampened with rum, brandy, or cognac. Repeat the applications of liquor periodically.

Date Nut Bread

Yield: 16 pounds (7.2 kilograms)

Dates	4½ pounds	2 kilograms
Nuts, chopped (walnuts, pecans)	1 pound	455 grams
Water	2¼ ounces	65 grams
Baking soda	1¾ ounces	50 grams
Brown sugar	2½ pounds	1.15 kilograms
Shortening	1⅛ pounds	510 grams
Salt	½ ounce	.5 grams
Eggs	1⅛ pounds	510 grams
Flour, pastry	5 pounds	2.25 kilograms
Baking powder	2 ounces	60 grams

1. Soak the dates and nuts in the water and soak them overnight.

2. Combine the baking soda, brown sugar, shortening, and salt. Mix them well.

3. Gradually add the eggs.

4. Add the flour and baking powder.

5. Scale off the batter into 1-pound, 14-ounce (850-gram) loaves.

6. Bake the bread at 350°F (175°C) until it is done, about 45 minutes.

Ladyfingers

Yield: 4 sheet trays

Eggs, whole, separated	13	13
Sugar	13 ounces	370 grams
Flour, cake, sifted	12 ounces	340 grams

1. Whip together the yolks with 4 ounces of the sugar until the mixture is thick.
2. Whip the egg whites with the remaining sugar to stiff peaks.
3. Fold one-third of the whites into the yolk mixture, then fold the lightened yolks into the rest of the whites.
4. Fold in the sifted flour.
5. Pipe out the ladyfingers onto prepared sheet trays lined with parchment.
6. Bake them at 350°F (175°C) until they are light-golden in color.

Bran Muffins

Yield: 5 dozen

Flour, bread	2⅓ pounds	1.02 kilograms
Baking powder	2½ ounces	70 grams
Sugar	1 pound	455 grams
Milk powder	2 ounces	60 grams
Salt	1 ounce	28 grams
Shortening	8 ounces	225 grams
Molasses	6 ounces	170 grams
Cinnamon	1 teaspoon	2 grams
Eggs, whole	3	3
Water	1 quart	1 liter
Flour, bran	4 ounces	115 grams
Raisins	1 pound	455 grams

1. Sift together the bread flour and baking powder.
2. Using the creaming method, combine all the ingredients except the raisins and bran flour.
3. Mix in the bran flour and raisins.
4. Scale the batter into muffin tins.
5. Bake the muffins at 400°F (205°C) until they are done.

Kugelhopf

Yield: 4 forms

Butter	2 pounds	908 grams
Sugar	1 pound, 10 ounces	737 grams
Lemon zest, grated	of 1 lemon	of 1 lemon
Eggs	1 quart	950 milliliters
Milk	1 quart	950 milliliters
Flour, bread	2 pounds	908 grams
Flour, cake	2 pounds	908 grams
Baking powder	5½ teaspoons	15 grams
Raisins	1½ pounds	680 grams
Fruit, candied, diced	12 ounces	340 grams

1. Using a mixer with a paddle, work the butter at medium speed until it is soft.
2. Add the sugar and lemon zest; cream the mixture for 15 minutes.
3. Combine the eggs and milk.
4. Sift together the flours and baking powder.
5. Dust the dried fruit with flour; shake off the excess.
6. Add the wet and dry ingredients alternately.
7. Fold in the dried fruit.
8. Scale the batter into prepared kugelhopf forms. Bake them at 350°F (175°C) until a skewer inserted near the center comes out clean.

Chocolate Sponge Cake

Yield: five 10-inch cakes or eight 8-inch cakes

Eggs	30	30
Sugar, granulated	30 ounces	850 grams
Flour, cake	17 ounces	480 grams
Cocoa powder	5 ounces	140 grams
Cornstarch	8 ounces	225 grams
Baking soda	½ teaspoon	1.5 grams
Butter, melted and cooled	10 ounces	285 grams
Lemon and/or vanilla	as needed	as needed

(continued)

1. Combine the eggs and the sugar. Heat the mixture over a water bath to 100°F (38°C).

2. Whip the mixture until it begins to recede, is very thick, and falls in ribbons.

3. Sift together the flour, cocoa powder, cornstarch, and baking soda.

4. Fold the sifted dry ingredients into the egg mixture.

5. Fold the butter into the batter.

6. Scale the batter into prepared pans.

7. Bake the cakes at 350°F (175°C) until they spring back when pressed.

Corn Muffins

Yield: 5 dozen

Sugar	1 pound	450 grams
Shortening	8 ounces	225 grams
Eggs	3	3
Cornmeal	1¼ pounds	570 grams
Bread flour	1¼ pounds	570 grams
Pastry flour	1 pound	450 grams
Milk powder	3 ounces	85 grams
Baking powder	2½ ounces	70 grams
Salt	1 ounce	28 grams
Water	1 quart	1 liter

1. Cream the sugar and shortening together until very light. Add the eggs and beat the mixture until it is smooth, scraping the sides and bottom of the bowl as necessary.

2. Sift all the dry ingredients together; then add them to the creamed mixture in two or three parts, alternating with the water.

3. Mix the batter just until all the ingredients are moistened. Scale it off into prepared muffin tins and bake the muffins at 400°F (205°C).

Chewy Brownies

Yield: 1 sheet pan (approximately 70 brownies)

Chocolate, bitter	1½ pounds	680 grams
Butter	2⅓ pounds	1.02 kilograms
Eggs, whole	1 pound, 14 ounces	850 grams
Sugar	4½ pounds	2.04 kilograms
Vanilla	1 capful	1 capful
Flour, cake	1½ pounds	680 grams
Pecans, chopped	2⅓ pounds	1.02 kilograms

1. Melt the chocolate with the butter in a double boiler.
2. Combine the eggs, sugar, and vanilla in a separate double boiler; heat them to 100 to 110°F (38 to 43°C).
3. Whip the egg mixture to medium peaks
4. Mix in the melted chocolate and butter.
5. Fold in the flour and half of the pecans.
6. Spread the batter in a greased, parchment-lined sheet pan.
7. Sprinkle the remaining pecans over the top.
8. Bake the brownies at 350°F (175°C) for 45 minutes.

Chapter *32*

Pastry Doughs and Cookies

All chefs should be able to prepare and work with a variety of doughs, and this chapter's techniques are not difficult to master, with some practice. Considerable precision is needed in measuring, working, and shaping the doughs.

Covered in this chapter are basic pie doughs, rolled-in doughs such as puff pastry, croissant, and Danish doughs, pâte à choux, and cookies. Instructions for filling and assembling various products made from these doughs are also given.

Pastry items are not exclusively prepared in the bakeshop; some, particularly puff pastry and basic pie dough, are used for savory dishes as well as sweet pastries.

BASIC PASTRY DOUGHS

Basic Pie Dough

Basic pie dough is often called 3-2-1 dough, because it is composed of three parts flour, two parts fat, and one part water (by weight). When properly made, the crust is flaky and crisp.

It is important to use pastry flour and to work the dough as little as possible. The larger the fat flakes before the liquid is added, the larger the flakes will be in the baked dough. If the fat is worked more thoroughly into the flour, the result will be a pie crust with a very small flake; this type of dough is sometimes described as mealy.

Fat and liquid should be at the proper temperature—both should be cold. Maintaining the proper temperature will ensure the correct results.

The fat may be shortening, butter, or lard. The liquid is customarily water, but milk or cream may also be used. Because of the fat in milk and cream, the amount of fat in the overall formula should be decreased if these ingredients are used. Cream cheese or sour cream may be required in some doughs, which also calls for a fat modification.

A finished dough's characteristics may be varied in several ways. Adding sugar will produce a dough known as pâte sucrée that is sweet and darker in color, with a crumbly texture. Eggs give doughs a golden color and a firmer texture. Some of a dough's flour can be replaced with ground nuts.

Mise en Place

1. Flour. In most cases, a pastry flour will be called for in the recipe. Pastry flour generally contains less protein than all-purpose or bread flour, and will result in a more tender product. Since it has a tendency to clump together, pastry flour must be properly sifted. Special flours may also be used to prepare a variety of pastry doughs and cookies, according to the specific recipe. In some instances, notably the dough for Linzertortes, the flour is partially replaced by ground toasted nuts.

2. Shortening. This is an extremely important component of all pastry doughs and cookies. The fat, shortening, butter, or oil used will contribute greatly to both the final texture of the product and its finished flavor. For flaky pastries and cookies, the fat should be cold and still plastic. For cake-like items, especially cookies, it may be desirable to have the fat at room temperature so that it can be easily creamed together with the sugar. Still other types of cookies may call for the fat to be melted. Refer to the recipes for specific instructions.

3. Liquid. Although this may be a small part of the dough for many items, it is nonetheless an important component, since it causes the ingredients to cohere into a homogeneous dough. In some cases, the liquid should be very cold to achieve the proper flaky texture in the finished item. It is a good idea in some formulas—notably for pie doughs—to completely dissolve the salt in the liquid to ensure that it will be evenly distributed throughout.

4. Leaveners. A variety of leaveners come into play when preparing pastry doughs and cookies, including physical (steam), organic (yeast), and chemical (baking soda or powder). Refer to the recipes for specific instructions.

5. Flavoring ingredients. Each recipe will indicate any flavoring ingredients that may be required. Nuts, seeds, spices, herbs, cheeses, and a number of other ingredients may be included to produce the desired flavor in the finished product.

Method

1. Scale all of the ingredients and keep the fat cool. It is a good idea to sift the flour to aerate it and remove any lumps. Cut or break the fat into large lumps, about the size of walnuts.

2. Dissolve the salt (if used) in cold water. This will ensure its even dispersal throughout the dough.

3. Combine the flour and the fat. Cut the fat into the dough either by hand, by using a mixer with a paddle attachment, or with a pastry knife. For flaky pie dough, leave the fat pieces rather large, about the size of nickels or dimes. For mealy pie dough, continue to blend the mixture until it resembles a coarse meal and has begun to take on a slightly yellow color.

4. Add the cold water all at once; mix it quickly into the flour-and-fat mixture. Keep mixing just until a shaggy mass forms.

5. Gather the dough into a smooth ball and chill it until it is firm. This allows the dough to relax and also firms up the fat.

6. Turn the dough onto a floured work surface. Lightly dust the dough's surface with additional flour.

7. Using even strokes, roll the dough into the desired thickness and shape. Turn it occasionally to produce an even shape and to keep it from sticking to the work surface. Work from the center toward the edges, rolling in different directions.

8. Cut the dough, if necessary, to fit the pan. Brush away all flour from the surface. (The flour could cause the dough to bake unevenly or to scorch.)

9. Transfer the dough to a pan and fit it gently into the pan's corners. Use a ball of scrap dough to press out any air pockets.

10. For a fresh fruit pie, add the filling, mounding it slightly over the pie pan's rim. Roll out the top crust in the same manner as for the bottom crust. Cut slashes in the top crust to allow steam to escape. Use clean hands to firmly pinch away any excess dough.

11. Brush the top crust very lightly with egg wash. (Be sure that there are no puddles of egg wash.) Bake the pie until it is done. For a description of baking blind and making lattice tops, see the next sections.

The steps in this method are demonstrated in Figures 32-1 through 32-3. For a quick summary, refer to the abbreviated method for basic pie dough.

Determining Doneness and Evaluating Quality

As with all baked items, the important characteristics are appearance, texture, and flavor. Refer to Table 32-1 for a listing of pie problems and their causes.

In general, pie doughs are baked just until they begin to take on a golden color. The presence of ingredients such as egg yolks, milk, butter, or sugar will contribute a richer golden to golden-brown color. The dough should appear dry. If the dough has been rolled out unevenly, the thicker portions may appear moist, indicating that the dough is not fully baked.

The texture will be determined in large part by the mixing method. If the fat has been worked into the dough completely, the finished crust should have a fine crumb.

Pie Dough (Flaky and Mealy)

Yield: 6 pounds (2.72 kilograms)

Flour, pastry	3 pounds	1.36 kilograms
Shortening	2 pounds	910 kilograms
Water, cold	1 pound	455 grams
Salt	1 tablespoon	15 grams

1. Combine the flour and shortening. Rub them together until the mixture resembles cornmeal if mealy dough is desired; the shortening should be left the size of hazelnuts if flaky pie dough is desired.

2. Dissolve the salt in the water. Add it to the flour/shortening mixture.

3. Mix the dough just until it catches.

4. Chill the dough.

5. Scale out the dough and roll it to the correct thickness.

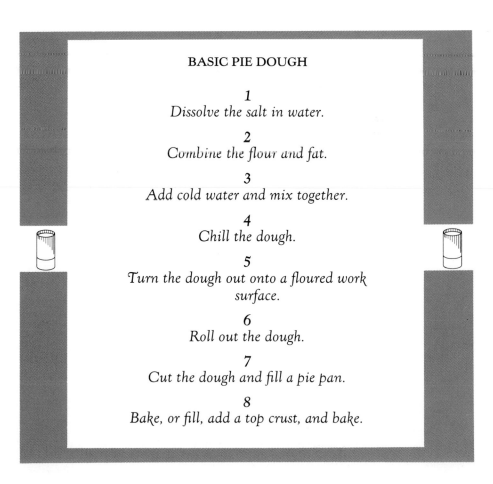

BASIC PIE DOUGH

1
Dissolve the salt in water.

2
Combine the flour and fat.

3
Add cold water and mix together.

4
Chill the dough.

5
Turn the dough out onto a floured work surface.

6
Roll out the dough.

7
Cut the dough and fill a pie pan.

8
Bake, or fill, add a top crust, and bake.

TABLE 32-1. PIE PROBLEMS AND THEIR CAUSES

Problems	Overmixed	Insufficient shortening	Too much shortening	Improperly mixed	Insufficient liquid	Too much liquid	Improper flour	Overworking of dough	Baking temperature too low	Baking temperature too high	No bottom oven heat	Excess acidity in filling	Hot filling used	Lack of opening on top crust	Improperly sealed crusts	Filling too thin	Wet pie plates	Boiling over of filling	Too much sugar	Insufficient sugar	Watery egg whites	Not beaten firm enough
Pie dough																						
Stiff		✓		✓		✓																
Crumbly	✓		✓	✓	✓																	
Tough	✓	✓		✓		✓																
Baked crust																						
Shrinkage	✓	✓			✓	✓	✓															
Solid crust		✓			✓	✓		✓														
Too light in color									✓													
Tough	✓	✓			✓	✓	✓															
Two-crust pies																						
Unbaked crust bottom				✓							✓	✓					✓					
Boiling of filling during baking									✓			✓	✓	✓	✓	✓						
Crust sticking to pans	✓										✓							✓	✓			
Crust soaked on bottom			✓						✓	✓	✓	✓	✓				✓		✓	✓		
Meringue																						
Watery or weeping				✓					✓										✓	✓	✓	✓
Tough				✓						✓									✓			

SOURCE: *The Baker's Manual*, Revised Third Edition, Joseph P. Amendola. New York: Ahren's Publishing Company, 1972, p. 91.

When the fat is briefly rubbed into the flour, the dough will be flaky. If the dough has been underbaked, the texture may be gummy or even rubbery. If it has been overbaked, the crust may be tough.

The dough's flavor will depend for the most part on the type of fat used. Pie doughs made with vegetable shortening will have a nearly neutral flavor. If lard has been used, the dough will taste slightly of that fat. Butter, or a combination of butter and shortening, may be used to introduce its flavor.

Filling Pies and Tarts

Although pies and tarts are alike in terms of the doughs and fillings that are used, there are some differences. Pies are generally double-crusted (having top and bottom crusts) and are baked in a relatively deep pan with sloping sides to accommodate large amounts of filling. Tarts are usually prepared in thin, straight-sided pans, often with removable bottoms. Tarts (and tartlets) most often have a single crust and are not as deep as pies.

Fruit fillings are used for pies, tarts, and strudels. They are generally prepared using sliced and peeled fresh fruit. The fruit is then either poached with liquid or allowed to cook as the entire pastry bakes, as in a fruit pie. Cornstarch or arrowroot may be added to the fruit to tighten the filling, giving it additional body and making the finished product easier to slice into portions. These fillings may be varied by combining fresh and dried fruits or by adding nuts and spices.

Most fruit fillings and some custard fillings are added to the pie

(1) Combining the fat and flour by hand.

(2) The proper consistency for flaky pie dough.

(3) Mealy pie dough resembles a coarse meal.

(4) Adding cold water to the flour and fat mixture.

(5) Combining the ingredients until a shaggy mass forms.

(6) Pie dough, ready to roll out.

32-2 ROLLING OUT DOUGH

(1) Rolling out the dough in one direction . . .

(2) . . . then in the other.

32-3 FILLING A TWO-CRUST PIE

(1) Transferring the bottom crust to a pie plate.

(2) Working out the air pockets.

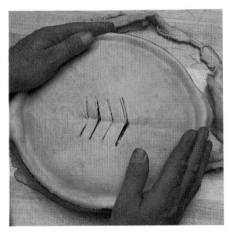

(3) Pinching away any excess dough.

(4) Applying egg wash to the top crust.

crust before it is baked. Cream fillings are usually added to pre-baked crusts. Fresh-fruit tarts are also generally made with pre-baked crusts. Once the shell is baked, it may be coated with chocolate to prevent the crust from becoming soggy. Various fillings may be used. In a typical example, pastry cream is added to the prepared shell and then covered with fresh fruit.

Pies, and less frequently tarts, may be topped with another crust or lattice, or they may be given a crumb topping. Another pie topping is a meringue, which is piped onto the pie in a decorative pattern or simply mounded and peaked. Meringues are quickly browned in

a very hot oven. If properly applied, they should not lift away from the filling, nor should there be visible moisture beads on the meringue's surface.

Fresh-fruit tarts are generally brushed with a glaze, such as apricot, to enhance their appearance and extend their shelf life.

The steps for preparing a lattice top for a pie are shown in Figure 32-4. Recipes for pie fillings and toppings are included at the end of this chapter.

Baking Pies and Tarts

Filled and trimmed pies and tarts should be placed on sheet pans and baked at a high temperature until

the dough is browned. To enhance the finished product's appearance, milk or an egg wash may be brushed on the dough to make a shiny, darker, and perhaps golden (if egg yolk is used) surface.

Baking Blind

The procedure for preparing a pre-baked pie shell is known as baking blind. The dough is prepared, rolled out, and fitted into the pan. The dough is pierced in several places with the tines of a fork (known as docking) to prevent blisters from forming in the dough as it bakes. The pastry is then covered with parchment paper and an empty pie pan is set on top of the paper (this is known as "double panning"). The pans are placed upside down in the oven. This procedure prevents the dough from shrinking back down the pan's edges and keeps it from blistering. The dough is baked in a moderate oven until it is set and appears dry, but not golden.

Another method is to place a sheet of parchment paper over the dough after docking and then fill it with pie weights or dried beans before baking.

Roll-in Doughs

Although the procedures for the roll-in doughs—Danish, croissant, and puff pastry—are the most technically advanced of the ones covered in this chapter, they are not difficult to master if the directions are followed carefully. Proper mixing methods, rolling techniques, and temperature control are important in order to produce doughs that are flaky and delicate after baking. Pastries based on these doughs, especially those made from puff pastry, are often referred to as French pastries.

32-4 CREATING A LATTICE

(1) Making an even rectangle from the rolled-out dough.

(2) Using a guide to cut even strips.

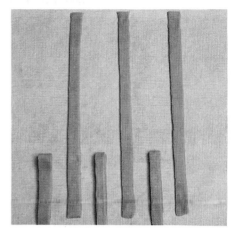

(3) Arranging parallel strips at even intervals on the parchment and folding back half of the strips.

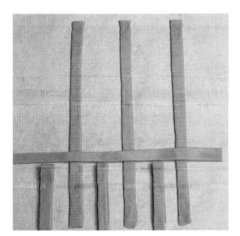

(4) Laying a strip at right angles to the parallel ones.

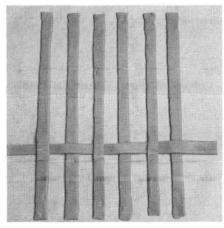

(5) Unfolding the strips.

(6) Folding back alternating, perpendicular strips and adding horizontal strips.

The techniques for preparing these three doughs are similar. Danish and croissant doughs include yeast; puff pastry (pâte feuilletée) does not include an added leavener. In all three, the dough is layered with butter (referred to as a "roll-in") in such a manner that several layers are produced after the dough is properly folded and rolled.

Mise en Place

Refer to the basic mise en place for pie dough, earlier in this chapter.

Method

1. Scale all the ingredients.
2. Combine the ingredients for the dough, and mix and knead them thoroughly. Puff pastry is made with a dough of flour and

(7) Transferring the lattice to the pie and crimping the edges.

water; croissant dough is essentially a lean yeast dough of flour, water, and yeast. Danish dough, a richer yeast dough, usually contains eggs and milk.

3. Allow the dough to rise, if it is a yeast dough, and punch it down. Dough made without yeast should be allowed to rest at room temperature.

4. To prepare the roll-in, combine butter with flour and work them to a smooth, cool, pliable paste. The roll-in should have approximately the same temperature and consistency as the dough.

5. Working on a floured surface, roll the dough out into a rectangle, about ½-inch thick. Use a brush to remove any excess flour from the dough.

6. Roll out the roll-in between two pieces of parchment paper to form a rectangle that will cover two-thirds of the dough; it should be the same approximate thickness (½ inch) as the dough.

7. Position the roll-in on the dough so that one-third of the dough is uncovered and there is a one-half-inch border on the other three sides.

8. Fold the uncovered dough portion in toward the rectangle's center, as for a letter. Once again, brush away any excess flour. Flour left on the dough will interfere with proper layer formation. Fold the opposite end over, and use the fingertips to weld the seams together.

9. It is essential to completely chill the dough between the rolling out and folding stages. If the dough is worked long enough for the butter (or other fat) to become warm, it will be absorbed into the dough, instead of remaining in a separate layer. This will reduce the number of layers and could give the finished product a rubbery or gummy texture.

Turn the dough 90 degrees before beginning to roll it out. This very important step insures that the doughs will have the correct number of layers. Using even strokes that do not extend over the dough's edges, roll out the dough into a large rectangle. Dust the work surface and the top of the dough lightly with flour while rolling it out. This completes the step known as the initial fold. It is done in the same manner for all doughs containing a roll-in. The dough may need to be chilled at this point. If it is still cool, continue with the next step.

10. Brush away all excess surface flour once the dough has been rolled out completely. For croissant and Danish, make three additional three-folds by folding the dough in the same way as described above for the initial fold. Remember to brush away excess flour from the dough. Mark the dough to indicate the number of completed folds, place it on a sheet pan, and cover and refrigerate it before making successive folds.

Puff pastry receives three or four four-folds after the initial fold to give the dough an even greater number of layers. The four-fold is also known as a book fold. (These folds—the three-fold and four-fold—create the layers that give these baked goods their characteristic texture, lightness, and volume.) Fold the narrow ends of the dough in to meet at the center, and then fold the dough in half again. Remember to brush away excess flour as needed. Mark the dough with a fingertip to indicate the number of folds, and cover and refrigerate it between folds.

11. Chill the dough between turns, and be sure that the dough is given a 90-degree turn before it is rolled out once more. This turn is the reason that successive folds are sometimes known as "turns."

12. Repeat step 10, making the

required number of three- or four-folds.

13. The dough should be allowed to rest overnight before being shaped.

Steps in this method are shown in Figure 32-5.

To work with these doughs after they are completely prepared, observe the following guidelines.

• Keep the dough chilled, taking out only the amount to be worked with at a given time. If the dough is too warm, the flakiness of the finished product will be reduced.

• Use a sharp knife when shaping or cutting the dough. Clean cuts will ensure that the baked item rises evenly. This is especially important for high, straight-sided items such as vol-au-vent and bouchée.

• Do not run the roller over the dough's edge; this will destroy the layers.

• Chill puff-pastry items before baking them. This keeps the layers of dough and roll-in separate, assuring the best rise and flakiness in the finished product.

• Save puff-pastry scraps. They can be piled together and rolled out to use for items such as napoleons where a substantial rise is not necessary.

For a quick summary, refer to the abbreviated method for roll-in doughs.

Determining Doneness and Evaluating Quality

Properly baked pastries should have a good volume and a deep-golden color, especially if they have been brushed with egg wash. Croissant and Danish do not usually rise as high as puff pastry, but they still should have noticeable volume.

Products made from puff pastry

(1) Brushing excess flour from the dough after it has been rolled out.

(2) Positioning the roll-in to cover two-thirds of the dough. (Note the margin left around the roll-in's edges.)

(3) The first fold of a three-fold has been completed.

(4) Sealing the edges of the first completed three-fold.

(5) Making a 90-degree turn so that the dough has its long edges parallel to the work surface's edge.

(6) The first stage of a four-fold.

(7) The completed fold.

(8) Marking the dough to indicate the completed fold.

(9) Refrigerating the dough until it is firm.

should have a crisp and flaky texture. Danish are usually more tender and croissants are more resilient.

The predominant flavor for these items should be a fresh, buttery taste. In some cases, puff-pastry shortening may be used; the flavor will be less buttery, but the rise of the item may be better.

Fillings

Nut- and seed-paste fillings are often purchased already prepared, as in the case of almond paste and poppy-seed paste. For the most part, they should be used sparingly. Frangipane, made from almond paste (marzipan), is commonly used as a filling for petits fours. Marzipan is also molded into various shapes (roses, for example) and used to decorate cakes and tortes. There are a number of other fillings that are appropriate for pastries made from Danish, croissant, and puff-pastry doughs, including fresh or cooked fruits, custards and other creams, jams, and savory ingredients such as cheese or sliced ham. Recipes for some commonly used fillings are included at the end of the chapter.

Various finished items made from roll-in doughs are shown in Figure 32-6.

OTHER PASTRY DOUGHS

Blitz Puff Pastry

This is essentially a pie dough that includes a greater percentage of fat than that required for pie dough. The fat is only very slightly worked into the flour before the liquid is added. Once mixed, the dough is rolled out and folded as for puff pastry. It can be used for pie and tart shells, napoleons, and other items where an even rise and discrete layers are not essential.

Puff-pastry Dough I (Butter)

Yield: 18 pounds (8.2 kilograms)

Dough

Flour, cake	1 pound	455 grams
Flour, bread	3 pounds	1.35 kilograms
Butter, chilled	8 ounces	225 grams
Water, cold	1½ quarts	1.4 liters

Roll-in

Butter	4½ pounds	2 kilograms
Flour, sifted	1 pound	455 grams

1. Mix the dough ingredients until they are combined and the dough forms a rough ball. Continue to mix the dough until it is fairly smooth. Pat the dough into a rectangle and let it rest briefly.

2. Mix the butter and the flour at low speed, or using on-off pulses with the food processor, until the roll-in is well-blended, pliable, and smooth. Refrigerate it, if necessary, to prevent the butter from softening too much.

3. Roll the dough into a long rectangle.

4. Roll the butter into a rectangle and position it so that it will cover approximately two-thirds of the dough rectangle. Make the initial three-fold to encase the butter.

5. Turn the dough 90 degrees and roll it to an even thickness. Make the first of four four-folds. Place the dough on a sheet pan and mark it to indicate the number of folds completed. Refrigerate the dough between succeeding folds.

6. Chill the dough well before cutting and shaping.

7. Chill the puff-pastry items well before baking them at 375°F (190°C).

32-6 ROLL-IN DOUGH ITEMS

(1) A variety of filled and baked Danish.

(2) Finished croissants.

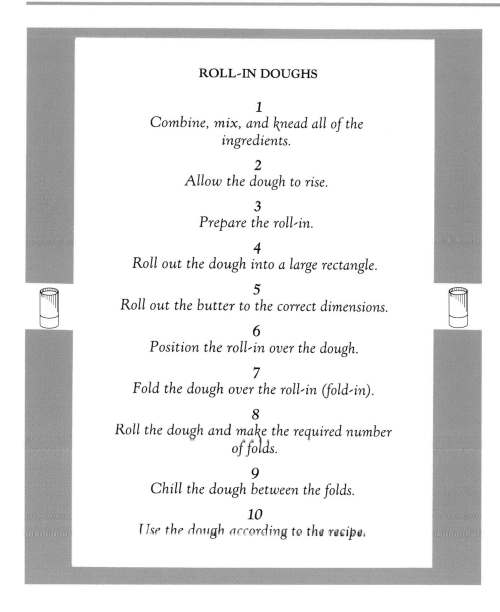

ROLL-IN DOUGHS

1
Combine, mix, and knead all of the ingredients.

2
Allow the dough to rise.

3
Prepare the roll-in.

4
Roll out the dough into a large rectangle.

5
Roll out the butter to the correct dimensions.

6
Position the roll-in over the dough.

7
Fold the dough over the roll-in (fold-in).

8
Roll the dough and make the required number of folds.

9
Chill the dough between the folds.

10
Use the dough according to the recipe.

Pâte à Choux

Pâte à choux is made by combining water, butter, flour, and eggs into a smooth batter. When properly prepared and baked, it will expand during baking, creating a delicate shell with an essentially hollow center, as can be seen in the first photograph in Figure 32-7. Pâte à choux is soft enough so that the chef can use a pastry bag to pipe it into different shapes. Among the most common shapes are cream puffs, profiteroles, and éclairs (shown in the second photograph in Fig. 32-7).

Method

1. Bring the liquid and fat to a full boil.

2. Add the flour and cook it until the mixture pulls away from the pan, forming a ball.

3. Place the dough in the bowl of a mixer. Use the paddle attachment to mix it for a few minutes, allowing the dough to cool slightly. This will prevent the dough's heat from cooking the eggs as they are worked into the mixture.

4. Add the eggs gradually, in three or four additions, working the dough until it is smooth each time. Scrape down the bowl's sides and bottom as necessary. Continue to do so until all the eggs are incorporated.

5. The dough is ready to use at this point. It should be piped onto sheet pans lined with parchment paper, according to the desired result. Figure 32-8 demonstrates the proper action; once the pastry is piped out, release pressure on the pastry bag, and drag the tip backward briefly to form an even shape without a "tail."

6. Bake the items until they are puffed and golden brown, with no beads of moisture on the sides.

Phyllo Dough

This dough, used to prepare strudel and baklava, is a very lean dough made only of flour and water and occasionally a small amount of oil. The dough is stretched and rolled until it is extremely thin. The butter, instead of being rolled into the dough, is melted and brushed onto the dough sheets before they are baked so that after baking it, the result is similar to puff pastry.

Most kitchens purchase frozen phyllo dough. This dough must be allowed sufficient time to thaw and come up to room temperature before it can be worked with success.

After phyllo is removed from its wrapping, it should be covered lightly with dampened towels and plastic. Phyllo can dry out quickly and become brittle enough to shatter otherwise.

For the best texture, bread crumbs, butter, or a combination of both are spread evenly over the dough to keep the layers separate as they bake. A spray bottle or brush is generally used to apply the butter or oil in an even coat.

As with items made from puff pastry, chilling phyllo items before baking them helps the layers remain distinct and causes the item to rise more as it bakes.

Begin by baking the item at a high temperature (375 to 400°F/190 to 204°C). Reduce the heat to 250°F (120°C) once the pâte à choux begins to take on color.

7. Remove the items from the oven and slash them with a sharp knife to allow the steam to escape. This will ensure that the products will not become soggy.

8. If the item is to be filled, slice it open and pull away any loose dough from the interior.

For a quick summary, refer to the abbreviated method for pâte à choux.

Determining Doneness and Evaluating Quality

The dough and the finished product have a definite golden color because of the high proportion of

Blitz Puff-pastry Dough I (Butter)

Yield: 10 pounds (2.5 kilograms)

Flour, bread	2 pounds	910 grams
Flour, pastry	2 pounds	910 grams
Butter	4 pounds	1.8 kilograms
Salt	1 ounce	28 grams
Ice water	1 quart	1 liter

1. Combine the flours in a large bowl.

2. Cut the butter into the flour as for pie-crust dough, until the butter is cut into 1-inch lumps.

3. Dissolve the salt in the water.

4. Add the salted water to the flour/butter mixture and mix them just until the water is absorbed.

5. Let the dough rest about 15 minutes, refrigerating it, if necessary, to keep the butter from softening.

6. Give the dough three four-folds, as in regular puff pastry. Chill it between folds as necessary.

32-7 PÂTE À CHOUX ITEMS

(1) An éclair cut in half after baking shows a hollow center.

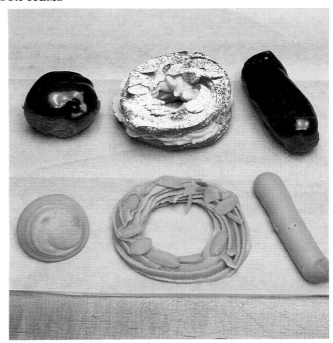

(2) A variety of desserts.

eggs. This color should not change drastically during baking. Properly baked items should appear perfectly dry, without moisture beads on the sides or top. These items should swell to several times their original volume during baking.

Proper baking should produce a dry, delicate texture. The moist interior should be removed before fillings for éclairs or puffs of any kind are added. The predominant flavor of pâte à choux is that of eggs.

COOKIES AND OTHER SMALL PASTRIES

The range of items known as cookies is so large that no single definition is appropriate. The recipes included in this chapter demonstrate the number of different styles possible, including drop, bar, spritz, filled, and icebox cookies.

In general, cookies should be bite-size. They contain a high percentage of sugar, so the oven temperature must be regulated during baking. Convection ovens, which produce evenly baked items, are especially good for baking many kinds of cookies.

32-8
Piping pâté à choux into éclairs.

Pâte à Choux

Yield: 6½ pounds (3 kilograms)

Water or milk	1 quart	1 liter
Butter	1 pound	450 grams
Bread flour	1½ pounds	680 grams
Salt	½ ounce	15 grams
Eggs, beaten	1 quart	1 liter

1. Bring the water or milk and the butter to a rolling boil.
2. Add the flour and the salt and cook the mixture until it pulls away cleanly from the sides of the pan when stirred.
3. Transfer the batter to the bowl of a mixer. Mix it with the paddle attachment briefly to cool it slightly.
4. While beating the batter on medium speed, add the eggs slowly until they are all incorporated and a medium-stiff paste has formed. The pâte à choux is now ready to pipe out and bake.

NOTE: Temperature and times for baking pâte à choux will vary depending upon the size and diameter of the item. Pâte à choux items are frequently baked at 400°F (205°C) until two to three times their original volume, golden brown, and with no beads of moisture on the exterior. After they are fully baked, pâte à choux items are normally slashed to allow any interior moisture to escape before filling, glazing, and so forth.

PÂTE À CHOUX

1
Bring the liquid and fat to a boil.

2
Add the flour and cook the mixture.

3
Mix it until it is cool.

4
Add the eggs gradually and stir them in.

5
Pipe out the batter.

6
Bake the items.

7
Remove them and slash the tops.

Cookies are often served at receptions, as part of a dessert buffet, or with ice cream or sorbet. An assortment of cookies might be presented at the end of a meal, as an appealing "extra." Cookies may be elaborate, with frostings and fillings, or plain. Some cookies—tuiles for example—are used as shells for various fillings.

SUMMARY

The proper manipulation of the fat determines the result in pastry doughs. Temperature control is crucial for most doughs, both in the mixing and shaping phase and during baking. Some of the doughs discussed in this chapter can be used for both sweet and savory items. A basic dough can be varied in many ways; for example, pie dough can be changed by adding different ingredients or by shaping it in a number of different ways to make a pie, a tart, or a tartlet.

Puff pastry, too, may be used to create a variety of products—cookies, turnovers, cases for savory fillings, and classic French pastries, such as the beautiful Pithiviers shown at the beginning of this chapter. This creation of puff pastry and almond paste, decorated with a pinwheel design, is a perfect example of the heights that pastry making can reach.

Croissant Dough

Yield: 12.5 pounds (6 kilograms)

Dough

Yeast	4½ ounces	130 grams
Milk, cold	3 pounds	1.36 kilograms
Salt	2 ounces	55 grams
Sugar	4½ ounces	130 grams
Flour, bread	5 pounds	2.25 kilograms
Butter, unsalted	8 ounces	225 grams

Roll-in

Butter	3½ pounds	1.6 kilograms
Flour	4 ounces	115 grams

1. Combine all of the ingredients for the dough using the straight dough mixing method; mix it for 8 minutes.

2. Roll out the dough in a rectangle and rest it in a refrigerator for one-half hour.

3. Combine the ingredients for the roll-in and beat them to a smooth consistency. (The roll-in should have the same consistency as the dough.)

4. Shape the roll-in into a rectangle that is two-thirds the size of the dough.

5. Make the initial three-fold and seal the edges.

6. Turn the dough 90 degrees and roll it out to the width of the sheet pan. Mark the dough and refrigerate it.

7. Complete the dough by making three additional three-folds. (The dough may be shaped as desired or frozen at this point.)

8. Cut the cold dough into triangles and roll it into shape. Let the croissants rise until their volume has doubled.

9. Brush the croissants lightly with eggwash and bake them at 375°F (190°C) until they are golden and baked through.

Linzer Dough

Yield: Eight 10-inch cakes

Butter	3 pounds	1.36 kilograms
Sugar, granulated	2¼ pounds	1 kilogram
Eggs, whole	6	6
Vanilla	1 teaspoon	5 milliliters
Filberts, toasted, ground	1½ pounds	680 grams
Cake crumbs, fine	8 ounces	225 grams
Cake flour	3¾ pounds	1.7 kilograms
Cinnamon	1 ounce	28 grams
Baking powder	1 ounce	28 grams

1. Cream together the butter and sugar until the mixture is smooth and light.

2. Add the whole eggs and vanilla; mix the dough until it is smooth.

3. Add the remaining ingredients; mix them in until they all are blended into the dough.

4. Chill the dough and then roll it out as desired.

Almond Cookies

Yield: 12½ pounds (5.75 kilograms)

Almond paste	3 pounds	1.36 kilograms
Sugar, granulated	1½ pounds	680 grams
Butter	1½ pounds	680 grams
Shortening	1½ pounds	680 grams
Lemon or vanilla for flavor	as needed	as needed
Egg whites	16	16
Flour, cake	2 pounds	910 kilograms
Flour, bread	2 pounds	910 kilograms

1. Cream together the almond paste, sugar, butter, and shortening.

2. Add the flavoring ingredients.

3. Gradually incorporate the egg whites.

4. Sift together the flours.

5. Add the dry ingredients and mix them well.

6. Spread the dough on sheet pans and bake until the cookies spring back when pressed. Cool and cut the dough to the desired shapes.

One-Two-Three Cookies (Regular)

Yield: 6 pounds (2.75 kilograms)

Sugar, granulated	1 pound	455 grams
Butter	2 pounds	910 grams
Lemon zest	as needed	as needed
Vanilla	as needed	as needed
Eggs, whole	3	3
Flour, cake	3 pounds	1.36 kilograms

1. Cream together the sugar and butter until the mixture is light.
2. Add the lemon zest, vanilla, and eggs. Mix them in until a smooth consistency is reached.
3. Add the sifted flour; mix it in until the dough is smooth.
4. Shape it as desired or refrigerate it.
5. Bake the shaped cookies on sheet pans at 325°F (165°C) until their edges begin to turn golden.
6. Cool the cookies on racks.

One-Two-Three Cookies (Special)

Yield: 7 pounds (3.2 kilograms)

Sugar, confectioners', sifted	1 pound, 6 ounces	625 grams
Whole butter	2½ pounds	1.15 kilograms
Vanilla or other extract	as needed	as needed
Egg whites	4 to 5	4 to 5
Flour, cake, sifted	3 pounds	1.36 kilograms

1. Cream together the sugar and butter until the mixture is light.
2. Add the vanilla and egg whites. Mix them in until a smooth consistency is reached.
3. Add the sifted flour; mix it in until the dough is smooth.
4. Shape it as desired or refrigerate it.
5. Bake the shaped cookies on sheet pans at 325°F (165°C) until their edges begin to turn golden.
6. Cool the cookies on racks.

Shortbread

Yield: One half-size sheet pan: 2¼ pounds (1 kilogram)

Butter	12 ounces	340 grams
Sugar	10 ounces	285 grams
Egg yolks	2	2
Amaretto	1 ounce	30 grams
Orange zest, grated	2 teaspoons	5 grams
Flour, cake, sifted	8 ounces	225 grams
Flour, bread, sifted	8 ounces	225 grams
Salt	pinch	pinch

1. Cream the butter and sugar together until the mixture is light. Add the egg yolks and beat them in well. Scrape down the sides and bottom of the bowl.

2. Add the Amaretto and orange zest and mix them in well.

3. Add the sifted flours and salt; blend them in just until the mixture forms a heavy dough.

4. Roll the dough out between parchment to an even thickness.

5. Bake the shortbread at 325°F (165°C) until it is golden brown.

6. Let the shortbread cool briefly and then cut it into the shapes desired.

Tuiles

Yield: 1 pound (455 grams)

Egg whites	4	4
Eggs	3	3
Sugar, confectioners', sifted	9 ounces	255 grams
Flour, bread, sifted	3 ounces	85 grams
Orange zest, grated	2 teaspoons	5 grams
Lemon zest, grated	2 teaspoons	5 grams

1. Whip together the egg whites, eggs, confectioners' sugar, and bread flour until they are blended into a smooth batter.

2. Fold in the orange and lemon zest. Let the batter rest overnight under refrigeration.

3. Using a template to create the desired pattern, spread the batter onto a greased and floured sheet pan.

4. Bake the tuiles, a few at a time, at 375°F (190°C) until the edges have just begun to brown.

5. Immediately remove the tuiles from the sheet pan and drape them over a dowel or rolling pin while they are still very hot in order to curve them slightly.

Cream Cheese Filling

Yield: 10 pounds (4.5 kilograms)

Cream cheese, softened	6 pounds	2.7 kilograms
Sugar	2 pounds	910 grams
Cornstarch	8 ounces	225 grams
Eggs	5	5
Butter, melted	1 pound	455 grams

1. Mix all of the ingredients until very smooth.

2. Refrigerate the filling until needed.

Hazelnut Filling

Yield: 6 pounds (2.7 kilograms)

Almond paste	1 pound	455 grams
High-ratio shortening	1 pound	455 grams
Sugar	1 pound	455 grams
Hazelnuts, slightly toasted, ground fine	3 pounds	1.36 kilograms
Cinnamon	1 ounce	30 grams

Mix all of the ingredients together until thoroughly blended.

NOTE: To give this filling a spreadable consistency, add a mixture of 1 part egg white to 1 part water as needed.

Cheese Filling

Yield: 9 pounds (4 kilograms)

Ingredient	US	Metric
Baker's cheese	5 pounds	2.25 kilograms
Sugar	1 pound	455 grams
Shortening or butter	1 pound	455 grams
Cornstarch	8 ounces	225 grams
Salt	1 ounce	30 grams
Eggs	1 pint	480 milliliters
Vanilla extract	½ ounce	15 milliliters
Milk	8 ounces	240 milliliters

1. Combine all the ingredients except the milk and mix well.
2. Gradually add the milk to avoid lumps.
3. Refrigerate the filling until needed.

Pithiviers

Yield: One 12-inch pastry

Ingredient	US	Metric
Puff pastry dough	24 ounces	680 grams
Frangipane	12 ounces	340 grams
Pastry cream	4 ounces	115 grams
Pears, apples, or raisins (optional)	as needed	as needed
Sugar	as needed	as needed

1. Roll the puff pastry out and cut it into two 12-inch circles.

2. Combine the frangipane and pastry cream and place in the center of one of the puff pastry circles, leaving a 1-inch border. (If desired, add the fruit to the filling at this point.)

3. Brush the rim of the filled puff pastry with water and top it with the second circle. Allow all the air to escape before pressing the edges closed.

4. Crimp the edges of the pithiviers and cut a spiral pattern in the top of the pastry.

5. Bake the pithiviers at 375°F (190°C) until it is browned.

6. Sprinkle the pithiviers with sugar and place it in a 450°F (230°C) oven until the sugar caramelizes and forms a glaze.

Lemon Filling

Yield: Four 10-inch pies

Water, total	4 pints	2 liters
Lemon juice, freshly squeezed	10 ounces	300 milliliters
Lemon rind	2 ounces	55 grams
Salt	¼ ounce	7 grams
Butter	4 ounces	115 grams
Sugar	2 pounds	910 grams
Cornstarch	6 ounces	170 grams
Egg yolks	8 ounces	240 milliliters

1. Bring 3 pints (1.5 liters) of the water, lemon juice, lemon rind, salt, butter, and half of the sugar to a boil.

2. Combine the remaining water and sugar with the cornstarch and egg yolks in a bowl. Mix until very smooth, then temper this mixture with the boiling lemon mixture.

3. Return the tempered egg yolk mixture to the remaining lemon mixture and bring the filling to a full boil. Pour the filling into prepared pie shells.

Almond Filling (Version 1)

Yield: 4½ pounds (2 kilograms)

Almond paste	3 pounds	1.36 kilograms
Sugar	1½ pounds	680 grams

1. Work the ingredients together until thoroughly blended.
2. Wrap the filling well and refrigerate until needed.

NOTE: To give this filling a spreadable consistency, add a mixture of 1 part egg white to 1 part water.

Almond Filling (Version 2)

Yield: 8 pounds (3.6 kilograms)

Cake crumbs	4½ pounds	2 kilograms
Macaroon or almond paste	1¼ pounds	560 grams
Sugar	1 pound	455 grams
Corn syrup or numoline	2 ounces	60 milliliters
Eggs	1 pint	480 milliliters
Milk	4 to 8 ounces	120 to 240 milliliters

1. Combine all of the ingredients except the milk.
2. Gradually add the milk until smooth.
3. Refrigerate until needed.

Holland Dutch Topping

Yield: 2½ pounds (1 kilogram)

Yeast	1½ ounces	40 grams
Warm water	24 ounces	600 milliliters
Rice flour	14 ounces	400 grams
Sugar	1 ounce	30 grams
Shortening	1½ ounces	40 grams
Salt	½ ounce	15 grams

1. Dissolve the yeast in the warm water.
2. Add the dissolved yeast to the remaining ingredients and work until smooth.
3. Let the mixture rise once and then apply it to rolls or breads.

Pecan Pie Filling

Yield: 13 pounds (6 kilograms)

Sugar	6 ounces	170 grams
Flour, bread	6 ounces	170 grams
Corn syrup, light	9 pounds	4 kilograms
Eggs	3 pints	1.5 liters
Vanilla	1½ ounces	60 milliliters
Salt	1½ ounces	40 grams
Pecans, whole	2½ pounds	1.15 kilograms
Butter, melted	10 ounces	280 grams

1. Combine the sugar, flour, and corn syrup.

2. Add the eggs, vanilla, and salt and stir to combine.

3. Add the pecans and the melted butter and mix until all of the ingredients are blended.

4. Scale the filling off to fill prepared pie crusts.

Pumpkin Pie Filling

Yield: 21 pounds (9.5 kilograms)

Granulated sugar	1 pound	450 grams
Brown sugar	1 pound	450 grams
Flour, pastry	4 ounces	115 grams
Salt	1 ounce	30 grams
Cinnamon, ground	1 ounce	30 grams
Ginger, ground	¼ ounce	7 grams
Nutmeg, ground	¼ ounce	7 grams
Pumpkin puree	7 pounds	3.15 kilograms
Corn syrup	24 ounces	720 milliliters
Milk	1 gallon	3.75 liters
Eggs	1 quart	950 milliliters

1. Combine the sugars, flour, salt, cinnamon, ginger, and nutmeg. Blend them thoroughly.

2. Add the pumpkin puree, corn syrup, and milk. Mix until smooth.

3. Add the eggs and blend until smooth. Scale the filling to fill prepared pie crusts and bake in a moderate oven until the filling is set and the crusts have browned.

Danish Dough

Yield: 12½ pounds (5.75 kilograms)

Dough

Sugar	10 ounces	285 grams
Salt	1½ ounces	40 grams
Butter	8 ounces	225 grams
Egg yolks	1 pound	455 grams
Milk	2 pounds	970 grams
Yeast	8 ounces	225 grams
Flour, pastry	1½ pounds	680 grams
Flour, bread	3 pounds	1.36 kilograms
Mace or cardamom	¼ ounce	7 grams
Vanilla, lemon, or other extract	to taste	to taste

Roll-in

Butter, beaten until elastic	3 pounds	1.36 kilograms

1. Combine all of the ingredients for the dough using the straight dough mixing method; mix the dough for 8 minutes.

2. Spread the dough onto a parchment-lined and floured sheet pan. Rest it in a refrigerator for one-half hour.

3. Roll the dough into a long rectangle.

4. Roll the butter into a rectangle that will cover approximately two-thirds of the dough rectangle. Make the initial three-fold to encase the butter.

5. Turn the dough 90 degrees and roll it to an even thickness. Make the first of the four three-folds. Place the dough on a sheet pan and mark it to indicate the number of folds completed. Refrigerate the dough between succeeding folds.

6. Cut the dough into the desired shapes. Fill and fold the Danish. Let the pastries rise until their volume has doubled.

7. Brush the dough lightly with eggwash and bake at 350°F (180°C) until golden and properly baked.

Puff-pastry Dough II (Shortening)

Yield: 15½ pounds (7 kilograms)

Dough

Flour, bread	4 pounds	1.8 kilograms
Flour, cake	1 pound	454 grams
Shortening, regular	1½ pounds	680 grams
Salt	1 ounce	28 grams
Water	3 pounds	1.36 kilograms

Roll-in

Puff-pastry shortening	5 pounds	2.72 kilograms
Flour, sifted	1 pound	455 grams

The method here is the same as that for Puff-pastry Dough I.

Regular Meringue

Yield: 3 pounds (1.36 kilograms)

Egg whites, room temperature	1 pound	455 grams
Sugar	2 pounds	910 grams

1. Place the egg whites in a bowl (copper gives the best volume).

2. Beat the egg whites until they are frothy.

3. Gradually add the sugar while still whipping. Continue whipping until the desired consistency is reached.

Italian Meringue

Yield: 3½ pounds (1.59 kilograms)

Sugar	2 pounds	910 grams
Water	8 ounces	225 grams
Egg whites	1 pound	455 grams

1. Combine the sugar and water in a pot over moderate heat and bring this syrup to 240°F (115°C).

2. Place the egg whites in the bowl of an electric mixer and beat them to soft peaks.

3. Add the hot syrup to the egg whites in a steady stream while continuing to whip them at medium to high speed until the desired consistency is reached.

Swiss Meringue

Yield: 3 pounds (1.36 kilograms)

Egg whites	1 pound	455 grams
Sugar	2 pounds	910 grams

1. Place the egg whites in a bowl (copper gives the best volume).

2. Beat the egg whites and sugar together, holding the bowl over a bain-marie until the mixture reaches 100°F (38°C).

3. Continue whipping the meringue in an electric mixer on medium speed until the desired consistency is reached.

Frangipane

Yield: 7½ pounds (3.4 kilograms)

Almond paste	4 pounds	1.8 kilograms
Butter	2 pounds	910 grams
Sugar, granulated	6 ounces	170 grams
Eggs	16	16
Flour, cake	6 ounces	170 grams

1. Combine the almond paste, butter, and sugar and cream until smooth.

2. Gradually incorporate the eggs and mix until smooth.

3. Add the flour and mix it in thoroughly. Store the frangipane under refrigeration until needed.

Marzipan

Yield: 13½ pounds (6.1 kilograms)

Almond paste	7 pounds	3.15 kilograms
Confectioner's sugar	5 pounds	2.25 kilograms
Corn syrup, light	1½ pounds	680 grams
Kirschwasser	to taste	to taste

1. Combine all of the ingredients and work them with a paddle until smooth.

2. Wrap the marzipan well and store it under refrigeration until needed.

Chapter *33*

Dessert Sauces, Creams, and Frozen and Fruit Desserts

The difference between a plain baked item and a fancy pastry often relies on the presence of a filling, a sauce, a glaze, or an icing. The ability to prepare a number of basic sauces and creams makes it possible to give basic cakes a great deal of variety without a great deal of effort.

The dessert sauces described here can also be used as a component for another dessert, either as a flavoring for a base or as the base itself, which may be lightened with whipped cream, stabilized with gelatin, or frozen. "Creams" is a broad category that includes such preparations as mousses, Bavarians, and buttercreams.

There are a number of new, lighter ways to approach desserts, such as replacing a vanilla sauce with a base of ricotta and yogurt or making a beautiful dessert of fresh or poached fruits. These items are not difficult to prepare and may be used as components in a range of desserts, from relatively simple ice creams and sorbets to elaborate pastry creations.

Pastry Cream for Hot Soufflés

Yield: 10 pounds (4.5 kilograms)

Sugar	18 ounces	510 grams
Flour	18 ounces	510 grams
Egg yolks	16	16
Eggs, whole	8	8
Milk	2¼ quarts	1.15 liters
Vanilla beans	2	2
Butter	9 ounces	255 grams

1. Combine half of the sugar, and the flour, egg yolks, and eggs in a bowl, and whip them together to a smooth consistency. Set the mixture aside.

2. Combine the remaining sugar, the milk, and the vanilla beans and bring the mixture to a simmer. Remove and reserve the beans.

3. Temper the egg mixture from step 1 with the hot milk mixture, and return the tempered mixture to the milk. Continue to cook over low to medium heat, stirring constantly, until the mixture comes to a boil.

4. Add the butter to the cream mixture and stir until smooth. Add a small amount of salt to taste. Let the cream cool by spreading it in a hotel pan. Sprinkle the surface with sugar or lay parchment paper directly on the surface to prevent a skin from forming. The pastry cream is ready to be used for dessert soufflés or other preparations at this point.

PASTRY CREAM

1
Combine the flour and part of the sugar; blend them well to remove all lumps. Add the eggs and/or egg yolks to this mixture.

2
Heat the milk with the remainder of the sugar to just below a boil.

3
Temper the egg mixture with one-third of the hot milk mixture. Return the tempered egg mixture to the pot.

4
Bring the pastry cream to a second boil, stirring it constantly.

---

soften the gelatin sufficiently. Be sure to combine the gelatin and vanilla sauce completely.

3. Cool the sauce by stirring it over an ice-water bath until it has gelled enough to form a slight mound when dropped from a spoon.

4. Beat the egg whites to a thick foam. Gradually add a small amount of sugar and continue to beat the egg whites to a medium peak.

5. Add the whipped heavy cream and fold it gently until it is combined.

6. Add the beaten egg whites and fold them gently until the mixture is combined. Refrigerate the Bavarian until it is thoroughly set.

For a quick summary, refer to the abbreviated method for Bavarian creams.

Mousse

Although quite similar to a Bavarian, a mousse usually does not contain gelatin as a stabilizer. Opinions vary as to whether the base should be added to the whipped cream, as done here, or the cream should be folded into the base. Both methods should yield a light, delicate mousse if all procedures are properly followed. A well-prepared mousse may often become the signature dessert for a restaurant. The presentation may be varied by using different containers, such as tuile cups, hollowed fruits, or special glasses.

Method

This method is demonstrated in Figure 33-3.

1. Measure all of the ingredients. Heavy cream should be whipped and held under refrigera-

Vanilla Bavarian Cream (Version I)

Yield: 2 quarts (2 liters)

Vanilla sauce	1 quart	1 liter
Gelatin	1 ounce	30 grams
Cold water	2 ounces	60 milliliters
Heavy cream	1 quart	1 liter
Vanilla-flavored sugar	3 to 4 ounces	85 to 115 grams

1. Prepare the vanilla sauce according to the recipe earlier in this chapter.

2. Dissolve the gelatin in the water and let it absorb the liquid (see note below). If the vanilla sauce is still hot, stir the dissolved gelatin into the hot sauce. If the sauce is cold, gently heat the gelatin over simmering water until all of the crystals are dissolved.

3. Stir the vanilla sauce and gelatin mixture over an ice bath until it is thick enough to mound slightly when dropped from a spoon.

4. Whip the heavy cream to medium peaks. Gradually add the vanilla-flavored sugar and continue to beat the cream to stiff peaks. Fold the beaten whipped cream into the vanilla sauce and gelatin base.

5. Use the Bavarian as desired for a filling, or place it in molds to serve as a dessert.

NOTE: Instead of water, the gelatin may be dissolved in a liqueur (Grand Marnier or Kahlua, for example) to add a special flavor to the Bavarian.

The Bavarian may also be flavored by adding melted and cooled chocolate, citrus zest, toasted and chopped nuts, or pureed and sweetened fruits such as raspberry sauce (see the recipe earlier in this chapter), or sliced bananas.

Refer to the recipe for Vanilla Sauce, earlier in this chapter.

tion. Egg whites should be allowed to come to room temperature and then beaten to stiff peaks. A percentage of the sugar is usually added to the egg whites to form a common meringue, which is more stable than plain egg whites.

2. Whip together the egg yolks and sugar until they are thick and light. The mixture will fall in ribbons from the whip when it has reached the correct consistency. (Some recipes will indicate the use of a warm sugar syrup instead of granulated sugar. This is done to ensure a finished mousse without graininess.) At this time, additional flavoring ingredients can be added to the yolk mixture (known as the base), according to the recipe.

3. Add the flavoring to the whipped cream and blend them.

4. Add the base to the whipped cream and blend them. Before continuing with the next step, make sure the mixture has a homogeneous color and texture. Do not blend the mousse too vigorously or some of the volume will be lost.

5. Add the egg whites to the base/whipped cream mixture. Fold them in gently with a whip to retain as much volume as possible.

6. The finished mousse should be well-blended but still retain as much volume as possible. Notice the texture and consistency shown in step 5 of Figure 33-3.

Buttercream

Buttercreams are made by several methods and are known as Italian, French, German, and Swiss. Most versions follow one of two basic formulas. In one method, a pastry cream or vanilla sauce is prepared, flavored, and allowed to cool. Softened butter is whipped into this base. The second method requires a syrup made by heating sugar and water. The hot syrup is beaten into eggs (whole, yolks, or whites) to make a meringue or foam, and then softened butter is added gradually, as shown in the step-by-step photos for Italian buttercream in Figure 33-4. Refer also to the recipes for French Buttercream and German Buttercream at the end of this chapter.

Method

1. Measure all the ingredients and assemble the mise en place: Allow butter to come to room temperature.

2. Combine sugar and water in a pot and bring them to a boil. Use a brush to wipe down the pot's sides; this will prevent crystallization of the syrup caused by undissolved sugar.

BAVARIAN CREAMS

1

Prepare a vanilla sauce. The sauce may be flavored as desired.

2

Combine the vanilla sauce with gelatin that has been bloomed and dissolved.

3

Cool the vanilla sauce over an ice-water bath until it mounds slightly when dropped from a spoon.

4

Fold whipped heavy cream into the Bavarian and pour it into prepared molds. Chill the Bavarian for several hours before serving.

33-3 THE METHOD FOR MOUSSE

(1)

(2)

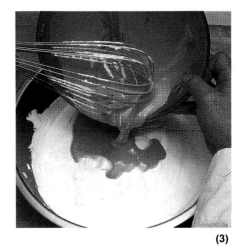

(3)

(4)

(5)

(1) Beating the egg yolks and sugar together.

(2) Adding flavoring to the whipped heavy cream.

(3) Adding the base to the whipped cream.

(4) Folding beaten egg whites into the base/cream mixture. Notice the action of the whip.

(5) The finished mousse at the correct consistency and texture.

Chocolate Mousse

Yield: *Twenty-five 4- to 5-ounce (115- to 140-gram) portions*

Semi-sweet chocolate, melted	2½ pounds	1.15 kilograms
Butter, melted, warm	6 ounces	170 grams
Sugar	8 ounces	230 grams
Egg yolks	20	20
Egg whites	20	20
Heavy cream, beaten to stiff peaks	1 quart	1 liter
Rum or vanilla extract	to taste	to taste

1. Blend the chocolate and the butter.

2. Beat half of the sugar with the egg yolks until the mixture is light, creamy, and has doubled in volume.

3. Beat the egg whites to soft peaks; while still beating the whites, gradually add the remaining sugar and continue to beat until stiff peaks form.

4. Fold the egg whites into the egg yolks, and then fold the chocolate and butter mixture into the egg mixture.

5. Fold in the whipped cream and the rum or vanilla extract. Chill the mixture until service. The mousse may be scooped out at service or piped into molds and allowed to chill directly in the mold.

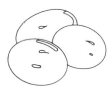

3. Continue to boil the sugar syrup until the temperature reaches 240°F (115°C). Step 2 of Figure 33-4 shows the use of a candy thermometer.

4. Beat egg whites to soft peaks. With the machine still running, gradually add the sugar syrup in a thin stream and continue to beat the mixture until a firm meringue is formed.

5. Gradually add softened butter to the meringue (as shown in step 4 of Fig. 33-4) and beat the mixture until a smooth, light buttercream is formed. Step 5 of Figure 33-4 shows the correct consistency and texture for an Italian buttercream.

FROZEN DESSERTS

Frozen desserts have always been extremely popular. The actual production of most of these desserts requires no special equipment. The aim actually is to produce an item that is semi-frozen; that is, it can be spooned up.

Some frozen desserts may be "still-frozen," which means that the basic mixture is prepared, placed in a mold, and then allowed to freeze. The presence of various ingredients, or the correct manipulation of ingredients, insures that the end result will be smooth, light, and not rock-hard. Ingredients such as sugar and alcohol will pre-

vent mixtures from freezing solid. Whipped cream and beaten egg whites will naturally introduce enough air to prevent the mixture from becoming too hard. An example of a still-frozen dessert is a frozen soufflé.

Other desserts are churned before they are frozen. This means that the mixture is agitated as it is cooled, incorporating additional air so that the end result is light and smooth. Ice cream is the classic example.

As is the case for the dessert sauces, none of the frozen desserts share a basic mise en place. The recipes themselves serve as the guidelines for mise en place.

Frozen Soufflés and Mousses

Frozen soufflés and mousses are made by preparing a mousse (as outlined in the section covering creams), using the mousse to fill an appropriate mold or other container, and then freezing it until it solidifies. In order to achieve the best texture, a frozen mousse often should be allowed to "temper" briefly under refrigeration before it is served.

Ice Cream

Ice creams may be made in various ways and with different equipment. Essentially, a custard base, cooked to nappé and chilled, is placed in an ice-cream freezer along with appropriate flavorings and garnishes. The freezer is chilled to temperatures below 32°F (0°C), and a paddle churns the custard as it freezes. This action incorporates air, preventing the custard from freezing into a solid mass. The result is a smooth, light, and creamy mixture.

Italian Buttercream

(1) Brushing the pot's sides with cold water.

(2) Cooking the syrup to the correct temperature.

(3) Adding the syrup to the beaten egg whites.

(4) Adding the softened butter to the meringue.

Yield: 21½ pounds (9.6 kilograms)

Sugar	5 pounds	2.25 kilograms
Water	1½ pounds	680 grams
Egg whites, whipped to medium-stiff peaks	5 pounds	2.25 kilograms
Butter, softened	10 pounds	4.5 kilograms

1. Combine the sugar and water and cook this syrup mixture until it reaches 240°F (115°C).

2. Continue to beat the whipped egg whites with the whip attachment of an electric mixer while adding the hot syrup in a thin stream. Whip the mixture until it reaches room temperature.

3. Gradually add the butter until it is all incorporated. The buttercream is ready for use, or it may be stored under refrigeration until it is needed. Whip the refrigerated buttercream until it is smooth and light before using it.

(5) The finished buttercream.

Frozen Orange Soufflé

Yield: 30 small soufflés

Egg yolks	15	15
Eggs	8	8
Granulated sugar	1⅓ pounds	625 grams
Grand Marnier, or another orange-flavored liqueur	6 ounces	160 milliliters
Heavy cream, whipped	3 pints	1.4 liters

1. Combine the egg yolks, eggs, and sugar in the bowl of an electric mixer. Heat this mixture over a hot-water bath, stirring frequently, until it reaches 140°F (60°C).
2. Place the bowl on the electric mixer and beat the mixture on the second speed until it is cooled and has reached its full volume. Stir in the Grand Marnier.
3. Fold in the heavy cream. Pour the soufflé mixture into molds that have been prepared with paper collars. Place the soufflés into the freezer immediately and freeze them overnight. Remove the collars before serving.

NOTE: Other liqueurs and cordials can be used to flavor the soufflé, as well as citrus zest, chopped toasted nuts, melted chocolate, and pureed fruits.

Basic Vanilla Ice Cream

Yield: 1 gallon (3.75 liters)

Milk	1 quart	1 liter
Heavy cream	1 quart	1 liter
Sugar	1 pound	455 grams
Egg yolks	16	16
Vanilla beans	3	3

1. Combine the milk, heavy cream, half of the sugar, and the vanilla beans in a heavy-bottomed pot. Bring the mixture to a boil.
2. Combine the remaining sugar with the egg yolks, and temper this mixture with approximately one-third of the boiling milk mixture. Return the tempered egg yolks to the boiling milk mixture and cook the mixture over low heat, stirring it constantly, until it is nappé.
3. Strain the ice-cream base and cool it over an ice bath. Split the vanilla beans and scrape out their interiors; add this to the ice-cream base.
4. Process the mixture in an ice-cream freezer until it is frozen. Store the finished ice cream in the freezer.

A variation on the traditional frozen, custard-style ice cream is a glace based on pureed and sweetened low-fat ricotta cheese and yogurt.

Sorbets/Sherbets

Sorbets are based on liquids such as fruit juices, wine, or coffee. The liquid is sweetened and may be combined with milk or cream and, in some cases, eggs. The base mixture is then frozen in the same manner as ice cream. The result is a sorbet with a texture similar to that of ice cream. The far lower percentage of butterfat and egg yolks, however, gives sorbets a more "icy" texture.

Sorbets that are not heavily sweetened and do not, as a rule, contain cream or milk frequently are served between a formal meal's courses as an intermezzo ("between the work") to cleanse the palate. Refer to the recipe at the end of this chapter.

Granite

In these "icy" preparations, the base mixture is prepared in the same manner as for a sorbet, although it customarily does not contain any milk, cream, or eggs. The mixture is placed in the freezer and allowed to still-freeze until service. At that time, the granite is scraped to produce large flakes or granules. Refer to the recipe at the end of this chapter.

FRUITS

Fruits play a number of different roles in any restaurant. In the bakeshop, they may be used as flavoring ingredients, garnishes, fillings, or the main element of a dessert.

This chapter will include some fruit desserts that do not fit into other baking categories.

Poached Fruits

The repertoire of classic desserts includes such examples of poached fruit dishes as peach Melba and pears Belle Hélène. Many restaurants with contemporary menus try to offer their patrons desserts that are low in calories, such as a variety of poached fruits. Poached fruits are also often used in other desserts as fillings or toppings.

Usually, fruits to be poached should be firm enough to hold their shape during cooking. Very tender fruits such as berries or bananas are generally not cooked using this technique. The greater the amount of sugar in the poaching liquid, the more firm the end result will be. The use of wine as part or all of the poaching liquid will have a similar effect.

Method

1. Prepare the fruit(s) as necessary. In some cases, it may be desirable to remove the peel, seeds, or pits before poaching the fruit. The peel frequently will be included with the fruit as it poaches to contribute additional flavor.

2. Combine the fruit(s) with the poaching liquid, often a mixture of simple syrup, spices, and occasionally wine, and bring it just to a bare simmer.

3. Reduce the heat and gently poach the fruit until it is tender. Test the fruit by piercing it with a sharp knife. There should be very little or no resistance.

4. Allow the fruit to cool in the poaching liquid, if possible, or serve it immediately.

Poached Peaches

Yield: 10 portions

Wine, white, dry	1 quart	1 liter
Water	1 quart	1 liter
Sugar	4 to 6 ounces	115 to 170 grams
Cinnamon stick	2	2
Cloves	2	2
Orange zest	1 piece	1 piece
Peaches	10	10

1. Combine the wine, water, sugar, cinnamon, cloves, and orange zest in a small rondeau and bring the mixture to a simmer.

2. Add the peaches and return the mixture to a simmer. The peaches should be completely submerged in the poaching liquid; if not, add more water to cover. Continue to simmer the fruit gently for 10 to 12 minutes.

3. Remove the peaches from the poaching liquid, peel them, and remove the stones before service. The peaches may be cooled and stored in the poaching liquid.

NOTE: Dry red wine may be used in place of the white wine.

OTHER USES FOR SAUCES, CREAMS, AND FRUITS

Many of the preparations discussed in this chapter are most often found as the icings, fillings, or decorations for a variety of special pastries, including tortes (or layer cakes, as most Americans know them). The steps for preparing a torte are outlined here.

Assembling and Decorating Tortes

Method

Steps in this method are demonstrated in Figure 33-5.

1. Prepare all the basic components and have them at the correct temperature. (Some will need to be warmed or held at room temperature in order to spread properly. Others may need to be held under refrigeration.)

2. Use a knife with a long blade to cut the sponge cake into layers. Be sure to use the entire knife to make the cut. Trim the cake's edges, if necessary, and brush away any loose crumbs.

3. Moisten the layers with simple syrup, if desired, and place the first layer on a cake circle to make it easier to work with. Spread the filling evenly on the top of the first layer.

4. Position the second layer on top of the first, and spread the filling evenly once again. In steps 2 and 3 of Figure 33-5, apricot jam and then whipped cream are spread on the cake. Notice that the filling is spread from the center to the edges.

(1) Splitting a genoise into layers.

(2) Spreading apricot jam on the cake.

(3) Spreading whipped cream on the cake.

(4) Applying whipped cream to the top after the cake's sides have been iced.

(5) Combing the sides on the cake.

(6) Creating a border.

(7) The finished cake has been marked into slices, decorated with dark chocolate circles and whipped cream rosettes, and topped with white chocolate circles.

5. Position the third layer on top of the second. Hold the cake on the fingertips of one hand and, using a palette knife in the other hand, spread an even layer of the icing or topping onto the cake's sides. Keep the icing's thickness as even as possible.

6. Set the cake on a turntable, as shown in step 4 of Figure 33-5. Spread an even layer of icing on the cake's top and use level, even strokes to smooth it out. Hold the palette knife parallel to the cake's edge and turn the cake into the palette knife to even the coating on the sides. Smooth the top surface once more. Occasionally dip the palette knife into hot water for the smoothest finish.

7. Use a cake comb to create a decorative edge. Hold the comb parallel to the cake's side and simultaneously turn the turntable, as shown in step 5 of Figure 33-5.

Various techniques for finishing the torte can be used alone or in combination:

• Use fine cake crumbs of a contrasting color to create an edge for the cake. Gently press them along the cake's bottom. Scatter the crumbs evenly over the top of the cake, if desired.

• Very lightly score the cake's top by pressing the edge of a palette knife into the icing to mark the slices. Place decorations, such as chocolate circles and whipped cream or buttercream rosettes, so that each slice will have a share of the decoration.

SUMMARY

This chapter has covered the preparation of a variety of sauces, creams, and frozen and fruit desserts. Many of these can be used to finish cake and pastry items. The complexity of the procedures involved varies greatly. Relatively simple techniques, such as combing a cake and decorating it with two sauces or glazes of contrasting colors, can be used to create a dramatic effect. More detailed precision work is required for such items as wedding cakes and petits fours.

Basic Custard

Yield: 1½ quarts (1.5 liters)

Milk	1 quart	1 liter
Vanilla bean	1	1
Sugar	8 ounces	230 grams
Whole eggs	6 to 8	6 to 8
Salt	to taste	to taste

1. Combine the milk and the vanilla bean and heat to just below boiling.

2. Blend the sugar, eggs, and salt until smooth. Temper the egg mixture with the hot milk and combine until smooth. Strain the mixture, then pour it into prepared molds.

3. Bake the custard in a water bath until set and firm. Remove the custard from the water bath and cool.

NOTE: If desired, this custard can be made richer by using 6 whole eggs and 4 egg yolks. The milk may be replaced all or in part by light or heavy cream. If a vanilla bean is not available, flavor the custard with vanilla extract. If desired, the ingredients may be blended cold, without heating the milk.

VARIATION

Bread-and-butter Pudding: Prepare the basic custard as above. Toss cubed bread with enough melted butter to very lightly coat the bread, and then toast the bread in a moderate oven until it is dry and very lightly browned. Combine the cubed, toasted bread with the basic custard and raisins and place in custard or soufflé cups. Bake the puddings in a waterbath until the custard is set. The pudding may be unmolded before service and accompanied with a custard sauce, if desired.

Ricotta Glace Base

Yield: 4½ pounds (5.5 liters)

Maple syrup	3¼ pounds	1.5 kilograms
Ricotta cheese, part-skim, pureed	4½ pounds	2 kilograms
Yogurt, low-fat or nonfat	6 pounds	2.75 kilograms
Vanilla extract	2½ ounces	70 grams

1. Combine all of the ingredients in a blender and puree them to a very smooth consistency.

2. Freeze this mixture in an ice-cream freezer according to the manufacturer's directions or use it as the base for a Bavarian cream.

NOTE: This dish is a reworking of a classic recipe in order to reduce overall calories, fat, cholesterol, and sodium.

(continued)

VARIATIONS

Fruit-flavored Glace: Add 4½ pounds (2 kilograms) of pureed fruit to the base before freezing.

Pumpkin-flavored Glace: Sauté 4½ pounds (2 kilograms) of pumpkin puree briefly to concentrate the flavor. Allow the pumpkin to cool completely before combining it with the glace base and freezing the mixture.

Pastry Cream

Yield: 2 quarts (2 liters)

Milk	1 quart	1 liter
Sugar	8 ounces	230 grams
Butter	4 ounces	115 grams
Cornstarch	3 ounces	85 grams
Eggs	4	4
Egg yolks	4	4

1. Combine the milk, half of the sugar, and the butter in a saucepan. Bring this mixture to a boil.

2. Stir together the remaining sugar and the cornstarch. Add the eggs and the egg yolks to this mixture and blend well.

3. Add the egg mixture to the boiling milk mixture; return the pastry cream to a second boil. Remove the pastry cream from the heat, strain it, and cool it over an ice bath.

Bavarian, Version II

Yield: 3 pounds (1.4 kilograms)

Fruit puree	14 ounces	400 grams
Glace base, ricotta	1¾ pounds	800 grams
Water	⅓ cup	80 milliliters
Gelatin	⅔ ounce	20 grams
Port wine, white	2½ ounces	80 milliliters
Egg whites	6	6
Sugar, white	2 ounces	60 grams

1. Combine the fruit and glace base and set aside.

2. Combine the water, gelatin, and port wine in a small bowl. Let the gelatin absorb all of the liquid, then heat it gently over hot water until all of the crystals have dissolved.

3. Add the dissolved gelatin to the fruit/glace-base mixture and stir well. Cool this mixture in the refrigerator or over an ice-water bath until it mounds slightly when dropped from a spoon.

4. Beat the egg whites to soft peaks. While whipping, gradually add the sugar, and continue to whip until a meringue with stiff peaks forms.

5. Fold the meringue into the cooled base mixture. Place the Bavarian in molds or use it as a filling. Chill it for several hours before serving.

NOTE: This dish is a reworking of a classic recipe in order to reduce overall calories, fat, cholesterol, and sodium.

Apple Ice Cream

Yield: 3 pints (1.5 liters)

Custard sauce	1 quart	1 liter
Whole butter	2 ounces	60 grams
Apples, Granny Smith, peeled and diced	2	2
Sugar	1 ounce	30 grams
Cinnamon, ground	½ teaspoon	1 gram

1. Prepare the custard sauce and let it cool.

2. Heat the butter in a sauteuse. Add the apples, sugar, and cinnamon. Sauté the apples until they are tender.

3. Freeze the custard sauce in an ice-cream machine, according to the directions. Fold the apples into the ice cream before placing the ice cream in a freezer to "ripen."

NOTE: Refer to the recipe for Vanilla Sauce, earlier in this chapter.

Baked Figs in Phyllo with Raspberry Glace

Yield: 4 servings

Figs, medium	4	4
Almond paste	4 teaspoons	20 grams
Phyllo dough	4 sheets	4 sheets
Raspberry sauce	¼ cup	60 grams
Glace base, frozen	2 cups	400 grams
Raspberries, fresh, for a garnish	¼ cup	30 grams

1. Spread the bottom of each fig with 1 teaspoon of the almond paste.

2. Fold each phyllo sheet into quarters. Place a fig in the middle of each sheet; pull the corners up around the fig and pinch the corners together just above the fig's stem. The pinch should resemble a small blossom.

3. Set the figs on a lightly greased baking sheet. Bake them in a preheated 450°F (230°C) oven until they are golden brown, for about 5 minutes. Remove them from the oven and let them cool.

4. Serve the figs individually or as a dessert centerpiece on a pool of raspberry sauce alongside the ricotta glace and fresh raspberries.

NOTE: This dish is a reworking of a classic recipe in order to reduce overall calories, fat, cholesterol, and sodium.

Strawberries Marinated in Grand Marnier

Yield: 10 servings

Strawberries (or other seasonal berries)	2 pounds, 4 ounces	1 kilogram
Grand Marnier	1½ ounces	45 milliliters
Sugar, brown	1½ ounces	45 grams
Crème fraîche	1 ounce	30 grams
Whipped cream	2½ ounces	70 grams
Almonds, toasted, sliced	¾ ounce	20 grams
Almond paste (colored red with food coloring)	1 ounce	30 grams
Phyllo dough	4 sheets	4 sheets

1. Rinse the berries and slice them if they are large. Combine the berries, Grand Marnier, and brown sugar. Toss them lightly. Let the mixture macerate for 1 hour or more.

2. Fold together the crème fraîche and whipped cream. Refrigerate it until it is needed.

3. Roll the almond paste into ten 3-gram balls. Stamp them with the Grand Marnier seal and reserve them.

4. Divide the berry mixture among 10 brandy snifters. Top each portion with ⅓ ounce (10 grams) of the crème fraîche/whipped-cream mixture. Sprinkle each with 3 or 4 sliced almonds. Set the glasses aside.

5. Cut 3 sheets of phyllo into 3 x 5–inch (7.5 x 13–centimeter) squares. Nick the corners off the squares to make octagons. Moisten the snifters' top rims. Lay one octagon of the phyllo on each rim, with an even overlap on all sides. Press it to attach it to the rim.

6. Fold the remaining sheet of phyllo in half and cut it into ¼-inch (½-centimeter)-wide strips. Cut a V-shaped notch out of the narrow edges (to look like ribbon). Lay two ribbons over the top of each glass, letting the notched edge of the ribbons hang over the side. (Moisten them lightly to attach them.)

7. Press the seal onto the glass's side, near the rim, to hold the ribbons in place. Hold the assembled desserts in a refrigerator until they are needed.

8. To serve, place them in a hot oven for 15 seconds, just until the phyllo is brown. Serve them immediately.

NOTE: This dish is a reworking of a classic recipe in order to reduce overall calories, fat, cholesterol, and sodium.

Apple Strudel

Yield: 20 servings

Apples, Granny Smith, peeled, cored, and sliced	4 pounds	1.8 kilograms
Butter	1½ ounces	45 grams
Raisins, golden	7 ounces	200 grams
Sugar, brown	3½ ounces	100 grams
Cinnamon	1 teaspoon	2.5 grams
Nutmeg	1 teaspoon	2 grams
Phyllo pastry	12 sheets	12 sheets
Butter, melted	1½ ounces	45 grams
Sugar, confectioners'	2 tablespoons	20 grams
Glace base, ricotta	1 quart	1 liter
Raspberry sauce	1½ cups	360 grams

1. Sauté the apples in the butter until they are tender. Remove them from the heat. Add the raisins, brown sugar, cinnamon, and nutmeg. Mix the ingredients together well and let the mixture cool.

2. Line a sheet pan with plastic wrap. Lay three sheets of the phyllo on the plastic; lay the remaining three sheets of phyllo on the plastic, overlapping the short edges in the center by approximately ¾ inch (2 centimeters).

3. Spray or brush the phyllo lightly with ⅓ ounce (10 grams) of the melted butter.

4. Place half of the apple mixture along the edge. Roll the phyllo up into a long roll.

5. Spray or brush the phyllo lightly with another ⅓ ounce (10 grams) of the melted butter. Score the top to divide it into 10 portions.

6. Repeat with the remaining phyllo to form a second strudel.

7. Bake the strudel at 400°F (205°C) until they are golden brown, about 8 to 10 minutes. Allow them to cool for 10 minutes before slicing them. Sprinkle the strudel with confectioners' sugar when they are cool. Serve them with a small scoop of the ricotta glace and raspberry puree.

NOTE: This dish is a reworking of a classic recipe in order to reduce overall calories, fat, cholesterol, and sodium.

SUBSTITUTION

Pear Strudel: Substitute Bosc pears for the apples.

Chocolate Whipped Cream

Yield: Varies according to need or use

Ganache	1 part	1 part
Heavy cream	1 part	1 part

Combine equal parts (by volume) of the ganache and heavy cream and whip them until the mixture is thickened and light. The whipped cream should be easy to spread and pipe out.

Sacher Torte

Yield: Two 10-inch cakes

Butter, unsalted	14 ounces	400 grams
Confectioner's sugar	14 ounces	400 grams
Egg yolks	10½ ounces	300 milliliters
Whole eggs	6½ ounces	200 milliliters
Chocolate, melted	16½ ounces	465 grams
Egg whites	14 ounces	400 grams
Flour, bread	5 ounces	140 grams
Almonds, toasted, ground	14 ounces	400 grams
Apricot or raspberry preserves	as needed	as needed
Ganache	as needed	as needed
Additional melted chocolate or marzipan for decoration	as needed	as needed

1. Cream together the butter and 10 ounces of the sugar until light.

2. Combine the egg yolks and the eggs, and add them gradually to the creamed butter and sugar. Be sure to scrape down the sides and bottom of the bowl.

3. Add the melted chocolate all at once and mix well.

4. Beat the egg whites to soft peaks. While still whipping, gradually add the remainder of the sugar, and continue to whip until a medium-peak meringue is formed.

5. Fold the meringue, flour, and almonds into the batter. Pour the batter into prepared pans and bake it at 325°F (165°C) until a cake springs back when lightly pressed.

6. Slice each cake in half horizontally and spread each half with preserves. Coat the cake with ganache.

7. Mark the cake for 16 slices, and decorate it by writing "Sacher" in chocolate on each slice or by placing a small marzipan circle with an "S" on each slice.

Dobos Torte

Yield: Two 10-inch tortes

Batter

Egg yolks	20 ounces	600 milliliters
Sugar	16 ounces	450 grams
Egg whites	28 ounces	840 milliliters
Flour, cake, sifted	1 pound	450 grams
Butter, melted and cooled	5 ounces	140 grams

Assembly

Buttercream, mocha	as needed	as needed
Sugar	7 ounces	200 grams
Lemon juice	to taste	to taste
Glucose	1¼ ounces	35 milliliters
Butter	1 ounce	30 grams
Chocolate, tempered	as needed	as needed

1. Whip together the egg yolks and half of the sugar until very light.

2. Whip the egg whites to a soft peak. Gradually add the remaining sugar while still beating to form a medium-peak meringue.

3. Fold the meringue into the yolk mixture; then fold in the flour and, finally, the butter. Mix just until combined.

4. Spread the batter onto parchment paper to cover fourteen 11-inch circles traced on the paper's surface. Bake the batter at 450°F (230°C) until the cake is golden. Cool.

5. To assemble, trim 6 layers per torte (for a total of 14 layers) and sandwich with the mocha buttercream. Ice the sides and top with buttercream, mark each torte into 16 slices, and pipe a dollop of buttercream onto each slice.

6. Combine the sugar and lemon juice, and cook the mixture over moderate heat to form a golden caramel. Immediately incorporate the glucose and the butter. Spread an even layer of this caramel on the two remaining layers of cake. Cut each layer into 16 equal wedges. When cool, dip the blunt end into melted chocolate. Lean the caramel-coated wedges on the dollop of buttercream on top of the tortes.

Assembly Instructions for Rum Truffle Torte

<u>*Yield:* 1 torte</u>

Filling Mixture

Cake crumbs	4 ounces	115 grams
Frangipane crumbs	2 ounces	60 grams
Hard ganache, warmed	3 ounces	85 grams
Raspberry jam	2 ounces	60 grams
Apricot jam	1 ounce	30 grams
Rum	as needed	as needed
Sweet chocolate, melted	as needed	as needed

For Assembly

Linzer dough round, baked	1	1
Raspberry jam	as needed	as needed
Sponge cake, chocolate	1	1
Simple syrup	as needed	as needed
Whipped cream, chocolate	as needed	as needed
Cake crumbs, chocolate	as needed	as needed
Truffles, rum	16	16

1. Except for the rum and melted chocolate, combine the ingredients for the filling to create a mixture of a slightly stiff consistency that will hold its shape readily. Add the rum and melted chocolate to taste to create a spreadable mixture.

2. Assemble the torte in the following sequence:

   Spread the linzer dough round with the raspberry jam. Add a layer of filling. Top with a slice of chocolate sponge cake and brush with simple syrup.

   Spread a sponge layer with filling, then add a second slice of sponge brushed with syrup. Add a third layer of filling and top the cake with a third slice of sponge brushed with syrup.

   Ice the cake with chocolate whipped cream, and mark it into 16 slices. Decorate each slice with a rosette of chocolate whipped cream and top it with a truffle. Decorate the torte's edges by combing and/or with cake crumbs. Refrigerate the tortes until they are ready for service.

Chocolate Sabayon Torte

<u>*Yield: Two 10-inch tortes*</u>

Filling

Egg yolks	9	9
Sugar, granulated	4 ounces	115 grams
Sherry	6 ounces	180 milliliters
Chocolate, sweet, melted	8 ounces	225 grams
Heavy cream, whipped	24 ounces	720 milliliters
Vanilla	to taste	to taste
Gelatin	½ ounce	15 grams
Brandy	2 ounces	60 milliliters
Sponge cake, chocolate	6 slices	6 slices
Simple syrup	as needed	as needed
Whipped cream, chocolate	as needed	as needed
Chocolate fans	32	32
Cake crumbs, chocolate	as needed	as needed

1. Combine the egg yolks, sugar, and sherry wine in a bowl. Cook over simmering water until thickened, and the mixture falls in ribbons from the whip.

2. Add the melted chocolate and blend. Fold in the whipped heavy cream and add the vanilla to taste.

3. Soften the gelatin in the brandy; then melt it over simmering water to dissolve all the crystals. Add this to the chocolate mixture.

4. Moisten the sponge cake slices with the simple syrup. Place one layer in the bottom of a springform pan, and add a layer of the sabayon filling. Add a second layer of sponge, followed by a layer of filling, and top this with the third layer of sponge. Repeat the procedure for the second torte. Refrigerate the tortes until the filling is firm.

5. Ice the tortes with the chocolate whipped cream and mark each torte into 16 slices. Trim the bottom edge of the tortes with cake crumbs. Pipe out a dollop of chocolate whipped cream onto each slice. Lean a fan of chocolate on each dollop.

Lemon Sorbet

Yield: 1 quart (1 liter)

Water	1¾ pints	420 milliliters
Granulated sugar	18 ounces	510 grams
Lemon juice, strained	8 ounces	240 milliliters
Egg white, whipped to a light froth	1	1

1. Combine the sugar and water and heat the mixture to dissolve the sugar completely, in order to form a syrup.
2. Add the lemon juice to the syrup and check the flavor. Let the flavored syrup cool completely.
3. Check the syrup's density by using the "floating egg" technique. (An egg should rise above the surface of the syrup enough to show only a nickel's worth of shell.)
4. Add the whipped egg white to the flavored syrup. Process the sorbet in an ice-cream freezer. Store the finished sorbet in the freezer.

Coffee Granite

Yield: 1 quart (1 liter)

Water	1¾ pints	420 milliliters
Sugar, granulated	18 ounces	510 grams
Espresso, strong-brewed	8 ounces	240 milliliters
Egg white, beaten to a light froth	1	1

1. Combine the water and sugar; cook the mixture until a syrup forms and all of the sugar has dissolved.
2. Add the espresso to the syrup and let the mixture cool.
3. Stir the beaten egg white into the flavored syrup. Pour this mixture into a shallow pan and place it in the freezer. As it freezes, occasionally scrape and stir the mixture to form large grains or crystals. The granite is ready to serve after it is completely frozen.

French Buttercream

Yield: 7 pounds (3.15 kilograms)

Egg yolks	12 ounces	360 grams
Whole eggs	1 pound	450 grams
Sugar	2¼ pounds	1 kilogram
Water	13 ounces	370 milliliters
Butter, softened	3 pounds	1.35 kilograms

1. Combine the yolks, eggs, and 2 ounces (60 milliliters) of water in the bowl of an electric mixer. Heat the sugar and the remaining mixture over simmering water until it reaches 238°F (114°C). Gradually add the hot syrup to the egg mixture.

2. Whip the egg mixture on the second speed of the mixer until it is light and has approximately doubled in volume. It should be nearly at room temperature at this point. (Any flavorings should be added at this point; see the note below).

3. Gradually add the softened butter until it is all incorporated and the buttercream is smooth and light.

NOTE: Add flavorings such as vanilla extract, rum, citrus zest, or melted chocolate to the egg mixture once it has reached full volume and is at room temperature.

French buttercream must be refrigerated at all times due to the presence of uncooked egg yolks.

German Buttercream

Yield: 3 pounds (1.4 kilograms)

Butter, softened	1 pound	450 grams
Pastry cream	2 pounds	200 grams

1. Place the butter in the bowl of an electric mixer and beat it until it is smooth and light.

2. Gradually incorporate the pastry cream until the mixture is blended and smooth. The buttercream is now ready to use.

NOTE: See the notes on French buttercream for information regarding flavoring and storage.

Appendix 1

Menu Development and Plate Presentation

There are many factors that cause a patron to select one restaurant in preference to another. It may be that a restaurant has a reputation for excellent food at reasonable prices or that the menu is considered outstanding for the type of cuisine served at a particular establishment. Location, proximity to parking, and price range often play a part in helping the prospective guest decide where to eat breakfast, lunch, or dinner. This appendix will cover two areas in particular where the chef can help sway the guest's opinion of the establishment.

MENU DEVELOPMENT

The first area on which the chef has an obvious impact is the menu. The way in which a menu is structured has both overt and subtle effects on the guest's impression of an establishment. A good selection of dishes should be offered, ranging from classic items to contemporary ones. The appearance of local and seasonal items is another way to increase the menu's appeal. Prices are important, too. The chef should write the menu with the potential customer's spending behavior in mind. A family-style restaurant usually offers traditional fare at reasonable prices; a white tablecloth restaurant can normally have a higher price range. A restaurant that features a regional style of cookery or ethnic cuisine will tailor its offerings to make sure that a reasonable selection of authentic dishes is central on the menu.

The menu is important for a restaurant that features healthful cooking. Many guests' immediate expectations are that the portions will be small and that the food will have no flavor. As shown in Figure A-1, a menu from The Culinary Institute of America's *St. Andrew's Cafe*, the chef needs to keep abreast of current food trends and feature items with special flavors, textures, and tastes to produce a menu that will tempt and intrigue the patron, without stressing nutrition to the exclusion of all else.

People are becoming increasingly sophisticated about food. Citizens of the United States eat away from home at an ever-increasing rate, but there is also stiff competition for the restaurant dollar. It is therefore essential that the restaurant have an appealing menu. One of the great challenges in developing a menu is putting together a list of offerings that will not only please first-time guests, but that will also encourage them to return over and over again to try new dishes or to enjoy old favorites. The following guidelines should be considered as basic principles for developing any menu, whether for an upscale "white tablecloth" restaurant, a small bistro, or a banquet hall.

Menu Guidelines

Base menu selections on quality ingredients. This is perhaps the most basic tenet of all. The chef must know the best available product, and should select preparations or special dishes to highlight the superior items he or she has purchased. This does not by any means imply that only expensive or difficult-to-find foods are the best. In all probability, the best product is locally produced and in season, whether the food is a fruit, a vegetable, game, or fish.

Keep menus grounded in the season as much as possible. This concept follows naturally from the preceding idea. There are certain times of the year when many foods—a vegetable such as sweet corn, for example—will be at their best. This is the natural time to use them. The menu should be designed so that the item can be handled in imaginative, creative, and, above all, appealing ways.

There will also be seasonal preferences that may have to do with a change of weather. For example, there is an increased demand for hearty, slowly cooked, savory dishes as the weather cools in the more northern parts of this country. Seasonal preferences exist throughout all of the nation's regions, reflecting the traditional availability of special foods at defined times of the year.

Some foods are traditionally associated with holidays although the significance of the holiday itself may not mean a great deal to every single patron. Many people, Irish and non-Irish, look for corned beef and cabbage on St. Patrick's Day.

Use locally produced products, where possible. Restaurants are part of the business community. It is important to try to work together with other businesses as much as possible. Buying locally may make good "political" sense. Far more important is the fact that locally produced things frequently will be much fresher than those shipped from long distances. They probably will also cost less because transportation costs may be significantly lower.

Use knowledge of classic preparations as a starting point. Some dishes are considered "standards" by which the caliber of the chef's food preparation can be judged. However, contemporary palates might find the heaviness of some classic dishes unappealing. The chef can elect to update or vary these dishes as appropriate to generate customer interest. For exam-

St. Andrew's Cafe

LUNCH

APPETIZERS

Pan-smoked Chicken Breast with Red Onion Marmalade and Baby Greens   3.50
Lobster Tortellini with Ginger-Lime Sauce   4.25
Salmon Roulade with Tomato-Basil Coulis   3.75
Rabbit Terrine with Corn Relish   3.25

SOUPS

Onion Soup Gratinée   2.50
Chicken Consommé with Fennel Ravioli   2.75
Cuban-style Black Bean Soup   2.00

ENTRÉES

Grilled Flank Steak with Polenta, Asparagus,
and Roasted Shallot Sauce   8.25
Sautéed Scallopini of Chicken with Risotto, Grilled
Eggplant, and Marsala Wine Sauce   6.75
Poached Fillet of Trout with Salmon Mousseline
Fine Herb Cream   7.50
Wood-fired Whole Wheat Vegetable Pizza with
Chevre Cheese and Garlic   5.95
Mesquite-grilled Mahi Mahi with Lentil Ragout
and Horseradish Cream   8.50

Seasonal Salad and a Variety of Breads are Offered with Each Entrée

DESSERTS

Glazed Pineapple Madagascar with Glace   2.75
Polenta and Banana Soufflé   3.50
Blueberry Glace with Almond Tiles and Fresh Fruit   3.25

St. Andrew's Cafe is a nonsmoking restaurant. Thank you for your cooperation. Reservations – 471–6608
St. Andrew's Recipe Sampler is available from your Maître d'Hôtel Instructor – $9.95

About St. Andrew's Cafe and
The Culinary Institute of America

At St. Andrew's cafe, we believe that eating wisely should be enjoyable. Menus are planned to follow guidelines of balance, nutrition, and taste. Our aim is that each dish be moderate in terms of the amount of calories, fat, cholesterol, and sodium, but also be prepared according to the good culinary principles of taste and presentation. All of the food and breads served at this and the Institute's three other public restaurants are prepared by our students under the supervision of our chef-instructors.   ❧   The Culinary Institute of America, founded in 1946, provides a culinary education for men and women seeking careers in the foodservice profession. The Institute has been in the forefront of many culinary advances, including the incorporation of nutrition into fine cuisine. The General Foods Nutrition Center and its St. Andrew's Cafe are examples of that commitment.

A-1

This lunch menu from *St. Andrew's Cafe* reflects a concern for healthful eating
and an interest in contemporizing both ethnic and classic dishes.

ple, pâtés and terrines are frequently considered too heavy and rich. A contemporary approach would be to prepare these dishes in a new way, such as a terrine of vegetables or a pâté of seafood. A number of other preparations lend themselves to new interpretations. Choucroutes can be prepared with seafood and heavy, cream-based sauces can be replaced with lighter vegetable coulis. These kinds of changes are showing up in all types of restaurants.

Select items that will offer the guest a reasonable range of options within a price range while still maintaining a good check average. Just as it is a good idea to have wines at a number of different price levels, it is also good to have a range of entrée prices. There will certainly be a general price range appropriate for the particular restaurant—varying according to restaurant type and general location—that will determine the upper and lower price limits. Within those boundaries, however, it is usually possible to offer a number of different options. Whatever the menu pricing strategy, it is essential that guests feel they have received top value for their dollar and that the restaurant is able to turn a profit.

Apart from customer appeal, menu development has other important effects on the restaurant's overall operation.

• Careful menu development ensures that the work load is balanced between the stations. An establishment's reputation is damaged if the customer feels that it consistently takes too long to get a meal. This can happen all too easily if one particular station is bogged down with too much work. Spreading the responsibilities throughout the kitchen by proper selection of menu items can often minimize this problem.

• Total utilization of product should be the aim wherever this is an effective way of keeping food costs in line. As an example, consider the possibilities from a whole salmon. The fish may be cut into fillets or steaks and then used as entrées. Instead of being grilled or sautéed, the same fish could be poached and used in a variety of cold preparations such as salads, spreads, or canapés. The trim might be used to prepare a mousseline forcemeat to stuff a fillet of sole or as a cold mousse appetizer.

• Menu items may also be designed to properly use foods in a timely fashion. If foods can be used as soon as they are brought into a restaurant, they will always be at their peak of flavor, freshness, and quality. Where possible, it is often advantageous to have the flexibility to create "specials" that can effectively sell the item quickly while it is still at its peak of quality.

• Menus should be created in such a way that the available equipment is properly used. If a kitchen is short on burners, but does have a large grill, the menu should reflect that fact. If there is little oven space, roasted or poêléed foods should be eliminated or kept to a minimum.

• Menus should be designed with an eye to the staff's capabilities in preparing the foods properly and consistently. Guests will come to expect a certain performance level from a kitchen, and although they will be delighted to receive food that is of a better caliber than might have been the norm, they will never forgive food that is not up to the level of their previous experiences.

PLATING TECHNIQUES

Once the guest has made a selection from the menu, the kitchen staff's duty is to be sure that the food that ultimately arrives at the table meets—or, better, exceeds—the expectations. The following principles are ways to make sure that food is correctly plated and presented.

Basic Principles

Serve hot food hot; serve cold food cold. Foods must be served at the correct temperature. Nothing is less appealing than tepid soup, salads that are not well chilled, sautéed items that are room temperature. Not only can the wrong temperature be disappointing in terms of taste, but it may actually pose a health hazard if the foods are in the danger zone.

Food should look neat and attractive; plates should be very clean. Food should look appropriate to the way it was prepared at all times. Sautéed or panfried foods should have a golden brown crust; poached foods should appear moist. Sauces should be the correct consistency so that they won't run on the plate; any skin or lump should be strained out and the butter should be properly emulsified. There should be no ragged edges or torn or misshapen pieces that give an impression of carelessly handled food.

Any drops of sauce or smudges should be wiped clean before the plate leaves the kitchen. Food that is simply slapped onto a plate gives the impression that the kitchen staff cares little about what they are doing.

The food must be properly cooked. If a steak is ordered rare, it should be sent out that way. If a sauce was requested on the side, it should be there, in a properly heated sauceboat or ramekin. Foods should be cooked in such a way that their flavors and textures are enhanced, not hidden.

Refinements

Beyond these common-sense instructions, there are additional refinements that can mean the difference between an acceptable plate and an exceptional one.

The plate should be attractive. This does not mean that one should elaborately garnish it simply for the sake of decoration, nor give the impression that the food was "played" with in the kitchen.

Contrast

The plated dish should have a variety of colors, cooking methods, shapes, textures, heights, and seasonings. All-white foods or all-pureed foods on a single plate can be boring to the eye or the palate. If garlic is used in one or two elements on a plate, it should not be used in the others. Too much repetition, be it foods of all the same size and shape or too much of the same flavor, is simply not appealing.

A simple entrée may be served with more complicated accompaniments—for example, a grilled chicken breast might be served with a panfried vegetable that has its own sauce. But an elaborately sauced and garnished entrée should be paired with very simple, perfectly prepared and seasoned side dishes.

Foods should be selected for their ability to contribute to the overall success of the plate in terms of appearance and flavor.

An accompanying vegetable can introduce the additional color. For example, use a green vegetable such as broccoli or snow peas rather than the "traditional" bunch of watercress or a sprig of parsley.

Harmony

The tastes and colors of the elements of a dish should harmonize to create a pleasing total effect. While an element of surprise may give some excitement to a dish, a flavor or texture that shocks and startles the palate is disturbing. There are no rules carved in stone dictating that one can only combine *this* sauce with *that* food; there is room for experimentation and personal expression in preparing a dish. First, however, it is important to develop a sense of balance and to educate both the palate and the eye.

Some foods may be mounded or piled up a little higher than other items to give the plate a pleasing appearance. This may take a little more care than simply dropping a spoonful of peas or ratatouille on the plate. Special techniques such as the one demonstrated in Figures A-2a and A-2b show how to create a dramatic effect.

The food appears to its best advantage on the plate if a certain amount of space can be left between items to prevent the overall effect from being busy or crowded. On the other hand, the food should not look lost on the plate, as this creates the unfortunate impression of small portions and gives the guest the feeling that he or she is not receiving full value.

The plate's border can act in the same manner as the frame of a painting. The food should not spill out into the border, nor should it look as if it is in danger of falling off the edge of the plate if a knife and fork are used to cut into something on it.

Special Techniques

There are some effective ways to enhance the overall appearance of a dish. A sauce is a good vehicle for giving a plate some drama. As is shown in Figure A-3, the sauce is first pooled on the plate and then evenly spread to create a field of color. The entrée is then placed on the sauce for the most dramatic appearance. Sauces or condiments of contrasting colors may be drizzled, "splashed," or dropped onto the background sauce. Dragging a thin blade through the second sauce can increase the visual appeal further by creating a marbelized look.

A-2a

A length of PVC pipe is cut to act as a mold. The mold is first positioned on the plate, then filled with ratatouille.

A-2b

The mold is lifted carefully away from the plate.

A-3

The pooled sauce serves as background for the entrée.

It is important to "feed the eye" and create the correct impression. Slicing pieces of meat on the diagonal and placing them strategically on the plate will give an impression of greater bounty. Shingled slices of a veal loin look larger and more generous than a single medallion, even though the entrée's actual weight may be exactly the same.

Simplicity

The final rule for plating is to keep the ideal of simplicity firmly in mind. If a food is properly cooked, it should not require fussing in order to look appealing. Elaborately garnished foods, sauces "painted" onto the plate, or architectural constructions can create an impressive effect. If it is nothing more than a way to hide the fact that basic techniques haven't been properly applied or that foods were not at the peak of freshness or quality, the effect is lost. Worse, the guest will feel cheated. The natural colors, textures, and shapes of foods are very often their own best garnish.

Appendix 2

Seasonal Availability of Produce

Fruit or Vegetable	Jan.	Feb.	Mar.	Apr.	May	June	July	Aug.	Sept.	Oct.	Nov.	Dec.
Apples	☆								☆	☆	☆	☆
Apricots				○		●	●	○				
Artichokes			○	○	○	○						
Arugula	○	○	○	○	○☆	○☆	○☆	○☆	○☆	○	○	○
Asparagus			○	○★	○★	○☆						
Avocados	○	○	○	○	○	○	○	○				○
Beans, shell			○☆	○☆	○☆	○☆	○☆	○☆	○☆			
Beans, snap					○☆	○☆	○☆	○☆	○☆	○☆		
Beets, gold							○	○	○	○☆	○☆	○☆
Beets, red							●	●	●	○☆	○☆	○☆
Berries						○	○	○	○	○		
Blood oranges	○	○	○									
Bok choy									☆	☆		
Boysenberries						☆	☆	☆				
Broccoli						○☆	○☆	○☆	○☆	○☆	○☆	○☆
Broccoli rabe	○	○	○	○			☆	☆	☆	☆	☆	○☆
Brussels sprouts	○	○	○						○☆	○☆	○	
Bulb fennel	○	○	○	○	○				☆		○	○
Cabbages	○	○	○	○	○	○	○	○	○	○	○	○
Cantaloupes						○	○☆	○☆	○☆	○		
Carrots	○	○	○	○	○	○	○	○	○	○	○	○
Cauliflower						○	○	○	○	○		
Celeriac	○	○	○	○	○	○	○	○	○	○	○	○
Chard	○	○	○	○	○☆	○☆	○☆	○☆	○☆	○☆	○	○
Chayote	●	●									●	●
Cherries						☆	☆					
Chinese cabbage										○	○	
Collards							○☆	○☆	○☆	○☆		
Corn						☆	★	★	★	☆		
Cucumbers	○	○	○	○	●	●★	●★	○	○	○	○	○
Eggplant, baby				○	○	○☆	○☆	○☆	○☆			
Eggplant, white						○☆	○☆	○☆				
Endive									○	○	○	○
Escarole	○	○	○	○	○☆	☆	☆	☆	☆	○☆	○	○
Fiddleheads		☆	☆	☆	☆							
Figs							○	○	○	○		
Frissée	○	○	○	○	○	○	○	○	○	○	○☆	○☆
Gooseberries									☆			
Gourds									☆	☆	☆	☆
Grapes						○	○	○	○	○	○	○
Herbs			○	○☆	○☆	○☆	○☆	○☆	○☆	○	○	○
Jicama	○	○	○	○	○	○	○	○	○	○	○	○

© 1990, The Culinary Institute of America.

California: ○   Local: ☆
California, Peak: ●   Local, Peak: ★

Fruit or Vegetable	Jan.	Feb.	Mar.	Apr.	May	June	July	Aug.	Sept.	Oct.	Nov.	Dec.
Kale								☆	☆	☆	☆	
Kiwi	○	○	○			○	○	○	○	○	○	○
Kohlrabi						●☆	●★	○☆				
Kumquats	○	○	○									
Leeks										○	○	○
Leeks, baby						○	○	○	○	○	○	○
Lettuce, baby			○	○	○	○	○	○	○	○		
Lettuce, bibb	○	○	○	○	○	○☆	○☆	○☆	○	○	○	○
Lettuce, iceberg	○	○	○	○	○	○	○	○	○	○	○	○
Lettuce, leaf	○	○	○	○	○	○	○	○	○	○	○	○
Mache	○	○	○☆	○★	○★	○☆	○☆	○☆	○	○	○	○
Mangoes	○	○	○	○	○	○	○	○				
Mustard greens							○☆	○☆	○☆			
Nectarines						○	●	●	○			
Okra							○	○	○	○		
Papayas	○	●	●	●	○	○	○	○	○	○	○	○
Parsnips			○	○	○	○	○☆	○☆	○☆	○	○	
Peaches							☆	★	☆			
Pears	○☆							★	★	★	○☆	○☆
Peas, green	○	○	○	○	○	○	○					
Peas, snow	○	○	○	○	○	○	○					
Peppers, bell						○	○☆	○☆	○☆	○	○	○
Peppers, red								○☆	○☆	○☆		
Pineapples	○	○	●	●	●	●	●	○			○	○
Plums						☆	★	☆				
Potatoes, baby red				○	○☆	○☆	○☆	○☆	○			
Radicchio	○	○	○	○		☆	☆	☆	☆	○☆	○	○
Raspberries						☆	☆	☆	☆	☆		
Romaine	○	○	○	○★	○★	○☆	○☆	○☆	○	○	○	○
Rutabagas									☆	☆	☆	☆
Salsify	○	○	○	○						○	○	○
Scallions								☆	☆			
Spinach	○	○	○	○	○★	○★	○☆	○☆	○	○	○	○
Squash, acorn									☆	☆	☆	☆
Squash, baby						○☆	○☆	○☆	○☆	○☆		
Squash, butternut									☆	☆	☆	☆
Squash, cheese									☆	☆	☆	☆
Squash, crookneck						○☆	○☆	○☆	○☆			
Squash, dumpling									☆	☆	☆	☆
Squash, neck									☆	☆	☆	☆
Squash, patty pan						○☆	○☆	○☆	○☆			
Squash, spaghetti									☆	☆	☆	☆

© 1990, The Culinary Institute of America.

California: ○ California, Peak: ● Local: ☆ Local, Peak: ★

Fruit or Vegetable	Jan.	Feb.	Mar.	Apr.	May	June	July	Aug.	Sept.	Oct.	Nov.	Dec.
Strawberries					☆	☆	☆	☆	☆			
Sunchokes	○	○	○	○	○						○	○
Tangerines	○	○	○									
Tomatoes						○☆	○☆	○☆	○☆	○☆	○☆	
Tomatoes, cherry							○☆	○☆	○☆	○☆	○☆	
Turnips	○	○	○	○	○	○	○	○	○☆	○☆	○☆	○
Watercress	○	○	●	●	○	○	○	○	○	○	○	○
Watermelons					○	○	○	○	☆			
Zucchinis				○	○	○	○☆	○☆	○☆	○☆	○	

© 1990, The Culinary Institute of America.

California: ○ California, Peak: ● Local: ☆ Local, Peak: ★

Appendix **3**

Basic Kitchen Ratios

Product	1	2	4	6	8	16	20	Misc.
Stocks	Water, gal.				Bones, lb.	Mirepoix, oz.		
Consommé	Stock, qt.	Egg whites	Mirepoix, oz.		Meat, oz.			1 tomato
Court bouillon	Water, qt.	Vinegar, oz.	Carrots, oz.					Onion, 4 oz.
Hollandaise	Vinegar, oz.	Water, oz.		Egg yolks				Lemon, 1 tbsp.
Mayonnaise	Egg yolk				Oil, oz.			
Plain royale	Egg, part	Liquid, parts						
Sauce anglaise	Milk, qt. Yolks, cup				Sugar, oz.			Vanilla bean
Duchesse appareil	Butter, oz.	Egg yolks, ea.				Potatoes, oz.		
Duxelle	Butter, oz. Shallot			←		Mushrooms, oz.	→	
Rice pilaf	Rice, part	Liquid, parts						
Noodle dough	Flour, lb.		Eggs					
Forcemeat, cold	Fatback, part	Lean meat, parts						
Forcemeat, hot	Fatback, part	Lean meats, parts						
Forcemeat, mousseline	Meat, lb.	Egg whites or 1 egg				Hvy. cream, oz.		
Pâte brisé	Water, part	Shortening, parts	Flour, parts					
Pâte à chou	Butter, part	Liquid, part Flour, part						1 egg per oz. butter

Appendix 4

Weights and Measures
Conversions

INFORMATION/HINTS AND TIPS FOR CALCULATIONS

1 gallon = 4 quarts = 8 pints = 16 cups (8 ounces) = 128 ounces.

1 fifth bottle = approximately 1½ pints or exactly 25.6 ounces.

1 measuring cup holds 8 ounces (A coffee cup generally holds 6 ounces).

1 egg white = 2 ounces (average).

1 lemon = 1 to 1¼ ounces of juice.

1 orange = 3 to 3½ ounces of juice.

METRIC CONVERSION TABLE

To Change	To	Multiply By
Ounces (oz.)	Grams (g)	28.35
Pounds (lb.)	Kilograms (kg)	0.45
Teaspoons (tsp.)	Milliliters (ml)	5
Tablespoons (tbsp.)	Milliliters (ml)	15
Fluid ounces (oz.)	Milliliters (ml)	30
Cups	Liters (l)	0.24
Pints (pt.)	Liters (l)	0.47
Quarts (qt.)	Liters (l)	0.95
Gallons (gal.)	Liters (l)	3.8
Temperature (°F)	Temperature (°C)	⁵⁄₉ after subtracting 32*

* Example: 9°F above boiling equals 5°C above boiling.

SCOOP SIZES

#	Approximate Weight	Measure/Tablespoon
30	2	1 to 1½ ounces
24	2⅔	1½ to 1¾ ounces
20	3	1¾ to 2 ounces
16	4	2 to 2½ ounces
12	5	2½ to 3 ounces
10	6	4 to 5 ounces
6	10	6 ounces

WEIGHTS AND MEASURES EQUIVALENCIES

Dash	less than ⅛ teaspoon
3 teaspoons	1 tablespoon (½ fluid ounce)
2 tablespoons	⅛ cup (1 fluid ounce)
4 tablespoons	¼ cup (2 fluid ounces)
5⅓ tablespoons	⅓ cup (2⅔ fluid ounces)
8 tablespoons	½ cup (4 fluid ounces)
10⅔ tablespoons	⅔ cup (5⅓ fluid ounces)
12 tablespoons	¾ cup (6 fluid ounces)
14 tablespoons	⅞ cup (7 fluid ounces)
16 tablespoons	1 cup
1 gill	½ cup
1 cup	8 fluid ounces
2 cups	1 pint
2 pints	1 quart (approximately 1 liter)
4 quarts	1 gallon
8 quarts	1 peck
4 pecks	1 bushel
1 gram	0.035 ounces
1 ounce	28.35 grams
16 ounces	1 pound (453.59 grams)
1 kilogram	2.21 pounds

Recommended Readings

FOOD HISTORY

De Honesta Voluptate, 5 volumes. Platine (Bartolomeo de Sacehi di Padena). Mallinkrodt Chemical Works, 1967.

The Diepnosophists (Banquet of the Learned), 3 vol. Athenaeus. Translated by C. D. Yonge. London: Henry G. Bohn, 1854.

Fabulous Feasts: Medieval Cookery and Ceremony. Madeleine Pelner Cosman. New York: Braziller, 1976.

Food in History. Reay Tannahill. New York: Crown Publishers, Inc., 1988.

Kitchen and Table: A Bedside History of Eating in the Western World. Colin Clair. London: Abelard-Schuman, 1965.

Much Depends on Dinner. Margaret Visser. New York: Grove Press, 1986.

The Pantropheon: or, A History of Food and its Preparation in Ancient Times. Alexis Soyer. New York: Paddington Press, 1977.

The Roman Cookery of Apicius. Translated and adapted by John Edwards. Point Robert, Washington: Hartley & Marks, 1984.

The Travels of Marco Polo. Marta Bellonci. Translated by Teresa Waugh. New York: Facts on File, 1984.

SANITATION AND SAFETY

Applied Foodservice Sanitation. The National Institute of Foodservice. Dubuque, Iowa: W. C. Brown Publishing, 1974.

Basic Food Sanitation. The Culinary Institute of America. Hyde Park, New York: 1986.

NUTRITION AND NUTRITIONAL COOKING

Choices for a Healthy Heart. Joseph C. Piscatella. New York: Workman Publishing, 1987.

Food and Culture in America: A Nutrition Handbook. Pamela Goyan Kittler and Kathryn P. Sucher. New York: Van Nostrand Reinhold, 1989.

Handbook of the Nutritional Value of Foods in Common Units. U.S. Department of Agriculture. New York: Dover Publications, 1986.

Jane Brody's Good Food Book: Living the High Carbohydrate Way. Jane Brody. New York: W. W. Norton, 1985.

The Living Heart Diet. Michael E. DeBakey, Antonio M. Gotto, Jr., Lynne W. Scott, and John P. Foreyt. New York: Simon and Schuster, 1984.

Nutrition: Concepts and Controversies (4th edition). Eva May Nunnely Hamilton, Eleanor Ross Whitney, and Frances Sienkiewicz Sizer. New York: West Publishing Co., 1988.

EQUIPMENT AND PRODUCT IDENTIFICATION

Equipment

Food Equipment Facts: A Handbook for the Foodservice Industry. Carl Scriven and James Stevens. New York: Van Nostrand Reinhold, 1989.

The Williams-Sonoma Cookbook and Guide to Kitchenware. Chuck Williams. New York: Random House, 1986.

General Product Identification

The Cook's Ingredients. Philip Dowell and Adrian Bailey. New York: William Morrow, 1980.

Tastings: The Best from Ketchup to Caviar. Jenifer Harvey Lang. New York: Crown Publishers, Inc., 1986.

The Von Welanetz Guide to Ethnic Ingredients. Diana and Paul von Welanetz. Los Angeles: J. P. Tarcher, 1982.

Meats, Poultry, and Game

The Meat Buyers Guide. National Association of Meat Purveyors. Tucson, Arizona: 1988.

The Meat We Eat. John R. Thomas and P. Thomas Ziegler. Danville, Illinois: Interstate Printers & Publishing, 1985.

Fish and Shellfish

The Complete Cookbook of American Fish and Shellfish (2nd edition). John F. Nicolas. New York: Van Nostrand Reinhold, 1990.

The Encyclopedia of Fish Cookery. Albert J. McVane. New York: Holt, Rinehart and Winston, 1977.

Fruits and Vegetables

The Blue Goose Buying Guide. Blue Goose, Inc. Fullerton, California: 1967.

The Foodservice Guide to Fresh Produce. Produce Marketing Association. Newark, Delaware: 1985.

Jane Grigson's Fruit Book. Jane Grigson. New York: Atheneum, 1982.

Jane Grigson's Vegetable Book. Jane Grigson. New York: Penguin Books, 1980.

Rodale's Illustrated Encyclopedia of Herbs. Claire Kowalchik and William H. Hylton, eds. Emmaus, Pennsylvania: Rodale Press, 1987.

Uncommon Fruits and Vegetables: A Commonsense Guide. Elizabeth Schneider. New York: Harper & Row, 1986.

Dairy and Cheeses

Cheese: A Guide to the World of Cheese and Cheesemaking. Bruno Battistotti. New York: Facts on File, 1984.

Cheese Buyer's Handbook. Daniel O'Keefe. New York: McGraw-Hill, 1978.

Cheeses of the World. U.S. Department of Agriculture. New York: Dover Publications, 1972.

The World of Cheese. Evan Jones. New York: Alfred A. Knopf, 1976.

Nonperishable Goods

The Book of Coffee and Tea. Joel, David, and Karl Schapira. New York: St. Martin's Press, 1975.

Spices, Salt and Aromatics. Elizabeth David. New York: Penguin Books, 1970.

PREPARATIONS AND RECIPES

The Art of Making Sausages, Pâtés, and other Charcuterie (orig. title: *Charcuterie and French Pork Cookery*). Jane Grigson. New York: Alfred A. Knopf, 1968.

Pasta Classica. Julia Della Croce. San Francisco: Chronicle Books, 1987.

Pâtés and Terrines. Frederich W. Elhart. New York: Hearst Books, 1984.

The Professional Chef's® Art of Garde-manger (4th edition). Frederic H. Sonnenschmidt and John F. Nicholas. New York: Van Nostrand Reinhold, 1988.

Salads. Veronika Müller. New York: Van Nostrand Reinhold, 1989.

Soups for the Professional Chef. Terence Janericco. New York: Van Nostrand Reinhold, 1988.

GENERAL/CLASSIC COOKING

The Art of Cooking. Jacques Pepin. New York: Alfred A. Knopf, 1987.

Classical Cooking the Modern Way (2nd edition). Eugen Pauli. New York: Van Nostrand Reinhold, 1989.

The Complete Guide to the Art of Modern Cooking. Auguste Escoffier. New York: Van Nostrand Reinhold, 1990.

The Cook Book. Terence and Caroline Conran. New York: Crown Publishers, Inc., 1980.

Cooking for the Professional Chef. Kenneth C. Wolfe. Albany, New York: Delmar Publishing, 1982.

Couleurs, Parfums et Saveurs de Ma Cuisine. Jacques Maximin. Paris: Editions Robert Laffent, 1984.

Culinary Olympics Cookbook. American Culinary Federation and Ferdinand E. Metz. Chet Holden, ed. Des Plaines, Illinois: Cahners Publishing Company and *Restaurants & Institutions* Magazine, 1983.

Dining in France. Christian Millau. New York: Stewart, Tabori & Chang, 1986.

The Grand Masters of French Cuisine. Selected and adapted by Celine Vence and Robert Courtine. New York: G. P. Putnam & Sons, 1978.

Great Chefs of France. Anthony Blake. New York: Harry N. Abrams, 1978.

James Beard's Theory and Practice of Good Cooking. James Beard. New York: Alfred A. Knopf, 1977.

La Technique. Jacques Pepin. New York: Wallaby/Pocket Books, 1976.

Paul Bocuse's French Cooking. Paul Bocuse. New York: Pantheon, 1977.

The Physiology of Taste. Jean Anthelme Brillat-Savarin. Translated by Anne Dreyton. New York: Penguin Books, 1970.

The Saucier's Apprentice. Raymond A. Sokolov. New York: Alfred A. Knopf, 1980.

AMERICAN COOKING/RECIPES

Chef Paul Prudhomme's Louisiana Kitchen. Paul Prudhomme. New York: William Morrow, 1984.

Chez Panisse Cooking. Paul Bertolli with Alice Waters. New York: Random House, 1988.

City Cuisine. Susan Feniger and Mary Sue Milliken. New York: William Morrow, 1989.

Cooking with New American Chefs. Ellen Brown. New York: Harper & Row, 1985.

Epicurean Delight: The Life and Times of James Beard. Evan Jones. New York: Alfred A. Knopf, 1990.

Jasper White's Cooking from New England. Jasper White. New York: Harper & Row, 1989.

The Mansion on Turtle Creek. Dean Fearing. New York: Weidenfeld & Nicholson, 1987.

The New York Times Cook Book. Craig Claiborne. New York: Harper & Row, 1990.

The Trellis. Marcel Desaulniers. New York: Weidenfeld & Nicholson, 1988.

INTERNATIONAL COOKING/RECIPES

A Book of Mediterranean Food. Elizabeth David. New York: Penguin Books, 1986.

Paula Wolfert's World of Food: A Collection of Recipes from Her Kitchen, Travels, and Friends. Paula Wolfert. New York: Harper & Row, 1988.

Asian

Classic Indian Cooking. Julie Sahni. New York: William Morrow, 1980.

Far Eastern Cookery. Madhur Jaffrey. New York: Harper & Row, 1989.

The Foods of Vietnam. Nicole Routhier. New York: Stewart, Tabori & Chang, 1989.

French

Cooking of the Southwest of France. Paula Wolfert. New York: Dial Press, 1983.

The Food of France. Waverly Root. New York: Random House, 1977.

French Provincial Cooking. Elizabeth David. New York: Penguin Books, 1986.

French Regional Cooking. Anne Willan. New York: William Morrow, 1981.

The Taste of France: A Dictionary of French Food & Wine. Fay Sharman and Klaus Boehm. New York: Houghton-Mifflin, 1982.

Italian

The Classic Italian Cookbook. Marcella Hazan. New York: Alfred A. Knopf, 1976.

Giuliano Bugialli's Classic Techniques of Italian Cooking. New York: Simon and Schuster, 1982.

Italian Food. Elizabeth David. New York: Penguin Books, 1986.

Greek/Middle Eastern

A Book of Middle Eastern Food. Claudia Roden. New York: Alfred A. Knopf, 1972.

The Art of Turkish Cooking. Neset, Eren, Izmir. Garden City, New York: Doubleday, 1982.

Greek Food. Rena Salaman. London: Fontana, 1983.

Mexican/Latin American

The Book of Latin American Cooking. Elizabeth Lambert Ortiz. New York: Alfred A. Knopf, 1979.

The Cuisines of Mexico. Diana Kennedy. New York: Harper & Row, 1972.

North African

Couscous and Other Good Food from Morocco. Paula Wolfert. New York: Harper & Row, 1973.

Russian

The Food and Cooking of Russia. Lesley Chamberlain. New York: Penguin Books, 1983.

Spanish

The Foods and Wines of Spain. Penelope Casas. New York: Penguin Books, 1985.

BAKING AND PASTRY

The Baker's Manual for Quantity Baking and Pastry Making. Joseph Amendola. Rochelle Park. New Jersey: Hayden Book Co., Inc., 1972.

The New International Confectioner (5th edition). Wilfred J. France. London: Virtue, 1987.

Practical Baking. William J. Sultan. Westport, Connecticut: AVI Publishing Co., 1986.

Understanding Baking. Joseph Amendola and Donald E. Lundberg. New York: CBI/Van Nostrand Reinhold, 1970.

CHEMISTRY OF COOKING

The Experimental Study of Food (2nd edition). Campbell Penfield Griswold. New York: Houghton-Mifflin, 1979.

Food Science (2nd edition). Helen Charley. New York: John Wiley & Sons, 1971.

On Food and Cooking: The Science and Lore of the Kitchen. Harold McGee. New York: Charles Scribner's Sons, 1984.

WINES/SPIRITS

Hugh Johnson's Modern Encyclopedia of Wine. Hugh Johnson. New York: Simon and Schuster, 1983.

Windows on the World Complete Wine Course. Kevin Zraly. New York: Sterling Publishing Co., 1985.

DICTIONARY/ENCYCLOPEDIA

American Food: The Gastronomic Story. Evan Jones. New York: Random House, 1981.

Books for Cooks: A Bibliography of Cookery. Marguerite Patten. New York: R. R. Bowker. 1975.

The Chef's Companion: A Concise Dictionary of Culinary Terms. Elizabeth Riely. New York: CBI/Van Nostrand Reinhold, 1986.

A Concise Encyclopedia of Gastronomy. André Louis Simon. Woodstock, New York: Overlook Press, 1981.

Culture and Cuisine. Jean François Revel. Translated by Helen R. Lane. Garden City, New York: Doubleday, 1982.

The Dictionary of American Food and Drink. John F. Marlani. New York: Ticknor & Fields. 1983.

Eating in America. Waverly Root and Richard de Rochemont. New York: William Morrow, 1976.

Food. André Simon. London: Burke Publishing Co., Ltd., 1949.

Food: An Informal Dictionary. Waverly Root. New York: Simon and Schuster, 1980.

Gastronomy. Jay Jacobs. New York: Newsweek Books, 1975.

The Gastronomy of France. Raymond Oliver. Translated by Claude Durrell. London: Wine & Food Society with World Publishing Co., 1967.

Gastronomy of Italy. Anna Del Conte. New York: Prentice-Hall, 1987.

Herings Dictionary of Classical and Modern Cookery. Walter Bickel. London: Virtue, 1981.

Knight's Foodservice Dictionary. John B. Knight and Charles A. Salter, eds. New York: Van Nostrand Reinhold, 1987.

Larousse Gastronomique (American edition). Jenifer Harvey Lang, ed. New York: Crown Publishers, Inc., 1988.

The Master Dictionary of Food and Wine. Joyce Rubash. New York: Van Nostrand Reinhold, 1990.

The New York Times Food Encyclopedia. Craig Claiborne. New York: Times Books, 1985.

The World Encyclopedia of Food. Patrick L. Coyle. New York: Facts on File, 1982.

MISCELLANEOUS

Food and Beverage Cost Control. Donald Bell. Berkeley, California: McCutchen Publishing Corp., 1984.

Math Principles for Foodservice Occupations. Robert G. Haines. Albany, New York: Delmar Publishing, 1988.

Math Workbook for Foodservice and Lodging. Hattie Crawford and Milton McDowell. New York: Van Nostrand Reinhold, 1988.

Menu Mystique. Norman Odya Krohn. New York: Jonathan David Publishing, 1983.

FOODSERVICE TRADE JOURNALS

Art Culinaire
Chef's Institutional
Food and Wine
Food Management
The Friends of Wine
Gourmet
Nation's Restaurant News
Nutrition Action
Restaurants & Institutions
Restaurant Business
Restaurant Hospitality
The Wine Spectator

Glossary

A

Abalone: A mollusc with a single shell and a large, edible adductor muscle similar to that of scallops.

Aboyeur (Fr.): Expediter or announcer; a station in the **brigade system.** The aboyeur accepts orders from the dining room, relays them to the appropriate stations of the kitchen, and checks each plate before it leaves the kitchen.

Acid: A substance having a sour or sharp flavor. Most foods are somewhat acidic. Foods generally referred to as "acids" include citrus juice, vinegar, and wine. A substance's degree of acidity is measured on the **pH scale;** acids have a pH of less than 7.

Adulterated food: Food that has been contaminated to the point that it is considered unfit for human consumption.

Aerobic bacteria: Bacteria that require the presence of oxygen to function.

Aïoli (Fr.): Garlic mayonnaise. (Also, in Italian, *allioli*; in Spanish, *aliolio*.)

Albumen: The major protein in egg whites.

Al dente (It.): To the tooth; to cook an item, such as pasta or vegetables, until it is tender but still firm, not soft.

Alkali: A substance that tests at higher than 7 on the **pH scale.** Alkalis are sometimes described as having a slightly soapy flavor. Olives and baking soda are some of the few alkaline foods.

Allumette: Vegetables, potatoes, or other items cut into pieces the size and shape of matchsticks, ⅛ inch x ⅛ inch x 1 to 2 inches is the standard.

Amino acid: The basic molecular component of **proteins,** one of the essential dietary components.

Anaerobic bacteria: Bacteria that do not require oxygen to function.

Angel food cake: A type of sponge cake made with egg whites that are beaten until stiff.

AP/As purchased weight: The weight of an item before trimming or other preparation (as opposed to **edible portion weight** or **EP).**

Appareil: A prepared mixture of ingredients used alone or as an ingredient in another preparation.

Appetizer: Light foods served before a meal. These may be hot or cold, plated or served as finger food.

Aquaculture: The cultivation or farm-raising of fish or shellfish.

Aromatics: Plant ingredients, such as herbs and spices, used to enhance the flavor and fragrance of food.

Arrowroot: A powdered starch made from a tropical root. Used primarily as a thickener. Remains clear when cooked.

Aspic: A clear jelly made from **stock** (or occasionally from fruit or vegetable juices) thickened with gelatin. Used to coat foods or cubed and used as a garnish.

B

Bacteria: Microscopic organisms. Some have beneficial properties, others can cause food-borne illnesses when contaminated foods are ingested.

Bain-marie: A water bath used to cook foods gently by surrounding the cooking vessel with simmering water. Also, a set of nesting pots with single, long handles used as a double boiler. Also, steam table inserts.

Bake blind: To partially or completely bake an unfilled pastry crust.

Baking powder: A chemical leavener made with an acidic ingredient and an alkaline one; most commonly these are sodium bicarbonate (baking soda) and cream of tartar. When exposed to liquid, it produces carbon dioxide gas, which leavens doughs and batters. Double-acting baking powder contains ingredients that produce two leavening reactions, one upon exposure to liquid, the second when heated.

Baking soda: Sodium bicarbonate, a leavening agent that may be used in combination with an acidic ingredient such as sour milk or as a component of baking powder.

Barbecue: A cooking method involving grilling food over a wood or charcoal fire. Usually some sort of marinade or sauce is brushed on the item during cooking.

Bard: To cover an item with slabs or strips of fat, such as bacon or fatback, to baste it during roasting. The fat is usually tied on with butcher's twine.

Barquette: A boat-shaped **tart** or **tartlet,** which may have a sweet or savory filling.

Baste: To moisten food during cooking with pan drippings, sauce, or other liquid. Basting prevents food from drying out.

Baton/Batonnet (Fr.): Items cut into pieces somewhat larger than allumette or julienne; ¼ inch x ¼ inch x 2 to 2½ inches is the standard. Translated to English as "stick" or "small stick."

Batter: A mixture of flour and liquid, with sometimes the inclusion of other ingredients. Batters vary in thickness but are generally semi-liquid and thinner than doughs. Used in such preparations as cakes, **quick breads**, pancakes, and **crêpes**.

Bavarian cream/Bavaroise: A type of custard made from heavy cream and eggs; it is sweetened, flavored, and stabilized with gelatin.

Béarnaise: A classic emulsion sauce similar to **hollandaise** made with egg yolks; a reduction of white wine, shallots, and tarragon; and butter finished with tarragon and chervil.

Béchamel: A white sauce made of milk thickened with light **roux** and flavored with onion. It is one of the **grand sauces**.

Bench proof: In yeast dough production, the rising stage that occurs after the dough is panned and just before baking.

Beurre blanc (Fr.): "White butter." A classic emulsified sauce made with a reduction of white wine and shallots thickened with whole butter and possibly finished with fresh herbs or other seasonings.

Beurre manié (Fr.): "Kneaded butter." A mixture of equal parts by weight of whole butter and flour, used to thicken gravies and sauces.

Beurre noir (Fr.): "Black butter." Butter that has been cooked to a very dark brown or nearly black; a sauce made with browned butter, vinegar, chopped parsley, and capers. It is usually served with fish.

Beurre noisette (Fr.): "Hazelnut butter" or "brown butter." Whole butter that has been heated until browned.

Binder: An ingredient or **appareil** used to thicken a sauce or hold together another mixture of ingredients.

Bisque: A soup based on **crustaceans** or a vegetable puree. It is classically thickened with rice and usually finished with cream.

Bivalve: A **mollusc** with two hinged shells. Examples are clams and oysters.

Blanch: To cook an item briefly in boiling water or hot fat before finishing or storing it.

Blanquette: A white stew, usually of veal but sometimes of chicken or lamb. It is served after the sauce has been thickened with a **liaison**.

Bloom: To soften gelatin in warm liquid before use.

Boil: A cooking method in which items are immersed in liquid at or above the boiling point (212°F/100°C).

Bolster: A collar or shank at the point on a knife where the blade meets the handle.

Boning knife: A thin-bladed knife used for separating raw meat from the bone; its blade is usually about 6 inches long.

Botulism: A food-borne illness caused by toxins produced by the **anaerobic bacterium** *Clostridium botulinum*.

Boucher (Fr.): Butcher.

Bouillabaisse: A hearty fish and shellfish stew flavored with saffron. A traditional specialty of Marseilles, France.

Bouillon (Fr.): **Broth**.

Boulanger (Fr.): Baker, specifically of breads and other nonsweetened doughs.

Bouquet garni: A small bundle of herbs tied with string. It is used to flavor stocks, braises, and other preparations. Usually contains bay leaf, parsley, thyme, and possibly other aromatics.

Braise: A cooking method in which the main item, usually meat, is seared in fat, then simmered in stock or another liquid in a covered vessel.

Bran: The outer layer of a cereal grain and the part highest in fiber.

Brazier/Brasier: A pan, designed specifically for braising, that usually has two handles and a tight-fitting lid. Often is round but may be square or rectangular.

Brigade system: The kitchen organization system instituted by Auguste Escoffier. Each position has a station and well-defined responsibilities.

Brine: A salt, water, and seasonings solution used to preserve foods.

Brioche: A rich yeast dough traditionally baked in a fluted pan with a distinctive topknot of dough.

Brisket: A cut of beef from the lower forequarter, best suited for long-cooking preparations like braising. **Corned beef** is cured beef brisket.

Broil: A cooking method in which items are cooked by a radiant heat source placed above the food.

Broth: A flavorful, aromatic liquid made by simmering water or stock with meat, vegetables, and/or spices and herbs.

Brown stock: An amber liquid produced by simmering browned bones and meat (usually veal or beef) with vegetables and aromatics (including caramelized **mirepoix**).

Brunoise (Fr.): Small dice; ⅛-inch square is the standard. For a brunoise cut, items are first cut in **julienne,** then cut crosswise. For a fine brunoise, 1⁄16-inch square, cut items first in fine julienne.

Butcher: A chef or purveyor who is responsible for butchering meats, poultry, and occasionally fish. In the **brigade system,** the butcher may also be responsible for breading meat and fish items and other **mise en place** operations involving meat.

Buttercream: A mixture of butter, sugar, and eggs or custard; it is used to garnish cakes and pastries.

Butterfly: To cut an item (usually meat or seafood) and open out the edges like a book or the wings of a butterfly.

Buttermilk: A dairy beverage with a slightly sour flavor similar to that of yogurt. Traditionally, the liquid by-product of butter churning, now usually made by culturing skim milk.

C

Calorie: A unit used to measure food energy. It is the amount of energy needed to raise the temperature of 1 gram of water by 1°C.

Canapé: An **hors d'oeuvre** consisting of a small piece of bread or toast, often cut in a decorative shape, garnished with a savory spread or topping.

Capon: A castrated male chicken, slaughtered at under 8 months of age and weighing 5 to 8 pounds (2.3 to 3.6 kilograms). Very tender, it is usually **roasted** or **poêléed.**

Caramelization: The process of browning sugar in the presence of heat. The temperature range in which sugar caramelizes is approximately 320 to 360°F (160 to 182°C).

Carbohydrate: One of the basic nutrients used by the body as a source of energy; types include simple (sugars) and complex (starches and fibers).

Carry-over cooking: Heat retained in cooked foods that allows them to continue cooking even after removal from the cooking medium. Especially important to **roasted** foods.

Casing: A synthetic or natural membrane (usually pig or sheep intestines) used to enclose sausage forcemeat.

Casserole/en casserole (Fr.): A lidded cooking vessel that is used in the oven; usually round with two handles. Also, foods cooked in a casserole.

Cassoulet: A stew of beans baked with pork or other meats, duck or goose **confit,** and seasonings.

Caul fat: A fatty membrane from a pig or sheep intestine that resembles fine netting; used to bard roasts and **pâtés** and to encase sausage **forcemeat.**

Cellulose: A complex carbohydrate; it is the main structural component of plant cells.

Cephalopod: Marine creatures whose tentacles and arms are attached directly to their heads; includes squid and octopus.

Chafing dish: A metal dish with a heating unit (flame or electric) used to keep foods warm and to cook foods at the table side or during buffet service.

Champagne: A sparkling white wine produced in the Champagne region of France; the term is sometimes incorrectly applied to other sparkling wines.

Charcuterie (Fr.): The preparation of pork and other meat items, such as hams, terrines, sausages, **pâtés,** and other **forcemeats.**

Charcutière (Fr.): In the style of the butcher's wife. Items (usually grilled meat) are served with sauce Robert and finished with a julienne of gherkins.

Chasseur (Fr.): Hunter's style. A mushroom-tomato sauce made with a white wine reduction and **demi-glace,** and finished with butter and parsley.

Cheesecloth: A light, fine mesh gauze used for straining liquids and making **sachets.**

Chef de partie (Fr.): Station chefs. In the brigade system, these are the line-cook positions, such as **saucier, grillardin,** etc.

Chef de rang (Fr.): Front waiter. A **demi-chef de rang** is a back waiter or busboy.

Chef de salle (Fr.): Head waiter.

Chef de service (Fr.): Director of service.

Chef de vin (Fr.): Wine steward.

Chef's potato: All-purpose potato.

Chef's knife: An all-purpose knife used for chopping, slicing, and mincing; its blade is usually between 8 and 14 inches long.

Chemical leavener: An ingredient or combination of ingredients (such as **baking soda** or **baking powder**) whose chemical action is used to produce carbon dioxide gas to leaven baked goods.

Chiffonade: Leafy vegetables or herbs cut into fine shreds; often used as a garnish.

Chili/Chile: The fruit of certain types of capsicum peppers (not related to black pepper), used fresh and dry as a seasoning. Chilies come in many types (for example, jalapeño, serrano, poblano) and varying degrees of spiciness.

Chili powder: Dried, ground or crushed **chilies**, often with other ground spices and herbs.

Chine: Backbone. A cut of meat that includes the backbone; in butchering, to separate the backbone and ribs to facilitate carving.

Chinoise: A conical sieve used for straining and pureeing foods.

Cholesterol: A sterol found exclusively in animal products such as meat, eggs, and cheese.

Chop: To cut into pieces of roughly the same size. Also, a small cut of meat including part of the rib.

Choron: Sauce **béarnaise** finished with tomato puree.

Choucroute (Fr.): Sauerkraut. *Choucroute garni* is sauerkraut garnished with various meats.

Chowder: A thick soup that may be made from a variety of ingredients but usually contains potatoes.

Cioppino (It.): A fish stew usually made with white wine and tomatoes, believed to have originated in Genoa.

Clarification: The process of removing solid impurities from a liquid (such as butter or stock). Also, a mixture of ground meat, egg whites, mirepoix, tomato puree, herbs, and spices used to clarify **broth** for **consommé.**

Clarified butter: Butter from which the milk solids and water have been removed, leaving pure butterfat. Has a higher smoking point than whole butter but less butter flavor.

Coagulation: The curdling or clumping of protein usually due to the application of heat or acid.

Coarse chop: To cut into pieces of roughly the same size; used for items such as **mirepoix,** where appearance is not important.

Cocoa: The pods of the cacao tree, processed to remove the cocoa butter and ground into powder. Used as a flavoring.

Cocotte (Fr.): Casserole. A cooking dish with a tight-fitting lid for **braising** or **stewing.** Also, a small ramekin used for cooking eggs. (*En cocotte* is often interchangeable with *en casserole*).

Cod, salt: Cod fish that has been salted, possibly smoked, and dried to preserve it.

Coddled eggs: Eggs cooked in simmering water, in their shells or in **ramekins** or coddlers, until set.

Colander: A perforated bowl, with or without a base or legs, used to strain foods.

Combination method: A cooking method that involves the application of both moist and dry heat to the main item (for example, **braising** or **stewing**).

Commis (Fr.): Apprentice. A cook who works under a **chef de partie** to learn the station and its responsibilities. A *commis de rang* is a back waiter or busboy.

Communard (Fr.): The kitchen position responsible for preparing staff meals.

Complex carbohydrate: A large molecule made up of long chains of sugar molecules. In food, these molecules are found in starches and fiber.

Compote: A dish of fruit—fresh or dried—cooked in syrup flavored with spices or liqueur.

Compound butter: Whole butter combined with herbs or other seasonings and usually used to sauce grilled or broiled items or vegetables.

Concassé/concasser (Fr.): To pound or chop coarsely. Usually refers to tomatoes that have been peeled, seeded, and chopped.

Condiment: An aromatic mixture, such as pickles, chutney, and some sauces and relishes, that accompanies food (usually kept on the table throughout service).

Conduction: A method of heat transfer in which heat is transmitted through another substance. In cooking, when heat is transmitted to food through a pot or pan, oven walls, or racks.

Confiserie/Confiseur (Fr.): Confectionery/confectioner. A **pâtissier** specializing in, and responsible for, the production of candies and related items, such as *petits fours*.

Confit: Meat (usually goose, duck, or pork) cooked and preserved in its own fat.

Consommé: Broth that has been clarified using a mixture of ground meat, egg whites, and other ingredients that traps impurities.

Convection: A method of heat transfer in which heat is transmitted through the circulation of air or water.

Convection oven: An oven that employs convection currents by forcing hot air through fans so it circulates around food, cooking it quickly and evenly.

Coquilles Saint-Jacques (Fr.): Scallops. Also, a dish of broiled scallops with any of several garnishes.

Coral: Lobster roe, which is red or coral-colored when cooked.

Essence: A concentrated flavoring extracted from an item, usually by infusion or distillation; includes items like vanilla and other **extracts**, concentrated **stocks**, and **fumets**.

Estouffade (Fr.): Stew. Also, a type of brown **stock** based on pork knuckle and veal and beef bones that is often used in braises.

Etouffé (Fr.): "Smothered." A cooking method similar to **braising** in which items are cooked with little or no added liquid in a pan with a tight-fitting lid. (Also étuver, à l'étuvée.)

Extrusion/Extruding machine: A machine used to shape pasta. The dough is pushed out through perforated plates rather than being rolled.

F

Fabrication: The butchering, cutting, and trimming of meat, poultry, fish, and game.

Facultative bacteria: Bacteria that can survive both with and without oxygen.

Farce (Fr.): Forcemeat or stuffing; *farci* means stuffed.

Farina (It.): Flour or fine meal of wheat.

Fatback: Pork fat from the back of the pig, used primarily for **barding**.

Fat: One of the basic nutrients used by the body to provide energy. Fats also provide flavor in food and give a feeling of fullness.

Fermentation: The breakdown of **carbohydrates** into carbon dioxide gas and alcohol, usually through the action of yeast on sugar.

Fiber/Dietary fiber: The structural component of plants that is necessary to the human diet. Sometimes referred to as roughage.

FIFO/First in, first out: A fundamental storage principle based on stock rotation. Products are stored and used so the oldest product is always used first.

Filé: A thickener made from ground, dried sassafras leaves; used primarily in **gumbos**.

Fillet/Filet: A boneless cut of meat, fish, or poultry.

Filleting knife: A flexible-bladed knife used for filleting fish; similar in size and shape to a **boning knife**.

Fines herbes: A mixture of herbs, usually parsley, chervil, tarragon, and chives.

Fish poacher: A long, narrow pot with straight sides and possibly a perforated rack, used for poaching whole fish.

Flat fish: A fish skeletal type characterized by its flat body and both eyes on one side of its head (for example, sole, plaice, and halibut).

Flat-top: A thick plate of cast iron or steel set over the heat source on a range; diffuses heat, making it more even than an open burner.

Fond (Fr.): Stock.

Fondant: An icing made with sugar, water, and glucose; used primarily for pastry and confectionery.

Food-borne illness: An illness in humans caused by the consumption of an adulterated food product. In order for a food-borne illness to be considered official, it must involve two or more people who have eaten the same food and it must be confirmed by health officials.

Food mill: A type of strainer with a crank-operated, curved blade. It is used to puree soft foods.

Food processor: A machine with interchangeable blades and disks and a removable bowl and lid separate from the motor housing. It can be used for a variety of tasks, including chopping, grinding, pureeing, emulsifying, kneading, slicing, shredding, and cutting julienne.

Forcemeat: A mixture of chopped or ground meat and other ingredients used for **pâtés**, sausages, and other preparations.

Formula: A recipe; measurements for each ingredient may be given as percentages of the weight for the main ingredient.

Fortified wine: Wine to which a spirit, usually brandy, has been added (for example, port or sherry).

Free-range: Livestock that is raised unconfined.

French knife: See **chef's knife**.

Fricassée (Fr.): A stew of poultry or other white meat with a white sauce.

Fritter: Sweet or savory foods coated or mixed into batter and deep-fried (also in French, *beignet*).

Friturier (Fr.): Fry chef/station. The position responsible for all fried foods; it may be combined with the **rôtisseur** position.

Fumet (Fr.): A type of **stock** in which the main flavoring ingredient is allowed to smother with wine and aromatics; fish fumet is the most common type.

G

Galantine: Boned meat (usually poultry) that is stuffed, rolled, poached, and served cold, usually in aspic.

Game chips: Potatoes sliced into thin circles and deep-fried.

Ganache: A filling made of heavy cream, chocolate, and/or other flavorings.

Garbure (Fr.): A thick vegetable soup usually containing beans, cabbage, and/or potatoes.

Garde-manger (Fr.): Pantry chef/station. The position responsible for cold food preparations, including salads, cold appetizers, pâtés, etc.

Garni (Fr.): Garnished.

Garnish: An edible decoration or accompaniment to a dish.

Gelatin: A protein-based substance found in animal bones and connective tissue. When dissolved in hot liquid and then cooled, it can be used as a thickener and **stabilizer.**

Gelatinization: A phase in the process of thickening a liquid with starch in which starch molecules swell to form a network that traps water molecules.

Génoise (Fr.): A **sponge cake** made with whole eggs, used for **petits fours,** layer cakes, and other desserts.

Germ: The embryo of a cereal grain, which is usually separated from the **endosperm** during milling because it contains oils that accelerate the spoilage of flours and meals.

Gherkin: A small pickled cucumber.

Giblets: Organs and other trim from poultry, including the liver, heart, gizzard, and neck.

Glace (Fr.): Reduced stock; ice cream; icing.

Glacé (Fr.): Glazed or iced.

Glaze: To give an item a shiny surface by brushing it with sauce, aspic, icing, or another **appareil.** For meat, to coat with sauce and then brown in an oven or salamander.

Gluten: An elastic protein formed when hard wheat flour is moistened and agitated. Gluten gives yeast doughs their characteristic elasticity.

Goujonette (Fr.): Fish fillet cut in strips and usually breaded or batter-coated and then deep-fried.

Grand sauce: One of several basic sauces that are used in the preparation of many other **small sauces.**

The grand sauces are: **demi-glace, velouté, béchamel, hollandaise,** and tomato. (Also called **mother sauce.**)

Gratiné (Fr.): Browned in an oven or under a salamander (*au gratin, gratin de*). *Gratin* can also refer to a **forcemeat** in which some portion of the dominant meat is **sautéed** and cooled before grinding.

Griddle: A heavy metal surface, which may be either fitted with handles, built into a stove, or heated by its own gas or electric element. Cooking is done directly on the griddle.

Grill: A cooking technique in which foods are cooked by a radiant heat source placed below the food. Also, the piece of equipment on which grilling is done. Grills may be fueled by gas, electricity, charcoal, or wood.

Grill pan: A skillet with ridges that is used to simulate grilling on the stove top.

Grillardin (Fr.): Grill chef/station. The position responsible for all grilled foods; may be combined with **rôtisseur.**

Griswold: A pot, similar to a **rondeau,** made of cast iron; may have a single short handle rather than the usual loop handles.

Guinea hen/fowl: A bird related to the pheasant. It is slaughtered at about 6 months of age and weighs three-quarters to 1 and a half pounds (350 to 700 grams). Its tender meat is suitable to most techniques.

Gumbo: A Creole soup/stew thickened with **filé** or okra.

Gumbo filé powder: See **filé.**

H

Haricot (Fr.): "Bean." *Haricots verts* are green beans.

Hash: Chopped, cooked meat, usually with potatoes and/or other vegetables, which is seasoned, bound with a sauce, and **sautéed.** Also, to chop.

Heimlich maneuver: First aid for choking; the application of sudden, upward pressure on the upper abdomen to force a foreign object from the windpipe.

Hilum: The scar on the side of a bean where it was attached to the pod.

Hollandaise: A classic **emulsion** sauce made with a vinegar reduction, egg yolks, and melted butter flavored with lemon juice. It is one of the **grand sauces.**

Hollow-ground: A type of knife blade made by fusing two sheets of metal and beveling or fluting the edge.

Hominy: Corn that has been milled or treated with a lye solution to remove the bran and germ.

Homogenization: A process used to prevent the milk-fat from separating out of milk products. The liquid is forced through an ultra-fine mesh at high pressure, which breaks up fat globules, dispersing them evenly throughout the liquid.

Hors d'oeuvre (Fr.): "Outside the work." An **appetizer.**

Hotel pan: A rectangular, metal pan, in any of a number of standard sizes, with a lip that allows it to rest in a storage shelf or steam table.

Hydrogenation: The process in which hydrogen atoms are added to an **unsaturated fat** molecule, making it partially or completely saturated, hence, solid at room temperature.

Hydroponics: A technique that involves growing vegetables in nutrient-enriched water, rather than in soil.

Hygiene: Conditions and practices followed to maintain health, including sanitation and personal cleanliness.

I

Infection: Contamination by a disease-causing agent, such as **bacteria.**

Infusion: Steeping an aromatic or other item in liquid to extract its flavor. Also, the liquid resulting from this process.

Instant-reading thermometer: A thermometer used to measure the internal temperature of foods. The stem is inserted in the food, producing an instant temperature read-out.

Intoxication: Poisoning. A state of being tainted with toxins, particularly those produced by microorganisms that have infected food.

J

Julienne: Vegetables, potatoes, or other items cut into thin strips; ⅛-inch square x 1 to 2 inches is standard. Fine julienne is ¹⁄₁₆-inch square.

Jus (Fr.): Juice. *Jus de viande* is meat gravy. Meat served *au jus* is served with its own juice or **jus lié.**

Jus lié (Fr.): Meat juice thickened lightly with **arrowroot** or cornstarch.

K

Kasha (Russ.): Buckwheat groats that have been hulled and crushed; usually prepared by boiling.

Kosher: Prepared in accordance with Jewish dietary laws.

Kosher salt: Pure, refined rock salt used for pickling because it does not contain magnesium carbonate. It thus does not cloud brine solutions. Also used to **kosher** items. (Also known as coarse salt or pickling salt.)

L

Lard: Rendered pork fat used for pastry and frying.

Lardon (Fr.): A strip of fat used for larding; may be seasoned. (Also, lardoon.)

Leavener: Any ingredient or process that produces air bubbles and causes the rising of baked goods. (See **chemical** and **mechanical leaveners, yeast, baking soda, baking powder.**)

Legume: The seeds of certain plants, including beans and peas, which are eaten for their earthy flavors and high nutritional value. Also, the French word for vegetable.

Liaison: A mixture of egg yolks and cream used to thicken and enrich sauces. (Also loosely applied to any **appareil** used as a thickener.)

Liqueur: A spirit flavored with fruit, spices, nuts, herbs, and/or seeds and usually sweetened.

Little neck: Small, hard-shell clams often eaten raw on the half shell.

Littleneck: A Pacific coast clam, usually steamed. (Also known as manila clam.)

Low-fat milk: Milk containing less than 2 percent fat.

Lox: Salt-cured salmon.

Lyonnaise (Fr.): Lyons style; with onions and usually butter, white wine, vinegar, and demi-glace.

M

Macaroni (It.): Pasta.

Madère (Fr.): A sauce made with demi-glace flavored with **Madeira.**

Madeira: A Portuguese fortified wine that is treated with heat as it ages, giving it a distinctive flavor and brownish color.

Mahi mahi: A firm-fleshed Pacific fish with a light, delicate flavor, suitable to all cooking methods. (Also called dolphin fish.)

Maître d'hôtel (Fr.): Dining room manager or food and beverage manager, informally called maître d'. This position oversees the dining room or "front of the house" staff. Also, a compound butter flavored with chopped parsley and lemon juice.

Mandoline: A slicing device of stainless steel with carbon steel blades. The blades may be adjusted to cut items into various cuts and thicknesses.

Marbling: The intramuscular fat found in meat that makes the meat tender and juicy.

Marinade: An **appareil** used before cooking to flavor and moisten foods; may be liquid or dry. Liquid marinades are usually based on an acidic ingredient, such as wine or vinegar; dry marinades are usually salt-based.

Marmite: See **stock pot.**

Marzipan: A paste of ground almonds, sugar, and egg whites that is used to fill and decorate pastries.

Matelote (Fr.): A fish stew traditionally made with eel.

Matignon (Fr.): An edible **mirepoix** that is often used in **poêléed** dishes and is usually served with the finished dish. Typically, matignon includes two parts carrot, one part celery, one part leek, one part onion, one part mushroom (optional), and one part ham or bacon.

Mayonnaise: A cold **emulsion** sauce made of oil, egg yolks, vinegar, mustard, and seasonings.

Mechanical leavener: Air incorporated into a batter to act as a leavener. Usually, eggs or cream are whipped into a foam, then are folded into the batter.

Medallion (Fr.): A small, round scallop of meat.

Meringue (Fr.): Egg whites beaten until they are stiff, then are sweetened and possibly baked until stiff. Three types are regular or common, Italian, and Swiss.

Mesophilic: A term used to describe **bacteria** that thrive within the middle-range temperatures between 60 to 100°F (16 to 43°C).

Metabolism: The sum of chemical processes in living cells by which energy is provided and new material is assimilated.

Meunière, à la: A cooking technique for fish.

Microwave: A method of heat transfer in which electromagnetic waves (similar to radio waves) generated by a device called a magnetron penetrate food and cause the water molecules in it to oscillate. This rapid molecular motion generates heat, which cooks the food.

Mie (Fr.): The soft part of bread (not the crust); *mie de pain* is fresh white bread crumbs.

Millet: A small, round, gluten-less grain that is boiled or ground into flour.

Milling: The process by which grain is ground into flour or meal.

Mince: To chop into very small pieces.

Mirepoix: A combination of chopped aromatic vegetables—usually two parts onion, one part carrot, and one part celery—used to flavor **stocks,** soups, **braises,** and stews.

Mise en place (Fr.): "Put in place." The preparation and assembly of ingredients, pans, utensils, and plates or serving pieces needed for a particular dish or service period.

Mode, à la (Fr.): "In the style" (usually followed by a descriptive phrase). Boeuf à la mode is braised beef; pie à la mode is served with ice cream.

Molasses: The dark-brown, sweet syrup that is a by-product of sugar cane refining.

Mollusc: Any of a number of invertebrate animals with soft, unsegmented bodies usually enclosed in a hard shell; included are clams, oysters, and snails.

Monosodium glutamate (MSG): A flavor-enhancer without a distinct flavor of its own; used primarily in Chinese and processed foods. It may cause allergic reactions in some people.

Monounsaturated fat: A fat with one available bonding site not filled with a hydrogen atom. Food sources include avocado, olives, and nuts.

Monté au beurre (Fr.): "To lift with butter." A technique used to enrich sauces, thicken them slightly, and give them a glossy appearance by whisking in whole butter.

Mother sauce: See **grand sauce.**

Mousse (Fr.): A dish made with beaten egg whites and/or whipped cream folded into a flavored base **appareil;** may be sweet or savory.

Mousseline (Fr.): A **mousse**; a sauce made by folding whipped cream into **hollandaise**; or a very light **forcemeat** based on white meat or seafood lightened with cream and eggs.

N

Napoleon: A pastry made of layered puff pastry rectangles filled with pastry cream and glazed with fondant.

Napper/Nappé (Fr.): To coat with sauce; thickened.

Nature (Fr.): "Ungarnished; plain." *Pommes natures* are boiled potatoes.

Navarin (Fr.): A stew, traditionally of lamb, with potatoes, onions, and possibly other vegetables.

New potato: A small, waxy potato that is usually prepared by **boiling** or **steaming** and is often eaten with its skin.

Noisette (Fr.): Hazelnut. Also, a small portion of meat cut from the rib. *Pommes noisette* are tournéed potatoes browned in butter. *Beurre noisette* is browned butter.

Non-bony fish: Fish whose skeletons are made of cartilage rather than hard bone (for example, shark, skate). (Also called cartilaginous fish.)

Nouvelle cuisine (Fr.): "New cooking." A culinary movement emphasizing freshness and lightness of ingredients, classical preparations, and innovative combinations and presentation.

Nutrition: The processes by which an organism takes in and uses food.

O

Oblique/roll cut: A knife cut used primarily with long, cylindrical vegetables such as carrots. The item is cut on a diagonal, rolled 180 degrees, then cut on the same diagonal, producing a piece with two angled edges.

Oeuf (Fr.): Egg.

Offal: Variety meats, including organs (brains, heart, kidneys, lights or lungs, sweetbreads, tripe, tongue), head meat, tail, and feet.

Offset spatula: A hand tool with a wide, bent blade set in a short handle, used to turn or lift foods from grills, broilers, or griddles.

Oignon brûlé (Fr.): "Burnt onion." A peeled, halved onion seared on a flat-top or in a skillet and used to enhance the color of **stock** and **consommé**.

Oignon piqué (Fr.): "Pricked onion." A whole, peeled onion to which a bay leaf is attached, using a whole clove as a tack. It is used to flavor **béchamel sauce** and some soups.

Omelet: Beaten egg that is cooked in butter in a specialized pan or skillet and then rolled or folded into an oval. Omelets may be filled with a variety of ingredients before or after rolling.

Organic leavener: Yeast. A living organism operates by fermenting sugar to produce carbon dioxide gas, causing the batter to rise.

Organ meat: Meat from an organ, rather than the muscle tissue of an animal.

Oven spring: The rapid initial rise of yeast doughs when placed in a hot oven. Heat accelerates the growth of the yeast, which produces more carbon dioxide gas and also causes this gas to expand.

P

Paella: A Spanish dish of rice cooked with onion, tomato, garlic, vegetables, and various meats, including chicken, **chorizo**, shellfish, and possibly other types.

Paella pan: A specialized pan for cooking **paella**; it is wide and shallow and usually has two loop handles.

Paillarde (Fr.): A scallop of meat pounded until thin; usually grilled.

Palette knife: A flexible, round-tipped knife used to turn pancakes and grilled foods and to spread fillings and glazes; may have a serrated edge. (Also called a metal spatula.)

Panada: An **appareil** based on starch (such as flour or crumbs), moistened with a liquid, that is used as a binder.

Pan-broil: A cooking method similar to dry **sautéing** that simulates **broiling** by cooking an item in a hot pan with little or no fat.

Pan-dressed: See **dressed.**

Panfry: A cooking method in which items are cooked in deep fat in a skillet; this generally involves more fat than **sautéing** or **stir-frying** but less than **deep-frying.**

Pan gravy: A sauce made by deglazing pan drippings from a roast and combining them with a **roux** or other starch and additional stock.

Papillote, en (Fr.): A moist-heat cooking method similar to **steaming**, in which items are enclosed in **parchment** and cooked in the oven.

Parchment: Heat-resistant paper used in cooking for such preparations as lining baking pans, cooking items **en papillote**, and covering items during shallow poaching.

Parcook: To partially cook an item before storing or finishing by another method; may be the same as **blanching.**

Paring knife: A short knife used for paring and trimming fruits and vegetables; its blade is usually 2 to 4 inches long.

Parisienne scoop: A small tool used for scooping balls out of vegetable or fruit. (Also called a melon baller.)

Parstock: The amount of stock (food and other supplies) necessary to cover operating needs between deliveries.

Pasta (It.): Dough/paste; noodles made from a dough of flour (often **semolina**) and water or eggs. This dough is kneaded, rolled, and cut or extruded, then cooked by **boiling.**

Pasteurization: A process in which milk products are heated to kill microorganisms that could contaminate the milk.

Pastry bag: A bag—usually made of plastic, canvas, or nylon—that can be fitted with plain or decorative tips and used to pipe out icings and pureed foods.

Pâte (Fr.): Noodles or pasta; dough or batter.

Pâte à choux: Cream puff paste, made by boiling a mixture of water, butter, and flour, then beating in whole eggs.

Pâte brisée: Short pastry for pie crusts.

Pâte feuilletée: Puff pastry.

Pâte sucrée: Sweet short pastry.

Pâté (Fr.): A rich **forcemeat** of meat, game, poultry, seafood, and/or vegetables, baked in pastry or in a mold or dish.

Pâté en croûte: Pâté baked in a pastry crust.

Pâté de campagne: Country-style pâté, with a coarse texture.

Pathogen: A disease-causing microorganism.

Pâtissier (Fr.): Pastry chef. This station is responsible for baked items, pastries, and desserts. This is often a separate area of the kitchen.

Paupiette: A fillet or scallop of fish or meat that is rolled up around a stuffing and poached or braised.

Paysanne/fermier cut: A knife cut in which ingredients are cut into flat, square pieces, ½ inch by ½ inch by ⅛ inch is standard.

Pesto (It.): A thick, pureed mixture of an herb, traditionally basil, and oil used as a sauce for pasta and other foods and as a garnish for soup. Pesto may also contain grated cheese, nuts or seeds, and other seasonings.

pH scale: A scale with values from 0 to 14 representing degree of acidity. A measurement of 7 is neutral, 0 is most acidic and 14 is most alkaline. Chemically, pH measures the concentration/activity of the element hydrogen.

Phyllo dough: Pastry made with very thin sheets of a flour-and-water dough layered with butter and/or crumbs; similar to strudel. (Also called filo.)

Pickling spice: A mixture of herbs and spices used to season pickles, often includes dill weed and/or seed, coriander seed, cinnamon stick, peppercorns, bay leaves, and others.

Pilaf: A technique for cooking grains in which the grain is **sautéed** briefly in butter, then **simmered** in stock or water with various seasonings. (Also called pilau, pilaw, pullao, pilav.)

Pincé (Fr.): To caramelize an item by **sautéing**; usually refers to a tomato product.

Poach: A method in which items are cooked gently in **simmering** liquid.

Poêlé: A method in which items are cooked in their own juices (usually with the addition of a **matignon,** other aromatics, and melted butter) in a covered pot, usually in the oven. (Also called butter roasting).

Poissonier (Fr.): Fish chef/station. The position responsible for fish items and their sauces; may be combined with the **saucier** position.

Polyunsaturated fat: A fat with more than one available bonding site not filled with a hydrogen atom. Food sources include corn, cottonseed, safflower, soy, and sunflower oils.

Port: A fortified dessert wine. Vintage port is high quality, unblended wine aged in the bottle for at least 12 years; ruby port may be blended and is aged in wood for a short time; white port is made with white grapes.

Prawn: A **crustacean** that closely resembles shrimp; often used as a general term for large shrimp.

Pressure steamer: A machine that cooks food using steam produced by heating water under pressure in a sealed compartment, allowing it to reach higher than boiling temperature (212°F/100°C). The food is placed in a sealed chamber that cannot be opened until the pressure has released and the steam properly vented from the chamber.

Primal cuts: The portions produced by the initial cutting of an animal carcass. Cuts are determined standards that may vary from country to country and animal type to type. Primal cuts are further broken down into smaller, more manageable cuts.

Proof: To allow yeast dough to rise. A proof box is a sealed cabinet that allows control over both temperature and humidity.

Protein: One of the basic nutrients needed by the body to maintain life, supply energy, build and repair tissues, form enzymes and hormones, and perform other essential functions. Protein can be obtained from animal and vegetable sources.

Pulse: The edible seed of a leguminous plant, such as a bean, lentil, or pea. (Often referred to simply as **legume.**)

Purée: To process food (by mashing, straining, or chopping it very fine) in order to make it a smooth paste. Also, a product produced using this technique.

Q

Quahog: A hard-shell clam larger than 3 inches in diameter, usually used for chowder or fritters. (Also called a quahaug.)

Quenelle (Fr.): A light, **poached** dumpling based on a **forcemeat** (usually chicken, veal, seafood, or game) bound with eggs that is shaped in an oval by using two spoons.

Quickbread: Bread made with **chemical leaveners,** which work more quickly than yeast. (Also called a batter bread.)

R

Radiant heat: See **direct heat.**

Raft: A mixture of ingredients used to clarify **consommé** (see **clarification**). The term refers to the fact that the ingredients rise to the surface and form a floating mass.

Ragoût (Fr.): Stew.

Ramekin: A small, oven-proof dish, usually ceramic. (Also in French, *ramequin.*)

Reach-in refrigerator: A refrigeration unit, or set of units, with pass-through doors. They are often used in the pantry area for storage of salads, cold hors d'oeuvre, and other frequently used items.

Recommended Dietary Allowance (RDA): A standard recommendation of the amounts of certain nutrients that should be included in the diet in order to prevent deficiencies.

Reduce: To decrease the volume of a liquid by **simmering** or **boiling;** used to provide a thicker consistency and/or concentrated flavors.

Reduction: The product that results when a liquid is **reduced.**

Refresh: To plunge an item into, or run under, cold water after **blanching** to prevent further cooking.

Remouillage (Fr.): "Re-wetting." A **stock** made from bones that have already been used for stock; it is weaker than a first-quality stock and is often reduced to make glaze.

Render: To melt fat and **clarify** the drippings for use in **sautéing** or **pan-frying.**

Ring-top: A **flat-top** with removable plates that can be opened to varying degrees to expose more or less direct heat.

Risotto: Rice that is **sautéed** briefly in butter with onions and possibly other aromatics, then combined with **stock,** which is added in several additions and stirred constantly, producing a creamy texture with grains that are still **al dente.**

Roast: A cooking method in which items are cooked in an oven or on a spit over a fire.

Roe: Fish or shellfish eggs.

Roll-in: Butter or a butter-based mixture that is placed between layers of pastry dough, then rolled and folded repeatedly to form numerous layers. When the dough is baked, the layers remain discrete, producing a very flaky, rich pastry. (See **pâte feuilletée.**)

Rondeau: A shallow, wide, straight-sided pot with two loop handles.

Rondelle: A knife cut that produces flat, round or oval pieces; used on cylindrical vegetables or items trimmed into cylinders before cutting.

Rôti (Fr.): Roasted.

Rôtisseur (Fr.): Roast chef/station. The position is responsible for all roasted foods and related sauces.

Roulade (Fr.): A slice of meat or fish rolled around a stuffing; also, filled and rolled sponge cake.

Round: A cut of beef from the hind quarter that includes the top and bottom round, eye, and top sirloin. It is lean and usually braised or roasted. Also, in baking, to shape pieces of yeast dough into balls to ensure even rising and a smooth crust.

Round fish: A classification of fish based on skeletal type, characterized by a rounded body and eyes on opposite sides of its head.

Roux (Fr.): An **appareil** containing equal parts of flour and fat (usually butter) used to thicken liquids. Roux is cooked to varying degrees (white, pale/blond, or brown), depending on its intended use.

Royale (Fr.): A consommé garnish made of unsweetened custard cut into decorative shapes.

S

Sabayon (Fr.): Wine custard. Sweetened egg yolks flavored with marsala or other wine or liqueur, beaten in a double boiler until frothy. (The Italian name is **zabaglione**.)

Sachet d'épices (Fr.): "Bag of spices." Aromatic ingredients, encased in cheesecloth, that are used to flavor stocks and other liquids. A standard sachet contains parsley stems, cracked peppercorns, dried thyme, and a bay leaf.

Salamander: See **broiler**.

Salé (Fr): Salted or pickled.

Saltpeter: Potassium nitrate. Used to preserve meat (a component of **curing salt**); it gives certain cured meats their characteristic pink color.

Sanitation: The preparation and distribution of food in a clean environment by healthy food workers.

Sanitize: The killing of **pathogenic** organisms by chemicals and/or moist heat.

Saturated fat: A fat whose available bonding sites are entirely filled with hydrogen atoms. These tend to be solid at room temperature and are primarily of animal origin. (Coconut and palm oil are vegetable sources of saturated fat.) Food sources include butter, meat, cheese, chocolate, and eggs.

Saucier (Fr.): Sauté chef/station. The **chef de partie** responsible for all **sautéed** items and their sauces.

Sauté: A cooking method in which items are cooked quickly in a small amount of fat in a pan (see **sauteuse, sautoir**) on the range top.

Sauteuse: A shallow skillet with sloping sides and a single, long handle. Used for **sautéing** and referred to generically as a sauté pan.

Sautoir: A shallow skillet with straight sides and a single, long handle. Used for **sautéing** and referred to generically as a sauté pan.

Savory: Not sweet. Also, the name of a course (savoury) served after dessert and before port in traditional British meals. Also, a family of herbs (including summer and winter savory).

Scald: To heat a liquid, usually milk or cream, to just below the boiling point. May also refer to **blanching** fruits and vegetables.

Scale/scaling: To measure ingredients by weighing; to divide dough or batter into portions by weight.

Scallop: A **bivalve** whose adductor muscle (the muscle that keeps its shells closed) and **roe** are eaten. Also, a thin slice of meat. (See **escalope**.)

Score: To cut the surface of an item at regular intervals to allow it to cook evenly.

Scrapple: A boiled mixture of pork trimmings, buckwheat, and cornmeal.

Sear: To brown the surface of food in fat over high heat before finishing by another method (for example, **braising**) in order to add flavor.

Sea salt: Salt produced by evaporating sea water. Available refined or unrefined, crystallized or ground. (Also *sel gris*, French for "gray salt.")

Semolina: The coarsely milled hard wheat endosperm used for gnocchi, some pasta, and couscous.

Shallow poach: A method in which items are cooked gently in a shallow pan of **simmering** liquid. The liquid is often reduced and used as the basis of a sauce.

Shelf life: The amount of time in storage that a product can maintain quality.

Shellfish: Various types of marine life consumed as food including univalves, bivalves, cephalopods, and crustaceans.

Shirred egg: An egg cooked with butter (and often cream) in a **ramekin**.

Sieve: A container made of a perforated material, such as wire mesh, used to drain, rice, or puree foods.

Silverskin: The tough, connective tissue that surrounds certain muscles.

Simmer: To maintain the temperature of a liquid just below **boiling**. Also, a cooking method in which items are cooked in simmering liquid.

Simple carbohydrate: Any of a number of small carbohydrate molecules (mono- and disaccharides), including fructose, lactose, maltose, and sucrose.

Single-stage technique: A cooking technique involving only one cooking method—for example **boiling** or **sautéing**—as opposed to more than one method, as in **braising.**

Skim: To remove impurities from the surface of a liquid, such as stock or soup, during cooking.

Skim milk: Milk from which all but 0.5 percent of the milkfat has been removed.

Slurry: Starch dispersed in cold liquid to prevent it from forming lumps when added to hot liquid as a thickener.

Small sauce: A sauce that is a derivative of any of the **grand sauces.**

Smoke-roasting: A method for **roasting** foods in which items are placed on a rack in a pan containing wood chips that smolder, emitting smoke, when the pan is placed on the range top or in the oven.

Smoking: Any of several methods for preserving and flavoring foods by exposing them to smoke. Methods include cold smoking (in which smoked items are not fully cooked), hot smoking (in which the items are cooked), and **smoke-roasting.**

Smoking point: The temperature at which a **fat** begins to break when heated.

Smother: To cook in a covered pan with little liquid over low heat.

Sodium: An alkaline metal element necessary in small quantities for human nutrition; one of the components of most salts used in cooking.

Sommelier (Fr.): Wine steward or waiter.

Sorbet (Fr.): Sherbet. A frozen dessert made with fruit juice or another flavoring, a sweetener (usually sugar), and beaten egg whites, which prevent the formation of large ice crystals.

Soufflé (Fr.): "Puffed." A preparation made with a sauce base (usually **béchamel** for savory soufflés or pastry cream for sweet ones), whipped egg whites, and flavorings. The egg whites cause the soufflé to puff during cooking.

Sourdough: Yeast dough leavened with a fermented starter instead of, or in addition to, fresh yeast. Some starters are kept alive by "feeding" with additional flour and water.

Sous chef (Fr.): Under-chef. The chef who is second in command in a kitchen; usually responsible for scheduling, filling in for the chef, and assisting the **chefs de partie** as necessary.

Spa cooking: A cooking style that focuses on producing high-quality, well-presented dishes that are nutritionally sound, low in calories, **fats, sodium,** and **cholesterol.**

Spider: A long-handled skimmer used to remove items from hot liquid or fat and to skim the surface of liquids.

Spit-roast: To **roast** an item on a large skewer or spit over, or in front of, an open flame or other radiant heat source.

Sponge: A thick yeast batter that is allowed to ferment and develop a light, spongy consistency and is then combined with other ingredients to form a yeast dough.

Sponge cake: A sweet-batter product that is leavened with a beaten egg foam. (Also called a **genoise.**)

Spring-form pan: A round, straight-sided pan whose sides are formed by a hoop that can be unclamped and detached from its base.

Squab: A domesticated pigeon that has not yet begun to fly. It is slaughtered at 3 to 4 weeks old, weighing under 1 pound (455 grams). Its light, tender meat is suitable for sautéing, roasting, and grilling.

Stabilizer: An ingredient (usually a protein or plant product) that is added to an **emulsion** to prevent it from separating (for example, egg yolks, cream, and mustard). Also, an ingredient, such as **gelatin,** that is used in various desserts to prevent them from separating (for example, Bavarian creams).

Standard breading procedure: The assembly-line procedure in which items are dredged in flour, dipped in beaten egg, then coated with crumbs before being panfried or deep-fried).

Staphylococcus aureus: A type of **facultative bacteria** that can cause food-borne illness. It is particularly dangerous because it produces toxins that cannot be destroyed by heat.

Steamer: A set of stacked pots with perforations in the bottom of each pot. They fit over a larger pot that is filled with boiling or simmering water. Also, a perforated insert made of metal or bamboo that can be inserted in a pot and used to steam foods.

Steaming: A cooking method in which items are cooked in a vapor bath created by boiling water or other liquids.

Steam-jacketed kettle: A kettle with double-layered walls, between which steam circulates, providing even heat for cooking **stocks**, soups, and sauces. These kettles may be insulated, spigoted, and/or tilting. (The latter are also called trunnion kettles).

Steel: A tool used to hone knife blades. It is usually made of steel but may be ceramic, glass, or diamond-impregnated metal.

Stew: A cooking method nearly identical to **braising** but generally involving smaller pieces of meat and, hence, a shorter cooking time. Stewed items also may be **blanched**, rather than **seared**, to give the finished product a pale color. Also, a dish prepared by using the stewing method.

Stir-fry: A cooking method similar to **sautéing** in which items are cooked over very high heat, using little fat. Usually this is done in a **wok** and the food is kept moving constantly.

Stock: A flavorful liquid prepared by **simmering** meat, poultry, seafood, and/or vegetables in water with aromatics until their flavor is extracted. It is used as a base for soups, sauces, and other preparations.

Stockpot: A large, straight-sided pot that is taller than it is wide. Used for making stocks and soups. Some have spigots. Also called a marmite.

Stone-ground: Meal or flour milled between grindstones; this method retains more nutrients than some other grinding methods.

Straight: A **forcemeat** combining pork and pork fat with another meat in equal parts that is made by grinding the mixture together.

Straight mix method: The dough mixing method in which all ingredients are combined at once by hand or machine.

Suprême (Fr.): The breast fillet and wing of chicken or other poultry. Sauce suprême is chicken **velouté** enriched with cream.

Sweat: To cook an item, usually vegetables, in a covered pan in a small amount of fat until it softens and releases moisture.

Sweetbreads: The thymus glands of young animals, usually calves, but possibly lambs or pigs. Usually sold in pairs of lobes.

Swiss: To pound meat, usually beef, with flour and seasonings; this breaks up the muscle fibers, tenderizing the meat.

Syrup: Sugar that is dissolved in liquid, usually water, with possibly the addition of flavorings such as spices or citrus zests.

T

Table d'hôte (Fr.): A fixed-price menu with a single price for an entire meal based on entrée selection.

Table salt: Refined, granulated rock salt. May be fortified with iodine and treated with magnesium carbonate to prevent clumping.

Tamis: See **drum sieve**.

Tang: The continuation of the knife blade into its handle. A full tang extends through the entire handle. A partial tang only runs through part of the knife. A rat-tail tang is thinner than the blade's spine and is encased in the handle and is not visible at the top or bottom edge.

Taper-ground: A type of knife blade forged out of a single sheet of metal, then ground so it tapers smoothly to the cutting edge. Taper-ground knives are generally the most desirable.

Tart: A pie without a top crust; may be sweet or savory.

Tartlet: A small, single-serving **tart**.

TCM/Tinted curing mixture: See **curing salt**.

Temper: To heat gently and gradually. May refer to the process of incorporating hot liquid into a **liaison** to gradually raise its temperature. May also refer to the proper method for melting chocolate.

Tempura (Jap.): Seafood and/or vegetables that are coated with a light batter and **deep-fried**.

Tenderloin: A cut of meat, usually beef or pork, from the hind quarter.

Terrine: A loaf of **forcemeat**, similar to a **pâté**, but cooked in a covered mold in a **bain-marie**. Also, the mold used to cook such items, usually an oval shape made of ceramic.

Thermophilic: Heat-loving. A term used to describe **bacteria** that thrive within the temperature range from 110 to 171°F (43°C to 77 °C).

Tilting kettle: A large, relatively shallow, tilting pot used for braising, stewing, and, occasionally, steaming.

Timbale: A small pail-shaped mold used to shape rice, custards, mousselines, and other items. Also, a preparation made in such a mold.

Tomalley: Lobster liver, which is olive green in color.

Total utilization: The principle advocating the use of as much of a product as possible in order to reduce waste and increase profits.

Tournant (Fr.): Roundsman or swing cook. A kitchen staff member who works as needed throughout the kitchen.

Tourner/Tourné: To cut items, usually vegetables, into barrel, olive, or football shapes.

Tourné knife: A small knife, similar to a **paring knife,** with a curved blade used to cut **tournéed** items.

Toxin: A naturally occurring poison, particularly those produced by the metabolic activity of living organisms, such as bacteria.

Trash fish: Fish that have traditionally been considered unusable. (Also called "junk fish" or under-utilized fish.)

Trichinella spiralis: A spiral-shaped parasitic worm that invades the intestines and muscle tissue; transmitted primarily through infected pork that has not been cooked sufficiently.

Tripe: The edible stomach lining of a cow or other ruminant. Honeycomb tripe comes from the second stomach and has a honeycomb-like texture.

Truss: To tie up meat or poultry with string before cooking it in order to give it a compact shape for more even cooking and better appearance.

Tuber: The fleshy root, stem, or rhizome of a plant that is able to grow into a new plant. Some, such as potatoes, are eaten as vegetables.

Tunneling: A fault in baked batter products caused by overmixing; the finished product is riddled with large holes or tunnels.

U

Univalve: A single-shelled **mollusc,** such as abalone and sea urchin.

Unsaturated fat: A fat with at least one available bonding site not filled with a hydrogen atom. These may be **monounsaturated** or **polyunsaturated.** They tend to be liquid at room temperature and are primarily of vegetable origin.

Utility knife: A smaller, lighter version of the chef's knife; its blade is usually between 5 and 7 inches long.

V

Variety meat: Meat from a part of an animal other than the muscle; for example, organs.

Velouté: A sauce of **white stock** (chicken, veal, seafood) thickened with white roux; one of the **grand sauces.** Also, a cream soup made with a velouté sauce base and flavorings (usually pureed) that is usually finished with a **liaison.**

Venison: Meat from large game animals; often used to refer specifically to deer meat.

Vertical chopping machine (VCM): A machine, similar to a blender, that has rotating blades used to grind, whip, emulsify, or blend foods.

Vinaigrette (Fr.): A cold sauce of oil and vinegar, usually with various flavorings; it is a temporary **emulsion** sauce. (The standard proportion is three parts oil to one part vinegar.)

Virus: A type of **pathogenic** microorganism that can be transmitted in food. Viruses cause such illnesses as measles, chicken pox, infectious hepatitis, and colds.

Vitamins: Any of various nutritionally essential organic substances that do not provide energy (noncaloric) but usually act as regulators in metabolic processes.

W

Waffle: A crisp, pancake-like batter product that is cooked in a specialized iron that gives the finished product a textured pattern, usually a grid. Also a special vegetable cut which produces a grid or basket-weave pattern.

Walk-in refrigerator: A refrigeration unit large enough to walk into. It is occasionally large enough to maintain zones of varying temperature and humidity to store a variety of foods properly. Some have **reach-in** doors as well. Some are large enough to accommodate rolling carts as well as many shelves of goods.

Whip: To beat an item, such as cream or egg whites, to incorporate air. Also, a special tool for whipping made of looped wire attached to a handle.

White chocolate: Cocoa butter flavored with sugar and milk solids. It does not contain any cocoa solids, so it does not have the characteristic brown color of regular chocolate.

White mirepoix: **Mirepoix** that does not include carrots and may include chopped mushrooms or mushroom trimmings. It is used for pale or white sauces and stocks.

White stock: A light-colored **stock** made with bones that have not been browned.

Whole-wheat flour: Flour milled from the whole grain, including the bran and germ. Graham flour is a whole-wheat flour named after Sylvester Graham, a 19th century American dietary reformer.

Wok (Chin.): A round-bottomed pan, usually made of rolled steel, that is used for nearly all cooking methods.

Y

Yam: A large tuber that grows in tropical and subtropical climates; it has starchy, pale-yellow flesh and is often confused with the sweet potato.

Yeast: Microscopic fungus whose metabolic processes are responsible for **fermentation.** It is used for leavening bread and in cheese-, beer-, and winemaking.

Yogurt: Milk cultured with **bacteria** to give it a slightly thick consistency and sour flavor.

Z

Zabaglione: See sabayon.

Zest: The thin, brightly colored outer part of citrus rind. It contains volatile oils, making it ideal for use as a flavoring.

Index